D0788181

DESCENTS
of MEMORY

DESCENTS
of MEMORY

THE LIFE OF
John Cowper Powys

MORINE KRISSDÓTTIR

OVERLOOK DUCKWORTH
New York • Woodstock • London

First published in 2007 by
Overlook Duckworth, Peter Mayer Publishers, Inc.
New York, Woodstock, and London

NEW YORK:
141 Wooster Street
New York, NY 10012

WOODSTOCK:
One Overlook Drive
Woodstock, NY 12498
www.overlookpress.com
[for individual orders, bulk and special sales, contact our Woodstock office]

LONDON:
90-93 Cowcross Street
London EC1M 6BF
inquiries@duckworth-publishers.co.uk
www.ducknet.co.uk

Cataloging-in-Publication Data is available from the Library of Congress

Book design and type formatting by Bernard Schleifer
Manufactured in the United States of America
ISBN-10 1-58567-917-8 / ISBN-13 978-1-58567-917-1
10 9 8 7 6 5 4 3 2 1

For Peter and "pour tous Pèlerins / Fous et Obstinés"

Many who bear this prince's mark have froze,
Tracking the vengeful stag.

—From a poem by Peter Powys Grey

CONTENTS

LIST OF ILLUSTRATIONS

It is almost impossible to determine who originally took the photographs that appear in this biography. The Powyses had the custom of making copies of particularly good shots and sending them to their relatives and friends, so I have found identical photographs in a number of different places. However, most of them were given to me by Peter Powys Grey, who inherited them from his mother Marian Powys, or lent to me by Francis Powys, who inherited them from his father Theodore Powys and from his uncle John Cowper Powys. The exceptions are the photograph of Frances Gregg, courtesy of Oliver Wilkinson; the photograph of Gamel Woolsey lent to me by Kenneth Hopkins; the photograph of Weymouth courtesy of the Dorset County Museum. I own the portrait of Phyllis Playter by Adrian Bury but have not been able to trace the present copyright holder.

PROLOGUE

"An Artfully Artless Work"

ONE OF JOHN COWPER POWYS'S FAVOURITE MYTHS WAS THE STORY OF the Uther Ben, the "Wonderful Head." When Bran the Blessed was wounded by a poisoned dart in the battle with the men of Ireland, he commanded his few remaining warriors to cut off his head and to take it to London for burial. He prophesied that "a long time you will be upon the road," but that his uncorrupted head would recite to them stories of such enchantment that they would forget the passing of time. They went first to Harlech, where they spent seven years, kept company by the magic birds of Rhiannon. It was said that the birds could sing the dead to life and the living into the sleep of death. Then the warriors went to the isle of Gwales, and found a spacious hall with three doors, two of which were open but the third was closed. They remained there fourscore years, feasting and listening to the enthralling conversation of Bran's head. But all joy came to an end when one of them opened the forbidden door, "to know if that is true which is said concerning it."[1] The spell that had kept them merry for eighty-seven years failed, and they were left as grieved about the death of their lord as though it had happened that very day. They could not rest for sorrow but went at once to London and buried the now dumb and corrupt head.

If not quite for eighty-seven years, I too have been on the road a long time, being sung to by the head of John Cowper Powys. I was perhaps twenty when my professor came up to me with a copy of *Autobiography* and said that it was essential reading for anyone specializing in both literature and psychology. I read his autobiography and then all his novels. They both attracted and repulsed me—they still do—yet the greatness of this wayward writer I have never questioned. My career took another path, but eventually I returned to Powys to write *The Magical Quest*. After another long gap, I was asked by Francis and Sally Powys, the copyright holders, to do a selection of his unpublished diaries. This came out in 1995 as *Petrushka and the Dancer*. Francis told me how they had gone to Wales to clear the house when John Cowper's companion died in 1982, and had brought back sack after sack of papers and letters. They put the bags in their attic and there most had remained for a dozen years. Now he asked me to take them away, sort through them, and if after doing so I wished to write a biography of Powys, I would have their full support. In the way of fairy tales, I became fascinated by the man behind the mythic masks, and I agreed to write his life as I saw it, although I was a little afraid that if I opened Bran's forbidden door the enthralment might come to an end.

It always seems as if a biographer either has too much material or not enough. This biographer had an *embarras de richesse*. I already had copies of the thirty-seven diaries. Sally Powys had laboriously typed out John Cowper's letters to Phyllis—there were eight hundred—before they were sold to the National Library of Wales, and these too I was given. In the sacks I found, in total disorder, many hundreds of letters from his brothers and sisters, letters from friends and strangers, typescripts, manuscripts, photographs, old dog licenses, income taxe returns, publishers' contracts, bills from years back. Other memorabilia was subsequently turned over to me by Peter Powys Grey, John Cowper's nephew, and John Powys.[2] It became very obvious as I sorted through all this material that a biography could not be written about Powys alone. He was one of eleven children in a family so closely knit that he called it incestuous. Nor could it be written without including Phyllis Playter, his companion of forty years. Her importance to his creative life—to his life—was inestimable. She was, he wrote, "my other I—my alter-ego."[3] He began writing stories at the age of sixteen and continued to write—poems, novels, philosophical books, literary criticism—until a few years before his death at the age of ninety. It was an eventful life filled with lecturing and writing; with illness and poverty; with rituals and sexual obsessions. The question was how to fit all this into four hundred pages in a form that would interest both the general reader and the scholar.

Powys made little effort to disguise the fact that most of his fictional characters were taken from his family and friends and that the hero in every novel was himself. He had little patience with those critics who point out the danger of seeing the creative work as a reflection of the life. So far as he was concerned, criticism of literature which has nothing to say about the impulses that drive a writer forward "becomes as dull and unenlightening as theology without the Real Presence."[4] He would have approved of the comment of another writer, John Fowles, who felt that "the academic world spends far too much time on the written text and far too little on the benign psychosis of the writing experience."[5] I am not sure that Powys's writing experience was benign; however it is the "impulses that drive a writer forward" that have interested me. John Cowper once said, "Every work of art is a purgation of the artist from something poisonous in himself."[6] This biography explores what poisoned arrow entered this singing head and when; the ways in which he tried to purge himself of the poison; whether the works he created out of the resulting misery were as entrancing as the melodies of Rhiannon's birds.

While he filled his invented world with characters resembling his family and Phyllis, they were, in the end, only aspects of a multifarious self. Powys had only one subject—his "I am I" in all its conflicting intrication. He constructed that self, he said, by revisiting nursery memories. But if these narratives from the crib were created out of memory, that memory was always skewed by defences against too much reality. John Cowper's stories of self were never straightforward or factual; transforming the personal and immediate into a mythic tale was always his most effective armor. One of his heroes, Wolf Solent, as he sits watching a bowling match at the local pub, finds that "everything disturbing and confusing sank out of sight for Wolf just then. Indeed his whole life gathered itself together with lovely inevitableness, as if it were a well-composed story that he himself, long ago and time out of mind, had actually composed."[7] It becomes a question whether not just his autobiography, but his life itself, was made into a "well-composed story."

From an early age, it was stories that entranced John Cowper, narratives that defined him. He told the stories superbly well, but with a prodigality that can seem like carelessness. "Words," one of his brothers wrote, "have often been a snare to him as well as a salvation."[8] Powys did not see it that way. He was a "conjurer with words," he was the "Henog," that storyteller of his last great novel:

> [He] had disciplined himself for half a century in restraining all emotions, save the emotional idea of getting his emotions completely out of the way, while he forced those eidola we call "words" to become dumb transparencies through which the lovely and terrible grotesqueries of the reality *beyond* words should be suggested *by* words and seen as he—the dedicated medium between man and man's life on earth—was allowed to see them.[9]

Powys concluded that by the time he was seventy, he knew himself "so very well," that he was "only held up & stopped in my quest for JCP by the completely inscrutable nature of everyone & everything!"[10] I expect that too is what has finally stayed me in my long quest for Powys, but in this biography I have taken the hint from the Henog himself:

> His method was to get these same troublesome words gathered and scattered, sifted and collected, like a flock of sheep by an imaginative sheepdog, till every ledge in the mental *clawdd-poncen* of his vision—that "upland dyke" connecting what he sees with all its associated ideas—fluttered with those magical wisps of wool out of which alone the manycoloured coat of the essential reality he sought could be woven.[11]

"It seems to me that it is the wisest and safest course to carry our 'madness,' our hidden Fear, about with us, and allow it to change, as it will, its outward form according to the age we have reached."
—*Autobiography*

"His kind gentle voice and his air of mild
forbearance ... so shockingly belied by his
wolf-like aspect and the grim resistant *Parta
Tueri* line of his mouth."
   —Louis Marlow, *Welsh Ambassadors*.

"She was a romantic, sensitive,
melancholy and morbid woman, indeed
of William Cowper's blood."
   —Louis Marlow, *Welsh Ambassadors*.

"It was an absurdly big place to house a man in, even a man who was the father, as he
became before we left, of five children considering that the village, of which he was the
parish-priest, never in his time exceeded two hundred souls."   —*Autobiography*

CHAPTER ONE

NURSERY MEMORIES
1872-1882

⟋

Revisiting today
my old familiar Weymouth
I struggle to revive my
nursery memories
waning as they are of the hours
when my recollections of
both my Parents and what
they liked me to do when
lying in Tiny Thin's soft
Bed under the big picture
there of the mountains including
Snow – Donia
Revisited often by both
my Mother and my Father
each full of separate memories
of the Weymouth Mountain of Snow
surrounded by Sea – Sand
Under which deep Descents
Went Down inviting visitation

THE CHILD AS BEGINNING AND END: THIS IS THE REVERIE OF A MAN OF eighty-eight, inviting one last visitation by his double-edged memories. Both a solace and a desolation, the memories are, in that haunting phrase, a "sunlit labyrinth of pain."[1] Powys knew all about labyrinths. When he was a child, he would sit for hours at the dining-room table, drawing mazes and setting himself the task of finding his way to their centre. He still remembered making these when he could remember little else.

> These consisted of pictures of narrow little paths which could be followed if you looked at them carefully until they either ended by entering their own track or by coming to a circular destiny resembling a lake or a pond.[2]

When he was a man he drew mazes for another little boy, Peter, who cried bitterly because he could never find his way out of the labyrinth his uncle had created. John Cowper learned to make structures, often apparently aimless, but of a pattern so complex that it was difficult to find the centre, and once inside, almost impossible to escape. He called them Romances.

Sometimes in his novels his hero found the pond in the centre; often enough, his stories were myths of failure, the Powys hero ending where he began, having found nothing. The pattern of his novels was based on the labyrinth of himself, and he was convinced the magic "clew," Ariadne's ball of thread,[3] to a "circular destiny" was to "remember back." At the age of sixty, after a life spent largely, he said, in self-analysis, he sat down once more to try to find the land and the child called Lost, never at peace inside his head. *Autobiography* was the result.

The story begins with a little boy in the garden with his father. The child is absorbed in "transferring tadpoles from the pond in the field to the puddles left by the rain at the side of the drive," where eventually they would die. The father comes over to see what his first born is doing and is outraged.

> It was therefore the merest coincidence that by noon that day, when he had so strewn the paths of the little spinney at the end of the garden with cloven laurel-boughs that a sweet savour of aromatic wood, in this cruel hewing and wounding, was carried across the lawn, my father should have been moved by a natural desire that his son should behold these deeds of devastation and glory in his begetter's skill and strength.
>
> Thus the tall figure of the Vicar of Shirley, in black trousers and grey flannel shirt sleeves, might have been seen that day dragging his protesting son away from his puddle-colonies and conveying him by force to his own devastated spinney.[4]

Powys remembered this scene all his life and it marked the beginning of what he called his "diseased conscience." He came to believe that this childish diversion was not an innocent game, but a deliberately sadistic act for which he had to atone. His expiation was to reverse the crime by rescuing young fish from shallow ponds and putting them into safer waters. He was still carrying out this self-imposed penance sixty years later.

His father makes an axe for the boy out of a piece of the laurel he cut down. This little axe becomes a "fetish" for Johnny, full of "magic power." He mourns its loss because he feels, from the distance of the forty years that separate the event and his retelling, that "I had lost—forever and forever lost—a mystery that would have guarded me all my days."[5] He associates this "enchanter's weapon" with "some magical Excalibur" that has disappeared into a deep lake. While it is "the merest coincidence" that the Vicar/Father is "hewing and wounding" the spinney at the same time as the grubby little boy is killing tadpoles, what is inextricably connected with this lost axe that has been "cloven" from the laurel by his father's axe is the memory of his first "wicked" act, and his father's rage. The axe becomes a double axe, a *labrys*, a symbol of a wound and the power to wound; a symbol of magic power; and a symbol of dismemberment.

However, the dominant memory of this interlude is "the cutting of those laurels." In his diary for June 1944, he notes that, to the dismay of his companion Phyllis, their Welsh neighbor is cutting down a beech hedge. "Les Lauriers sont Coupés—another trouble, for Phyllis loves as my Mother did a bit of

Wilderness left in gardens."⁶ Much of what is left unsaid in the autobiography is said years afterwards in his unpublished diary, sometimes exploding in the biographer's face like a long-submerged bombshell. The association between this nostalgic phrase and the early scene of spinney devastation is finally made: his mother may have loved a bit of wilderness in a garden; obviously the father did not. Another source of guilt is forged; because of his desire for that "enchanter's weapon," the son and the father are bound in double-natured implication.

Powys next describes another wounding incident he says occurred when he was three. He hung his baby brother, born only eighteen months after Johnny, from "the great bell-rope . . . that hung in the passage at the top of the stairs." The toddler began screaming for help only when "Littleton's face had suddenly assumed a swollen and purple aspect."⁷ In his diaries he remembers that at this time he also hung Littleton by his belt out of a window and tried to "strangle him with my fingers." His mother is no longer his sole possession, and he reacts with jealousy and rage, not only against the usurper, but also against the mother who has abandoned him. Then he feels terrified by what he has done, or fantasized that he has done: another cleaving, another loss, another source of guilt.

He remembers that at this same age his nurse Maria showed him "the most horribly sadistic-homicidal illustrations" of tortures in Foxe's *Book of Martyrs* and while they were waiting for a train "in the Second Class Waiting-Room at Dorchester," his father would read to him "about what Latimer & Ridley did in the flames."⁸ However, it was an innocent, no doubt religious, picture book that made the greatest impression. The picture of the eagle seizing the lamb, an allegory of the victory of the spiritual principle over the lower instincts, instead of striking the fear of God into him, gives him pleasure—sexual pleasure.

> It must, I presume, have become known to my father at a very early epoch of my Shirley life that I was in the habit night by night of making my little cot shake with the feverish intensity of my infantile eroticism. I recollect well that I would be asked every morning if I had been "doing that" . . . and since it invariably happened that I *had* "done that" I was accordingly punished, and had the fever of my childish viciousness cooled, by having ice-cold water poured over me.⁹

All small children seek the comfort of self-stimulation in whatever form, but for Powys, infantile masturbation was "premature perversity," "abnormal eroticism." This "viciousness," which he says was "insatiable" and of "savage intensity," was irrevocably connected with sadistic images: "And these intense orgies that—in my excited mind—shook not only my guilty bed, but all the pillars of my whole small cosmos, were without exception free from every sort of sensuality except pure sadism!" From then until he was fifty, "this deadly vice transported and obsessed me."¹⁰ He says he "could not have been more than three years old" when he began to masturbate while imagining the eagle swooping on the lamb. That would have made it some time after October 1875. Theodore, the third child, was born in December 1875. Little Johnny would not know (although big John the maze maker would) that the eagle is also identified with the male sun fertilizing female nature. Still, even a three-year-old recognizes the swollen belly of a mother about to give birth to yet another child.

Johnny's "viciousness" was punished—not by the nurse, as might be expected —but by his father. It is possible that C. F. did not like seeing his own strong sexuality, carefully concealed except in the one obvious outcome, so blatantly inherited and displayed by his eldest son. However, his reaction was not unusual. For both medical and moral reasons, masturbation was viewed with horror in the Victorian period. There were any number of household medical manuals advising parents how to prevent it, ranging from tying the child's hands to the bedposts to applying a kind of straitjacket under the nightshirt, to threatening the child with "cutting it off."[11] Pouring ice-cold water over Johnny was not therefore as severe a punishment as it might have been. Nor did it work.

> I can well remember when we were driving one day into Ashbourne—my father had a tall dog-cart in those days and . . . as we passed a little stuccoed cottage—ah! how long a memory our vices have! . . . I caught sight of an old woman through the window holding a young woman—as it seemed to me—by the throat. . . . My father drove on, and the vision left this world. But though leaving this world it was not annihilated. On the contrary it transferred itself to that invisible "Book of Perdition" the nightly turning of whose pages condemned me, though without their self-imposed impulse of penitence, to the freezing cure for such temptations welcomed by the ancient Saints of the Thebaid.[12]

Two more incidents in early childhood are intensely remembered. Again, he must have been about three or four because Littleton was still in the pram.

> I can remember nothing of the church at the foot of the hill; but of the narrow lane between high hedges leading down to the church I recall to this day, and it is one of my vividest memories, the exultation that poured through me like quicksilver, when walking once a little ahead of the perambulator, which carried my brother Littleton, I turned to the nurse-maid who was pushing it and announced triumphantly that I was "the Lord of Hosts."[13]

By his own admission, he was an anxious child. Johnny's declaration of omnipotence functioned almost like a defensive second skin—psychic rather than physical—to contain the now almost unbearable tensions. It was the earliest manifestation of the "I am I" defence that Powys was to use again and again in later years, but it was also an understandable "desire for some obscure magical power,"[14] which eventually developed into a fascination with magician figures. Immediately after this in *Autobiography*, he records what appears to be divine retribution for this little display of independence and power, although in reality the following event must have happened when he was several years older.

> We had been taken to a private lake in the middle of Osmaston Park . . . and after our picnic in this secluded spot I had flung into the water a considerable-sized dead branch! . . . One of the grown-up persons of our small picnic party uttered, as foolish grown-up people will, the senseless remark that Johnny had better look out. The police would have him for throwing things into the pretty lake! Alas, poor Johnny! He not only "looked out," but he looked round, night after night, after night, from his cot opposite Littleton's cot, thinking to himself: "They'll come for me. They'll come and take me away."[15]

The episodes of killing tadpoles, trying to hang his baby brother, and throwing a stick into a lake coalesce into a terrible Fear (always capitalized in his mind and his writing) that he carried with him always. "My whole life—yes! up to this very day, when in my hiding-place in the New York hills I recall these things!—has been one long struggle with Fear, self-created fantastical Fear."[16] He suggests that on this occasion what he feared was punishment by imprisonment but, as he gradually reveals, his fear was really an ingeminated terror—a fear of confinement and, at the same time, of abandonment.

> I should under all conceivable circumstances, being the person I am, have suffered from Fear. It might not have been Fear because of a stick thrown into a pond; but Fear of some sort it would have been; and a magician not yet seven is able to call up but few protecting Spirits from "the vasty deep."[17]

So skilfully constructed is *Autobiography* that the father becomes both the protecting spirit *and* the fear, a twofold force arising from a watery underworld, that a budding magician is powerless against. Everything about the father seemed to the child larger than life. His pleasure was "massive," even the gold seals hanging from his watch chain were "massive." His personal pride was "stupendous" but, says Powys, "it was nourished upon a simplicity that was equally majestic." Powys uses the word "simple" often in relation to his father. Charles Francis was an Evangelical Anglican who preached simple sermons, regulated his "very simple political ideas" by reading the conservative daily paper, ate and drank abstemiously and simply. Again and again in these early chapters, he refers to his father's apparent emotional control, even as he undercuts his own words. "The man's force of character was so deep, so formidable, so majestic—and incidentally so restrained—that in a thousand little things which touched his life he was liable to burst out with an intensity of emotion that was terrifying." In a page and a half of description, the word "volcanic" is used four times to describe his father: "volcanic intensity," "volcanic pleasure," "volcanic pride," "volcanic contempt." C. F.'s rigidly held control over his explosive anger just made it more frightening when suddenly it burst out, particularly as the inarticulate rages were "sustained by an inaccessible reticence." To a fearful little boy already full of self-doubt and covering it with excitable chatter, this must have been a bewildering combination, but he says he well understood the "tone," "as a dog understands things by the inflexion of the voice." And yet,

Powys insists, "never once—no! not once—have I known him to indulge in physical violence. He never struck us when he was angry. That boxing of our ears—which he gave up when we left Shirley—was done 'for our good' quite judicially, and in cold blood."[18] He does not mention that it was probably one of these judicial blows that left him deaf in one ear.

In *Autobiography* the father becomes a towering hero of primitive myth. Possibly the Reverend Charles Francis Powys saw himself in such a light. Powys remembers when he was five and Littleton four their father took them on the ferry that crossed from one side to the other of the inner harbour at Weymouth. The ferry was in reality a rowboat and the distance a very short stretch of water, but to the boys it must have been an awesome adventure. It seems to have been to the father as well: "I cannot describe to you . . . the primordial pride—like a Neanderthal parent guiding his progeny along untraversed shores."[19] The father exalted in his athletic prowess and loved to tell his boys stories of his great rowing ventures and "his dangerous climbs up trees, up walls of ruined castles, up sea-cliffs, down the sides of quarries, among precipitous rocks."[20]

A vivid memory is sitting beside him on the dining-room sofa after tea and being told "an interminable story about two mythic personages called Giant Grumble and Fairy Sprightly. All I can remember now of this never-completed tale was that its villain, the devil of the piece, was always a scientific pedant, called by the narrator 'the *Professor*' whose sinister activities required all the arts of both Giant and Fairy to circumvent and neutralize." These stories "were imprinted on my imagination through a mythological haze of enchanted wonder."[21] It might be said that this imprint was the archetypal pattern for many, if not all, of Powys's sophisticated novels. The father would also read to them; his favourite book was an illustrated edition of Aytoun's *Lays of the Scottish Cavaliers*. It was an unusual choice of story to read to a four-year-old and a three-year-old, but there is no doubt of its significance to Powys as a writer.

> I fancy it was in winter, for the great green curtains with red embroidered tassels covered the windows, that my father read to Littleton and me—Theodore being asleep in his crib upstairs—a war like poem called "The Passage of the Rhine." . . . The important point—at least to me—is that I received my first impression of the enchantment of literature in connection with exiles, and with exiles whose own cause seemed irretrievably lost.
>
> Aytoun's *Scottish Cavaliers* stirred up, down deep in the central pit of my stomach where the umbilical cord must have been, that peculiar Celtic emotion . . . which, like the spirit of Wales itself, is always returning, like water seeking its level, to its own proud, evasive, ingrown, interior being.[22]

Another favourite author was Sir Walter Scott. Johnny used to "listen with entranced absorption" and these romantic novels were to become "by far the most powerful literary influence of my life." Not only did the first stories his father read to him turn him "once and for all into an obstinate, incurable romanticist,"[23] he was also profoundly influenced by his father's pride in his ancient

Welsh descent: "My father's eyes used to burn with a fire that was at once secretive and blazing, like the fire in the eyes of a long discrowned king, when he told
us how we were descended from the ancient Welsh Princes of Powysland."[24] The
theme of exile very early on became connected in John Cowper's mind with a
pride in "irretrievably lost" causes. He saw his father as an "exiled wolf" with "a
savage intensity of emotion rising up . . . from some submerged level of Cymric
pride in defeat."[25] Whether "savage intensity," "passion for exile," "pride in defeat"
were actual characteristics of C. F. Powys hardly matters; what matters is that he
identified closely with this father at an early, impressionable age. It had profound
implications both for his life and his writing. The father's perceived personality
characteristics were incorporated into "that half-conscious self-creation" that
the adult John called his "life-illusion."

The first chapter of *Autobiography* is one of the most complex and beautifully
sustained pieces of prose about early childhood ever written, but there is something distinctly odd about it. Clearly it could only have been written by someone who had a profound knowledge of the ways in which a very young child
develops, so it seems curious, to say the least, that in a chapter that delineates
beginnings, there is no mention of the person who is arguably the most important person in a baby's first years—the mother. She is never mentioned in the
entire *Autobiography*.

It is left to the second son, Littleton, to give us a portrait of Mary Cowper
Powys.

> Our mother . . . was as complex as our father was simple. She was independent,
> but at the same time very dependent; she was morally courageous, but physical-
> ly timid; eager for freedom, yet so dominated by a sense of duty, that she never
> enjoyed it; full of imagination and romantic ideas, but they were suppressed by
> the life she had chosen; in her early years a lover of life but always afraid of it;
> proud of her children and zealous for their success, yet possessed with a horror
> of publicity and a fear of disaster; a devoted supporter of her husband's faith, but
> with a mind as active as hers there may well have been questionings and doubts
> which she shared with no one. . . . As a young girl, so her sisters used to tell us,
> she was gay and the life of the party. She was full of fun and a most entertain-
> ing narrator of incidents in the village life. She entered regularly into local
> social life and was very keen about croquet and archery. She had a deep love of
> poetry and literature and a voracious appetite for reading. Drawing and paint-
> ing appealed to her, and when staying with her aunt at Esher she had lessons in
> London and used to go to art galleries and exhibitions. Her sketch books show
> she had no small gifts in this direction. She loved music. . . .
>
> With these tastes and gifts she seemed made for an artistic life. But
> when our father came and claimed her for his own, she willingly diverted
> her burning zeal for the arts into the channel of her devotion to him and
> the life that was his. Every now and then in her early married life she would
> make a sketch or paint some bird or butterfly or shell, but her busy domes-

tic life soon made this impossible. And how could her love of music thrive
with a husband who knew not one note from another?[26]

While Littleton's loving description reveals much, it gives little of her ances-
try. Fortunately, a cousin, Mary Barham Johnson, wrote a family history which
includes some thoughtful comments on the Powyses' mother as a young woman.
Mary Cowper Johnson was born in 1849, one of seven children. Her father, the
Reverend William Cowper Johnson, was Rector of Yaxeham in Norfolk. His
ancestors included the poets William Cowper and, more distantly, John Donne
on his father's side, and on his mother's side, rich Jamaican plantation owners.
He is described as "a good burly fellow, well-visaged, though something like a
negro in his contour," and prone to bouts of "nervousness." Although at times he
could be "a most enchanting companion," on other occasions "he sat moody and
silent, and laughter ceased when he entered the drawing-room, and no-one disturbed him."[27] Mary Cowper's Dutch mother, Marianne Patteson, is described as
"an affectionate mother," but rather "stolid and unimaginative." Although her
husband found Marianne's "somewhat domineering ways" irksome, Barham
Johnson points out dryly that he was "very lucky financially" in his marriage. Her
father was a partner in a flourishing brewery and her mother was the daughter of
a Rotterdam diamond merchant.[28]

William Cowper and Marianne had one son, Cowper, and six daughters:
Kate, Dora, Gertrude, Mary, Annie, Etta. The eldest daughter was given some
schooling in Brussels, then became the governess for her younger sisters, so Mary
Cowper had no formal education. She was susceptible to colds and coughs and
the family became concerned that she would contract the tuberculosis that killed
her sister Gertrude. At age nineteen, she was sent to London to be under a doctor's care while she stayed with her aunt and uncle. Letters to her brother
Cowper, who was at that time on the customary grand tour after coming down
from Cambridge, indicate that, under the influence of lively relatives, Mary blos-
somed. She attended public lectures and concerts, learned to dance, and took
painting lessons.[29] Her health also quickly improved but her deeply religious parents, rather alarmed that she might be "quite contaminated," soon had her
returned home. According to the scant information available therefore, before
marriage Mary Cowper appears to have been sensitive, artistic, open to new situations, fairly lively if always rather serious, and prone to self-doubt. Only gradually, over the years, do other aspects of Mary Cowper's personality become clear.

A good deal more is known about Charles Francis and his background. His
"ancient Welsh descent" is dubious but faintly possible. However, since the sixteenth century at least this branch of the family lived in Shropshire. By the early
eighteenth century, they were even further from their putative Welsh roots. The
family seat was firmly established in the middle of England when Sir Thomas
Powys, Attorney General under James II, acquired the manor of Lilford in
Northamptonshire. A later Thomas Powys was raised to the peerage for political
services in 1797 and became 1st Baron Lilford. His younger brother, Littleton,

entered the Church and did well under his brother's patronage. He had one son named Littleton Charles, John Cowper's grandfather. Littleton Charles graduated from Corpus Christi College, Cambridge, was elected Fellow of the College, and became its Bursar. He abandoned this comfortable existence in 1838, when, at the age of forty-seven, he resigned his fellowship to marry thirty-five-year-old Amelia, a widow with a young daughter. This may well have been a romantic gesture, but one eased considerably by the fact that the widow was wealthy and the college gave him, (or, according to family tradition, he gave himself) "the Richest Living the College held"—the living of Stalbridge, Dorset. Littleton Charles remained Rector of Stalbridge for thirty years, an apparently conscientious, beneficent man of God who always made sure the cook put out the used tea leaves by the back gate so the poor could fetch and re-use them. Amelia Moilliet, the daughter of a Swiss banker, was a clever, imperious, and artistically rather gifted woman. By her first marriage she had a daughter, Philippa, and by this second marriage two sons. Her diaries indicate that the eldest, Littleton Alfred, was her favourite child. He went to Sherborne School in Dorset—the first Powys to do so—but instead of going on to university and ordination, as was expected of him, chose instead a military career. The second son was the father of John Cowper.

Charles Francis, born in 1843, showed none of the cleverness of his brother. There is a suggestion that Charles was what is now known as dyslexic, but whatever the case, his parents had to send him to a series of private establishments and later to a variety of crammers to be educated.[30] As fate or chance would have it, one of those was William Cowper Johnson, who as well as being Rector of Yaxeham coached boys of fifteen and sixteen in maths and theology. He must have been good at his job; C. F. managed to gain admittance to Corpus and even to graduate with a second class degree, although as the college historian points out, at that time admissions were "fairly haphazard," and "the reputation of the college for learning was far from high."[31] It was, however, reputed to be the leading evangelical college in the University. C. F. was ordained in 1867 and took the curacy of Bradford Abbas, ten miles from his father's parish. In 1869 he was invited to spend a week at Yaxeham with the Johnsons. A visit from a bachelor to a household with five unmarried daughters, in a neighborhood that suffered a dearth of eligible men, would no doubt have aroused a certain anticipation. Although the Johnson daughters privately made fun of his physical ungainliness,[32] Mary's parents evidently liked him because his manner was "solemn and devout" and while at Yaxeham he preached a "simple, earnest Gospel sermon." Charles Francis and Mary Cowper were married on October 4, 1871. She was twenty-two and he was twenty-eight.

They were in Bradford only a few months when the new husband was presented the living of Shirley in Derbyshire, an event closely followed by the death of his father. On the flyleaf of an address book C. F. noted briefly the relevant dates: "Received the presentation to the Living of Shirley Wednesday 31st Jan^{y},

1872. 11th Feby 1st Sunday at Shirley. Few people in Church. The Church cold & damp. 13th Feby 1872 Returned to Bradford met by Mary at Yeovil—very sad time. 19th Monday Funeral of my dear Father at Stalbridge. 25th Instituted by Bishop Hobhouse to the Living of Shirley. 27th Returned to Bradford. 29th Van packed Messrs Taylor &Co." The rich living of Shirley was in the gift of the prestigious Shirley family, and almost undoubtedly his half-sister Philippa, now the widow of Walter Waddington Shirley, had a hand in the negotiations. Mary was two months pregnant with her first child when they moved early in March. A protected younger daughter, she had no experience in managing a very large house, much less coping with the duties of a vicar's wife. She may still have been in delicate health; for whatever reason, her cousin writes "when she faced the birth of her first child, she was full of foreboding and did not expect to survive. This fear never left her, and she dreaded each birth, though when the babies arrived she loved them all dearly."[33] John Cowper was born on October 8, 1872. We have no direct evidence of how difficult this first birth may have been, but there is a novelistic hint that it was a potentially dangerous breech or "footling" birth. Fortunately her second born, Littleton, was born quickly and easily, arriving before the midwife did. The nurse, Susie Maskery, remembers C. F. saying "Another little boy? Well, well, Susan; and I hope his movements will always be as swift and sure as they have been this morning."[34]

John Cowper had firmly held ideas about the effect of birthing on the subsequent character of a person, although this does not come out for many years after the writing of *Autobiography*. He is commenting in his diary on the neighbors' two little boys, Barry, the elder, and Martin, the younger. "Martin a happy kid was born in 20 minutes while poor Barry an unhappy anxious boy took 48 hours and this was due they say to the Nurse not sending for the Doctor. . . . And hence a lifetime of neuroses for little boy B. However like Brother Littleton Martin (what a good gallant defiant fairy supporting wine women & song loving Name Martin is!"[35] He does not end the sentence, but interestingly, Littleton, in his circuitous way, says something similar in his own autobiography, *The Joy of It*.

> Let us see what enormous part chance does play in giving happiness to man. First comes the chance of birth. . . . He may be a healthy child with a happy temperament, or one nervous, restless and unhappy: this no doubt largely depends on the parents, but their lives and affairs have been affected by this chance or that chance over which they have had little or no control.[36]

John Cowper was even more intrigued by the possibility that he was "vaguely aware of existence"[37] while in his mother's womb at Bradford Abbas, and that his mother's feelings before and immediately after his birth profoundly influenced his personality. If that is the case, Mary's anxiety would have been caught, and perhaps even transferred to the foetus, if only as memories in feeling. His interest in his prenatal past echoed that of Coleridge, who considered that "the history of a man for the 9 months preceding his Birth would probably be far more interesting & contain events of greater moment than all the 3 score & 10 years that follow it."[38] Powys wondered if his "darkest, most anti-social instincts [were] nothing but the pure material accidents of some prenatal jolts and agitations, of some trifling pathological chances of birth and inheritance,"[39] but ultimately decided that they were no accident, but determined at conception. What was intuition on his part has been confirmed by modern ultrasound techniques, which have demonstrated that not only does each foetus relate differently to its uterine environment, but each appears to have its own distinctive personality, preferences, and reactions.

Whatever Mary Cowper's fears and forebodings, she found herself perpetually pregnant, bringing eleven children into the world in less than eighteen years. While at Shirley, she had five children, all under the age of seven. John Cowper was born on October 8, 1872; Littleton Charles, April 25, 1874; Theodore Francis, December 20, 1875; Gertrude Mary, October 6, 1877; Eleanor, August 20, 1879. There were, of course, always nurses, undernurses, later a governess for the children, a housekeeper, cook, maids, and gardener for the house, but Mary seems to have learned to run this large household with efficiency, dignity, and reserve.

Although Littleton was only five when they left Shirley, little incidents remained quite clear in his mind. "I can see the little village church standing clearly outlined on a hill; I can see a pathway leading to it across the fields; I can see our two cows, Spot and Beauty." He goes on, "Of the inside of the Vicarage I can remember little, but that little is all connected with my mother. I remember her tucking me up in bed at night and often singing a hymn to me; and I can remember the first lessons in reading which took place in the anteroom, a room which led into the drawing-room; and there, too, I used for the first time the paint-box which she had given me. I can remember going to church, and sitting near her while she played the organ." He remembers his father showing them birds' eggs and how to catch newts and tadpoles in a net, teaching them the folk names of wild flowers. Osmaston Lake had none of the terror it held for Johnny: although he remembers that "at its edge were many old dead branches," it was simply the place where he watched his father skating.[40] Shirley, Littleton says, "left in my mind not a memory that is not a happy one." On the other hand, John Cowper says bluntly,

> I, for one, would sooner have almost any continuous seven years of my life ... than have my early childhood over again. .... And, in this matter, nothing in heaven or earth—not even if my father had been God, or had been able to walk from Mount Cloud to Osmaston Park in Seven-League Boots—could have reassured me.[41]

When Littleton read his brother's version of their childhood, he was struck "to see how completely different was the reaction to life of these two little boys, born of the same parents within eighteen months of each other. The one, myself, unruffled and happy . . . the other, Johnny, as he was always called in those days, even then made restless by the workings of his powerful imagination."[42] Johnny *was* different, and neither parentage nor a shared environment accounted for it. What was happening in that "Shirley childhood of mine," the adult John believed, was that "a wavering human soul is gradually taking shape, gathering to itself curious and conflicting signs and symbols and tokens of what its blind urge is driving it towards."[43] Powys used the word "soul" often and deliberately, not in any conventionally religious sense but in the sense that Plato does in his myth of Er, according to which the soul of each individual [was] given a unique daimon before it is born, and this daimon has selected a defining image or pattern that encompasses the person's entire destiny. The soul companion, the daimon, chooses the body, the parents, the place and the circumstances that best suits the soul. That, as the myth says, belongs to its necessity, or what Powys called "the logic of temperamental destiny."[44] Furthermore, he believed that all an individual's experiences have a drive, "through all the twists and turns of accident, towards some implied fulfilment in accordance with some deeply-involved entelechy."[45] Accidents belong to the pattern or the image, and help to fulfill it. A character in one of his late novels decided that "accident and chance only provided the occasions out of which his self-tormenting soul invented its own obstinately-returning secret horror."[46] The stick in the water was therefore an accident waiting to happen. If it had not, the child or his daimon would have found another equally trivial experience, in order, as W. H. Auden expressed it, "to find a necessity and direction for its existence, in order that its life may become a serious matter."[47] What Littleton called his "restless imagination," John called listening to his daimon.

When young Johnny was seven, Charles Francis made what Powys describes as "a rapidly conceived and rapidly executed move to Dorset."

> My father seems to have felt, after his only brother's death, that it behoved him to reside within call of that bow-windowed house in Weymouth where our aged relative lived. So he accepted—a rather unworldly move in a young priest's life—the subordinate position of a small-town curate, after having enjoyed for seven years the sweets of an authority that was practically despotic. . . . My father became then the hard-worked curate of the Rector of St. Peter's, the chief parish-church . . . of the old Roman town of Dorchester.
>
> With a characteristic gesture . . . he now took, on some sort of a lease, an enormously large dwelling in an extensive garden, quite heedless of the fact that the house was still being built and that the garden still being dug. This was Rothesay House, the birthplace of three more of his eleven children. . . . Mr. Knipe, the elderly Rector, used to point out to his amazed friends this brick-and-mortar castle arising so near the South Walk for the lodging of a Curate. Poor Mr. Knipe! He must have felt sometimes that it was his destiny—good, easy man—to be the clerical superior to a veritable "Giant Grumble" whose disturbing pretensions were only matched by his astounding and disconcerting simplicity![48]

Whatever the reasons behind the departure of Charles Francis from Shirley, it was not the death of his elder brother that prompted it. Littleton, a major in the army, died suddenly of cholera in Afghanistan in August 1879 but C. F. was already negotiating a possible move to the West Country as early as June. Nor was this father as totally unworldly as John Cowper suggests. He had a tidy income from the beginning of his marriage and accumulated a good deal more money very quickly. Charles Francis's father had left an estate of £34,780.11.10, of which the two sons immediately got £9,000 each. The rest of the estate was left in trust to his wife Amelia. Various documents indicate that very shortly thereafter, on the advice of C. F., Amelia made over the income from the majority of the stocks and bonds to both her sons, keeping only enough to live on. In Littleton's will (of which C. F. was executor) his half-sister Philippa was left £5,000 and the residue of his estate went to his brother. The probate indicated an estate of £16,500. Shortly thereafter, the mother's brother, in a most unusual and unexplained move, disinherited his two sons and left half *his* large estate— about £20,000—to C. F., who was (again) acting as the executor. With the death of his brother and his uncle, therefore, the Powys father was worth at least £46,000.[49] In today's terms that represents a "purchasing power" of more than three million pounds. He could well afford to be a curate, or nothing at all, and certainly he could afford to purchase a "brick and mortar castle."

Despite knowing the house would not be ready for another six months, Charles Francis moved his family from Shirley in December 1879 and took up his duties as curate in Dorchester. He put his wife and five children (Nellie, the second daughter, was only three months old) into lodgings in Weymouth, the seaside town eight miles away, where his widowed mother Amelia had moved after the death of her husband. John Cowper was never fond of his grandmother, and the feeling appears to have been mutual. She thought him a tense, demanding little boy compared to the affectionate and happy Littleton. But for the rest of his life, Weymouth was the place "where I was more *at home* than anywhere else in world."[50] Always in John's memory was the pebbled seashore opposite Brunswick Terrace, which shelved so quickly that the fisherman drew in their nets there, and from where you could see Portland, the White Nose, and St. Alban's Head. He remembered the peculiar smell of Penn House, where his grandmother lived, "that pathetic and beautiful smell of old fragrant carved wood" which mingled with "the smells of sea-weed and fish and sun-warmed pebbles that came in through those large bow windows." There was the "dry" sand where the donkey-stand was, and the "wet" sand out by the bathing-machines where he was sometimes allowed to play. Digging with a wooden spade in the wet sand near the sea's edge, watching the yachts racing across the bay, seeing the glitter of the sun upon the water—all became felicitous symbols of enchantment.

They finally moved into Rothesay House in May 1880. John Cowper declared that the years from the age of seven until ten, were "years of extraordinary and exultant satisfaction," and "the most important, most significant, and certainly most happy of my whole life."[51] Significant they were, but given the temperament of "extreme psychic intensity" that was emerging in these latency years, it was inevitable that the moods of exhilarated happiness alternated with feelings of tense dejection. The active little boy would wake up every morning "with a tremendous life energy pulsing through me."[52] Every event was a "high-ly-pitched occasion," and imprinted on his memory. The adult John couldn't remember his "less agitated, less excited, less troubled moments," and wondered if there ever were such times for young Johnny. He decided that "except when I was asleep, I lived such a nervous, strung-up life that my only relapses were changes from one kind of tension to another."[53] The "tremendous life energy" was the sexual energy still bubbling beneath the surface, and although the child struggled against his eroticism, the "nightly orgies of sadistic imagination were never for long intermitted."[54] Very early on, the father who poured cold water over him became, in effect, an internal censor, into whom he projected much of his own aggression and punitiveness. Johnny became convinced that he was "an odious little boy" and the smallest display of innocent mischief became for him a sign of his own "badness."

> Oh, what a number of queer memories come back as I think of those Chestnut Walks of Dorchester! It was in this same secluded South Walk that we used often to overtake a fellow pupil at our own Dame's School, whose father was none other than the Governor of the County Prison. This little boy was always escorted by a nurse-maid, and, as it happened, by a nurse-maid of Spanish origin. . . . We used to hide behind the chestnut-trees and rush out like a pair of unconscionable gamins shouting in our shrill young voices: "Spanish maiden! Spanish maiden! Spanish maiden!" . . . The "Spanish maiden" complained to her mistress, the Governor's lady, and Master Johnny—though he did not go to prison—was put to bitter shame and something like public ignominy.[55]

The very earliest fear of imprisonment for throwing a stick in the lake was reactivated, as it would be many times in his life, but Johnny was acquiring ways of circumventing the anxiety. The unnamed fear transformed its shape into a fear of his own aggressive thoughts, and the crucial defence he was learning at this time was to turn the aggression against himself. He began to use even his most happy times as ways of making himself appear even more unlikeable.

> It was a wonderful day for me when once walking with my teacher—who loved Littleton and detested Johnny—along the hot Weymouth pavement . . . and I recollect exactly how I felt at that moment, I experienced the first conscious "ecstasy" of my life. . . . Such a flood of happiness raced through me that I did not scruple to invite the confidence of my teacher. . . . My teacher was Littleton's friend but not mine; therefore my enemy! Such was my psychology. And oh, what voluptuous joy . . . to cry out shamelessly to my enemy just those very aspects of my feelings which would most of all

excite contempt! . . . I bade my teacher guess why I felt so happy. My teacher of course—and what a priggish, incalculable, unlovable little boy I must have seemed!—murmured some reply that indicated complete indifference to whether I was happy or not.[56]

He became a great tease, intuiting that teasing was an almost-acceptable substitution for aggression. He remembered how his father boxed their ears when he and Littleton "danced round Theodore calling out 'Flabby Fat! Flabby-Fat!'"[57] Once he taunted Littleton into such a "paroxysm of anger" that it was Littleton who got into "serious trouble." Powys's nascent conscience demanded immediate penance. He decided to find Littleton an ammonite because he had heard about them from his father and "every phenomenon [my father] referred to, whether animate or inanimate, became a sacrosanct thing, a privileged object like those objects in fairy tales that travellers carried to work magic with."

> Well, my great ammonite was embedded in the cliff's edge . . . and this small repentant Prester John was soon occupied in gouging it out with his fingers. But the grand act of penance, for it was twice as large as a human skull, was to go staggering under the weight of this terrific fossil all the way home. Past Lodmoor Hut I had to go, past the clipped evergreen hedges of Victoria Gardens, and along that sandy pavement beneath the pebbly wall that enclosed the garden of the turreted stucco house where the great Doctor Smith lived.[58]

Such childhood memories became as firmly imbedded in his imagination as the great ammonite, one day to be revivified in the landscapes of his novels. The reader of *Weymouth Sands* will immediately recognize all the places and spaces he went by that day in his penitential walk.

John Cowper relates two events, one immediately after the other, which make it clear that in the Rothesay period his brother Littleton was acquiring a new role and significance. Emulating their father's love of long walks, they decided one day to walk the eight miles from Weymouth to Dorchester. He thought they might be nine and eight at the time but they were more likely eight and seven.

> We advanced sturdily enough till we were about half-way up the main ascent of the high, grassy, tumulus-crowned ridge, and then quite suddenly my heart and strength failed me and I sat down on the sunburnt, thyme-scented grass, and . . . gave myself up to despair. We had gone so far that to return seemed as impossible as to advance. . . . It was then that Littleton showed "the rock from which he had been hewn and the pit from which he had been dug" by doing what anyone would have supposed absolutely impossible. He took the collapsed "Johnny" upon his small unconquerable back and actually staggered under this burden up the remaining portion of the ascent! Thus it came to pass that my first crossing of the South Downs was not upon my own feet but upon the feet of my younger brother.[59]

The second incident became a touchstone in his mind of past and future failure.

> I remember how my father loved to take us both, our weariness of the way forgotten as we followed the adventures of that unwearied Giant and Fairy, past Lodmoor Hut, past the coastguard cottages, to the little beach where Preston brook ran, and I suppose still runs, into the sea. There was one place here where a spirited boy could just succeed in jumping over this small stream; and this feat Littleton invariably accomplished. As invariably, and without one single redeeming exception, I used to make frantic and desperate runs to the challenging spot, but always pulled up at the last second, fearful of the leap into the air.

Here was the younger brother who was lovable when he was not, who was courageous when he was not, who could please the father when he could not. Here was the baby he had wanted to kill for depriving him of his mother's breast, but here also, suddenly, was an unthreatening father substitute who, by taking the vulnerable Johnny on his sturdy back, had proved he would never abandon him. It was the beginning of a "singular relation."[60]

It was at this period that another brother impinges on his consciousness and conscience—Theodore, born a year and a half after Littleton.

> At this time of our living in Weymouth lodgings all I can recall of the future hermit of East Chaldon was his tendency—not to fall asleep as one might have expected of so young a child during family prayers—*but to faint*, and fainting slide down upon the floor! This was the beginning of a long series of not always very considerate compulsions, into which the little Theodore—like a unicorn in a lion's den—was dragged here and there by my father and me. . . . Oh dear! how well I can see little Theodore, white in the face and with great forlorn eyes like an over-driven animal, as he was dragged along some dusty road where the very flies joined forces to persecute him![61]

Theodore could not have been more than four and a half when his father took him for these walks. Johnny himself would be no more than seven and a half; nonetheless he identifies himself with his father's cruelty. What he does not mention in *Autobiography* or indeed at any time, is a further cruelty toward this other little brother who, like Littleton before him, was a usurper of his mother's attention. Theodore remembered that "when he was a little boy he had been half-smothered, experimentally, by a brother with a pillow."[62] A persecuted Theodore-like character was to appear often in Powys's novels, almost as if he were expiating his "sin" by so immortalizing him.

It was during the Dorchester years that his relationship with his brothers and sisters became a way of sorting out his relationship with his parents, or rather, the parental inhabitants of his internal world. If he was not likeable, perhaps he could impress them with his verbal precocity. If he could not jump Preston Brook, with his imagination and cleverness he *could* assume a leadership role in the games he played with his younger siblings. Littleton, in *The Joy of It*, has a delightful and revealing reminiscence of John as leader.

> The garden provided us with an ample playground. The first single-wicket match I played was against my brother John, and in it I proved that at that game at any rate I was to be his master. But in every other game we played and there were many of them, he was always supreme, for they were games he invented himself. He was our leader, whether as Red Indians we were engaged in trapping wild beasts, always hoping to find our gardener in one of our deep-dug pits covered with sticks, leaves and soil, or as soldiers of the de la Volentiä army warring against imaginary enemies we found on all sides, or when playing at trains we would go puffing up and down the garden paths, stopping at imaginary stations and picking up passengers. I shall never forget our amazement when upon one occasion a boy neighbour of ours, who was being initiated into the mysteries of one of these games, actually put the question, stammering as was his wont, "Wh . . . at's the ob . . . ject of this G . . . ame?" Well might he ask it; but to us led by this brother, brimful of imagination, it was indeed an impertinence. . . . On Sundays John was no longer a general; but, as the clergyman of his parish, he ruled the nursery. If we did not go to church, he insisted on our having a service at home; he would read the prayers, and preach long extempore sermons, a chair being the pulpit. After a while I became tired of being always only one of the congregation; and I insisted on being allowed once and away to be the parson myself. John gave me permission. . . . Not a word would come. . . . Finally I surrendered, defeated, and came down from the chair, which was promptly occupied by John who in a sermon of unusual length harangued his small brothers and sisters on the sufferings caused by sin.[63]

If only in the nursery, Johnny could assume the mantle of his beloved father. More lastingly, he had discovered that the secret of power was to invent his own rules, and he learned that he had the gift of words by which he could exercise that power.

> It must have been in my ninth year that I established—like a young Mussolini—what I called the "Volentiä Army." This organization played an overwhelming part in my life at that time; and, such was my hypnotic energy, I forced it upon every one of my fellow pupils at that Dame's School near the Great Western Station. . . . Oh! with what an incredible sense of importance, as the enchanted chief of an occult revolutionary régime, I used to sit in the lathe-and-plaster "roof-room"—it was not really a "room" at all— that the workmen employed by Mayor Gregory had left half-boarded under the slates of Rothesay House! I dragged—I presume with Littleton's help— a little table up there, and on this table I placed two lit candles—it is

extraordinary what amount of licence I was allowed in these enterprises!—
and there I sat, in exultant state, feeling like a re-incarnation of Owen
Glendower, a toy pistol, loaded with real explosive "caps" *in both hands*, and
the ferocious scowl of a dealer-out of life and death on my misanthropic
countenance.[64]

This was a game whose rules *he* invented, and over which he could exert full
control. As importantly, the boy vaguely realized that the amorphous destructive
anger of infancy, which seethed still under the surface, could be contained, or at
least channeled, into a warlike pursuit that his father, the lover of Sir Walter
Scott and Aytoun's *Lays of the Scottish Cavaliers*, would have found morally and
socially acceptable. There had to be an enemy, of course, and Johnny now
invented one: "a whole tribe of extremely powerful but rather dwarfish men,
called 'Escrawaldons' whose role was to be the official enemies, in my History of
the World, of the 'Volentiā Army.'" There had to be a secret language and he set
out to compose one. Perhaps his love of words and "the magical significance of
words" began with several half-penny notebooks. Words gave him the deepest
pleasure, not for any "merely scholarly" reason, but because with them he
obtained "the sense of power in an Arch-Medicine-Man, or a Super-High-Priest,
who invents a ritual for subsequent generations to follow." This as-if game, translated into the sophisticated symbols and language of his adulthood, was to
become the recurring plotline of his novels, the strangeness of which echoes the
borderline between the real and the unreal.

> I set to work, bit by bit, fragment by fragment, to invent a mythology! I did
> this with a thoroughness that showed I had not forgotten my father's inter-
> minable fairy-story; only this was not a "story." This was a way of life. . . .
> The "Volentiā Army" became in fact a sort of multiple Logos, standing mid-
> way between the visible and the invisible. In its realistic aspect it entered
> constantly into my daily life whereas in its ideal aspect it became part of an
> imaginary history that had no counterpart in reality.[65]

He dragged Theodore, then six, into this Midgard, for he suspected that
"Littleton always regarded the activities of the Volentiā Army with certain
shrewd reservations" but "the small Theodore gave himself wholly up to them."[66]
It was at this time that he felt he had "reached a quite peculiar understanding
with Theodore, an understanding of a totally different kind from any I have ever
had with Littleton, and one that may be said to have consisted in a fantastical
'rapport' between our most extreme and least communicable personal peculiarities."[67] He found in the imagination of this third brother "a quick response to
some of my most devilish games." For some reason, the sight of "a grave, self-pos-
sessed little girl, with long straight fair hair" walking on the South Walks, the
pathway near their home, "roused the very devil" in Johnny and he tried in vain
to get Littleton to join in teasing her. Most oddly, Powys does not remember, or
does not choose to remember, that Theodore was also there. Perhaps by the time

he wrote *Autobiography*, John knew that his "most devilish games" were in his imagination, but that this brother never understood the "as-if" play. Theodore *was* there, and this is what he remembers:

> The first feeling a boy child has to a girl child is hate; there is lust in this hate, lust that would tear and beat and leave its victim in tears and deflowered.
>
> When people talk about the innocence of childhood, they always mean something quite different, they mean primitive instinct. I am as innocent today as when my brothers and I attacked that little girl in the Walks. I wanted to hold her throat, to hold it tight, I longed to beat her face with my hands, I wanted to pull handfuls of her hair in the road.[68]

Johnny was already learning the ways of dissipating his sexual/sadistic imaginings, but Theodore had few defences except withdrawal. The other brothers and sisters were already beginning to feel an extraordinary bond of closeness with each other that would one day be described as the "Hydra-Headed Powys." Theodore was the only Powys who, from the beginning, wanted nothing to do with these clanlike feelings. When surrounded by the others, "he would shrink into himself, and grow physically frailer and slighter, and even move and speak in an indrawn muted manner, as if he were only disguised for the nonce in our Powysian flesh and blood and would very willingly put it off. At such times, as he withdrew himself into himself an expression of stricken, smitten, *terrible* melancholy would rise up, like an ice-cold film from the silt at the bottom of the sea and diffuse itself over his grey eyes."[69] Theodore's only protection was to hide himself away in a variety of secret places. In the grounds of Rothesay House, he built a solitary retreat in the bushes, into which none of the children, not even Johnny, dared to intrude.

In the meantime, the Powys clan went rampaging on, with their eldest brother always in the lead. However, John's as-if games did not always take the form of masculine aggression; the feminine side of his nature was evident even at this early time, although it was always to take some strange forms.

> Try to envisage an odd-looking, untidy, surreptitious little boy, in muddy knickerbockers and navy-blue jersey, putting on an expression that he believed was ethereal and Ariel-like. . . . Our aged Penn House relative had given me a small musical box, no bigger than a half-penny bun; and with this in my possession, turning the handle with one hand while I held it, as I supposed, in an airy feminine manner in the other, I used to hurry on tiptoe from room to room of Rothesay House. . . .
>
> I wish I could recall the half-indulgent, half-scared expression with which Littleton, at the dining-room table, industriously drawing ships, for he was loth to rouse Johnny's irrational anger, and yet found it difficult to see the despotic Head of the "Volentia Army" in the light of a butterfly-winged Ariel, must have turned to greet my perambulating tinkle of sweet sound.[70]

The same "aged relative"—Amelia, his grandmother—also gave him a small cedar-wood cabinet, which he says "became a fetish of mine." In it he placed a picture of a girl's face which he wrapped up carefully in "about twenty paper wrappings, all carefully fastened with sealing waxe," and "only on very ritualistic occasions did I so much as open this sacred drawer and contemplate the outside wrapping!" In another drawer of this cabinet he kept some of his own "very ambiguous, although extremely decent writings."[71] Possibly all highly introverted and sensitive children have such fetishes. Carl Jung has a strikingly similar story to relate. He was almost the same age, nine or ten, when he secretly carved a manikin, and wrapped the idol up as carefully as Johnny did his. Jung also wrote down "something in a secret language of my own invention," and in a "solemn ceremonial act" hid both in a pencil box which he then put in a forbidden attic.[72]

What Powys called "my dominant obsession" appeared in this same tenth year. His obsessiveness already took the form of ritualistic acts and fetishism—it was a way of keeping in control. The Volentiā Army was not, in his eyes, a game of cops and robbers but a "sort of secret Rosicrucian or Thaumaturgic society" of which he was the head. Accompanying the struggle to be in command, of himself and of others, was now an emerging desire to become a magician. His "longing to possess supernatural powers" had become, he insists, "a perfectly conscious and clearly articulated thing."[73] It was a desire to impose his world on the world of adults, to perform "some fantastical transaction that broke up the normal world." What he needed to accomplish this was a magical object, a double axe, like the laurel axe of infancy, "which would immediately thrust into the world of grown-up people's reality a wedge of *my* reality, so that it would be forced to come to terms with it! I am convinced that I *knew*, without question or doubt, that my world—the world in which I was a magician—was a great deal more than mere pretending."[74] But at night, the ten-year-old magician became once more "little Johnny, in his white night-shirt" who "cried aloud when Fear glared at him."[75]

CHAPTER TWO

THE SCHOOLING
1883-1893

⮑

THE "ENCHANTED NINTH YEAR" PASSED INTO THE "FATAL TENTH."[1] John and Littleton entered Sherborne Preparatory School in May 1883 when Johnny was ten and a half and Littleton nine. From the protected freedom of their Dorchester life, they were catapulted into an environment of enforced sociability and conformity. In the discrepant accounts of their school years, it sometimes seems as if the two boys inhabited two different worlds, but then, as Powys observed, "interest, drama, meaning, purpose are qualities given to events by the individual mind."[2]

This is what John remembers about the day of arrival. "Indelibly is it branded on my mind the day when my Father took Littleton and me to Sherborne and left us at the Preparatory School."[3] He says that his father "characteristically enough" cut short the Headmaster's attempts to make the boys feel welcome, and carried them off for one of his dearly loved walks. All the rest of his time at the school Johnny would take the same path across Sherborne Park, "simply because it was here he came with us that day." He goes on to say: "I cannot remember, I fortunately have forgotten, the actual moment when we saw that tall dignified figure take leave of us."[4]

Littleton's memory of that day is rather different: "The 9th of May 1883 arrived, when Father and Mother and Johnny and Littleton set off for Sherborne, where these two first born were to be left in charge of William Heitland Blake, a Norfolk friend of the family, headmaster of Sherborne Preparatory School."

> After being taken to Westbury House . . . we set off into the Town. I can well remember the bitterly cold east wind we faced as our father led us along Long Street to a little post office at the further end of it where there lived some old lady from his native Stalbridge. . . . Little then did I realize all that my mother was going through; John knew far better than I. . . . That was the only occasion in my life that I saw my mother weep. John shed not a tear. His feelings were far deeper than mine.[5]

Why John chose to leave out of his story the fact that his mother was with them that day and that she cried, or why the moment of leave-taking has been

"fortunately forgotten," remains a mystery. What is clear is that the earlier anxieties about separation, abandonment, imprisonment now returned. He felt
"left,"—"deposited." Littleton, on the other hand, loved the prep school life, and
marvelled at their temperamental dissimilarities. John, he wrote, "went his own
unconventional way regardless of the opinion of those around him. I loved the
approbation of others and strove to win it; the school games of cricket and football, on which boys set so much store, meant little to him, to me they were things
to live for; fashions of dress, which some boys count important, were despised by
John, who seemed to love wearing odd and ill-fitting clothes, and boots of gigantic size."[6] Littleton concluded that this was "unintentional offence." This conventional man loved and defended his brother at school and throughout life, but
Littleton never apprehended the intricacies of his brother's labyrinthian nature.

It did not take Johnny long to attempt to regain the ascendancy he had
enjoyed within his family. He tried the teasing technique that he had perfected
at home, but here at school he was confronted by someone as clever as he, and
was humiliated—or felt himself so.

> What must I do, in my nervous volubility and eager impertinence, but begin
> trying to "tease" this child, after my accustomed manner, by pressing him
> with challenging questions as to whether he was a *Fenian*, a word that in my
> Father's newspaper was synonymous with the Devil. . . . Mansel, without
> resorting to fisticuffs, made a complete fool of me. . . . How strange it is that
> what bites most deeply into our consciousness and lasts the longest in mem-
> ory should be neither great pleasure nor great pain—but simply *shame*, some
> intolerable hurt to our self-respect![7]

A second mortification quickly followed. His father had purchased a football
for him from Mr. Pouncey, the Saddler's in South Street. Johnny proudly went
off with it to the Preparatory playing ground on the very first afternoon.

> As the General of the "Volentiā Army" and the inventor of magic formulae
> for controlling "Dromonds" I had no conception of the etiquette of football.
> . . . I fancied that in giving this football to *me* rather than to anyone else my
> father dedicated it to my private enjoyment. . . . The sequel I need hardly
> relate. In the first place the ball was not the right kind of ball. It was round;
> but a Rugby ball, like the earth, is not round. . . . But whatever it was when
> it entered that field in Powys Ma's arms when it came out it was a crumpled-
> up, indistinct mass of shapeless bladderlessness.[8]

This was the beginning of a lifelong distaste for organized games—or games
that he did not organize. However, recalling the Volentiā technique of divide
and rule, eventually Johnny "persuaded all the bigger boys to form themselves
into two hostile bands and play-act a sham battle, a battle full of ambuscades,
hiding-places, fortresses, retreats, and circuitous flanking movements."[9] For the
younger boys he organized treasure hunts, drawing maze-like maps for the clue to

his hidden treasure. The maps were so complicated that the boys complained they never could find the three-penny bits he hid in tree stumps. While Littleton remembered these battles and treasure hunts, he felt that where his brother really excelled was in telling stories: "His imagination was such and his power of description so vivid that often the boys in his dormitory would be so terrified that they would disappear beneath their bed-clothes. And when not so long ago I read some of the reviews of the *Glastonbury Romance* I could not help feeling that the same thing was happening as had happened before, the little boys now grown men were again wanting to hide their heads."[10]

Telling stories was a way of keeping the game in his own hands, but the ritual was also important for his own comforting.

> I invented the childish and singular pastime of creeping down under the bedclothes to the very bottom of our beds. Such was the hypnotic power I possessed of extending the domination of my manias that if Mr. Blake had entered our room after "lights out" he might on occasion have found the whole six of us entirely concealed from view, as we turned our bedclothes into rabbit-burrows; but what does seem odd is that even now, as I approach my sixty-first birthday, I can exactly reproduce the mystic ecstasy with which I thus burrowed—as some would say—in search of pre-natal concealment, but certainly to escape the real world.[11]

There were other compensations in this period between childhood and adolescence. On Sunday afternoons they were allowed to wander about the country at their will. He and Littleton explored every lane, pond, and spinney around Sherborne, and the memory of that landscape was to provide the vivid evocation of place that characterizes his best-known novel, *Wolf Solent*. The Headmaster allowed him the freedom of the school library, and books became "a more complete escape from the real world"[12] even than exploring the countryside. Rather grudgingly Powys admitted that the Prep period was not totally unhappy. Nor was he as disliked as he makes out. Although John himself does not mention it, Littleton says that "before very long John became a leader in his peculiar way" and in his last year "John was head of the Prep, and a most conscientious head he made."[13]

Toward the end of their time at Prep, another momentous move occurred when their father succeeded in becoming the vicar of Montacute. Why C. F. left his prestigious position at Shirley in the first place for a lowly curacy in Dorchester is perplexing, but once there, almost immediately he was looking about for advancement. He thought he had found it when, in August 1880, William Cowper Johnson left Yaxeham to accept the living of Northwold in Norfolk. Johnson offered Yaxeham, the family living, to his son Cowper and when the son hesitated, he offered it to "Charley"—as his father-in-law called C.F. Although he had only been in Dorchester seven months, C. F. indicated his interest; Cowper promptly accepted, and C. F. remained a curate.[14] For whatev-

er reason, in the summer of 1885, when the rectorship of another church in
Dorchester—All Saints—fell vacant, he was again passed over. Fortunately the
embarrassment was alleviated in September when W. R. Phelips presented him
with the living of Montacute in Somerset. This most advantageous appoint-
ment appears to have come through the influence of his mother. The family
(there were now eight children) moved into the ten-bedroom early Victorian
house just before Christmas 1885, and C. F. began a ministry that lasted for
thirty-two years.[15]

The vicarage and the village has passed into Powysian mythology. Littleton
called the vicarage "the inner circle of our home life," and described in loving
detail the rambling house built of the local golden stone, the stables, the walled
kitchen garden, the apple orchard, the paddock, the terrace walk, the tennis
lawn, the ivy-covered summer house. It must have been an idyllic setting for the
Powys children who were permitted to roam freely in the fields, woods, and hills
of the surrounding countryside, all of which belonged to the Phelipses. In summer, the Ham Hill quarries were "a glorious playground." In winter, one of their
greatest delights was a day's skating on nearby Pitt Pond. In the evenings the
mother would read to them or John would dragoon his brothers and sisters and
the Phelips children into acting Shakespearean plays, with "Johnny-Moony"
playing the tragic heroes. Christmas was a special time, culminating in present-
giving and a grand "Volentiā tea." These small epiphanies were remembered
obsessively in the next four years when school, always a purgatory, now became
for the adolescent John "an endless hell."

. . . .

Littleton and John entered the Big School together in September 1886.
Powys Minor, gregarious and a natural athlete, slipped into the new regime with
ease; Powys Major loathed it with a passion that lasted a lifetime. He was neither
the first nor the last supersensitive boy to write about his misery at school; someone has said that English literary autobiography seems to have been invented
expressly to accommodate them. But certainly for John Cowper, his time at the
Big School made "a dent on my mind from which I shall never recover."[16] The
emotional tensions of earliest childhood at Shirley, which seem to have disappeared during the Dorchester years, were in truth merely rumbling away in the
background and now erupted again in adolescence. Powys was convinced that
during that period he was enduring stresses and tensions "far more crucial" than
anything he could possibly encounter in the future.[17] Already driven by a secret
Fear that he would be taken to prison for some misdemeanor, and remembering
his punishment for making his crib rock with his "erotic fervour," the onset of sexual maturity had its special horrors. For the next sixty years, Powys never failed to
observe the First Whit Sunday as the beginning of "my adolescence or puberty of
the hours of emitting a lot of the child-or-foetus-creating SEMEN or Spunk."[18]

There was no lack of medical warnings about the disastrous effects of youthful
incontinence. One of the most popular manuals in the Victorian period was by

Dr. William Acton, who described a boy who habitually masturbates thus: "The boy shuns the society of others, creeps about alone, joins with repugnance in the amusements of his schoolfellows. He becomes careless in dress and uncleanly in person. If his evil habits are persisted in, he may end up becoming a drivelling idiot." Acton considered "nocturnal emissions or pollutions" as dangerous as masturbation and warned that both could cause impotence, consumption, curvature of the spine, and chronic dementia. As if this pronouncement were not terrifying enough for a youth like John Cowper, Acton insisted that cases of dementia "chiefly occur in members of families of strict religious education."[19]

For the tormented teenager, unappeasable sexual longings warred with feelings of shame and a dread of retribution; he had "Portnoy's Complaint" with a vengeance.[20] He hunted "feverishly" for pictures of slender girls with exposed limbs to assuage his "erotic obsession," and found them in unlikely places, such as copies of the old Addisonian *Spectator* in his parents' house and in the illustrations of certain editions of the works of Rider Haggard. He was especially attracted to the "long legs of the Houris"[21] he found in the popular comic of the day, *Ally Sloper's Half Holiday*,[22] cutting out the impossibly slender figures of Tootsie and her actress friends and carrying them about in his pocket. His only happy times at Sherborne Big School were on Sunday afternoons when he could hide away in the school library, perusing bound editions of *Punch*, from which he would get "great erotic satisfaction." From the beginning, it was a "sylphid type of feminine loveliness, evasive, aerial, characterless as flowing water," that came to be "the type that appealed most to my intense, if sterile desire." [23]

In the meantime, in the flesh, it was the limbs of boys that aroused him. Although the "wretched Powys Ma" found the swimming pool "a kind of icy Giudecca," when the Lower School was bathing, he would always find a place of undressing and drying next to a "delicately beautiful" boy in his house. He never so much as spoke to him, but his delight in this boy's loveliness "was so intense that when I stole timorous, nervous, furtive, and yet ardently satyrish glances at him . . . I was totally lost to the world."[24] The adolescent John felt he could safely indulge his attraction to boys as long as he did not actually embrace them, "save in those scribbled *perdita erotica* which I kept in my treasure-box."[25] When there were no beautiful boys available to stare at, he would "embrace velvet-embroidered cushions or pillows dressed up in my own vests," in a "forlorn spasm of unsatisfied longing."[26] Even these most innocent pubescent occupations he decided were sins sufficient to have him "boiled alive like a Lodmoor eel in eternal Hell" and that "abstinence"[27] was the only salvation. However, his burgeoning conscience did not stop his gaze but merely filled him with guilt and fear.

Twenty years later, another Sherborne boy, Alec Waugh, wrote *The Loom of Youth*, in which he tackled the issue of homosexuality in public schools. The book caused a scandal now difficult to understand, but Littleton, who was to become a headmaster, was still indignant about this book thirty years after it was published. Waugh observed that homosexual romances were "the inevitable consequence of a monastic herding together for eight months of the year of thirteen-year-old children and eighteen-year-old adolescents."[28] Equally inevitable in this closed-in world was the bullying of boys who were deemed "different." Waugh recalled that a group of them would regularly "ship" the study of one tall, thin, scholarly boy who wore untidy clothes and "did not play footer."[29] For John Cowper, who was similarly "different," it was the bullying that went on at Sherborne that made his life there "bitten." He found it intolerable that the authorities were so preoccupied with the suppression of "a fault that would have merely amused Socrates," but allowed bullies to carry on "with their infernal cruelties in complete immunity." Powys writes that during his time there, "one of the very worst of these bloodthirsty ogres flourished."[30]

> In our dormitory on the third floor we kept hearing horrid rumours of the cruelties practised by that devilish brute . . . in the dormitory on the second floor; and it once occurred to some of my worst enemies in *our* room to compel "Powys Ma." to take a certain big sponge belonging to one of them, and descending in his night-shirt to the floor below enter the bully's room and fling this missile at his head! Do you think I have forgotten the sick terror that this command sent shivering through my bones? What *was* I to do? To obey was hell. To disobey was hell. It was then that great creative Nature put it into my inventive skull—why had not the brute's victim, down below there, thought of such an escape?—to *pretend to be mad*. I therefore began— with that fatal sponge in my hand—to dance a Bedlam dance, while I chanted in shrill and piercing tones my childish lines about Corfe Castle. My reputation as a half-witted Loony was by this time so well established, that not one of the dozen boys in our big dormitory questioned my pretence, or doubted for a minute the fact that Powys Ma. had quite lost whatever feeble intelligence he once had; and the result was that somebody fetched the matron and I was transferred for nearly a week to a room by myself.[31]

There are several peculiarities about this story. The bully and the victim, referred to in *Autobiography* discreetly as D– and P–, were Henry Robert Deacon and Harold Downe Puckle. Although Powys continued to insist in his diary for years afterward that Puckle died as a result of this "heavy-handed insensate brutality," the *Sherborne Register* indicates that Puckle went on to become a successful London stockbroker. Deacon, bully or not, proceeded to R. M. C. Sandhurst, served in Mesopotamia in the war, and was decorated three times. Perhaps ironically, he was given France's highest decoration, the *Légion d'honneur*, awarded for gallantry in military action. Littleton, who kept track of all the "old boys," would have known this and presumably told his brother, but Powys had his own reasons for wanting the story to end *his* way. Littleton quietly contradicted another aspect of this story of victims and torturers. He indicated that "things were made easy for us" because, from the beginning of Big School, they had a bedroom to themselves. He thought "this privilege was due to the fact that for some reason or other John was considered a delicate boy."[32] Littleton's opinions may sometimes be suspect, but in questions of fact he is totally reliable. John's insistence that they slept in a dormitory is a *méconnaissance*. Why did he remember it this way? For that matter, why were they given the most unusual entitlement of a bedroom to themselves? Why was John considered to be "delicate"? Photographs of him at this age suggest a tall, well built, well fed teenager. It is possible that this privilege had more to do with the influence of Squire Phelips of Montacute House, who was a governor of Sherborne School.[33] However, by the time he wrote *Autobiography*, John Cowper preferred not to remember that he was, in every sense, privileged. Above all, he wanted to be a person he was one day to identify as the "ill-constituted," the "born pariah." He was convinced that at his house, Wildman's, he "excited the sort of disgusted distrust that country boys feel for a grass-snake when they stone it to death."[34]

The big finale to the bullying stories comes at the end of the Sherborne chapter of *Autobiography*.

> It was a Sunday afternoon; and after tea, before setting off to chapel, as Littleton and I amused ourselves in our study . . . there were obvious indications of an *emeute* in the passage outside. . . . Finally our sacred study-door itself was thrown open; and the mob outside, full of both malice and fear began pushing one another in. . . .
>
> One single honest blow with the full force of my bony fist at the handsome, derisive countenance of D—Ma. would have done the trick. But in place of such an air-clearing gesture, a contemptible scene followed. . . . Haverings and hoverings ensued, blows that were no blows, hits that were no hits, abuse that did not dare to rise to effective vituperation, combined with a confused barging and hustling and jostling and threatening. . . . But our athletic head of the house . . . intervened at last, and we all drifted off ignobly enough to prepare for evening chapel. . . .
>
> And then it came about as the service proceeded that a strange and startling resolution took possession of me, so that the heart within me was stirred to its depths. I was unable to use my Derbyshire fists, why should I not use my Welsh tongue? . . . This very night I would utter to the whole of Wildman's house my accumulated and long-smouldering apologia! . . . This was to be my last official night in that Saxeon school. And before I left why should I not imitate Owen Glendower and "call up spirits from the vasty deep?" . . .
>
> Well, the moment came; and I stood up. The extraordinary, nay! the unique nature of this revolution held all the boys spell-bound. . . . Beginning lamely enough, but quickly catching my cue, I poured forth a flood of tumultuous speech. Out of my foolishness it came, out of my humiliation, out of my inverted pride. It came literally *de profundis*. . . . I dragged in every single detail they derided me for, I exposed my lacerations, my shames, my idiocies. . . . I referred to the great dilapidated umbrella I placed such stock in. I referred to my obscene fashion of chewing my food with my front teeth. I stripped myself naked before them. Taliesin himself could not

have prophesied to such a tune when he celebrated the procession of his planetary metamorphoses.

> When I sat down there was a moment's dead silence. I did not dare to look at Littleton. But I had not failed. A hullabaloo of applause, puzzled, bewildered, stupefied, confounded, rose up around me. . . . Next morning I was in the sick-room with an attack of my gastric trouble.[35]

This is superb theatre; unfortunately, not the strict and particular truth. Littleton tells the same story but, once again, it comes out differently. He calls the episode "ragging," not bullying, and he does not call Deacon a bully but "an unimaginative well-meaning youth." Furthermore, as Littleton remembers it, not only did brother John ridicule *himself*, he also poked fun at the aggressors, then heaped coals of fire on Deacon by offering to shake hands with him.[36] John Cowper was convinced that his life "would have been different at every point, not only at school but long afterwards, *now* in fact, if I only had the power to stand up to people and speak out, or strike out, boldly."[37] In fact, he *had* struck out most effectively; it was at Sherborne that Powys learned the art of the indirect hit.

Although John says that this dramatic episode "was to be my last official night" at the School, Littleton makes it clear that his brother did not leave Sherborne until much later—two years after Deacon and Puckle had gone. Moreover, Littleton gives an account of why and when John *did* get quit of the hated School.

> In the spring of 1891 my brother John left; he had suffered from dyspeptic trouble for a long time, and one day the doctor had said that to diagnose the cause of his illness properly he would have to use a stomach-pump. The thought of this was more than John could stand; so he sent for me just after our mid-day dinner, and told me that I must run over to Montacute that afternoon and tell them that he must be taken away the first thing next morning. Montacute was ten miles away; but . . . off I went, and told my story so well, that by nine o'clock next morning my father arrived in a hired carriage, and John became an Old Shirburnian.[38]

Powys collapses the two separate incidents in his telling—the end of the bullying and the end of his incarceration at Sherborne become the literal end of the chapter in *Autobiography*. Was this conflation simply to make the whole business more spectacular? It was perhaps not sufficiently dramatic to mention that he was afraid of a stomach pump when he had just compared himself to his heroes, the warrior Glendower and the poet Taliesin. However, in the deepest sense, the merging of episodes had to occur in his mind. He had, in effect, just made the supreme inventive gesture and there was nothing left but to go off. In later years, when he was on the lecture circuit, he would enthral his huge audiences with his theatrical words and gestures and then head immediately for the train to the next city and the next engagement. He was well aware by the time he wrote *Autobiography*, and possibly even by Sherborne, that his was a "play-acting ego"

with the deepest of needs "to heighten the intensity of its normal life-experi-
ence."[39] In any case, who knows best, Johnny or Littleton, what "really happened?" *Pseudologia* belong to a shadow land where the two worlds of fact and
fable collide. Biographical confabulations belong as much to the Powys narrative
as do the facts, but they are not mere cover-ups or grandiose fantasies. It is as if
the fictions, disguises, and denials of the adolescent Johnny (and the adult John)
were saying "I will not let what is strange in me, my mystery, be extinguished by
a world of social and environmental realities." He was always aware that there
were two subjects in his life story: himself and the mysterious other—his soul
companion or daimon. In this story and in all his future stories he sought to
create a borderland space in which both could live.

Powys says truly that his character was "forming, rapidly forming, during
those years at Sherborne."[40] For the rest of his life, Powys used with great efficacy all the defensive measures he learned there. He discovered at this critical period that extreme eccentricity, if not madness, was a way of escape—not only from
bullying, but from everything in the "real" world he feared or detested. He
learned that the spoken word, especially his own spoken word, was the route to
that escape. He says he composed his first poem about Corfe Castle at the age of
ten, had it by heart, and by chanting it at School, "in the wildest and most
terrifying manner," he got what he wanted—"placed at night in the Housekeeper's room, which was the escape from a certain cruel bully that I above all
desired."[41] Johnny had learned gain from illness. Complicating his response to
bullies was his awareness that his own childhood "sadistic" fantasies remained
with him. Although he says he was a coward and went "in deadly fear of several
much smaller boys" at the prep school, his wrists were so strong that he could and
did put boys on the ground. His school report recorded "a decided tendency to
bully." Littleton, too big now to be hung from a bell-rope, nonetheless often got
the brunt of his anger and frustration. Most of the time John kept his destructive
urges to himself, but his "indurated sadistic vice was always seething in the background of my nerves" and more than once on his solitary walks around
Sherborne, he went "looking for something to tear to pieces."[42]

The rearrangement of events and the skimming over of facts in *Autobiography* can also be seen as an imposition of his carefully thought-out psycho/
philosophical beliefs on the happenings of forty years before. By the time he
wrote his autobiography, he had dedicated himself to the helper role, the protector of the pariahs of the world. Powys needed to recreate Puckle as the delicate
one tormented by a bully in a dormitory full of taunting boys, although perhaps
the strangest thing about this story is that far from attempting to deflect the
bully's attentions from Puckle, Johnny used his "inventive skull" to escape being
made a victim himself. He never forgave himself for this "cowardice," as his diary,
rehearsing this long-ago event again and again, makes abundantly clear. There is
therefore another possibility—that he needed to rewrite this part of his past to
suit his own lifelong psychic preoccupation with guilt and retribution. The bully

and the victim were the representatives of his own conflictual inner world, and they could, and did, sometimes sliver the self that became John Cowper Powys. Still, he learned another indispensable defence at Sherborne School. Deacon and Puckle become fictional characters onto which he can project those aspects of self he found unacceptable, the scapegoats for that which he most despised about himself.

The "gastric trouble" was real enough, and seems to have begun as early as the Prep. What also began at Prep, he says, was "a savage greed for sweet-meats" and to his relief he discovered that there was "something in greed as a vice that can mitigate sexual self-indulgence."[43] He extended its supposed efficaciousness to anger as well as masturbation.

> I recollect perfectly how one night after some quarrel with Littleton, and when, too, I was burning with an erotic fever that none of the treasures in my gold and ebony chest could assuage, I tried to overcome the two most formidable of human passions—anger and desire—by abandonment to the vice of pure gluttony. In that one night I ravenously devoured a whole sponge-cake.[44]

It only gave him a stomach ache, but for the first time the constellation that was to play such a large part in his personality and his writings had come together: his sexuality, his "sadism," and his need for punishment. All the stories he tells of the bullying at Sherborne seethe of anger—his own anger. It is as palpable as the rage he felt as a child when he beat the heads off daisies and tried to hang the rival baby brother. If acting out aggression and desire was forbidden, equally unacceptable was cowardice. His evangelical parents' profound belief in hellfire for sins of omission and commission had early on been internalized. Powys says he "cannot remember a time when Conscience was not a trouble to me, ordering me to do what I didn't want to do and to refrain from doing what I wanted to do."[45] A friendly enemy was to tell him that "what Jack needs is a good sound flogging every morning!" Powys wasn't "flogged" physically as a child, unless pouring cold water on him every morning to dampen his erotic urges could be considered as a sadistic act by his father, but since then he had learned "the art of inflicting this flogging on myself."[46] In his imagination, poor Puckle "died"—whether from bullying or from cowardice hardly mattered. The "internal parents" demand punishment, and what fitter punishment for a cowardly bully than internal pain? The Powys family called his lifelong ulcers simply "Jack's pain."

. . . .

Despite his hatred of it, John had been at Sherborne for four and a half years, longer than most of the boys who entered with him at Michaelmas 1886. However, after a week in the school sickroom, John was sent home on 3 April 1891. According to his mother's diary, it was two full weeks before the boy was well enough to "go out in the garden." Joining him there was Theodore. John

Cowper was not the only one who had learned the uses of ill health. Theodore was sent to Sherborne Prep in January 1888, at the age of twelve. He was there for less than a year before he was removed and sent to his grandmother in Weymouth to recuperate from an illness.[47] For rather more than a year Theodore remained at home, taking lessons with Gertrude under the governess Miss Frances Beale. In September 1890, when he was almost fifteen, he was sent to a private school at Aldeburgh. He was evidently much happier there but made little progress scholastically, and by the age of fifteen and a half his haphazard formal education was over.

John Cowper spent the summer at Northwold, his grandparents' home, cramming for the Cambridge Little-Go. After Weymouth, Northwold had always been a favourite holiday destination for the Powys children, and in later years they constantly reminded each other of its joys.

> I always think of that little round pond in the rose-garden Aye! and that makes me think of the green finches nests we used to find . . . in those rose-espaliers & also of the salperglosses which Aunt Dora wd sometimes put into cut glass vases along with verbenas and those little phloxes. Aye! what a life that was & how beautiful that house was. I can see those red leather chairs now, and Manning with manure on his boots & the stable "boy" & Grandfather putting cream into his porridge & looking over the lawn to the Lime-trees—& that big picture of the Livius grandfather & grandmother. Dear dear how it does all return! . . . Aye! & how I can now smell the lemon-verbena on the porch what time grandmother with purple pansies in her bonnet was preparing for church. And that funny game wh stood in the passage upstairs—& the look of the dough & treacle & the taste of those particular rock-cakes.[48]

However, he added in this letter, "the last time I was there was when I was preparing for the Little go . . . but that was not the same thing at all." John could recall very little of that summer except "a vague sense of undisturbed well-being and a peace like that of an unruffled sea." The remark has that curious quality of convalescence and interval so often noted by those who are recovering from a long illness, and there is little doubt that Sherborne had been exactly that for him.

Corpus Christi, Cambridge, was the inevitable choice for the firstborn son, partly because it was the family college, and partly because it had been, and Charles Francis assumed it still was, a stronghold of Evangelicalism. The Powyses always relied on family precedent or connections, and C. F. was related by marriage to a Corpus Fellow, Henry Ernest Fanshawe.[49] He also knew the tutor Charles Moule, who was the son of a friend, the Reverend Henry Moule of Fordington, Dorchester. C. F. would probably have been unaware of the feud between Moule, an ardent Evangelical, and Fanshawe, a leader in the movement against the dominance of Low Church Evangelicalism. When John entered

Corpus, Fanshawe had just replaced Moule as tutor, but by then the College's reputation had sunk very low. It was undistinguished socially and academically with few undergraduates and even fewer B.A.'s.[50]

Although John was by then nineteen, his father took him up and bought the furnishings for his room. The sense of continuity pleased the young man.

> They were such objects as seemed to me to bring all Stalbridge Rectory—from which *his* father had taken *him* to Corpus—into my room. And I have no doubt that this yet older gentleman had been himself in his day brought by *his* parent to this college of the generations from yet another rectory!

His rooms looked out on the Old Court whose walls at that time were covered with ivy "which my father always averred *his* father had planted," and he felt he was living in "some enchanted ruin in a fairy-like forest of old romance."[51]

The close tie with his brother was broken when Littleton stayed on at Sherborne[52] and John began to reach out, albeit tentatively, to new friends. He said that in those days there were three sets of students—the fast set, the pietistic evangelical set, and the athletic set. Despite his raw awareness of what he had suffered at the Big School because of his total unathleticism, he immediately took up the sport of rowing "simply and solely because all my days I had heard my father tell stories of his rowing." He recognized how ludicrous this was but attributed it to "the timorous conservatism of my deepest character."[53] He not only rowed, but joined the rowing society. Indeed, despite his insistence that "there were very few people I knew at Cambridge; and I did not desire to know more,"[54] the Corpus records suggest the opposite. He was a member of a play-reading society, the debating society, the chess club, the boat club and the rugby club. The "Gravediggers" was a reasonably serious society that met to read the plays of Shakespeare; however, two at least of these were undisguised social clubs. The chess club restricted its members to "athletes of some kind," and was more involved in playing whist than chess. There are two extant photos of the "Fireflies," a small dining club, and Powys is in both photos, looking not unhappy. Both Littleton and John are in another photo, taken in December 1893 of the "Rugby XV." John looks self-conscious in his rugger cap and sweater, as well he might.[55]

The self-confessed solitary was equally sociable outside the college. His mother's diary and the few letters of hers extant often refer to "dear John's engagements"—tennis with the Phelips daughters, dances at the "big houses" nearby, holidays with the hospitable Shirley cousins at Oxford, weekend visits with college friends to their country estates.[56] It may be that John was simply discovering the protection of masks, learning that "wisdom" is made up of "paradoxes and contradictions, of shifts, compromises, transformations, adaptations, adjustments, balancings, calculated blindness, artful avoidances, premeditated foolishnesses, cultivated simplicities!"[57]

Formal education impinged no more on his consciousness at Cambridge than it had at Sherborne; furthermore, he found Corpus singularly lacking in imaginative, poetical, or intellectual students to converse with. In the absence of any young Phaedruses, he "beat up out of my own crazy wits" all the poetical idealism he craved. Just as once he harangued his brothers and sisters with impassioned sermons, before his first term was over he was inviting "anyone who liked to turn up to come to my rooms and listen to a weird prophetic denunciation I had composed, entitled 'Corpus Unveiled.'"[58] Mostly it was "anonymous pariahs" who came to these "crazy monologues" and thus began in earnest Powys's singular ability to attract acolytes with impassioned words. He himself recognized that it was at this time that he "began to develop my gift for pierrot-like oratory."[59]

Other nascent personality characteristics emerged at Corpus. One was what Powys called his "asceticism" and, in a franker moment, his "self-persecution." Instead of walking alone as was his preference, or with someone with whom he could have an interesting conversation, he would deliberately choose as the companions of his walks "the particular young persons of my acquaintance who were the least esteemed in the college."[60] Fond of sweets at Sherborne, he now became abstemious to the extreme in his diet. As so often later in life, this vein of austerity with its "fussy, pharisaic exactions" made life equally difficult for those around him who had to endure it. And it had its humorous side, as he was aware.

> I can recall, during one of our walks—and as always with these notable occasions when I made a fool of myself I can see the very spot where I made the remark—gravely observing, after half an hour's intense silence, that I thought I might continue to allow myself *one egg* for breakfast. To such a conclusion as this—and there were not a few of them—Littleton would always reply by the same indulgent and not in the least quizzical stare, opening his mouth a little and his large grey-blue eyes a good deal, and wrinkling his forehead.[61]

Many of these exactions were harmless enough, but they were the forerunners of something more serious. Leaving any "especially delicious" porridge for the cleaner may not have thrilled the servant, but obviously gave Powys some sense of self-worthiness that he desperately needed. He was into his twenties but, as he freely admits, all these tendencies arose from the desire to be in his father's "good graces." Parsimony and abstention were "the shortest cut to this end."[62] His self-denial extended to his "deepest and most congenial vice" which suddenly vanished while he was at Corpus. Maybe it was the endless walking that did the trick—it was a much-favoured prescription in Victorian sex manuals to lessen "self-abuse." Connected with this dispensation, something of greater importance occurred at Cambridge. Walking until he was exhausted not only kept his hands "out of plackets" (as he put it), it also temporarily put his fear (in whatever form it took) into abeyance. Long walks were to become daily essentials for Powys.

> The truth is, it is as a rule only by constant physical movement, even when alone with Nature, that I can escape those self-created, self-torturing incar-

nations of Fear, which, like that luckless stick thrown into the lake in Derbyshire, rise up from Hell to torment me.[63]

It was on these lonely walks on the flat country roads around Cambridge that he developed the idea of "sensation-thought," which he sensed was "the deepest and most essential secret of my life."

> The field-dung upon my boots, the ditch-mud plastered thick, with little bits of dead grass in it, against the turned-up ends of my trousers, the feel of my oak-stick "Sacred" . . . the salty taste of half-dried sweat upon my lips, the delicious swollenness of my fingers, the sullen sweet weariness of my legs, the indescribable happiness of my calm, dazed, lulled, wind-drugged, air-drunk spirit, were all, after their kind, a sort of thinking, though of *exactly what*, it would be very hard for me to explain. Did I share at such times the sub-thoughts, or over-thoughts, that the old earth herself has, as she turns upon her axeis, or that the vast volume of the ocean has, as his tide gathers along his beaches or draws back hoarsely into his gulfs?
>
> They were at any rate what might be called sensation-thoughts. They had to do with the impact of the wind on my face and with all those vague, obscure half-memories that the wind can bring with it, full of half-realized impressions from days far off, days perhaps *so* far-off that they actually belong to previous reincarnations. . . . Even as I try to seize upon them they dissolve and melt away; but in their vanishing they leave a lovely residue, a mysterious satisfaction, that seems to well up from the inner being of old posts, old heaps of stones, old haystacks thatched with straw. . . . What gave me these sensations seemed to be some mysterious "rapport" between myself and these things. It was like a sudden recognition of some obscure link, some remote identity, between myself and these objects. Posts, palings, hedges, heaps of stones—they were part of my very soul.[64]

Powys was a firm believer in the Romantic creed that "the Child is father of the man"; that his taste, intelligence, philosophy, and character had been "created at Shirley, enlarged at Weymouth and Dorchester; and then had been finally branded into me—by harrowing necessity—at Sherborne."[65] It annoyed him to confess that it was not until Cambridge that he became conscious of "what has now come to be my most obstinate cult, I mean the conscious drinking up of all the various sense-impressions which the Self receives as it embraces the Not-Self."[66] It could be argued that this sensuous response to nature did not come into play until he was an adult because it was a learned response, acquired to mitigate the worst effects of his terrors. Learning to escape the unknown fear by "Sensation-Thoughts" while walking was Powys's ultimate defence mechanism. It was, he said, "the conjuring trick by which life can be adequately handed."[67]

Although the idea of connecting both with "the old earth herself" and perhaps even with "remote ancestors" went far beyond his father's simple love of walking and nature, it was close enough to family mores and traditions to be acceptable to his sense of attachment both to his parents and to his brothers and sisters. Montacute was still "home" and he returned there at every available opportunity while he was at Cambridge. There were now eleven children (all with nicknames) in the Powys clan. In 1893, John Cowper (Johnny) was twenty, Littleton (Tom) was nineteen, Theodore (Bob) almost eighteen, Gertrude (Gert) was fifteen, Eleanor (Nellie) thirteen, Albert (Bertie) eleven, Marian (May) ten, Llewelyn (Lulu) eight, Philippa (Katie) six, William (Willie) four, and Lucy a baby. The family position in the village as well as their minor gentry status tended to isolate them from the rest of the world, and the parents encouraged this sense of a "house set on a hill."[68] Over the years, the closeness became more than the usual family intimacy. John thought that the "grotesque singularity" of the attachment they felt for each other qualified them as an "insane family."[69] Littleton was to write that "though in tastes and interests no two members of the family were alike, in affection for each other they were bound together by bonds which nothing in this world could ever loosen."[70] The boys would bring school friends home, of course. These were made welcome enough but always made somehow to feel outsiders. One indignant young man felt that to see them gathered in one place was to see a Powys phalanx: "It stood there blasphemous against the solidarity of the human race."[71] This all-enveloping clannishness was broken into the year before John left Cambridge. On April 12, 1893, the second-born daughter, Eleanor, died suddenly at the age of thirteen. Nellie was a delicate, talented girl, full of poetic fancies, with whom JCP felt particularly close. She died an agonizing death from peritonitis,[72] following appendicitis that the old family doctor tried to treat with leeches. Most of the children were at home when it occurred and they remembered the event with startling vividness for the rest of their lives. In that large house, where everything had been stable and predictable, they suddenly fragmented into isolated groups, like a shield wall that had mysteriously collapsed. At the time, Llewelyn was a "small child drifting in and out through the tall French windows" but many years later he wrote about the event in that far-off spring.

> It was as though the countryside was under some strange enchantment that year. The cuckoo began calling before ever March was out and by the beginning of April the gorse was already filled with linnets' nests, some of them with young birds nearly fledged. The smell of gorse in the sun! Could there be any smell more reminiscent of the life-giving earth? That particular scent has haunted me ever since—a whiff of it anywhere at any time, and I am back again bird's-nesting with that child who has now lain under ground for close on thirty years.
>
> An evening came, a spring evening full of the promise of summer, when, as we played at hay-making at the end of the tennis lawn, cutting the fresh long grass and setting it out in little heaps to dry, she complained of a hurt in her side. . . . Four days went by and she was dead.

Llewelyn remembered that during this time his mother quietly continued her duties. "She was in the dining-room at the appointed hour, in the nursery, in the school-room, her face articulate as a cry in a frost-bound forest, though never a tear fell."[73] It was only after her own death in 1914 that any of the children learned what Mary Cowper was thinking as she went her rounds. They read the entries in her laconic diary.

> 23 March: John comes home
> 10 April: J. dined at Montacute House
> 13 April: May has a bad cold
> 15 April: John goes to Sherborne with Miss Harding to see the sports
> 16 April: My beloved Nellie taken ill in the night of Saturday
> 17 April: Sent for the doctor Very feverish and wandering
> 18 April: Nellie very ill & feverish
> 19 April: My darling worse. Dr Liddon called in to consult
> 20 April: My pretty Nellie taken to her Saviour at quarter to 11
> 21 April: "Thy will be done"
> 22 April: My pretty pretty Nellie My beloved child

Nothing has been entered for the next week but across the pages for April 25 to 29, she has written: "I cannot remember much about these days."[74]

In August Llewelyn and Katie came down with scarlet fever, then Lucy, then little Willie. At that time scarlet fever was still a potentially lethal disease. A few weeks later, May became very ill with a pain in her side that her mother must have feared was another case of appendicitis. This time a doctor was called promptly and came often. Katie was in quarantine six weeks, and Llewelyn was "upstairs" for almost two months. Eventually all the children recovered, but it was an anxious period. Yet another break with the past and the unity of the family occurred that autumn. Six months after her child's death, Mary's father also died. This death meant, amongst other things, the end to the idyllic summers they had spent in Norfolk. Mary's spinster sisters moved into Norwich Close, and Powys did not see Northwold again for another thirty-five years.

John says that it was "taken for granted that as the grandson of two clergymen, and the great-grandson of at least two more, I should, as the phrase ran, 'enter into Orders.'"[75] It was probably some time in the months following Nellie's death that the young man told his parents he would not follow in his father's footsteps and become a clergyman. To John's surprise, his father made "not the faintest protest."

"He, then in 1901, was twenty-eight, and unknown, except to his University Extension lecture audiences. He had written nothing except lecture-syllabuses and a little verse. But he had complete faith in his own genius."
—Louis Marlow, *Welsh Ambassadors*.

"Well I remember, O my sweet,/How first beside your native wood/I found you, like a flower complete/In perfect flush of maidenhood"
—JCP, *Poems*, "To MA"

"the formidable phenomenon of that Powys phalanx"   —Louis Marlow, *Swan's Milk*.

"It was one of those early Victorian houses with a slate roof, and sash windows, which seem to have been made for homely comfortable country life."

—Littleton Powys, *The Joy of It*.

CHAPTER THREE

THE EXTENSION LECTURER
1894-1901

P OWYS LEFT CORPUS IN JUNE 1894 WITH A SECOND-CLASS DEGREE IN history and "not the least idea" how he was going to earn his living. He applied to an employment agency with the Dickensian name of Gabbitas and Thring and totally by chance, or so it seemed, he fell into a life of lecturing. His first position was to give a few lessons a week at two girls' schools in Hove, Sussex.[1] He established himself in lodgings above a grocer's shop in Southwick and, with little to do beyond six hours of class work a week, proceeded to educate himself in literature, reading right through the "English Worthies" and the "English Men of Letters" series.[2]

A rhythmic pattern was becoming evident in Powys's psychic life: a period of turmoil succeeded by an interval of relative calm. Just as the confused feelings and painful conflicts of early childhood were temporarily suspended during the Dorchester years, so the tumult of adolescent sexuality he experienced at Sherborne receded while he was at Corpus. Cambridge, like Dorchester, seems to have been another "breathing space" for him, a second latency. Nature can sometimes be kind to those who worship her, especially when that veneration is combined with exhausting walks and cold baths. But this protective carapace of what he called his "poetic idealism," while it gave necessary shelter to the vulnerable aspects of his personality, must have been exceedingly fragile, for suddenly it shattered. For the next nine years he "gave complete rein to so many manias and aberrations that those who knew me best must often have wondered how far in the direction of a really unbalanced mind I was destined to go."[3]

External circumstances were partly to blame. The move away from protracted childhood was particularly hard for these protected Powys children. Their cousin, Mary Johnson, wrote bluntly that "they were an unusually close-knit family, at the same time self-centred and slow to mature, so that most of them found the problems of adult life difficult."[4] Witnessing a child being "taken away" would have roused all John's old Shirley fears.[5] Short but revealing entries in his diaries of many years later give the meaning of that death to him. He remembered being in his father's dressing room and hearing through the wall Nellie cry

out to her mother, "Why don't you say Good-bye to me?" when she was dying.[6]
He remembered his father's response to the death: "When my sister died [he]
took all his sons walking walking walking leaving my mother alone in the
house."[7] Even the scarlet fever incident must have disturbed the young man who
so badly needed the protection of the family. While the three sick children were
in quarantine, the four older ones were sent away from May until October 1893.
Gertrude and Bertie were sent to Seaton, John Cowper and Littleton to
Weymouth. A necessary precaution felt like a banishment. Littleton wrote about
the Weymouth interlude and in his circumspect way indicated that even then
"John's mind was full of various problems." Poor Littleton—despite his devotion
to his eldest brother, it must have been a difficult ten weeks: "He would say to
me, 'You never think, Littleton: why don't you think? You must think'; but he
never gave me any idea as to what I was to think about."[8]

The mother, centre of that childhood universe, was worn out with nursing
and anxiety and in deep mourning for her beloved father and young daughter.
She continued her domestic rounds efficiently and tearlessly but must have
seemed, to her more sensitive children, in some way to have withdrawn herself.
Her eldest son's decision not to enter the Church would have been a further blow
to Mary Cowper, though it may not have come as a total surprise. Possibly both
parents by then had realized that his particular personality was totally unsuited
to such a profession. Powys said he went back to his last year at Cambridge "without the problem of my future career receiving a thought from anyone." However
casually he stated this, it is very possible that he saw this "indulgence" in reality
a proof that his parents did not care about his future or about him.

The close family ties had both protected and inhibited him. Suddenly on his
own in a strange town on the south coast, he became aware not only that the
bonds were finally loosening, but that he had no idea what he was to do with this
new freedom. As he embarked on his first real independence, all hell broke loose.
As well as external events, internal factors contributed to an eruption of buried
impulses and tormenting thoughts. At Cambridge, his long rambles brought him
"mystical ecstasies," but now on his solitary walks, instead of finding rapture at
the sight of branches "as they made a delicate tracery against the sky," a "Demon
within me" would torment him with "revolting images."[9] Even at this early
period, John Cowper's mind was predominantly an image-making one, and this
talent would one day serve the novelist well. For the time being, it only caused
him suffering. Immersed in the poetry of William Cowper, he would walk along
a certain picturesque road, thinking it was just the kind of road that would have
pleased the poet, and all he would see was a road strewn with "bullock's blood
and black snails!" Cowper, a distant Powys relative, being insane for extended
periods of his life, would not have been surprised by this hallucination. Nor is it
after all so odd that John began to think of this ancestor at a time when he was
concerned for his own sanity. The Powyses were only too aware that there was a
tendency to psychotic illness on the Johnson/Cowper side of the family.[10]

The other torment was his own body. At Southwick, Powys was "for ever struggling to make my real life correspond to a mental and sensual fastidiousness that was an appalling tyranny." Unfortunately, his real life consisted of the "little necessities of nature" which "just because I desired to imagine a life entirely free from them and was for ever trying to *think them away*, were always imping-ing irrelevantly upon me." He recounts the pleasure he took in crossing a cer-tain bridge, which he considered "symbolic and sympathetic." He intended to give this bridge a romantic name but one day the "little necessities of nature" forced him to urinate on it, and from then on he could only think of it as the Pissing Bridge.[11] Possibly every extremely sensitive young person sooner or later is confronted by the conflict between his "poetic idealism" and his reality, par-ticularly the reality of his body. For Powys, this particular battle was never resolved. In a late letter to a young friend, he admitted, "The deepest mania I have is what I call ANTI-NARCISSISM, though I only have invented that term and you won't find it in Freud or Adler or Jung. It means a neurotic shrinking, a maniacal shrinking from any thought or contemplation of myself as a PERSON WITH A BODY. The odd thing is that I'm a terrific one for SENSATION, but I like their medium to be non-existent." He added, "this peculiarity I inherit from my mother."[12]

He did not stay long in lodgings. His idealism extended to houses, and soon he began searching for his "Platonic idea of a house." He thought he found it in a "French-looking house," which appealed to him because it was "hidden from all the rest of the world, but revealed to the railway passengers who travelled, and there were not few of them, between Worthing and Brighton"[13]—a rather neat aphorism for his own developing personality. He was soon dissuaded by relatives and friends and instead rented, for £40 a year, a farmhouse on the outskirts of Offham, West Sussex. He moved into Court House in the early months of 1895,[14] but finding it difficult to manage alone, went home to Montacute in July. His mother arranged for the widow of their former gardener to keep house for him.[15]

> Mrs. Curme was an old woman then; but she remained extremely hand-some, and her manners were those rather of a lady-in-waiting than a ser-vant. She was just the person for me at that juncture, when in my crazy folly I was carrying half the milder aberrations, mentioned in "Krafft-Ebing," on my obstinate shoulders.[16]

Psychopathia Sexualis, which only appeared in English in 1892, three years before this, might have frightened any young man worried about what Krafft-Ebing called an "hereditary taint." Powys may have wondered if he was as "degenerate" as some of the patients who appeared in the psychoneurologist's lurid case histories of sexual perversions. Whether or not it was the power of sug-gestion, what had begun as harmless eccentricities and rituals now developed into something slightly more serious. It was during the summer of 1891 before he went up to Cambridge that he acquired a dislike of certain fabrics. This distaste now became an aversion. He couldn't bear to eat off a tablecloth and it was "hateful" to him to be in contact with bedding. To this fairly harmless obsession, he added several more. He became a compulsive hand-washer and would stand outside doors "calling to people to open them for me lest by contact with the handle I should make my hands dirty." His diet became increasingly eccentric. At Sherborne he had learned to assuage his "erotic fever" by the primitive but effective defence of greediness for sponge cake and apricot paté, but as he grew older and the "violence of my erotic obsession increased," this "lust for sweet-meats" lost its efficacy.[17] His landlord at Southwick, a ship's chandler with a shop full of provisions, must have been slightly bemused to be asked to provide the young man only with "great bowls of bread and milk." His decision to become a vegetarian, made at the time of Nellie's death, can hardly be called an aberration, but he imposed his fastidiousness on others. When he moved to Court House, he would not allow meat in the house, so old Mrs. Curme had to console herself by drinking hot beer. When he acquired yet another "mania" (as he referred to it)—insisting on "changing my shirt and all my underclothes every day"—it was of course Mrs. Curme who did the laundry for him, as well as opening doors for the "perambulating Pilate."[18]

Despite the "the gad-fly grubs of neurosis under the skin"[19] which must have made everyday existence rather trying, he performed his teaching duties satisfactorily and continued to read omnivorously. Using the £200 his father gave him to furnish Court House, he bought leather-bound quartos of Dryden, Virgil, Milton, Beaumont and Fletcher, and Baskerville's Latin authors. But, as he says, "as has happened before in human psychology, correct opinions continued to run parallel with secret vices,"[20] and he began to frequent pornographic shops. He found one in Eastbourne that had a private lending library of "fantastical erotica." He would bring the books home to read, carefully concealing the "dubious matter" from Mrs. Curme when she came into his study to say goodnight. Fortunately the old housekeeper never presented herself without knocking and always asked permission to address him. Before taking his erotica to bed with him, he would read Swinburne to her and then ask her how she liked it. "'Mr. John,' said Mrs. Curme gravely; 'I do thank 'ee, Mr. John, from my poor heart. It does me good to hear the dear Lord's name mentioned so frequent!'" After saying goodnight, upon leaving she would "always walk a few steps backward, making as she did so not exactly a curtsy, but a sort of obeisance of her whole aged frame."[21] As well as pornography, he also tried prostitutes, and at one point was sleeping with "three sisters of the same family," one of whom was only twelve, in a Brighton flop-house. Even the Madame was impelled to remark, "you like them young."[22] He gave that up because, to his chagrin, "my desire, directly I became friendly with the girl herself, changed into a sort of ideal attachment."[23] John Cowper knew what the trouble was, or at least he knew by the time he wrote *Autobiography* in 1934. His "poetic idealism" was contending with his bodily needs, and more specifically, with the violent upsurge of his sexual needs. It was difficult for him to know how to deal with what he called his "fastidious eroticism." He began searching for a "fantasy of femininity, a kind of Platonic essence of sylph-hood . . . the state of being-a-Sylph carried to such a limit of tenuity as almost to cease to have any of the ordinary feminine attributes."[24] Many of the ritualistic compulsions of this period seem to have been developed to bolster his own internal arguments that he is too "fastidious" for normal love and sexuality. Masturbating (appropriately called in those days "the convenient vice") while indulging in a sexual fantasy about imaginary sylphs seemed to be the answer.

Powys gives the impression that the emotional upheaval and phobic reactions that were occurring at this time were uniquely his own, and so they were. However, many of his particular behavioral responses, beliefs, and attitudes had a social and cultural context. So too did the stories he began to write at this time. Powys was catapulted out of the protective cocoon of family, school, and college into the last tumultuous years of the nineteenth century, a period when it seemed to many that all the laws governing identity, class, and behaviour were breaking down. The late Victorian, Karl Pearson, founder of modern statistical theory and professor of eugenics, saw the "two great problems of modern social life" as "the problem of women and the problem of labour."[25] The Powyses had grown up in a mid-Victorian time warp, but Montacute village was the home, not exclusively of the squire and the vicar, but of the workers of the Ham Hill quarries above the town. The family could not be totally oblivious of the distress of the unemployed and chronically poor; indeed, C. F. *was* aware of the poverty of most of his parishioners and responded with charity and prayers. The "problem of women" was less apparent to the family on the hill, or to the male members of it, but the suffragist movement, the feminist reform legislation of the 1880s, and the "New Woman" were all challenging the traditional institutions of work, marriage, and the family. Father Powys may not have noticed, but England's patriarchal system was in the process of being dismantled.

The inevitable shoring up of defences against these profound changes was a noticeable, sometimes virulent, antifeminism and a concomitant promotion of the idea of "manliness." Politicians and medical men warned of the moral and psychological dangers of the new order and psychiatrists identified a new kind of male neurotic, the "borderliner": young men from the upper and middle classes, freed from the controls of a patriarchal society and uncertain of their role. A popular medical text, *The Borderlands of Insanity*, warned that these young men would find their minds "first stiffen from disuse and then rot from the decay of a vitality which is never properly brought into play."[26] Pronouncements about virility, degeneracy, effeminacy were abundant in this period; the not-so-coded message as usual was that the degeneracy was caused by "the solitary vice." However, avant-garde male artists, writers, and intellectuals were also challenging the entire system of patriarchy—its class structures and roles, its compulsory heterosexuality and marriage, and its cultural authority—and they too were roundly castigated. Maxe Nordau, physician, journalist, social critic, and defender of morality, famously opined in 1895 that "degenerates are not always criminals, prostitutes, anarchists, or outright lunatics, they are often writers and artists."[27] Powys decided he must be "a weak, cowardly, fastidious degenerate,"[28] and consequently, perhaps on the basis that he might as well be hung for a sheep as a lamb, he joined forces with "they artists." To that end he set about establishing a coterie, gathering around him a diverse group of men he called his "Circle." They met in pairs or as a group for long walks on the Sussex downs and coast and then repaired to a pub for boisterous discussions that ranged through the centuries of literature, religion, sex, art, politics, philosophy. It was a veritable Brighton School of Peripatetics.

Shortly after arriving in Sussex he was introduced to Alfred de Kantzow, and immediately Powys was "linked with hoops of steel" to this man who was over seventy when they met. They shared "ruminative, almost mystical walks" and on them de Kantzow would quote his poetry, talk about his early days in the East Indian company and his marriage of forty years. Why Powys devoted five pages to this man in *Autobiography*, other than for the sheer joy he takes (and gives) in painting a memorable portrait of this trampish old aristocrat, is baffling. For that matter, why did he remain de Kantzow's "devoted henchman" for nearly ten years? It was, Powys says, his need for "hero-worship" of "a great man" but he then goes on to make it clear that it was his own heroic efforts that got the man "the public recognition that he deserved." Powys was of course responding to Carlyle's call to take "the great ones of the earth" as models for imitation,[29] but, not seldom, those who look for a messiah also dream of becoming one, even as they deny it. Possibly the point of his story, and perhaps of his friendship, was that de Kantzow had a forlorn need for success as a poet and for public acknowledgement, whereas Powys wished to impress on himself and his readers that he had "not the remotest interest in my career," and indeed "nourished some weird Saturnian contempt for the judgments of men."[30] To prove this, he lavished more effort, he says, to get de Kantzow's poems published than ever he did on his own. This is nothing less than the truth since it was his cousin Ralph Shirley who undertook to get Powys's first two volumes of poetry published and it was his father who paid for them.

A Cambridge friend, Thomas Henry Lyon, was another member of this seaside Lyceum. Powys considered Lyon his most intimate friend at Corpus, although they had little in common. Lyon was three years older and had already served two years as an apprentice architect when he went up to Cambridge. Small, with delicate, almost girlish features, he was self-assured and sociable—in short, everything that Powys was not. At university, Harry's "unequalled charms had held him spellbound," as it held many young men and boys throughout Lyon's life. Now, they engaged in such "long, intricate, and I might say furious arguments, that the delicate charm, full of all manner of chivalrous nuances, of our earlier contact was bruised." Powys told a correspondent late in life that he tried hard once to become "a homo." It may be that much of the ambivalence that now emerged between them had a sexual frisson to it, but Harry was, nonetheless, an indispensable member of the circle. Both had strong convictions, and their arguments helped them, "not so much in the direction of modifying our basic assurances as of clarifying them to ourselves."[31]

One of the most important of these new friends was the slightly older John William Williams, whom John nicknamed "The Catholic." Williams had also been to Corpus but had fled to Oxford when he converted to Catholicism. They would meet in inns on the days Powys lectured in Eastbourne, quote at each other "lines in Shakespeare, in Homer, in Dante, in Milton" and spend the hours in excited discussion of their "favourite authors from Rabelais down to Dickens."[32] It was Williams who kindled Powys's lifelong flirtation with Catholicism.

> J. W. W. was the first real *Papist*—that race of beings regarded by my father as in some especially close conspiracy with the Devil—whom I had ever spoken to in my whole life; and I was simply spell-bound by a *wisdom* that seemed like a deep rich earth full of divine nourishment. . . . My nature at that time simply craved this kind of nourishment—something with a real tradition behind it, where the myths I loved, and the ballad-poetry I loved, went down deep into the soil of history.[33]

This "scholastic thinker" instilled in Powys a "passion for the great gnostic heresies," the doctrines of which Powys would incorporate so successfully into his later romances. For now, Williams provided an intellectual justification for the tentative move away from his father's evangelical religion.

> His favourite word—long before Einstein—for you must remember I am describing events that took place ere the nineteenth century was over—was the word "Relative." By the help of this magic word J. W. W. would evoke a body of rich and subtle thought that served as a sort of covered bridge between conservative orthodoxy and the most rebellious modernism.[34]

The fourth member of this charmed circle was Dr. Bernard Price O'Neill, who became Powys's "best and life-long friend." O'Neill was seven years older and a qualified physician when they met. O'Neill immensely extended Powys's literary and artistic knowledge, particularly of the fin de siècle. Powys says that Bernie, as he was known, was "an adept in the extremist pages of all the Cagliostros of modern literature. He knew every drawing of Beardsley, every quip of Whistler, every paradox of Wilde."[35] John was able to "confide quite freely" to this medical man about his various aberrations, and O'Neill was "invariably sympathetic with the most convoluted turns and twists of my perversities." Eventually Bernie became a close friend of the entire Powys family. His nonmoral outlook had a benign effect on these morally constipated children, and he opened up the closed world of the Montacute vicarage to the realities of the new world that was beginning at the end of the nineteenth century. John maintained that O'Neill "supplied our Powysian life-cult—so rustic, so earth-bound—with overtones and undertones drawn from the erudition we suspected, the popular slang we avoided, the art we despised."[36]

No four friends could have been more dissimilar in personality and training but each of these men gave Powys something he craved, not least intellectual companionship and the reassuring bond of masculine identity. Perhaps Powys saw them as the equivalent of the numerous London male writers' clubs flourishing at this time—a rural Rhymers Club or the Sussex branch of the Athenaeum.[37] Certainly he was very proud of his circle, although on the face of it was a rather pathetic little group. One seventy-year-old poet manqué; one unemployed, congenitally deaf medical man; one failed Catholic priest; one homosexual architect—gathered round one phobic who scratched a living lecturing at girls' schools. Sceptical outsiders twitted Powys for inflating the literary significance of this small assembly of friends and for seeing himself as the pivot of the group. It is the case that while later he had every opportunity to become a member of any of the distinguished literary circles that grew up during his lifetime, Powys avoided them, possibly preferring to be the proverbial large frog in a small pond.

This small band of brothers soon found their way into stories that Powys now began to write. He brought all of these "disreputable puppets" into a book, and the writing of this eased his heart, and "more than my heart."[38] He gives no further details in his autobiography of this "interminable and totally unpublishable story." However, in March 1954, the bookseller George Sims knocked at Powys's door in Corwen, Wales, and for £125 carried off an attic-ful of early manuscripts and notebooks. Eventually these unpublished pieces found their way into three archives: the University of Texas at Austin, Syracuse University, and the National Library of Wales. There they have lain, largely ignored, much as they had moldered in their author's attic over the years. Internal evidence indicates that they were written while he was living at Court House.[39]

Two of these segments, which he calls his "Bedlam compositions," deal directly with his "Krafft-Ebing fantasies" of this period.[40] Both are unnamed and unpaginated, however the first begins "How Philip Warton came to Godbarrow." It is more a series of disconnected vignettes than a story. The Catholic appears as Cousin Taxeater, de Kantzow as Mr. de Woztnak, Harry Lyon as Hugh Bigod, and Bernie O'Neill as Christopher Touzeler. Also present is Powys himself in the guise of Philip Warton—the first of many Powys-heroes to appear in his novels.[41] Philip Warton is an "eccentric young man" who has been working as a journalist but who has come to Godbarrow at the invitation of his college friend Hugh Bigod, to "realise his poetic tendencies in peace and become . . . a second Wordsworth or Wm Cowper." There are three main strands to the story: Philip meeting the Runnymede children, Philip talking with new male friends, and Philip attending an orgy. The children Warton encounters, Ora-Ray and Littleton, are clearly modeled on Powys's sister Nellie (Eleanora), who would have been the same age as Ora—fifteen—had she lived, and his much younger brother Llewelyn, who, like Ora's brother, was eleven in 1895. There is a charming description of the children's rural pursuits, bird-nesting and tree-climbing, which closely echoes those childhood activities at Montacute.[42] Rather less beguiling are the descriptions of the "narrator" peeping on the sleeping girl, admiring her "dark wavy hair all loose on the pillow," "her fresh red lips a little open," and "the whitest slenderest limbs in the world." This particular storyline peters out after the hero rescues the children from drowning when they lose their balance and fall into the dam pool. There follow several chapters describing the protracted "symposia" held on Brighton Beach and elsewhere, presumably a pastiche of the many discussions Powys had with his circle of friends.

The last strand in the story is the most carefully worked out. Philip meets the Squire of Godbarrow (his friend Hugh's father) and a "poor relation" the Squire has adopted. This is Annette, a young girl "under sixteen" who is "a slender creature" with "large childish eyes" and "dainty ankles peeping out from under her short print skirt." Later, Philip and his friends are invited to the Squire's manor for dinner. After a good deal of talk and "brimming glasses of Canary sack" they are joined by seven beautiful little boys and seven girls who troop in and begin dancing wildly. After more wine, the men throw off their clothes and "soon that Old Georgian hall was the scene of an orgy." Taxeater and Hugh retire with the loveliest of the little boys, while Touzeler, sitting on the floor, leers up at the little girls' "quivering thighs and the demesnes that there adjacent lie."

> As for Philip he stood stock still in the middle of the room—absolutely naked—his head thrown back his arms stretched out and his eyes shining with an almost supernatural light as one who was mad with joy. The Squire hesitated no longer before them all and in the eyes of his own son to throw the slender Annette upon the floor and to pluck with brutality and cruel violence the flower he had so long toyed with.

One can understand why Powys called this "totally unpublishable"; less understandable why he kept it for sixty years. Most of it is appallingly badly written. Even at this early stage in his writing career, he was more comfortable with description than dialogue, but his descriptions are ponderous in the extreme. The oyster-sellers on Brighton beach are "loud-voiced sons and daughters of Nereus" who offer "the spoils of their watery hunting grounds in exchange for certain mineral appendages of the land." Nonetheless, there is some rather more lively writing, an example of which is an account of a meeting of the Ladies' Intellectual Discussion Society. Among those present is Mrs. Swinksby Swinks, "a large plump woman with weak watery eyes, a double chin, breasts bigger than the udders of any ordinary cow." In her right hand she holds a little volume of Matthew Arnold's *Culture and Anarchy* and in her left a smelling bottle. The president is Mrs. Body Smith, who "had been head-mistress of a large private School and was possessed of a smattering of the sciences, a few chips and fringes of the Arts, six or seven Latin words, Herbert Spencers Principle of Sociology, and an English translation of a French translation of a German Compendium entitled Sceptical Thought after the Time of David Hume."

This derisive sketch echoes *Punch* parodists of the time who satirized as "literary dames" the women's professional clubs that had sprung up in protest of being excluded from men's clubs. Powys spent the rest of his life giving lectures to just such women's societies, and at this period he was dependent financially on the very headmistresses he describes here—another reason for putting the manuscripts into a drawer. Other morsels of rancor come even closer to the bone (or home), and perhaps closer to the hidden anguish that must be written out.

> See the Parson preaching on self-control and going home to sow the seeds of his fifteenth offspring and drink the port upon which poor pale Mrs. Parson casts such longing eyes as she says in the oft-repeated formula "No thank you my dear I am quite well and you are tired after your service."

In a second narrative which looks to have been written at this same time, the orgy theme is dropped but Powys's fantasies about children are explored in more detail. Philip Warton becomes Philip Davenant in this next tale,[43] and like the first Philip, has come to the country to discover himself as a poet. He meets a young girl, called Ray Runnymede, and falls passionately in love with her. Powys's use and re-use of the same names for his characters and places in his early writings causes confusion but also a strange sense of shifting implication. A character in one fragment shares the same name as a character in another, but with disconcerting differences in personality. It is as if he were following through to its conclusion a thought that might be unacceptable if stated clearly. In the Warton tale, it is the old Squire of Godbarrow who rapes Annette. In a disturbing twist, Powys makes this latest Philip the Squire of Godbarrow. Although this Ray is even younger than the first Ray, she is another tomboy, exulting in the natural world.

In one scene Ray and Philip Davenant walk through the spring woods, the child innocently collecting insects while he has "the strange half-sick excitement of a lover." In another fragment, Philip and Ray stretch out next to each other in the long grass, and Philip wishes for a return to "the old Pagan days" when he would have followed his instincts, but he is fearful of "living out his nature" and satisfies his sexual need only with "eye-lust." At this point the story of Davenant and Ray breaks off abruptly. When it resumes, Philip is berating himself: "Men of his disposition, he knew very well, were regarded both as madmen and profligates. No child was safe, so parents thought, for one moment within three miles of such a monster." Philip apparently has "never touched those little hands, that wavering hair," so why does he call himself "the Ogre of the old fairy tales"? When this story was acquired by the National Library of Wales it was accompanied by other short pieces of manuscript which appear to be connected

in some way with it. One such segment gives an alternative reading. In this fragment, the action takes place in the same wood, but the man who meets Ray is
not Philip, but his friend Hugh. Hugh suffers none of the compunctions of Philip,
and with "simple animal desire" he rapes the little girl. It is impossible to tell
whether this fragment was intended to be part of the original story; however,
when the main narrative is once again taken up, Ray has been sent away to the
home of her uncle. She writes to Philip to say her uncle is cruel to her and she
wishes to run away with Philip. In the first "orgy" story, the hero rescues Ora-
Nellie from drowning, thus becoming a savior rather than a child abuser. In the
second story, Philip hurries off to save this Ray, but she drowns in a pond trying
to get to him, and Philip commits suicide.

Napoleon's dictum that to understand a man you have to know what was
happening in the world when he was twenty was certainly true of Powys. Like
many a writer of the 1890s, Powys was rebelling against the stifling social and
moral values of high Victorianism. Bernie O'Neill introduced him to authors
who were publishing stories which were virtually case histories of deviance,
rebellion, and anarchic sexuality. This is what Powys was trying to write, albeit
with little skill and unconvincingly. In these two early pieces of sexual fantasy,
he was allowing himself to "go to the extreme limit"[44] in his prose in much the
same way that he was giving free reign to his phobias and obsessions in his daily
life. The orgy at the Squire's mansion represents a freedom, a release, for Philip
Warton who feels that "hitherto he had never lived."

> [Warton] had been overburdened . . . with theories and ideas. But now in
> this strange eccentric company he felt for the first time . . . that kind of sym-
> pathy for physical joy however obtained which strikes boldly at the root of
> all the traditions customs conventions and moralities of society.

Powys had found Richard Burton's unexpurgated translation of *Arabian
Nights* in his favourite pornography shop. Burton delineated a latitude which he
called the "Sotadic Zone" where androgeny, pederasty, and every other sexual
perversion was the norm.[45] Never having been out of England when he wrote
these first pieces and knowing nothing of exotic places, John wisely confined his
transgressive space to the dining room of a Sussex manor house. While it was
an age when the art of shocking the middle class came into vogue, it was also a
period of increasingly strict legislative measures against the burgeoning homosexual subculture, prostitution, and pornography. Powys would have been fully
aware that publishing his stories was too dangerous a rebellion, but rebelling he
was. Both his behavior and his writings at this time represented the first cracks
in the ice of his evangelical upbringing and his own highly developed conscience. It was still an adolescent rebellion, although Powys was by this time in
his mid-twenties. His hero, Warton, indulges in orgies involving children while
he is being tended by a housekeeper (provided by his parents) who looks after
him as a nurse—or a mother—would a child. The long-suffering Mrs. Curme,

the Court House housekeeper, is transplanted into a story ostensibly about the young hero's search for sexual freedom and joy. Was she introduced to make the transgression more difficult and therefore more exciting, or was she indicative of his ambivalence about the whole adventure into freedom and of his need for backup protection?

Given the episodic nature of these two pieces, it is easy to conclude that love of little girls, rape of children, and sexual orgies are all connected. To our twenty-first century politically correct sensibilities these themes are distasteful and/or hopelessly immature. But if the various strands are unraveled, it is easier to see that Powys was attempting to deal artistically, albeit self-consciously and clumsily, with ideas that he would address again and again in his later writings. Nourished and informed by his constant reading of the Romantics, he embraced their seminal beliefs that children have the same non-moral, innocent, unfettered freedom as nature, and that physical joy and relief from responsibility can be found, or regained, through children.

> [Philip] loved with a poet's passion whatever was young, beautiful and fresh. . . . He himself became a child again, regarding life with innocent careless joy. He felt wonderfully attracted by the freedom and boyish courage of Ora and as an admirer of Greek art he could not but enjoy the perfect physical development of the boy Littleton. . . . In their society he found an escape from himself from his own thoughts from all his elaborate ambitions and literary schemes. They made for him a world quite apart—a world where he could take refuge when his poetic endeavours failed.

Philip Davenant is convinced that nature holds the key to his quest to become a great poet, or alternatively, the recompense if he does not. John Cowper believed that Wordsworth's "cerebral mystical passion for young women is intimately bound up with his abnormally sensual sensitiveness to the elements,"[46] and his hero, Philip, considers that his passion for the little girl is the same as Wordsworth's. The natural world is not only the woods and the fields; it is also the ten-year-old child Ray whom he desires "less for herself than as a door or gate through which he might enter into the recesses of nature." It is rather ironic that Warton feels overburdened with theories and ideas but Davenant is indulging in these very theories, possibly to make the break with convention and morality less radical. His passion for Ray is an acceptable passion to him for the very reason that she *is* a child, "a sexless, unclassified being, a bright spirit flittering."

Powys was brought up in a society which discouraged and distrusted sexual desires. Because intercourse with a child was taboo, the presexual, innocent girl or boy became the focus of fantasies that gave emotional satisfaction without threatening the ideal of chastity. In our post-Freudian age we may feel slightly dubious about the motives of someone like Lewis Carroll who could write the mother of one little girl he photographed that, "It is good for one (I mean, for one's spiritual life, and in the same sense as reading the Bible is good) to come into contact with such sweetness and innocence," and to another, "Would you kindly let me know what is the minimum amount of dress in which you are willing to have her taken."[47] Even so, estimable men who idolized pretty little girls were not uncommon in nineteenth-century England. John Ruskin fell in love with Rose la Touche when she was nine years old. Powys's portrayal of the sleeping Ora-Ray is most circumspect compared to the diary entry for July 13, 1875, of the English clergyman Francis Kilvert: "One beautiful girl stood entirely naked on the sand . . . there was the supple slender waist, the gentle down and tender swell of the bosom and budding breasts, the graceful rounding of the delicately beautiful limbs and above all the soft and exquisite curves of the rosy dimpled bottom and broad white thigh."[48]

John may have thought that so long as a girl remains a metaphor, an innocent idealization, this would be one way in which he could wed his father's love of nature and his own powerful eroticism without transgressing his own "diseased conscience." It worked, but only if the artist remained an onlooker, a voyeur. It is the old Squire who rapes young Annette; it is Hugh who rapes little boys in the first story and Ray, the little girl, in the second. Philip Warton pays his respects to homosexuality as represented by Hugh and Taxeater, but he makes it plain that this is not his way. Nor is heterosexuality. The Powys-hero is a textbook definition of a voyeur—one who obtains sexual gratification either from watching the sexual acts of others or from erotic fantasy. The other Philip wants to lose himself in nature, "to grow more and more wedded to the inanimate world of grass and stones," but it is the child Ray who "embodied the most exquisite revelations." As Philip and Ray lie innocently together on the ground, Philip is engulfed by the "indescribable musky odour" of the grass. The "deep breaths he had been drawing from the bosom of the virgin soil" turns into a "passionate pressure from his lips" and his prone position becomes "an actual caress." Philip Davenant rubbing himself against the ground is Johnny rocking himself in his crib as a little boy; the only difference is that the adult Philip can fantasize that the earth is a girl. This is no longer a pre-sexual innocence; it is homoerotic orgasm.

While respectable Victorian society avidly read the novels of Dickens and gave their children Lewis Carroll's *Alice* books, at the same time an enormous amount of pornography was flooding the publishing market. Powys was certainly reading Dickens and other Victorian novelists, but he was also reading the kind of books Rousseau described as being written to be read single-handed. In much of this pornographic literature, every sexual deviation was catered for— incest, flagellation, lesbianism, communal sex, sadomasochism, homosexuality, pedophilia. Child pornography in particular was as much a feature of Victorian erotica as it is today on the Internet. It might be argued that Powys recognized this mixture of hypocrisy, repression, and innocence in himself and in the literature of the time, and this is why he juxtaposed the rural idyll of the Runnymede children with the Squires' orgy. On the other hand, it is possible he did not notice the incongruity. A favourite theme of the time was the spiritual rehabilitation of an adult man by an innocent little girl. Inevitably, the counterimage in pornographic literature was of the girl-child who is as sexually desiring as her violator. For example, in the "Little Miss Curious's Tale," the child is only ten when her father's servant begins to masturbate her. Before long she is returning the favour, and by the time she is twelve, she is begging the man to "complete her education" and "snatch the last favour."[49] While Powys's brief scene of the defloration of Annette is mild compared to the stories he was devouring at this time, he followed the pornographic convention that the innocent, shy child has a disconcerting way of becoming a consenting female. In the Warton piece, there is the suggestion that Annette is not totally devastated by her rape: "The shrieks of poor Annette had been changed to sobs and sobs to something that resembled laughter."

Powys read Nabokov's *Lolita* in 1959 and found it "dull beyond words," but *Lolita* is Ray Runnymede to a turn, and Humbert Humbert's description of himself as a nympholept clarifies what Powys was coming to terms with in this earlier phase of his life. Humbert says that in his twenties and early thirties his body knew what it craved but his mind rejected its pleas. He was fearful that it was a "forerunner of insanity," that for him "the only objects of amorous tremor were [nymphets]."[50] In *Autobiography*, Powys was more defiantly sure of his fate: "To be a nympholept, or 'sylpholept' I then was, seemed to be so absolutely inevitable that it never crossed the threshold of my consciousness . . . that I could struggle against it."[51] In another scrap of early manuscript Powys describes a nympholept as a man in love with "the powers of nature." This is a bizarre definition but understandable, given Powys's identification of children—nymphets—with nature. Nabokov's Humbert is convinced that "between the age limits of nine to fourteen there occur maidens who, to certain bewitched travellers, twice or many times older than they, reveal their true nature which is not human, but nymphic (that is, demoniac)."[52] The menace of the nymph is that it is Janus-faced. The mystical merging with nature through the child may be the road to creativity, but the nymph may also be demonic—the road to madness. It was a discordance that Powys constantly tried to resolve in his writing and in his life. After his two earliest stories, he dropped the girl-child nymph for the quest for a sylph, who would be "so much less substantial than any real feminine persons."[53] It is fairly obvious that Powys's sister Nellie is the prototype both for Ora-Ray and for Ray. Since Powys later privately admitted to having incestuous feelings towards this sister, this mixture of incest and nursery may have been too threatening to him to continue the theme.

In one discarded section of only a few pages, Powys introduces his Brighton porn seller. Here he is "a dealer in Decadent prints and books" and he is in agony because the young girl he loves has turned sixteen: "the child in her is

dead . . . buried . . . alive in the horrible body of a woman!" The Powys-hero
echoes this revulsion.

> He could marry indeed in after years a woman called Ray Runnymede, but
> the child he loved would be gone forever. . . . Better, O far better, that she
> were dead. This strange woman, the Ray of the future, tortured his imagi-
> nation.

Nellie did of course die, and therefore remained both a child and the unattainable ideal. It was the grown-up Ray, who might end up with breasts like Mrs.
Swinksby Swinks, "bigger than the udders of any ordinary cow," that was causing
Powys such anguish at this time. It is said that a crystal smashed to the ground
comes apart along the lines of cleavage that are predetermined by the crystal's
structure. The eruption of tormenting thoughts and obsessions at this time was
part of a pattern of unresolved conflicts that went back to his earliest childhood,
and if the crystal analogy is relevant, earlier still. Yet it is easy enough to overlook, in this whirl of manias and fantasies, the probable cause of the smash. The
fact is that at this time Powys had engaged himself to marry Margaret Alice Lyon,
sister of his best friend at Corpus.

There is a play in the archives of Syracuse University which, most unusually, has a definite date—1894—in Powys's own hand. Written while he was still
at Cambridge, with none of the sexual fantasies of the Philip stories of 1895, it
is old-fashioned melodrama. However, it does give a clear indication of Powys's
preoccupation at this time. The hero, Count Ravenstein, is torn between his passion for Violante, a beautiful gypsy girl with a "lustful light" in her eyes, and his
devotion to nature and philosophy. "Why must I choose between the life of the
spirit and the life of the lower love?" Powys solved this particular fictional crisis
by having both of them die.[54] Even while he was writing this, his courtship of
Margaret continued. Powys had met her shortly after he came up to Corpus in
1891. He visited Harry Lyon at his family estate and Margaret visited her brother at the university on festive occasions. It is not known when acquaintanceship
became romance, but she was invited to Montacute three times in 1894—an
indication of its seriousness, at least as far as the parents were concerned. In April
1895, his brother Littleton with him to lend support, John went to the Lyon
home in Devon and proposed marriage to Margaret.

It has always been a mystery why Powys chose this time to marry, or to marry
at all. He might have followed the example of his uncle—his father's brother, the
affluent Victorian bachelor. Until now, John had enjoyed great freedom to
pursue his own path. He was looked after by his mother in childhood, by his
brother at school, by college servants at Cambridge, then his housekeeper at
Court House. Choosing *not* to marry would have been an affirmation of this
freedom, yet there were forces pushing in the opposite direction. There is
absolutely no evidence to suppose that Powys's outpourings were anything more
than fantasies—the product of an erotic imagination. However, following the

exposé of child prostitution by W. T. Stead in 1885 through to Oscar Wilde's trial and conviction in the year of Powys's engagement, there was mounting public concern about sexual deviation and demands for restrictive legislation. While the possibility of John being involved in a public scandal would not have occurred to his parents, they would have encouraged his marriage for other reasons. He was the beloved eldest son who was to carry on the ancestral line. He was also manifestly disturbed at this period, and his parents may have felt that a wife and children would be a stabilizing influence.

The engagement precipitated a further flurry of phobic behavior. He was determined to become a "master writer," preferably a great poet like Wordsworth, and his ingrained romanticism linked nature with creativity. He had convinced himself that the entrance both to nature and to poetry was through the feminine body; unfortunately a child's body was off limits and mature female sexuality was repulsive to him. With the excuse that he is "half-drunk already after two glasses of claret" Philip Warton shouts, "there is poetry in everything that is more than a thousand years old. Women, sir, have existed for a period longer than that, women have suffered from a hundred and twenty thousand repulsive necessities of Nature for a period longer than that and therefore women are poetic—their petticoats are poetic, their under-linen is poetic, everything about them is at the same time repulsive and poetic!" To complicate matters further, he was reading voraciously the writers of the nineties and many of his apparent psychological peculiarities as well as his future literary themes have a disconcerting similarity to those of the French Decadents. He was to explore again and again in his own novels their fixations with sadism, androgyeny, and incest. However, it was the polarities that were set up in the last decades of the nineteenth century between nature and art that particularly preoccupied him at this time. Men were dedicated to the inner life of sensation and the imagination; women were closer to nature, to the outer life of the body. He was much attracted to Huysman's hero, des Esseintes, whose fantastic plan of life was to divorce himself as far as possible from ordinary existence,[55] but it was the more brutal version of this aesthetic by the earlier Baudelaire that spoke most directly to his present conundrum. "Woman is hungry so she must eat; thirsty, so she must drink. She is in heat, so she must be fucked. How admirable! Woman is natural, which is to say abominable."[56] That is, woman is entirely governed by her biological and physical impulses. Needless to say, the theme of devouring female sexuality was not new, but calling himself a *nympholept* gives a clue to Powys's thoughts at this time. *Nympholepsy* is, according to the NED, "a state of rapture supposed to be inspired in men by nymphs; hence an ecstasy, a frenzy, especially that caused by desire of the unattainable." On the other hand, a *nymphomaniac* is "a feminine disease characterized by morbid and uncontrollable sexual desire." For men the frenzy is *un amour de l'impossible*—in other words, a desire that is never consummated and therefore never satiated; for women, the frenzy is a sexual disease. For a fastidious, aspiring poet/writer pursuing an unattainable ideal, the earthy desires of a woman who is no longer a child could only inspire terror and disgust.

Another phobia which developed immediately after his engagement makes it obvious that he was close to a state of panic about his forthcoming marriage. Margaret gave him as an engagement present a beautiful retriever. To his horror, he soon realized "that the companion of my walks belonged to the feminine sex, that fatal sex."

> The realization that until this dog's death all my walks upon the surface of the grain-bearing earth were to be, so to speak, "feminized" caused me an epoch of extraordinary suffering! A gulf of femininity opened beneath my feet. It made me shudder with a singular revulsion. Everything I looked at in Nature . . . presented itself to me as a repetition of the feminineness of Thora! I could no longer enjoy the singing of the birds. They might be feminine birds! I loathed the thought that so many of the trees and the flowers possessed feminine organs. The thing went so far with me that I became panic-stricken lest I myself should develop feminine breasts, breasts with nipples, resembling the dugs of Thora. . . . I began to feel as if there were no longer any real solidity left in Nature, as if, whichever way I turned, the firm substance of the earth would "go in."[57]

The half-jocular, half-serious tone of this distracts the reader from noticing the sheer illogicality of his argument. Within two sentences he goes from "breasts with nipples" to fear that "the firm substance" of the "grain-bearing" earth would "go in." Nipples stick out, they don't go in—unless of course they go into the mouth of a baby or a lover. Penises stick out, until they go into the vagina. But the illogicality is only apparent. The penis and the nipple not only look alike, they share similar functions; they engorge when stimulated, yield life-giving fluids, and link one person to another. However, what is causing the panic is his awareness that the breast and the passageway to the dark interior of a woman's body—the earth mother "going in"—comprise the essentials of female sexuality. Like the breast that can either nurture or deprive, thereby arousing great longing and terrible hostility, the womb becomes a symbol of desire and dread. It is a lilting Lorelei urging a return to the beginnings of life, to a state of blissful envelopment, yet it is something that may drain, devour, destroy whoever or whatever might enter.

Nevertheless, his terror about the imminent demands of genital sexuality was associated with a more encompassing issue. Although much of the sixth chapter of *Autobiography* is concerned with his manias and his fears, he begins it by recounting an episode which tends to get ignored in the general flood of his sexual confessions. As a graduation present, his father gave him a trip to the Lake District with an "unequalled companion"—his sister Gertrude. One day, Powys goes off alone with the intention of climbing to the top of Helvellyn, but about a mile from the top he was suddenly seized by "fear."

I came pelting down like a frightened beast. All the way home . . . my magic stick "Sacred" seemed to utter speech, as I grasped it by its curved handle. It kept repeating at every step I took "Recreant—recreant—recreant!" And my impression now is—or my fancy, if you will—that it departed after that and removed itself from me, so that I saw it no more! Whether it vanished in the bosom of some mountain tarn, or whether, as a counter-talisman to that fatal stick in the Shirley lake, it still floats, like the "rod and staff" of the heavenly shepherd, in some fairy limbo of the spirit, I know not. I only know that . . . after my *gran rifiuto*, in refusing to carry it to the summit of Helvellyn, "Sacred" disappears.[58]

The stick, Sacred, accompanied him on his "road to Damascus" at Cambridge, when he felt for the first time that he could and would become a poet and a medium. It now calls after him that he is a coward and then disappears like the wounded Arthur's sword Excalibur into the "bosom of some mountain tarn." Powys explicitly associates the incident of losing his stick with his Shirley fear of imprisonment, and in a sense this "Sacred" happening echoes his earliest fears of being himself the stick that disappears into the lake. However, it indicates more than a fastidious fear of "normal" sexuality, of "going in." He blames the disappearance of his magic stick into "some fairy limbo of the spirit" on his inability to carry it to the summit of Helvellyn. He calls this his *gran rifiuto*, that is, his refusal to, or inability to, rise to the Platonic idealism which was so much a part of his "higher nature," with the implication that he too will end in limbo. In Dante's words, he is "that man / Who out of cowardice made the great refusal." Dante threw Celestine V into his Inferno for saying no to the world and yes to the spirit, but Powys appears here to be saying no to the world of spirit and poetry and yes to the material world and marriage. The Greek poet Cavafy, in his lovely "Che fece . . . il gran rifiuto," writes that there comes a day when certain people must say either the great Yes or the great No. "And yet that no—the right no—crushes him for the rest of his life."[59] The incident is bound up with Powys's vision of himself as a poet and a possessor of magical powers. He has now lost, or thinks he has lost, his "sacred" stick, just as he once lost his "magic" laurel axe—the axe that was given to him by his father, the "heavenly shepherd." And there is the rub. This spiritual father, the maker of magic axes, was also the maker of eleven children, though no doubt with a shudder of distaste at the duty. So John has failed on two counts—he cannot rise to the world of the spirit and he cannot rise to generative sexuality. He is indeed in limbo.

They married on April 9, 1896, at the Lyon home in Ilsington, Devon. Margaret's father, a wealthy retired businessman from Manchester, had bought a farm in 1864 and set himself up as a country gentleman. It was a large and ornate wedding, jointly officiated by the Reverend Charles Francis and William Lutyens, a friend of John Cowper from Sherborne and Cambridge. Gertrude was a bridesmaid and Littleton the best man. Mary Cowper is in one of the wedding pictures, looking drawn and old, although she was only forty-four and her last child, Lucy, but five. She is dressed in deepest black, still grieving the loss of her daughter Nellie three years before. The rest of the Powys clan was there *en masse*, except for Theodore. The littlest ones, Lucy, Katie, and Will, were now being schooled at home by a governess. Llewelyn was at the Sherborne Prep; Marian was attending a high school in Norwich; Bertie was intending to apprentice as an architect; Gertrude was studying art at the Slade. Littleton, down from Corpus, was about to begin his career as a schoolmaster. Only Theodore gave some cause for parental worry. There was no question of Cambridge for this boy. C. F. had also been a "late developer" but *his* parents had got him through Cambridge by dint of concentrated coaching and cramming. Apparently Charles and Mary felt that even this would not get Theodore through. This decision meant the end of any possibility of his entering the professions, not even the church. It is difficult to know whether it was his emotional fragility or his mental acuity that concerned them. Whatever the reason, after less than a year at the school in Aldeburgh, and a period at home, in March 1892 he was sent to a friend of the family at Rendham, Suffolk, to learn farming.

John and Margaret settled into Court House and, on the surface, they led the usual domestic and social life of newlyweds. He obtained more work at other girls' schools, and attempted to break into public lecturing. He wrote a good deal of poetry, and more prose. The stories, or the five fragments that have survived, are plainly attempts to articulate his anxieties about this marriage.

The Powys-hero has changed little in these new pieces. He remains unconventional in clothes and behavior, and still sees himself as an outsider. The hero's name has changed from Philip Warton and Philip Davenant, to Philip Bleddyn, then Philip Glendower, and finally to Owen Glendower. No longer wanton Warton, a sexual libertine, the hero's liberty is now symbolized by his race. He becomes a Welshman, an outlander remote from middle-class English society. In a sense this was an important first step in a distancing technique and gave Powys his first inkling of a possible alternative emancipation. However, the stories are not about independence, but enslavement. The theme of all of them is the trap set by the conventions of society and, not accidentally, all of them deal with an engagement.

In one, Philip Glendower is engaged to Elspeth, who is portrayed as a woman with an interesting mind and a boyish figure. Philip explains to Elspeth that he is fond of her but does not want to marry and believes that people would be happier if they just lived together. At this point another character from the earlier stories is re-introduced—Hugh Bigod. Elspeth, upset by Philip's attempt to break off the engagement, goes off to swim naked in a pond. While there, she overhears Philip tell his friend Hugh about the discussion. Unaware of Elspeth's presence, Hugh throws a heavy stick into the pond and hits her, dazing and wounding her. Powys now employs a device he has used more than once in these early stories. He abandons further dialogue about the dilemma facing Elspeth and Philip and reverts to a long and frank description of Mr. de Woztnak's unhappy marriage and his attitude toward his wife. It is not a pleasant picture. "He felt compelled to call upon all the miserable blank hours he had spent in her society—they rose, they fluttered around him squeaking like bats. . . . Day after day year after year bound hand and foot to one he hated—one who embodied for him all that his shrinking flesh and his disgusted spirit most loathed and abhorred."

In a second fragment[60] the hero, Owen Glendower, is the orphaned son of a Welsh landowner. He has been engaged for a year to Elspeth Runnymede, who lives with her two sisters, Bess and Ray, and their father, the Vicar of Godbarrow. Owen has been away in Brittany, translating Welsh verse and writing his own poetry, but as the story begins he has returned to England in an attempt to break off his engagement. Elspeth in this version no longer has a sylphlike figure— "Everything about her was charged with the spirit of domesticity, practical efficiency and propriety." She is specifically contrasted with her older sister Bess, who is a tomboy, and her younger sister Ray, a sensitive child who "might have been a child of Southern Deserts; fevered, passionate and volatile." Elspeth has no intention of letting him break off the engagement.

> Elspeth as a matter of fact had never loved Glendower; it was not in her nature to love. But she was shrewd and far-sighted and she knew well enough that to a clergyman's daughter in a remote country village, young men with even small independent patrimonies do not often offer themselves. She saw also, though with an unsympathetic eye, that the youth had intellectual powers of no common order—might indeed one day become famous; and Elspeth, like many other shallow, worldly and narrow-minded people, had an overweening respect for intellectual Fame.

In the third version of events a shift occurs. Owen is no longer an orphan but the son of the Rector of Godbarrow Church, and financially dependent upon his father. His fiancée is now called, puzzlingly, Ray, but they are as incompatible as the previous couple. Ray urges him to abandon his poetry and take up a career. The hero retorts, "How often must I tell you that I have no intention of sacrificing myself to what is called 'getting on.' The idea of a little suburban house with a neat servant at the door and a couple of flower beds gives me a hopeless feeling of dreariness." In another fragment this awareness of what marriage would mean to the hero is driven home.

> Owen Glendower looked as far as he could into the future of his life and it seemed to him that existence became ever narrower and narrower until almost contracted away into nonentity. . . . He saw himself entangled in a web of soft domesticity—shut up, as it were, in a labyrinth of thornless roses. He saw with horrible, clarified distinctness the conventional world with which his marriage would surround him.

This story introduces another dimension. Ray/Elspeth may be conventional and Owen/Philip may be fearful of adult sexuality, but they both feel "the carnal primeval attraction." Possibly in a retreat from this realization, in yet another short piece, Powys introduces a totally new character, Lacrima Colonna—a young sixteen-year-old girl who is not a child but also not yet a sexually mature woman. She is only sketched in at this point, and it is not until later novels that Powys develops so successfully the triangle of a man in love with two different types of women. However, in a fifth fragment, Philip not only seduces Lacrima but breaks Elspeth's heart by corrupting her little sister Ray. Briefly, but only briefly, he was tempted back to the child seduction theme. These drafts, rehearsing the possible ways in which the hero could escape from a marriage, were written anywhere from two to five years *after* his marriage. By the time John was writing them he had indeed taken up a career at his wife's urging, and he had "a little suburban house with a neat servant at the door."

While the sentiments expressed in these stories are hardly the stuff of taboo-breaking, they certainly would have been shocking to the Powyses and the Lyons, and to Margaret herself. In fact, they almost surely did not see them, although the Circle may have. Powys seems to have kept double journals as well, one for his wife's and his relatives' perusal, and one for his male friends. At Syracuse there are eleven notebook journals containing more unpublished fragments of stories and pages of unfinished verse, as well as notes for lectures. One journal in particular contains several love poems addressed to Margaret, extolling her "golden locks" and "sweet eyes," and the beginning of a story which is quite different, both in style and content, from the ones quoted above. It is only six and a half manuscript pages but contains a description both of the man and the wife, Jack and Alice Meredith: "Jack Meredith is an enthusiastic and timid youth of great idealizing tendencies, strongly imaginative and with no small conceit of himself and his attainments. Meredith's lady love (not yet converted into a busy housewife by the care of children) is chiefly remarkable for the delicacy of her complexion and the slenderness almost sylph-like of her youthful figure. In disposition Alice Meredith presents a charming contrast to her husband."[61] In another discarded segment Owen appears to have found a way out of his dilemma, comforting himself that perhaps he can have marriage and freedom too: "I do not see why I should give up my freedom. Even though I am married. There are plenty of men who lead double lives."

Powys not only kept double journals, he led a double life both before and after his marriage. In this he was not alone of course, but unlike those who had a respectable daytime world involving marriage and family and a night world of homosexual or heterosexual encounters, both, Powys's lives were conducted in broad daylight. After teaching he would head for Brighton Beach to look at "provocative feminine forms basking in that blazing sunshine." He acknowledged that "this maniacal pursuit of the sensations of impersonal lust increased rather than diminished after my marriage."[62] However, the sylph fetish now became more specialized. Perhaps aware that trawling the beach for children or even young women of a suitable slimness would rouse public suspicion, he refined his staring at "the anonymous and if possible the *unconscious* bodies of feminine representatives of my race" to parts of the female body—preferably the legs or ankles. Even at Sherborne, when it was still young boys who attracted him, it was their "beautiful legs" that were the object of his sexual drive. Powys was later to elaborate what he called his voyeurism into a complicated philosophical construct, although his penchant for staring at body parts was not technically voyeurism but fetishism. Unlike a character in one of his later novels, Powys seems to have avoided the attention of the police, possibly because he had taken to wearing large, loose, and concealing overcoats even in the depths of summer, or possibly because, as one psychiatric text dryly points out, for some fetishists, simply to look at the fetish is sufficient to produce orgasm, "without supplementary overt stimulation."

His first trip outside England came in 1896 when he and Margaret went to Paris and Rome, with the brother of Bernie O'Neill acting as their guide. His generally eccentric behavior and his debouchings into "lust-drugging erotic bookshops" must have been, to say the least, irritating, and he wondered "how my companions and my relations ever tolerated my erratic and wayward humours in those days."[63] Returning to Sussex to a "virtuous and settled life" left him gloomily rebellious. He decided he must become a scholar-gypsy like Hazlitt, "wandering about the world as he pleased, and completely selfish in all the ordinary human relations."[64] It took him some years to achieve, but achieve it he did.

In January 1901, he travelled to Hamburg, Germany, to give a set of English lectures.[65] How he obtained this commission he does not say, but it was while there that he had a phobic experience that was psychologically more ominous than any of his previous aberrations. Hoping to find in Germany the romantic sensations and cultural life he longed for, instead "the especial Demon, in the lunatic asylum which I kept locked up in my cat-head" presented him with " a vision of loathsomeness."[66] Once again, it was breasts that attacked his equilibrium. It was his terror of his dog's "dugs" that first sent him hunting for "some sylph-like figure recumbent on Brighton beach, at whose knees and ankles I could glare like a mad ogre, while I forgot that there were such things as breasts in the world."[67] Now in Hamburg he sees, or imagines he sees, "a stream of blood from a woman's livid breasts."

> It was a picture that had a woman's breasts in it and in some way connected with these breasts a great deal of blood. But this blood, at least to my morbid imagination, was not ordinary blood. It was very pale, but it was also very vivid. . . . It seemed to have the power of leaping from the page and of splashing over my face; yes! even into my mouth and down my throat. Nor did this bloodstained Milky Way stop at my throat. It sank into me until it reached some deep-buried "loathing-nerve" that licked it up with frenzy. . . .
>
> Yes! I was followed about by those breasts and that blood. I used to go down to those black canals and those cinnamon-scented warehouses with hurried and eager steps, trying, as I trudged through the discoloured snow,

to avoid, if possible, all the innumerable shops, and book-stands and paper-stalls which made me feel as if from the paps of the whole round world issued forth milk and blood![68]

More than six pages in *Autobiography* are devoted to this episode, albeit with many digressions and interpolations. Often to fathom what Powys is driving at the reader has to ignore the diversionary asides to concentrate on his images and, above all, on his intertwining of images. He begins by comparing his quest for new cultural experience with "sucking the dugs of the world" just as he sucked sweets at school. He follows this by describing his difficulty in finding a toilet while he is out walking. This rather innocuous-seeming insert becomes part of the "loathsomeness" of the experience, although why that may be he does not say. (However, many years later, in his diary, he refers to his "loathsome dreams" which are always of dissolution. He connects the terrifying dreams with his chronic constipation and his feeling that he is filling up with "white excrement.") Suddenly he sees a picture in a paper. He says in one place it may have been a comic paper, and in another hints that he may have seen it in one of the many shops selling pornography, which in Germany at that period was fairly hardcore. He sees a woman's breasts spouting blood, but not ordinary blood—very pale blood. The liquid splashes from her breasts over his face and into his throat, and he licks it up "with a frenzy."

This is a powerfully controlled recounting of an experience he several times calls loathsome. Powys links images of sucking with breasts, breasts with pale blood, blood with "the milky way." He does not speculate why the liquid is bloodstained. Nor does he suggest any connection with, or memory of, breast-feeding, baby-bitten nipples, or mothers. He never, in fact, refers to milk at all, until an isolated comment several pages later, after he has managed to introduce Swift's quotation—"Go, go; you're bit!"—when he then universalizes the experience by saying it made him "feel as if from the paps of the whole round world issued forth milk and blood!" The use of the phrase "Milky Way," prefacing it with the adjective "bloodstained," is an example of Powys's allusive, not to say elusive, erudition, leaving the reader to make of it what he will. As a reader of erotica Powys would have been familiar with its slang meaning referring to a man's semen or a woman's come. He would also have known some of its more poetic meanings, such as Sidney's "thy eyes were starres, thy breasts the milken way."[69] He would have known, "The path to Heaven is a milky way; not a bloudy," from *The Wandering Jew*[70] and, given his imagery, he may well have known the even more apposite: "When those two Milky Mountains become one double bag full of Blood, they are no more desired by men."[71] The question remains why these breasts spout both milk and blood. "You're bit" indeed.

The Hamburg episode reads as if it were a case history appearing in a psychoanalytic journal, and it begs consideration of the various possible stresses at this time, when he felt he had a "lunatic asylum" locked up in his head. But did he? Or was this just another romantic idea that associated insanity with genius?

As if aware that the question might be raised, he points out when describing the Hamburg episode that,

> This morbid and indeed almost monstrous sensibility is something that you pay a heavy price for. . . . Nor does a person with a terrible imagination get much pity. I know well what I am talking about; for my vitality is so terrific, my constitution so adamantine, my will so strong, that it is difficult for people to believe that so galvanized a Jack-in-the-Box, making such lively gesticulations should be completely skinless and raw under its motley jacket.[72]

Powys certainly had a remarkable ability to live in two worlds. Almost immediately after his return from Hamburg, he was in Montacute giving a talk about the history of the town, "In Aid of the Re-Hanging of Montacute Church Bells,"[73] with, I should imagine, his mother and father looking proudly if somewhat quizzically on. Powys does not mention this in his autobiography; perhaps it did not fit in with his image of himself as "verging on madness." In a photograph of him taken at this time, he is lounging in a chair, appearing perfectly relaxed, smoking a cigarette, impeccably dressed. There is no sign of madness. Spoiled? Probably. Immature? Almost certainly. Insane? No.

CHAPTER FOUR

AMERICA

1902-1911

⌣

THE BLOOD-AND-BREASTS STORY RAISES THE QUESTION WHETHER POWYS was an inspired psychologist or a trickster figure who fooled not only the reader but himself. Or was he a born storywriter who happened also to be both of the above? The more that is brought to light about his life—apart from the evidence that Powys himself supplies—the more tempting it becomes to see *Autobiography* as one of his most imaginative novels: Powys as anti-hero; Powys as accidental success. One of John Cowper's most sustained life-illusions was that he was totally unworldly, completely devoid of ambition. He suggested that in this he was following faithfully in the steps of his father, but he surely must have known that this ardent Evangelical, while giving the impression of otherworldliness, had nonetheless managed to secure through influential friends and rich relatives a pleasant living and an excellent income. John insisted that he had no idea what he was going to do when he left Cambridge, and that it was totally by chance that he fell into a lifetime of lecturing.

> My mind has always had a tendency to be what might be called "a Foreground Mind," that is to say a mind absorbed in the present and totally unconcerned about the future. . . . I assure you I never gave one serious thought to my future career.[1]

When he wrote that, Powys would not have been aware that universities are assiduous collectors of archives, and that their institutional records would tell a different story. Not only did he give "serious thought" to his future career, he intended from the beginning to go into extension lecturing. Extension education was a burgeoning movement by 1894 and an attractive career opportunity for someone not likely to become a Fellow or Tutor of a University College. Immediately after he graduated in June 1894, Powys wrote the secretary of the Cambridge extension office, A. J. Archbold, who happened also to have tutored him for the History Tripos. Powys asked if he would "have any chance of getting any sort of University Extension Lectures," and assured the secretary that he could get "elaborate testimonials from my College people and if ambition and

aspiration is any test of power I am a modern Addison." Archbold recommend-
ed him to the authorities as "a nice gentlemanly sort of man who is very fond of
ladies," and Powys sent in his formal application, along with a testimonial from
his relative, Fanshawe, now in the influential position of college tutor.[2] However,
the extension office turned him down in July, and it was only then that he went
to Gabbitas and Thring and found a job teaching in girls' schools. But by no
means had he given up the idea of extension lecturing. His next opportunity
came in 1896, when he went to Rome with his new wife.

Powys says that to make a little extra money he gave "lectures in one of the
Roman hotels to an exhausted group of young ladies from Eastbourne."[3] The year
before he had managed ("I must have had nothing less than a miraculous power
with these excellent ladies") to obtain five more schools at Eastbourne, and in
fact, these were his own pupils, on a tour of Italy with their headmistress, a Mrs.
Barber.[4] Although he creates the impression that he had inadvertently stumbled
upon them, he must have arranged beforehand to give a series of lectures to
them. Evidently, he also invited any other residents in the pension who wished
to listen. One of those private guests happened to be Canon Moore Ede, one of
the first organizers of Cambridge Extension Lecturers. Powys does not refer to
Ede in *Autobiography* nor does he mention that he must have asked Ede to write
a letter to the Extension Authorities. Ede did so, noting that Powys had been
"holding forth on Julius Caesar M. Aurelius Dante Raphael &c. He is really a
very fair lecturer. . . . It wd. strengthen your staff of lecturers if you could put him
on."[5] For whatever reason, even this recommendation went no further, but he
applied again two years later. In the meantime, he had been hiring town halls
and giving public lectures in Sussex. The first, in Hove, was not an outstanding
success; the box office receipts amounted to "three shillings and sixpence" and
the audience consisted of "three women and one child; the child being let in for
the sixpence."[6] Despite this disheartening beginning, he had persevered and his
renewed application to the Extension Board contained testimonials to "the success of lectures which Mr. Powys had given privately at different places in the
South of England."

The story gets a little complicated at this point. Oxford and Cambridge
dominated the extension field at this time, and potential lecturers normally
applied to belong to one or the other list. However, Powys's November 1898
application to Cambridge referred to the local secretary of the Oxford extension
centre at Brighton and also to Dr. J. G. Bailey, a prominent lecturer on the
Oxford list. Bailey had been engaged in the autumn of 1898 to give a six-month
course of fortnightly lectures on Tennyson to the Brighton centre. In January
1899 the extension press suddenly announced a revision to the schedule. Bailey's
lectures were to be augmented by an additional twelve lectures, to be given by
"one J. C. Powys." This was most unusual. If class numbers proved unexpectedly
large, an assistant might be appointed, but only to correct the written work.
However it happened, in January 1899 he had suddenly become a recognised lec-

turer for Oxford without having applied or been formally appointed.

The Oxford Delegacy next invited him to deliver a lecture at their vacation school "summer meeting" in August 1899.

> It was from Court House that I set off one summer to give my first trial lec-
> ture at Oxford before the University Extension authorities. Incidentally I
> had to speak before a considerable audience; but this audience had no idea
> that the speaker was on his trial, and this ignorance made everything easier.
> By some occult destiny . . . I was called upon by Mr. Marriott, then the head
> of the Oxford Extension Society to lecture upon the Arthurian Legend. For
> this lecture it was only necessary for me to buy *one book*, namely the work
> on the subject published by the Professor of Celtic Literature, the
> Welshman, Sir John Rhys.[7]

Powys was writing about an event that had occurred almost thirty-five years before, which might account for certain factual inaccuracies. The spin he put on it was not accidental. First of all, he knew very well that it was a "trial" lecture in name only. The summer lectures were essentially a promotional device, used by the extension authority to give favoured lecturers a chance to display their wares before an audience composed mainly of members of regional committees who were responsible for selecting lecturers for the next season. Moreover, far from being ignorant of the situation, the audience was perfectly aware that they were headhunting.[8] Secondly, his lecture was not on the Arthurian Legend, but according to a published press report it was on "Tennyson's Attitude towards Nature." Powys gave a number of so-called "trial" lectures at summer meetings— in 1899, 1901, 1903, and 1905—and, indeed, one of those later lectures was on Malory's *Morte D'Arthur* and another on Tennyson's *Idylls*. It was not until 1929 that he read Rhys's *Arthurian Romance*. Even so, it is the case that by this time, he was interested not only in the Arthurian legend as popularized by English poets but in its Celtic antecedents. The 1890s saw the rise of the "cult of the Celt," although it was particularly the Irish Celts who were "discovered." Characteristically Powys took advantage of a vogue but made it peculiarly his own by ignoring the Irish and concentrating on Welsh literature and myth— sieved through his own imagination. Lady Charlotte Guest's translation of *The Mabinogion* was not half so loose as Powys's future gloriously anarchic interpretations of the characters and events in those tales.

From the beginning Powys was very popular with extension audiences and by the autumn of 1901 he was teaching courses for Oxford as far apart as the Lake District in the North and Kent in the South. In the meantime, Cambridge, impressed by his success as a lecturer, had finally accepted his application, and Powys was alternating his engagements—working one term of three months in Oxford territory, the next for Cambridge. In 1902 he switched to all Oxford centres, while negotiating with Cambridge to work exclusively for them in 1903 *if* they increased his fee. Cambridge dithered, and since there was a certain amount of competition between the two university systems, the Oxford delegacy, seeing their chance, offered him a promotion to their senior division with significantly higher fees. Powys simply resigned altogether from the Cambridge list. For someone who was totally unworldly, he had proved quite adept at working the system. Either that, or his wife Margaret had taken over the management of his business affairs.

The next years of extension lecturing in England taught him skills that would stand him in good stead for his later successful career in America. They also reinforced personality and intellectual traits already present in his character, particularly his perception of himself as an outsider. Extension work was another way of rebelling against the established order. He saw himself as bringing culture to the masses and hugely enjoyed being labeled "unscholarly," even fraudulent—being the opposite, in other words, of his father's despised "professor." He says that he had no sooner begun his "life of peripatetic philosophizing," than the cry of "charlatan" arose.

> When they cry "Charlatan!" what they really mean is: "How dare this fellow talk about Dostoievsky's Christ, and about Plato's Eros, and about Goethe's 'Mothers,' and about Wordsworth's *Intimations of Immortality* and about the 'art' of Henry James, and about the 'critical values' of Walter Pater, and about the 'cosmic emotion' of Walt Whitman, as if these recondite subjects, complicated enough to fill the whole span of several real scholars' life-work, could possibly be lugged into an address to working-men and tradesmen's assistants!"
>
> These natural enemies of mine, these "Philistines" of Culture, as Nietzsche calls them, *dare not*, for the life of them, bring Christ and the Mothers and the Grail and the Over-Soul and the secret of Jesus and eternal recurrence and being-and-not-being and the monochronos hedoné of Aristippus and the pleasure-which-there-is-in-life-itself of Wordsworth and the absolute of Spinoza and the mystery of the Tao and Fechner's planetary spirits and the mythical elements of Empedocles and the natural magic of Shakespeare's poetry into an interpretation of the Sleeping Beauty or of the Castle of Carbonek.
>
> To parade such topics before an unacademic audience is to give yourself away as no better than a vulgar conjurer. Thus would speak my father's ancient enemy, the scientific professor; and I . . . regard the magic of the *Mabinogion* as a nearer approach to the secret of Nature than anything you could learn by vivisecting dogs.[9]

His leaps of logic are sometimes breathtaking, but what he is doing in this apologia is clear enough. He is setting himself up as a conjurer and a clown-actor—who happens to be impressively erudite—in opposition to scholars who are variously "Philistines," "scientific professors," and vivisectionists. Behind Powys's defence lies the tension not only between his methods and those of "scholars," but between a career within the college walls and without. Powys glories in his "charlatanism," all the while somehow giving the impression that it was a unique and lonely quest. In fact, it was common for extension lecturers at this time to be given such labels as "traveling salesmen of knowledge," and "literary bagmen." The labels bothered not at all men of such caliber as Sir Bernard Pares, the foremost authority on Russia, or Philip Wicksteed, the famous Dante scholar, or Ramsay Muir, the renowned historian, all of whom were regular extension lecturers. Probably such a word as "charlatan" would have simply amused one of the very first to give an extension course—Alfred Tennyson, who lectured on Shakespeare to an audience of a thousand working people at Shoreditch.[10]

Without a doubt, the way the "peripatetic university" (as the extension movement was called) was organized suited Powys's skills and personality. From its beginnings in 1873, the movement operated on the assumption that universities could and should extend education everywhere in England. Eventually all universities sought to expand their teaching outside their walls, but in Powys's time Oxford and Cambridge dominated this system. Voluntary groups would organize themselves into local centres and request a lecturer to teach a course of six to twelve weeks. The university would then coordinate these centres into circuits so that the lecturer could deliver a talk in one town, catch a train to the next centre, and return to the first town on the same day the following week. It was highly organized educational itinerancy. The location of the centres ranged from manufacturing cities to seaside resorts and the people attending were equally varied. Powys's audience might contain manual workers, certificate seekers, schoolteachers, senior pupils, but the majority of students in any course would be middle-class females seeking cultural stimulation. (The recommendation of Powys's original referee that he "was very fond of the ladies" was not as irrelevant as it first appears.) Since the courses had to be self-supporting, the authorities had little choice but to offer popular subjects (and lecturers) capable of attracting large numbers. Although Powys graduated in history, he attempted to give a history course only once. After it was judged to be "technically incompetent" he concentrated on English literature, particularly Shakespeare and Victorian prose and poetry writers. Fortunately, at a time when literature was virtually ignored in universities, it attracted a good deal of public interest. His subject matter and his lecturing technique combined to make him highly sought after by far-flung centres.

It was, inevitably, a grueling life. The Cambridge circuit offered twelve weekly lecture courses; the Oxford practice was to give "short courses" of six fortnightly lectures. While resigning the Cambridge circuit may have given him a certain vengeful satisfaction, under the Oxford system he had to lecture at twice as many centres to make the same amount of money. Financial survival meant catching the right train at the right time and keeping travel expenses to a minimum. Powys received a third-class fare and five shillings for each centre visited. He would walk to his lodgings from the station, which both saved money and made him feel closer to his father, who "always preferred to walk where it was humanly possible" ("I like to be *independent*, John, my boy!")[11] but he then confesses that he always secretly traveled by first-class train. It is one of his most

endearing and essentially honest traits that Powys very often first turns necessity into a philosophical or emotional construct, and then demolishes the whole
elaborate structure by undercutting it with such admissions. Although he rose
through the Oxford grades with amazing rapidity, going from probationary status
to staff lecturer in three years, it was a financially uncertain life. His high grade
meant that he could demand higher fees, but his income was totally dependent
on these fees. There were no faculty privileges, there was certainly no accident
or illness insurance, and there was no guarantee of work. If he did not attract
large audiences with popular lectures, he simply would not be asked again to that
centre. "Independence" was not an option—Powys had to sell himself to survive.
It must have been a difficult lesson for his father's son to learn.

An aspect of Powys's extraordinary ability to turn disadvantage to brilliant
advantage was that he evolved a dramatic and attention-arresting technique that
was perfect for an audience which demanded a blend of education and inspiration. He called it "a new art, the art of 'Dithyrambic Analysis'" after the wild,
impassioned Greek choric hymn originally in honor of Dionysus.[12]

> It is the way I always go to work in literary criticism, and it gives me the
> power, I will not say of *becoming* the personality I am dealing with, but at
> least of diffusing my identity through its identity and of realizing myself
> through the medium of its sensibility. The thing in its essence is a kind of
> spiritual eroticism and in my case it is intimately connected with my vice
> as a *voyeur*. Does not all literary penetration spring from some subtle sub-
> limation of our deepest vice? From a *voyeur* I become a *clair-voyeur*.[13]

Calling himself a voyeur and a charlatan was part of his "life-illusion," but
there is every evidence that he was a thorough professional. His "dithyrambic
analysis" may not have pleased everyone, but Powys would not have been
invited back again and again to the local centres if he had been in any sense a
fraud or not totally conversant with his subject matter.

Extension work was an essentially lonely occupation. The lecturers knew
each other by name, but the set-up ensured that they seldom met. A contemporary of his remarked that his colleagues of those days were "like commercial travellers, passing each other on various routes with a common experience and an
augur's wink."[14] True, while on circuit lecturers stayed with local families who provided overnight accommodation and hospitality. It was a system not unlike the
Methodist custom of "entertaining the preacher"—a comparison which would
not have been lost on Powys. Given John Cowper's professed "misanthropic
avoidance of my fellow-creatures,"[15] it might seem surprising that he chose to pursue a career in which enforced familiarity was a necessary part of the job, but
apparently "this perpetual talking to strangers helped to deepen my congenital
ego-centric isolation."[16] Although he had to be sociable with people he did not
know, and whom he would not have considered to be his class, he was now learning the invaluable art of appearing genial without being so. It could even be said

that this career provided an admirable *raison d'être* for escaping intimacy. During the Cambridge and Southwick years he was able to give free reign to his sense of "proud and vicious loneliness."[17] However, with marriage he had to become accustomed to the company of someone who, unlike Mrs. Curme, the housekeeper, would not bow herself out when John wished to be alone. Extension lecturing solved that problem admirably: he was only home every second weekend. The clairvoyance he perfected for his art, the art of solitude for his personal life.

In 1902, he and Margaret moved from Court House to a cottage in the village of Burpham, near Arundel, West Sussex. Bought at the instigation of his brother-in-law, Harry Lyon, Bankside remained—nominally—his home for twenty-five years. Powys asked his father for a loan of £550 to buy the property. C. F. refused, although not for reasons of economy as three years later he lent Littleton £3,000 interest-free to buy Sherborne Preparatory School.[18] He also told John at this time that he was replacing him with Littleton as the executor of his estate. It was a symbolic gesture indicating the father's complete confidence in his second son, and by implication, his lack of trust in his eldest. The father's refusal to lend him any money may have been a covert revenge for John threatening to become a Roman Catholic convert. Theodore wrote with asperity that he was just playing with conversion in order "to annoy your father";[19] Bertie, always the plainspoken one, called it bull-baiting. It was rather more than that. He was stirred by the "occult mysteriousness" and the "sensuous beauty" of the Roman liturgy but admitted that "the fact that it was all ritual too, and in a profound sense all *acting*, satisfied my dramatic nature as nothing had ever done before."[20] Under the influence of "the Catholic's convoluted metaphysic," Powys actually got as far as calling on the local priest as the first step to conversion. He could remember "the uncomfortable sensation that seized me, as if I were an actor who had suddenly discovered that his imaginary role was turning into a formidable reality, as I waited outside that priest's door." He seems to have concluded that the priest's absence was "a deciding omen"; certainly when his father said what a blow it would be "in my old age" Powys yielded at once.[21] Still suspicious, C. F. insisted John put this capitulation in writing to his friend Williams.

Perhaps Theodore's word "playing" best described John Cowper's interest in Catholicism. He was equally fascinated by Buddhism, Hinduism, Neoplatonism, and Theosophy.

> In the drawing-room at Montacute—knowing perfectly well how it would annoy him—I expatiated at exhaustive length upon the *Seven Principles of Man*, as interpreted by Annie Besant. I went on till he lifted up his head from his netting—he used to make our lawn tennis sets then—and burst out, trembling with fury:
> "She is a Demon—John—a Demon! *The woman is a Demon!*"[22]

Powys would always be attracted by esoteric religions but this teasing was more indicative of a movement away from parental influence than any serious commitment to theosophy. Gradually the strong emotional ties to his father were loosening.

The ties to his wife Margaret were another matter. From the earliest stories, he had used his writing as catharsis, allowing "all the seething suppressions of my inner life [to] come pouring forth."[23] Now the difficulties with his marriage, his sexual obsessions, his anger, are worked out in cheap notebooks on pencilled page after page. With each succeeding story, however repetitious they appear, he further clarifies the conflicts and, as importantly for his future as a writer, clarifies his expression of them. Two of the notebooks at Syracuse each contain a short story of about a hundred pages. A note attached to one indicates it was written shortly after he moved to Burpham. The story reverts to the conundrum outlined as early as 1894. Like Count Ravenstein and the gypsy Violante in his melodrama *With Love Away*, this latest hero, Sebastian Laud, a curate in a village recognizably Montacute, is passionately in love with an exotic and seductive woman, Lydia/Lileth Hornsey. She is described as "willowy and voluptuous, full of amorous solicitations." Laud is torn between his sexual desire and his spiritual aspiration. He marries Lydia, although "possessed as he was by his mad desire, Laud could not conceal from himself the knowledge that a desire so absorbing was in itself wrong . . . and that no marriage ceremony could really make it right." The bishop disapproves of the marriage and forces the couple to leave the village. The rest is sadly predictable: "Sebastian's relations to his wife varied now between moods of amorous servility, when he was simply her slave, and moods of bitter recrimination, when he heaped upon her cruel and pitiless words as the sole cause of their ruin." The story ends with Laud standing by a pond contemplating his disastrous marriage when, as if in a vision, an old man, leaning on a stick, appears. After the defrocked curate leaves, the ancient throws himself and his stick into the pond which closes over him.

Ponds and sticks were never far from Powys's mind. While on one level the story is rehearsing the troubled relationship with Margaret, on another it is pointing to something that will preoccupy him more deeply and for much longer. In a passage in *Autobiography* where he describes his life during his long trips on the lecturing circuit, a further twist is introduced to the old Shirley Fear.

> For hours and hours I would sit up reading *The Return of the Native* or *Far from the Madding Crowd* or *The Woodlanders* or *Jude the Obscure*, till by degrees as I listened to the wind in the chimney the genius of Hardy would drive my demon away and some formidable Spirit from Stonehenge would come rushing out of the Magic West into this dark house and my whole inner being would change. Then I would sit with my bony knees close to the red coals and feel myself to be as formidable and as powerful as that south-west wind itself! I would feel myself to be what the great Magician Merlin was before he met his "Belle Dame Sans Merci."[24]

Reading Hardy evoked all the old desire to become "formidable," whether as a writer or as a magician, or both. Like the ancient who drowns in the pond, Merlin lost his power when he succumbed to Nineue and the seductions of the white-thorn maze in the forest of Broceliande. "The perils of the deep" are oblivion, loss of identity—a kind of spiritual castration. So far as Laud/Powys is concerned, it is the absorbing male lust for a woman that makes a man powerless and imprisoned. The motif of self-generative, self-creative potency will become one of Powys's most illuminating themes in his future great novels.

Ironically, he wrote the Merlin passage as he contemplated the fact that after six years of marriage, Margaret was pregnant. Their only child, a son, was born on August 30, 1902. They called him Littleton Alfred. For reasons best known to himself, Powys in later years assiduously promulgated the myth that he was unable or unwilling to have normal sexual relationships, and that in any case, he was particularly frightened of sexual intercourse with a virgin. Margaret, obviously determined to have a child, went into hospital to be surgically "deflowered."[25] Nonetheless, since even "the least reference to normal sex functions turned my stomach,"[26] he considered her subsequent pregnancy a "miracle."[27] This myth was trotted out any number of times during his life, convincing friends and followers that he was psychologically if not physically impotent. As unpublished diary details show, he was perfectly capable of normal intercourse, but preferred masturbation—which had the added advantage of avoiding conception. In a letter written in 1923 when he was twenty-one, Littleton Alfred rather sadly refers to himself as "the creature whom you had the misfortune by an unhappy accident to create out of your loins!"[28] Whatever the complicated reasons John may have entertained for not wanting a child, Littleton Alfred eventually became a focus of a convoluted pattern of love, guilt, and reparation. For the time being, Powys's lecturing schedule meant that he saw very little of the baby. From the beginning, Margaret doted on her son; unfortunately this did not bring the couple any closer. John found the maternal instinct "destructive of the sylph-nature."[29] Worse still, maternal love was a threat to "the inmost flame of my soul, the vital leap of my life-force," which flees "at the faintest approach of any warm maternal lovingness."[30] For Powys, the fear of paternity was associated not only with his sexual inversion but his belief that his "life-force" should be channeled into creative, not procreative activity; that it should result in a work of art, not a child.

Once again, this idea was not unique to himself. Gerard Manley Hopkins, for example, wrote in 1886 that "the begetting of one's thoughts on paper" was "a kind of male gift."[31] It was a celibate enterprise that required no contact with the maternal body. John Cowper's dislike of coitus was in part an aversion to female sexuality, but it was also bound up with the myth of male creativity. He did not want to be a father in the usual sense, his father's sense, but a father in the celibate, self-creating, homoerotic sense. His son therefore had to be a "miracle." In a late novel, *Porius*, the miraculous child is a product of masturbation, grown not in a womb but in a magician's alchemical retort. In his first published novels, a youth appears as the hero's savior and muse—not an inspiring goddess but a masculine muse, looking suspiciously like John Addington Symonds's vision of the beautiful young man with large blue eyes and wavy yellow hair emitting a halo of misty light.

As if on cue, his brother Llewelyn—a beautiful boy with "a wealth of bright golden curly hair"—now took centre-stage in his life. In October 1902, Lulu (the diminutive by which he was always called) was at Sherborne, a schoolboy of eighteen going through the usual teenage agonies of religious doubt and sexual awakening. Until this time, the older Littleton had been Lulu's especial hero. He was very proud of this brother's athletic prowess, and Littleton took time to go long walks with the boy, sharing with him his deep pleasure in nature lore and in Romantic poetry. When Llewelyn was fifteen, Littleton, then twenty-five, took him for a fortnight's holiday on Exmoor, and even thirty-five years later Lulu remembered every incident of that holiday together. It was in this time of "utter happiness" that he began tentatively to question the virtue of the denial of such happiness. Two years later, he was even more doubtful of the Christian teaching of life-denial, having fallen in love with a school friend.[32] He turned to Littleton for advice. Now a schoolmaster, Littleton could only warn him against intimacy with another schoolboy and counselled him on "economy of semen." Lulu then wrote to John, who, no doubt remembering his own adolescent turmoil, respond-ed promptly and with quirky common-sense. He told Lulu he must not feel too unhappy or guilty: "You must expect to have difficulty in keeping control over that more unruly member even than the tongue. Though the tongue is a fire, that is a furnace—and when your amorous and affectionate heart with its desire for love is added to these volcanic crater-vents of animal desire the difficulty becomes double." John then goes on in this very long letter to assure the boy that "wishes—glances—touches" are acceptable so long as "the last embraces are not reached." He ends by saying "when you have to choose any afternoon between the wild pleasures of lust and the calm pleasures of books and philosophy, think of J. C. P. and for his sake choose the latter."[33] Knowing the "J. C. P." of *Autobiography*, this may come across as flagrant hypocrisy but Lulu never forgot his loving concern and remained devoted to John for the rest of his life. Llewelyn may have been remembering that time when he wrote Littleton in 1937 congratulating him on his book *The Joy of It* but going on to say, "You place 'liberal opinions' as important, but then you qualify this declaration by insisting upon diplomatic reticences and this confirms a reader of my kind in his suspicion of an educational system that is largely in the hands of those who are intent upon leaving the more troubled water smooth upon the surface." In another letter, as if to rub it in, Llewelyn refers to John as "that elder brother of mine who is by far the most exciting and God-like figure I have ever had to do with in my life, and whose inspirations have illuminated my life from the days when I sat like a little frog upon his navel!"[34]

That "God-like figure" was having a rough time of it in 1902. Margaret felt she required not only a maid and a nanny but an addition to the house after the birth of Littleton Alfred. John expanded his grueling schedule of lectures around England for the next two years to meet the increased expenses. Most of his time was spent on the northern circuit between Manchester and the Lake District. He would return home only for a day on alternate Sundays to see "Mag and her kid" as he refers to them in a letter to his sister Gertrude. It was a truly terrible exis-tence, trailing across England from one industrial city to another for months on end. When he wasn't lecturing in Manchester, Derby, Coventry, Leeds, Birmingham, Halifaxe, Sheffield, he would spend all his free hours wandering for miles through "the most wretched and sordid streets hunting for little squalid news-paper-shops, that sometimes contained provocative, if not pornographical pictures in their windows."[35] The "desperate lust-starved walks," he noted wryly, may have been good exercise, but not much else. Only once did he pick up a street girl. She took him into her poor home, past sleeping children and a man cleaning harness, to her bedroom. He was so disconcerted when she lay on the bed without even unlacing her muddy boots that finally he just gave her some money and left. "The man in the room below bade me good night without lifting his eyes."[36]

In the midst of such "famished desolation,"[37] he encountered a life-giving refuge in the form of Tom Jones, who now became an important addition to his circle. Jones was a "passionate and secretive Welshman" who worked as a clerk in the cotton exchange in Liverpool. How they met is not known—possibly it was at one of Powys's courses, but for many years thereafter John made Liverpool an unofficial northern base, staying with Tom Jones in whatever Merseyside lodging house he happened to be in. They would sit for hours in the "Kardomah Cafe" discussing Nietzsche's philosophy and Keats's poetry. Jones was immensely generous, sharing his bed, his meals, and his innumerable girlfriends. After John's abortive experience with the streetwalker, "Tom Jones's girls" were "an oasis of paradisiac happiness,"[38] and he remembered those visits to Liverpool as "among the happiest times of my whole life."[39] It would seem that the enjoyment he derived was largely due to the fact that the girls were not "intellectual Bohemians," but "lower middle-class" shop girls. Above all they were not his wife. The girls were "enjoyed with no afterthoughts of emotional agitation, no complicated responsibilities, no tragic jealousies."[40] Powys suggests that these encounters were essentially innocent, consisting of "every kind of dalliance they liked, short of the final consummation," and that Jones taught him "to diffuse my impersonal craving over a thousand and one little *accompaniments* of erotic desire."[41] Whatever that may mean, Powys seems to have got his greatest trans-port when the sweet-natured Liverpool girls sat on his lap and he caressed them, while he felt they received their biggest thrill when he recited "Lycidas" and "Ode to a Grecian Urn" to them.

Although he says that for the first five years after his son's birth he began "to get better control over my nerves," he continued to have "deep moods of rebel-lion against all responsibility."[42] Now in his thirties, he was also aware that he had not fulfilled his early creative promise. Before marriage, both Margaret and her brother Harry had been as confident as Powys was that he would be a master writer and that his forte was poetry. They were now dubious, as was Powys himself. Although he persisted in writing poetry for the rest of his life, he was beginning to wonder if he was not "a mere imitating copy-cat, repeating, repeating, repeating the rhythms of men of genius."[43] He was writing more stories, but was conscious that they were of a kind that could not be shown to his wife or family and decidedly not publishable. He feared that he was "destined to be as ego-centric in my writings as I was abnormal in my eroticism and diseased in my conscience."[44]

On the evidence of the stories that he was writing at this time, it is apparent that his sense of creative frustration was as strong as his sexual frustration. Escape seemed the only answer, and in January 1905 he got his chance. The American Society for the Extension of University Teaching (ASEUT), founded in 1890 and based in Philadelphia, was always eager to employ the best Oxford Delegacy lecturers—their accents and their gowns were very popular with American audiences. Powys was invited to lecture in the eastern United States for three months, an arrangement that suited his circumstances admirably. He was paid twice as much as in England, and because the term times were different, he was able to lecture in the U.S.A. for the first three months, and in England or Europe for the rest of the year. Judging from the letters he wrote to his family, that first trip was both stimulating and bewildering. He found the look of the houses and streets "very foreign," the landscape strange in appearance, the men "a very queer race," and the women "like olives—an acquired taste." However, he hoped he would "survive."[45] He did. It was the beginning of a twenty-five year lecturing career in America.

He was back in England at the end of March and went directly to London. Undaunted by his Birmingham experience, or perhaps emboldened by his Liverpool education, he had struck up a friendship with a prostitute called Lily. Over the next years, Powys was to have much to say about prostitutes, whom he romanticized shamelessly. In a study of Keats, written about 1910 but which deservedly remained unpublished for eighty years, he opined: "One of the chief tests of a man of genius is his invariable preference for 'fallen' over 'unfallen' women. . . . How else is a man of genius, unless born in a hovel, to escape from 'Ladies?' How else is he to encounter real women—that is to say, women of the people?" He went further in an essay penned the same year entitled "The New Paganism," writing, "It is well known that the only women that poets and artists feel really at home with—to say nothing of saints—are the women of the street, and this is not only because the others are so cold and so formal, but because they get so dissociated from reality that they have got, by reason of their contemptible virtue, so artificial that it is rapidly becoming impossible to have anything to do with them."[46] Needless to say, this is more about his relationship with Margaret at this period than cutting-edge sociological theory. Lily not only proved that his was an artist's rebellion against convention and class but, even better, her consumption rendered her a veritable sylph. Amazingly, Margaret, despite her "contemptible virtue," once allowed him to invite his "pet whore" to Burpham. Apparently, she was polite to the prostitute, but the maids "of the people" refused to wait on her.[47]

Lily provided him with new inspiration—or at least new copy. Powys came back from America determined to "stop writing my huge unprintable book, and begin on a proper, a normal—or as normal as I could make it—Romance."[48] Although in the end he apparently managed only six chapters of this, the writing was less stilted than previous attempts, and he cut out the orgies and the long philosophical discussions with his male friends.[49] The first chapters of "Owen Prince" are about Glory Raven, aged fourteen, the younger daughter of a drunken woman who wants Glory to follow in her older sister's footsteps and "start the game." Glory works for a pittance for a second-hand bookseller of fifty who has hired her to dust his books (and so he can watch the "blooming" girl up a stepladder). Glory's boyfriend is Lopsy Turk, a boot-black. Possibly becoming aware that his knowledge of what two young Cockneys are likely to say and do was minimal, J.C.P. soon drops them, and from chapter four onward we are back in the village of Godbarrow with the same characters and conflicts that he has rehearsed so often before. A discussion is taking place between the Vicar of Godbarrow, the Reverend Randolph Runnymede, and the widow of Captain Prince about a possible marriage between his daughter Bet and her son Owen. Owen had spent three years at Oxford and lived a year in Paris. He has come home with a burning desire to express in English "those fleshly and spiritual subtleties" of French prose. Bet has been to a "modern High School" and developed a "deep respect for intellect, for talent, for genius" although her "proclivities" tend to the athletic and open-air. The two young people have been "brought up, you might say, like brother and sister" but since both have returned home they have been seeing much of each other and the parents, concerned about "the world's opinion," wish to see them married.

Owen is "as little suited for domestic life, or anything approaching what is called 'settling down' as any youth could be." Instead, he "cherishes literary ambitions." Bet is "not in the ordinary sense of the word in the least in love with him" but her great ambition is to marry "a great man," and a great man "was the especial human product she was yearning to help to produce." Powys hints that what is hidden both from herself and others is that "the primary instinct of the woman to secure, at any price and by the nearest means, a chance of obeying Nature's tyrannical mandate." In other words, Bet wants to produce a child, not to help create a great poet, although Powys insists in several ways that she is not aware that she is being used "as a tool by the Great Mother so insatiable of offspring." A difficult conversation between the vicar and Owen ensues in which the vicar asks bluntly whether Owen wants to marry his daughter or not. Owen is angry that he "should be pressed into a corner in this bald and brutal way" and asks if he can postpone his answer until the next day. There follows several paragraphs in which Powys analyzes why the personality of Owen makes the situation almost impossible for him.

> He was so devoted to his mother, depended so much upon her love for him and more than that, upon her respect for him, that to do anything which would cause her distress or shake her confidence seemed almost impossible. . . . He had done nothing in this case that any one could lay hands upon as definitely wrong, and yet he was as much afraid of a "scene" as the most guilty, the most secretive of criminals. It was partly the cowardice of his temperament and partly also the fact that, though of a wandering and adventurous spirit, he was extremely dependent upon the attitude towards him of those he loved. It was necessary to him to have a life of his own apart from this inner circle, but it was also necessary that when he returned to the inner circle he should be received with triumphal honours and without the least shade of disapprobation. . . . To be shut up in a prison at the very out-set of his life . . . how could he, for any one's sake, submit to such a destiny.

The story ends when his mother misunderstands a careless remark he makes as meaning he will marry Bet, and Owen is left in "speechless dismay . . . as though contemplating the performance of an extremely absurd play." It is impossible not to see this story as the first coherent and undisguised explanation of why he married Margaret, even if it was ten years and a child later before he found himself able to do so. Margaret was determined to marry a "great man" and, possibly unconsciously, also determined to have a child. The marriage was the dearest wish of his mother, Mary Cowper (or at least so John thought). It is also strongly hinted here that his engagement came as a result of the urging of his father, C. F. (Although in this draft the vicar is Betty's father, in other fragments he is Owen's father.) Powys finally makes it clear that he knew from the beginning that the marriage would be disastrous, but his own personality was such that he had no choice except to go ahead with it. This is the best piece of psychological self-analysis that Powys had yet achieved in his writing. He depended not only on the love of his mother and the approval of his father, but the adoration of his brothers and sisters. The story is strangely prescient: his "wandering spirit" eventually led him to spend most of the year in the United States, but he expected to be welcomed ecstatically by his family, if not by his wife, when he returned once a year to home ground.

On the May 20, 1905, his brother Bertie married his cousin Dorothy in London. Considering that Owen is convinced his own calamitous marriage to Bet was "arranged," it is curious that Powys never ceased trying to arrange marriages for his friends and relatives. John had met Dorothy on one of his trips north and decided she would make Bertie a good wife. Possibly because he was largely responsible for the union, he organized the wedding breakfast and invited the guests. It must have been a fairly bizarre event. Neither the parents of the bride or the groom were present, nor was Littleton. Bertie had been working for

Harry Lyon, now a highly successful architect with his own London firm, since at least 1901. However, Harry also did not attend, perhaps because Lily the prostitute, wearing a grotesquely large hat bought by John, was a member of the wedding party. Theodore had been married less than two weeks before but came without his wife. Two others of his circle were there—John William Williams and Bernie O'Neill—as was Llewelyn, now at Cambridge.

Also at the wedding was Louis Umfreville Wilkinson. John had met Louis through Bernie O'Neill in the summer of 1901 and described him as a "most resplendent invader of my life."[50] That is a fair description of what was to become an intensely equivocal relationship. Louis was another family connection. His mother, a girlhood friend of Mary Cowper, had married the Reverend Walter George Wilkinson. Wilkinson ran a school at Aldeburgh, Suffolk, and it was here that Theodore had been sent for special attention. Louis, born in 1881, was nine years younger than John. The only son, he was adored and indulged by his mother and his nanny: "Whatever Master Louis wants, Master Louis should have."[51] He went up to Pembroke, Oxford, but was expelled for blasphemy in December 1901. No doubt the irreverent pantomimes and mock masses which led to Louis's expulsion would have amused and interested John Cowper, then preoccupied with his own more concealed rebellions. The charges created a certain publicity and it was only by some luck and a good deal of pull that the Reverend Mr. Wilkinson managed to get his son into St. John's, Cambridge, in the autumn of 1902.

Powys promptly nicknamed Louis "the Archangel," describing him as "a strangely beautiful youth, all of chemical reds and greens and golds and scarlets entirely inhuman." That hint of the Wildean hermaphrodite may have been misleading but Louis was very much the nineties aesthete at this time. With his long hair dipping over an eyebrow, his extraordinary eyelashes, delicate complexion, scarlet lips, he described himself as having "an elegance of a rather perverse kind . . . rather suggestive of the strange allure of those long lines of the bodies of Beardsley's women."[52] Possibly it was this sexual ambiguity which led John to avoid introducing his young brother to Louis, but when Llewelyn went up to Corpus in the autumn of 1903, he promptly introduced himself. For a few years the two young men became inseparable. Louis in his autobiography called it a romantic friendship, pointing out rather ambiguously that "it is possible for one man to be preoccupied by another, in loverlike fashion . . . without his being 'in love' completely, as with a woman; though of course in the two kinds of love the same elements exist."[53] John, having established his close relationship with Llewelyn after the birth of his son, may have felt rather jealous of this friendship. In any case, when Bertie invited the three of them to join him for a weekend in Grantham shortly before the wedding, John made an abrupt decision. The American lecture authorities had asked him to recommend someone to lecture for them for six months beginning that September. Powys persuaded them to take Louis although he was only twenty-three and had not yet sat his Tripos. As Llewelyn said wistfully, "*It is* good of Jack!"[54] but the charitable act also got rid of

Louis, at least temporarily, and left Llewelyn to find consolation once again with
his elder brother.

In England, Powys continued his grueling schedule of lecturing for the Oxford
delegacy but collapsed with ulcer pain in February 1907 while on tour. He was in
hospital for three weeks and then returned to Burpham. There was a further crisis
and it was found that his ulcers had now blocked the duodenal cavity. He was operated on in a nursing home in Harley Street, "being an incredible number of hours
on the table." Llewelyn came constantly to visit him in the following month of
hospitalization, and John was touched by the young man's attachment to him. He
could understand Littleton's, "for it is like mine for him," but "Llewelyn's has something else in it, like a trouble in the Sun at some chasm appearing in the rondure
of the Moon."[55] When he was released from the hospital he went to Bognor to
recuperate over the summer. Harry Lyon was present much of the time, and there
were some heated discussions with his wife and brother-in-law, who wanted young
Littleton (nicknamed Tony) to be brought up as an Anglo-Catholic. Lyon had
married off his eldest sister, Caroline, to another Corpus friend, Percy Wise, who
became a leader in the Anglo-Catholic movement in Australia. In 1902, when
Harry visited Australia, Wise was having a new church built and gave Lyon his first
major commission to design it. Harry had come back a convert. Another Corpus
friend, Edmund Courtney Pearce, now married to a third Lyon sister, Connie, had
also become an Anglo-Catholic. Pearce was admitted to Corpus two years before
John Cowper, graduated brilliantly, and became a Fellow in 1895 and Dean in
1901. As Margaret no doubt pointed out from time to time, Pearce was altogether
more successful both as a scholar and in worldly terms than John ever was, becoming Master of Corpus in 1914 and then Bishop of Derby in 1927. However, his
importance at this time was that, as the College's influential Dean, he was leading
Corpus further away from Evangelicalism toward a liberal Anglo-Catholic theology.[56] With his eldest son flirting with Catholicism and spiritualism and his beloved
college cutting its evangelical roots, C. F. must have wondered—out loud and loudly—what the world was coming to. His refusal to lend John the money to buy
Burpham had many roots.

The anger and frustration on both sides of the marriage, as well as the vexed
problem of the son's education, is addressed in a play called The Entermores,
which was written during that recuperation period of 1907.[57] The plot is undisguisedly based on real events. Madeline Entermore has inherited a large fortune
from an uncle in Australia which her husband Roland, an unsuccessful poet,
wants to use to fund a magazine, The Black Pierrot. The publishers, Florian Fay
and Theophilus Groteus, modeled after Bernie O'Neill and Louis Wilkinson,
are two misogynistic fin-de-siècle types who are contemptuous of Roland's
poetic ambitions and talent, but eager to take the money. Madeline has other
plans for her legacy. Deeply religious, she wants to use the money to help build
a church, of which her brother would be the architect. She is very dependent
on the Anglo-Catholic curate, Pontifex, who wants to take charge of the edu-

cation of the Entermores' son, Tony. To Pontifex she confesses: "I have found out lately that I do not love my husband as much as I used to. And I want to ask you, is it wrong to feel this—this coldness when he makes advances to me? . . . O, sometimes when he spends whole evenings with his friends and comes home late—I am sitting up and I feel as if I almost hate him." Roland's friends include the young prostitute Bess Round, and in a scene which has a distant (very distant) Shavian echo, Roland and Madeline quarrel. He tells her that his flirting is "pure amusement": "Come, Madeline, I will be quite honest and candid with you. All husbands, without a single exception, feel these passing desires for other women.' She asks, "Why do women submit to such a degradation?" He responds: "Partly because Society is organized to make them submit by keeping them dependent on men for their own and their children's support—and partly because of their incredible ignorance." This goes on for some time, with Roland telling Madeline that she should be "gratified at having won the permanent and spiritual affection of an honourable man" and "allow him these little lapses." She flounces off, and he says to himself: "It's bad enough to be married at all, but to be married to a—nun!"

Powys tried once again to utilize his Lily-inspired knowledge of the lower classes and introduces into the play a barmaid, a coal heaver, a pimp, and several prostitutes. It is all very bad stuff, but he does manage to get another hit at Margaret by having Flo the barmaid say about Madeline Entermore: "Depend on it, 'ee was sorry when 'ee was married. A man who's faithful to a shrew wot 'ooked 'im into marriage, ain't anything less than a shrew." The play ends with a highly unlikely scene where the two prostitutes argue over the pimp, and Bess throws herself out the window, crying "I thought I 'eard my old mudder callin' me. Mudder!" For some inexplicable reason this death leads to the reconciliation of the married couple, who decide they will not invest the money either in building a church or funding a literary magazine, but in their son's future.

By 1907, Louis Wilkinson was a part of the circle, but he proved a divisive member, for Wilkinson was an astute judge of character with an acerbic way with words. The letters exchanged between Powys and Wilkinson during the time the play was being written make it clear that although Louis by now had an "unqualified dislike" of Harry Lyon, his relationship with Jack (as Powys was now being called) also was not without rancor. In one letter Powys writes, "Your enemy may be unsatisfactory and disagreeable person but you mustn't be allowed to call his emotions 'spurious.'" Powys chose to dwell on Wilkinson's contempt for Lyon, but Louis pointed out that "spurious" and "sentimental" were the terms he had applied to Jack himself.[58] A few years after this, Wilkinson wrote a novel, *The Buffoon*,[59] which deals in part with the events that took place between 1905 and 1907. Although it was published in 1916, when events had created an even more convoluted love-hate relationship with John/Jack, the novel throws an interesting light on the three men. In the book Powys is Jack Welsh, Harry Lyon is called Reggie Tryers, and Louis Wilkinson is Edward Raynes.

The description of Jack Welsh is near caricature, but it is perceptive and witty. Dressed "in what looked like cast-off clothing," with "little co-ordination between his body and his mind," Welsh could "look like an imbecile" at one moment and at another "almost noble." But Raynes decides that despite the "sprawled effect," Jack "was not a charlatan." In a few brief sentences Wilkinson blows away at least two of Powys's most cherished personae. Raynes/Louis asks Reggie/Harry if Welsh has written anything, and Lyon replies: "nothing but stray poems and a few chapters of a disgraceful novel," which "if he ever gets it published, it will break his mother's heart."[60] Raynes accuses Welsh of being a flatterer to enhance his own ego.

> You heighten the character—abilities and vices—of every one you meet, because that makes it more interesting and sensational for you. So you're always moving among remarkable men: the plan works magnificently into the hands of your egoism. It works all round.[61]

Wilkinson is not any easier on himself as the character Raynes: "His existence was agreeable and superficial." Active in mind and body, "Edward's balanced variety of well-toned interests conspired to prevent him from going intellectually or emotionally too far, and so kept him safe." Above all, "he did not enter upon painful self-analysis."[62] From these portraits, it is difficult to imagine two people less alike than Welsh/Powys and Raynes/Wilkinson, and the events in the novel point to the clashes the two would have in the future.

However, it is the relationship between Powys, his brother-in-law, and, by indirection, Margaret, that catches the attention. The hostility between the two men may have had a continuing sexual component, although Jack always denied any homosexual proclivities. Alternatively, Powys may have become aware that Lyon, rejected as a lover, had tricked him into marrying his sister. By the time *The Buffoon* was written in 1916, John had played the same if-I-can't-have-you-my-best-friend/sister-can joke on Louis. Louis has Welsh say of Reggie Tryers, "His spleen against me is quite terrific. . . . I have treated his sister badly I know, but he always encourages me—said she wouldn't mind, it was what she expected . . . and that women had no souls."[63] Tryers, on the other hand, is convinced that Welsh has deliberately set about to destroy both him and Margaret. "I can't leave her alone to Welsh. His cruelty is appalling—you can't conceive of it—not ordinary cruelty. He tortures the soul. Everything with him is in the brain. Nothing you can take hold of. That's why he maddens me. He suggests to me abominable vices—he doesn't act them himself. He can only enjoy them by getting other people to act them." Tryers says Welsh is dangerous "because he seems such a fool," but "he has a kind of hypnotic power—hidden away."[64]

As Reggie Tryers explains what he means, the reason for the unusual enmity between Wilkinson and Lyon comes out, albeit in an oblique fashion: Lyon was at one of the mock masses Louis held in his rooms at Oxford for which he was sent down. Subsequently, Wilkinson asked Lyon to intercede with the college authorities over whom Lyon had influence, and Lyon refused. Wilkinson never forgave him for that, but in fairness, here he gives the other side of the story.[65] It seemed strange that Lyon, always so heedful of his career, should be at such an event, but in *The Buffoon*, Lyon/Tryers suggests that it was *Powys* who, under the guise of introducing him to a friend, "an Oxford man," had deliberately set out to undermine his faith.

> He knew my passions were strong. He knew it was only my religion—my belief in immortality—that saved me from them. He knew that the one sure way to ruin me was to take away my Faith and let my passions have full swing. . . . And then when I yielded . . .
>
> "Are you sure," he'd say, "that this free Pagan life is the best after all? Won't you be sorry in the end?" . . . Curse him! He wouldn't let me enjoy even that life, though it was he who had seduced me![66]

Clearly the relations amongst the three men were complicated and venomous, but in the novel there were two things about which they are in total agreement: the imbecility of women, and the constraints that middle-class convention places on man's freedom. All for pagan freedom, these men sing from the same hymn book. For Tryers a woman is "like some sort of disturbing insect" and marriage is "servitude: it is degradation." Jack Welsh is slightly more circumspect, complaining that "there is certainly something gross and unfastidious about the feminine temperament."[67] Edward Raynes rails against another aspect of femininity that repels him: "the peculiar grossness of maternal lust" and the "emotional blackmail" of the mother.[68] This may be Louis's reaction to his own mother; another indirect hit at Powys; or it may simply be an idea imbibed from the decadent ethos.

The Buffoon ends with Welsh dying during his ulcer operation. Raynes goes to visit him the day before and thinks as he looks at him, "He should have been a genius, was a genius perhaps. What was it, though, that had failed him? Something—some interfusion of substance that he had just missed—another of Nature's tricks?"[69] In real life Powys survived the operation but his ulcers were to become the pivot around which his emotional and physical life revolved. The first attack occurred at Sherborne School and except for the remission during the Cambridge years, ulcers and dyspepsia plagued him for the rest of his life. The latest medical theory suggests that more than ninety percent of ulcers are caused by a bacterium spread through fecal-oral contact. Given the primitive toilet facilities of Montacute Vicarage this is perfectly possible, although it does not account for the fact that the sisters did not suffer from them. It may have been a genetic weakness, inherited only by the males in the family. All the sons suffered from duodenal ulcers, with the exception of Theodore. Littleton was harassed by them, Will had a number of life-threatening operations for them, and both Bertie and Llewelyn died as a result of perforated ulcers. Whatever the original cause of the ulcers may have been, Powys himself was convinced that it was his "sylpholepsy"—in other words, his eroticism—that inflamed them. Louis Wilkinson is fairly circumspect in *The Buffoon* about Powys's dislike of penetrative sexual intercourse. He has Welsh say,

> "'I admit that I find it a little fatiguing—a trifle tiresome, to deal with—er—objective matter. It's not in my line. I find it so much easier, more satisfactory, simple to imagine. . . . The beach at Littlehampton in the summer, for example. It is quite enough for me to sit there."
>
> "Holding a silent orgy?" inquired Edward.

Tryers/Lyon breaks in : "That's why Welsh has this frightful nervous dyspepsia. It's all through that cursed Cerebralism of his."

"It's worth it!" cried Welsh.[70]

The chorus of three chants the conundrum of pain. What is "worth it"? Is it worth having pain in order to indulge in voyeurism with resulting sexual release, or is the pain worth it if it provides sufficient punishment demanded by his "diseased conscience"? Whatever "it" was, pain had a continuing appeal for Jack Powys.

Despite the major operation, he was back lecturing in England by September and in the U.S. during the first three months of 1908 when the Philadelphia Society engaged him again for the spring tour. He wrote often to the young Llewelyn during this period. Earlier letters had been slightly condescending in an elder brother way, but they now became more confidential, or rather, more man-to-man or lad-to-lad, recounting to Llewelyn when he is "resisting those perilous calls of the lower lord," and when he cannot. In America he soon discovered that burlesque shows gave him a new outlet for his voyeurism, but his rampant sexual needs occasionally oppressed him and at times frightened him. "His serene magnificence the Lord of the Ascendant" was, in more ways than one, his prick; it goaded him "to think of the years and years yet to come—and never never free from the Brutish Sting. What I wish is that by some single effort—not possibly quite as bloody as Origens—. . ." His purist zeal, however, did not rise to castration, and seldom could he resist "the delicious peril."[71]

He returned to England in early April, but by the twenty-fifth he was in Dresden and Leipzig giving a series of twelve lectures on "Representative poets and prose writers of the Nineteenth Century." The university extension method had been introduced in Germany ten years earlier but this was considered an important pioneering venture by the Oxford delegacy, partly because the lectures were not intended simply for English expatriates, but for highly educated Germans with a professional interest in modern languages and literature.[72] It was a mark of the delegacy's high regard for him that they asked John Cowper to be their representative. As it turned out, the series attracted much attention and praise. He wrote Littleton from Dresden a nicely sedate description of the German royalty who had come his lecture, of how he and his cousin Alice (who was with him during this trip) had gone to see *Hamlet* and taken a trip down the

Elbe on a steamer, of listening to the blackbirds in the gardens of the Zwinger palace.[73] He wrote Lulu on the same trip a much different letter. It is an amusing story of a typically inept Powys who can nonetheless laugh at himself. He told Llewelyn that "in the matter of all matters" he has had a three-day orgy reading pornography, and especially a book "bound in plain blue cover like a government report, entitled 'Pearl.'"[74] While he refers at the beginning of the letter to a book, toward the end of the letter he refers to books. *The Pearl* made its debut in 1879, a monthly journal of erotica for every taste. It flourished on the subterranean market until 1880, when it vanished as mysteriously as it had appeared. The eighteen issues were subsequently republished in a variety of editions; the version Powys read would probably have consisted of three fairly hefty volumes. When he "recovered" he tried to get rid of the incriminating books by tying them together and fastening the bundle to a stone with a piece of string, intending to throw it into the river Elbe. However, he became convinced he was being watched and that when people heard the splash they would report him. So he walked a long way along the river to avoid detection but was afraid to get close enough to the slippery edge to throw them. He next crossed a high bridge and thought he could throw the books from there, but just as he raised his arm "someone looked at me." After that he got on a ferry, thinking he could quietly slip them over the side, but feared the splash would be heard and an attendant "hook it out all open and clear to the eye." So he paid the fare, leapt to the land, and bolted.

> I fled, fled, fled, along the river Elbe, but always I seemed watched, watched, and I thought if I am seen, if I am heard and the splash will be terrific, I shall be cobbed. I got half crazy, I have been reading the books so madly and they burnt my hands—such books—Pearl! Everyone looked at my bundle. It grew larger and larger. The contents showed themselves in flaming letters through the damned blue paper covers. I observed an official following me.

He finally found the courage to throw the pornographic bundle into the river but,

> Horrors of horrors the thing floated. Yes, the devil made all that condensed sardism light as dove's feathers and in power like a barge, so that it actually floated, a great cursed blue island with that fucking stone still hanging beneath it at the end of the string—for the stone wasn't big enough to drown such a book. . . . I ran away and left it as it was.

He ends his letter with "Bless you my dearest Lulu I am now quite calm and happy." Exhausted might have been a more accurate word. Ragged copies of the raunchy *Pearl* can still be found floating around (although on the Internet, not the river). For a man who insisted that all normal sexuality sickened him, he would have found the stories in the *Pearl* disappointingly "normal." There are, however, enough stories of young girls masturbating each other to quiet him.

He explored Germany for the rest of the summer and in the autumn of 1908 he was back in England on the lecture trail. Llewelyn said that it was at this time that he "fell more completely than ever under the influence of my brother J. C. P."[75] Llewelyn had been ploughed in the History Tripos but after a summer of cramming, in November 1906, took a second-class pass degree. He finally got a job at a boys' prep school at Broadstairs. He hated it, terrified that the boys were cleverer than he was—which, quite possibly, they were. His next position was at Bromsgrove, where he coped slightly better, but apparently not well enough, as the headmaster suggested he try another profession. He then tutored a rich boy for three months, but "playing the sedulous ape"[76] was not to his taste either. John rescued him by convincing the secretary of the American University Extension Society to invite Llewelyn to lecture for three months beginning January 1909. Obviously worried that his "reputation as a recommender"[77] was on the line, John advised Llewelyn to prepare his lectures and practice reading them, then from August to December Lulu followed his brother around northern England being coached and listening to him lecture.

Despite the best efforts of John, who actually wrote some of his lectures, Llewelyn failed abysmally as a lecturer in America. Louis, who was also there and attended one of his earliest lectures in New York, wrote that "listening to it was one of the most acutely embarrassing and distressing experiences I have ever had."[78] Before they left for America, John had advised Lulu to apply for admission to the Oxford List. Although his application was politely deferred "for further information" not even John's high standing with the extension authorities could convince them to take on a person with an inferior degree and no lecturing skills. When they returned to England in April, the circle rallied around with various ideas of what to do with Lulu. Cousin Ralph Shirley had a controlling interest in the publishing house Rider & Son, and had offered Bernie O'Neill a directorship in the company. Bernie declined because John hinted that Llewelyn would take it if he did not want it. Llewelyn turned it down because he disliked the idea of working routine office hours. John then suggested that Llewelyn join Tom Jones in the cotton trade, an even more improbable idea.

Littleton, who was by this time the headmaster of the Sherborne Preparatory, now stepped in and offered Lulu a position as an assistant master. Shortly after his marriage to Mabel Bennett on August 4, 1904, an opportunity arose to buy the Sherborne Prep. Littleton borrowed the large sum from his father, and to his great joy, found himself back in Sherborne in April 1905. It was a successful venture and from accounts left by his pupils, he and his wife were greatly loved and respected. Llewelyn was not enthusiastic about another round of schoolmastering, but his father put a halt to further procrastinations and Llewelyn was at Sherborne by the first of May. Despite his lecturing fiasco, he had some faint hopes that the American Society would employ him again. When they declined, he returned to the Prep for the autumn term. In November he was diagnosed with consumption. It was an event that changed the course of

Llewelyn's life; it was also an acceptable if drastic way out of failure.

In the meantime, Jack made his third trip to Germany, returning to Dresden and Leipzig, this time to speak on Shakespeare. After the course ended, he went on another sightseeing tour, travelling with Miss Jane Heatley, the headmistress of his first girls' school. The question arises whether he could speak or at least read German. He always insisted he could not, but he appears to have got along very well with his German hosts, not all of whom would have spoken English, and he read a good deal of German literature at this time. The question is not an idle one, because certain of his writings strongly suggest the influence of German novelists and philosophers whose books were, at the time untranslated. Perhaps his wife or his sisters Marian and Gertrude, all of whom were fluent in German, translated for him.

By the first of June he was back at Burpham with his wife and son. He told Littleton that there was a "remote chance" that he would be asked to lecture next May in Heidelberg and hoped that it "might lead to something permanent." To that end he began writing a biography of Keats, and wondered if it would be "a good thing with a view to settling down somewhere as a professor, to claim a Litt.D at Cambridge?"[79] Despite his public stance of belittling ambition, and his father's scorn for such beings, becoming a professor was a possibility that he discussed often over the next years with Littleton. He never did get the degree, but, ironically, it was at this time that Louis "accidentally" got a degree of Doctor of Letters from St. John's College, Annapolis. According to Louis, it was an accident because he was actually trying to get the honorary degree for "a friend." The incident must have been doubly galling to John Cowper.[80]

He had returned from Germany once again very ill with his ulcers and on June 25 went into a nursing home in London. On the advice of the specialist, he resigned from the lecturing staff of the Oxford agency and also from the ASEUT (the American Society). He proposed to Oxford that Louis should take over his courses being planned for the autumn term. This was accepted, and Wilkinson was given his chance at last to begin lecturing regularly in England. John also asked Louis to meet the emissaries from Saxeony at the summer meeting, and thus it came about that it was Wilkinson, not John, who acquired the sought-after German connection. Llewelyn set to work to persuade his brother to write "light literature for the papers—thrilling stories, sentimental poems—critical articles."[81] John agreed, and by the end of July had written some verses, which he sent to A. R. Orage of *The New Age*. They were rejected. He also wrote two short stories, "The Incubus," and "The Spot on the Wall." He told Llewelyn that Jane Heatley, Bernie, and Louis "do not think much of them" and "away from you I do not think quite so highly of their merit."[82] Presumably written to Llewelyn's prescription of light reading for the masses, in fact, under the guise of a horror story, "The Incubus" revisits all his old preoccupations and adds a few more. The nerve specialist, Doctor Windlas, tells his friends, the middle-aged Marcus Fittleworth and Major Shales, the story of attending the death of Romer Mowl in Brighton. He describes the bloated ruddy-faced man, looking "like some horribly-engorged leech." The patient's forehead is covered with scabs, his mouth "like the mouth of a Pit," and his eyes "scaley cavernous Holes," in which "baffled yet insatiable Desire seemed to burn and smoulder in them like death-fires in a lime pit." The lurid description owes much to Krafft-Ebing and other leading psychiatrists of the late nineteenth and early twentieth centuries who described in detail the physical stigmata resulting from "degeneracy." Mowl's wife thinks he has the evil eye: "He used to walk up and down the Beach," she said, "at Brighton and other places, not speaking to a soul but staring, staring, with that dreadful look."

"Did he treat everybody like that?" I asked.
"O no," she said, "only children and most of all little girls."

Powys was drawing on his experiences at Brighton Beach. By this time he had realized he is not the only voyeur on the beach.

I ultimately became aware of certain other men—and their eyes, eyes that had almost lost all human expression, shocked me and terrified me—who had evidently reached a point of obsession far beyond my own. No heartless seducers of women, no neurotic perverts, that I have ever encountered have had such a look of being hopelessly *damned* as these elderly gentlemen. . . . Did the people they stared at ever grow conscious of the eyes of these spiritual hyaenas?[83]

In *Autobiography*, Powys calls himself a "cerebral voyeur "—presumably having a "cerebral" orgasm, and intimates that the "sylphs" he stared at were slim young women. Although there he disassociates himself from these "spiritual hyaenas," in the unpublished writings his characters are precisely that, and the sylphs are clearly children.

In a second part of "The Incubus," Fittleworth goes on a little holiday— coincidentally to the same seaside village where Romer Mowl is buried. There he meets a little girl of eleven called Kid Catchway, who is crying because she is convinced that Mowl killed her friend Katie. Fittleworth is "drawn in the most powerful manner to this beautiful little child." "That day and the next day, and the day after that, the middle-aged Scholar and the eleven year old child met and talked and played together. After her school time was done she would race down to the shore, where between the Tamarisks and the sea-bank, for he would love Tamarisk bushes, he told her, to the end of his life, she would find him waiting for her." Another little friend of Kid's has a vision of "gigantic paws, scales of pestilential protrusions and yawning leporous cavities." When she dies, Fittleworth is convinced he must dispose of the body of Romer. He and "the Village Fool" dig Romer up and drop the coffin and corpse into the sea. Unfortunately he does a poor job of it, and soon the corpse is washed up again (rather like Powys's pornography books). The parson appears and warns the parents that it "was most improper for their little daughter to make friends with strangers from London." Now Kid grows gravely ill, and in a quick ending—Powys is obviously bored by this time—Fittleworth obtains the help of the Major, who, when the apparition appears, strikes out at him "as though he had the very Sword of the Lord in his hand." The girl lives. End of story.

It is astonishing that Powys decided to write for publication a story with subject matter virtually the same as the ones he previously felt could not be published. Perhaps it was Llewelyn pressing him to write "for the papers," perhaps his illness was lowering his usual guardedness, or perhaps it was simply angry defiance. Powys appears to make a distinction between Mowl, whose voyeurism is evil, and Fittleworth, the "scholar," who feels idealistic love for a child. However, it is about the same time this story was written that he confided to Theodore that he "had had difficulty with my little pupil Margerie Edwardes of Burpham" and had made up his mind that "the only alternative to erotic obsession was writing romances."[84] It was, so to speak, a seminal decision. Although it was another six years before his first novel was published, for the rest of his life he was, he says, "driven on by a terrific 'libido' to write book after book."[85] "The Incubus" can hardly qualify as sublimation, but Powys had hit upon the Freudian-approved way to channel his strong erotic energy.

Despite his dislike of Harry, whom he called "the Christian crocodile,"[86] Llewelyn had made several trips to the Lyon estate in Devon, hoping to convince him to help out financially so John would no longer have to lecture. Harry could well afford to, being the sole inheritor of a fortune when his father died in 1898. In July, Lulu had left John writing these short stories while he went to visit with Louis at Aldeburgh. To his dismay, when he returned the cry had become "back to the platform"; in his absence Margaret and Harry had convinced John that he must continue to make his living from lecturing. Powys rescinded his resignation with the ASEUT but *not* with the Oxford delegacy. He was about to embark on a full-time career in the United States.

However, he was still very unwell, and when he joined the customary August family gathering at Montacute, his father agreed to pay for a trip to Florence and Venice. It was arranged that Gertrude should go with him to look after him. By this time Gertrude had been to the Slade, entering in 1894, the same time as Augustus and Gwen John. She had subsequently gone to Paris to further her studies and was beginning to show an accomplished talent. But there were already indications that the family had decided on her appointed role, and it was not that of artist. Jack and Gertrude were in Paris on the way home when, on November 4, they heard that Llewelyn, now back schoolmastering at Sherborne, had had a hemorrhage. He was diagnosed as having pulmonary tuberculosis. Llewelyn's 1909 diary[87] and his later *Skin for Skin* describe the first shock and how "in every possible way I dramatised my situation." His father prayed over him and went out and bought him a "black serviceable rug." His mother brought him flowers from home, but Llewelyn knew in his heart that she would rather he had died at Montacute under her care "clinging to the Christian hope," than fight for life. John had no intention of allowing that to happen and persuaded his parents to pay to have Lulu treated in a Swiss sanatorium. On December 10, he accompanied his brother to Clavadel Sanatorium, Davos Platz, where Llewelyn was to remain for seventeen months.

The relationship between John and Llewelyn, particularly after their time in America, had became closer. It was Llewelyn who had escorted him to the specialist in London, Llewelyn who had "acted as private secretary and nurse" to Jack, copying out and sending the stories to various magazines. When his attempts to "free Jack" ended in failure and Powys decided to return to lecturing, Llewelyn felt that his love was not appreciated or even acknowledged. He wrote in his diary, "Because I love Jack, I do not ask that Jack should love me in return." But when he contracted consumption, John's response was all he could ask for: "Jack comes—'not Lulu, not Lulu ill.' Jack shows that he, like me, can love fiercely & selfishly."[88] John only stayed with him at Davos for two days, but his letter written on the return journey would have satisfied any lover's heart:

> 12 December 1909: O my son Absalom, my son, my son! I recall now how often when together your hand has been slipt caressingly into mine as we walked along so many roads! . . . No one I believe loves me now like you do. . . . You my darling demand nothing and give all and therefore I love love love you.

Such lover-like letters would continue: "I seemed to see your white hands toying so luxuriously with the soft outside of your ice—moist, as it were, with lovely amorous perspiration. I could see your beautiful lips (surely quite uniquely beautiful) lips lap up the moderately satisfactory lake surrounding your Mount St. Michael of oatmeal cereal."[89] Powys thought that "Llewelyn never minded these large grandiose inaccurate gestures of mine. 'John in his translunar mood,' or 'John in his planetary mood,' he would say to himself, reverencing me in his hero-worship; when really it was 'Sawney John,' the King's jester, at his familiar antics, paying himself with the tinkle of his own gold, and feeding himself with the smell of his own goose."[90]

Gertrude was dispatched to Switzerland and stayed with Lulu for the next six weeks. John reassured him, "You can pack the old girl off (bless her devoted and fierce championship of her brothers!) as soon as you are really well enough to do a bit of tarting."[91] Marian, now twenty-six, spent May and June at Clavadel, and Mabel and Littleton visited him in August. There appears to have been a veritable stream of concerned relatives, including Aunt Dora, who, though older than her sister Mary, went back and forth several times. While the parents were grateful to Dora for her "full and circumstantial letters," they declined to go themselves. John admitted to Llewelyn that "they both have a slight tendency to treat you as if you were already dead, but at the same time mother seems irritated with us all because your funeral is so very expensive."[92]

The focus was, understandably, on Llewelyn, but Mary Cowper was just as concerned about another son—Theodore. Always protective of this sensitive, vulnerable one, it was largely on her initiative that he had been sent to Suffolk to learn how to farm, and after two and a half years, on the recommendation of her brother Cowper, he was sent to Norfolk for a further year of practical experience. C. F. loaned him £2,000 in October 1895 to lease and stock a 120-acre farm at Sweffling, Suffolk. The hope that this time he might succeed shines through in Theodore's retrospective account of the experience. He writes that he "felt the same delightful feeling of possession that I had felt as a child when I crawled under the wood that I piled against the wall."[93] At first, all went well. He invited his beloved Gertrude to come and housekeep for him. He travelled about the country a good deal, joined the local tennis club, enjoyed shooting, had visitors, involved himself in the community to the extent of being on the parish council and even being made treasurer of it. But it was low-lying marginal farm land, difficult to work profitably; in any case, it was a bad time for all farmers, right in the middle of that long period between 1870 and 1914 which agricultural economists term "The Great Depression." Characteristically, he took the blame for his failing on to himself: "For a year I worked early and late and every work that I undertook convinced me that nothing done by me could prosper, my garden of Eden was beginning to grow thistles." In 1902, he sold the operation at a loss, determined never to farm again. "I wished to get away from the worry of losing . . . I wanted to take a new part in the play." He decided to go to Studland, near Swanage, hoping that "the white cliffs and blue skies" would bring him joy. Inevitably, he found that "the same grey colour was still around me; I had not moved away from myself."[94] Perhaps the full enormity of his failure at farming, or his perceived failure, hit him then, for he felt "ashamed that I had not the courage to go and cast myself from the deepest cliff into the sea."[95] From Studland he moved inland. As Llewelyn explained in his inimitable fashion, "he took his stick from the corner and set out to find some unpretentious village, where he could be altogether free from molestation."

He found East Chaldon, "possibly the most hidden village in Dorset,"[96] and in 1905, at the age of twenty-nine, he married eighteen-year-old Violet Dodds from the village. They had two sons, Dicky and Francis,[97] and for a few years Theodore was happier than he had ever been. He cultivated his garden, read, began to write stories and dialogues, and existed on the £100 allowance his father gave him. But the mental depression was never far away. In April 1908, he wrote to Louis Wilkinson: "In my work now I seem to be getting into the regions of much ice, where thoughts are few and bitterly cold, but there seems no other way, and what is beyond must be reached at last." The man who as a child had longed for silence had found it. "I am in the walls now, the walls of silence; I cannot break again into life."[98]

At the end of 1909, John travelled to America for his three-month lecturing tour. He returned to Burpham in April 1910 but made a decision that summer to spend as much time as possible out of England in the future. His justification, if one were needed, was that the local doctor admitted that if he lived in California or South Africa he would be cured of his stomach problems. He wrote Llewelyn,

"I certainly shan't put up with another summer with as much constant pain as I have endured this one. Why should I? when I know it is the climate. . . . Why shouldn't I get lectures out in Australia, S. Africa, or California for the summer and only pay quite short visits home to Burpham . . . but how to get such work? . . . I can't endure this constant pain."[99] Climate was never an issue when in future he decided to live in upstate New York and later in Wales. Either he was fooling himself or searching for a valid reason to escape a failing marriage.

He wrote Llewelyn regularly that summer, letters intended to cheer and amuse. He told him that C. F. had lent Will, the youngest boy, £700 to buy a farm at Witcombe, a few miles from Montacute. Philippa and Lucy were sent to live with him, and John "thoroughly approved of the situation." He thought it would be the saving of "these two lost lambs." He was vastly amused at the sight of his father approaching Willy as he milked: "Dad looked so inevitably reduced to the position of second fiddle as he stood paces off behind the swishing tail." He continued with a description of his father's "pride," an account that has none of the exaggerated deference of that in *Autobiography*. "Dad spoke of parish troubles and that he went on very quietly. He said this with more pride than you can possibly conceive—all Nature seemed to echo the words as though celebrating the Glory of God. He goes on very quietly said the Ditch—he goes on very quietly cried the dunghill—he goes on very quietly repeated the Cuckoo."[100]

Powys left England in mid-September 1910 on the *S. S. Lusitania*, determined somehow to remain out of England for most of the year. The difficulty was that the Philadelphia Society, as the ASEUT was also called, was so organized that he could lecture in the States at most for six months. In order to escape, he had to convince Margaret he would make enough money in America to keep up Burpham and pay for their child's education. The 1907 discussions about Littleton Alfred's education resulted in the decision that in due course the boy would go to Littleton's Preparatory School at Sherborne, as John wished, *not* to an Anglo-Catholic school. Having won that battle, however, he needed more work and more pay. The first hint of a change came in October, when he wrote Littleton, "Various other agencies are considering the possibility of offering me more than Atkins [the Society's secretary] does for next year but it remains to be seen what actually emerges. I remain passive and permit these speculators to bid for me. I may end employing young Arnold Shaw at a fixed salary to act as a Secretary and Organizer in which case no agency or Bureau would be necessary. Or perhaps a group of lecturers might join together and hire Arnold Shaw as their secretary and so get rid of the middleman who at present steals so large a percentage of the profit."[101]

For some reason, he does not mention Louis Wilkinson in this letter. From 1906 until 1909 Louis also worked for the Philadelphia Society. However, when Atkins offered him less than he thought he should get for the three winter months of 1910, Louis simply left the Society and, as he puts it in *Swan's Milk*, "got a young Englishman, Arnold Shaw, to run his lectures for him."[102] Louis began lecturing for the new association, which was called The University

Lecturers Association of New York, in January 1910, while Powys stayed with the ASEUT. Wilkinson wrote, "Arnold Shaw soon got other lecturers to manage" and that "after a while" he and Shaw "persuaded John Powys to join them."[103] Powys did not actually join the new organization until October 1911. His relationship with Wilkinson was by now fairly ambivalent. Louis, a bachelor with a comfortable independent income (as well as the work in England and on the continent that Powys had generously handed over to him in 1909), had an ease and freedom which John in his present state of financial and marital "bondage" must have envied. It is also evident that it was *Louis* who made the courageous break with the Philadelphia Society, and Powys who fell in behind when he was reassured that the business was viable. This prudence may have been Margaret's, not Jack's, but it would have been a further cause for rancor.

John Cowper met Arnold Shaw on the ship carrying both to the U.S. in December 1904. Powys was then thirty-two and Arnold only twenty. He had spent only one term at Balliol when, according to family tradition "something occurred" which led to a decision to send the young Shaw off to the colonies—specifically, to Canada. The "something" was probably a liaison between the boy and a Catholic girl called Lizzie. Shaw's father, like Powys's father an evangelical minister, was as anti-Catholic as was C. F., and the family's disapproval only increased when Shaw himself became a Catholic convert and married Lizzie in 1905. Powys would at once have seen the similarities between them: his own flirtings with Catholicism, their joint evangelical background, their rebellion against the world these fathers represented. It is appealing to think of two excited Englishmen looking forward to a new world and freedom from the old. Powys says that the man who became "my life-long friend and bosom-crony" was a "complete stranger" when they met on board ship. While this is likely true, it would not have taken him long to realize that Arnold was the son of Hudson Shaw, the eminent Balliol fellow, and one of the earliest and best known of extension lecturers in England and America. Powys was highly regarded as a lecturer but Hudson Shaw was known as "the doyen" of the extension movement, so it was with glee that John informed Lulu in 1908 that "I have been invited again for next year—a triumph over old Hudson Bloody Shaw my venerated Rival."[104] The triumph was an empty one since by 1908 Hudson Shaw had transferred all his energy to lecturing in England with the new Workers Educational Association, of which he was the first chairman. The extension movement had become more and more a middle-class cultural movement, but the WEA, founded in 1903, had as its specific object to provide university courses on subjects which would help the working classes improve their conditions. The courses were intended for more prolonged and serious studies and therefore based on small tutorial classes rather than large audiences. By 1908 the Oxford delegacy had taken up this new trend and the WEA in a big way.[105] It is rather odd that there is no sign in his writings or in the institutional records that Powys, despite his professed and indeed sincere admiration of the "dispossessed," took any interest in the WEA. It may be that another reason, as well as illness, prompted Powys to resign in 1909 from the English extension circuit and move into the American market. His method of teaching was cultural-inspirational, not earnest tutorial, and he knew that his lecturing style was still the preferred one in the States. It was a style that appealed to the flamboyant personality of Shaw as well; and a frenetic if eccentric business relationship was about to begin.

In the meantime, Powys continued lecturing for Atkins and the ASEUT for the winter months of 1911 and then returned to England in time for Lucy's wedding at Montacute on April 22, 1911. Although John thought that Hounsell Penny was "really not at all a bad chap," Littleton protested strongly against her marriage to a miller's son. However, it was a lavish wedding and five days later Lucy borrowed a large sum from her father, presumably to assist her new husband to set himself up with his own mill.[106] As always, John's arrival was eagerly awaited. His mother never failed to note his returns—the simple "J home" in her diary is as close as she would allow herself to admit that he was her favourite. His sister Marian remembered that when she and Llewelyn were little, "there was a favourite game called 'Johnny coming home from school.' This game seems now to have great significance as our brother John's coming into our lives was the most important thing that ever happened to us."[107] At the time of Lucy's wedding, Marian was a strikingly attractive twenty-eight-year-old. All the Powys girls were educated by a governess, but Marian had the good fortune of attracting the notice of Aunt Dora, who, seeing she had a good mind, carried her off to study in an excellent High School at Norwich. Marian had always been an independent spirit, but under the guidance of the school's headmistress, one of the "new women," May (as she was called by the family) became determined to have a career. She decided on lacemaking, studying both technique and design at Taunton and Yeovil School of Design. She then went to Hanover to perfect her German and subsequently taught there to earn money to further her lacemaking skills in Brussels. John now offered to pay her fare to America and to support her until she could find a job. She arrived in New York just before Christmas, 1911.

John returned to America in the autumn to begin a new career with the University Lecturers Association of New York. Arnold Shaw had a flair for promotion and advertising, and for the first few years Powys made much more money than he had either in England or in the U.S. under Atkins. There were always the ubiquitous ladies' clubs and they had another ready market in the Chautauqua Movement, an immensely popular form of adult education begun in 1873 in New York State. Thousands attended the eight-week summer program which offered courses in the humanities, arts, and sciences. Other communities formed local Chautauquas, bringing in authors, explorers, musicians, political leaders, and lecturers like Powys on a contractual basis. The Chautauqua started out as a Methodist camp meeting and always retained something of spirit of the revival meeting.[108] Powys felt right at home and they in turn loved him. His astonishing career as an independent lecturer had begun.

Marian Powys, this very beautiful
dandelion sister, with her "self-
assertiveness, independence and
granite-based will-power."
—JCP letter to Llewelyn,
22 October, 1914.

"This marvel of personality; so
rich, so varied, with its maniacal
passions, emotions, desires, in
the thrall of the most articulate
spirit that ever dominated mortal man."
—Frances Gregg, *The Mystic Leeway*.

"Then *you* came,
passing through my senses
and soul like a storm
with hidden icebergs."
—JCP letter to Frances, 28 July, 1914.

"What a meeting of the various coloured beasts it will be! A proper background,
O a very proper background—How will we be able to conduct ourselves under
so much scrutiny!"
                                                    —JCP letter to Frances, 16 July, 1912.

CHAPTER FIVE

MEETING FRANCES GREGG

1912-1915

POWYS, EXHILARATED AND EXHAUSTED FROM THE FIRST THREE MONTHS
lecturing under this new regime, was back in Philadelphia in January
1912 to give a series of talks. After one lecture, a very lovely, very thin girl came
up to him and shyly gave him one of her poems. Powys thought he had found his
real-life sylph. He was vastly mistaken, but in the process of discovering what she
was, he learned a good deal about himself. The relationship began predictably
enough. A few days after this lecture the forty-year-old John invited himself to
tea at the tiny house on Pulaski Avenue where Frances Josefa Gregg lived with
her mother Julia. He subsequently either wrote or visited the twenty-six-year-old
constantly for the next three months. It is difficult to know what emanations she
threw out that encouraged him to believe he had not only found his sylph, but
that he could safely extend the sexual-sadistic images he had hitherto kept
locked up in his "cat-head" onto her. Shortly after their first meeting Powys sent
her a poem in the Swinburnian mode, addressing her as Sadista.

> Is it not strange?
> That a shy white body like yours, Sadista,
> Should only grow more and more delicious
> The more it is made to quiver under the lash—
> The more it is bruised by the Panther's tongue?[1]

The poem ends with the speaker's blade "pointed, pointed forever" at the
breast of Frances/Sadista. Presumably this was in the way of a psycho-sexual joke
between them, but in letter after letter to her he describes his fantasies of the
ways of "delicate punishment." What her immediate response to this kind of
lovemaking was will never be known because, although she kept his letters, he
later destroyed all hers from this period. It was not until she wrote her autobiography in the years just before her death that the rage and grief in her all those
years poured forth. If he was looking for a sylph, she was looking for a saviour—
not for a lover. She already had two lovers, Ezra Pound and Hilda Doolittle, both
of whom she met in Philadelphia in 1910. When she attended that fateful lec-

ture, she was more than half in love with Ezra; Hilda was totally in love with Frances. Into this triangle, all unknowing, came Powys. Frances had already attended many of his lectures with another friend, Amy Hoyt, and found the experience "maddening, exalting, incredible." She and Amy sat, "my thin fingers entwined in her soft square little hands, while the boundaries of our souls fell like the walls of Jericho."

Powys thought he had chosen her. It was equally true that she had chosen him with great deliberation. In fact, in a letter written in 1925 she admitted she was "considerably less than twenty when I first fell in love with you,"[2] which means that she must have heard, and become entranced by, one of the first lecture series he gave in America. Troubled by the sexual confusions of her upbringing and her feelings for both Ezra and Hilda, she was looking for the "chaste" angel Gabriel and was enraged by what she found.

> After Ezra and Hilda and their mountainous evoking of little god-mice, I cried to the universe that there must be something better than that, a god-like, noble being, . . . a tragic lonely figure, chaste—and, by all that was ironic, I chose a Powys. I crooked my staff and drew in to me—John Cowper Powys, who, with a few well chosen ape gestures drew me to his bosom—"My darling, this is what I wanted." Whereupon my darling joined the sisterhood who were to minister to the "divine and evil moods" of that dark Merlin. I forgave him, but not at once. I forgave him, but perhaps not yet.[3]

What Frances became to him is fairly clear in a letter dated January 9, 1912, but probably written a year later on the anniversary of this first meeting. "On January 9th this strange being . . . sought out and marked down for her prey that unfortunate poet. . . . It is hardly possible . . . to decide which was really the victim and which the devourer."[4] Who indeed? But in the meantime, he was "completely enslaved by this boy-girl's beauty."[5] A large part of her enchantment was that she appeared to be the androgynous figure of his earliest fantasies. It is difficult to know at what point he became aware of the reality of her bisexuality, but when he did it only excited him further. Frances wrote that when she met Powys she was completely ignorant "of the phallic in life."[6] She was hardly innocent in the ways of a woman's love. As an adolescent she discovered that her mother had three female "satellites," as Julia called them, although, as Frances said, "Had I hissed 'Lesbian' at her, she would have yelled the house down." In 1909 Frances met Hilda Doolittle, who in the next few years was to become H. D., the imagist poet. H. D.'s biographers assume that Frances was Hilda's "first woman lover." Whether it was a lesbian relationship or not, there was a most intense love between them. The "girl with the hyacinth-blue eyes" became for Hilda the most important thing in her life, as she makes clear in the story "Her" which she wrote in 1927 but kept unpublished. As for Hilda's attraction-repulsion to Frances, the following makes clear:

Hilda was entrancing. Hilda was ridiculous. Hilda was exquisite. Hilda was hideous.... My heart turns over in my breast as I remember her.... Hilda had no traffic with love. She had invented a state of the soul that I can only describe as "lecherous." There emanated from her a constant ethereal drumming, like the communications beyond the bounds of the meagre senses of humans, sight, hearing, that insects have as part of their sexual equipment.[7]

They called themselves "the wee witches" and were inseparable.[8] Although Hilda's parents were disturbed by this, in 1911 they allowed the young women to go to Europe together providing they were accompanied by Frances's mother. Julia was also agitated by what she thought was happening: "My mother wept, wailed, and gnashed her teeth across two continents, accusing Hilda of robbing the widow of her orphan, destroying its morals, besmirching its innocence."[9]

Ezra Pound was by 1911 in London, and he and his musician friend Walter Rummel escorted Frances, Julia, and H. D. around the galleries and museums of Europe, introducing them to artists and writers. Frances became more and more resentful as Hilda was wooed as the "American poet" and she was left on the periphery. They also had arguments about the primacy of art, for Frances even then was the "born moralist." But it was Frances's mother Julia who was most of all responsible for the break-up. Hilda told Frances she intended to remain in England and that she wanted Frances to stay with her as "satellite and protégé," but that Frances would have to send Julia back to America. It was not the last time that her mother's adhesive presence would interfere with Frances's life. She returned to Philadelphia with her mother, but told Hilda, "I will return in April," although her autobiography states that she had no "idea how that fantastic promise could be fulfilled."[10]

Frances had only been back a few months when she met John Cowper. Whatever she may have felt later about his methods of lovemaking, she accepted them at this time; he, in turn, was infatuated with her. Unfortunately he was married. So, employing his new Merlin-like powers, he introduced her to his friend Louis Wilkinson, "like a visible god" to a goddess. Less than a month later Frances and Louis were married. Why these two intelligent, independent-minded people of opposite temperaments fell for his magic with words is, on the surface, incomprehensible. Louis, at least, knew John Cowper's predilection for marrying off relatives and friends. He has his Jack character in *The Buffoon* admit, "'It is unpardonable, this mania for drawing others into one's own net just to see how they look when they're there! And I'm always doing it. I lead my friends on to marriage—even my brothers. Then I have a sudden panic, a mad reaction, when it's too late. Well, at least I suffer.'"[11] He was to suffer all right. On the other hand, both Louis and Frances had reasons of their own for marrying someone, almost anyone.

Frances wrote of herself, H. D., and Ezra Pound, "But there you have us, two girls in love with each other, in love with the same man, and making our plans for the waylaying and the snaring of nice, safe husbands in due course."[12] Frances needed to capture a "safe" husband. She had grown up watching the domination of her grandmother over her mother, and she could see that the pattern was repeating itself if she did not get away from "the Mother." She also must have realized that marriage was the best way of taunting Hilda for sidelining her. She had said she would be back in April and so she would be—with a husband. Marriage was a revenge, but it was also a refuge. She called it "the leeway of marriage."[13]

Louis had his own reasons. In *The Buffoon*, published in 1916, Wilkinson has the Louis-character, Raynes, decide that although it might interfere with his bachelor life, marriage allowed for "regular sex in a situation which is least dangerous and least effort to arrange." In 1934, in his autobiography, *Swan's Milk*, Louis in his alter-ego, Dexter, offered another motive for marrying.

> In the autumn of 1911 he began to feel that this unromantic, disjointed, sensually spasmodic way of life of his could not go on, must not go on. He began to want one, one only: one to be loved, to love him, to be everywhere with him. He longed to be constant in love. . . .That was what Dexter longed for towards the end of his thirtieth year, and he wrote to John Powys, who was then in America, to tell him so: indeed, almost asking him to bear it in mind. He left England at the end of 1911 determined to love and to marry, and in three or four months he did get married. We know what came of that.[14]

By the time he wrote *Swan's Milk*, Louis had been long divorced from Frances and was bitterly angry toward her and even more toward Powys. It is possible that he was rewriting the script, insisting that *he* asked John to find him a wife, rather than admit that he had been tricked into marriage. Or was this a retrospective slap at Powys, in effect saying he, Louis, had tricked *him*? Whatever the case, the antagonism and malice was deep in both of them—as well as the friendship.

Llewelyn, in an autobiographical fragment in which he gave Louis the name Leopold, was to provide another reason for this marriage.

> It had always given Leopold the greatest satisfaction to possess what we have wanted. No sooner do we set our eyes on a rare particular flower . . . but he must needs rush in and pluck it for himself. . . . He had won Josephine in just this way. . . . Of course, as my brother was married, the girl would not consent to give herself up to him. He talked to Leopold about her, but for weeks refused to let him know where she lived. At last one day . . . he took an envelope out of his pocket and wrote on it. . . . That afternoon Leopold called at the house and three weeks afterwards had married her.[15]

The "we" suggests that Louis's actions affected both the brothers. John told Lulu by letter of this new love of his, hinting that "there are exquisite and rare experiences to be related" though teasingly refusing to name Frances.[16] This news would have come as a shock to Llewelyn, who thought he was first in his brother's affections. He wrote in his diary, "I was bitter at heart. Ah! why, Daddy Jack, do you love these Ultima Thules more than me!"[17] He was even more upset by the laconic note he got from his former lover Louis: "Dearest Lulu, I am to be married on April 8th in Philadelphia to Frances Josepha Gregg, whom I met through Jack. . . . Eternal love, dear Lulu, from Louis."[18] Frances appears to have been something that had to happen, the next act of a long play.

The whole business now became even more outlandish. Louis thought that they were going to be married on April 8 and sail to England on the eighteenth. They married instead on the tenth and went directly to the ship, accompanied by John Cowper and his sister Marian. Somehow between them, John and Frances's mother had extracted a promise from the couple that the marriage would not be consummated for a year. From the ship Jack wrote Julia a blow-by-blow report of how, for the entire sea crossing, he kept Frances safe from her husband and as much as possible in close company with himself. They were met at the docks by Hilda, who, seeing the elegant, well-bred, sophisticated Louis, felt that "Frances had triumphed over her,"[19] which no doubt was what was intended. Louis was due to lecture in Dresden so there was little Powys could do to prevent their going to Germany alone, but he arranged to meet them in Venice a month later.

John went on to Montacute to be confronted by an envious Lulu. Llewelyn had returned to Montacute in mid-April 1911, apparently cured of his tuberculosis. He basked briefly in the attentions of his mother and sisters then went to stay with Theodore for a few months in the autumn, with the intention of learning to write for a living. He decided to return to Switzerland for the winter in the hope of finishing his cure. In February he made a foolishly reckless fifteen-mile journey on foot over a snow-covered pass from Arosa, the village where he had been staying, to visit Clavadel. It was intended to be a conquering-hero reunion with friends at the sanatorium; instead he had to be admitted as a patient once more. He returned to England in March 1912, this time to less welcoming parents.

Jack promptly invited Lulu to join the party in Venice, writing to Frances that "Poor Lulu—he is jealous of you child." He was no doubt perfectly aware that Lulu was jealous as much on account of Louis as of him. In the same letter, John asked her to get them hotel rooms and "please get mine next yours and Louis."[20] Taking Llewelyn to Venice when he was still convalescing from his consumptive relapse was a risky business. The parents were not even told about the proposal until the day before, but in any case, they had, in John's words, "washed their hands of their mad wilful children and all their ways."[21] The brothers and sisters however loudly objected; Bertie bluntly accused Jack of acting "'as I always did'; of sacrificing others with reckless unscrupulousness to my lust for dramatic excitement." Powys admitted that Bertie was correct, that he "*was* at his old trade of a cerebral Pandarus."[22] He knew full well not only that the convoluted business with its heated sexual/sensual atmosphere had been deliberately set up by him, but also that in some way it pandered to his emerging belief in himself as a powerful magician. He felt he had created an "enchanted spell," "and no doubt our white-admiral's flutterings, now in the direction of Llewelyn, and now in that of Louis, helped to bind it faster."[23]

What John apparently did not know was that Frances had also invited Hilda to accompany them on this Venice trip, and Hilda had agreed, only to be stopped at the boat by Ezra Pound. H. D. was later to write at least two different versions of this time in *Asphodel* and *Paint it Today*.[24] In *Asphodel*, Fayne/Frances has sent Hermione/Hilda a letter which "burns," announcing her marriage. It is George/Ezra however who has been told the real truth, that Fayne is not in love with her husband Maurice/Louis but with the lecturer "John Llewyn." George tells Hermione she is not to go with them. In *Paint It Today* the sense of betrayal is even stronger, and it is clear that H. D.'s relationship with Frances colored her whole life. In this fragment she has Frances write that in the past she had told her nothing but lies, and that "theirs was an impossible love." Although Powys seldom referred to Ezra Pound, when he did, his jealous dislike was clear. Pound in turn had no affection for Powys, referring to him in 1912 as "Jesus C. Powys."[25] Oddly, John never mentions H. D. at all, not even in his private letters to Frances. Frances presumably would have given him some version of their friendship, and Mrs. Gregg would have supplied him with the explicit details. Eventually bisexual women would appear as characters in his novels; for now his thoughts were on the trip to Italy.

Seldom has an interlude in Venice been so fully described by all the parties involved, albeit long after the event. Louis was to write his interpretation of it in *Welsh Ambassadors* and *Seven Friends*, and John in *Autobiography*. Llewelyn's version is possibly the most trustworthy of them all. A fragment he called "Venice2" appears to be a continuation of the diary he kept, although unaccountably he stopped writing in the diary proper just before the trip. He may have felt that the story was too frank even for the unflappable Powys siblings who regularly read each other's diaries.

Llewelyn was as ensnared by Frances as John could have hoped. He was struck by her "equivocal desirable body" with its "exquisite contours—her breasts small and rounded and pointed—her waist slender and delicate." He explicitly identifies her beauty with Lilith, "beautiful not with an ordinary beauty but with the fascinating beauty of the serpent in the orchard, the beauty of goodness degraded and evil transfigured. She might have been some courtesan of Babylon. . . ." According to Llewelyn, one night the two brothers took Frances for a gondola ride while Louis was dining with another friend. They sat in the boat, "like two kestrel hawks" on either side of her, each holding one of her hands. Llewelyn then suggested that he and John live with her in some cottage in the West of England, and Frances replied that she would have an intrigue with Ebenezer

Shelling (Pound) and "get a divorce that way." "We two brothers did not demur but like billing stock doves nestled closer to her."

Having reduced the predatory hawks to a pair of cooing doves, she rounded on them: "Do you really expect to win me for yourselves without any trouble, without any revelations and scenes? . . . Do you imagine for a moment that I would leave Leopold for you? With him at least I know where I am—. . . God, what lovers you are! You who would give your girl into the arms of another to escape social exposure. . . . I am glad I have married him. Your world is a world of words and sensations and I am looking for facts and strong arms to shelter me."[26]

This has the ring of an actual conversation. As attractive as she apparently found Llewelyn, he was merely an added fillip to the situation. She was speaking directly to Jack, accusing him of cowardice, of procuring, and of living in an illusory world. Not surprisingly, John does not mention this *scène de chasse* in *his* version of the Venice trip. He preferred instead to concentrate on Frances's "girl-boy" aspect and the sexual kick he got out of her wearing boy's clothes.

> I remember going alone to Verona one day and being so elated by the thought of Juliet in her tomb, by the vast stone Amphitheatre, and by that gondola-loving boy-girl. . . . Alone in that Roman circle, . . . the thaumaturgic element in my nature rose to such a pitch that I felt, as I have only done once or twice since, that I really was endowed with some sort of supernatural power.[27]

There are several interesting elements in his account. First of all, he says that Frances "insisted on dressing up as a boy" but it was John who had bought her the boy's costume. He had purchased something similar previously for his young Brighton prostitute, thinking it "looked like the attire of one of those enchanting boy-girls, or girl-boys, in Shakespeare's comedies," but the girl was indignant, declaring that it "would have suited a postman."[28] John may have felt that by wearing it, Frances was catering privately to his boy-girl fetish, but it is equally possible that she was dressing for the delectation and delight of Hilda, or rather, the absent Hilda. Secondly, he did not go "alone to Verona" to be "elated by the thought" of Frances. Frances was with him in Verona, as is clear in a letter he wrote to her shortly after. His boy-girl was not the real Frances at all, but an image in the mind. The image arouses his erotic excitement which in turn triggers a feeling of "supernatural power." Powys in Verona was one step closer to the clue of magicianship, but that would be of little consolation to the gondola girl who wanted "strong arms to shelter" her, not a "world of words." What must have driven her to further distraction was the knowledge that he knew exactly what he was doing. A few pages later in his autobiography he says "it was even as if, in his erotic delirium, he was forever mixing her up with all the other thaumaturgistic figures who had made him dance," and that this would seem "to her own proud intelligence to be doing her secret original identity only a very dubious kind of honour."[29]

No honour. She wrote sadly in *The Mystic Leeway*, "So far, in all my life I have met no single Man . . . nor has any man encouraged me, or indeed been willing for me, to be a Woman. Mumbo-jumbo, superstitions, muddled mythologies, have been my fate amongst these artists and prelates and magicians, these escapists from life—from Life!"[30]

In Venice he had a recurrence of the "revolting images" which had so distressed him in Hamburg.

> There must be a veritable Demon of Auto-Sadism dwelling within me; for the more thrilled I became with the ambiguous beauty of our boy-girl companion the more rigorously did this Demon within me set himself to spoil my pleasure. Do you know what this Demon used to compel me to do in my perverted mind? And it was clearly a mental proceeding that could only be regarded as sadistic *towards myself*. He used to compel me to smear her beautiful form from head to foot with some grotesque sticky substance![31]

The ways of self-punishment are strange, but it was hardly *auto*-sadism that made him imagine he was smearing Frances with a "sticky substance"; it was erotic malice—pure aggressive sexual fantasy—that was making him twist in the wind.

Predictably, both Llewelyn and John became ill on the way home from Venice. In Milan, Llewelyn began to cough blood and had a severe attack of kidney stones. John's ulcers flared up. Gertrude had to be dispatched in mid-June to nurse them both and then bring them home. On their return, Louis and Frances went to Aldeburgh to visit Louis's mother. John promptly followed them. She was still his "Sadista, little incestuously loved sister."[32] He devised a plan whereby he would hire a horse at Ipswich, and the two of them would elope, but as Frances dryly told her son in later years, "In the event he was unable to find a horse."[33] However, he began to sign himself with the name Heathcliff to her Cathy. Presumably he had decided Louis was Edgar Linton.

In August a further blow fell on the Powys family. Philippa (or Katie as she was called) had a psychotic breakdown. Since childhood, the brothers and sisters had broken into groups of three according to age; as the youngest ones, Katie, Will, and Lucy were particularly close. When in 1910 Will began farming, the two girls joined him, Lucy doing the housework and Katie learning to do dairy. Katie, and perhaps all three of them, seem to have assumed that they would always be together. This dream of an ideal future ended when Hounsell Penny fell in love with Lucy, "a great glorious buxom strapping round-armed wench." Their marriage left Katie bereft. She wrote in her diary, "She crossed the bridge and now we can only talk over it."[34] Several years before this, on the annual Powys holiday to Sidmouth, they had met Stephen Reynolds, a young man who, after a nervous breakdown, had retired to this fishing village to live a working man's life. In 1908 he published *A Poor Man's House*, and by the summer of 1909, his literary fame and his good looks greatly attracted the female visitors to Sidmouth Beach. As was the custom with all the fishermen, for a fee Reynolds would row them in his boat. He was particularly kind to Katie and discussed religion and literature with her as with an equal—something that seldom occurred in her male-dominated family. Katie convinced herself that there was great affinity between them, began a correspondence with him, and wrote ecstatically of her passion in her diary. In August 1912, Katie went again to Sidmouth with Llewelyn and Gertrude for a few days. Reynolds by now realized her state of infatuation and when they met this time he hit upon the ruse of telling her that he felt his destiny was always to be alone, "loved only by the natural world around him."[35]

When Katie returned to Will's farm, her behavior became so strange that she was taken back to the vicarage to be nursed by Gertrude. On the twenty-second of August, Powys traveled up from Sussex to be by her side. The fullest and most unreserved account of this period comes in John's letters to Frances. They hired a nurse but Katie became violent when the medication wore off. John could well understand the nurse being terrified of her. "Her arms strengthened by work at Willy's farm are as strong as a labourer's and her face is sometimes convulsed with rage till it looks like a combination of all the most terrifying wild beasts."[36] A few days later, at three in the morning, she got on to the window sill of her room and threatened to throw herself out. Since the parents "only stand aside and let things drift," Jack and Gertrude were left to make the decision whether to put her into an institution. In 1912, it was a difficult call to make: to be certified and labelled "insane" would make Katie's future life in a small village very difficult—always assuming she was ever released. However, she became impossible to manage and was admitted to Brislington Lunatic Asylum, near Bristol.[37] C. F. had always escorted his children in important rites of passage and now this elderly priest was to perform one last disastrous ceremony. Katie finally told her own story of her love for Stephen Reynolds and its outcome in the late 1920s in a prose poem "Phoenix or Driven Passion."[38] Overwrought and overwritten, it is nonetheless a moving, at times wrenching, recital.

As they set off from the vicarage for Bristol, her father, in a "gesture fantastical" presented her with a bouquet. She writes in "Phoenix," "Hastily, without thought, he pushed into my hands those delicate blooms—blooms of white Myrtle—the flowers of the bride." Peter Powys Grey, Katie's nephew, was very close to her in later years and she told him that they had dressed her in a wedding gown to persuade her into the carriage. While there is no doubt that she would have resisted going to an asylum, that would seem too cruel and too bizarre a stratagem even for this unusual family. Nevertheless, she was convinced that her father was escorting her to her wedding. "The further we went, the more sure I became, and when we reached the journey's end I advanced trembling, but the church and the altar were wanting. The bridegroom was missing. Instead of the joyful pealing of the bells, it was the moaning of the mad. Instead of the scattering of rice, it was the uncanny dance of the demented. . . . I cursed my Father and my Mother, and the day of my delivery."

All this must have caused John huge anxiety, not only because he wondered if he too had inherited the maternal family history of madness, but because it re-aroused his childhood fear of imprisonment and confinement. Katie was going to have to be "confined"; indeed the family may have decided that the only way to get her to the place of confinement was by the subterfuge of marriage. By "the day of my delivery" Katie may have been referring to the day of her birth or the day of her delivery to the institution, but equally she may have meant the day of the birth of her child. A child is never mentioned, and of course there was no possibility of one, but Katie may have had delusions that she was carrying Reynolds's baby. John's reaction to Katie's psychosis was telling. He wrote to Frances that he wished he could "either give up the time to go right away with her—or had the power to kill her and finish it."[39] In fact, what he did was run away. As the eldest and the one in charge, John should have been the one to take her to Brislington. Instead he went to Paris to be with Frances and Louis, leav-ing the father, who all the family knew was losing his mental faculties, to take the young woman to "prison": the unhinged leading the unbalanced.

Katie was confined to the asylum for six months. Afterward she was sent to an agricultural training school at Studley College, Warwickshire, then to a woman's cooperative farm in Sussex. Eventually she had a small dairy farm in Montacute. She saw farming as her penance rather than a vocation: "In the care of cows was my separation contrived." She never saw Reynolds again. In her poem she says she accepted the fact that he could not possibly marry someone who had been mad. "Who would walk with one who smelt of the mad-house? / Who would gather among roots blackened by fire? / None can give birth whose dreams are a furnace." For the rest of her life she believed that he did not love her because of something lacking in her. Evidently it did not occur to anyone to tell her what must have been obvious—at least to the Powys boys, experienced as they were in identifying homosexuals. Nor was she ever told. Who can know whether it would have eased her lifelong sense of failure or simply destroyed the only comfort left her—the idealized image of him she carried with her always.

Katie had inherited the strong sexuality that John himself found such a bur-den until he learned how to channel it into his "magicianship" and his writing. As an unmarried woman in a vicarage family, she had no such outlet, as John himself recognized. "The real cause of all this is our present cursed system which permits no freedom to a child of unhappy and hopeless passions like Katie, he wrote."[40] Gertrude had another theory. "Gertrude says that the cause of it is not unsatisfied passion but . . . that Katie's brain has always been small, her emotions fierce, and that she ought long ago to have been separated from such people as most of us are and have lived an absolutely placid and commonplace life." Perhaps Gertrude intuited even then that this was to be her role; she was to spend much of the rest of her life protecting Katie in the seclusion of an isolat-ed cottage on the Dorset downs. But John's further analysis is possibly the more perceptive, opening up as it does the whole saga of the family romance. "I think that we are too many. That is the really fatal thing."[41] It was not the first time that John had touched upon the theme of "too many" and would not be the last.

The escape to Paris did nothing to ease his feelings for Frances, merely leaving him more uncertain than ever what she felt for him. He would not know for some time yet. In mid-October Powys returned to the States, but the Wilkinsons stayed in London for the autumn, seeing a good deal of Pound and H. D. They were in the U.S. for the January to March term of 1913, but propinquity did not make John's jealousy any less. In February 1913 he was writing to Frances, "Does it give you pleasure to know that at this moment I am experiencing a suffering of a quite damnable kind because you belong to dear little Louis instead of me?" However, she must have permitted him to continue his kind of lovemaking or at least allowed him to write her his sadomasochistic fantasies. The following letter is characteristic of those he wrote her during this period.

> And then the Evil one who a little while ago loved her so gently—must needs loosen her hair and shake it free . . . and when he has done that—he must lift her up and bend her backwards over the heavy oak table holding her hair in one hand. And then with the other hand he gathers her flesh— between armpit and breast—as one might gather a bunch of wood-anemones and crush it in his fingers . . . and her body, he can feel it all the way down, pressed between his and the heavy table quivers in little trembling vibrations and little quivering resistances . . . and her mouth twitches and her lips move—but he does not kiss her—he only looks at her waiting—while his fingers tighten on what he holds—waiting till the long pent-up tears cannot be held back any more—and when they begin to appear, not one of them (were there ever such big tears!) is allowed to get very far on their way down for he drinks them all—all—all for that is his peculiar thirst and the only quenching of it. Enough? We are good again now.[42]

Jack intended to go to Spain with Frances and Louis in April, but Louis, whose tolerance or indifference to the ménage was massive, finally said, "I wish—we wish—to be alone." In May he received a letter signed by both of them which was a fairly brusque attempt to shake off his constant pursuit. He responded by saying that their letter had "almost precisely the effect upon me that you intended,"[43] but he continued to write to her. In August he told her that his anger against her "has been due to any movement of yours to escape from that idealistic prison," which he now recognized was the result of his "substituting my own Imagination, or rather Image, for you yourself." How *much* he recognized is debatable. In the same letter he wrote: "I would willingly foreswear anything else . . . if destiny would let me live with you & Louis forever."

John disconsolately spent the summer at Burpham with Margaret and "the little boy" who was now eleven. He decided that "poor Margaret's nervous irritability of temper . . . is no doubt really a desire for a tender considerate affectionate and amorous mate," and pitied "this poor high-strung egoistic lady almost as much as I pity myself."[44] Frances suggested he try to "achieve a rapport" with his wife, so in August he took Margaret to Paris and bought her a ten-volume edition of *Jean Christophe*. With this added to the parrot he had brought back for her when he was in Paris with Arnold Shaw and his wife in April, and his wretched attempts at planting out geraniums for her, Margaret must have felt the well-beloved. However, just before he left again for America in September, he wrote Lulu: "Isn't it curious that I should find myself more in love with [Frances] than ever? One would have thought that it would be impossible for 'love' to have outlasted the blows I have received."[45]

Although they remained a clan emotionally, by the end of 1913 most of the brothers and sisters had gained at least some physical independence from their Montacute home. With Katie still incarcerated, Gertrude was freer to further her art studies in Paris. Will decided to emigrate to British East Africa. Marian had returned to England in 1912 because she could not find a job in New York, but she had no intention of being the next daughter delegated to look after aging parents. She took a typing course and left for New York again in December. Jack spent several days between Christmas and New Year with the Wilkinsons and Mrs. Gregg at the mother's home in Philadelphia. When Louis and Frances told him that they planned to remain in England the next year and then to live for a time in Italy, he decided it must be an attempt to evade the "trying" Mrs. Gregg! He continued to dream of having Frances to himself and proposed to her "a little Cerebral ceremony. Frances' Second Marriage!"[46]

Powys was a firm believer in astrology and noted with concern that his fortune, as well as Frances's, for 1914 was "sinister," and that the "Ace of Spades the Death Card," continually turned up for Louis (although that may have been more wishful thinking than Tarot). As it happened, 1914 did not begin well for either John or Louis. Their manager/agent Arnold Shaw had left his wife Lizzie and their child, was neglecting his work, and was showing the first symptoms of the mental instability that was to overtake him later. Louis, always the pragmatist, was afraid that "his immoral revolution may not confine itself to the erotic, but extend to the financial sphere!"[47] In late March, a more immediate and heavy blow struck: John heard that Mary Cowper was terminally ill with cancer. In his immediate reaction to the news, he was more direct about his feelings of love and guilt toward his mother than ever before, calling her one of the "daughters of darkness and the spirits of the night." He felt that he was a traitor to his inheritance of her "black blood," having "curried favour with the Sun—her enemy." It is a strange way of saying—if he is—that he had chosen to emulate the father, but it is clear that John felt he had somehow "completed the work of our Leonine progenitor, in blocking up vistas and corridors (full of shadows but also of night-air) from this sensitive and troubled spirit."[48]

Powys sailed for England on the seventh of April. He went immediately to see his mother, but instead of staying with her, he joined Louis and Frances in Toledo and Seville, and then in May took his brother Bertie to Rome for a week.[49] In the meantime, it must have been plain to Llewelyn that he was no longer the primary focus of the affections of either Jack or Louis. While they were in Spain, he began a romance with a cousin, Marion Linton, and in very short order proposed marriage to her. Then in mid-June, when he was in Seaton with his mother and father on their usual summer holiday, he made another abrupt decision. Will was now in Kenya managing a sheep farm owned by a syndicate and suggested that Llewelyn join him. Llewelyn accepted, hoping that the climate in Africa would cure his consumption so that he could marry. He was also bored and frustrated at home. The family for most of the year was now composed only of Gertrude, when she was not in Paris, himself, and his parents. He found himself irritated equally by his father's "monstrous egoism" and his mother's "self-abnegation."

Jack returned from Europe the third of June and on the nineteenth he and Margaret joined the group at Seaton. Mary, although by now close to death, characteristically was more concerned about her eldest son, writing daughter Marian that John was "tired and in pain and unable to walk." He was in pain from more than ulcers. He was shocked by the news of his beloved Lulu's impulsive engagement and equally sudden decision to go to Africa. He was even more stunned by a letter from Frances revealing that she was pregnant. He responded on the twenty-first of June: "it has the same queer shock as if you had by a sudden effort of will transformed yourself into a different being, climbing up as it were through a hole in the roof, of our subjective cave—into an ampler region. . . . Then a quite distinct feeling . . . a sudden angry and irrational jealousy—it is *my girl* & some damned other person has shot in & done this—almost as if it had been rape—& our friend *a drifting high-road Tramp*."[50] Years later he had convinced himself he was in the next room when Oliver was conceived and by long-distance, so to speak, was the father. For the present, Jack was furious with "tramp" Louis and "*his triumph over me*." He was even more angry with Frances, who was "now carrying a heavy burden that I couldn't relieve you of." No longer a sylph, Frances had become the hated maternal body. Frances also told Hilda of her pregnancy and Hilda promptly became pregnant as well, although the child was still-born. In memory of the lost child and the lost Frances, H. D. named her next child Frances Perdita. In the continuing complicated inter-relationships, Powys appeared at times almost peripheral, metaphorically as well as physically in the next room.[51]

The Powys parents returned to Montacute vicarage, and John, Margaret, and the boy went on to Exmouth for a further holiday, then back to Burpham. On July 28, Llewelyn wrote in his diary that his mother suddenly said to him "I am afraid of the spirits." But on the twenty-ninth, when he cried to see her pain, "she looked at me in such a queer way—quite coldly, with an expression of surprise, almost of contempt."[52] She died on the thirtieth. Strangely, although the family now gathered at Montacute knew her time was short, apparently they did not telegraph John. In fact, two days before he and Margaret had taken Littleton

Alfred to school at Sherborne and were only a few miles away. For some reason, they did not come on to Montacute but returned to Sussex. He wrote on the thirtieth, unaware that his mother was already dead. "I shall come down at once if she gets worse. It is frightful to me how little I have appreciated her or made any real effort to let her talk about these things."[53]

Mary Cowper's funeral was on the fourth of August, 1914. Great Britain's declaration of war on the same day was welcomed as a "distraction" to the assembled family. Only Charles Francis appeared "quite unmoved" by his wife's death.[54] Gertrude was dreading being left alone with him at the vicarage and becoming rather afraid of his "peculiar temper."[55] There had already been family discussions whether the father should resign and "have done with Act 3 of the Powys Comedy,"[56] but C. F. had refused. John, busy at his customary matchmaking, hoped that Katie would be able to look after her father in order to free Gertrude so she could marry his friend John William Williams.[57] It was a totally impractical idea since his friend "the Catholic" was impecunious, physically unwell and on the way to being an alcoholic. John was cheered by the fact that at least "Gertrude was no longer nervous of him"[58] but nothing came of the proposed match. In the end Gertrude was left "holding the hands of the Old Prophet."[59] Lulu sailed for Africa and Bertie decided to join an Officers' Training Corps. As he returned to America, Jack had "the sense that in leaving Montacute I am leaving it forever."[60]

A few weeks after the funeral, Gertrude sent him their mother's diaries. Singularly barren and unrevealing as they are, John was nonetheless deeply moved by them.

> What a pathetically monotonous and uninspiring existence it reveals! Poor dear, how she seems to have been separated even then from the instinctive impulses of her own soul. How C's "serious" sermons and "tiredness" and "Johnny's" diabolical colds, and School School School School, seem to have narrowed her in, and blocked up, in a sort of Kiel Canal, every large and noble vista! . . . Her mind went ferreting inwards and inwards—until these daily events seem like the little earth-heaps, left by moles, whose real interests are so hopelessly unseen![61]

In a letter to Frances and Louis he went further in his forthright analysis of Mary Cowper's personality:

> She was remote, ironical, submissive, and very cold; at the same time teased by a thousand objective cares for her family which she lacked the affectionate warmth to turn from annoying duties into friendly pleasures. She had cold deep obstinate romance, secret and almost savage, a romance that tunnelled itself inwards, and—like a reed with roots under water—was happier by night than by day. She had a look sometimes wistful—like a planetary spirit vexed and fretted—and laughing, and imprisoned. She had a fragile merriment, like a wounded deer watching in deep water the reflection of

the arrow in her flank. She hated, with an abysmal hatred, sunshine, prosperity, healthy energy, and above all <u>success</u>. When she was happy at rare times it was like one of those fragile and enchanted moths that go from hedge to hedge with a dread even of moonlight. She lived always in a large cool dark cavern—and alone—and when anyone came near she hated them though when they went away she loved them—and even while she hated them she knew the sun was on their side and that her resistance was hopeless & mad. But it was then that she <u>went</u> <u>on</u> and the more hopeless and mad and wicked it was—the more she did it—her defiance of the "All" that <u>ought</u> <u>not</u> to have come forth from the "Nothing"—& yet she was doomed—she who had a madness for being left alone— to have eleven earthy great children![62]

He was to regret his candor, writing to Lulu, "Frances has got me 'on the hop' . . . over a letter I was foolish enough to write her about mother, in which she was pleased to discern a 'flicker of sincerity.'"[63] His analysis was more than sincere; it was a coming face to face with those aspects of his mother that he saw in himself: the apartness, the submissiveness, the inherent coldness, the disdain for success, the irony, the romance, the need for confinement, at the same time, a resistance to that need that was both "hopeless and mad."

Back in New York, John felt "now more alone than I have ever been in my life." The death of his mother, coinciding as it did with Frances's pregnancy, impelled him to call up the extensive armoury of defensive tactics that had served him so well in previous traumatic weanings and loss. His first move was to turn to his sister Marian for consolation. As he pointed out to Llewelyn, "we must be prepared to follow the tide, and make hay of dandelions if there are no marsh-marigolds." He was gradually to recognize the qualities of this very beautiful dandelion sister, her "self-assertiveness, independence and granite-based will-power."[64] He added in a further letter, "I love her well—as well as we can love girls we can't have."[65] Marian was to become emotionally very important to him in the next six years that they lived together; her love for her brother allowed him to regain some sort of equilibrium. The writing he now plunged into provided another psychic second-skin defence, helping to create a sense that the disjoined parts of his personality could somehow be made to cohere.

When John returned to America he found that Arnold Shaw had regained his high spirits. He announced to John in early October that he had decided "overnight" to become a publisher. All he needed was a book to publish, so Powys sat down and wrote one in less than ten days. The book was called *War and Culture*. It was a reply to a book by Professor Hugo Munsterberg entitled *The War and America*. War was an unlikely subject for his first book, but Shaw, if not Powys, would have known that it was a topic of more intense interest than a book on Keats. It was printed as quickly as it had been written, and by the twenty-eighth of October the small book was in its second printing. Powys used a laundry basket to deliver copies to New York booksellers, and Shaw went off to arrange a series of lectures in a "huge hall" in Boston.

As was to happen often in future, Powys's *War and Culture* issued from a personal reaction. Munsterberg was a prestigious academic, head of the psychology department at Harvard and the acknowledged forerunner of modern behaviorism. Powys had "always disliked" Munsterberg, for no apparent reason other than that he was the archetypal "scientific professor" Father Powys had warned his little boys against. He begins his polemic by stating that the professor's remarks were "deliberately designed to mislead public opinion in America," and that the reasons for war lie deeper than "the immediate and superficial causes of war." Characteristically, Powys puts his own slant on the subject, making the war a question of different cultures and opposing mind-sets. "This terrible war, caused primarily by the natural egoism of races, has become, by the logic of events, and by the invisible pressure of the system of things, a war of Ideas. The Idea of Germany is to force upon the world, by means of an omnipotent and irresistible State-machine, a certain hard, scientific, unimaginative and efficient culture. The Idea of the Allies is to protect the individual against the State, the little nations against the empires, and the drama, colour, passion, beauty, and tradition of the various races of the earth, against a monotonous and murderous uniformity!"[66] As a piece of slick propaganda, this is hard to beat, but his scorn of Germany and the German personality has a certain irony, for the German people, from the very beginning of his career, have appreciated and honored Powys's flamboyant genius in a way that no other nation, including both his own and the U. S., has.

The influence of Nietzsche's writings on this book is obvious. It was Bernie O'Neill who, at least fifteen years earlier, first introduced the Powys brothers to this philosopher, and John now put his reading to good use. On a tour of Eastern Canada early in 1914, a newspaper report dated 24 March 1914 quoted him as saying: "Nietzsche holds that the secret of life is contained in hardness, in assertion, in domination, in the will to be cruel, to have and to dispense power. . . . Nietzsche teaches that there are two sets of people in the world, with different moralities governing each. They are the slaves and masters."[67] As the war progressed, however, he began to emphasize Nietzsche's capacity for pity, and "his affinity for non-German European culture." The *Toronto Daily News*, on February 24, 1915, reported that Powys described the Nietzschean Superman not as "the Blond Beast" but "the classical ideal of distinction, beauty, magic and grace."[68]

This radical change of emphasis may have been due less to a shift in his view of Nietzsche than to his (or Shaw's) acute sense of what would draw audiences. In a letter to Llewelyn, he admitted, "I can tell you this war produces a fine state of nervous tension over here. . . . I have scandalised some. . . . [Arnold] chuckles day and night over the situation."[69] It certainly helped the financial situation. He had nine lectures a week in November and December of 1914. An indication of his approach was a debate held on the twenty-eighth of November 1914 at

Boston's Twentieth Century Club on "Nietzsche and the War" which attracted
an audience of 500. Powys argued that Nietzsche was a noble and exquisite spirit, and "if on any side at all, on our side." Professor Jay Hudson of the University
of Missouri retorted that Nietzsche was "dangerous if believed literally and the
sooner we kill him intellectually, the better, and I am going to start now."
According to the newspaper "the discussion waxeed so warm at times that
women in the audience stopped knitting for Belgian babies long enough to
applaud the defender and the denouncer of Nietzschean doctrines."[70] While
Powys was not above fooling his audience, or later, his readers, in this instance
he did not attempt to fool himself or his brothers. He wrote Littleton in
December that he is lecturing in Boston again on the war: "Your little Johnny is
the great authority on the War in Boston! The subject is to be the Saxeon,
Teuton, & Slav Ideals. I wonder if these honest soldiers in the trenches know as
much about their 'Ideals' as we do in Boston."[71]

   Powys said the war had "two very drastic psychological effects" on him. It
started him off "at a break-neck pace writing books" and it caused him "to make
a vow to give up all erotic pleasures until the War was over." He wondered if this
repression "was a great incentive to literary creation" but decided that "the real
reason for my becoming an author was simply that Arnold had become a publisher."[72] Although his mother's death and Frances's perceived defection no doubt
provided the impetus, he never forgot that it was Shaw's enthusiasm and courage
that put his first books into print. The success of the *Reply* pamphlet emboldened
them to publish some of Powys's most popular lectures, a project he had had in
mind for some time. On February 9, 1915, *Visions and Revisions* came out. These
were essays on the perennial favourites, both his own and his audiences':
Dickens, Rabelais, Shakespeare, Milton, Lamb, Arnold, Shelley, Keats,
Nietzsche, Hardy, Pater, Dostoevsky, Whitman. The book went through four
impressions in sixteen months. Powys was by then filling large halls with his lectures on these authors and Shaw knew he had a captive readership.[73] Powys was
on a roll, but sometimes those in his wake drowned.

   Hyman Weiss was a young socialist and artist, eking out a living for himself,
his wife, and little boy by doing stamped-leather work and hawking it around to
department stores. He and his wife attended a lecture on Dostoevsky and Hardy
in Philadelphia in March 1913. Mrs. Weiss wrote in her diary that at first she
thought the coupling of these two authors was "a trick" but Powys "reached" her
when he argued that both writers were distinguished by "their sympathy for the
poor and the defeated, the underbelly of the world, the dispossessed." She noted
that his audience consisted of "middle-aged ladies eager for self-improvement
and culture" and "pale young men who wish to change the world but are not
quite sure how." Powys visited the Weisses the next day, asking Hyman to do the
illustrations for his next book, which would be on "European Writers and Their
Influence on American Thought." Weiss was convinced it was the beginning of
a change in his fortunes; his wife was both hopeful and dubious. "Hyman needs

recognition and money now, not later, not tomorrow. But for my idealistic hus-band the cord has been tied. . . . Powys has told him that his [sketches] will smash Victorian art into rubble and it is the stimulus he desires." She was worried that there was no mention of money or of a written agreement, but her husband said, "Powys and I have an understanding that is more binding than any law. We are kindred spirits."

They did not see Powys again until October, when he breezed in to say his new book had been postponed. "I'm silent while Hyman is dismayed." He looked at what Hyman had drawn and asked him to make it "more symbolic." Handing him a list of ten authors, Powys then requested Weiss to have all the illustrations ready by the time he returned early next year, adding, "We are just at the begin-ning of our collaboration." Rebecca Weiss wrote in her diary, "Yet while Powys states this with conviction I wish there were more than promises. Hyman has invested so much already in this prospect that if anything should go wrong, it could be devastating." Weiss completed all ten sketches, but his wife noted omi-nously, "the work is striking, the line and detail clever and self-assured, but the tone is mocking." She could see that the portrait of Charles Dickens was a cari-cature "which shows the self-dramatising nature of the man. His head is enor-mous, he is virtually all head and no body, and he holds a pen that is shaped like a sword, and his expression is one of righteous indignation, as if he, personally, must right the follies of the world." She wondered whether the Englishman devoted to Dickens would accept it. Her intuition was correct. Who knows why Powys did not use them. Possibly the caricature was too close to the bone—his own bone—but the book, *Visions and Revisions*, was published with no illustra-tions. Hyman Weiss died in 1914, at age twenty-six, apparently of typhoid. Powys hoped his death wasn't caused by "sheer starvation."[74] Another cause for guilt.

John returned to England for the summer of 1915. C. F. had lent Katie the money to set up a smallholding in Montacute but she was having difficulty. Her nerves were irritated by the business aspect of it, and by C. F.'s "rather helpless attempts to give her advice with her work." John wrote Marian from Montacute, "Poor old egoist found out by the last of his daughters—by the mad one!"[75] He was full of admiration for Gertrude: "How well she manages Father the Village—and everything—and yet she hates it so!" He went on, "Well, I am glad you at least are out of all this—what an escape! I think of our happy flat & carefully arranged parties free from all discordant elements with such relief now."[76] A now pregnant Lucy was visiting Montacute, John noting slyly that she was "evidently more fond of Hounsell than formerly." On Llewelyn's behalf, John devoted con-siderable time during this trip trying to persuade Marion Linton, now hesitating, to marry Llewelyn. She decided that she would prefer to go into a nunnery instead and did so.

Undeterred in his helper role, John made his customary visit to Chaldon to visit Theodore. Chaldon suited Theodore; its landscape echoed his life-illusion.

He described it as a place of stone: "not smooth shining pebbles—sharp zigzag flints. And the chalk of the hills in places broke through the thin covering of grass, like the skin of a beggar showing through her ragged clothing."[77] The few years of happiness with Violet and his sons had not lasted long. When Llewelyn stayed with him in 1911, he found this brother "sunk in one of his worst moods of despair. His features had the same dreary look that was presented by the patient window-panes with the grey rain trickling down them."[78] Living solely on his father's allowance, he and his family were desperately poor. He wrote, story after story. Friends tried to interest publishers in his work, but the stories always came back.

The rancor, as well as the depression, flared out in his writing. Theodore had always seen his parents' vain attempts to settle him in a quiet farming life in Suffolk not as love but rejection. In 1913 he wrote an unpublished short story about this time. Charlie Blackburn was "one of those castaways thrown out by the upper classes and allowed to drift into a kind of madness." Because "he could not pass his exams as a boy," he was "thrown away among the boars and serfs when he was a man." He added bitterly, "Though the father had a good fortune, his children were so many that each received only a little."[79] The other Powyses wrote openly about their mother's death. Theodore seems to have remained silent except that about the time of John's visit in 1915 he was writing the story of another Charley, an outcast with whom he used to walk when he was at the Suffolk farm. "He could remember how his mother used to pet his brothers and hate him because he was ugly. And the ugly duckling does not in real life become a swan. . . . I felt sure he would be treated just as cruelly wherever he went. . . . If he had been sane as his brothers he would have got on just as they did."[80] The outbreak of war, his poverty, his continuing lack of success at anything, added to his depression. Violet's half-sister, Georgina, who in 1915 was fourteen years old, was his only consolation. Two years later, he was to write John drearily that he had held Georgie "so present—so very present for 10 years. As though she— ignorant and foolish and selfish as she is—was worth holding."[81] Georgina was "stolen away from us by a soldier for three packets of woodbine cigarettes and two tins of potted salmon."[82] Theodore wrote her into two stories, neither of which ever saw the light of day.

In the meantime, John was hoping to cheer him with news of his latest "stunt." The success of *Visions and Revisions* encouraged Powys and Shaw to attempt more ambitious publications. John would write a novel; they would also arrange a publication that was to put the Powys clan (or rather, the Powys brothers) on the literary map. They dreamt up the idea of a book of "confessions" by all six of the Powys brothers. John "loved the idea of all of us going down to posterity together" and besides "the novelty was bound to make the book sell."[83] Will and Bertie were on active service and Littleton was struggling to keep his prep school going in wartime conditions; nonetheless Powys wrote them, "instructing" them to contribute, and was astonished when his eldest-brother directive was turned down flat. However, Theodore and Llewelyn agreed and the abbreviated project went ahead. On this visit, John could tell Theodore that the book would be published as soon as he had completed his novel. He spent the rest of the summer finishing *Wood and Stone* which came out November 5, 1915. Shaw was proving to be an excellent publicist, taking out a number of large newspaper and magazine ads and putting a catchy blurb on the dust cover. The book sold well.[84]

John wanted to call the book *The Pariah*, but the name was taken. His second choice was *Planetary Opposition*. Once again using Nietzsche's ideas, or his interpretation of them, as windmills to tilt against, Powys asks in a grandiloquent preface what "secret" governs the universe and proposes several "antipodal possibilities": self-assertion or self-abandonment; fate or chance; the will to power versus the will to love. He then gives his own answer, "In a universe whose secret is not self-assertion, but self-abandonment, might not the 'well-constituted' be regarded as the vanquished, and the 'ill-constituted' as the victors? In other words, who, in such a universe, *are* the "well-constituted"?[85] On the side of the "well constituted" is the rich businessman industrialist, Mortimer Romer, who owns the stone works of Leo's Hill and the people who work the stone. He and his daughter Gladys are portrayed as sadists who get erotic pleasure from their sense of power. The "ill constituted" are represented by Maurice Quincunx and Lacrima Traffio who are "born pariahs." As the story opens, the Italian girl, Lacrima, is Gladys's paid companion but the Romers are forcing this "fragile, hyper-sensitive, absolutely dependent" pariah/sacrifice/love object to marry the brutal farmer Goring. Lacrima loves Maurice, who is financially dependent on Romer. Powys has the Romers "lose"—the father ends up humiliated and the daughter pregnant and abandoned by her lover.

The concomitant story of the Andersen brothers presumably is another example of the opposites of love and power, which Powys attaches vaguely to other antipodes such as light/dark and self-sacrifice/self-indulgence. James, the elder, is black haired, black of personality, a moon worshipper. Luke is a sun worshipper—a fair haired, fair minded "life enamoured youth."[86] James is bent on a life of sacrifice, like his dead mother. He loves Lacrima but is prepared to surrender her to Quincunx if that will give her happiness. Luke, on the other hand, just wants to enjoy life. In Luke, Powys sets up another hypothesis about the secret of the universe. It may be that "there is no inner fatality about it at all, that the whole thing is a blind, fantastic, chance drifting chaos."[87] The only response if this is the secret, suggests Luke, is neither self assertion nor self abandonment but sceptical epicureanism.

Readers unaware of his earlier stories have assumed that *Wood and Stone* was Powys's first work of fiction. In many ways, however, it is a continuation of the preoccupations of his previous stories. The same themes of sadism, masochism, fondling of children, and misogyny recur, as do many of the characters. Lacrima Traffio has appeared before as the mysterious Italian girl that Powys-heroes have been attracted to. Romer and Mole, the two boys at Sherborne who became the composite villain Romer Mowl of "The Incubus," now reappear as the evil Mortimer Romer. The narrative of the Andersen brothers, too, is a more accomplished version of the rejected 1909 tale, "The Spot on the Wall." In that, John and James Hare are two brothers who "lived in complete harmony with each other" until the younger, James, "realized that he did not quite understand his brother John." John goes about staring at women and "diving into little post-card shops and purchasing innumerable pictures of up-to-date actresses and singers." These (shades of the adolescent Johnny) he keeps in his pocket and ponders on, "always with the same unsatisfied, disappointed air." James concludes that "his brother is mad" when John becomes obsessed with a spot on the wallpaper in his room.[88] This was John Cowper's earliest attempt to portray his relationship with his brother Llewelyn; in *Wood and Stone*, the Andersen brothers are a second assay. Mary Cowper herself is fleetingly introduced as their dead mother; the village gossip says that the elder is exactly like his "poor moon-struck" mother who "suffered from more than one distressing mania." The old trot also hints darkly that "the whole village do say" that they are "more than brothers." They "lived, worked, ate, drank, walked and slept together" in "devoted attachment to one another." However, Luke's irresponsible behavior angers James and they quarrel. James begins to hear voices in his head and eventually, completely mad, he falls between two precipices in the quarries. Luke briefly feels guilt for his brother's death, even more briefly mourns, then marries a village girl, and sunnily continues to be Luke.[89]

Despite the similarities, *Wood and Stone* is more focused and plausible than his earlier stories. It is also considerably strengthened by his use of a landscape he knew intimately. The action takes place in Nevilton, which is Montacute, and in a sense this novel is a farewell to the home represented as idyllic by the rest of his family. Not, apparently, by Powys himself. He has James Andersen say, "I have always hated Nevilton, and every aspect of it." John Cowper, having newly discovered the light of Italy, has James continue: "These English vicarages are dreadful places. They have all the melancholy of age without its historic glamour. And how morbid they are! Any of your cheerful Latin curés would die in them, simply of damp and despair."[90] His observations of human relationships can be astute. For example, a mother quarreling with her daughter, "with that perverse self-punishing instinct, which is one of the most artful weapons of offence given to refined gentle-women"[91] does the one thing she most dislikes to do as well as the most likely to upset the entire household and make her daughter feel guilty. However, it is the portrayal of the pariah personality that is the most accomplished piece of characterization John Cowper had so far achieved. His depiction of Quincunx and Lacrima is almost clinically authentic. Lacrima makes no effort to escape either from bondage to the Romers or marriage with the brutal Goring.

> It would seem almost incredible to a healthy minded person that Lacrima should deliberately let herself be driven into such a fate without some last

desperate struggle. Those who find it so, however, under-estimate that curious passion of submission from which these victims of circumstance suffer,
a passion of submission which is itself, in a profoundly subtle way, a sort of
narcotic or drug to the wretchedness they pass through.[92]

Maurice Quincunx is also "a true Pariah in his miserable combination of
inability to strike back at the people who injured him, and inability to forget
their injuries. He propitiated their tastes, bent to their will, conciliated their
pride, agreed with their opinions, and hated them with demoniacal hatred." For
Quincunx, work is a "hideous purgatory" and a small bequest has allowed him
freedom from this. The sadistic Romer first tells him this unearned income has
ceased and henceforth he must work as a clerk, and then proposes that if Lacrima
marries Clavering, he will arrange for Quincunx to go back to his reclusive ways
and steady income. Because she loves Quincunx, Lacrima agrees to this, and one
pariah says to the other: "It is noble, it is sweet of you to think of marrying that
brute so as to set me free," and comforts her: "For you to be married to a man you
hate, would only be like my having to go to this . . . office with people I hate."[93]

At this point in the plot, Powys returns to the nymphet theme of his earlier
attempts, only now he has Theodore's Georgina as a model. One of "those small
wandering circuses" comes into town and sets up on the village green. They have
acquired a twelve-year-old Italian child, very beautiful with dark curls, long eyelashes, a scarlet mouth, and an "ivory pallor" on her skin—a "dainty bit of
goods." Quincunx happens by and is smitten. "Perhaps to all extremely sensitive
natures of Mr. Quincunx's type . . . the electric stir produced by beauty and sex
can only reach a culmination when the medium of its appearance approximates
to the extreme limit of fragility and helplessness." In an excess of courage he has
never previously shown, Maurice Quincunx sweeps the child off to his home,
determined to adopt her.[94]

Powys has added some new characters. One, the "boyish," charming, rich
artist, Ralph Dangelis, is modeled on an American friend. Vennie Seldom, for
whom "the idea of sex is distasteful and repulsive" and who ends up in a nunnery,
is obviously Marion Linton. These two are the saviours of the "ill-constituted"
ones. When Vennie Seldom finds Quincunx fondling the little girl sitting in his
lap, with Lacrima watching them with "an expression of despairing hopeless-
ness," she—"like St Catharine herself"—whisks them off to Weymouth where
she knows Ralph Dangelis is holidaying. Vennie convinces the American artist
to settle a handsome sum on the couple so they can marry and escape with the
child Delores to the Channel Islands to live happily ever after. This resolution is
based on another of Powys's hypotheses in the preface, that "the true secret lies
in some subtle and difficult reconciliation between the will to Power and the will
to Love." His version of this "reconciliation" is to have the pariahs rescued from
the Romers by Dangelis. An angel indeed, but hardly a disinterested one. Ralph
has been trying to find an excuse to escape from his engagement with Gladys and
makes the generous gesture when Vennie provides him the excuse by telling him

of Gladys's affair with Luke. If Dangelis is simply a gentler version of the power of money, what is between the two pariahs can only be described as a perversion of the power of love. They will marry but Quincunx fantasizes that Lacrima will catch a fever or drown so that "he and Delores would be left alone."[95]

It is one thing to introduce his beloved Llewelyn into his fictional pantheon but another to use Theodore as the model of Quincunx.[96] In *Autobiography*, written nineteen years after *Wood and Stone*, Powys insisted that his own "most instinctive affinities" were with "the oddities and queer ones and half-mad ones."[97] He makes it clear that the affinity arose, not out of a Nietzschean philosophical construct, or a evangelical imperative to favour the despised of the world, but out of his Sherborne experience: "I expect I still think of that well-constituted torturer, in the dormitory below ours at Wildman's, and of his ill-constituted victim." They were in every sense never out of his mind, or rather, his "diseased conscience." Powys developed his belief that he had magical powers for many reasons. But one reason was so that he could protect the "funny ones" from "the brutality of the normal." Quincunx is brutalized by the "normal" Romer, but Powys may well have been thinking of all the times that Theodore was persecuted by normal people, and the normal people were himself and his father. *Wood and Stone* is not a convincing novel, but it marks the beginning of a lifelong literary penance, bringing together in Powys's mind his feelings of cowardly failure for not going to the rescue of the "pariah" at school and the guilt he shares with his father for the torment of little Theodore. As an author, he can play the magician by orchestrating a plot, however unlikely, whereby Quincunx gets his heart's desire. The grown-up Theodore would never have to work again, would live in a country where he would never have talk with strangers, would have a wife to look after his practical needs and a little girl to satisfy his sexual fantasies. What more could a pariah wish for? The malice with which this pariah is portrayed is a more complicated matter.

Powys's imaginative life may have been set firmly in Somerset, England, when he wrote *Wood and Stone*, but his working life was very much centred in the midwest United States. Arnold Shaw soon increased the geographical range of the lecture tours, and by the autumn of 1912 Powys found it more convenient to make Chicago his headquarters for five months of the year. This period, which lasted perhaps four years, was a "very happy and a very exciting epoch" in his life, and he was always "a little sad" when he had to leave Chicago.[98] This is a surprising remark, because he always disliked cities and Chicago was not only the largest in the west, but was proud to be, in the poet Sandburg's words, "Hog Butcher for the World, / Tool Maker, Stacker of Wheat, / Player with Railroads and the Nation's Freight Handler. "[99] Notwithstanding, it was also in the midst of what the novelist Sherwood Anderson, called the "Robin's Egg Renaissance." Chicagoans boasted that the Fine Arts Building was "the only skyscraper in the world devoted solely to the arts." The Chicago Symphony Orchestra was flourishing and the Chicago Opera under way. Isadora Duncan danced on the Chicago stage, and the Art Institute brought the Armory Show of avant-garde paintings to town. The Windy City became the magnet which drew aspiring novelists, poets, playwrights, and journalists from the small towns of Illinois, Indiana, Wisconsin, and Iowa: Theodore Dreiser, Sherwood Anderson, Maxewell Bodenheim, Vachel Lindsay, Edgar Lee Masters, Carl Sandburg, Eunice Tietjens, Arthur Davison Ficke, Witter Bynner, Ben Hecht, Floyd Dell. Powys was acquainted with all of them; some were to become close friends. For a time, it was not only a literary and artistic bohemia, it also attracted such political and social radicals such as Jane Addams, Clarence Darrow, Eugene Debs, Emma Goldman—all of whom Powys admired, debated with, and in his lectures courageously defended. All in all, Chicago was at that time an exhilarating place to be.

Aspiring writers were fortunate to find outlets in the many literary magazines that sprang up all over America between 1910 and 1920. Two of the most famous were based in Chicago. *Poetry* was founded by Harriet Monroe in 1912. She published Robert Frost, William Carlos Williams, Vachel Lindsay, Carl Sandburg—the poets who would become famous as the "Western School" of American poetry. On Monroe's early list of possible contributors was Ezra Pound. To her astonishment and initial delight, he wrote back suggesting himself as her foreign correspondent to keep her "in touch with whatever is most dynamic in artistic thought" in England and France. He sent her poems by W. B. Yeats, D. H. Lawrence, Richard Aldington, and H. D. in quick succession. It was in *Poetry* that Hilda Doolittle published her first poems in 1913 and became not Hilda from Philadelphia, Pennsylvania, but "H. D.—Imagist." Pound also sent Monroe T. S. Eliot's "Prufrock" but she didn't like it, preferring to publish Joyce Kilmer's "Trees."

Pound soon decided that Monroe was "a bloody fool" for publishing "rotten poetasters,"[100] and switched his attention to another Chicago-based literary magazine, the *Little Review*. This iconoclastic magazine, founded in the winter of 1914 by Margaret Anderson, reflected the many political, social, and literary enthusiasms of the bohemian avant-garde: feminism, anarchism, symbolism, the back-to-nature movement, the Hellenistic revival, and Nietzsche's philosophy, to name a few. For more than a decade the *Little Review* attracted many of the leading modern writers and was a showcase for the most controversial writing of the period. Given its modernist stance, it is somewhat startling to read that Anderson considered Powys "the Little Review's godfather." She had heard him lecture and was determined "to reflect something of his attitude, his critical appreciation in a magazine."[101] Powys contributed a number of articles and reviews to the *Little Review*, mainly during 1915-1916, and his Chicago lectures were fully announced and commented on in the magazine. Anderson was publishing the magazine on a shoestring so that when Pound wrote to her in January 1917, offering to find the cash-strapped magazine a "prospective guarantor," she was duly grateful. In return, Pound was made contributing editor, insisting on the

right to have his work and that of his protégés published promptly in the magazine, and to have a say in the selection of other contributors. That agreed, he
promptly told her that, "Your dear Powys is a wind-bag lacking both balance and
ballast" and "not reliable intellectually."[102]

Not only was Pound proving to be an astonishing sniffer-out of new writing
talent, he was also an aggressive self-promoter, which may be why Powys wrote
Lulu sourly from Chicago, "What a demon of esoteric influence Ezra must be. He
has the genius of pulling wires if he has no other kind."[103] Their mutual animosity was not surprising; Ezra remained very much part of the complicated web
woven about Frances. As much as they disliked each other, both were pursuing
similar paths—writing articles and reviews, poetry, and lecturing. Pound never
relucted at making extra cash by giving literary lectures for society ladies in
London and apparently intended to milk this cash cow further by lecturing occasionally in the States. According to Frances Gregg's son, Oliver, it was during
this period that Powys prevented Shaw from signing Pound on as a lecturer, an
act which Frances understandably interpreted as jealousy and never forgave.

It was of course Ezra Pound who had found James Joyce in Trieste and proposed this author's new work to Anderson. An enormously courageous woman,
willing to challenge censorship, she published in the *Little Review* the
"Lestrygonians" episode of *Ulysses* in January 1919, the "Scylla and Charybdis"
in May, and the "Cyclops" in January 1920. The United States Post Office con-
fiscated and burned the entire three issues of the magazine because of Joyce's
text. But it was the July–August 1920 issue, containing the "Nausicaa" episode,
that proved to be crucial. Although the 1933 trial of *Ulysses* was the decisive
one, it was first brought to court thirteen years earlier. In September 1920, the
secretary of the New York Society for the Prevention of Vice, lodged an official
complaint.[104] Anderson's steadfast admiration for Powys must have been balm to
his Ezra-ridden soul, and he repaid the compliment fully by appearing as an
expert witness in the subsequent trial. Her lawyer decided to use three "literary
experts" to "testify that *Ulysses* in their opinion would not corrupt our readers"[105]—Scofield Thayer, editor of the *Dial*, Phillip Moeller of the Theatre Guild,
and John Cowper Powys. Moeller tried to explain that the objectionable chapter was an unveiling of the subconscious mind, and one of the judges called out,
"Here, here, you might as well talk Russian. Speak plain English." Powys testi-
fied that "*Ulysses* was too obscure and philosophical a work to be in any sense
corrupting." As described ruefully by Anderson in her autobiography, *My Thirty
Years' War*, the trial was a ludicrous episode in the farcical history of obscenity
law, but in February 1921, she and her co-editor were convicted of publishing
obscenity, fined, and instructed to stop publishing *Ulysses*. Anderson and her col-
league Jane Heap moved to Paris and tried to continue the magazine but in 1929,
the year of the stock-market crash, the last issue of the *Little Review* came out.

At the same time as the heyday of little magazines, there was a sudden flush
of little theatres all over America. The flowering was brief and by 1920 most had

disappeared. The Chicago Little Theatre opened on November 12, 1912, and closed five years later; yet, while it lasted it was, according to the dramatist Cloyd Head, "the foremost experimental theatre in America."[106] It was through Louis Wilkinson that Powys met the founder and director, Maurice Browne, his wife Ellen Van Volkenburg, and their troupe of players in the newly created Little Theatre. Louis and Browne had been friends as Cambridge undergraduates. For a period, Browne, his ideas, and his theatre (not to mention his actresses) became immensely important to Powys.

Browne was attempting to establish an "art theatre," by which he meant an intimate playhouse in which "important" drama, creatively staged, was performed. The Chicago Little Theatre was certainly intimate—in truth a *little* theatre. It was situated on the fourth floor back of the Fine Arts Building in downtown Chicago, with a stage a mere fifteen feet across, eighteen feet deep, and eleven feet high. The auditorium only held ninety-three seats, so that every member of the audience was in close proximity to the stage. The term "little" also meant for Browne stripping the stage to essentials; his motivating idea was to eliminate everything that interfered with the play being able to speak for itself. Most theories originate in necessity, and Browne's were no exception. His emphasis on minimal staging, costumes, props, and lighting—and his rejection of star actors for amateurs he could train himself in the principles of art theatre—corresponded nicely with the fact that the company began with virtually no capital and had to depend on patronage and membership to cover their operating costs. The chief aim of the Chicago Little Theatre, Browne wrote, was to "create and produce poetic drama." To that end he put on plays by Euripides, Ibsen, Schnitzler, Strindberg, Synge, and Yeats. Browne was convinced that the public would come to the theatre if it offered intelligent drama. Unfortunately, he was wrong. With the exception of *The Trojan Women*, the plays were usually box-office failures. As one unregenerate reviewer wrote after an evening of Schnitzler, Yeats, and Dunsany, "If that's high-brow drama, give me a cowpuncher movie every time!"[107]

It is difficult to know how much of the "new movement" ethos Powys accepted. Certainly he was grateful to the Brownes for allowing him to be part of their bohemian life, and proud to be "the only privileged outsider in this remarkable Little Theatre group."[108] He lived with them and the rest of the troupe when he was in Chicago and sat for hours at their rehearsals. At this period in his life, Browne was, "as far as *aesthetics* went, almost my whole world of environment and experience."[109] Yet in another passage in the same "America" chapter of *Autobiography* John Cowper makes it clear that he never derived from theatre the "intoxicating pleasure" he got from burlesque shows: "I don't go so far as to say that I despise *all* acted plays . . . for I sometimes have felt myself, when I was lecturing, to be acting like Sir Henry Irving, and I have an almost religious idolatry for Charlie Chaplin, but, speaking roughly, it is certainly true that the American burlesque represents the only art of the stage, if it *be* an art, from which I have

MEETING FRANCES GREGG : 1912-1915 137

got thrilling delight."[110] His reference to Sir Henry Irving points out one crucial area where he would have disagreed with Browne. Irving was champion of the star system. His productions were artistic spectacles with emphasis on scenic detail, and as an actor he was most successful in the "realistic" melodramas of the day. Maurice Browne was revolting against all of this, and in his attempt to build an ensemble of anonymous players, he was in the new wave of dramatist-directors who were displacing the individual star performer as the creative centre of American theatre. This was simply not Powys's style. He was the flamboyant individualist par excellence.

Nonetheless, John Cowper was admiring of Maurice's real genius for gathering people about him. Browne wanted the theatre to become the centre and focus of Chicago's intellectual life, and so, for a brief period, it must have been. As well as producing plays, Browne invited guest lecturers—playwrights, poets, musicians, singers, social reformers, feminists, anarchists, architects, city planners. Powys called it "Maurice's Pedagogic Province."[111] What he found appealing was the idea that this kind of theatre was to be accessible to all; it fitted well with his idea of the secretive culture of the dispossessed that he was beginning to formulate. Unfortunately, it was not his "pariahs" who attended the plays and joined in the discussions, but more often the artistic elite of the city who gathered in the little tea room adjacent to the auditorium to discuss everything from art to some current social or political issue. Powys was one of their favourites.

Although he lectured at a number of different venues in Chicago and to different audiences, he was undoubtedly at his most fulfilled and powerful during the period of association with Maurice Browne and the Little Theatre. He gave thirteen lectures there during January and February of 1915 on the literary giants of the past. The *Little Review* faithfully reported the lectures and their enormous impact on the audience.

> I was present at the transubstantiation of Oscar Wilde, performed by John Cowper Powys. Was it a lecture? . . . What a dwarfish misnomer for the solemn rite that took place in the dark temple, the "catacomb" of the Little Theatre! I close my eyes, and see once more the galvanized demi-god vibrating in the green light, invoking the Uranian Oscar. We, the worshippers, sit entranced, hypnotized, bewitched. . . . To quote Powys is as impossible as to tell a symphony.

One of Browne's most passionately held beliefs was the concept of performance as ritual and incantation. In a 1914 essay he wrote, "Art, in common with all religions, needs its rituals and priesthood,"[112] and Powys fully recognized the significance of what Browne was trying to achieve. In an encomium that itself reaches incantatory heights, Powys wrote in the *Little Review* in March 1915 that "What the Little Theatre is doing is nothing less than a restoration to the worship of Eternal Gods of an Institution which has been bastardized, perverted and profaned!"[113] It is therefore not surprising that in the review quoted, Powys is called a "sorcerer," his lecture a "solemn rite," and his "worshippers" bewitched. Another reviewer referred to Powys gradually lifting himself into a "Dionysiac frenzy," his audience catching the infection and "careering along after the wine-god," and feeling afterwards as if they had been "under the influence of a drug."[114] Even a sophisticated admirer, Henry Miller, would say in later years that "leaving the hall after his lectures, I often felt as if he had put a spell upon me."[115] It is possible that what John Cowper loved most about the Chicago Little Theatre was that he was given complete freedom to perform his own rituals and incantations and that it was here, for the first time, he felt that "the ritualistic and symbolic elements in my performances, that had hitherto only been recognized by the devoted instinct of Nuns and Communists met with a subtle aesthetic response."[116]

Above all, the lectures were "one continuous performance of the Actor in me."[117] And Maurice Browne, despite his strictures on star performers, encouraged and promoted this. Powys always lectured in a black university robe which he had borrowed from "a very nice maiden lady who ran a school for girls," after he lost his Cambridge one on the train.[118] He wore it at the beginning of his American career because the audiences he was attracting then paid good money to be taught by an English Oxbridge man. In later years, he wore the black gown because, as Will Durant—no mean actor-lecturer himself—said, "it was a stratagem to arouse a curiosity that would alert attention."[119] A friend recalled "this effect as it flapped and gyrated to his stridings and turnings, working its own necromantic spell."[120] Browne and Raymond Jonson, his brilliant art director, now proceeded to make Powys into a priest performing a religious function. "A demi-god vibrating in the green light" is a startling image, but Browne was a pioneer in the field of lighting. His equipment may have been primitive but the effects were always spectacular. In March 1915 his wife Ellen played Medea in Euripides's tragedy and Browne kept her face in a spot of green light while the rest of the cast was illuminated with rose floods. Browne used the same techniques to allow Powys full reign as a dramatic actor. An accomplished professional actor himself, Browne paid tribute to Powys's tremendous skill.

> Once I heard him talk on Hardy for over two hours to an audience of over two thousand in a huge auditorium in the heart of Chicago's slums; throughout those one hundred and thirty-odd minutes there was not a sound from his listeners save an occasional roar of applause or laughter; and when he had finished speaking we rose like one person to our feet, demanding more. The man was a great actor.[121]

Powys did not always take everyone with him, particularly when he ventured beyond the tried and true path of famous writers. In another article in the *Little Review*, the reviewer, Margerie Currey, while admiring the technique and acknowledging his "cult" status, advised him to stick to a subject he knew something about and resist the temptation "to revel in obvious and facile romanticisms." The cause of her ire was a debate in November 1915 between Powys and Browne when Powys took a pro-war stance.

> The great one, appearing robed in black, through his Delphic releasing blinding vapour clouds of infallible utterance, was to devastate the suggestion that war is evil, avoidable, and should not be prepared for by military methods. . . . The master himself was the glorious vulture of war. Looming there on the stage of the Little Theatre, black, huge, alone under a vast orange sky heavily streaked with black, a violet light from somewhere touching the crimson of his face—and beside him in that great lonely cosmos an iridescent emerald bowl upon a high ivory pedestal. . . .
>
> "War a great evil and an unmitigated wrong? I cannot see it. A pacifist struggle for existence is only a meaner struggle. They are fools who think it advisable or possible to stamp out war; they are knaves if, thinking this possible or advisable, they still go on a pacifist crusade." Followed then the picture of a well-managed nation during war, a regime of exalted socialism—the pooling of all moneys, the raising of the income taxe, the rich paying for the needs of the poor; she who was once thought a bedraggled hussy of London's east end now become a saviour of her country, in her potential gift of a son to the recruiting officer.
>
> Well, after all this heroic joy and thin-ice socialism, it was announced at the end of the evening that the week after the subject would be Walt Whitman. Thank heaven! Let his people listen to John Cowper Powys on Walt Whitman. Of these he should speak—of Walt Whitman, of Oscar Wilde, of Huysmans and Richepin and Milton and Ficke and Baudelaire and Goethe and Shakespeare. On these he speaks divinely. Peace and war indeed![122]

Powys admitted that "a certain power of rapid and logical assimilation tempts me to pass off as my own conclusions views and visions which are really quite alien to myself," but both Powys and his manager Arnold Shaw knew precisely what effect this encomium to war would have on a largely pacifist audience. Shaw, particularly, knew full well the value of being "heartily suspected, feared, disliked, detested, by the usual type of ethical person," and that "violent altercations" resulted in bigger crowds turning up the next night, attracted precisely for that reason.[123] Powys also loved to "stir up a fine row" and blow his "poor audience sky-high."

> I managed to divide my audiences into two opposite camps, one of agitated lovers, and one of implacable enemies. . . . This arousing of conflicting currents of psychic chemistry in my silent "reservoirs of magnetism" was never, as you may suppose, displeasing to my misanthropic guile.[124]

This was, of course, a motivation totally different from putting bums on seats. Claude Bragdon, the man who was to publish his next book, *Confessions of*

Two Brothers, asked Powys once why he continued to give lectures. "He answered that it enabled him to rid himself of certain hates and loathings which, undischarged, would poison him, mentally and physically. He lectured to please himself more than to please his audiences, but people flocked to witness his fireworks, even when they got singed by them. . . . Sometimes while pacing up and down the platform, clad in his flowing Oxford robe, or grasping the back of a chair with his long, nervous fingers, intent upon the precise formulation of some envenomed thought, he seemed like a big black spider spinning a web of words with which to ensnare the minds of the unwary; while at other times and in other moods he was a black-robed priest, his lips as though touched by a coal from the altar, communicating the eternal truth of things."[125]

Powys seems always to have been a natural lecturer, his talent emerging in early childhood when first he harangued his brothers and sisters from his nursery "pulpit." Not for the first time have the sons of preachers become teachers or actors. When he was an extension lecturer in England he developed the technique he called "dithyrambic analysis" but under the aegis of Arnold Shaw he thought up a "new stunt" which he called "Histrionic Psychology." He confided to Lulu:

> I shall dress up as Nero, Heraclitus, Marlowe, Byron, Goethe, etc etc . . . and, as these actual people, returned to life, defend my historic loves and murders! . . . Don't you think it will make our fortune? Can't you see Arnold and I touring the cities of Europe with the New Art? . . . And how charming to employ Marian to make the costumes![126]

What dreams he had. He was still thinking how to put this "new art" into practice when he met Frances a year later, and soon he had fantasies of her as part of the act. Here was someone with whom he could play dress-up as he had with his brothers and sisters, and where he always played the lead. In her autobiography Frances described the abortive attempt.

> John Cowper was inventing a new art. Why, with his clairvoyance, lecture? He could be—who could he not be, if he gave up his personality with sufficiently lowering of all boundaries between present and past, between soul and soul. No one had fathomed as he the illusion of personality. . . . Modestly, he chose Lorenzo, and I was to be his sister Lucrezia. . . . When the night came, Lucrezia, in a hired costume—hired by Jack without regard to the structure of his Lucrezia—caught to her form by a myriad of safety pins, made fruitless endeavours to gather her scattered wits together after the first sight of Lorenzo in tights. Those legs were out of a nightmare of Durer's. They suggested a monstrous offspring of Don Quixote and Rosinante. Lucrezia could, and did, fold her garments round her in swathes, but I don't know what held those tights up.

After getting tangled up in the velvet curtains, she finally made it on stage, "bearing a most unconvincing phial of poison which she endeavoured to persuade Lorenzo to imbibe, with the air of a competent Nannie with castor oil. When it came to parcelling out occult inspiration Miss Borgia just wouldn't play, and John Cowper did not invent a new art."

Nevertheless, Frances goes on to say: "Not that he needed to, for his lecturing was an art on its own such as, one feels, the world will never see again."[127] She was right. His lecturing passed beyond sympathetic analysis or acting to something much more powerful. He felt he became a medium for the revelations of the great writers: "The protean fluidity of my nature is such that I could give myself up so completely to the author that I was analysing that I *became that author.*"[128] This in itself was a "new art" although quite possibly all the best lecturers have this ability to a greater or lesser extent. But Powys seems to mean more than an empathic identification with his subject.

His many references to his lecturing in his writings are complicated and often contradictory, but the following account is the clearest and most honest explanation of what he finally achieved. Before a lecture he would squat down on anything that was available behind the stage and "proceed with deliberate Tibetan craft to make my mind a blank." This was not, he said, to think about his subject ("for that I always left till the Lord should tell me what to say") but in order to "sink into I know not what fathomless depths of sub-Being." He would then proceed to dip his ladle into "the great reservoir of human magnetism." It was not his own energy, but that of his audience, which allowed him to speak for several hours at a time.

> The curious thing was that I derived renewed strength, vitality, magnetism, electric force, and even some kind of mysterious planetary energy, by giving a lecture. Instead of being vampirized by my audience, I vampirized *them.* . . . I renewed my life-sap by drinking the blood, and I do not speak altogether figuratively, of older men and women as well as of young men and young women! . . . What really paid me for lecturing was not the fees I shared with Arnold, but the actual *sensation* I got from it and the life-energy I imbibed from it. Such sucking up of crowd-magnetism I found to be one of the most marvellous of human restoratives. When I stopped, after lecturing for an hour and a half, or even sometimes for two hours, I felt light, airy, frivolous, gay and butterfly-like; whereas my audience were so wilted, so drooping, so exhausted, so wrung-out, that they were like people who had spent a night of the extremest form of erotic debauch![129]

What he is describing here has nothing whatever to do with the subject matter. Indeed, some less generous members of the audience would complain that it did not matter whether he lectured on d'Annunzio, Ibsen, Gorky, Maeterlinck, or Hauptmann, he would say "practically the same thing about all of these men." What he was doing to his audience was closer to the technique of crowd manipulation used by the primitive Methodist preacher or the modern American television Evangelist, and, as disillusioned journalist Burton Rascoe says, Powys was fully aware "of the meretricious motives of some of his most eloquent oratorical flights and gestures."[130]

This was, in a sense, another aspect of what Powys called his "voyeurism." Arthur Ficke wrote a poem which appeared in the *Little Review* in April 1916 in which he addresses Powys as "Old Salamander": "Impenetrably isolate you stand, / Tickling the world with a long-jointed straw."[131] It is a shrewd description of the shape-shifter's techniques, his effect on audiences, and his essential disengagement from that audience. However, there were times when Powys would himself be "swept away, out of my own methods and consciousness, on the tide of some invisible force."

> Some would say that I have the power, under certain conditions, of drawing upon what certain psychologists call the subliminal consciousness and that the inspiration of this consciousness, flowing from a source more general and impersonal than the individual brain of one speaker, shows a clairvoyance and an energy beyond what would be possible for me to reach in any normal moods.[132]

He was not sure at this stage whether he was tapping into an impersonal source or the mental vibrations of his audience, or whether they were one and the same. He was later to locate this "subliminal consciousness" in "the deep vases of the mind." This ability, if that is what it was, was to have a profound effect on what and how he wrote, when he turned away seriously from lecturing to the writing of novels. For now he seemed to need an audience to suck up the necessary energy to tap this source. It is little wonder that the audience felt it had taken a drug or participated in some Dionysian rite. Whatever it did to the audience, or to himself, lecturing was essential to him. "Yes, the platform has been everything to me. It has been the bed of my erotic joys. It has been the battlefield of my fiercest struggles. It has been the gibbet of my execution. It has been the post of my scourging. It has been my throne. It has been my close-stool. It has been my grave. It has been my resurrection."[133]

CHAPTER SIX

LOW EBB
1916-1920

⌒

JOHN NOTED GLOOMILY ON THE TWENTY-SECOND OF FEBRUARY 1916, "This is a dark hour in our horoscope." The continuing war and "a sim-ple lack of spirit to go through the bother about passports," made him decide to cancel the customary summer in England and his proposed trip to Africa to see Llewelyn. His duodenal pain worsened, and X-rays in January indicated that another operation was inevitable sooner or later.[1] A bad case of flu did not improve his mood. He concluded that Americans were "good-natured enough" but "staggering illiterates,"[2] and he felt an "indescribable loathing of my exis-tence as a lecturer."[3]

Eager to follow up their publishing successes, Shaw was urging him to write another volume of essays. Powys was afraid the strain would make his stomach worse; in any case, he was not well-disposed toward Arnold at this time. It was the "Confessions" project that was causing the coolness. Theodore had punctiliously completed his part and sent it to Shaw. Llewelyn, who had taken over Will's job as manager of the African stock farm at Gilgil while his brother was fighting, had little time to write, so in early October 1915, he sent John some autobiographical fragments and his diaries, asking his brother to select extracts. John did so and then wrote his own, much longer, confession in three weeks. Unfortunately, Shaw disliked both Llewelyn and John Cowper's essays and refused to publish them. He decided instead to publish Theodore's separately. Theodore's contribution came out in January 1916, entitled *The Soliloquy of a Hermit*. At the same time, Shaw produced an advertising pamphlet written by Louis Wilkinson called "Blasphemy and Religion." Presumably Shaw intended it to promote both the *Soliloquy* and the recently published *Wood and Stone*, but it did not have that effect. Louis praised *Soliloquy* as a "perfect work of art," and the author "a man of genius." He went on to say that one sentence of Theodore's—"I have tried to hide amongst grassy hills; but the moods of God have hunted me out."—had "more weight than all the seven hundred pages of *Wood and Stone*." Not content with this, Louis con-tinued his criticism of the novel: "The Mythology of Power and the Mythology of Sacrifice; a couple of Rocking Horses. He went out and bought them," adding,

"He is forever breaking into spiritual sweats. They water his forehead: his soul keeps dry." As a gratuitous further hit, to remind John of what he lacked, for the first and last time in a publication Louis included his own degrees—M. A., Litt. D.—after his name on the title page.[4]

Wilkinson's praise of Theodore was understandable. His love and admiration for this brother was sincere and enduring. Louis had been trying unsuccessfully since 1906 to get Theodore's stories published, and it may have been he who convinced Shaw that Theodore's piece should stand alone. But that hardly explains the virulence against the author of *Wood and Stone*. Possibly Louis was angry at John's portrayal of Theodore as Quincunx, but a less honorable motive would have been the increasing tension between Louis, Frances, and Jack. He knew that John could not answer back; all Theodore's relatives and friends were eager for Theodore to have the recognition he so desperately craved. Indeed it was John and Louis who had paid for the private printing of Theodore's first book, *Interpretation of Genesis*, in 1908. Shaw could therefore quote John Cowper on the book cover for *Soliloquy* as saying that "compared with the deep originality of his hermit brother, his own work is a mere matter of receptivity and repetition."[5] Theodore also may have suspected Louis's motivation, but encumbered with a wife and two small boys and barely surviving on his father's allowance, he was more interested in whether "this banging together of Jack's head and mine [will] produce gold?"[6]

Powys had no luck finding another publisher for the leftover essays until Claude Bragdon, an architect who had attend his lectures in Rochester, offered to publish them as *Confessions of Two Brothers*. When Llewelyn saw his portion in print he said he wished he had taken more trouble. He may have regretted giving John carte blanche to put together a selection from the materials he had sent. Certainly the job was sloppily done. Moreover, Llewelyn had instructed him to "cut out anything insipid."[7] Instead, John had excised some of the more indiscreet entries. The entire gondola episode, for example, which Llewelyn had described with admirable clarity and frankness, was reduced to one banal sentence: "At night we glided through the city in a gondola."

Llewelyn made it clear in his foreword that he did not consider his contribution was a "confession" but rather "vague autobiographical ramblings." John's apologia was another matter. His personality almost demanded a periodic confession of his sins—if not to a priest, then to an audience. More than once with an audience he would deliberately "wither, blight, freeze, devastate and bewilder the souls of some 500 double-dyeds, with a kind of mock-serious pseudo-wistful Apologia."[8] Powys was always a more astute seller of himself than he ever admitted, either to himself or to others; he knew that there was no form of literature likely to sell better than the unveiling of a writer's inner self. Inevitably, this early confession compares unfavourably, both in style and content, with his later autobiography, but in it he makes a statement which his reader, and above all his biographer, must always keep in mind in an encounter with John Cowper Powys:

In reading what follows the reader must be on the lookout for indirect betrayals·and unmaskings. He must follow me suspiciously, guardedly, furtively. He must be prepared for that invincible human trick of using language to conceal rather than to reveal. I am ready to confess myself, as a man may be ready to throw himself into the water. But once *in* the water, the instinct of self-preservation compels him to swim. So I swim—on words—unless the reader's imagination is shrewdly alert to thrust me down into the truth.[9]

His "self-preservation" instincts in *Confessions* lead him to make pronouncements which contradict almost everything he has written previously and much of what he would write in future. For example, on his childhood: "I cannot bear to recall my childhood." His attitude toward pariahs: "I observe as an interesting physiological fact, that the society of nervous and ill-constituted people throws me, inwardly, into a reaction of hard, clear, and even philistine capacity." Of his Wordsworthian nature quest: "Those wonderful second-thoughts and earth-escaping ecstasies, which I am able to describe only too eloquently in words, never come to me in life."[10] There are a number of other apologetic declarations which, in their dramatic self-analysis, hint that this confession has a subtext, but, for what it is worth, this is his image of himself in 1916: "A figure struggling beneath the burden of its wretched contradictions, yet looking for no issue from its dilemma, save in the narcotic power of critical analysis, and the obliterating power of death."[11] The only defence that seemed to release him from this bind of conflicting personalities was this: "My whole life has been one long running-away; and the years have given me swiftness and agility."[12] It was a strategy that served him well in the years to come.

Some of the assertions take the breath away. At one point he insists that he *thinks* by books but he does not *live* by books.

> For instance, because books upon Greek Art assure me that the exquisite limbs of boys and girls are more important objects of contemplation, and more revealing of the Platonic ideal of Beauty, than trees and flowers, I do not therefore leave my solitary valley in the Sussex Downs, and rush to the beach at Brighton.[13]

This strangely reads as if he were playing with himself, his reader, and those who knew him. He states one true thing about books, then tells a lie, but which most readers would not know was a lie. Yet why use the example at all, except to anger and annoy those who knew the truth? Neither reader nor biographer can ignore another assertion in *Confessions*: "When I write a book, I never write for posterity. . . . I write with quite definite people always before me."[14] This is certainly true of his next book of poems, *Wolf's Bane*, which came out in March 1916. While the poems might be taken simply as a general lament about the illusoriness of love or the desire for death, many have clue words which indicate that they are directed specifically at persons to whom he wishes to give either a "certain thrilling caress" or a "certain malicious prod." There are several that obviously are addressed to Llewelyn, at least seven to Frances, one to Louis, and a bitter one that refers to "the pond-newt" who is "silky and soft and lewd." Poor Ezra! As artificial and conventional as most of the poems are, there is an occasional directness of hurt. The poem "Reversion" must have been written after he had been with Frances and Louis in Spain, when he "thro' the rose-parterres / Caught Babylonian airs." Now he is back at Burpham planting "geraniums in a row."[15] Other poems miscarry because they use imagery which is obscure except to the person in on the secret. The sudden unexplained reference to "the witch-girl's window" in "Compensation" makes no sense, except to those who know that H. D. called Frances "witch-girl." There is another reference to the "witch-girl" in "Knowledge" as well as to the "rook-boy," which was a private name for himself in the letters to Frances. However, one verse of this poem, presumably a reference to Katie's madness, is a rather lovely thing:

> The wild owl over the mad-house knows
> In what padded place
> The loveliest form that ever breathed
> Lies on her face.

A month after *Confessions* was published, in April 1916, *The Buffoon* came out. Ostensibly written by Louis Wilkinson, their son Oliver was certain that much of it was written by Frances herself. It probably was. Frances wrote a short story in 1915 entitled "Two Brothers." The brothers are undisguisedly Jack and Lulu, and the story is patently her bitter version of the events surrounding her marriage to Louis. The elder brother is dying (an echo of the scene in *The Buffoon* where Jack dies after an operation) and he has a last conversation with the younger about "the invisible third." The young man blurts out, "Why did you marry her to him?" The dying brother responds: "Why? . . . She was so frail, so chaste. . . . I watched her seduction, her destruction. To see her shame and humiliation was exquisite to me." The Lulu character then asks, "Why did you bring me into it?" The response: "Did I not see it all from the beginning—how you would yearn for her, when you saw her like a bruised white petal in the hollow of his great hand! And she turned to you as to the sun. But I did not let her mistake. . . . I brought to her mind her mutilation. And in the midst of her pain I caressed her. . . . And you were jealous, you, our young conqueror of women, were jealous of your elder brother. . . . Shall I ever forget your suffering? . . . Ah, I have been a God—I have played as a God with your emotions!" The story ends with "She,"—Frances—sending a letter of "concentrated bitterness" to the dying man: "Here was vengeance."[16]

In *The Buffoon*, Frances and Louis did not confine their ire to John Cowper but lashed out in all directions. The portraits of Pound as Raoul Root and H. D. as Eunice Dinwiddie are more vicious than anything the Wilkinsons say about Powys. However, their lampoon of him in *The Buffoon* angered the entire Powys family, with the exception of Theodore, who called it "a most honest book."[17] Littleton and Llewelyn were especially incensed, feeling, quite correctly, that Louis owed a great deal to John. Jack Welsh is portrayed as timid, physically ungainly, slovenly, cruel, naive, class-ridden, and with "an encased personality." Witty and cruel it may be, but in *Confessions* Powys describes himself in much the same terms, saying he "love[d] nothing better than to be the butt of my friends' ethical and intellectual indignation." He admits that there is in this defensive mechanism "much more malice than is usually supposed": "One some-times does it simply in order, in a queer perverted way, to be *revenged*."[18] It was as if he already knew what would be in *The Buffoon*, and got in first.

Nonetheless, he was hurt by it—not so much by the description of physical and personal characteristics that he himself emphasized, but by those benign-seeming, glancing blows buried throughout the book that could only be made by a woman who knew him intimately. For example, in one scene the three of them are at a party hosted by an American woman who lionizes Welsh. She describes ecstatically being at one of his lectures when he confided to his audience all about his "summer home," his little boy, the dog, Mrs. Welsh and—yes—the geraniums. However, it might have been Louis's hits at his lecturing that would have hurt most: "First he hypnotised them by incantations of some genuine power; then he would reel off clap-trap, launch joyously into bombast, strike out shamelessly for naked melodrama."[19]

John's riposte to *The Buffoon* was to write a review of it in which he says that Wilkinson "takes the humours and frailties of humanity and sets them upon a Fancy-stage that has no point of contact with the little realities of life,"[20] but the aftermath was serious. The irony was that it was John who had helped Louis get the book published by appealing to his new friend Theodore Dreiser. Dreiser got his publisher, Knopf, to take the book. Knopf had in turn talked Shaw into buy-ing 200 copies of it before Arnold had read the book. John wrote Llewelyn, "Louis feels as though Arnold is silly to think the book could hurt us. Arnold thinks Louis is mad to think it won't. . . . Knopf wants us to push the book. Arnold wants the book to die down. . . . I don't want to be unfaithful to Louis who has what Frances calls a pathetic assurance that I will do what I can to help him out, but on the other hand I'm indissolubly linked up with Arnold who has been working himself thin and nervous over my books."[21] There was more to this than divided loyalties and business sense. Jack had met Theodore Dreiser in October 1914 and immediately felt a special bond with him. He subsequently introduced him to Louis, who captivated Dreiser—as he had charmed Llewelyn, Frances, and so many other of John's friends. In a disarmingly candid letter to the man himself in 1907, John confessed his jealousy of Louis, long before the advent of Frances had exacerbated it.

Bernie O'Neill when he was down here with Lulu said, "You Powyses are always speaking as though Louis was a cunning sort of dog, as cunning a dog, in fact, as you are yourselves"—and then the word "worldly" as applied to you led on to an unaccountable outburst of fury on my part, in which I denounced you in so scandalous a manner that even those impenetrable psychologists were shocked. However, after this outburst . . . I speedily returned to my normal and rational condition and then was only anxious to find the explanation of this explosion of subliminal feeling. The explanation which I gave to them in public was that I must have been latently and unconsciously jealous of your literary and lecturing gifts, but the real explanation which I only whispered to Lulu afterwards was that my devotion to Bernie and my almost absurd desire to engross his affection made me jealous not of your literary powers but of your personal attractions.[22]

Despite all this, he invited the Wilkinsons to join them when he and Marian rented a cottage on Rodmor Lake in Vermont at the beginning of May.[23] Marian was recovering from a bad back caused by a fall, and he was attempting to write a book of essays, another of verses, and a novel for Arnold who was now in serious financial difficulties. The combination of closeness to Frances and the sexuality of the summer scene proved too much and, leaving Marian to her own devices, he fled back to New York in August. In all likelihood he was close to a breakdown when he took refuge with Marian's doctor, but for purely practical reasons, the move was convenient. Dr. Thomas and his wife found him an empty apartment in their building, gave him his meals and let him work in peace. Begun in July, *Rodmoor* was finished by September and Arnold had it published by October.

In an almost defenceless fashion, Powys's early novels set up not only symbols, but themes and characters which will recur in increasingly complex patterns in the later romances. In *Rodmoor* many of the characters and the discussions in the unpublished stories are back, albeit handled more skilfully. The Powys-hero is Adrian Sorio, portrayed as a nervously incompetent, hypersensitive forty-year-old who has had one bout of madness and is obviously heading for another breakdown. As the novel opens, Adrian has been invited by his old friend Baltazar Stork to live with him in Rodmoor, a coastal village in East Anglia. Baltazar, "delicate and dainty" as a girl, is the Harry Lyon who has appeared in so many of his previous stories. The other old friends who discussed life, time, and women on the Brighton seafront are also back. At one of their drinking sessions, Powys has Sorio expand on the familiar theme of women and nature. "The sentimental writers always speak of women as so responsive, so porous, to the power of Nature. . . . Of course they're porous to it. They're part of it! They've never emerged from it. . . . No woman who ever lived could understand the pleasure we're enjoying now—a pleasure almost purely intellectual. . . . They haven't the remotest idea that, as we sit in this way together, we enter the company of all great and noble souls."[24]

The theme of a man in love with two women, only touched upon in previous tales, is now explored more fully. Before coming to East Anglia, Sorio has met and proposed marriage to Nance Herrick, who follows him to Rodmoor.

Nance is a conventional, practical young woman with a "deep maternal pity, infinite in its emotion of protection."[25] Sorio is content with her until he meets Philippa Renshaw, "this insidious 'rose au regard saphique,'" and "the revelation of Philippa . . . altered everything."[26] Philippa is the sylph figure of Sorio's imagination: "the boyish outlines of her body gave her the appearance of one of those androgynous forms of later Greek art."[27] In this novel the sylph is given body, so to speak, by being modeled on Frances Gregg. The sadomasochistic relationship documented in their letters is now turned into fiction: "Something radically cold and aloof in her made it possible for her to risk alienating him by savage and malicious blows at his pride. But the more poisonous her taunts became, the more closely he clung to her, deriving, it might almost seem, an actual pleasure from what he suffered at her hands."[28]

In a scene which curiously echoes the childhood episode when he almost strangled Littleton, Sorio and Philippa find themselves at a deserted windmill. Sorio wants them to go up a dangerous ladder to the floor above. She refuses, and he proposes to tie a rope around her and pull her up. She again refuses, and his face "darkened to a kind of savage fury." He starts to tie the rope around her and when she resists, he strikes her across the breast with it. Only when she becomes "docile and passive" does he suddenly stop and begin to talk about his son and "the bond of abnormal affection which existed between them."[29] This son, Baptiste, unaccountably left behind in America and presumably the product of a previous marriage, is out of sight throughout the action of the novel, but Sorio is convinced that no one except this boy "understands" him. For the first time Powys's son, Littleton Alfred, enters his fictional world—the son that John Cowper was sure would "grow up to take my side against the world."[30]

The novel ends when Sorio makes an apparently unmotivated attack on Philippa's brother Brand (who bears a pronounced physical resemblance to Louis Wilkinson). Sorio then tries to strangle Nance (who has many of Margaret's characteristics) and is incarcerated in the local insane asylum. The attack on Brand is totally unconvincing so far as plot is concerned, but Powys was still using the novel form as therapy—punching-bag fiction. After a week, Philippa gets the Powys-hero released from the asylum, but after drifting together in a barge on the river Loon, Sorio suddenly decides he must reach the sea and be alone. He begins to run, and then "something seemed to break in his brain or his heart."[31] Blood rushes into his mouth and he dies, crying "Baptiste!" Philippa ties him to herself and drowns in the sea.

More convincing than the plot is Powys's portrait of Helen Renshaw, the mother of Philippa and Brand. It is as if we are seeing Mary Cowper herself, so vividly does he describe this mother. In the novel, Helen Renshaw is an enigma not only to her own family but to everyone, her personality a combination of depression, masochism, and "unusual and almost terrifying power."[32] Baltazar asks her, "I wonder whether it is I or you who is the most unhappy person in Rodmoor!" and she replies: "What we suffer seems to me like the weight of some great iron engine with jagged raw edges—like a battering-ram beating us against a dark mountain."[33] Nance has wanted to be of "some service to this unhappy one," yet "she felt shut out and excluded."[34] Now when Nance goes to Mrs. Renshaw to tell her of Sorio's illness, Mrs. Renshaw's sympathy dispirits rather than encourages Nance, just as Mary Cowper's once dismayed the tubercular Llewelyn. "Her attitude seemed to imply that it was better, wiser, more reverent, not to cherish any buoyant hopes, but to assume that the worst that could come to us from the hands of God was what ought to be expected and awaited in humble submissiveness."[35] She tells Nance that the more you love a person the happier you are when "they are set free from the evil of the world." Nance wonders if Mrs. Renshaw had "actually secured some strange and unnatural link with the dead which made her cold and detached in her attitude towards the living." Mrs. Renshaw goes on to lay down the law to Nance about a woman's duty in marriage. "God has ordained, in his inscrutable wisdom, that there should be a different right and wrong for us women, from what there is for men. . . . A woman is *made* to obey. . . . We were made to bear, to endure, to submit, to suffer."[36]

While there is guilt evident in this portrait of Mrs. Renshaw, guilt that "the boys" did nothing to alleviate the dreariness of their mother's life with C. F., there is also a suggestion that "this strange being was diseased and perverted" when it concerned "religion or the opposite sex."[37]

On the other hand, Mrs. Renshaw's attitude is not dissimilar to the earlier one expounded by the band of brothers. The inferiority of women was not an idea that John Cowper had imbibed solely from his reading of *The Yellow Book*, but something he had been brought up with. In 1928, when he wrote Marian, "the independent one," to congratulate her (she had just been called to Washington as a lace expert—"the expert of the land"), he went on to note that Marian was "the lady who was treated so casually & cavalierly in the days when only the Six Hulkers <u>counted</u> as living Persons at all!" All the Powys boys were raised to believe they were the superior sex. It was a difficult lesson to unlearn; some of them never did.

What makes this novel particularly interesting is that Powys was attempting to put into fiction the immediacy of his own depression of that summer. The coastal village of Rodmoor and the people in it are dominated by their passions or by the North Sea, one or the other of which destroys them. Everyone is afraid and most of the characters are "rather morbid." Those who are not insane have either protected themselves with neurotic obsessions or stand immobilized before the "appalling terror of the unconscious."[38] Confusingly he gives the Frances Gregg character his sister's name (the only time he ever used the name in his novels), but it is his terror of Katie's insanity, the family "taint," that he is rehearsing once again. He confessed to Llewelyn that when he wrote this novel he was "a little mad." Yet his Powys-hero is unconvincingly mad. Sorio is in and out of an insane asylum in exactly one week, unlike sister Katie who was incarcerated for many months. A brisk therapist would likely say that Sorio's "madness" was not a serious psychosis at all, but a way of escaping intolerable tension caused by an unresolvable conflict in relationships.

Powys would not be the inspired writer he became had he simply continued to write stories about old friends and relatives or as a form of self-therapy. *Rodmoor* is not a convincing novel, but it is an advance on *Wood and Stone* because of its more advanced wedding of philosophical and personal concerns. Sorio and Baltazar may be John and Harry Lyon, but they hold, and try to articulate, opposing life views which Powys spent the rest of his life hoping to resolve. Adrian is writing a book which will explain what he calls his "philosophy of destruction." It is, he says, the philosophy espoused by "the great terrible minds of antiquity," and it calls for the destruction of the self, the destruction of the duality of good and evil which arose with consciousness. To reach that "absolute white light" the individual must drown. Baltazar Stark, on the contrary, worships consciousness because it offers him a "temporary freedom" before he falls into "the depths of his soul" which is, to him, a "bottomless crevasse." Consciousness is the veil we spin to hide the void. Stork therefore considers that Adrian's suicidal struggle "to reach the ultimate horror of that frozen Sea" is a sign, not only of "moonstruck mysticism," but of insanity.[39] Despite this belief, Baltazar, one day, (in a state of mind perhaps similar to E. A. Robinson's Richard Cory) "without haste or violence, and with his brain supernaturally clear, drowned himself in the Loon."[40] Baltazar apparently becomes convinced that there is no horror "behind" in the unconscious that is worse than the horror that conscious life can offer; that there is, in fact, nothing behind. Adrian's vision too is of nothingness, emptiness, but his nothing contains everything. Death for him is an ecstatic release: "He was there at last—safe from everything—safe from love and hatred and madness and pity—safe from unspeakable imaginations—safe from himself!"[41]

All this can of course be mocked. Louis immediately wrote a "jeu d'esprit" which he sent around to family and friends. Llewelyn wrote Louis from Africa, "Jack has just sent me your parody on Rodmoor. I think it far the most witty and clever thing I have seen for a long time."[42] In truth, his *Bumbore is* amusing.[43] Purporting to be one of John's chapters (Chapter DCCCXCIX), Louis ridicules Jack's propensity for long novels, his repetitiveness, his clumsiness with dialogue, his over-the-top psychobabble, his sexual predilection for masturbation, and his fetish for the slender legs of girls. The hero Sorio becomes "Sadio," nicknamed "Onan," "a mental masturbator, a cerebral shagster." When Gremia (Nance) asks Sadio if he has got work yet, "by some singular psychological association, the intricacies of which Sadio at that moment was wholly unable to disentangle or unravel, at that very instant when Gremia's lips enunciated the word 'work,' he was conscious of an extraordinary and indescribable antagonism towards the girl: he noticed immediately that the calves of her legs were thicker than he had always supposed they were. His whole spirit suffered a profound atavistic revulsion, unspeakably petrifying to him." Wilkinson makes a mockery of Powys's Baptiste, and "the bond of abnormal affection." The savior-boy becomes

"Pappiste"—"the most desirable, the most desired, the most exquisite, the most wonderful white goat in the world!" So far as Louis was concerned, and probably Frances also, *Rodmoor* was a bum bore.

Whatever his friends may have thought, the public liked *Rodmoor*. The first edition of 3,000 copies sold out almost immediately and John wrote exultantly, "we've sold extraordinary numbers of the book—as many as ever old Hardy sold of Tess." For some reason, he and Shaw made no money out of it, but John was optimistic that they would as time went on and "we hit on another vein."[44] He began a further book of essays on September 24, finished it in November, and Arnold published *Suspended Judgements* on the fifth of December, 1916. John had intended to give these essays to "one of the big publishers" but either none wanted it or he realized that he owed a good deal to Arnold, who was now "struggling desperately to keep up his end." They are incisive and discerning essays, but Powys could never resist hitting back when he had been hurt. On the very first page of *Suspended Judgements*, he wrote, à propos of nothing that goes before or after, "the cultivation of what in us is lonely and unique creates of necessity a perpetual series of shocks and jars. The unruffled nerves of the lower animals become enviable, and we fall into moods of malicious reaction and vindictive recoil. And yet . . . the very betrayal of our outraged feelings produces no unpleasant effect upon the minds of others."[45] This echoes Baltazar's astute comment about Sorio: "That's always the way with you touchy philosophers. You stir up the devil of a row with your bad temper and make the most harmless people into enemies and then think you can settle it all and prove yourself right and everybody else wrong by writing a book." Adrian's response is bewilderment. "His air at that moment was the air of a very young child that suddenly finds the world much harder to deal with than it expected," and this gives Stork "secret pleasure."[46]

Although it is done covertly, with no names ever mentioned, almost every essay contains a sharp poke at Ezra Pound and H. D. ("shallow and insensitive spirits who make use of these new forms"). He takes potshots at the "novelty-mongers," at the new criticism with its "cult of the unique phrase," and at the literary magazines that did not take his poetry—asking the gods to "deliver us . . . from the hypocrisy of judicial condemnation!" His essays on the literary greats are fine criticism, although weakened by personal pique. The perceptive essay on Byron's poetry, for example, becomes an excuse to scold his own enemies.

> Our modern poets dare not touch the sublime naiveté of poetry like that! Their impressionist, imagist, futurist theories make them too self-conscious. . . . They cannot do it—our poets—they cannot do it; and the reason of their inability is their over-intellectuality, their heavily burdened intellectual conscience. They are sedentary people, too, most unhealthily sedentary, our moderns who write verse; . . . whose environment is the self-conscious Bohemia of artificial Latin Quarters. They are too clever, too artistic, too egotistic. They are too afraid of one another; too conscious of the derisive flapping of the goose-wings of the literary journal![47]

It turns out that the great writers of the past have the very attributes that Frances and Louis laugh at in him. He complains that "they do not see, these people, that the very carelessness of a great poet like Byron is the inevitable concomitant of his genius."[48] In an essay on Rousseau, he hopes for the "appearance upon the earth of genuinely dangerous writers, of writers who exploit their vices, lay bare their weaknesses, brew intoxicating philtres of sweet poison out of their obsessions and lead humanity to the edge of the precipice!" He adds, "There is something peculiarly stimulating to one's psychological intelligence when all this is done under the anaesthesia of humanitarian rhetoric and the lulling incantations of pastoral sentiment."[49] The essay on Rousseau is as much about himself and his future program for writing; the essay on Balzac gives fair warning of the long novels he intended to write: "I maintain that in the broad canvas of a nobler, freer art there is ample space for every kind of digression and by-issue."[50]

Despite his depression throughout 1916, he managed to write an astonishing five books. Unfortunately, after a brief flurry of attention on publication, they did not sell and the war hit the lecturing business badly. In an attempt to recoup their fortunes, Shaw stitched together a California tour in early 1917, but it was not a success. John wrote Littleton that "Californians are a gay, frivolous set, not much addicted to lectures."[51] He was franker in his letter to Lulu: "I wish a tidal wave wd. drown the whole country."[52] Part of the reason for the outburst was sheer fatigue. He gave two lectures a day on the three-month tour of the Pacific Coast, and at the end of it he had not made enough money to keep him through the summer, much less send his wife the money she required to keep up Burpham with its two housemaids, a cook, and a gardener, as well as to pay Littleton Alfred's school fees. However, the main reason for his depression was his health. He had been warned that adhesions from his previous operation together with a new ulcer had almost totally blocked the entrance to the duodenum from the stomach. In an attempt to control the pain and prevent an occlusion, he was eating virtually nothing. This in turn made him "nervous and incapable of effort."[53] Arnold borrowed money to pay the expenses of another California tour, but by the end of September Powys realized he must have another operation. He used Shaw's money for the operation and Harry Lyon, who was in New York at that time, lent him a further £250 for the surgeon's fees. He explained in a letter to Lulu on October 17, as he was recuperating: "I had a new entrance made, eliminating all necessity for the accursed duodenum; all sorts of adhesions cut away. . . . With this new entrance, sewn to one of the main intestines, I ought to get on." The operation, a gastroenterostomy, is no longer performed because surgeons eventually realized that it caused innumerable complications to the patient as time passed, but so far as Powys was concerned, at the time it was "a really miraculous success."[54] He was assured by the doctor that he could eat anything within reason and was encouraged to do so to regain strength. However, the diet favoured by his father—bread, milk, and tea—obviously satisfied some requirement that superceded any physical need.

Complaining of "whoresome lethargy" he nonetheless began lecturing again as soon after the operation as he could stand up, grateful that he no longer had to "speak leaning against the desk like an animal with a spear stuck thro' it."[55] It was becoming difficult to get any lectures at all, and he was frantic, knowing that not only were Margaret and his son depending on his support, so also were Arnold and his family. He wrote Littleton, "I daresay it is only the war. But it may be that my books have hurt me with the sort of persons who arrange lectures."[56] Arnold and John must have realized when they began to publish that it was going to be a risky, even reckless move. Setting aside the possibility that novels like *Rodmoor* put off the typically conventional organizers of lectures, the effort they spent on writing and publishing meant less was spent preparing tours and giving lectures. It may be, in part, for that reason that he wrote nothing for several years, except a slim book of verse, *Mandragora*, which came out in September 1917 and was promptly panned by both Llewelyn and Frances. He had little energy for another novel and in any case Arnold had no money to publish anything else. John also realized, with discouragement, that everything he had so far written was "all too hurried—all too patched up and rushed through."[57]

In January 1918 he started out for a month's tour of the midwest, but he had only two lectures a week and immense distances between venues. He traveled 1,400 miles to give one lecture to an audience of zinc miners. This was probably when Powys met the mining magnate, Franklin Playter, who would play a significant role in his future life. In desperation, he continued to try to get to get "a permanent place as a lecturer in some potty provincial university . . . but the university circle suspect me as a dangerous radical." The whole situation depressed him and made him wish that he had "quietly sunk into oblivion under those beneficent anaesthetics."[58] Harry Lyon and Louis Wilkinson stood on the sidelines and jeered, "all nerves and no stomach."[59] One of the few events to raise his spirits in those dark months was meeting Isadora Duncan. This renowned dancer and choreographer had been so impressed by his *Visions and Revisions* that she sent him "so many red roses that they filled the little flat" and when he was recuperating in November 1917 she danced for him alone. "It was as though Demeter herself, the mater dolorosa of the ancient earth, rose and danced."[60] They "harmonised at once," and he listened carefully to her revolutionary views—she was an outspoken socialist and a strong supporter of the liberation of women. She went on tour to California shortly after and from San Francisco sent him a telegram, dated November 26, 1917, "remember I am waiting for you here."[61] She had a fruitless wait, for he did not get back to the West Coast until the spring of the following year and by then Isadora had left for France.

However, once he got to California, there were other distractions. In 1918, Los Angeles was another American boom town like Chicago, with an artistic and intellectual milieu fuelled by a steady influx of actors, writers, set designers, and potential movie stars heading for Hollywood. It was a heady mix of epic theatrical productions, fundamentalist tent revivals, eastern mysticism, all-night

cabarets, prohibition, and attacks against Communists, anarchists, and minori-
ties by the Ku Klux Klan. Powys was always rightly fearful of the "lynchers" but
courageously spoke out against them. Prohibition meant he drank bootleg
whiskey or spirits of ammonia as a necessary "pick-me-up." He plunged into Los
Angeles life, describing himself as a "radical," a "lover of poetry," and a "Parlour
Bolshevik." His lectures, as always, attracted the bohemian element. Tina
Modotti and Edward Weston, both acclaimed photographers, met him at this
time, as did Modotti's partner, who had the unlikely name of Roubaix "Robo" de
l'Abrie Richey. Powys was particularly attracted to the "tall, slender, and rogu-
ishly handsome" Robo, and it was easy to see why. According to Modetti, Robo
had "a clear disregard for convention. . . . There was a deeply spiritual, almost
mystical side to his character, borne out of his constant search for the exotic and
beautiful in life and an aversion to the realities of the material world."[62] Powys
welcomed this Southern California coterie of literary admirers and would-be
poets to his lectures and he attended their parties. Their rebellious individualism, their anarchical stance, their sexual freedom, their idealization of poverty,
all appealed strongly to him and chimed with his ingrained romanticism.
Possibly he wanted to be one of them, but his vicarage background, his middle-
class marriage, and his own innate conservatism militated against it. He was an
outsider in outsider-land. His own eccentricities of dress and behavior were more
those of an actor than a committed maverick. Perhaps the only thing he authentically attained was the poverty.

The bohemian crowd flocked to his lectures on this tour but they did not pay
well. Powys noted that he was "reduced to accepting the most rotten lectures at
25 dollars a time" (compared to his usual $100 fee),[63] but told Littleton, "I must
get what I can these days."[64] He had hoped to obtain some work at the University
of California, but "some damn 'embusqué' has cut me out over that job."
However, a new friend in Portland, Charles Erskine Scott Wood, offered to
arrange a lecture series for him, promising him a class of fifty "leisured ladies in
San Francisco" paying twenty-five dollars a month each. Perhaps feeling that he
himself would be considered an "embusqué," instead of taking up this proposal
John suddenly decided in May 1918 that it was his "destiny" to return to England
and enlist.

Powys's attitude to World War I was a mixture of idealism and guilt.
Although his stern theory was that all who went to the front were brave, and all
who did not make desperate efforts to go to the front were unheroic, he did not
consider himself either brave or heroic, so he had postponed for four years any
effort to get near "the burning crater."[65] In 1914, after his mother's funeral and
the outbreak of war, he spent the remainder of the summer at Burpham. Margaret
became secretary to the local commandant of the Red Cross, and posted a notice
in the local shop saying "England expects every man and woman to do their
duty." His wife assigned *him* the duty of keeping their little boy amused and opening the garden gate to lady helpers. He noted wryly, "How the war puts 'men of

letters' in their place!"[66] Despite the German warships, that autumn Llewelyn got to Africa to join Will, and John got back to America. Bertie joined the Officers' Training Corps, although his brothers felt this was more a desperate move to escape an unhappy marriage than anything else. Theodore said he was "not so much afraid of the smell of the dead but the smell of the living," and that he'd rather "run away." John supported him in this; he thought Theodore drilling on Salisbury Plain was as absurd an idea as "Aubrey Beardsley looking after the boy-scouts."[67] Despite his athleticism, Littleton suffered from "nerves," insomnia, and stomach problems; in any case he felt it was his duty to keep the prep school going. Nonetheless, he was passed grade A and it took several tribunals and a protest from the Department of Education before the military granted him a discharge.[68]

When John returned to England briefly in 1915, he wrote Marian that the British government might introduce conscription, which, he was sure, "will send Louis off to America post-haste."[69] It did—Louis arrived in New York with Frances and their son Oliver in July 1915—and it sent John Cowper back to America as well. Powys, then forty-three, reassured sister Gertrude that he would be back to enlist as soon as "the age is raised to 45—but so far it is 41."[70] Saying he would return would have appeased his "diseased conscience," even while he would have guessed that in the early stages of conscription at least, his married status, his age, and his poor physical health meant that he would not likely be accepted. However, his decision not to return in 1916 may have added to, or even caused, the depression he suffered that summer. He remained in America in 1917 when he had the gastroenterostomy. In 1918, Bertie was taken prisoner of war, and the age of conscription was raised from 41 to 50. By this time, even the timid Theodore had presented himself several times only to be rejected because of a weak heart. Llewelyn, still with active tuberculosis, had been examined and declared "absolutely unfit," but Will had volunteered to join the East African Mounted Rifles shortly after Lulu arrived in Africa. Even Isadora Duncan, "my one and only true love,"[71] had gone to tour in the midst of war-torn France, and John had written her, "I seem to see you always with a secret of courage."[72]

His friends were all "fiercely opposed" to his taking the risk of returning to England, but, announcing dramatically to Llewelyn that he could not "drink grape-juice in California while these barbarians overrun the earth," John decided that it was time to take a risk: "After all I have lived a protected life, ever since I was at Sherborne."[73] He went first to the British Recruiting Office in New York on May 29, 1918. He wrote in *Autobiography* that to his astonishment he was not rejected on grounds of his truncated stomach but because of an old tubercular scar.[74] He couldn't have been that amazed, since the doctors found that "one of his lungs was affected" when he had his first ulcer operation in 1907.[75] This raises the possibility that John had given consumption to Llewelyn, but that has never been mentioned. It is more likely that the damp bedroom at the end of the north wing of Montacute Vicarage, where all the boys slept, was responsible for their susceptible lungs.[76] John Cowper made the dangerous crossing to England in June 1918 "in a regular fleet of eleven great liners, all sailing near one another." He applied again but was similarly turned down due to the evidence of former tuberculosis. He was exempted from service and told he could return to America, but he decided instead to give lectures up and down the country for Lloyd George's Bureau of War Aims.

> Judging from the Versailles Treaty my "War Aims" differed in several respects from those of the Prime Minister but no one interfered with me; no one gave me any instructions; and at the Government's expense I lectured—or rather made soap-box speeches, for these addresses were always in the open air—upon my own personal ideas as to what the War was about and how it ought to end. . . .
>
> The local political agents, taken casually from both the big parties, were made responsible for all the practical arrangements; and, on my soul, these arrangements were sometimes as quaint as if we had still been in the time of Charles Dickens. One worthy gentleman . . . made use of his trip with me to a remote portion of his county to collect eggs. In a dog-cart stuffed with eggs we sought out the particular village-green where I hoped to increase Mr. Wilson's fourteen points from fourteen to forty.[77]

Powys soon recognized that he could not pay his son's school fees at the Big School or keep up Burpham from a dogcart and returned to America in the autumn. He wrote to Llewelyn as he crossed the Atlantic, "neither of our lots is as bad as Bertie's in a German prison, or of Theodore's in the prison of his own depression, or of L.C.P. in the prison of (and that is the worst!) a bourgeois marriage!"[78] The armistice was signed on November 11, 1918.

Like John, Louis Wilkinson felt then, and long afterwards, a sense of guilt about the war. In his *Forth Beast*, his alter ego says, "Almost anyone in your position and of your temperament would have done the same." Dexter/Louis replies, "If I had simply said to myself, 'I want to live and I'm not going to let this war stop me living if I can help it. . . .' But why did I have to convince myself that the war wasn't a good one, why did I have to slip sideways like that?"[79] Louis had stayed in America during the war with Frances and his children—Oliver and a second child, Betty, who was born in Philadelphia, on March 28, 1917. Two events which must have made the marriage increasingly untenable occurred during this time. Firstly, Louis had become increasingly violent toward Frances and had knocked her down shortly before she gave birth to her daughter. Frances's mother, Julia, who had lived with them almost continually since their marriage, and whose presence was a constant irritant to Louis, extracted a written confession from him about this incident and used it as a weapon against him. Betty was born badly retarded.[80] Secondly, Louis spent most of his time during the war with British expatriates and had become friends with the notorious Aleister Crowley, who also spent the war in America. Crowley, who liked to be known as "the great beast" and "the wickedest man alive," had been expelled from Italy because of rumors of drugs, orgies, and magical ceremonies. Possibly Frances felt that her husband's uncharacteristically violent behavior was due to this man's influence, for she accused Crowley of having a malign influence on Louis. Crowley reciprocated by trying, and almost succeeding, in having Frances committed to an insane asylum. Louis did nothing to prevent this. Partly as a result of this trauma, partly as an aftereffect of the Spanish flu that she and her son Oliver contracted in the autumn of 1918, Frances developed a lesion on the lung, thyroid trouble, and a bad heart. She was in hospital, close to death, the whole of February 1919. John had been unsuccessful in protecting her from these events, but he now took her for three weeks to Lakewood, New Jersey, to recuperate before she returned to England with Louis. It was this interlude that made him realize that he wanted "nothing so much as to live with you."

What this time and the succeeding months meant to him is documented in a series of open-hearted letters from California to his sister Marian, who had by then become his main confidante. He wrote, "I had those three weeks [with Frances] which were like those funny exquisite dreams when people, like mother for instance, that one had thought lost forever, are really alive again!" This time he was determined that he was "not going to be fooled by death again as I was in the case of Mother."[81] His guilt at leaving his mother when she was dying to go to Paris to be with Frances had never subsided. Now in an ironic twist, Frances was very ill, and this time John was determined not to fail her. He began to plan for them to live permanently together. For perhaps the first time in his life he felt a deep physical desire for a woman. His letters at this time make it very clear that his love for her was not "platonic" but "normal" in the sexual sense; they were "made to fit into each other like a classic knife into a classic sheath." He wrote the eighth of May that the previous night had been "a night of thought but . . . then I stopped thinking and made love to you . . . and then with my mouth upon your right breast I drank up your soul till our souls mixed together."[82] After he had "stopped thinking," matters moved quickly. Frances sent him a telegram: "If you telegraph again I shall come to San Francisco I will. So let that terrify you." However terrified, he replied, and then wrote Marian that "it is not outside the bounds of possibility that I may be able not to have to be separated from Frances any more. . . . Louis is well aware that I have such a hope in my mind but he thinks it would be impossible for me to carry it out because of lack of money over & above my own family's needs."[83]

He then asked Louis if he would give Frances up permanently. Louis telegraphed on May 17: "Permanent arrangements impossible. This arrangement purely fraternal. These things being understood wire if you still want California plan." John bitterly agreed to this arrangement, rented a tiny house in Sausalito, and sent $200 for her fare.[84] Frances arrived in early June 1919. She also brought her mother, two small children, a nurse, and a large dog. John wrote Marian that he was hoping to secure a permanent newspaper job in San Francisco and with the lecturing might be able to support two households.

> I think if I were even moderately sure of this, as I practically am, Frances would cast her lot with me & turn Louis down. But have I the courage to announce to Margaret & my son that I have taken on another family? . . . Have I the hardness and drastic resolution to announce this change to my son? Have I the initial spirit to make this plunge—and then the tact & energy & patience to carry it out? . . . You know my weakness in these things, my cowardice, or whatever it is. . . . Frances fears my nature in these things lest I should suffer remorse, if I were bold enough to do it, and uncon-sciously—you know?—vent my uneasiness on her. I think it is more my emotional undependableness she fears than the economic difficulty.[85]

Frances knew him well. Incredibly, he was already suggesting that Margaret and his son could join them, and possibly Llewelyn and even Louis, although as he said to Marian in this same rambling letter, "I don't know whether I could bear again the appearance of Louis on the scene with a right to divide us. I don't know that Frances could bear such a half-and-half affair as it would be." Even Marian's ample tolerance toward her beloved brother's dithering ways stretched only so far and it must have snapped at that, for he wrote apologetically on the fifth of August,

> Shall I never see the limit of my clumsiness and stupidity and gross blunder-ing in these delicate personal relations? . . . I hold tight on to her, who is after all what I want with all that is freest in me. But selfishness and cow-ardice are forever dragging me back; and it seems so cruel that a nature like hers, who has already suffered so much from life, should be perpetually com-ing up against such walls of gross earth as I seem automatically to build. It is the war in me of what I have of CFP with what I have of MCP. Neither will let me give myself up to the other. . . . Well—there it is! I love her; but I am selfish.

Matters were not made easier by the fact that they were very poor. Frances was writing but could not get her stories published, and his lecturing audiences were small. The hoped-for job with the newspaper turned out to be a "fiasco." In desperation and in a repeat of the summer of 1909, he dashed off a number of sto-ries in the shortest possible time, all of which were rejected. At the same time he was writing a "serious" book of philosophy which he should have known would never bring in the money they so desperately needed. The five short months they had together must have been tumultuous. Powys was sure that "in spite of mis-understandings" they were "profoundly linked together."[86] Nonetheless, Oliver, then only four years old, had a vivid memory of huge arguments. He wrote that "Jack and Frances argued as fiercely as they made love; and their discussions sometimes reached a pitch of excitement that was like physical love."[87] There were other reasons why living together must have been hellish for them both. Frances was convinced that John had it in him to become a great writer, but she saw, too clearly, the personality characteristics that would prevent his growing into greatness, and she made the mistake of pointing them out to him. She flayed him with all the intellectual acuity and emotional intensity at her command. He tried to be "the way you wish me to be," without anything "guarded." But he found this extraordinarily difficult—"so alien a thing from my constructed self of years." Ultimately he could not. The mythic mask and personae he had created so laboriously to protect himself from the world and himself were too firmly fixed. In another letter toward the end of that summer he wrote hopelessly to Marian that "my queer inhumanity seems to hurt every person that comes into my existence."[88] For all these reasons, and no doubt more that were private between them, Frances and her menage returned to Louis now in England, sailing on the *Mauretania* on November 22. John borrowed the money to pay for their passage.

The "serious book" he wrote that summer was turned down by Liverwright and finally published by Dodd, Mead in September 1920. *The Complex Vision* is almost unreadable, partly because Powys is attempting to describe a state which is, by its nature, indescribable, partly because it is highly theoretical and abstract, and partly because his logic is faulty. But his aim was clear: to explore the means by which great poetry comes into being. It can be created only when the "constructed self" allows a greater consciousness to realize itself within. This is the daimon of old, of which he had always been somehow aware, but which now he accepted was the companion whose voice he must obey if ever he was to be the artist he was convinced it was his destiny to become.

> There come moments in all our lives, when, rending and tearing at the very roots of our own existence, we seek to extricate ourselves from ourselves and to get ourselves out of the way of ourselves, as if we were seeking to make room for some deeper personality within us which is ourself and yet not ourself. This is that impersonal element which the aesthetic sense demands in all supreme works of art so that the soul may find at once its realization of itself and its liberation from itself. [89]

Almost immediately he turned against *The Complex Vision*, calling it a "mythological tour de force." Possibly after his experience of living with Frances for five months in enforced "suppressed lust," the abstract image of the complex vision as a "pyramidal wedge" of flame "cleaving the darkness like a point of a fiery arrow," struck him as altogether too real—closer to a wet dream than a symbol of poetry.

The remainder of 1919 passed in depression, withdrawal, and suppressed rage. In a long letter to Lulu he bemoaned his "incapacity for dealing with life."[90] Money worries did not lighten his mood any. He had to borrow money from Littleton to keep Margaret and his son going as lectures continued to be lamentably few. Arnold Shaw's increasing mental instability seems to have been both cause and effect ("When things go down Arnold goes down"[91]), however, in early 1920 Arnold hired Archie Spring, the son of Shaw's father's gardener. Despite his physical disability—he was a "hunchback"—Spring proved to be an ideal clerk. A trip to the midwest was sufficiently successful that John was able to send Margaret the money she was urgently demanding to keep Burpham going with its staff of four. Nonetheless, he had to borrow a further £200 from Littleton in order to send his son to Corpus, Powys's old college.

After Frances left him, he felt fairly hopeless about his writing, telling his brother, "I don't weigh enough mentally speaking. I pose, I pretend, I play games. I have always been the Captain of the Volentiā Army."[92] However, in 1920 he began another novel. *After My Fashion* is unlike anything he had written before or would write again.[93] The disastrous attempt to live with Frances appears to have jerked him into a new understanding both of himself and of the relationship between men and women. It begins, as did an earlier unpublished tale, with the hero returning to England after a long period abroad. Richard Storm has spent twenty years in France, sixteen of them in Paris and four of them doing war work. He has left France to escape his love affair with a dancer, Elise Angel. The war and Elise have "pulled him up by the very roots out of his old pastures." Although Richard has a fair reputation as a critic of modern French poets, he wants to be a poet himself. He thinks that if he "digs himself" into English soil he will be able to write a new kind of poetry. Feeling guilty that he has survived the war in which other men have died, he intends it to be a kind of offering of wisdom to the world. "He wished to take the many poignant 'little things', bitter and sweet, tragic and grotesque, common and fantastic, such as the earth affords us all in our confused wayfaring, and to associate these, as each generation is aware of them before it passes away . . . with some dimly conceived immortal consciousness that gave them all an enduring value and dropped none of them by the way."[94]

Richard's long explanation of what he wants to achieve in his poetry is, in part, an echo of *The Complex Vision*, but more importantly, it is a credo. Powys's poetry never reached the hoped-for cradling of the everyday in the protective arms of the immortal, but his later novels magnificently did.

Richard goes to Sussex because his grandparents are buried there. There he meets Nelly Moreton and is attracted to her "fragile face and fair silken hair." Despite the fact that she is betrothed to Robert Canyot, an artist and a war hero, there is something about Richard, although he is twice her age, that appeals to Nelly's maternal instinct. "This man from Paris . . . began to look like that grown-up child which, once in every woman's life, becomes her most fatal attraction."[95] Richard and Nelly marry; her senile father, the Vicar of Littlegate, who has been forced by the authorities to retire, moves in with them. The Reverend John Moreton is an unvarnished portrait of C. F. Powys. Moreton's "fierce fanatical pride made him . . . remain as he chose to remain," and he goes "quietly on my own way."[96] This vicar is, in his "quiet" way, as selfish as C. F., simply assuming his daughter Nelly would do, as his wife had done, whatever was necessary for his comfort.

The couple are happy at first. Richard knows that he has consciously married Nelly to be "a living symbol" of what he was aiming at in his work: "In embracing Nelly he was embracing the very body of the sweet earth which, just then, was so luxuriously responsive." Gradually, Nelly "becomes more of an obsession to him in a physical sense and very much less of an inspiration to him in a spiritual sense." Nelly too plunges "recklessly into the mere material thrill of the chemical attraction that existed between them."[97] However, Richard gets himself in a philosophical and logical pickle when he starts on the idea that his "erotic obsession" is sapping "the life-blood of his soul."[98] In the meantime, a few months after his marriage, Richard receives a letter from his lover, Elise. The dancer has accepted an engagement at a New York theatre from October to Christmas and suggests he come over. Coincidentally (Powys was never very good at plots) Canyot is successful with his paintings and has been asked to have several large exhibitions in New York. He asks Storm to bring Nelly to New York: "I can't work without her. I can't cope with existence without her. . . . Without seeing her I can't do my work." This fits nicely with Richard's desire to see Elise again. He feels "extremely pleased with this queer turn of fate but prepared to get the full credit for magnanimity."[99] They move into a flat in Greenwich Village, and Robert looks after Nelly in a brotherly fashion, introducing her to the bohemian crowd. Richard is serene about this. He feels "thoroughly sorry for his defeated rival," and it "eased his conscience" to give Canyot "every facility to make the best of the rind, so to speak, while he enjoyed the fruit."[100] Indeed, the situation suits Richard perfectly.

> If he had analysed his feelings down to the bottom he would have found that it was not at all disagreeable to him to have Canyot there, somewhere about, so that when he was in a mood for solitude he could hand over Nelly to him and go his own way. . . . There *were* moments, especially after he had made love to her a great deal, when he was decidedly bored with her society. The companion he really loved best was, after all, none other than Richard himself. Richard alone with Richard was what really gave him the deepest satisfaction.[101]

Soon after they arrive in New York, Nelly discovers she is pregnant. Richard becomes "vaguely aware for the first time in his life" that a "certain human warmth" is lacking in him. He does not want the responsibility of a child. "He wanted his name to be perpetuated not by children but by poetry. Children were nature's will and pleasure. Poetry was the attempt of the spirit of mankind to rise above nature and extricate itself."[102] Matters are made worse by events. Canyot finds his paintings are successful and he is accepted as "a desirable personage by the whole aesthetic fraternity of that enterprising cosmopolitan city."[103] Richard, on the other hand, gets word from Paris that his publisher there has gone bankrupt; his poetry is unsuccessful and he cannot find any work. When he resumes his affair with Elise, Nelly finds out. He does not understand why she is so upset.

> For one moment Richard seemed to catch a glimpse of what women meant by love. For one moment he seemed to see that mysterious bond, the unbroken attachment of a man and woman, like a visible thread of light over a dark gulf. Then his masculine logic broke into this sudden vision; and he reasoned with himself that this fierce claim of hers for absolute loyalty was a wild demand of insane possessiveness that no human soul had a right to make upon another.[104]

Nelly finds his attitude as incomprehensible as he finds hers: "Sometimes I doubt whether you've ever grown up. You seem so blind to certain things; as if you actually *didn't* understand."[105] Nor does he get any comfort from Elise when they go off for a few days to Atlantic City. There are "violent quarrels and passionate reconciliations," both of them "exchanging words of cruel and wounding bitterness, such as only those who are physically attracted without being temperamentally congenial are capable of flinging at one another."[106] Elise tells him he is a creature of "masks and screens": "You're scared of losing something of your precious personality." He makes matters worse by responding, "I can't help my nature. I was made like that." Elise hisses, "Oh, how English you are, Richard! That's what we other races have to accept is it, and just conform to? *Made like that*. And we have to unmake *ourselves* . . . so as to adapt ourselves to this thing that cannot alter!"[107]

Elise then goes on to give him a few home truths about his poetry. When he says "I've only done in my poetry what English poets have always done . . . tried to get the magic of the earth soul into words," she laughs at him and tells him he is no Shelley or Keats.

> Surely the whole purpose of art is to make such impressions universal, so that everybody feels them? If you're content to write about ponds and ditches for the benefit of English people—well! you must please yourself of course; but I cannot allow you to call such a thing art. It's the merest personal sensation of one individual! . . .
>
> I think you *have* great powers. But I cannot say I think this poetry of yours has done justice to them. . . . It is too self-satisfied, too unruffled. It's as if you had never really wrestled with life!

This stirs him to the "very depths of his self-love," but he soon comforts himself by thinking: "She is only a woman. . . . Her art is instinctive, not intellectual. She does not understand the quieter, cooler, more magical kinds of poetry." And with this, Richard's "vanity is completely reinstated upon its secret throne."[108] Elise does not allow this self-complacency for long.

"You talk of bringing your philosophy into your poetry. My good man, you must realize once for all that your poetry is a fraud, a fake, a piece of rank charlatanism."

"If my poetry isn't real," said Richard, "nothing in my existence is real."

"Nonsense! . . . You're capable of doing very good honest literary work. But you're so ridiculously proud. . . . You must be the great poet of the age— or you will sulk in your tent."

"No one can tell for certain where their power is until they—"

"Until they stop lying," she interrupted. "Don't you understand that art is a thing connected with character?"[109]

These are wonderfully vivid scenes, which must have been lifted directly from the many turbulent discussions John and Frances had about his poetry and his character. The time with Frances in California had inestimable consequences, one of which was that Powys finally had to face the fact that if he was going to be anything more than a third-rate poet he would have to find another medium. This is what he was working through in this novel, with honesty and a certain self-mockery. The "masks and screens" of his nature were another matter. He has his hero, Richard, make "a genuine effort to break the crust of egoism which imprisoned his soul."

His analysis of his real inmost reaction to all these events revealed to him that he had been all the while, secretly and without any self-forgetful suffering, dramatizing his situation. He had been making it all a part of one long stream of not wholly intolerable occurrences, in the flowing tide of which the figure of Nelly herself, the figures of Elise and Catharine and all the rest, were there to be exploited, were there to be contemplated subjectively, as scenes in the human play which after all remained *his* play— whereof he was not only an actor on the stage but an appreciative critic in the gallery! . . .

Was he actually wanting in some normal human attribute; and did everything that occurred to him approach his consciousness through some vaporous veil like a thick sea mist? He began naively to wonder what the great artists of the world were like in these complicated human relations. It occurred to him that they must have the power of transfiguring the results of analysis and forcing the issue by the use of some sort of creative energy which the gods had completely denied to him. Where was *his* place in the world then, he who was neither a normal human being nor a creative genius?[110]

This was the question that Powys himself was confronting at this time, for which he has no answer. Suddenly a "great Paris specialist" is called in to finish off the plot. Richard had been warned that "any extreme physical strain will finish off a bad heart," and the hero decides this "would be a better way than morphia." Nelly goes back to England to have her baby, and he follows her.

When she refuses to have him back he apparently hurts his heart fatally by trying to rescue a "luckless sheep" that had slipped into a dew pond.[111] It is obvious
that Nelly and the baby will end up with Canyot.

In all his future novels, Powys would rely heavily on landscapes and people
he knew intimately, and this novel is no exception. His descriptions of the life
in Greenwich Village are marvelous, culled directly from his own existence in
New York with Marian. Powys insisted that he "never shared the Bohemian
life"[112] of Greenwich Village. While it is strictly true he never shared a collective
life with any group, since 1913 he and the outgoing Marian had lived in the East
Village and had many bohemian friends in the area. The flat he and Marian
moved to in December 1919 becomes Nelly and Richard's flat; the walks he took
daily and the sights he saw become Richard's.[113]

> In this particular quarter were artists of all the nations of the earth, writ-
> ers, painters, journalists, bric-à-brac dealers, revolutionists, virtuosos,
> charlatans, dilettantes, actors, bachelor women, women workers, wealthy
> connoisseurs of the theatre, aesthetic dabblers, art-book dealers, literary
> recluses, imagist poets, futurist sculptors, popular mystics, cranks, faddists,
> philosophers, humbugs, devoted humanitarians, art-movement leaders,
> and many quiet solitary thinkers living between uptown fashion and down-
> town greed.[114]

Like most thrifty novelists, Powys never wasted an experience. At the beginning of the story he introduces, rather incongruously, a scene where a hydro-
cephalic child is hit with a stone by bullies. This was taken straight from an incident in which he and Frances were involved in San Francisco. The characters in
After My Fashion are also drawn from life. Richard Storm is the Powys-hero,
Nelly is Margaret, Elise is ostensibly Isadora Duncan but her personality, her
ideas, her incisive critical faculties are Frances's. Louis is Canyot. A new friend,
Theodore Dreiser, makes a cameo appearance as Pat Ryan with his "large and
powerfully molded head." However, Powys scatters events and conversations
among the characters, so that they become curiously inconsistent. For example,
Canyot (Louis) begs Richard (John) to come to America with Nell because he
cannot do his creative work or even exist unless he has her "within reach."[115]
Canyot is not here Louis, but Powys, begging Louis to allow him to be a third in
their marriage. Nell then becomes for the nonce Frances. It seems as if the characters don't really matter, only the feeling. Nell is mostly his wife Margaret, but
there are glimpses in her of his dead sister Nellie, and she is passed around
between Storm and Canyot just as Frances was. The painter has nothing of Louis
in his character, but in a sense Robert, by giving up Nelly to Richard, and then
getting her back, does what Louis did in the case of John and Frances. The only
consistently drawn character is Powys himself as Richard Storm. It is a beautifully drawn portrait of a man who has finally learned the true nature of malice,
and of its effect on self and others.

It was one of Richard's weaknesses to dislike beyond everything else the flick or sting or smart of a well-placed rebuke; especially if administered by a woman he cared for. . . . Externally he kept his temper, to avoid looking a fool; internally he revenged himself out of all proportion to the affront. And he never really forgave.[116]

Powys sent the novel to Dodd, Mead, who had published *The Complex Vision*, but they turned it down. For whatever reason, he did not try another publishing house.[117] Dodd, Mead was the first big publisher he had had; his only other publishers were Arnold and his cousin Ralph Shirley. Perhaps the rejection dispirited him. Or Margaret may have objected to it, although Nelly is sympathetically portrayed. It is even possible that the novel represented a moment of self-revelation and he found it rather too difficult to confront. But the most likely reason is that three months later he met someone whom he would not have wanted to see his love for Elise/Frances. In any case *After My Fashion* became another one of those unpublished manuscripts in his drawer.

"I have never seen anyone
even remotely like you except
in my imagination."
    —JCP letter to Phyllis,
        20 March, 1921.

"Watched Lulu re-join Alyse and Gamel. . . .
Like Odysseus with Calypso and Nausicaa."
—JCP Diary, 1 July, 1929.

CHAPTER SEVEN

PHYLLIS FOUND

1921-1925

W ITH FRANCES GONE, POWYS TURNED ONCE AGAIN TO MARIAN. DURING
his illness and depression of 1916 and 1917, she became his "wise
and resolute & formidable angel,"[1] and by 1919 he was addressing her as "my dear
companion and wife of 5 years," ending a letter with "I love to think of renew-
ing our marriage as soon as possible."[2] Whatever her private feelings, Marian was
tolerant of his flirtations with his actress girls and gave him her astute advice during the much more serious relationship with Frances. She also tried her best to
find someone she could love as well as she loved her brother. Theodore Dreiser
proved elusive, Arthur Ficke evasive, and Rollo Peters, the actor, a good friend
but a faithless lover. John wondered if, in a previous incarnation, he had been
"content to have long talks through the grating with a Marquise May married to
the Doge of Venice," but he feared that there was "something most fatally deriv-
ative from the Vicar of Montacute—no monk it is true!—about me!"[3] The closeness of their "marriage," whatever form it may have taken, was disrupted when
John Cowper returned to England in April 1920, for his usual summer visit.

The Powys father had finally resigned as vicar of Montacute in 1918 and
Gertrude found a large house for them in Weymouth at 3 Greenhill Terrace.[4]
Llewelyn had returned to England in August 1919, after five years of exile in
Africa. His initial reaction was joy, but he soon realized that he had only
exchanged one cage for another, and that he was now trapped in a small seaside town with only the company of a spinster sister and a senile father who
was always "ready and waiting to sally out for a walk like some large harmless
importunate dog." John urged him to write, and Llewelyn tried, but "I hold my
head in my hands, spend long hours thinking of nothing, simply howling, try
to write, fail, sit on my chair, try to write, fail, go for a walk with father, water
the flowers."[5] He thought his despondency was caused by "prolonged sexual
repression" and he was determined to escape to America. A concerned Jack
agreed to this but convincing Marian that this was a good plan was not so easy.
By this time she had established herself as a lace maker and an authority on
antique lace, and had just opened the Devonshire Lace Shop, in Manhattan at

54 West 57th Street. As well as the flat she shared with John, she also rented a small cottage in the Palisades of New Jersey. John wrote her from Weymouth, reassuring her that Lulu had promised to live most of the time at her cottage and only to come into New York "one night, say every week, to make friends with people and look around," and when there, he would "house-keep and cook for us." He ended the letter by assuring Marian, "I don't think our Lulu will come between us."[6] Despite May's vigorous objections, when John returned to New York in August 1920, Lulu was with him. John went on tour almost immediately and, as Marian knew would happen, Llewelyn did not stay at the cottage and did not housekeep. Instead, stimulated by New York life, after a slow start, he finally succeeded in his ambition to "write for the papers." The *New York Evening Post* commissioned him to do some sketches about Africa which, for a time, were very popular. He also met and ingratiated himself with many of Jack's women friends, thereby achieving his second aim, the longed-for sexual fulfilment.

By November, John was in Chicago on a long wait-over before beginning a winter tour. It was no longer the Chicago of excitement and companionship it was a few short years before: Browne's Little Theatre had folded in 1919 and his actresses scattered; Margaret Anderson had moved her *Little Review* to Greenwich Village; many of the writers and poets had also migrated east. Louis Wilkinson had decided to stay in London and France that autumn, so Frances too was inaccessible. John was forty-eight, getting to an age, he thought, "when I feel it to be wonderful for any girl to be interested in me."[7] The midwest tour in the early months of 1921 included the states of Illinois, Kansas, and Missouri. Powys had previously met Franklin Playter, a retired businessman and lawyer with cultivated tastes, and on March 18, 1921, when Powys gave a lecture in Joplin, Missouri, Playter attended with his twenty-six-year-old daughter, Phyllis. Jack had found his sylph—again. This time, he was determined to have "a 'real one' to make things real & true and not just a creature of my brain."[8] At a reception after the lecture, John found Phyllis on the balcony, "laid hand on her maiden zone,"[9] and asked her to be his pet hare. Presumably she got the Poseidon and Tyro reference if not the Cowper. She was similarly, but more uncharacteristically, forthcoming. The next day she invited him to the Playter summer home in near-by Galena and showed him the cabin where she slept. They went for a long walk, talked constantly, and sheltered in a cave against the rain. He left for St. Louis on the twentieth and from a hotel there wrote the first of a total of 400 love letters.

> 20 March 1921: Damn! how many things we didn't have time to say! . . . It annoys me that I talked so much and didn't make you say more things in that language of mortal men which is not natural to you. . . . I have never seen anyone even remotely like you except in my imagination. . . . There <u>must</u> be some gods or powers abroad who arrange these things. . . . I have been hunting for you up hill & down dale and now I've got you you've

got to take me into protection and guard me. . . . I cling to you and you
mustn't betray me. . . . I don't know what you have done to me.

The gods had given him his elemental, his otherworldly creature, but she
was also a real girl, his "bint" that he could make love to in anyway he desired.
He admitted that "it is a queer thing—this chemical selection,"[10] but the chemical selection was inviolable. Despite their age difference of twenty-two years, his
marriage, their conventional upbringings, and their highly individual and anti-
thetical natures, they were to live together—they apparently could not *not* live
together—for the rest of his long life. What was to happen in the next years was
as much an outcome of Phyllis's personality and family background as his, but
until recently almost nothing was known about her earlier life, except what
could be gleaned from newspaper reports about her father and hints that John
dropped over the years. She was almost pathologically averse to drawing attention to herself, and her letters to Powys, which would have provided many
answers, she burned in 1951.[11] Now some of the crucial blanks have been filled
in with the fortuitous discovery of a few of her lost diaries, along with a cache of
early letters to her parents and some fragmentary writings found in a folder she
had marked "precious, precious."[12]

With records going back to the early fifteenth century, the Yorkist Playters
of Sotterley had roots in Suffolk at least as deep as the Powyses in the Welsh
Marches. However, in the eighteenth century, George Playter, an officer in the
British Army, settled in Philadelphia and married Elizabeth Welding, a Quaker.
Although he lost his considerable property when he fought for the King in the
American Revolution, he was rewarded for his loyalty with a vast tract of land
in Canada. The Playter males had the Midas touch. His eldest son Watson married Priscilla Waterman, who came from a wealthy, aristocratic Philadelphia
family and they moved to Newmarket, Ontario, where Watson and his son,
another George, built up large business concerns. Phyllis's father, Franklin, one
of eleven children born to George, studied law at Toronto University but
quickly saw that his fortunes lay in the "Wild West" of the United States.
Franklin Playter was a true entrepreneur. Deserving of his name, "the empire
builder," he made (and lost) several fortunes in ranching, railways, real estate,
and banking. By 1890 he had assets conservatively estimated at $250,000 (in
today's money, almost five million dollars).[13] Most of this was wiped out in the
financial panic of that year, but he started again, buying a waterworks, a brick
plant, and a foundry. He then went to Washington which gave him further business opportunities, including real estate development. Later on he established
the famous Conqueror mine and the United Zinc Company.

When his first wife died, Franklin married Mary Hawley, daughter of his law
partner. Mary was vivacious and beautiful, her dark hair and eyes revealing the
Spanish blood in her background. She was twenty-five years younger than
Franklin. Three years after their marriage, Phyllis, their only child, was born on
the twenty-ninth of November, 1894, in Kansas City, Missouri. The Playters

moved to Boston, where Phyllis grew up in a palatial house at 44 Pinkney Street and received her education at an exclusive girls' school. Their summer home, Wildacre, was built in the foothills of the Ozarks, some three miles southwest of Galena, where the young mother and her daughter kept horses and dogs. According to relatives she was a bubbly, happy child, extravagantly indulged by doting parents. There is a charming newspaper photograph and caption of her at age eight, going up in a hot-air balloon with her father. When Phyllis was fourteen, her mother took her for a year to Rosporden, Brittany, where she took art lessons and perfected her French. They returned from France to find that Franklin had lost another fortune in the depression of 1907. The father once again tried to recoup his losses but by 1910 decided to return to Kansas. Franklin, almost seventy by then, may have finally felt defeated; who knows what the mother—then only forty-four and accustomed to wealth and ease all her life— must have felt. They sent Phyllis, who turned sixteen in November of 1910, to boarding school in Boston until she was eighteen, and then to art school in Boston for a year. There, according to Powys, "she wrote poetry at the back of all her drawings & discovered that her real taste was rather for Literature than Art."[14] Only one of these poems survives from this period but it is indicative of events to come: "A thing of flesh am I / That knew content / And not without integrity / My firm white bones resist vicissitude / But in the end the utter lassitude / Of dust, the futile dust, prevails in me."[15]

From her own account, she returned to her parents in 1914 when she was twenty, and it was at this time she fell into a more serious depression. In his diaries, Powys at first refers to it as her "unhappiness" but later becomes more explicit, saying that in fact it was "a mental state that was really Deranged."[16] Phyllis herself says clearly, in one of her found fragments, that her depression lasted for five years—that is, until she was twenty-five in late 1919. The deepest point was in April 1917 when she was twenty-two and seriously considered committing suicide. In August of that year, presumably in an attempt to break free of the depression, she answered an advertisement for a waitress job in a railway hotel in Needles, California. She gives an account of her interview in an unfinished piece entitled "The Needles." What is significant about this is her conviction that she was "certain to be rejected—and to return in a few hours to my family—from whom I had so incredibly managed to effect my escape the day before—in a manner that I still regarded with admiration and amazement." In another, she is on the train to Needles, travelling through New Mexico, and while loving that landscape, finding distasteful everything connected with the day coach she is forced to travel in and especially the people in it. She lasted at the job only a few weeks. There are three extant letters to her parents from this time. She was treated kindly by the employers who wanted her to stay on, but "I think I shall come home and sew my silly handkerchiefs and lie on the grass and listen to the Victrola and get terribly bored." She then asks her father for the return fare. In a rather breezy second letter she discusses very knowledgeably (as

the daughter of a mining engineer) whether to buy some rough turquoises and
other gemstones. The third letter says, with no profuse gratitude, that his money
order had come. The letters bespeak a sensitive young woman who is not obviously homesick, not particularly loving, but very accustomed to being indulged.
She subsequently lived with her aunt in Kansas City while she took a secretarial
course, then rejoined her parents at Wildacre, patently still depressed. Each year
on her birthday she would place a white flint beneath a tree in their woods. After
one such excursion she wrote,

> Looking at these stones she had come as near thinking the matter out as she
> had ever done. First she had thought—when you're young your mind has to
> be active—and if it has nothing but nothingness for five years to gnaw it
> turns on itself and devours that. . . . She had wanted a great many things
> from life. That was the way it had begun, chafing because there seemed no
> possibility of getting any of them. And now her despair lay like a cold
> shroud on the fact that there was nothing she wanted, nothing that seemed
> to matter. . . . Only death, so that the miseries which one went on feeling
> were gone, no longer able to reach one. In the earth—safe—absolutely
> safe—with the rain seeping through to one's white bones—which would
> gradually free themselves from this revolting sentient flesh—that was hurt
> and crushed and crushed and hurt other flesh in its turn.[17]

That despair and misery was to become the recurring motif of her life, but
in 1921, on the balcony in Joplin, she did not know that. She may have felt
then that anything was better than "nothingness," anything better than life in
a small mining town with an old father and an unhappy mother. If not
Needles, then Powys. Jack was as necessary a happening to Phyllis as Phyllis
was to Jack.

In the meantime, there was Llewelyn. A few days after John's meeting
with Phyllis, Lulu joined him in Chicago and they traveled to California,
where John was lecturing for six months. This was to be the uninterrupted
interval of closeness both had looked forward to, although John confided in
Frances that "I am not quite as thrilled by our journey together to California
as I once was when I went to Venice. But he is thrilled at it himself—the
babyish kid that he is."[18] The brothers settled into a hotel in Sausalito and he
introduced Llewelyn to his many Californian acquaintances. Theodore
Dreiser, whom John had met in 1914, was there with his latest woman friend,
Helen, an actress. Helen wrote about that first encounter with the two
Powyses in her biography of Dreiser.[19] John Cowper struck her as "cosmically
and psychically old and yet so eternally young." Even so, that day it was
Llewelyn who attracted her: "like a beautiful and trusting child; he had won-
der-loving eyes, and his head was covered with curls." But beneath the sur-
face, she detected that he was "much more the realist than his brother John."
Dreiser took to Llewelyn, as he had to Louis, and offered to write a preface to

his African stories. This generous gesture by a well-known novelist undoubtedly contributed to the collection being published in 1923 as *Ebony and Ivory*.
Llewelyn dedicated it to "John Cowper Powys, whose cold, mysterious, planetary heart I have had the audacity to love."

Very soon after their arrival John introduced Llewelyn to Charles Erskine
Scott Wood. Wood, then sixty-eight and semi-retired, had been a highly successful maritime lawyer. During the later years of his law practice he became increasingly interested in civil liberties and in social and political reforms. Since 1918
he had lived with Sara Bard Field, a well-known suffragist, newspaper reporter,
social reformer, and poet, who was thirty years younger than Wood. They
became close friends of John Cowper, and at the home of this hospitable couple,
he met writers, artists, and political activists, among them Ansel Adams,
Robinson Jeffers, William Rose Benét, and Lincoln Steffens. Llewelyn had
already met Sara when she was in New York in the autumn of 1920, recovering
from a severe illness. It was Sara who had talked John into taking Lulu with him
to California, promising to pay his room and board and to find a cure for his
tuberculosis. Whether it was Field or another friend of John's, the poet George
Sterling, who was responsible, Llewelyn was introduced to one Dr. Abrams,
whose unorthodox treatments rendered his tuberculosis quiescent for nearly
three years. A rejuvenated Llewelyn wrote rather coyly in his *Verdict of
Bridlegoose*, "I made many friends" in California.[20] That summer he had affairs
with a number of women, including Sara Bard Field.[21] Possibly it was while Lulu
was pursuing his friendly relationships that John found the privacy to write two
and sometimes four letters a day to Phyllis. She was still a secret from friends and
relatives alike, including Llewelyn.

The letters to Phyllis, uniquely beautiful as letters of love and longing, are
also invaluable for the information they give about Powys's life from 1921 to
1930. Almost from the beginning, his letters to her were almost as frank as
those to Frances, to whom he was writing at the same time a similar tale of woe:
"Frances, I can deal with dead books, dead pictures, dead leaves—dead girls you
will be tempted to add!—but *living* people in *real* life—oh how a cold panic of
incompetent wretchedness overtakes me then!"[22] This candid assessment of
himself was to prove valid in almost every area of his personal, financial, and
professional life, but this particular lamentation was in connection with the
imbroglio with literary agents that he got into during this spring of 1921.
Llewelyn and Wood had talked him into abandoning Shaw and signing a
contract with Jessica Colbert, who had acted as an informal manager on his
previous California tours. However, when John returned to New York briefly in
May to do a series of lectures, he found that Shaw had already booked most of
his next season's lectures. He wrote Phyllis on May 23, 1921: "I ought never
to have signed that California contract in such haste without first finding
out how far his bookings had gone. It was anyway an unkind and indeed a
dishonourable thing to do. I have been miserable since I did it—my brother

over-persuaded me. But I was weak and too easily influenced. So here I am with two contracts!" He ends the long plaint by saying to his new love: "Never did I want my wife over here as much as now! I would then put all the responsibility of the decision on her!" He was still fussing about the situation when he wrote her again the next day: "It was a scandalous thing to contemplate doing—just deserting my old manager without a word of warning. . . . My sister says it would have been a dishonourable thing & not at all what 'a Powys' ought to do! . . . It isn't a question of honour—to the devil with that—it is a question of Arnold's whole existence. He is 37 and hopelessly unable to get a new job, and after all tho' incompetent enough he has published my books and he has managed my lectures—somehow—for 10 years. To drop him without warning—I cannot think how I was ever hypnotised into thinking such a thing!"

John then convinced himself that by staying with Arnold he would make more money, or enough "to ease up the lives of everybody dependent on me." At that time it was not only Margaret and his son he was supporting; he was sending both Frances and Theodore a not-inconsiderable amount every week.[23] He also wanted to "be able to help Lulu to stay in California—if he only will consent to that & not punish me by coming East." Then Wood told him that if he broke the contract with Colbert she would demand heavy damages. On the other hand, if he left Shaw he would owe him $1,500 (about $15,000 in today's currency) in lost commissions. To make matters worse, he was getting letters from his friends saying that "Lulu is very unhappy and upset—and it is bad for his health to be so." Marian made the practical suggestion that he compromise: work with Arnold until Christmas and then enter into the two-year California contract. He found it "awful" to have "my friends and managers tugging at me with angry threats contracts and promises on both sides" but acknowledged that "of course it is my own fault—I am a hopeless blunderer."[24]

Needless to say, even at this early stage, the blundering had implications for his relationship with Phyllis. He had already persuaded her to come out to San Francisco, on the basis that he would be in California full-time. Phyllis was at that time a timid, fearful woman, not totally recovered from her severe depression, but she went out in July, telling her possessive parents that she was visiting a friend from boarding school, Adele Stackpole. Then Powys decided that after all he must honor his commitment to Arnold and left for New York in October. He urged Phyllis to stay on until February, when he hoped to return to California. In the meantime, they did have a happy few months together that summer, and it was then that he hit upon two of the most evocative of their many pet names. She had a room on Telegraph Hill so she became "Jill" to his "Jack." They were also the "Associated Terminals," then simply "the Terminals." Initially, this came of their habit of taking the trolley to the farthest terminus and then walking in the country. But as so often with Powys, the term had many nails, each one pinning down a different meaning. One was that they were literally poles apart in their interests, their personalities, their life illusions.

However inadvisedly, John Cowper urged all his friends and relatives to write stories or poetry, and Phyllis was no exception. Both found reasons why this proved so difficult for her. It was not for lack of verbal facility or intelligence. Indeed, Powys remarked more than once, even in this early period, that he found her letters "a bit too subtle" for him, and admitted that he could not always "quite keep pace with every swift nuance of your strange thoughts."[25] Those pieces of her writing that have been found are intellectually sophisticated, philosophically complex, and, in some strange way, emotionally flat. When he left for the East, Phyllis found a job waitressing in the restaurant at Foster and O'Rear, and there are several pages about this and about San Francisco, but no mention of "Jack." His letters to her, when he began writing her again in October, were also more ambivalent. He expects that they were not destined "to see each other long & long & long at a time, such wanderers are we both," and he refers often to his "faithless heart."[26]

It was in that autumn of 1921 that John Cowper began yet another novel he never completed. James Goring, age forty-nine, loves his cousin Bridget, who is twenty-two years younger than he is (the ages Jack and Phyllis were in 1921). Goring hesitates to declare his love for a variety of reasons: the age difference, their incompatible temperaments, and, not least, his jealousy of his younger brother Frank, who, unlike James, is handsome and flirtatious. Bridget wants "life, freedom, liberty," but is afraid of taking on the world by herself. Contact with strangers "paralyses her." She accepts Goring's offer of marriage because she feels she has no other choice.

> Her body remained cold and passive under his hands . . . her brain worked with terrible lucidity. "If I say 'no,' she thought, "I shall go on living with Cousin Elizabeth till my hair is grey. . . . If I say 'yes' . . . we might go to London, to Paris, to Rome. I might see Spain before I die. . . . And she gathered the force of her will together and issued a fierce quick sudden mandate to her body.

The younger brother is disconcerted when Bridget tells him she would have married *him* had he asked her, that she would have married anyone. Frank feels that James "wasn't very honourable . . . snatching at a girl like that before she'd had her chance or seen any fellows of her own age. . . . It's—oh damn it all—it's a kind of prostitution."[27] Setting aside the complicating possibility that Frank is Lulu, it seems fairly obvious that John is rehearsing here his own doubts. He is wondering if Phyllis loved him as he loves her, or whether it is indeed a kind of prostitution. The unfinished story raises a larger issue. Powys admired Marian's ruthless determination to make her own way in the world, but she was unusual in his circle. He had seen the effect of economic dependence on the lives of his mother, of his other sisters, his wife, and also on Frances. What choice did the women he knew have to buy freedom from their dependency on parents, except in selling themselves in one way or another, usually through marriage? He had already explored the problem in previous novels, most successfully in *After My Fashion*. Nelly Morton is fully aware that "in these days of women's freedom" she might be able to find a job, but she has no training and no experience. For Nelly, marriage is the only escape from "a struggle for bare life with a helpless parent on her hands."[28] Powys was to write even more perceptively in later novels on the plight of the dependent woman. In his own life, he wanted Phyllis to become independent so she could make her own choices; on the other hand, he was afraid that if she became independent, he might lose her. Giving his woman to a friend had proved calamitous in the case of Frances. He considered the possibility, or the impossibility, of marrying Phyllis, and several letters in the following year refer to this.

> It does seem crazy to submit to separation—because after all—my son is grown up—and—and well you know! I really haven't the least idea what Mrs Powys really feels, apart from pride and economic dependence, with regard to me—a certain "old lang syne" feeling I suppose & our common interest in our son—but I doubt if she has any emotion left, that my wandering ways haven't long ago killed. . . . Well—there it is!—but, I fear, cowardness, and hatred of shocks and scenes, and that curious traditional feeling of a dislike of interrupting the continuity of one's past—do you know what I mean?—will not let me be brave & drastic as perhaps would be the true path. No! I suppose I am not brave enough—forgive me.[29]

In the event, he was not brave enough. He never did ask his wife for a divorce, nor did he, after his wife's death, marry Phyllis. Indeed, he managed to keep Phyllis a secret from both his son and his wife until 1934, eleven years after they began to live together. Llewelyn and Marian were a different matter. They had to be told, and both reacted to the news in fairly extreme ways.

A few days after they had met, John wrote Phyllis that he would not reveal to Lulu "a single faintest shade of your existence!" There were plausible reasons for this uncharacteristic reticence: he had confided frankly to Llewelyn about previous entanglements with various women—Mabel Hattersley, Helen Wylde, Margaret Mower, Isadora Duncan, and, above all, Frances Gregg. He may have felt this relationship was different, or perhaps he just felt embarrassed. The other reason, as he explained to Phyllis, was that he and Lulu were "much more like lovers than brothers—our relation is very unusual." Still, it was impossible to keep Phyllis's existence secret from his brother once she arrived in San Francisco in July. In order to honor his agreement with Shaw, John returned to New York in October and then left almost immediately on a midwest tour that lasted until December 1. As John feared, the jealous Lulu "punished" him by returning with him to New York, and while he was away on tour, Lulu met and promptly made love to a woman called Alyse Gregory. In retaliation for his brother's secrecy, neither did he tell John when he moved into her flat on Patchin Place, in Greenwich Village, early in 1922, while John was again on tour. Alyse was to become another important character in the Powys family romance. She was thirty-seven when they met, the same age as Llewelyn. Born on the nineteenth of July, 1884, in Connecticut, she came from a scholarly and musical middle-class background. She had a fine voice and was given operatic training in France. After a period of travel in Europe and several unhappy love affairs, she returned to America and began working for the women's suffrage movement. Her passion for social reform became a lifelong commitment and during the First World War she also became a fervent pacifist. She moved to New York to make a living as a journalist and by 1918 her apartment at 5 Patchin Place in Greenwich Village had become the social focus for a group of well-known writers and artists. For some time she ran a tea shop, which was near the offices of the *Dial*, one of the most avant-garde and prestigious literary magazines of the time. She came to meet the new owners of the *Dial*, Scofield Thayer and Sibley Watson. Impressed by her literary acumen, intelligence, and facility in four languages, they asked her to be managing editor, offering her "almost complete control of the paper."[30] Llewelyn too was impressed by her "poise" and "intellectual intensity" although perhaps more so by her fair hair and her round white arms "as delectable as dairy junket."[31]

If telling Llewelyn about Phyllis had been difficult, telling Marian was even more so. Marian quickly realized that Phyllis would usurp her place as even Frances had not succeeded in doing, and, reacting in her own characteristically vigorous way, she deliberately became pregnant that October by a married neighbor at Sneden's Landing where she had her cottage. Lulu was "bitterly hostile"[32] to her pregnancy and to uphold the family honour, John concocted an ornate stratagem whereby in October, 1921 May married someone in the diplomatic service who had died of malaria while travelling in Italy in the spring of 1922.[33] They took great delight in calling the putative father Peter Grey after "an exceedingly naughty boy" of that name in *Holiday House*,[34] a favourite storybook their mother read to them in their childhood.

John had not mentioned Phyllis's existence to Frances either. Juxtaposing the now-published letters to Frances with the unpublished letters to Phyllis is a curious experience. To Frances he would write, "Never ever are you quite out of that subconscious mind which underlies everything—nor ever will be, I suppose. . . . But it is all beyond my analysis, what I feel for you—such a tumultuous wood-flood under the dead leaves."[35] To Phyllis he was writing at the same time: "What a good thing I found you & we found each other! And like a sudden melting of two streams so easily into each other—without surprise without hindrance."[36]

His professional life remained as confused as his personal life. To his consternation, having decided to return to Arnold Shaw's management with the promise of lucrative work and a full schedule of lectures for the autumn, he found he had only two lectures a week. He decided after all that he must leave Shaw, and wrote his brother Littleton in January 1922 that even his "wavering & inconsistent mind has stiffened itself at last."[37] Powys returned to San Francisco on the first of February and he and Phyllis had a month together before she left for her parents' winter home in Joplin. He remained in San Francisco, feeling "more desolate than I have felt since the summer when I wrote Rodmoor." He found a room with an Italian family which was cheap, but "noisy and claustrophobic." He would often flee to a hotel, always his anonymous refuge, to write his daily letter to her. However, in the first few months under Jessica Colbert's management he felt great "relief at being adequately managed at last & with a feeling of material security—at last. . . . My vanity, my ambitious pride, my babyish sense of finding wonderful treasure . . . is a sort of Jack & the Bean Stalk mood." He compared himself to "a terra-cotta satyr, gorged with the thought of impossible beech-nuts & forests of boy-girl oreads like humanized orchids, and all the gold of Syracuse in conquered triremes." Colbert was talking expansively about a "grand tour next May—not only Australia but Honolulu, Hong Kong, the Philippines, Java and then right round the world thro the Suez canal & Egypt back to England." In the meantime she was motoring around the town to cajole an audience together.[38] His bean stalk optimism never left him, although his "ambitious pride" was knocked out of him in subsequent years. Sadly, there never *were* any conquered triremes, or gold or beechnuts, but he *did* capture a boy-girl oread.

In May, he stopped off at Joplin on his way back to New York, and he and Phyllis had four days together, although he had decided that they must be "wisely conventional over that other mad yet delicious frankness we dreamed of or rather you dreamed of." Back in New York, he felt rather differently. He found Marian heavily pregnant, "like a vessel with full-bellied sail." Llewelyn confided that Alyse was also pregnant, although this "little Lulu" never came to term (or possibly never existed except in Lulu's imagination). John was astonished that "this very marked progenitive tendency in the Powys clan at this juncture does not turn away my own touchy & finikin inclinations—so evasive & wilful & capricious & nervous—altogether from such 'country matters' but apparently it doesn't." He sighed to Phyllis, "if only I had had the courage—waiting with you there only a day or two longer till—to risk that great experiment! Damn! Isn't it odd how I have changed over that? I used to dread the thought of it as something that would in a way not exactly 'divide' us but divide your interest, but now I seem to want anything that makes you more definitely belong to me."[39]

He had done his best to give emotional support to Marian during her pregnancy; she was finding her courage and sturdy independence severely tested. In her seventh month, the cottage she rented at Sneden's Landing was suddenly sold. She found a house for sale nearby—Hagen House—but it cost $1,500. She asked the father of her child to lend her the money and he refused. John commiserated, "Men are not very brave when it comes to paying the piper or very generous either and few women there are who have the wit to realize this fact in advance as you have always done—& discount it—making the moment all that matters."[40] Undefeated, Marian appealed to Littleton, who by now had power of attorney, and he advanced her the purchase price against the settlement of C. F.'s estate. Hagen House became her beloved home for the rest of her life. Later that month, she was faced with having to give up her shop due to poor sales, but another bit of luck came her way and she sold an important lace consignment to Mrs. Pierpont Morgan. This contact led to other influential clients and her business career was assured.

Although Marian was due at the end of June, John left in early June for his customary visit to England, going first to see Frances. Frances had written him that she and Louis were divorcing. Louis had fallen in love with another woman, Nan Reid, and told Frances he had no intention of supporting her and the children. Louis warned her that if she sued him for maintenance, he would bring a countersuit naming John as co-respondent.[41] They met in London, where, with her mother and two children, she had gone to find work, and it was at this time that John made "a full confession openly and candidly" to her about his new love. It would have been a difficult meeting, with what might have been lurking in both their minds. He spent the remainder of his time at Burpham, with brief visits to friends and relatives. The letters to Phyllis and Marian were mainly filled with an analysis of his son, Littleton Alfred, now twenty. He found him "extraordinarily beautiful," but "his mind . . . is evidently developing very slowly." Although John had once dreamt of the son joining him in America, he now saw that Littleton Alfred had "so little iron in him that it would be just like transporting Gaston de Latour to the United States."[42]

When John Cowper visited East Chaldon, he found a much happier Theodore. Until the year before, despite all their efforts, friends and family had not succeeded in getting Theodore into print. He expected a good deal of them, assuming that the Wilkinsons or Marian or Llewelyn or John would type his manuscripts, revise them, if necessary rewrite them, and scout for publishers. When he felt they were not making sufficient efforts on his behalf, he would complain, "You don't value my work enough to spend the time over it, old prejudice—that's what it is."[43] However, in 1921 three new friends joined the band of loyal supporters. On a walking tour of Dorset, Stephen Tomlin, a young sculptor, discovered both Chaldon and Theodore. Tomlin told his friend Sylvia Townsend Warner about this "most remarkable man . . . a sort of hermit" who read Dostoevsky.[44] Theodore soon showed Tomlin the unpublished stories that lay in a drawer. The first of his stories that Warner read was "Mr. Tasker's Gods," written about 1915. She was "enthralled" but "frightened and oppressed by this genius," and shocked by "the grinding insistence upon human lust," and "the ruthless hatred with which he pursued the peasant characters." The pair solicited the help of David Garnett, who took a story of Theodore's, "Hester Dominy," to Charles Prentice, senior partner at Chatto & Windus. He knew it would have a sympathetic reading as Garnett's mother, Constance Garnett, was published by Chatto, and David's *Lady into Fox* was about to be published by the same firm. So it turned out: Prentice became a devoted admirer of Theodore's works, a friend, and, most importantly, his publisher.

Powys landed back in New York in August and went immediately to see Marian and her infant son Peter, who had been born on the fourteenth of July. While Jack was there, May asked him to be the boy's official guardian.[45] He then took the train to Galena to visit Phyllis and her parents. He told Llewelyn that it was intolerably hot in Kansas and that "Phyllis and I could do nothing but sit side by side . . . with our feet in the river" but that he had "looked at Cassiopeia calmly enough." Rather more than that happened. In subsequent letters Jack tenderly teased his Jill about the night she came to the cabin where he was staying, looking for her dog: "I keep thinking of when you came to call Peter & 'not for that'—never in your life have you been less of a philosopher, Jill, and more of a girl than you were then!"[46] He wrote her a story about the night he looked "calmly" at Cassiopeia.

> "Is that Peter? Where is Peter? It is for him I came." It's the only time Jill has resisted but it isn't difficult to push her into her house across the threshold. How clear the stars are. I won't light a candle because I can see Jill quite clearly. How thin she looks! There, I'll hang up her dressing-gown—now she does look so slight a figure! I don't think I have ever seen [her] without her dressing-gown. What's that? Jill's shivering. You're not cold Jill are you? It is a warm still night. No—go out Peter! She shall come presently but not quite yet—presently Peter—there! go & lie down!
>
> No she isn't cold, not cold, and yet she's shivering still. Let me take her to the window so that she can look out over the valley at the stars beyond the river and the sycamore trees. How thin she is! But that's her hip-bones! There—now I have got her just as I like having her—my hands are quite free and can take one of hers so that she can feel the length of the bow of Sagittarius herself; so that her hand in my hand can feel how long that bow is and her hand in my hand can lift the clouds out of the way herself. There I've got both her hands now—but now I let them go because the length of the bow of Sagittarius is so exciting that I cannot hold her hands anymore—now I am wandering towards the Gemini the two children of the Swan. Let your head fall more back, Jill; and give up to me these Swan-born—deliver up to me these Swan-born so that I can make them more sensitive and responsive. Give them up to me. I must have both of them. I can only have one of them and Sagittarius at the same time—but I want everything, everything! Give me everything Jill will you? You're shivering again. . . . There—you can turn round now and lean against the window-post while I look at your face a little. . . .
>
> Lift up your chin now and let me look at you. Are we really at last in the middle of the story? Is that a leaf tapping at the wall or is it another lit-

tle Jill beating at the too-long closed door? Well? perhaps! How long have we got before dawn comes—Hush! Where are we? Out of space—out of Time? Don't cry Jill darling it's all right.[47]

That night, to which over the years he referred to again and again, seems to have been the defining point for both of them and thereafter it became a question of not whether, but how they might live together.

When he returned to San Francisco in the autumn he found that the new agent on whom he had pinned such hopes was involved in a theatre venture with "a swinging rough and ready art-exploiter." Powys feared that this would sidetrack "the chief magnetic rush of her energy,"[48] and this proved to be the case. He had only four lectures a week and Margaret was once again agitating for money. Possibly as a sop for not finding him any lectures, Colbert asked him to write a play. He fell for this, as he had before in Chicago when he tried, unsuccessfully, to write plays for Browne's Little Theatre.[49] This new play, he informed Lulu, was "as good as any of those Ibsen things."[50] Both Ibsen's *Rosmersholm* and his play have a clergyman, a putative politician, and a woman who commits suicide, but otherwise this ego-boosting reference to Ibsen is a bit of a red herring. He gave Phyllis a clearer description of what he had in mind. "I've got a thrilling idea—an old degenerate English family near Chesil Beach at Portland, Dorset. The mother & an Oedipus-son, the father and an Electra daughter—crosscurrents—and then their lovers coming in; but in the end going off <u>together</u> mystified & glad to escape![51] He wrote the play, *Paddock Calls*, in six days, and Colbert talked of the company touring California with it and then selling it to New York. As it turned out, Colbert and her partner quarreled in January 1923, and the theatre venture ended unceremoniously, as did Powys's playwriting career.

Whatever its minimal virtues as a play, *Paddock Calls* is indicative of how interested he was at this time in psychoanalytic theories. His philosophical roots, embedded in Wordsworth and Rousseau, would have led him almost inevitably to these latest reformulations of the unconscious mind and of the importance of childhood memories. His concern with the workings of his inner self and with his sexuality likewise prompted him to read whatever he could find concerning sexual deviations and neuroses. Like so many others, he was intrigued by the Freudian theory of the Oedipus complex. He wrote Llewelyn in November 1920: "I dreamt about mother so vividly, so very vividly last night. I love her. I am in love with her. I am Oedipus—and she is dead. The psycho-analytical books—those huge mysterious sibylline books—say that this is incest, and the clue to everything. It is! It is! I know it. I saw her face so clearly last night and in my dream I said to myself—'Yes!'" Powys's study of the writings of Freud probably began in his Chicago period when the artists and writers whom he met at this time were absorbing and expounding Freudian ideas. Sherwood Anderson wrote of Chicago in 1913: "At the time Freud had just been discovered and all the young intellectuals were busy analyzing each other and everyone they met."[52] Nor could he have avoided the subject when he was in New York, where, as Floyd Dell said, "everyone at that time who knew about psychoanalysis was a sort of missionary on the subject, and nobody could be around Greenwich Village without hearing a lot about it."[53] Tradition has it that the Village was first introduced to Freudianism at Mabel Dodge's salon in the winter of 1913, when the psychoanalyst A. A. Brill gave a talk about unconscious behavior and its giveaways. Brill was one of the earliest and most active exponents of psychoanalysis in America, and between 1910 and 1914 translated Freud's three seminal works: *Three Contributions to the Theory of Sex*, *The Interpretation of Dreams*, and *The Psychopathology of Everyday Life*.

If Powys needed any further encouragement to explore Freudian theories, his friend, Theodore Dreiser, would have provided it. Dreiser knew both Brill and Horace Frink, another neurologist and psychiatrist who was to play a role in the lives of John and Phyllis later on. In 1920, Dreiser published a book called *Hey Rub-a-Dub-Dub*, and in a chapter, "Neurotic America and the Sex Impulse," he railed against the hypocrisy of middle America in respect to the sex instinct: "We continue to assert, as a nation and as individuals, that everything sexual is wrong, while at the same time having sexual feelings and impulses which we can scarcely disguise even to ourselves." He went on to argue that the concept of sublimation was simply a bribe to moralists and that, on the contrary, "via sex gratification—or perhaps better, its ardent and often defeated pursuit—comes most of all that is most distinguished in art, letters and our social economy and progress generally."[54]

A booklet that Powys began writing in February 1922, and which Colbert finally published in 1923, was almost certainly influenced by Dreiser's chapter.[55] However, *Psychoanalysis and Morality* goes far beyond anything that Dreiser attempted in positing the pervasive influence of the "much-maligned impulse." This little-known work, now long out of print, reveals not only of the depth of John Cowper's psychoanalytical knowledge by this period but the origin of many of his most deeply held theories. He begins by saying that "the importance of what is now called 'Psychoanalysis' has hardly been fully realized even yet," but "it throws such startling side-lights upon the nature of sex and man's relation to sex as to go a long way towards creating a complete revolution in our Western attitude to these things."

Sex invades "every thought we have, every animosity, every sympathy, every vague and obscure assertion of pride, every plunge into humiliation and self-effacement." He argues, moreover, that "an exhaustive analysis of the subtle and complicated ramifications of the emotional aberration known as incest" means it will no longer be considered "an abominable and unspeakable crime" and that other sexual perversions such as homosexuality will no longer be thought of as sins. Then, in a reference to a subject close to his heart:

"It means that in the midst of a society, founded on the theory that pleasure derived from sex has no justification except as a means to the lawful propagation of the race, there exist virtuous and reputable men absorbingly engaged in an analysis of sterile and unproductive sexual imaginations."[56]

Psychoanalysis, he contends, calls into question one of the major tenets of civilization—that "by the drastic suppression of certain pleasurable sensations we can attain higher levels of human consciousness." The answer of psychoanalysis is clear: "If we do attain such levels it is at the risk of morbid and violent reactions, carrying us back . . . by a terrible swing of the pendulum, into lamentable disorder." He looks forward to a time when "this two-thousand-year-old adamantine chain, dark with the rusty blood of infinite cruelty, is struck at last from the beautiful limbs of Eros!" but notes sadly that "it requires a superhuman effort to detach oneself from a moral imperative that has eaten into one's very bones." For no one was this more true than for Powys himself.

Freud's work on the link between mental and physical disorders struck another responsive chord in the ulcer-ridden John Cowper. By now he was well aware that his gut was his dark second brain.[57]

The fatal power of suppressed sex-libido, acting on the human mind with such overpowering force, is one more proof of the intimate association between the nerves and the intellect, between material vibrations and mental consciousness. Berman's glandular theories, supported by so much strange evidence, add still further weight, from another direction, to this terrible dependence of mind upon body.[58]

This is the only reference to Louis Berman that Powys makes in *Psychoanalysis and Morality*, but in fact, the most original ideas in his booklet are expansions of, or reactions against, Berman's little-known theories.[59] Berman pointed out that Freud's ideas, however revolutionary, did not answer the question why, when two individuals are exposed to the same situation, "one will develop a complex, the other will remain immune?" Berman's own answer was:

"The internal secretions (endocrine glands) with their influence upon brain and nervous system as well as every other part of the body corporation . . . have been discovered as the real governors and arbiters of instincts, dispositions, emotions and reactions, characters and temperaments, good and bad. . . . A derangement of their function, causing an insufficiency of them, an excess, or an abnormality, upsets the entire equilibrium of the body, with transforming effects upon the mind and the organs. In short, they control human nature."[60]

Berman was aware that a person instinctively rejects the idea that he is dominated not by his mind or consciousness or soul, but by his gland chemistry and even more clings to the conviction "that he is something apart, inherently, and therefore infinitely different."[61] While Powys was fascinated by this idea as a possible answer to his own difficulties of temperament, his reverence for the uniquely individual mind and its infinite possibilities made it difficult for him to accept such a possibility, and he uses his particular interpretation of psycho-analysis to refute Berman's "materialism," arguing: "Not only does psychoanaly-sis suggest that there are unfathomable mine-shafts, so to speak, in the person-al soul that reach out and beyond the sphere of material phenomena; it also seems to suggest that these mine-shafts of personality remain *individual* and do not lose themselves, as Oriental mysticism implies, in any over-soul or world-consciousness."[62]

The medical man also touched a nerve with his concept of memory. Powys, even at this early period, understood that while psychoanalysis may have liber-ated mankind from the "mort-main" of many taboos in positing the unconscious, it had created its own terrifying kingdom: "If the mind of a man or a woman is henceforth to be regarded as a vast universe in itself, full of deep black holes that descend into unfathomable mystery, why then, what was once cosmic-panic becomes the self-panic." Only by a "certain heavenly magic," Powys became con-vinced, could a person "overcome the demons of our own mental inferno." This magic against bad dreams was what he called "the art of forgetting," and it became the most important weapon in his defensive armory.[63] Berman had a response to the idea that we could avoid the "this unsloughable remembrance of the past."

> You can no more think of getting rid of these unconscious memories of pro-toplasm than you can think of getting rid of the wetness of water. They are embedded in the most intimate chemistry of the primeval ameba as well as in our most complex tissues. The memories of the cold lone fish and the hot predatory carnivore who were our begetters, may haunt us to the end of time. . . . The powers of unconscious memory and unlearnable technique of reaction to experience, once grooved, thus prove the great gift and the eter-nal curse of protoplasm.[64]

Another Berman idea was to obsess Powys: the mystery of man's impulse to separation, to disjunction, which is constantly being subverted by his need for junction, assimilation. Every living being, Berman argued, is separated from all other living beings by inorganic dead masses, and yet driven to contact with them by a fundamental impulse to assimilate them into itself and make them part of itself. "That assimilatory urge is present in every activity from coarse ingestion as food to the moral metabolism of the hermit-saint who would influence others to do as he."[65] Powys presumably picked up this idea of the assimilative urge and gloriously made it the basis of what he called "identity-lust"—a concept that in *Psychoanalysis and Morality* covers everything from creativity to lovemaking, and eventually was made to explain his relationship to nature and indeed the uni-verse. The relevant sections deserves to be quoted fully.

We actually do caress and possess with the obscure flow of our polymor-
phous "libido" every single external thing to which our attention is attracted. Or, if we do not lust after it, we reverse the movement, and shrink from
it with sex-saturated loathing. . . .

It might be maintained that every living organism instinctively—like
the human infant—stretches out every sense-nerve it possesses in order to
satisfy its identity-lust by appropriating to itself as much of the external
world as it can reduce to submission to its mastery. . . . And behind the sex-
functioning of both men and beasts and their blind pursuit of nourishment
there stirs and moves the same centrifugal and centripetal force—this persistent identity-lust—aiming to bring about as complete an inter-fusion
between themselves and the object of their desire, as the submissiveness of
the object or the margin of its own satiety makes it possible to achieve. . . .

The inherent Narcissism of our identity-lust can easily be tested. . . .
We instinctively select among objects of food, for example, those which
answer in some mysterious manner to the secret chemistry of our sub-conscious souls. We are drawn towards, or repelled by, certain fabrics and substances, certain soils, certain earth-formations, certain minerals, trees,
plants, certain atmospheres and climates. And over and over again, the outward and apparent texture of our nature, its conscious pose or mask to the
world, is quaintly refuted and exposed by these deeper, more instinctive
preferences.[66]

Psychoanalysis and Morality is a dexterous amalgam of the theories of Freud
and Berman, albeit with a uniquely Powysian slant. While he may be arguing
from the basis of his own highly distinctive temperament and individual manias,
he nonetheless manages to shed light on some of the most obscure—and universal—governors of human behavior. He referred to "chemical selection" in one of
his earliest letters to Phyllis, and he now expands on this. For a love affair to be
lasting, each lover "must find something in the object of their desire that corresponds to their choice in these other occult reciprocities. The person must
represent the preferred climate, the preferred scenery, the preferred food, the preferred fabrics, substances, materials, elements! . . . Thus what all lovers seek is
nothing more or less than an objective shadow of their hidden soul, materialized
and substantiated."[67] In a rather chilling addendum to his theory of identity-lust,
he wrote Phyllis a few months later: "If you cannot use a person as a door to go
through into Nature and into that reciprocity in Nature of your own mental
landscape . . . well then you just hate them."[68] In other words, erotic attraction
is the trigger by which a door is opened—whether it is the door of the mind or
the door into nature. It is "narcissistic" because it is assimilative. You *use* the person to whom you are sexually attracted to open up the creative mind, to release
you into another world. Jack knew by now that Phyllis's "peculiar submissiveness" would answer well to his "assimilative urge" and that she would become the
necessary entry through which he would finally enter into a creative life.

In the meantime, with all this newfound psychoanalytical knowledge, he felt he could help Phyllis with her own psychological problems, writing on September 22, 1922: "Jill, you will tell me if you suffer from any of these nervous fears or dreads or psycho-analytical compulsions and miserable terrors? Because I have known them—well! of course, you know, I obviously would be bound to! but they are better now—and I really could exorcise yours." And when she reports to him difficulties with her parents, he analyses them in terms of the classical Electra complex: "There undoubtedly is some deep obscure hostility that goes on between parent & child except when some still obscurer sexual attraction blots it out, and your father being so much older than you has prevented what wd have been a natural cure for all this. I mean a beautiful incestuous subtlety towards you on his part—you see, in *that* sense you've never had a father & it accounts for a lot!"[69]

I think it was at this time—the advent of Phyllis, corresponding in time with his deep study of psychoanalysis—that he began to see himself seriously in this priestly role of helping others. Just as the analyst was seen as a non-judgmental figure who could assuage guilt and free the victims of neurosis, Powys was finding his way to assuming the role of his father, *the* father, not as a priest of religion but as a priest who could relieve the unhappiness, the suffering, the neuroses of others. As it turned out, Jill would have none of it, but in the next few years, he would write a number of self-help books for the Theodore/Puckle pariahs.

When Phyllis was in San Francisco, her friend Adele Stackpole had talked about taking her to Paris, but the plan never materialized. In October 1922, despairing of ever getting to France, Phyllis considered a job with Haldeman-Julius, the publisher of the "Little Blue Books," based in Girard, Kansas, a few miles from her parents' home. Powys was against it, sure she would be miserable and would hate working for "those people." He felt guilty about not finding her a more congenial job in New York, but he soon realized that there were advantages to her working for this small firm. Haldeman-Julius subsequently published a number of Powys non-fiction booklets, which helped to keep him financially afloat in this difficult period, and it was Phyllis who saw the first of these through to publication. Although she found the job too exhausting and resigned after six months, the experience she gained as editor, condenser, and proofreader was very useful to him. Unknowingly, Phyllis had embarked on a lifetime's work as copy-editor of John Cowper's writings.

During their long separation in this period, he wrote her virtually every day, and letterwriting became lovemaking: "Surely it is possible to make such marks and scrawls on a bit of paper that when your girl reads it she has to shut her eyes & lean against a tree, a door-post, a bed-post, a wall—& feel you take her & take her."[70] However, when she had an "attack" of crying when she went home to her parents for Christmas, he knew well what the problem was: "The long strain of cerebral imaginations going so far back has left your nerves at a point at which your actual [word scribbled out] virginity, as if it were a drooping wood-plant that must be picked by the fumbling satyr-fool who keeps kneeling down and [word scribbled out] caressing it, but leaving it on its stalk. . . . I too keep helplessly & vainly wishing—as I have not done—and could not do—except for you—that [words scribbled out] that—oh damn! these words!—that I might really 'take' my Jill!"[71]

Llewelyn was also the recipient of many letters from John in the autumn of 1922. He told his brother how lonely he was for Phyllis, how he wished Llewelyn and Alyse could find her a job in New York, and that it was her "noble and distinguished intelligence" that he loved. "I am in love with her Mind, brother; with her Mind."[72] At the same time he was also reassuring Phyllis that he loved her mind, "as a listener & half-creator of my thoughts," but clearly it was not the only thing that attracted him: "I always imagine you lying by my side stripped of all your clothes and lying on your face so that I can caress you from head to ankles—all your shoulders & waist & back and flanks—oh damn!"[73] Inevitably, Phyllis became the focus of what Powys called "the perpetual discord" between Marian and Llewelyn, which came to a head in March 1923. Marian was still very important to John; he missed their "queer peculiar customs; our lingered-out epicurean joys, our gossips, our jests, our historical chatter."[74] At some point he confided to Marian his true feelings for Phyllis. Llewelyn was furious when he found out that it was Marian and not himself who was Jack's confidante. He wrote a stinging rebuke early in 1923, chastising Powys for writing too many letters to Phyllis, for writing too many letters to too many girls over the years, for being too sentimental, and for being sexually "abnormal." These charges angered John, and he fired off a barrage of letters to his brother, accusing Llewelyn of being "narrow and bigoted and self-satisfied." He defended his preference for masturbation over "rogering" in his lovemaking, and tried to explain to Llewelyn the larger issues that arose from his particular type of personality: that the abuse of self was an aspect of the search for self.

> When you say "but so many" don't you recall the idea of Hardy's *Well Beloved*, what the Freudians now call the Narcissistic hunt for "his own self" of the true Don Juan! I grant the "onanism," I confess to the "self-abuse," the spiritual "shagging," but these things have more mysteries and wonder in them than you guess. . . . And if Nature makes a feeling thrilling and lovely to me, why should I try & suppress it because Lulu calls it "aesthetically displeasing"? Perhaps it is no more aesthetically unpleasing to Nature than Billy Pod's encounters with his Suffolk goat! . . . But don't you see I am an epicene queer abnormal pervert in everything—when I write poetry I "make love" in my "unpleasing" way; when I lecture I "make love" in my unpleasing way; when I walk on the hills, the same! by the sea, the same! when I drink coffee, the same! and I don't "cheapen" or "vulgarise" these things! It is the Moon "in trine" with Venus, I expect, in my horoscope. . . . I am a born perverted sensationalist.[75]

The letters Jack wrote to Lulu at this time are rather moving in their frank self-analysis, but they raise the tiniest suspicion that his old "lust for dramatic excitement," as brother Bertie once called it, was again in operation. He knew better than anyone that confiding in Marian would infuriate Llewelyn and that his *apologia pro vita sua* would in turn cause Lulu to feel remorse. In any case, the unintended—or intended—result of this Powys tempest was that a contrite Llewelyn offered them the room above their own flat in Patchin Place for the summer. An excited John began to think of money-making plans for when they were together in New York. Phyllis would "proof-read for a New York Jew—for you & I can't escape from the House of Israel," and he would lecture to "East-side little Jewish Bolsheviki."[76] In the meantime, almost all his money continued to go to his wife and his son, who was now at Corpus. He paid this uncomplainingly, although he admitted to Llewelyn that the last two Cambridge terms were the greatest financial strain, with Littleton Alfred "floating lightly through his pleasures." Margaret was sending John "piteous begging letters" while the son, "the dear rogue, is now shooting at something manor . . . and then off to Devonshire and back again for the great Ball at the Castle."[77] He regularly sent Margaret £50 a month and he also paid Littleton Alfred a generous allowance and his Cambridge fees—a further £350 a year. It is difficult to assess the value of this allowance of almost £1,000 a year to his family in today's terms, but it would be about £35,000.[78] Possibly a better comparison was what Louis Wilkinson settled on Frances in 1924 for her support and the support of their two children: only £112. However, the astonishing sum John sent was still not enough. Harry Lyon lent him money to pay Margaret's income tax for the year, and a further £100 to pay the son's tailor. John Cowper wrote brother Littleton (now frequently called "Old Littleton" to distinguish the two Littletons) in April, telling him of his financial worries. "I am working hard & lecturing some five times a week & the audiences are slowly improving here in Los Angeles, but it takes a good many lectures to raise a hundred pounds."[79] He ended his letter by telling Littleton that he had dedicated *Psychoanalysis and Morality* to him, a rather strange thing to do given Littleton's conventional nature. However, the begging letter (for it was nothing less) did the trick, and Littleton cabled him that he would look after Margaret's outstanding debts. Jack admitted to Phyllis, "You see I tend to use as my only weapon to get what I want a 'babyish candour' with them both as I am so used to having the outward events of my life arranged for me by more competent hands than my own."[80] This was nothing less than the truth. Until now, someone had always arranged his outer life—his wife, Littleton, Marian, Llewelyn. From now on it would be Phyllis's turn.

Just when he had managed to bring about this longed-for meeting in New York, Adele Stackpole once again proposed Paris to Phyllis, offering to pay her fare and expenses. Phyllis initially refused, then accepted. Although he had encouraged this trip since 1921, when it was first mooted, by now it was obvious that Powys did not want her to go and was fearful that Adele would corrupt her. For the first time in his letters, he hinted that Phyllis had lesbian sympathies, or rather, attracted lesbians. Adele became "my Rival," "the little Lesbian"; in a letter to Lulu she was "that little boy-girl rogue Adele Stackpole."[81] In a somewhat circuitous manner he warned Phyllis, "Remember that, with your nature, there is pleasure in submitting even to what with your intelligence you know the limitation of! And remember that however lovely it is to yield to a strong generous feminist, it may yet prove more lovely to yield to a weak masculine sadist!"[82] Phyllis sailed for France on the sixth of April, 1923. They arranged to meet in New York on the first of July in "the upper room" at Patchin Place. His letters of the next few months are filled with fantasies about what would happen when they were finally together. "I hope that our long long expectations won't end when that 'goodnight Lulu' has really been said in our dying of happiness. . . . Think of Lulu hearing two thumps upon the floor a heavy one and a light one, and coming up to find the terminals really terminal! . . . Here lie the bodies of J. P. & P. P. who died of happiness July 1st 1923."[83]

While she was in Paris, both began to worry, as lovers do, if they would be able to cope with living together. He wondered if she would hate him for taking so long to wash in the morning, and she was fearful of sharing a small room with someone else. By the middle of May she was quite scared and confessed that her concern about intimacy had as much to do with sexual familiarity as with spatial closeness. He gently reassures her: "Take heart little Phyllis! . . . There shall be no more of that 'appalling intimacy' . . . than by slow stages you can be gently seduced & beguiled into!" He was genuinely tender of her fears, but they also suited his own sexual fantasies and predilections. A large part of that fantasy was that she was a little girl and a virgin. He reminds her of their first meeting when she held her lips together "and pouted them like a young child," and exults, "To have a virgin of this hyper sensitive kind for my own! There she will be, bare and unresisting!"[84] Phyllis represented to him "all the girl-children in the world whose ways have attracted me so terribly—their silences, the way their long legs are & their thin arms."[85] His old horror of mature female sexuality was circumvented by yet another illusion was that she was an "elemental," a "half-born," and therefore "only half-human and never to be a grown-up terrible woman—never never never!"[86] His other dream, of incest, was also imaginatively satisfied in her. "I get such a quaint feeling as if you weren't my girl so much as my daughter," and he refers again to the fact that "your father being so much older has meant that a certain delicious incestuous relation has never protected and guarded and comprehended your weakness & helplessness."

From the beginning, he encouraged and reinforced this "weakness and help-lessness," which was, undoubtedly, a part of her personality. "When you are sad & at your very weakest then is when your Jack loves you the most!"[87] In her first

letter from Paris she told him that she felt like a "transplanted little object," and
he responded, "I adore it when you call yourself a little object or a little anything," adding, "I know it is deep, deep in your queer Flora de Barral inferiority
complex."[88] By the next letter, he had changed the "o" to an "a" and another pet
name was born. She was now his "little Abject." Like Flora in Conrad's *Chance*,
Phyllis aroused both sexual excitement and protectiveness in her lover. Whether
Phyllis, like Flora the only daughter of a bankrupt tycoon, *did* need the protection is an open question. What matters is that in Jack's imagination she suddenly became the suicidal, desperate Flora whom Conrad described as "dreadfully
and pitifully forlorn," with a thinness that was "appealing and—yes—she was a
desirable little figure."[89] John had written in his *Confessions*, "I surround everything that occurs to me by a bookish atmosphere. Books make a fine, mellow,
imaginative mist, through which I see things and people thrown to an enchanting distance."[90] He must therefore echo the words of Antony Roderick in *Chance*,
who tells Flora, "Whatever your troubles, I am the man to take you away from
them."[91] Powys knew his Conrad and knew himself. The narrator, Marlow, puzzling out "the suddenness of the affair," concludes that men like the captain who
are timid and chivalrous have "a great need for affection": "At the least encouragement they go forward with the eagerness, with the recklessness of starvation.
. . . With all her inexperience this girl could not have found any great difficulty
in her conquering enterprise. She must have begun it."[92] Suddenly in Jack's letters, it is Phyllis who made the first move in March 1921, who had "come straight
up to me & given yourself to me—the very first time we ever spoke to each
other! I didn't know that such a thing as you—with your particular kind of Flora
de Barral nature ever really existed."[93] How Powys was again and again to make
his life fit literature.

Presumably Powys saw other similarities between their romance and that of
Conrad's novel. Captain Anthony of the *Ferndale* is a passionate suitor and idol-
ator, but he is so fantastically chivalrous that he is unwilling—or unable—to
consummate his marriage when he is led to believe that Flora has married him
out of desperation. This "unselfishness" almost destroys both of them. On their
long marriage journey, all the captain can do is stand on the bridge of his ship
and stare at Flora, gradually disintegrating under the torture of a powerful sexual appetite that he can neither release nor control. Powys was eventually to create equally powerful portraits of the sexual voyeur. Whether or not he took on
board Marlow's final comment is debatable.

> If two beings thrown together, mutually attracted, . . . voluntarily stop short
> of the—the embrace . . . then they are committing a sin against life. . . .
> And the punishment of it is an invasion of complexity, a tormenting,
> forcibly tortuous involution of feelings, the deepest form of suffering.[94]

Phyllis arrived on the first of July, as arranged, but they did not stay long at
Patchin Place. By the end of July they had moved to an apartment on nearby

Bedford Street—the first indication that the "passive" Phyllis had a will of her own. John would say that both their life-illusions were based on Grimm's fairy tales; she was the "lonely funny goose girl who held the dog so that it shouldn't bark when the mad beggar John came into the village."[95] The reality of living together proved rather more difficult. He had to adjust to her "oceanic moods." She, in turn, found his ways so disconcerting that once she ran out at four in the morning to find a policeman, although what she intended to report is never divulged. On the other hand, their sexual fantasies dovetailed nicely. Together they elaborated a touching fantasy of sex and bondage, beating and submission. She is a virgin about to be "delivered up" into his bandit hands. He grabs her by the hair, forces her to kneel on the bed while he slips the ribbons off her shoulders, and fondles her breasts (called Daisy and Daphne). He holds both her wrists in one hand until she is completely "docile" and cries. Then with her back to him so she becomes "such a romantic unearthly anonymous thing," he masturbates to orgasm.[96] They have another rather lovely fantasy—he imagines that his virgin is the mother of "Glauk," and she is sewing "something made of starlight and nothingness for your little daughter." He often teased her gently about that hot September of 1922 "when, in so mythological a manner, I begat Glauk for you—and indeed to say the truth—on you."[97] An immaculate conception, so to speak.

Powys always maintained that he did not start to live until he was fifty. His life with Phyllis coincided with the death of his father; it is difficult to disentangle the significance of the two events. C. F. Powys died on August 5, 1923, at the age of eighty. Old Littleton, as executor, joined Gertrude in Weymouth to carry out the terms of the will. It was a considerable task. There were many securities to be disposed of, the big house in Greenhill Terrace to be sold, and furniture, pictures, silver, and china divided among them. When the Estate was finally settled at the end of the year, each of the children received £2,896 16s. 9d. The money allowed Gertrude to go to Paris to further study her art, Katie to come to New York for six months, Littleton and his wife Mabel to spend six months in Italy, Marian to expand her lace business, and Will to buy more land in Kenya. To the dismay of his brothers and sisters, John Cowper immediately signed over his entire share of the estate to his wife. He had already made over the Burpham house and his valuable library when he left England in 1905. At the age of fifty he most truly began his life again.

In November 1923 he embarked on a new novel, finishing it in June 1924. He called it *Ducdame*. The New York scenes in his previous novel were particularly graphic, and he may have considered setting this next one wholly in New York City. He had abundant material, having lived for more than a decade only a few blocks from the tenements of the Lower East side where new immigrants worked out their lives in sweatshops and factories. Given his professed interest in "pariahs" and the underdog, he would have had an unequalled opportunity to write about those alien immigrants and their struggle for survival. His own strong feelings of alienation in America were, in some sense, not so different from the thousands of outsiders who were also confronting the "American Way of Life." He never did write about them; possibly he realized he was not capable of doing so. Eastsiders were themselves already writing about their pariah-hood, their sense of estrangement, with an authenticity that he could not equal. Nonetheless, some years later, when the novelist Dorothy Richardson asked him again why he had not written about New York, he sketched that part of New York he knew in such a way that one regrets the unwritten novel. He described "the peculiar Sunday morning silence with a vast hole in space," the milk-cart horses, the buoys in the harbor, the sirens of the great liners, the "cracked one-bell jangling that you hear tell the Angelus sometimes with a faint little sound that you can almost watch making its hurried thin way between the tall buildings like a nervous little old dwarf-nun." He told her about the "fish-monger who's a miser & who always talks about reading Dickens on the strength of once having been left a legacy of 3 books that were too dilapidated to sell" and "an umbrella-mender and a dairy shop-man who keep up the secret tradition of being human beings." Then in a throwaway remark in which lies one of the keys to the peculiar power of the novels he was to write in the next ten years, he went on: "I've lived here for 25 years, lady, did you know that? For a quarter of a century. No one knows the <u>nuances</u> of America better than I do— none as well! But do you think I'll write about it? Sideways I always must—for I must see England like a daydream, a brown study, an onanistic (forgive me) ecstasy."[98]

So, instead of a novel about New York or Chicago or San Francisco, Powys turned once again to his own past landscapes, characters, themes, and preoccupations. The plot of *Ducdame* is simple. Rook Ashover lives with his widowed mother and his mistress, Netta Page, in the ancestral home in Dorset. His younger brother Lexie lives nearby, as do several idiot children, fathered by the dead Mr. Ashover. Rook's mother has invited his cousin, Lady Ann Wentworth Gore, to stay with them, in the hope that Rook will marry her and produce an heir to the estate. Eventually Rook marries Ann and Netta disappears. The story ends with the drowning of Rook and the birth of his son. Although Powys rehearses once again his relationship with his brothers and with his mother, the unfinished business of his marriage, the role of the mistress, the themes of nature as woman, death as liberator, *Ducdame* is not entirely recycled juvenilia. Rook Ashover is still recognizably the hero of his previous stories, "this master of manias and inhibitions,"[99] who loves his life-loving younger brother Lexie, dying of tuberculosis. However, Rook's mistress, Netta Page, although another pariah figure, is no longer the unlikely prostitute of earlier attempts, or the even more improbable if real Lily whom Powys once took home to Burpham. Netta is convincingly alive with all the ways of Phyllis, right down to the way she cries. Lady Ann, the young aristocrat Rook reluctantly marries, is Margaret in appearance and determination, but his unusually tender description of the "strong, capable, high-spirited" Lady Ann in her pregnancy relies on his more recent observation of his courageous, gay, and steely-willed sister Marian, enceinte.

Indeed, *Ducdame* is a considerable advance on previous novels. For one thing, Powys had been immersing himself in a study of mythology, which interested him as much as or more than psychoanalysis. Not only was he now learning to weave his personal experiences more seamlessly into his philosophical preoccupations, increasingly he was using mythological motifs to give a reverberative significance to his fiction. The metaphysical battle between dualities that has played such a large role in his writings reappears—this time as an ambiguous combat between creative and destructive forces—but Powys has now grounded it in the larger psychological conflict of wills between man and woman. Furthermore, he skillfully embeds his story in the myth of the Mother-Goddess and the hero/son struggling for autonomy. Rook Ashover is struggling against the will of his mother, who, in her "insanity of devotion to so impersonal a thing as the survival of a family,"[100] is determined that the ancient Ashover line will continue. Rook has resisted and lives with a woman who is barren. "It was defiance; since he had chosen their very resting place to flaunt his sterile malice. Into this very shrine of their vitality, of their hope, of their unconquerable life urge he had come to parade his disillusionment, his alliance with . . . the eternal *No* of the abyss."[101] Rook feels "a blind repulsion" at the idea of being married to Lady Ann and that "his life-illusion was outraged by this marriage."[102]

> He felt as if Lady Ann's personality were actually adhering to his own; and not only adhering to it, but sucking it up. . . . He felt as though this female creature . . . were some sinister living growth, fungus-like and carnivorous, that devoured his flesh and drank his blood.[103]

Nature echoes this devouring aspect: "It was perhaps because of the millions and millions of dead leaves that were dissolving back into the flesh of their great drowsy mother that, with this air from the woods and meadows, there came a perceptible savour . . . of the very sweat of death itself."[104] Rook calls this December day "a woman's day," and he "hated the day." Struggling to free himself from the "unconscious necessity" of the feminine nature, the endless circle of dissolution and a new life, Rook has developed some defences. He has evolved a "philosophic scepticism," a "detachment of his brain," a "cold clairvoyance," but it does not save him. Although believing that "it's like death to make love,"[105] Rook nonetheless makes love to, impregnates, and then marries the Lady Ann.

There is a good deal of theorizing in the novel about the nature of women which may have been influenced by some recent reading. On April 28, 1923, he had written to Phyllis, referring to a phrase she has used of herself—"this disillusioned little soul." He wonders if "your mind felt itself to be little."

> So that Weininger is right when he says that the essence of the feminine is to be absolutely nothing! How furious that Weininger doctrine wd make my sister Marian and my sister Alyse. . . . When one thinks of the silent will-

power of one's mother! . . . Egoism of a tenacity & unscrupulousness that makes the "selfishness" of the male appear like the peevish snatching of a child compared with the inhuman fatality of nature herself!

Otto Weininger's *Sex and Character*,[106] a metaphysic of sexual love and feminine psychology, was alternately praised by admirers such as Strindberg as "full of truths," and denounced by detractors as "vehement misogyny." Powys appears to give Rook Ashover some of Weininger's ideas as well as some of his pathological fear of women. Even more interestingly, a description of the brilliant Weininger, who committed suicide at the age of twenty-three, might be a description of Powys himself: "Weininger's nature forced his mind on long expeditions into psychology, biology, literature, and philosophy, journeys from which he never returned. Dissatisfied with scientific research, discontented with his own restless nature, he went farther and farther along the paths of speculative thought until he was, at the end, quite alone."[107]

Freud had refused to recommend Weininger's book for publication, telling him that the world wanted evidence, not thoughts, but his depreciation may have risen from the fact that Freud was himself intending to write on another topic in Weininger's book—bisexuality. In *Rodmoor*, just before the insane Adrian Sorio dies, he has a vision of his son, Baptiste, the first of many androgynous figures that will appear in his novels. From Plato's description of a bisexual spherical being to the androgyne of the Gnostics, the hermaphrodite has always been a symbol of the original divine perfection. He is the Primordial Child of myth—Hermes, Eros, Dionysus—the god who leads the way to wholeness, who *is* wholeness, and yet is in some mysterious way oneself, or the self one is struggling to become. Baptiste is the "angel" of the nothingness that Sorio craves. Just before *his* death, Rook Ashover is also rewarded with a vision of a young man on a gray horse with a face "so unmistakably resembling his own but with a beauty and power in it beyond anything he had ever approached."[108] Powys's love for his own son verged on idolatry, and his portrait of him in these boy-girls is a charming compliment to Littleton Alfred. But these fictional sons are, in a larger sense, evanescent visions of some future reintegration.

The unhappy hero of *Ducdame*, frantic to escape what John Knox called the "monstrous regiment of women,"[109] holds fast to the idea of an Elysian Fourth Dimension. "It was almost as if . . . there really did exist something corresponding to the old Platonic idea of a universe composed of mind-stuff, of mind-forms, rarer and more beautiful than the visible world."[110] Witch Betsy calls this place "Cimmery Land," the place where "folks do live like unborn babes,"[111] and Rook, like Adrian, comes to believe that this land can only be attained by drowning:

> Drowning! That was the ultimate sensation he craved. . . . That mysterious country of the underworld of which the Greek wanderer had his vision,

coming to it at last through those Cimmerian mists, may after all have held a shadowy correspondence with something that really did exist![112]

It was Phyllis who introduced him to the land of Cimmeria. On July 25, 1924, he reminded her of how "the very first day we met you quickly and hurriedly told me about Cimmeria just as a child who at last finds someone who can understand them rushes off to their treasure-box and brings out something that no one else has ever seen and flings it on their knee and can hardly speak because it is giving them the thing that is like their very soul such as they themselves don't often take out of its box!" When Powys was at his most misogynistic in his fiction, he could also be as delicately perceptive as this of a woman's "soul." It is no accident that he is describing the secret treasure box he had as a child as well. Cimmery Land became a visionary place where *both* he and Phyllis, male and female, might live "like unborn babes." However, in the world that Ashover and John still inhabit, the merging of male and female traits remains a distant dream.

There is another myth closely connected with the Mother-Goddess: the myth of the hostile twins. In the age-old technique of splitting, the only way for the hero to break free of the absorbing power of the Great Mother is to create another male hostile to him who represents the destructive aspect of the mother. A motif that has appeared in previous novels is the loving relationship between two brothers or friends who nonetheless hold opposing world views. James and Luke Andersen of *Wood and Stone* reappear in *Rodmoor* as Adrian and Baltazar, and now as Rook and his younger brother Lexie. Although the personalities of James and Luke are radically opposite, the brothers are extremely close. In *Rodmoor*, some ambiguity begins to appear. It seems as if Baltazar, out of sexual jealousy, deliberately drives Adrian mad. In *Ducdame*, once again the relationship between the two brothers is loving, but now a third character is introduced into the twin dialogue, and this third "twin" is overtly hostile to one of the other two. It is as if a third is necessary to absorb the latent conflict between the two. *Ducdame* is largely an exploration of this triad—Lexie, Rook, and the new "twin," William Hastings, the vicar of Ashover. Powys has hit upon a new and powerful way of exploring not only his inner tensions but the tensions between himself and Llewelyn and Theodore.

All the qualities of Adrian Sorio in *Rodmoor* are now divided between Rook and William. Both Adrian and Rook have the mystic dream of finding through death some fourth dimension, but Rook is quite sane and he has no "philosophy of destruction." The insanity and the philosophy of destruction are taken on by Vicar Hastings, who wants to get "behind the scene and pull up the dam, so that the death force can flood the whole field."[113] Nonetheless, Rook and Hastings are drawn together almost against their wills. They are strangely alike; both hate the material world, the idea of sexual procreation is loathsome to them, and "life" is disgusting to them both. So alike, there nonetheless develops between them an intense hatred. The vicar's wife, Nell, puzzled by this obscure hostility, remarks "I've always known that the real opposite to William was Lexie Ashover and not

Rook Ashover." She is correct—Lexie is the life lover, but Hastings ignores Lexie and concentrates his hostility on his fellow death lover. Nell again tries to point out their essential sameness and differences.

> There's something hateful in William—something wicked and cruel—that wants to destroy things. Rook doesn't want to destroy anything. He only wants to escape, to get away, to let everything go. Things are only half real to Rook; and people too. They're real to William; and that's why he wants to blot them out.[114]

Rook and William, the hostile twins of world mythology, are in Powys mythology John and Theodore. "Things" were always real to Theodore too, as they never quite were to John. John continued to feel that there was an "indescribable bond, or covenant, or understanding" between the two brothers, and there was. Cousin Ralph Shirley would have said their strong sense of connection came out of their astrological kinship, with Theodore's sun and moon in Sagittarius and Libra respectively and John's in Libra and Sagittarius. Theodore's astrological function was, quite literally, to throw light on John's hidden demons. But the hostile twin does not want to see; it is easier and psychologically safer to project the demons onto a brother/twin. "This devilish Proteus," wrote Powys in *Autobiography*, referring to his fear, "thus persecuting his poor brother-Proteus." In myth, the earth mother's deathly aspect becomes an animal which the hero fights but which is essentially his own self. Powys uses the symbolism and imagery of this motif to describe the struggle between Hastings and Rook:

> The struggle between them had by this time become one of those primeval struggles between two horned animals. . . . It seemed to Hastings . . . as if their hostility to one another, this sullen obscure wrestling that was going on in the darkness, occupied an arena that sank down into the very navel of the earth.[115]

Rook's life has been extremely unhappy, but the defences he has painfully evolved—his scepticism, his detachment—have kept him free of madness and this is hateful to the self-enclosed vicar who has no such defences. The insane Hastings brings "to an end [Rook's] Pyrrhonian scepticism"[116] by stunning him with a garden rake; Rook falls into the river and drowns, thereby achieving his desire. Hastings dies the next day, of brain fever. The dying Lexie lives on. The sublimely ridiculous garden-rake death leaves open the question whether Rook has succeeded or failed, reached the desired Cimmery Land of the spirit, or returned to the hated womb of the Mother-Goddess.

Powys finished *Ducdame* in June 1924 and sent it off to Doubleday. Phyllis went to her parents for the summer while he began another extended tour of the southern states. Despite being heavily in debt again, he went ahead with his plans to visit England for the summer, even though his son had already written to say he would be away much of the time grouse shooting. As usual, Jack had left his passport and tickets to the last minute, and was greatly agitated to find that under the new immigration act, he would no longer be able to return to the U.S. as a "resident alien." Indeed, without a permit, which he had also neglected to get, he would not be allowed back at all. In Phyllis's absence, he turned to Alyse, who was "wonderfully competent," filling out his passport form, accompanying him to get his photo taken, getting the forms for the required permit.[117] She was glad of the distraction. Llewelyn had gone off on an expedition in the Rocky Mountains, and having heard nothing from him, Alyse was increasingly worried. It was in this anxious time that John began to know and understand better the conflicting personality traits of this highly intelligent, reserved feminist. He felt that given her prickly nature, Alyse had few friends who gave her affection, or even dared to. He felt indignant that her boss, Scofield Thayer, treated her like a loyal paid servant, but speculated to Phyllis that it was Alyse's fault. "She likes flattering & waiting hand & foot upon the men she respects; I suppose it's the reverse side of the great medal of Alyse the Liberator." He had the grace to acknowledge that "of course Alyse flatters me & is prepared to run upstairs, downstairs, here & there," and concludes that she is the kind of woman "especially appealed to by rather spoiled rather selfish rather helpless intelligent men."[118]

Understandably concerned about the fate of *Ducdame*, John asked Alyse to phone Doubleday while he was in South Carolina. She spoke to Russell Doubleday, who reported that he was confident they would accept it. Powys was back in New York by July 18, and, to much relief, Lulu returned safely from his expedition the following day. What happened next is comical, ludicrous, and totally characteristic of the way Powys consistently mishandled his professional career. Two days after Llewelyn returned, the publisher wrote John about *Ducdame*. The letter, which he quoted to Phyllis in full, was a cautious acceptance, but Powys read it as "a polite, civil, tactful, roundabout, refusal of the book." He asked Llewelyn to go with him to retrieve the manuscript. Despite his knowledge of Alyse's business acumen and experience with publishers as managing editor of the *Dial*, apparently it did not occur to him to ask her to accompany them. Both Llewelyn and John were convinced they had inherited their "Powys caution" from their father, who, according to his eldest son, always sat on his financial documents when he visited the bank manager. In fact, the father had the greatest craft in business affairs—a trait not shared by either of these brothers.

Off they went, John in his winter overcoat despite the heat of a New York July, and Llewelyn still in his expedition gear. On the way, Lulu was mistaken for a tramp.

> 22 July 1924: We were waiting on 33rd St for our train (for an hour) and Lulu was sitting on the pavement under a wall and I was walking up and down when I saw a woman looking so oddly at me & I took her for a whore and looked away and came back to Lulu—and he said she had taken him for a beggar or a tramp and he showed me a nickel wh she had

given him. . . . It was Lulu's battered straw hat and old clothes & his sitting on a newspaper on the pavement that made her do it—oh and his beard too!

With their characteristic Powysian sang-froid snobbishness, they arrived at the Garden City station and were taken to lunch by two men John described to Phyllis as "subordinates of some sort." These individuals escorted them back to the train after lunch and were "very unwilling to let us take the manuscript away." It was not until they got home that they wondered if there might have been some "misunderstanding." The next day he received a second letter: "We wrote that we would like to publish *Ducdame* so I do not quite understand—" Powys was "simply puzzled by it all," but eventually the manuscript went back to Doubleday, which published the novel the following spring. He ended the long letter to Phyllis with, "And do you know, Jill, one of those Employees as Lulu & I thought them, or superior clerks, turns out to have been Mr. Frank Doubleday, the head of the firm."[119]

The proposed trip to England became the focus of serious conflict between John and Phyllis. She thought such a long separation was "madness," and he wrote anxiously to her "Jill, we won't have anything ever again 'between us' will we? However selfish and exploiting and Powysian Jack is—or however restless and rebellious and longing for 'Extras' thin Jill is?" The "extras" she longed for were modest enough—money for "vanishing cream," cigarettes, some badly needed shoes. In the meantime, the fare to England cost him $326 with Cooks. Arnold managed to get him a summer school job in South Carolina which covered some of the price, but he had sent Phyllis off with no money at all, and her parents were by this period themselves living in straightened circumstances. He forwarded her some of his old manuscripts to sell to Haldeman-Julius for fifty dollars, so she could feel "at ease and independent."[120] She managed to get twice as much for the manuscripts but she sent it all to Jack because he needed the money for the remaining fare and expenses during his two-month stay in England. Totally broke, she agreed to do a French translation for Haldeman for an advance of thirty dollars and responded with "black fury" when John suggested he grudged her doing this kind of work when she should be working on what he called her "novelette." She was equally upset when he told her that if he did not get the permit, he would have to stay in England and resume lecturing for Oxford and Cambridge Extension. He felt aggrieved that his friends and relatives were not doing more to help him get the permit since "it is my happiness; it is my fate that is at stake!"[121] He seemed totally unaware that the whole sorry business had been created by his own determination to visit England.

Once at Burpham, he had to face the full implications of Harry Lyon's long influence on his son. Littleton Alfred was now apprenticing in his uncle's London architectural firm, had been made his heir, and was living with Harry. The son did not come home until a week after John arrived, and then Uncle Harry was with him. Powys confided to Phyllis, "Certainly Harry Lyon clings as pathetically to my son as the author of 'animula vagula blandula' did to Antinous! But I trust the issues will be different."[122] Powys tactfully omitted the second line, "hospes comesque cororis,"—"My body's comrade and its guest."

In September, he went to Dorset to visit brother Theodore and his sisters Gertrude and Katie. At loose ends after her return from America, Katie decided she wanted to live near Theodore and found an isolated cottage on the downs a mile and a half from Chaldon. The family decided that Katie could not possibly manage to live by herself, and Gertrude, who had been studying and painting in Paris since the death of her father, was summoned to live with and look after her sister. They had been there only four months when John came to stay with them at "Chydyok," as their cottage was called. To Phyllis he describes this magical, marooned place.

> 11 Sept 1924: The view from this window stretches away down the steep valleys with a winding grassy road (no other approach except across the down-turf) disappearing & re-appearing over one crest of a ridge & then over another & right above them all (over the very top of the Five Maries) you can see the expanse of Egdon Heath. Three minutes walk up the hill southward you can see the whole stretch of the sea-cliffs with the isle of Portland & Chesil Beach on the extreme right & St. Alban's head and the Isle of Purbeck on the extreme [left] and precipitous chalk-cliffs with seagulls and cormorants & guillemots whirling round the edges—"ragged gusts of wings blown from off the beaked promontories." Yesterday night with the moonlight on the water & the great flickering light-house on the Portland Bill, and the wind whistling thro' the bracken, Gertrude & I had a walk together but we came upon a field where there was an animal Gertrude thought was a Bull—the famous "Blue Bull of Wool" come to life—and retreated and then met a tramp; a tinker—grey bearded & with rain-soaked shoes to whom we gave eighteen pence & directed him to Lulworth Cove wh I hope he reached safely. How the wind does howl round this hut. Lucy was frightened & says she will never come here again. She said she heard a voice all night on the wind calling "Gertrude! Gertrude! Gertrude!" Gertrude has just been out to pick onions in this wind-blown garden where the clothes on the clothes-line flap like a schooner's sails!

Littleton, Bertie, and Lucy also took the opportunity to see the sisters' new home and to visit with their eldest brother. It was a regular Powys clan gathering, with all the attendant tensions. By this time Chatto had published two of Theodore's novels, three of his novellas, and were preparing to publish two more novels in 1925. Although his success as a writer had given him some reassurance and a certain financial ease, it was obvious that this brother, as always, had to be handled carefully. The rest of the family made sure that Theodore saw only positive reviews of his books, but Bertie, incapable of such tact, immediately infuriated Theodore by defending a critical review that appeared in J.C. Squire's

London Mercury. "Theodore will take years to quite forgive that!" It is possible that John did not fully comprehend the source of anger on both sides. Bertie, now the highly respected secretary of the Society for the Protection of Ancient Buildings, had a regular architectural column in the *Mercury.* He was intensely loyal both to Squire and to the literary editor, J. B. Priestley. Priestley had panned both *The Left Leg* and *Mark Only,* calling the characters in Theodore's novels "creatures somewhere between human beings and horrible and obscene little clockwork dolls."[123]

However, it was the friction between Theodore and Katie, the family scape-goats, that was most troubling to Jack. Katie seems to have worshipped all her brothers, and she was delighted to be living within easy distance of Theodore, but Theodore had written to their friend Bernie O'Neill that he was "afraid of Katie." John reported worriedly to Phyllis that "Theodore was ready to be angry with Katie as if with an ordinary person who ought to know better . . . but Theodore is always a little 'funny' and scarcely within the scope of blame any more than Katie herself."[124] Katie had sent John a manuscript of a story she called "The Tragedy of Budvale" and he thought it an "amazing production." The whole family encouraged her to write, possibly as a kind of therapy. The only exception was Theodore, who forbad Katie "not so much as even mention her writings!"

It was left to Gertrude to attempt to keep the peace in this new situation. She was a remarkable woman. She cooked, cleaned, gardened, kept bees. She somehow even found time to do a little painting, and John was struck by "a lit-tle painting of my father in his extreme old age drinking a cup of tea with both hands which has the story of Gertrude's life in its mixture of tenderness and unconquerable gaiety." She had, he said, a large calmness that extended itself to everyone "like the touch of a healing 'goddess of the infant world.'" Even Theodore could not keep "a hidden anger against her."[125] Katie was always unpre-dictable and, as Bertie put it in a typical Powysian understatement, "inclined to a frolic of rage at times if the jam is not properly at half past four upon the table,"[126] but apparently Gertrude could keep Katie calm as no one else could. Katie's gratitude to her sister was expressed in a handwritten poem which was found in her diary of the war years, a few lines of which are: "Though like a rest-less bird / I fly from field to field / You stand the same / A living tree / Upon whose branches / I may hide." "Goddess of the Infant World" was a fair descrip-tion of Gertrude's destined role as protector, not just of Katie and Theodore, but of all these Powys siblings who never grew up.

John returned to New York just in time to attend the wedding of Alyse and Llewelyn on the thirtieth of September. The sudden marriage appeared to be purely a matter of convenience, since Llewelyn had no intention of giving up his extramarital affairs and marriage was against Alyse's deep-seated feminist princi-ples. John suspected that the fact that Alyse "in the depths of her heart doesn't always feel opposed to it only teases & provokes her the more."[127] A few months earlier Llewelyn had a hemorrhage, indicating that the tuberculosis had returned after a three-year remission. After the wedding, they rented an isolated farm-house in Vermont so that Llewelyn could continue his recuperation.[128] This meant Alyse had to travel three hours by train each way to her New York office and Llewelyn urged her to give up her position at the *Dial*. She was loath to do so; it was her badge of independence. However, she worried constantly about Llewelyn and was grateful that John stayed for ten days with him after the wedding. During that time together, the brothers discussed Jack's finances, his future as a lecturer, and his living arrangements. He reported these conversations at length to Phyllis, seemingly without realizing their effect on her, still more than 1,500 miles away with her parents.

When Powys arrived back in America, he had no money to bring Phyllis back from Kansas. Feeling that John would "act more wisely" if Phyllis were with him, Llewelyn offered to lend him $100 and insisted that they should live in Alyse's furnished Patchin Place flat. John accepted Llewelyn's offer before consulting Phyllis, but, vaguely aware that he was on thin ice, he asked her pardon "for all the unknown 'bricks' I have dropped." Several letters later, he was assuring her that he would soon get some decent lectures and all would be well. "After all, it is not so very much to have to raise $30 a week for England & $20 for ourselves. If it weren't for England we would be in no anxiety at all—but there it is." He ends the letter with: "I beg you Abject of my Soul not to let the least thinnest wedge of Grievance enter your dear mind about that proportion of $30 to $20!"[129] Considering he had not had a letter from her since his return, he must have known that something was amiss, but when she finally wrote a "grievance letter" on the ninth of October, he was "staggered—bewildered—hit in the face." "Now let me think what it could be. That you didn't want us to be in Patchin Place?" He asks her not to "for God's sake get into that awful mood about my family." Then he gets angry: "If my letters were blundering ones at least they came to you—one after another—every day. But you remained silent. . . . Well, I've always said I didn't fully understand you didn't I? & I've tended rather to glory in such mystery haven't I? But by the gods this goes a little too far!"[130] He ends this twenty-seven-page letter with an outpouring of love and ink splashed every-where. By the twelfth of October, he had calmed down a little, and tried to reassure her in a letter that, uncharacteristically, was confined to financial matters. He told her he had eighty-five dollars in hand and he would send the money for her fare and wished he had done it on Saturday—only he had forgotten and Monday was Columbus Day and everything was shut. He explained that because he still owed Alyse sixty dollars and another thirty for the month's rent, he didn't want to borrow the hundred from Lulu, and Marian was being "hard & marbly." However, he assured her he had managed to get five "Briefer Mentions" from the *Tribune* to review, and that "I've got my most competent and iron vein upon me—fighting for my Jill."

With such a letter of incompetence and reassurance, she would have found it hard not to return to him, and she wrote apologizing and suggesting she find a job. He refused to allow this, saying he wanted her to help him write some short articles and proofread *Ducdame*. By November he was writing Lulu happily that "we play Chess o'nights and it is like C. F. P. and M. C. P. playing chess as anything you can imagine." By now, Powys had convinced himself that Phyllis bore a striking physical resemblance to his mother, with her oval face, deep-set brown eyes, her wide brow, and her long brown hair. Presumably he saw himself as his father. Such a méconnaissance had implications for their future life.

Powys had ascribed her sense of grievance solely to the question of living quarters, but it is more likely that what had upset her was a combination of things: his leaving her to go to England for two months, the long letters about Alyse's feelings about marriage when Phyllis was only too aware of her mistress status, his overly generous payments to an already financially comfortable wife and son, and not least, the unceasing anxiety about their own poverty. Of even more concern to her would have been the fact that once again he was negotiating a change of agent. After his calamitous experience with the California manager Jessica Colbert, he went back—again—to Arnold Shaw, but when, on his return from England, he found that Arnold had arranged only two lectures for the remainder of the year, he decided that he must be "firm and drastic"[131] and find a new manager. He interviewed four different agents, hoping to find one who would also employ the destitute Arnold to whom he felt loyalty and guilt in equal measure. In several rambling letters to relatives and to Phyllis he outlined other considerations, all of which were crucial to his professional and personal life: which agent had the most prestigious client lists which would get him the most work, who paid expenses, length of tours, etc. The Pond Agency, suggested by Marian, made by far the best offer, but John took a dislike to the owner. He ended up signing a contract with the Lee Keedick Bureau, some years later ascribing this decision to "an exaggerated worldliness of a queer snobbish bourgeois kind."[132] Actually it was Llewelyn who convinced him to go to Keedick, and this before Phyllis had been consulted. It was a disastrous decision in all respects. He signed a "50/50" contract. It is always possible that Powys thought that this was the same deal that Pond had offered. Pond agreed to pay all expenses himself and split the lecture fee equally, but Keedick, as it turned out, meant Powys divided *everything* 50/50, including all his advertising, hotel, and travel costs. Out of a $100 lecture fee, by the time he had paid his share of expenses John Cowper often netted no more than $27.50, compared to the $50 he would have received from Pond. It took him some months to work this out, and he complained that he could not understand why he was lecturing more but making less than ever before.[133] It was too late by then. He had already signed, not the two-year contract he was seeking, but a *five-year* contract with Keedick *and* found himself on far-flung tours that took him away for months on end. When Keedick suggested that Powys also give him ten percent of any earnings he made on his books, Marian was "fiercely opposed" and told him that "it is only just weakness and once more being exploited by a manager as I've always been before."[134] Keedick himself was "surprised and pleased"[135] when Powys agreed to do so, again at Llewelyn's urging.

When Phyllis returned to New York on October 18, they moved into 4 Patchin Place. Patchin Place was—is still—a short cul-de-sac off West Tenth Street in Greenwich Village. The alley, enclosed by a tall iron gate, is lined with small Georgian houses divided into flats, and was then overlooked by a jail.[136] Their apartment consisted of one room and an alcove, with a toilet and sink two flights below. He remained confident that he would be able to give her "a lovely thrilling beautiful and happy existence!"[137] What she thought is a mystery. She had lived with him for a year and, intelligent woman as she was, must have known him by then fairly thoroughly. But what were the alternatives? She was thirty years old and unlikely to meet someone else if she remained living with her elderly parents in small-town Joplin, Kansas. Besides, whatever Powys gave her she apparently needed, just as he needed her. As he put it, their "universes of discourse" coincided.[138] More prosaically, their fantasy lives coincided. He felt that it was his destiny to "heal" her: "it's such a funny feeling, Jill—it's a wish to be bruised & beaten and endure aridness & desolation, instead of thin Jill. It's the oddest feeling—it's as if all you'd gone through was gone through for me and that nothing I could do could make it up!"[139] As touching as the sentiment is, it is difficult to know who is saving whom here. It became still more difficult to know as the years passed.

CHAPTER EIGHT

THE LONE WOLF

1925-1930

I N SIGNING UP WITH THE LEE KEEDICK BUREAU, POWYS'S LECTURING CAREER entered a new and disappointing phase. "The King of all Managers" only dealt with his first string of lecturers, so it was his booking clerk, Mr. Glass, who made all the arrangements for Powys's tours. Glass's itineraries had him traveling long distances by rail between lecture stops and were so badly structured that he would find himself crisscrossing states several times in a tour. The Bureau soon discovered that Powys was hopeless with money, and instituted a procedure that left him baffled, humiliated, and out-of-pocket. All the fees went directly to the agent's office, which would give John an advance for expenses before he began a tour. The advance was invariably too little, and he dreaded having to wire for more. He always felt, he said, like Oliver Twist and Glass like "Mr Bumble with the porridge." After days of agitation and vacillation, he would send the wire, the money would be sent, and then the check could not be cashed unless "some upstanding citizen of the town" accompanied him to vouch for him. Not until the end of a long tour was Powys paid, and then only after he sent in an itemized list of his expenses. Since he often forgot to write down an expenditure, he cheated himself abominably. Furthermore, he was getting much less than under his previous agents—an average of $100 a lecture, compared to Keedick's imported lecturers, such as G. K. Chesterton, who would receive up to $1,000.

Powys's first tour under the new auspices was a month long and he lectured, mainly to "ladies clubs," in Illinois, Indiana, Louisiana, Florida, Tennessee, and Virginia. When he returned to New York on March 12, 1925, the news greeted him that Llewelyn had decided to return to England to live. This was so unexpected that John could not "bring it home to my realising consciousness."[1] It is difficult to know when Llewelyn made this decision. He had written an old friend, Rivers Pollock, on the thirteenth of February that he intended to stay in the U.S. another year, but less than a month later he wrote his sister Gertrude that he and Alyse would sail the end of April. He asked her to send him information about houses to let near Chaldon and instructed her to make sure his share of the furniture from the father's estate was kept safe. "I want *everything* I can lay my hands on. . . . Let some of Theodore's share come my way. He won't notice." He added, "It's disgraceful of me to have persuaded Alyse to give up the *Dial* but *I want to come home*."[2] Gertrude found them a coastguard cottage over-looking the White Nothe—a thirty-minute walk from her and Katie at Chydyok and Theodore and his wife at East Chaldon. John thought it was "most lovely and single-hearted of Alyse to chuck her native-land and follow Master Llewelyn."[3]

During the second tour of 1925 he finally achieved his ambition of lecturing at universities, but they were not exactly Cambridge. His week at Norman, Oklahoma, was fairly typical of the summer schools he would lecture at for the next few years. The campus consisted of "absolutely new buildings in a burnt-up bit of sort of prairie-grass with a few beds of petunias." He found the town "a regular little Main St." and confessed that getting acquainted with "real rustic western America" was a little alarming. "I've never felt quite so far away from the old world as I do here. No one seems to understand what I say nor do I understand what they say."[4] He had begun a new novel but lack of privacy and the overpowering heat made it impossible to do any writing. However, he was always immensely generous with his time when the young male students would come up to him after a lecture "dumb, nervous & silent." These were the thirsting youngsters who craved the cultured life his lectures so vividly communicated and who would soon be further parched by the prairie dust-storms and the depression of the thirties. "The look in the eyes of Mr Owsley of the Kentucky Mountains is what most of all I shall convey away from here. Like an infinitely sad faun who has had a glimpse of some dryad who can never be found again."[5] He went directly from Norman to the Agricultural and Mechanical College at Stillwater, Oklahoma. He was surprised to be given a carte blanche on any subject; the only drawback was that at the end of his lecture he had to listen "to a long discourse from the President on breeding cattle!" "The Dean of Arts & Sciences who always introduced me had never heard of Pater. He called him Paton & he had to learn syllable by syllable to say Dost—oy—ev—sky."[6] He returned briefly to New York and then did another southern tour from November 14 to December 17, covering Virginia, South Carolina, Tennessee, Louisiana, Texas, Arkansas, ending in New Orleans. He had a long wait-over in New Orleans but when he finally did give his lecture, it was to a huge audience and some of the old magnetism, dissipated by weariness and poverty, came back: "I felt tossed on an extraordinary wave of power, as if I could say anything & do anything with those people. . . . I am like one who has been sent to utter an oracle."[7]

His letters to Phyllis, always one a day when he was on tour, he compared to the "descriptive letters" he once wrote to Montacute—"as my mother can hear no more." Yet Montacute vicarage never had such letters. His adventures, his reactions, his miseries are conveyed in a vivid prose which increasingly shows his mastery of the imagery that would give his novels much of their intricate beauty: "The minds of southerners differ from the minds of middle-westerners in the kind of stupidity simplicity & ignorance which they have, so weighed upon by the forces of Nature as to form little angry touchy round pellets of emotionalism, like the hard dung of so many un-stuffed owls, lying among dead leaves where the tree-trunks obstruct the winds."[8] With Phyllis he could drop his propitiating mask and reveal "this wicked malicious touchy crazy angry loneliness of mine & so much pride & hate—& hate—hate!"[9] But along with the lists and schedules and worries about finances, the pages were filled with his love for her. He was constantly reassuring her that it will be "all right." "That we have met & loved each other—that is the thing. All the rest is the price paid."[10]

Both paid the price. He wrote to her from New Orleans on her thirty-first birthday. "I have now come to lean on you so. You have put the thin body of the Abject between me & the troubles of life so that when you are not there I feel so lost."[11] He in turn protects her, although from what is never very clear. He has, however, by this time the abiding image of himself as "the wise, the enduring Centaur Chiron who goes trampling on with the little Thin holding tight to his back!"[12] This image of himself as Chiron encompasses many meanings, astrological, mythological, and sexual. The half-animal, half-human Chiron was accidentally wounded in the knee by one of the poisoned arrows of Hercules. With his great knowledge of healing, he knew that the wound was incurable and that being immortal he could only suffer but not die. Prometheus offered to take upon himself Chiron's immortality, and the Centaur was transformed into the constellation Sagittarius. It was probably after he returned to New York in the previous spring with a wounded knee of his own that Powys first made the connection. Nor would he have missed the tradition that the bow of Sagittarius is a symbol of the phallus, emblem of animal and godlike power. Thus, in a lonely hotel room, the fantasy of making love to her, "makes a centaur feel little electric shocks in his spine and in the hand which holds the great Sagittarian Bow."[13]

Phyllis's "quite abnormal" sensitivity, her mood swings, her angers, her depression must have been the price *he* paid. Her rages, because they seemed to him to be childlike, he encouraged.[14] It was when she began to show signs of growing up that he felt panic. Despite his conviction that she did not like big cities, she exulted in New York. When she had any money at all, she went to the theatre and concerts. But in letter after letter at this time he urged her not to go out at night and to "be careful crossing the streets. It wd be so serious for you to be tossed down & up & away—like a feuille de ça de là—from the wheels of a great dray or truck."[15] It is difficult to know whether he was aware of the extraordinary violence his worries display here, or whether his many references to beating her was merely a shared fantasy. Both of them had deep wells of suppressed rage. The letters often startle with their singular evocations of childhood, memories, love, and sadism, all intermixed. As the last tour of 1925 ends, he says he has "that same excited feeling I used to have on the last day of the term at Sherborne. Just the same kind of trembling excitement & a dim vague delicious sort of sense of frozen roads & lit up candles and mud & holly-bushes & signposts! . . . Oh Thin when I think of various aspects of your character & of your ways & various looks, gestures, words, expressions, I could just kill you I love you so—beat you to death with my big great heavy stick crying out I love you! I love you! I love you!"[16]

The winter of 1926 was bitterly cold, and their only heating in Patchin Place was an open fire. The coal man's "inordinate charges," which amounted to as much as the rent, meant that while Powys was on tour from January 12 to February 21, Phyllis had to resort to tearing up strips of newspaper for fuel. Despite their poverty, Powys was determined to make his customary trip to England. Phyllis returned to her parents and remained with them until August. He was in England by early April and, as usual, he was caught between his loyalty to his son and wife, and the demands of his brothers and sisters. Llewelyn was anxious that his brother see them in their new setting, but John went first to Burpham. Lulu was furious and wrote John that he should not treat his family as if they were still children at Montacute, taking them "for kind little walks in turn."[17] John answered that all he cared about was keeping people happy and avoiding violent and agitating scenes. In any case, he was anxious to see his son, who in 1925 had decided to abandon architecture and become an Anglican priest. Powys was glad of this, "for all manner of reasons," as he put it cryptically. On this trip, however, he began to accept that while it was "lovely" to be with his son, "it is all kind of outward & external to me—like an outer dream going on over an inner dream."[18] He admitted to Phyllis that she had been right when she had "burst out with your grand grievance of my going to England." To take off almost three months from lecturing was not only personal folly but financial madness.

When he returned to New York, he was again heavily in debt and without work. If Will Durant had not given him three lectures at the Labor Temple in October, they would have been hard put to it.[19] Phyllis tried unsuccessfully to get a job waitressing at Childs, and when Alyse suggested that she ought to take a more intellectual or executive job, John replied that "she dreads that kind of mental responsibility." Once again, because we see Phyllis only as she is filtered through Powys's letters, it is difficult to know if this is true or whether something else is going on. The "self-disparagement" myth of Phyllis was part of his fantasy of her as a princess in a secret room.

> When you disparage yourself in this insane way I get so happy (it's scandalous) just as if I had invented some spell to make you do it like a circle round you of crazy self-disparagement to keep all the world from seeing you or noticing you like one of these "clouds" that the gods throw round their "pet animals" to hide them.[20]

It was an odd state of affairs. He was becoming ever more dependent on Phyllis to manage his everyday life, but vaguely aware that his fantasies made it more difficult for her to act in the way he demanded. "It's a shame a little girl-child like you born for imagination & a lovely passive life, by well-sides! to have to be clung to so tight & heavily by a necessitous & helpless & incompetent bug-ger & hulker like me! . . . You have to be such a lot of things Thin."[21]

As they found themselves increasingly in debt, Powys began writing short articles and reviews—something that constitutionally he was ill-suited to doing and which paid little. Having to give Keedick ten percent of the fee made the exercise even more pointless. However, it was all that kept them afloat. Marianne Moore, Alyse's successor at the *Dial*, gave him a number of reviews which, at thirty dollars each, at least paid the rent. He wrote articles on Emerson and Longfellow which Phyllis typed and sent to various journals, but they were rejected as too long. In desperation, he turned again to Haldeman-Julius, who took the Longfellow article and paid $300. Although Phyllis was reluctant "to give the rogue any such goods for his whirling printing presses," Powys decided they had to "keep in touch with this not exactly fabulous but still very timely oil-mine."[22] He relied on Phyllis to comment on each piece he wrote, and increasingly he also used her experience and skill in editing; as he wrote each essay and review, she would condense it and copyedit it. Clearly they were trying to write articles that would boost his lecturing engagements. In February 1927 he wrote an article on "Oklahoma and its scenery and its inhabitants," and when it was accepted by H. L. Mencken, he wrote buoyantly to Littleton, "I shall certainly be invited to lecture at the University of Oklahoma this summer." It was published as "Elusive America" in the *American Mercury*, and he praised Phyllis's revisions and additions. "Your imagination & critical power just seems made to add the right touches & cut out the lapses of your lover's work."

In January 1927, Phyllis's eighty-six-year-old father became critically ill with pneumonia. Her parents now lived in a small flat in Joplin during the winter. Returning to a place she hated, to help nurse an ill and depressed father in cramped quarters, soon left her "beset by misery." John's responses must have confused her. He would insist "if there was any danger of your coming even towards the margin of that terrible 'unhappiness' it would be a wicked thing to stay [in Joplin]," then in another letter he would give reasons why it was impossible to return—she must think of her mother, she would feel remorseful if she returned and her father died, he is embarrassed to ask Glass for the money necessary to send her a ticket to come back, and so on. He would recount in the greatest detail everything that was certain to worry her, while imploring her not to get nervous: "you are not a strong human-being for this harsh-scraping world—so do take care—& here you are acting so Henry-James like; & everything." He seemed to have a deep need to perceive her as weak and nervous even while he faintly recognized that in her Jamesian way she coped. And did so for the rest of their lives in appalling circumstances.

All the while he was writing worried letters imploring her not to have the kind of breakdown she had in her early twenties, he was writing to her about sending more money to his wife. By January 1927, in default of any lectures, Keedick was giving him fifty dollars a week as a kind of "salary." Powys always sent two-thirds of this to his wife. Then came the cheering news from Margaret that she intended to let Burpham and live with her son when he was ordained and obtain a curacy in June.[23] Powys was jubilant and wrote Phyllis that eventually he might be able to reduce his payments from six pounds to five pounds a week "if in our strange complicated non-moral circumambient manner we felt we were being unfair to the Abject beyond that subtle little dot on the barometer wh. is so difficult to see!" Even Powys with his poor eyesight should have seen that the barometer would move to stormy at this remark, but he was "bewildered" and "startled" by her response that he was being "unfair" to her.[24] In a late novel Powys has the hero say, "I am amazed at the amount of 'stupid being' as that American lady in Paris calls it, with which man's self-complacency muffles his natural mother-wit."[25] John was constantly asking Phyllis not to have a "grievance" and begging her to forgive him if he says something wrong, but in some region of his "stupid being" he surely knew what he was doing. In mid-February 1927, he was trying to get himself organized for a long tour without her help. He assured her that he can deal with all the necessary arrangements and then in letter after letter related in detail a series of incidents which illustrate how totally incapable he was of managing anything: He accidentally cut off a sleeve from a fur coat Mr. Playter sent him to combat the intense cold in their flat; he hopes she will not "collapse" when she sees that he has done nothing to the room in six weeks, "not even washed the dishes or swept," and the sheets are "black as coal"; he goes to the office to get an advance for travel expenses, then loses the cheque and has to get it reissued; the advance makes him feel "bloatedly rich" and when she writes to remind him of their debts, he admits, "Proportion in anything but especially in money seems to be peculiarly hard to me. But you'll see! I'll get it by degrees."[26] After many letters to and fro, they decided she should stay on in Joplin until he returned to New York after his tour at the end of March. They had only five months together in 1926, and 1927 was shaping up to be another long exile.

Then came another crisis, which, despite its seriousness, had its amusing aspects. He wrote Littleton about it: "Arnold Shaw has now been put into the State Lunatic Asylum of Maryland because he bought automobiles by the dozen, pinned all his ties to his window-blind, tried to throw a lady out of a window, and finally walked into the street in his night-clothes and a cricket blazer of his old school days."[27] He admitted to Phyllis that he was "naturally inclined to understand his desire to throw Mrs. Sullivan [Shaw's mother-in-law] out of the window," but he was sincerely concerned about his old friend, his wife, and their newborn child. Inevitably Arnold's incarceration in an insane asylum reminded him of his sister's. "Katie was in just such a place like this & after six months she was cured, or cured enough to come out. People are, tho' one wouldn't suppose it."[28]

Worried about the fate of Arnold, his own prospects also increasingly distressed him. He wrote to brother Theodore "the American public is tired of my voice."[29] It was not really that so much as the times; by the mid-1920s, advancements in film and radio provided new alternatives for cultural enrichment and entertainment, and circuit managers encountered increasing difficulties in getting bookings for lecture tours. It was the disastrous decline in income that caused him the most anguish. Under Shaw's management he used to take home clear £1,000—£800 for Margaret and £200 for himself—with expenses in the region of £600.[30] By the end of 1926 his total income had dropped from £1,600 to less than £600. Although occasionally he still drew large crowds in the bigger cities, by 1927 his audiences were increasingly of the small-town variety, and he was often reduced to giving commencement addresses at undergraduate ceremonies. However, when he did encounter an appreciative audience, he could still excite them and the breadth of his knowledge and the flexibility of his lecturing skills remained remarkable. On one occasion Glass gave him the wrong subject to lecture on, so "in the middle of my lecture one of the young men came up to me on the platform stopped me to explain that I was to lecture on something else! Well! I gave them really the two lectures in one & they seemed quite pleased & satisfied & all went well after that small contretemps!"[31]

Something that does not come across so clearly in his novels as in his letters to Phyllis is his sense of humor. Amidst the details of his financial and lecturing woes, his lovemaking and his "bricks," are the vignettes of the places he ends up in and the people he meets. Wherever he went, he would walk before a lecture and usually see something that appealed to his sense of the ludicrous: "I stopped by the Mortuary where there are wonderful Petunia-beds & written over the door 'Walk In.'"[32] When teaching summer school at the nascent University of Oklahoma, to save money he stayed at Mrs. Davis's boarding house. "Mrs. Davis is a nice old lady whose husband (now with God) used to be the night watchman of a Lunatic Asylum. This fact has fitted her to let rooms to teachers of the University."[33] His descriptions of "the funny ones" as he called them, were always tender and often compassionate. Lecturing to a group of young men in a small college in Atlanta, Georgia, "their stern earnest Lacedaemonan silence & attention made me feel terribly responsible." "The more literary ones came on the platform afterwards & stayed there dumb & nervous & silent as if I had been really the Centaur Chiron, & they were young Myrmidons, who didn't know what to do or to say, until their chief Achilles came. In this case he never did come!"

He seemed unaware that his eccentricities aroused wonder, if not suspicion, in small southern towns, reporting to Phyllis, "Two little white girls I passed yesterday almost fell down off their porch, such were their convulsions of laughter as I passed by. What aspect of my appearance excites this laughter I can't say." He particularly disliked smart young hotel desk clerks, with whom he had to deal daily, and wished when they asked "what name" he could say that he had forgotten for the moment, but suspected if he had he would have "ended in the Memphis Lock-Up." On the other hand, his humor is affectionate when he encounters "the feeble pulse of Kentucky."

The bookseller I called on, Mr. Garvin, conveyed me across the square to call on the Insurance man, Mr. Herdman, and . . . it was like sitting round a Franklin stove in Lincoln's time only they were all so very frail & shaky & nervous. . . . Then there was a Captain Cover a venerable but very proud old gentleman who as far as I could gather had formerly been an engine driver. . . . How Mr. Garvin ever sells a book I can't think or Mr. Herdman ever insures anyone or Captain Cover ever conceivably got a locomotive to even start—I cannot think! I visited the local cemetery and found crowds and crowds of infants' graves. . . . The moss was certainly of Vergilian softness under the old Maples there but really the pulse of this little place is so feeble that to lie in that moss can be no very great change.[34]

As time passed, he felt increasingly that the Keedick Bureau treated him "as if I were the Circus Elephant going to stop at some corner for buns."[35] He admitted that the disconcerting way in which he veered from "sheepish propitiation" to "serpent's malice" made it difficult for the Bureau. "I suppose I have, by long suppression, acquired a reserve store of almost insane & savage maliciousness that a certain <u>look</u> from a type especially hostile to my type is liable to tap with alarming results." He lost badly an important debate on morality with a certain Dr. Bridges, a man he particularly disliked, before an unusually large audience of two thousand and the next day the papers accused him of "not having given a thought" to this debate. Although he privately admitted to Phyllis that this was true, he was seething with anger and his response was to give a lecture the next day to an unsuspecting religious women's club where he launched into "a crazy-crazy defence of Proust's 'Sodom & Gomorrah'." He called this malice dance his "art of 'indirect reaction.'" It was an art that by this time he had perfected.

Looking on the bright side of a dismal start to 1927, Powys wrote to Frances that he had had a hard winter financially, but the absence of lectures meant he could write "my huge book which has now reached 1250 MSS pages."[36] He still did not have a publisher for this novel, but later that month, he had a public debate in Chicago with Will Durant. Simon and Schuster had published Durant's book, The Story of Philosophy, in May 1926, and rather unexpectedly had made Durant "a small fortune." Durant spoke to his publishers, and by the end of March, Simon and Schuster had written Powys several times "eager to know how my novel is progressing." Llewelyn wanted him to use Doubleday again but he wanted "more daring & less conservative publishers and ones that wd advertise." He decided, as he put it to Littleton, that he would "go to the Jews" with this book.[37]

However, the novel was by no means finished and his living was dependent on lecturing. In the summer of 1927 he was in Las Vegas, New Mexico, for six weeks. There are twenty-five letters to Phyllis for this period. It is an important run because it gives more clearly than ever before what his lecturing career had descended to, the kind of audiences he encountered, the humiliations he endured, as well as his honest opinion of the people he met, rather than the published propitiations of *Autobiography*. This was a job he got himself. Through friends in Chicago he met a Mrs. Bacon who had been hired by the Las Vegas Chamber of Commerce to create a new Chautauqua there. He soon discovered that it was the Santa Fe Railway bankrolling "this Chautauqua & its development into a "'Fiesta del Artists,'" and that it was not going to be the kind of Chautauqua he had known. He was initially flattered. "I've been brought here as a 'star lecturer' to throw a sort of high-brow atmosphere over the whole thing." Then he was told that he was expected to participate in the "cultural activities."[38]

> O dear! to propitiate Mrs. Bacon I went to hear Mrs. Cocke of Dallas give a dramatic recital in her own words of a novel called "If I were King". . . . This audience was of good size in fact all Las Vegas turned out & were spell bound. There was, to me, something weirdly affecting about it because Mrs. Cocke "arrayed or rather disarrayed" in shimmery filmy attire was at least as stout as Mrs. Binderin. . . . I praised her performance as extraordinary & it really <u>was</u> extraordinary. . . . The other "stars" are mostly musicians of various kinds. You should have seen Mrs. Bacon and me sitting together last night while the man from the coast taught us how to sing "There's a long long trail" and "America the Beautiful" etc etc all of us holding great sheets of songs and being encouraged to believe that in these exercises of the community spirit the culture of the South West wd be attained and that the spirit of unison etc etc adapted to these beautiful hills etc etc.

Worse was to come. After giving two lectures he was told he would not have any more for three weeks, and he realized "it's not for the lectures that they want me. It's just to have this particular kind of Barnum animal in a cage."[39] He disliked the "sort of bubbling gay-sentimental chirruping, like a million drunken sparrows, drunk on elderberry wine" of southern women, but he found Mrs. Bacon worse.

> O I am accumulating such anger at these humiliations. And really Mrs. Bacon is the limit. . . . I referred to that great green wood-pecker that we call "the Yaffle" to Mr. Dixon and now whenever I see the woman on the streets she bends her head about and cries aloud "here comes my yaffle—I call him my Yaffle!" and takes my arm—think of poor crusty Mr. Powys, in his harried hunted old age, becoming Mrs. Bacon's Yaffle! But what can a person do? . . . I can't be rude or uncivil to the woman when I've got to last it out—and she knows that well enough the bitch!

What seems to have agitated him most was that he could not escape. "The whole of this visit I've had to deal with people every day and with the same ones over & over. This is a new thing for me. Generally in my occupation I give my lectures & sheer off—I've always just <u>gone off</u>."[40]

He did not encounter many people this summer who pleased him, but one was Arthur Ficke, whom he had previously met in Chicago and then again in

New York. Ficke and his new wife Gladys were living in Sante Fe and invited him to visit. He found completely "soothing to my mind" Ficke's "peculiar kind of earthy naturalness and benevolent common-sense." He had a carefree few days with them and took photographs of Arthur and Gladys bathing naked: "Happy I was under those fir trees drinking whiskey and watching those two, like Adam & Eve splash about in their waterfall!"[41] He also met a distant cousin he did not know existed, Warwick Gurney Powys, a nephew of the late Lord Lilford. In the next few weeks Phyllis received letter after letter about this man. In some nebulous past, poor cousin Warwick had been wickedly robbed of all his money, books, silver, and even clothes by a pair of Irish villains, the lady of whom having practiced on his "emotions." How Warwick ended up in New Mexico remained unclear, but he was at the time of their meeting a "sort-of gentleman-janitor"[42] on a ranch owned by some Easterner, guarding it from robbers in its owner's absence and "living as solitary as Robinson Crusoe" with a horse called Cuss and a cat called Anxiety. John was immensely drawn to this quaint eccentric because he was, or appeared to John to be, a "Sir Walter Scott character." Above all, his "selfish Powysian sensitiveness" and his "fierce mythological Welsh prince pride" reminded Powys constantly of his father. Phyllis no doubt could see what was happening. Warwick's romantic story of loss, his solitariness, his ancestral pride appealed to one side of John, but he could also fit the man who was like "a very aged wounded heron," into his pariah category. Powys was sure that Phyllis would like him. As it turned out, she loathed him.

Powys and Phyllis had two months together before he had to leave again on another tour of the hated South on the first of November, 1927. Those eight weeks seem to have been particularly chaotic as they had to arrange both for a place to stay for niece Isobel, Bertie's daughter, who arrived in New York September 12, and also to find a room for Alyse and Lulu in Patchin Place. Irita van Doren had asked Llewelyn to be "visiting critic" for the *New York Herald Tribune*. John was away most of the time that Llewelyn and Alyse were in New York but had six weeks with them before he left on another extended tour on April 18. Phyllis waved goodby to Lulu and Alyse and then, on April 22, 1928, she packed up the top copy of his completed novel, *Wolf Solent*, and sent it off to the publisher Simon and Schuster. His previous novels had been written at breakneck speed, but *Wolf Solent* took five years to complete. The sheer need to survive by other means was partly responsible for its long gestation, but it is possible that he did not want it to end. The writing became a necessary escape during those years when Powys was enduring constant financial, professional, and personal humiliations. Gradually his sense of failure had broadened into an all-encompassing guilt and, acute psychologist that he was, Powys knew that if he were not to have another breakdown similar to the one of a decade earlier, he must summon up whatever defences he could find.

In August 1924, making one of his summer visits to England, he walked up the steps of Waterloo Station on his way from London to Burpham. As so often

with Powys, the present is an opening into the past; present afflictions are incorporated into past misery. He would be remembering, as he walked up those twenty-
three steps built of Portland stone—the stone of his beloved Dorset—that it was
precisely ten years before, the fourth of August, 1914, that Britain declared war
on Germany and his mother was buried. The massive steps and triumphal
Victory Arch that formed the new entrance to Waterloo Station were formally
opened on March 21, 1922. Although intended to be a memorial to the war
dead, they were, even more, a symbol of the industrial might of the British
nation. In an ironic twist, the steps soon became a place where beggars, many of
them mentally or physically crippled ex-servicemen, gathered. Powys, himself
beleaguered, and in a sense crippled, would have known immediately that he had
an opening to another story. A few days later he wrote Phyllis that he was "med-
itating on the possibilities of a new novel."[43] He did not begin *Wolf Solent*[44] until
early 1925, but during the following months what he saw that day must have
haunted him.

Wolf Solent is a thirty-five-year-old history teacher who, one January afternoon, suddenly "found himself pouring forth a torrent of wild, indecent invec-
tives upon every aspect of modern civilization." The apparent trigger for this
long-suppressed emotion is "the inert despair upon the face" he had seen on the
steps outside Waterloo Station. "It was just the face of a man . . . against whom
Providence had grown as malignant as a mad dog. And the woe upon the face
was of such a character that Wolf knew at once that no conceivable social read-
justments or ameliorative revolutions could ever atone for it—could even make
up for the simple irremediable fact that it *had* been as it had been!" What "it had
been" remains vague, but for Wolf/John "it" gradually expands from a vision of a
suffering figure to "the monstrous Apparition of Modern Invention," then to an
evil First Cause. Because that face "turned towards him" Wolf cannot evade it.
Nor could Powys. It entered into his "diseased conscience," and out of it came a
magnificent novel about the many faces of "inert despair."

Unusually, not once in the novel does Powys mention the actual year in
which the events are supposed to take place. However, at carefully scattered
points in the story, he gives precise information which allows a curious reader to
work out that the story must begin Thursday, March 3, 1921 and end fifteen
months later, in May 1922. There is no direct reference to the Great War that
ended only three years before, nor is there any indication that Wolf, who would
have been twenty-eight years old when the war began, had seen service. Neither
had Powys, of course. Was this also suddenly back in his mind, another source of
guilt? While the war and its aftermath are never mentioned in the novel, they
are embedded in the metaphors and imagery—the earth is being "steadily assas-
sinated"; the silent lanes "invaded" by the "hard snorting and snarling" of motor
cars; the skies are filled with "aeroplanes spying." Wolf's detestation of all things
mechanical and modern, his immense malice toward a new world that he found
detestable, is the keynote throughout the narrative. The novel is in fact about a

world after that great war—a world in which everything is irrevocably changed. This new reality is not only hated by Wolf, it is almost incomprehensible to him. The question that the novel poses is, with a personality like Wolf's, if you do not escape into madness, or commit suicide, how do you defend yourself? And what do you do when the coping mechanisms fail?

Although the first chapter is entitled "The Face on the Waterloo Steps," after those few striking opening sentences the focus shifts immediately from the anonymous face to the Powys-hero. Up to that point, Wolf has built up more than adequate defences against what he calls "reality." His first defence is to ignore it by escaping into his own imaginative fantasy world. However, the image of the gouged face causes a temporary collapse of what he calls a "mental screen or lid or dam in his own mind," and he suddenly bursts out into a "malice dance" sufficiently serious to warrant his dismissal from his position at a small school in London. Through the influence of Lord Carfaxe, a family connection, he gets a position as a "literary assistant" to the squire of King's Barton in Dorset. Solent was born in nearby Ramsgard (Sherborne), but when he was ten, his father died—"a byword of scandalous depravity" in the local workhouse. In the twenty-five years that follow, Wolf has lived "peacefully under the despotic affection of his mother." Now he is escaping not only *from* the horrors of London, but escaping *to* "the very region where the grand disaster of his mother's life had occurred."[45]

Another "mental device" Wolf resorts to in times of great stress is something he calls his "mythology," his "life-illusion." As he travels to the source of his birth, Wolf goes over and over what he means by his "mythology." This is the belief that he has a "magnetic strength" which he can pit "against the tyrannous machinery invented by other men," which has "scooped and gouged and harrowed," and left the "whole round earth . . . bleeding and victimized" like the face on the steps. He believes that "this secret practise was always accompanied by an arrogant mental idea—the idea namely that he was taking part in some occult cosmic struggle—some struggle between what he liked to think as 'good' and what he liked to think of as 'evil.'" Wolf believes that this "extreme dualism" descends "to the profoundest gulfs of being" and that he can influence the outcome of the battle, not by any overt gesture, but by an imaginative device whereby he conjures up the healing forces of nature. Imagining himself "a sort of demiurgic force, drawing its power from the heart of Nature itself," gives Wolf an "intoxicating enlargement of personality." It is the same defensive enlargement of self that Powys struggled to attain when, as a little boy, he declared himself "the Lord of Hosts." It is easier and safer for the Lord of Hosts to take on the guilt of what Powys called "the First Cause" than to deal with the immediate and possibly irremediable reasons for guilt. This "life-illusion" of Wolf's effectively removes everything hurtful to the safe distance of an imaginary world of his unconscious: "Outward things, such as that terrible face on the Waterloo steps . . . were to him like faintly-limned images in a mirror, the true reality of which lay all the while in his mind—in these hushed, expanding leaves—in this secret vegetation—the roots of whose being hid themselves beneath the dark waters of his consciousness."

Wolf has these thoughts as he is travelling in one of those despised mechanical inventions—the train—as Powys did constantly. Wolf, enjoying the journey, apparently does not get the joke. But he *does* begin to worry "whether the events that awaited him . . . would be able to do what no outward events had yet done—break up this mirror of half-reality and drop great stones of real reality—drop them and lodge them—hard, brutal, material stones—down there among those dark waters and that mental foliage." He wonders if "this new reality" will smash up his "whole secret life" and speculates what it will be: "perhaps it won't be like a rock or a stone . . . perhaps it won't be like a tank or lorry or an aeroplane. . . . Some girl who'll let me make love to her."[46]

His intuition is correct; it is not war machines but a girl who destroys his "whole secret life"—two girls, in fact. One short day after his arrival he has met Gerda Torp, the beautiful eighteen-year-old daughter of the local gravedigger and tombstone maker, and Christie Malakite, the daughter of a pornographic bookseller. Events then move swiftly; within a week he has seduced Gerda, settled his mother into a cottage when she unexpectedly arrives from London, and begun work on Squire Urquhart's project. Urquhart wants Wolf to help him write a "History of Dorset" in "an entirely new genre," which turns out to be nothing more than a "monument of scurrilous scandal." Wolf, "in that mysterious mythopoeic world in which his own imagination insisted on moving" decides that Urquhart is "an antagonist who embodied a depth of actual evil such as was a completely new experience in his life."[47] He soon finds that Urquhart's "History" is less scurrilous than his own hitherto unknown family history, which is now revealed to him. He discovers that he has a half-sister and that his father had several other women in the town in love with him, including the old maid Selena Gault. He learns that his father, once a respected history master, died in obscure circumstances after some "depravity" which appears to be more serious than merely fathering bastards, and which is somehow connected with his friendship with the bookseller Malakite. Wolf also finds out that Malakite had an incestuous relationship with his elder daughter and the child Olwen was the result. Eventually he also learns that his mother had as a lover her rich cousin, Lord Carfaxe.

"Reality" further breaks in with his marriage to Gerda. Gerda has "the swift, unconscious movements of a very healthy young animal" and it is her "startling beauty" and the "simplicity of her nature" that attracts him. Just as Margaret knew thirty different bird songs,[48] it is Gerda's ability to whistle wild-blackbird notes that completely enchants Wolf. John Cowper has portrayed his wife Margaret unkindly and at times bitterly in earlier novels. However, Gerda is a lovely tribute to the young woman of the early poems whose "form so fair" was expected to "bring release" to the poet's "world-wearied heart."[49] Gerda is a final working out

of what attracted him to Margaret so long ago, and in part why he continued to
feel such responsibility toward her. Wolf has romantic visions of marriage in "an
enchanted hovel where he would live with this unparalleled being, free from all
care,"[50] but Gerda soon tires of Wolf's eccentricities and his determined lack of
ambition, and turns for comfort to her childhood friend, Bob Weevil. Wolf in turn
is clear in his own mind that he had married Gerda for her beauty and not because
"he could . . . be said to have fallen in love with her."[51] While Wolf takes erotic
delight in this young wife, when he meets Christie Malakite he feels that they are
"two long-separated spirits . . . rushing together." Christie is a carefully drawn portrait of Phyllis. She has a "honey-pale oval face," smoothly parted, silky brown
hair, quaint pointed chin, "abstracted brown eyes," a drooping underlip, and she
contains, with her slender figure, "every secret of girlhood that had ever troubled
him."[52] Even before he meets Christie, Wolf has built a fantasy of her that proves
illusory. His new friend, Darnley Otter, has told him that Christie "lives so completely in books that I don't think she takes anything that happens in the real
world very seriously."[53] This immediately seems to connect them: "talking to
Christie was like talking to himself." He knows that if he gives up Christie for
Gerda, it will mean "that the one unique experience destined for me out of all
others by the eternal gods has been deliberately thrown away." He thinks now
that marrying Gerda was a "blunder," that he had only married her "because he
had seduced her." However, he concludes that "if his soul was Christie's, his life
must go on being his mother's and Gerda's."[54] Having made this decision, he tries
to persuade Christie that theirs is a "special love." He reasons, "All lovers in our
position I know very well would be desperate to make love, to live together, to
have a child; but here we are, in this field, perfectly content just to be side by side.
You don't want anything more than this, Christie, do you?"[55] This sums up magnificently Powys's long balancing act between Margaret and Phyllis. Wolf learns,
with the loss of his "mythology," that this is not possible.

On Good Friday 1929, Powys wrote Littleton, "Theodore is one of the chief
characters in it as a poet and his poetry given in the story for the reader to enjoy,
criticize or abuse. Marian too is a chief character—the rest is imaginary." This is
a typical Powysian dodge. Still not knowing of Phyllis's existence, Littleton
would not have made the Christie connection, nor would he have recognized
some of the other characters that John drew from a life kept carefully secret from
this brother. However, without difficulty he would have discerned Theodore in
Jason Otter. Jason has large "overly sensitive" gray eyes, a "grim and massive
countenance," a "morbid timorousness" that assorts strangely with his terrible
rages and a suspiciousness of everyone. Like Theodore, he has the habit of wearing a cabbage leaf under his hat for fear of the sun, and of sitting in a ditch for
coolness and seclusion. Jason is averse to work, spending his days drinking and
writing poetry, while expecting his brother Darnley to support him. Wolf is
drawn toward Jason and somehow feels a responsibility toward him, even while
he feels antagonism toward this man who has "deliberately stripped himself of

every consolatory self-protective skin."[56] Wolf thinks that Jason's head "resembled that of some lost spirit in Dante's Inferno, swirling up out of the pit and crying, 'Help! Help! Help!'"[57] However much Wolf resists, as the months pass, "the peculiar nature of this man's pessimism began to affect him as if he had been forced, till his hands were weary, to push away great stalks of deadly nightshade."[58] Once again, Powys addresses the uncomfortable correspondence in his nature and Theodore's and reflects it in the relationship between Jason and Wolf. Theodore had also long recognized the link. He wrote in 1917: "The matter is simplicity itself, one has only to sit in the sun to be happy. But that is not what I can do. . . . I can see you sitting as I am, as we damned ones always are, with no peace in your heart but at the best only a pretended peace."[59]

Powys insisted in *Autobiography* that he never burst out in a blind rage at Theodore as he did with Littleton and Llewelyn, "however his *bon mots* may hit the weak spot in your armour," because "I have seen a degree of suffering in Theodore's face that I have never seen in either of theirs."[60] It did not prevent him from lashing out in his fiction. Wolf recognizes that Jason's "concentrated vindictiveness" allows him to spot "just where my life-illusion is weakest. It's because he sees this weak spot, like a raw scratch in the hide of a bear tied to a pole, and it somehow gets on his nerves, so that he wants to poke at it."[61]

Powys continued throughout his writing career to use himself, his family, and his friends almost exclusively as the characters in his stories. Using those he knew intimately had advantages. Although he often makes his people unusual or even eccentric to the point of disbelief, because they are drawn in such meticulous detail, they are convincingly alive. However, there were obvious drawbacks. While the ordinary reader may not know, or care, that he was portraying family members, *they* did—and this penchant must have intensified the love-hate relationships in that family. Interwoven with the rest of the action is Wolf's struggle to decide whether his loyalty lies with his mother or his father. As in *Ducdame*, Powys again sets up the situation of a sexually dissolute father, long dead, and a possessive mother, very much alive. This should be about as distant from John Cowper's real parents as is possible, but he brings this fictionalized mother/father relationship perplexingly close to his own life by setting the main action in "King's Barton," which, as he explains to Llewelyn in a letter, is Bradford Abbas, C. F.'s first post, and where John was conceived—"so it does seem appropriate to take it as the background."[62] To confuse matters more, Powys gave Wolf's mother all his sister Marian's characteristics. Powys often remarked on Marian's similarity to his mother. She was, he said, "like the desperate woman who bore her, with the same strained merriment, the same bowed head, the same terrible irony."[63] In a rather puzzling inscription in a book he sent to Marian in 1917, he wrote "your way her way resembles / And the Veil of Isis trembles." He does not call himself Osiris, but the portrait of Mrs. Solent hints at the mother/sister/son/brother of incestuous fantasy. In any case, when he wrote to Marian on May

23, 1926, he said "I have an idea that you will like my picture of you as Mrs.
William Solent in my new book."

Whatever the complexities, Mrs. Solent, with her "high spirits," her "recklessness," her "despotic abruptness," her "warm, ironical, half-mischievous
glance," her "shining wood-animal eyes," her handsome face and wavy mass of
splendid hair, her "savage eroticism," and her "primeval passion," is an acute,
admiring, if somewhat disconcerting portrait of Marian. Wolf and his mother
have always been very close. While he wishes she hadn't come to Dorset and that
she would "interfere with his plans," as he meets her train "he recognized in a
flash that existence without her . . . would always be half-real."[64] There is a
remarkable scene in which Wolf and his mother are quarreling about Gerda.

> She towered above him there with that grand convulsed face and those
> expanded breasts; while her fine hands, clutching at her belt, seemed to
> display a wild desire to strip herself naked before him. . . . In the storm of
> her abandonment, the light irony that was her personal armour against
> life seemed to drop from her, piece by glittering piece, and fall tinkling to
> the floor.

Mrs. Solent then flings herself down on the sofa with a "physical shameless-
ness" that shocks Wolf. He pulls his mother into a sitting position and then falls
to his knees in front of her. "She let her tousled forehead sink down until it rest-
ed against his; and there they remained for a while, their two skulls in a happy
trance of relaxeed contact. . . . Wolf was conscious of abandoning himself to a
vast undisturbed peace . . . a peace that flowed over him from the dim reservoirs
of prenatal life." Then she kisses him "with a hot, intense, tyrannous kiss," and
they both get up, make tea, spreading "large mouthfuls of bread-and-butter with
overflowing spoonfuls of red current jam. . . . Wolf felt as if this were in some way
a kind of sacramental feast . . . as though their enjoyment in common of the
sweet morsels they swallowed so greedily were an obscure reversion to those forgotten diurnal nourishments which he must have shared with her long before his
flesh was separated from hers."[65] Later, when his mother and Gerda have a violent quarrel, Wolf, although he feels torn in two by their struggle, decides that
he had spent "longer nights and closer caresses" with his mother than with
Gerda. When Miss Gault begs him to take his dead father's side against his mother's, he replies angrily, "We've lived together more closely than anyone knows.
Do you understand? More closely than anyone knows."[66]

While the incest theme between Malakite and his daughter is clearly articulated, any such feelings between mother and son are only hinted at in the
novel. However, other perversions abound—Urquhart and the vicar's love for little boys, Wolf's own homoerotic attraction to Darnley, and Wolf's fascination
with the "passionate perversity" of two girls he is convinced are lesbians. Unlike
some of Powys's heroes, Wolf is capable of, and takes pleasure in, normal sexual
relationships, but his intense sexuality is tempted by other forms of release which

his dualistic morality forbids. "Sex-aberration" was "the medium through which unspeakable emanations of evil . . . flowed up into the world."[67] Spying on a supposed lesbian encounter sets "his heart beating and his pulses throbbing," and to cool himself off Wolf escapes into the darkness of Gwent Lanes. "Lying upon that rank, drenched grass, he drew a deep sigh of obliterating release. . . . He had fallen back into the womb of his real mother. He was drenched through and through with darkness and with peace."[68]

Nature is for Wolf a refuge from reality. Possibly what is more important, intercourse with nature gives him ecstasy. By now Powys is a master at evoking images that conflate the sexuality of nature and the self. However delicately and circumlocutory Powys's description of this is, the imagery connects nature specifically to the womb and the ecstasy to orgasm: "With a desperate straining of all the energy of his spirit, he struggled to merge his identity in that subaqueous landscape . . . as if he were seeking to embrace in the very act of love the maternal earth herself."[69]

Merging into this "vegetable flesh" gives psychological release and sexual relief. If it is an "act of love," it has nothing to do with what is ordinarily defined as "love." For Wolf, "love was a possessive, feverish, exacting emotion. It demanded a response. It called for mutual activity."[70] This argument and imagery have appeared in previous novels but never expressed so powerfully or so clearly as here. Merging oneself in nature is morally acceptable. The onanistic "obliterating release" that comes of it is not just an escape from possessive love, but also an escape from the unhappiness of the world, from the drudgery of work. It is a way of "losing oneself"; more importantly, this kind of ecstasy "demands nothing in return." Many passages in the novel describe Wolf's passion for nature, which is one shared by all of Powys's heroes and reflected his own deeply held beliefs. *Wolf Solent* is replete with nature imagery—glorious descriptions of plants, flowers, sky, ponds, birdsong, which at first glance is romantic nature worship and, at second glance, erotica. After Gerda has whistled her blackbird song for Wolf the first time, Wolf "found her a different being. . . . She had lost something from the outermost sheath of her habitual reserve, and like a plant that has unloosed its perianth she displayed some inner petal of her personality that had, until that moment, been quite concealed from him."[71] The metaphor, tucked between bits of moss and twigs, is easily missed, but for anyone who knows a little botany, the meaning is clear. The perianth is the outer protective sheath which encloses the sexual organs of the flower. Put bluntly, Gerda is sexually aroused and ready to be penetrated. How consciously aware Powys was that his images were intensely sexual is unknown.

Wolf is Urquhart's second secretary. The first was a beautiful young man called Redfern, who has died in mysterious circumstances. The village folk are patiently awaiting Wolf to share the same fate. Wolf is resisting—he still has his defences more or less intact, one of which is to retreat into a world of poetry. It is another way of distancing himself. In one scene, Gerda and Wolf's mother are quarreling about what may have been digging a hole by Redfern's grave, Mrs. Solent insisting it is a mole. Wolf bounces back a line about moles from *Hamlet*.[72] Mrs. Solent then says that Gerda "looks like the pretty girl leaning over her Pot of Basil." The effect, deliberately or not, shuts out the illiterate Gerda and probably contributes to her angry outburst: "I've always been an outsider to both of you. . . . You've always despised me and my family." Wolf, with his "inhuman detachment" contemplates "the angry consciousness of Gerda and the supercilious consciousness of his mother; but below them both—down there on the quiet river-floor—was the discoloured, decomposed, unrecognizable face of the young Redfern."[73] There is no apparent reason why Wolf should suddenly have this vivid image of Redfern's face, or at least not one that Powys makes clear. But Wolf has followed through the few innocuous lines his mother has quoted from Keats's "Isabella," and completed the poem in his own head. In fact, Keats's romantic tale triggers such fantasies in Wolf's mind that eventually he is convinced that Urquhart and Urquhart's servant are engaged in a necrophilic act of digging up Redfern, just as Isabella and her servant dug up Lorenzo, and that Urquhart intends to take back Redfern's head to "his secret chamber" in the same way Isabella carries away her lover's head and puts it in a pot of basil. It is possible that Powys uses this as an example of Wolf's delusive imagination, to point out the gap between Wolf's imagination and reality. Equally it is possible that the stray lines of a poem he knew well had passed through Powys's head and provided him, just as Bocaccio had provided Keats, a complete narrative plot which enables him to create the long and slow build-up of horror which ends with Wolf contemplating suicide in Lenty Pond.

The entire novel is studded with images taken from poetry, plays, classical myth, folklore, nursery rhymes, and he often uses these to structure scenes and forward plots. This vast literary undercurrent is in part what gives his novels their richness and complexity, but the technique (if such a dazzling gift can be so described) makes considerable demands. Occasionally, the movement of the plot is puzzling and a character's motivation is inexplicable unless the reader himself has at least some of this background and can provide his own analogical context. For example, in one scene, Wolf, after much dithering, tells Urquhart that he will complete his scurrilous book. Later they share a bottle of Malmsey, and when Urquhart gets "hopelessly drunk" and begins to gibber "incoherently" about the soft skin of "a boy not twenty-five" who is buried three-feet-deep in Dorset clay, Wolf realizes he is referring to Redfern. Then Urquhart cries, "It falls off—it falls off—the sweet flesh!" and "The lips—the lips—where are his lips now?"[74] What is the reader to make of this? If, that is, he wants to make anything of it. He can take it simply as a reference to the decay of Redfern's body. However, to read Powys in a literal fashion is to miss much. Urquhart, or rather Powys, is recalling the words of the eighth Julian Revelation: "For his Passion shewed to me most specially in His blessed face (and chiefly in his lips) . . . Thus I saw the sweet flesh dry in seeming part after part, with marvellous pains. . . . How might any pain be more to me than to see Him that is all my life, all my bliss, and all my joy, suffer?"[75] In another scene, Wolf has a "passionate dispute" with the skull of his father and tells the skull that the world is made of "mental landscapes," not "the sweet flesh of girls." The skull answers scornfully, "I am alive still, though I am dead; and you are dead, though you're alive."[76] Later, he goes to the grave of his father again and imagines his soul becomes a mole that burrows down to his father's skull until it "had fumbled and ferreted at that impious, unconquerable grin!"[77] We are watching, in Wolf's meandering stream of consciousness, the collapse of the dualities in his philosophy, and with them, the certainties which sustained his life-illusion. Powys accomplishes this by the insistent linkage of images of skulls, graves, faces, moles, and lips and through imagery from widely different contexts that connects the suffering, pain, and passion of mankind with Christ and the saints. Images of this kind are what Powys called "mystical vignettes in the margin of an occult biography."[78] The problem, if it is a problem, is that the reader must either tease out the allusions, or ignore them, or judge them in the category of Edith Sitwell's "Emily-coloured hands." One admirer called Powys's mind "a vast echoing chamber." Certainly it was a mind that constantly made connections and sometimes the connections were not immediately obvious.

And does Powys really want the reader to see where he is coming from? Did he ever expect the "common reader" for whom he had convinced himself he was writing, immediately or even eventually, to understand these analogies? Is it possible that he is playing the same game Wolf and his mother play with Gerda— they are Jack's secret laugh with the chosen few, or even just with himself? Or is it that Powys lived almost exclusively in his interior life of symbolic connections, using images in the mind like stepping stones through an interior and caring little who followed him.

The relentless beat of the novel is the stripping away of Wolf Solent's defensive armour. Despite the intricate and confusing subplots which Powys delighted in detailing, the steps in the loss of these defences and the consequences are distinct enough. The local inhabitants become more insistent that he is "Redfern Two" and wait for him to drown himself in Lenty Pond. He does not do so, but when he tries to "summon up that formidable magnetic mystery" he realizes that his mythology would never help him again. "That ecstasy, that escape from reality, was gone. Dorsetshire had done for it!"[79]

Two superb scenes in this tale of destruction are Jason's warning and the night with Christie. In the first, he has been walking with Jason, and Jason has been attacking Miss Gault by saying, "She only wants to stir things up, because she's never slept with a man." Wolf falls into the trap and answers irritably, "Sleeping with people isn't everything in the world . . . I should have thought that being a poet you'd know that, and wouldn't go putting such importance on these material accidents." Jason gives "a swift, bitter malicious blow, aimed where the opponent was most vulnerable." He tells Wolf, "You'll walk into a material accident that'll stir *your* quills, master. . . . *You'll* walk into the wood where they pick up horns.'[80] They part, and almost immediately Wolf hears a "rustling in the grass by the side of the road." It is a hedgehog, and as he bends to investigate, a bramble thorn cuts his finger. He mistakenly thinks this is the "material accident" but Jason was referring to horns, not thorns, and his stronghold is breeched.

Wolf has spent his life imagining he could alleviate the suffering of the needy ones—Jason, the beggar on the Waterloo steps. Now he is one of them. As he sees Bob Weevil hurrying away from their cottage, the distancing ends and the pain begins: "No alert, self-watchful demon in him cried out, 'What is this?' or 'What does this mean?' He just suffered; and his suffering was such a completely new thing to him that he had no mental apparatus ready with which to deal with it." Wolf knows that from now on Weevil will "be always there," "that there'll always be a slit in her thoughts through which his eye will be on me."[81]

Wolf makes no connection with Gerda's supposed unfaithfulness and his wanting to spend a night with Christie. He is only concerned that in some way making love to Christie will be the final blow to his "mythology." However, he doesn't want to give up the chance of seeing "the tiny blue veins just above those slender knees." In any case, he has decided she is another one to be saved.

> Men of his type make their girls into anything. He had made her what he wanted her. He had satisfied his sensuality with the other one and gone to Christie for mental sympathy. He hadn't considered *her* side of it at all. But now—tomorrow night—he would be a magician! He would turn this Ariel, this Elemental, into a living girl![82]

As the evening progresses, he asks Christie to take down her hair; then asks her to take off her dress. As she begins to do so, he looks into her mirror and "it seemed to be reflecting the mysterious depths of Lenty Pond," then it seems to reflect "the lamentable countenance of the man on the Waterloo steps." He is about to sink "into nothingness, into a grey gulf of non-existence" when his "will gathered itself together in that frozen chaos and rose upwards—rose upwards like a shining-scaled fish." As he returns to "full awareness," he calms himself by reading her Sir Thomas Browne's *Religio Medici*. Even Wolf realizes that "I have hurt her feelings in the one unpardonable way." He tries to explain to her: "The day I left London, from Waterloo Station, I saw a tramp on the steps there . . . and the look on his face was terrible in its misery. . . . I have remembered that look. It has become to me like a sort of conscience." Christie is not impressed by this explanation of his withdrawal and tells him, "Everything that happens is only something to be fixed up in your own mind. Once you've got it arranged there, the whole thing's settled—What you never seem to realize, for all your talk about 'good' and 'evil' is that events are something outside any person's mind. Nothing's finished—until you take in the feelings of everyone concerned! And what's more, Wolf," she went on, "not only do you refuse *really* to understand other people; but I sometimes think there's something in you yourself you're never even aware of, with all your self-accusations. It's this blindness to what you're really doing that *lets you off*, not your gestures, not even your sideways flashes of compassion.'"[83]

This scourging seems to have no effect on him whatsoever. And when Gerda then calls him a "monstrously selfish man," he is simply "bewildered and non-plussed by this unexpected outburst." He goes to his mother for sympathy and only gets another whipping, "Will you never face the facts of life, my son? . . . That's what you do, Wolf. *You look the other way!*" Wolf uses the same technique he has used with everyone: "Wolf was listening to his mother at this juncture very much as an unmusical person listens to music, making use of it as a raft whereon his thoughts are free to cross far horizons."[84] He simply does not believe that events are "something outside any person's mind." "I don't believe in any reality. . . . Everything is as I myself create it."[85] However, sexual jealousy is what finally makes "a hole in his armour which never, to the end of his life, quite closed up." He is sure that not only is Gerda allowing Bob to make love to her, but that Christie Malakite is allowing her father the same privileges. As well as feeding Wolf's imagination, stray lines of poetry lead him to conclusions that may or may not be illusory. When the dying bookseller tells Wolf "she pushed me," lines from "Goosey Goosey Gander" pop into his head and leads him to the totally unwarranted (except by a nursery rhyme) conclusion that Malakite had transferred his incestuous intentions to Christie and had been "in his lady's chamber." In the end, the reader wonders if Wolf is not imagining everything that happens to him that year. Possibly that is what Powys intends; possibly it was not intentional.

Whatever the case, Wolf finally realizes "that until the last two or three days he had never faced reality at all." He knows his "mythology" is dead; the question now is: "How did human beings go on living, when their life-illusion was destroyed?"[86] However eccentric, egocentric, and adolescent Powys's hero may be, the question is one of utmost importance, not just to Wolf, but to Powys, and presumably to most human beings. Wolf tells himself a story.

> He had imagined himself meeting Jesus Christ in the shape of the man of the Waterloo steps. He had imagined the man stopping him . . . and asking him what he was doing. His answer had been given with a wild, crazy laugh. "Can't you see I'm living my secret life?" he had said.
>
> "What secret life?" the man had asked.
>
> "Running away from the horrors!" he had cried, in a great screaming voice that had rung over the roofs of Blacksod. But immediately afterwards he had imagined himself as becoming very calm and very sly. "It's all right. It's absolutely all right," he had whispered furtively in the man's ears. "You needn't suffer. I let you off. *You are allowed to forget.*"[87]

Wolf decides he must "have the courage of my cowardice" and determines to enjoy life "with absolute childish absorption in its simplest elements."[88] This gives him the release he needs to carry on living, and to remain sane, to bear "the long future stretch of the days of his life." The last sentence of *Wolf Solent*, "Well, I shall have a cup of tea," has confounded many a reader who has been led through the romantic *sturm und drang* to expect something else. Powys tried to explain to Llewelyn in a letter dated August 16, 1928.

> I confess I am faintly conscious now and then that with a terrific gathering up of my forces, the general situation of this book—centreing round Urquhart's necrophilism and Wolf's "mythology"—might have been made to mount up and mount out and finally break in a great crashing catastrophic King-Lear-like, Possessed-like finale with Urquhart's death taking place in some wild storm . . . and Wolf torn from both Gerda and Christie and tossed back miserably to London or committing suicide in Lenty Pond, etc. etc.

However, he has decided he cannot "bring myself to sacrifice them in cold blood to an artistic finale, unless I were heroic enough to be prepared—if you catch my meaning—for such a suicide or for such a tragic end for myself." Instead of sacrificing Wolf, Powys brings in Lord Carfaxe.[89] Wolf "knew perfectly well that what he was yielding to now was an insane desire to make this man responsible— as if he had been fate itself."[90] It is left to Lord Carfaxe, who suddenly appears, to accomplish effortlessly all the good that Wolf has been unable to achieve: he buys up the entire stock of pornography in the Malakite bookshop, thus allowing Christie to go away to live in Weymouth; he arranges to have Jason's poems published; he saves the man on the Waterloo steps, or at least the waiter Wolf has identified as the incarnation of that suffering face; "by his glowing sympathy" he restores Gerda's "unique gift" of birdsong. He reduces Wolf's sense that he has been engaged in "a supernatural struggle with some abysmal form of evil" to an assuaging belief that Urquhart's evil is simply an old bachelor's dotage.

By bringing Carfaxe in, Powys deflates all Wolf's fantasies, but is Powys not also using him as a mechanism of self-deflation? This raises the whole complicated issue of authorial intention and distancing. Is Wolf intended to be a portrait of Powys or is Powys using various devices to indicate his ironic distancing from this very selfish, egocentric man, with his "wild self-pity"?[91] Certainly the numerous examples of traits, manners of speech, subject matter, concerns, that Powys was discussing with Phyllis in his letters in the period of writing suggest that not just similarity but close identification was intended. The way in which both John and Wolf struggle to defend themselves from their awareness of their own incapacity is also similar—they use humiliation as armor. There *is* a distancing that goes on, but it is a subverting and self-flagellation mechanism. Creating a hero so closely identified with onself, and then presumably exaggerating the defects of that hero to the point that the reader in his own mind makes the disconnection between the two, is a defensive mechanism of a rather clever sort.

Carfaxe is a not a convincing *deus ex machina*, nor is he a very satisfactory artistic solution. He *is* a passable psychological solution. Powys calls Carfaxe in his letter to Llewelyn his "scapegoat." Carfaxe lets Wolf off, just as Wolf lets Christ off. But the real scapegoat was the publisher who allowed Powys to escape from the threatening implications of scenes he had himself written. What happened was this. They sent the typescript of *Wolf Solent* to Simon and Schuster in early May 1928. On the fifteenth of July, he wrote Phyllis that he had received "an immense & very important letter from Schuster!" and he went on to quote extensively from it. "He gives a pretty long list of individual passages and then he says "if you are prepared to make these condensations we shall deem it a privilege and honor to make an immediate publishing proposal for this book." Since he desperately needed the money Powys had little choice but to cut.

He removed a total of 350 manuscript pages in six weeks and signed the contract with Schuster on the fourteenth of September 1928. It is *what* he cut that remains problematical. He ignored the suggestion of cutting "individual passages" and instead eliminated the whole middle section of the book of six chapters. An examination of the deleted manuscript chapters (now at the University of Syracuse) makes it clear that his excisions changed the complexion of the whole novel.[92] For example, Wolf distances himself from the incestuous Malakite in the final version, calling him a "senile nympholept"—but in a deleted passage he imagines himself beginning "to slide into some ghastly reciprocity with Mr. Malakite. To be suddenly able to catch that quivering light of desirableness— that perilous sweetness of girlhood—falling on limbs oneself had begotten, too well he could understand that fatal provocation! Just as the desire of girl for girl, by reason of its quivering ineffectualness, had proved so maddingly a thrust so now the worse obsession of the old bookseller began to pierce him to the quick. He seemed to be able to share at that moment every vibration of its perversity."[93]

There was an even more important deletion. He told Llewelyn that "I do know that from the beginning of the book I intended to avoid tragic external incidents." This is simply not true—he intended to disfigure Gerda. In an eliminated chapter, Wolf and Christie go out for a day's outing on Melbury Bubb and he finally gets around to telling her that Gerda and Bob Weevil "had some terrific quarrel." He explains that Gerda had run out to the backyard, fallen full length, and "her cheek was terribly cut and the nail must have been rusty."[94] Wolf had come home to find her bleeding, did nothing for a few days, then took her to hospital, by which time "the Doctor says she's bound to be disfigured—badly disfigured—whatever they do."[95] This disfigurement of Gerda's "flawless beauty" is strangely shocking, not least because so much in the novel is taken from actual events in his life. There is no indication that Margaret ever had such an accident, but sister Katie did. In 1922 Katie had a fall from her horse, which, according to the adopted daughter of Theodore, "damaged her face irreparably. . . . Before that she must have been strikingly good-looking."[96] While he was writing this section of the novel, Katie had another accident to her head. Whether it was another riding accident is unclear, but in any case it was probably Katie's damaged face that gave him the idea of hurting Gerda's face.[97] He apparently had no compunction about using Katie in this way, and the scene and its aftermath was part of the final typescript sent to the publishers. However, when the publishers insisted on "condensations," he may have realized, belatedly, how much it would hurt Katie to see her own "despoilation" in a novel by her beloved brother.

The question remains: Why did he choose to disfigure Gerda and why did he then decide to remove any reference to such an accident? Its removal made the motivation for later events unnecessarily mysterious. As will happen in his later novels, often the motivation for the actions of his heroes is left out, perhaps deliberately—like a carefully constructed maze which lacks the essential clue for successful navigation. It is either that, or he did not know himself. In fact, such a defacement had a necessary fictional function for Powys. By this means he could make a connection and switch-over of pity from the Waterloo beggar to Gerda—face to face. In the original version he had written, "The shape that remained most persistent was not, today, that face of the Waterloo steps; but, on the contrary, the face of Gerda . . . patched and plastered with abominable strips of lint-bandage—the face of Gerda despoiled and disfigured perhaps for life."[98] Now Wolf can transfer his ineffectual world pity from the anonymous face on the steps to the face of Gerda and concentrate his pity on her. The accident is actually a better motive for what happens in the bedroom scene with Christie. "The face on the Waterloo steps" in the final version is what stops him from making love to Christie, but it is actually Gerda's disfigured face that does so. Equally, the *removal* of this defacement may have been necessary to Powys himself, certainly to Wolf. In the uncut version, it is Gerda who, albeit accidentally, has hurt her face so badly. If Powys had left Gerda disfigured, then this would have been a very good reason why her whistling stopped, whereas in the cut version, Wolf himself can now take on the guilt: it is Gerda's unhappiness with her life with Wolf that puts an end to her whistling. Powys/Wolf insists that Gerda is intimately connected with nature and the primitive world and when she whistles she *is* nature. "That strange whistling was the voice of those green pastures and those blackthorn-hedges." He is therefore as guilty as the motor cars and planes that are "assassinating" the beauty of Dorset's land. In some labyrinthian way, Wolf is responsible not only for the loss of her birdsong, but his own life-illusion. He has violated the nature that is his escape and his mythology.

As important as the deletion of the disfigurement is the deletion of Christie's reaction to the news. The typescript reads: "'Poor Gerda!' he murmured, sighing again. . . . 'Poor Gerda!' echoed Christie with the barest perceptible movement of her lips but with a sarcasm that was blighting." Wolf asks, "'What's the matter, Chris?' . . . 'You look as if I'd done this thing to Gerda.'" In the manuscript, he has Christie say, "I don't mean with your stick. But you *did* it all the same."[99] Powys modified this in the typescript to: "It isn't what you've done. I don't believe you know what it *is* to feel—to actually realise another human being's feelings."[100] When they meet again some weeks later, she tells him, "Something's happened now, that's changed everything. . . . You've changed. . . . Gerda and I are sharing your pity. That's what it is! And pity's the only kind of love you're capable of! And now we are sharing it. She so much—I so much!"[101] Her decision to go away to live in Weymouth would have arisen naturally out of this brutal assessment of Wolf, but in the final version, Powys has Christie leave Blacksod a defeated woman. The total effect of deleting these chapters is to focus all the attention back on Wolf. Christie (uncut) is passionate, jealous, and worldly wise. This was not what Wolf wants. So what can he do to crush the spirit of a passionate woman? He can pity her—as Christie predicted—and he can refuse to have sex with her. What has always remained somewhat mysterious in the novel makes sense if the removed chapters are replaced. He can both punish Christie for blaming Gerda's accident on him and humiliate her at the same time.

Wolf being Wolf, he has it both ways—he has taken on the heavy burden of world guilt and personal guilt while managing to punish those who hurt him. There is still the question of why Powys removed those chapters. When Arnold was admitted to the asylum, he wrote Phyllis that it is all "so exactly like one of my craziest stories that I feel as if I ought to be able to change everything for these poor 'characters' & make it all nicer for them."[102] Phyllis, on the other hand, smiling her "most Christie-like & spirit-like smile," was constantly pushing him to make his characters more "real."[103] In his letters to Phyllis, he often refers to "this work of ours."[104] I think it was Christie/Phyllis who, at this period, was trying to lead Wolf/Powys to "reality." Both Christie and Phyllis lost. The Christie Powys conjured up in the manuscript was lively, acerbic, independent—rather like the woman that the shy, passive Phyllis was becoming by the late 1920s. Christie in the cut version is Phyllis as he unconsciously wanted her. One side of him wished Phyllis to develop and flourish. The other side was very fearful of any independence, or, as he put it: "a lover likes to see the plant growing—as long as it stays where it is."[105]

Once he had done the proofreading, there was little to be done but to wait anxiously for the publication of this book they set their hopes on. It was a gamble. Dick Simon and Maxe Schuster were destined to revolutionize the publishing business in America, but at this time they were just two young men in their mid-twenties whose only publications were crossword-puzzle books until the best-seller success of Will Durant's book.[106] The initial gamble (on both sides) paid off. They remained Powys's publishers for many years, and when *Wolf Solent* came out on May 16, 1929, it was an instant success in America. It was sent to Jonathan Cape in England for consideration, and in late April John received a letter from Cape's reader, "the great Edward Garnett the most authoritative of all English critics," who expected that "after the first shock" Cape would accept the book.[107] Powys wrote happily to Theodore a week after publication that the novel had had wonderful reviews and that "Mr. Schuster is a grand one for advertising . . . though the only certain advertisement I suppose would be if I dressed up and walked up 5th Ave with a board on my back saying 'Buy Wolf Solent—this is how he walks.'"[108]

The success of the novel emboldened Powys to approach publishers with another project. He knew that the lecture circuit was changing, "the old academic regime" being replaced by single talks delivered by writers and critics "who have recently published one book or article that has been the subject of conversation." He and Phyllis dreamt up the idea of a book of essays which would serve a threefold purpose: "something that would be circulated widely and by discussion bring back my lost audiences," be a "condensed culture-breviary for Main Street Libraries," and be "what many youthful 'Reds' crave & require."[109] The publisher, W. W. Norton, had begun something called The People's Institute Lectures-In-Print Series, and they wanted a companion volume to Everett Martin's book on education, *The Meaning of a Liberal Education*, which had sold 15,000 copies. Powys knew Martin as a popular fellow lecturer at the Cooper Union and other centres of adult education in New York. A staunch defender of liberal education, Martin was best known for taking often abstruse material and making it available to a heterogeneous audience, and for understanding the need to write for adults striving to move beyond the boredom of their work and their everyday lives. Powys quickly saw that he could write a culture book on the same lines. At Phyllis's insistence, John asked for a $300 advance from Norton, which he got without "the least demur." Powys had the idea that "this sort of book ought to have a good academic sale over here if no better than that." In fact, it had little academic sale but it proved hugely popular with "the common reader" and was one of the few books of his that remained in print for many years.

He began *The Meaning of Culture*[110] in May 1928 and had almost completed it when he left for his customary English trip "home" the end of May 1929. Phyllis suggested that he write a diary in lieu of the daily letters he wrote to her on tour. He countered with the proposition that she begin to write a diary as well. John's diary writing continued daily, without fail, for more than thirty years. Phyllis appears to have kept hers with regularity for three years only—1929, 1930, and 1931. Until this point Phyllis can be seen only through his letters to her, except for the very brief fragments of her juvenilia. Her prose style, replete with short dashes, is not easy, and as Powys often remarked, her thought processes are subtle, but these diaries are of inestimable help in filling in many missing pieces in the jigsaw of their relationship. She wrote the first entry after receiving the letters he had written aboard ship.

> Monday June 17th [1929]: When I opened them—it struck me all the more—this tide of emotion—that seemed as bottomless as the ocean—and that once it began to rise would submerge everything. It is strange with anyone as queer and unnatural as I am—with my funny ways of feeling—so—on the fringe —so fantastic—so strong and poignant sometimes over such odd sources—that would fail to arouse the least flicker of response in other people—and perpetually aware of my feelings as I am—constantly living in

a set of burning hot or sharp or quivering points of contact to be avoided—all a little insane and unnecessary—and non existent—that there could be any <u>area</u> of feeling left—I was not self-conscious of—but apparently—in me—the great tides—the great depths—the really essential emotional transactions—well up—accumulate—soundless, bottomless—without my knowing. Over Jack there is a region as infinite as space—that is always there like the Fourth Dimension and sometimes comes into communication with my usual world—my mind always witnesses these inundations with a kind of respectful astonishment.

What comes across most insistently in the few entries she made in 1929 is her depressive personality. She is at her parents' summer home and realizes that seeing the landscape golden with ripe hay should "fill one with a kind of ecstasy of contentment." Instead she feels "an unutterable desire to be in some dark barren place where there was no <u>growth</u>." In a sense, her childhood was much more golden than Powys remembers his being, but unfailingly, any reminder of it leads her on to think of the period when it all came to an end with her breakdown. She finds an old music box she had in the days of "44 Pinkney Street and my doll Adelaide."

> 1 July 1929: I opened the lid and pulled the lever. It began to play creakily and falteringly—with terrible sounds now and then in the machinery—a thin mechanical tinkle—so infinitely sad—and like vanished times. I began to cry—and as it played on and on I sat down on a log in the storeroom and sobbed—with that terrific deep tearing away—of something in the depths of your body—that I remember when I was so unhappy.

John went first, as he always did, to visit his wife and son. It was this trip when he finally realized that "these two have no need for me. My son is <u>very</u> beautiful & of a lovely nature—but altogether mysterious to me—something, I know not what, of his mother about him seems to make a gulf wh it is very difficult for me to cross."[111] However, the affection of his brothers and sisters reassured him: "they <u>are</u> so affectionate and <u>so</u> <u>glad</u> for us all to meet." He and Littleton had a happy trip to Norfolk in Littleton's new car. They stopped at Stonehenge where he dipped his stick in the hollow of the Stonehenge altar so "my stick will possess an immense ancient Magic henceforth."[112] At Northwold, they stayed once again in the house that had been their grandparents' and spent their days reliving their childhood adventures, visiting Dye's Hole, Harrod's Mill pool and Oxboro Ferry, and one day had "the most heavenly drift down the river." This was an intimate time when he could have told Littleton about Phyllis, but he did not, although somehow he managed to talk Littleton into trying to find Sotterley, the home of Phyllis's Playter ancestors, without telling him why. The trip was in part a sentimental journey back to golden days of childhood, but it was also intended to provide material for another novel he was contemplating. In his newly begun diary we immediately get the strong sense of the way in which every person, every experience, every landscape—past and present—was grist for his creative mill. Much of what he did, thought, read in these summer months was eventually transposed to "the modern grail legend"—*A Glastonbury Romance*. He hoped to visit Glastonbury several times when he came to visit them at Chaldon, and he wanted "Gamel" to go with him as she "knows most about such matters."[113]

"Gamel" was Gamel Woolsey, an exquisitely beautiful American woman of thirty-three who once lived across from John and Phyllis on Patchin Place. They had come to know her well, and during this trip to England in 1929 Powys was to witness the outcome of a plan he had himself largely engineered. Reconstructing the sequence of events has been difficult—each actor in the drama had his/her own version, and until recently some critical information was unavailable. Gamel was born in South Carolina on her father's cotton plantation. She was expensively educated and early began to write poetry and read voraciously, particularly poetry, mythology, and early romances. After contracting tuberculosis in her twenties and spending a year in a sanatorium, she went to New York where she mixed with painters and writers in Greenwich Village. She met an actor and journalist, Reginald Hunter, and they became lovers. When she told Hunter she was pregnant, they married, but shortly after, she had an abortion on "medical grounds." The marriage lasted perhaps four years, and by 1927 they were in the process of separating.[114] When Llewelyn and Alyse were in New York that autumn, John had introduced them to "the poetess," as John called her. Llewelyn was immediately attracted to this frail, romantic figure, and in early April, when Alyse was briefly away visiting her parents, Llewelyn made love to her.[115] In his only direct reference to this, Llewelyn commented on "the few hours . . . that we spent together."[116] That is probably all they had, since Gamel's husband was continually visiting her at that time. Presumably either Llewelyn or Gamel told John, for in a letter he wondered to Phyllis "what the upshot of that occurrence is destined to be!"[117]

On April 25, Lulu and Alyse returned to England. Later in July, they visited Holland in the company of New York artist Reginald Marsh, and his wife Betty. While there, Llewelyn received a letter from Gamel, forwarded from England, which was no doubt a letter saying she was pregnant, but since her side of the correspondence is missing, there is no way of knowing if she told him the child was his. His response was hardly that of an excited expectant father, however, and he did not tell Alyse until three weeks later. By then they were in Bellay, France, where he wrote the first draft of a novel which, with characteristic Powysian malice, he entitled *Apples be Ripe*. In September, John wrote Llewelyn to say he was busy copying the cuts he had made in *Wolf* but did not mention that Gamel was helping Phyllis do the retyping. In October, he wrote to tell them that Gamel had had an accident "& because of her tubercular history, the doctors had insisted on an abortion."[118] She would have then been almost six months pregnant if it were Llewelyn's. By this time, Llewelyn had decided he desperately wanted to have a child. Before and after marriage, Llewelyn had had a number of affairs. An ongoing one was with Betty Marsh; she had come to Europe in July specifically to continue her unsuccessful attempts to conceive a child by him.[119] There is, in fact, despite Llewelyn's reputation as an overly free spirit, no indication that he ever impregnated any of his women friends. On October 28, Powys wrote Lulu to "give the wench another chance."[120] He wrote again in November, urging them to allow Gamel to come to England and live near them. In her Journal entry for November 30, Alyse refers to "the last few days before the letters began to come were so exquisite. . . . It is not so much that a child will separate us as that she, like B., is so passionately in love with him."[121] The letters from John that so upset Alyse would have been written while he was on tour that autumn. Although he always wrote Phyllis every day, never does he refer to writing such letters. Still, Phyllis may have been expecting some such maneuver. In two letters to Phyllis in November, it became obvious that Powys was thinking as much of himself as he was of Llewelyn. In them he makes broad hints about Gamel's lesbian tendencies and his own barely suppressed jealousy: "I don't grudge that poor mermaid her thrill in following you up that ladder of rope to that garden of petals."[122] Certainly Phyllis and Gamel enjoyed going to the theatre and concerts together, and discussing modern poetry. Gamel was talking about the two of them going to Europe together in the spring. Whatever the actual relationship was between Phyllis and Gamel, it was clearly a close friendship. Phyllis wrote Gamel a note just as Gamel was leaving for England:

> Dearest Gamel, this is just to let you know whenever you open it how much I love you. . . . I have just seen you walk out of the alley from the window— as you have passed out of sight a hundred times—and so you might have passed out of sight without my ever having known you. O Gamel dear— nothing that happens will ever be as sad as that would have been and that can now <u>never never</u> happen. I cannot bear to have you go."[123]

Many years later, in 1954, Gamel wrote to Phyllis about that autumn: "Though I never felt that I had lost you or even that I could lose you, it was as if you had gone immensely far away & that there were barriers set up between us."[124]

An entry in Alyse's Journal in early January 1929 suggests that Alyse also suspected that Jack had reasons of his own for forcing this through. "John says that I am both noble and subtle. . . . But I think he says this to reconcile me. In this sad world who is whose friend? And what is nobility? To accept defeat in silence? And what is subtlety? A kind of inspired cunning? It is he who is subtle, not I."[125] John Cowper was correct in perceiving that Alyse's intellect was finely nuanced; her motivation for allowing Llewelyn his sexual "freedom," if not "noble," was certainly convoluted. But her defeated silence was not total. In the next years she wrote several novels in which she not only describes a Lulu character with an incisive scorn but outlines a revenge strategy. Even before Gamel's arrival, Alyse had finished her novel, *King Log and Lady Lea*, in which the heroine, discovering that her husband has had an affair, deserts him and lives with that same woman in a covert lesbian relationship.[126]

Alyse and Llewelyn returned to White Nose on May 10, 1929, after a winter in Anacapri. In early June Gamel arrived from America, staying at nearby Ringstead, a ten-minute walk away. Gamel seems to have known she was pregnant as early as the twelfth of June, canceling a proposed trip to Russia. When John arrived in Chaldon in July, he wrote Phyllis that Llewelyn had told him "that our mermaid is once more."[127] Nothing of this is mentioned directly in his newly begun diary; even at this early stage, he strains information through the sieve of his imagery. He writes instead: "After lunch we walked in a terrific wind to meet Gamel at the Obelisk. . . . The wind was so high that it made Gamel feel funny almost faint & so Alyse took her home to White Nose. . . . Down in Scratchy Bottom we saw a pregnant lizard with a scorched tail."[128]

As usual, the circle had gathered at Chaldon to greet him. Louis was there with his latest wife, Nan Reid; Bernie O'Neill, who regularly spent his holidays with Gertrude at Chydyok; Bertie with Faith Oliver, the woman he was to marry when his divorce came through in October. John wrote with vexation to Phyllis of "so many inordinate & vital egoists" and "such cross currents of alliances & secret disfavours." Katie, who referred to herself as "Phyllis's sailor-boy," was jealous of Gamel "because no doubt of you as well as Lulu." Llewelyn did not want Bertie and his mistress to stay anywhere near them in case of "talk" in the village. "We know well how these social situations get to be taken <u>so</u> <u>very</u> <u>hard</u> and with such gingerly niceness & elaboration by the Master of the White Nose!" This was rather rich, considering the relationship between Lulu and Gamel, and Llewelyn was happy enough to stay with Bertie and Faith in London while Gamel went into hospital in mid-August for another abortion. Gamel's "tubercular history" was again given as the reason for the termination. John and Alyse appeared to have been more concerned by the effect of the news on Llewelyn's health than on hers. Gamel was reported to be "calm and resolute," but Llewelyn was devastated that again he had been defrauded of a child. This dramatic episode, which was to pass into Powysian family mythology, had its puzzling aspects. By all accounts, Gamel had a tender heart and told people what she felt they wanted to hear; Lulu wanted to hear that he could father a child. The pronounced Powys features, which always emerged in the children, would have proved it was Llewelyn's; equally, had the child been born, their absense might have proved it was not.

The journals of John, Alyse, and Llewelyn create differing portraits of this woman, but the strengths of their own personalities and desires tend to suppress her reality. Gamel seemed destined to be seen through the eyes of others, but she did write an autobiographical novel. *One Way of Love* was probably written in the early months of 1929, but the publisher's fear of libel meant that it was not issued until after her death. In it, Gamel analyzes her own character with acuity—her drifting quality, her sense of waiting for something to happen which never does, her fear of loneliness. She is a woman "who had almost a courtesan's desire to please, even at the sacrifice of her own pleasure."[129] In the novel, her heroine, Mariana, conducts two more affairs in quick succession after her separation from her husband. The first is Holworth: "She had let Holworth, for whom she had only felt friendliness, make love to her. It had been wrong for her to do so because she had not loved him. It had only been a refuge and a respite from the loneliness of her life."[130] If this is Llewelyn, it is not a particularly flattering portrait. As the heroine waves good-by at the train station to the first lover, she meets John Linschoten, "a man she had known for several years." Gamel gives quite a bit of detail about this man and his background—educated, rich, married but a virtual separation. They soon make love. Afterwards, Mariana "thought it sad enough to have one casual affair with Holworth, but to have two within a few months was shocking to her."[131] There seems to be little doubt that Gamel *did* have an affair with this man after Llewelyn had left New York, and that he was as likely to be the father of the aborted child as Lulu.

John returned to America in September to be confronted by another crisis. He wrote Littleton the full details of his latest contretemps with his manager, Lee Keedick.

> 22 November 1929: I signed up a contract with this Mr. Keedick 4 and a half years ago which is due to end next Sept 1930. I thought when I signed it . . . it left me free at this time to renew it, with him, or not as I pleased. Instead of this—by the wily introduction of the word "option"—I now learn that legally . . . I am bound to him for another term of 5 years if I lecture at all in America or Canada! . . . However my great and kind & sagacious Hebrew Publisher the incomparable Mr. Schuster wants me to fight this contract & go to law about it in order to be free to choose another less avaricious and less stick-in-the-mud manager. . . . You might at once say "why not . . . leave America and come back to England?" Well, Littleton darling . . . circumstances into which I cannot enter just now make it seem necessary to me to remain in America. . . . Here I've got my unequalled friend and publisher Mr. Schuster. Here I know and am known. Here I could make my living if I were put to it by writing. The point to be decided is shall I eat dirt & allow Mr. K his tricky victory over an Englishman & a fool or shall I risk having a lawyers fees to pay and the court costs to pay & go to law on it?

1929 ended with a grand debate on the 13th of December with Bertrand Russell on Marriage. Powys argued in support of marriage and narrowly lost, but two less suitable men to discuss the pros and cons of marriage it is difficult to conceive. Much against his will, a very short clip was done for publicity purposes. Russell is totally at ease, speaking naturally; Powys, despite the fact that he was once described as having a voice and a delivery that Demosthenes might have gained pointers from, stands with shoulders hunched, speaking in a high-pitched artificial tone that he used when he wanted "to cover a spasm of irritation."132 It was the only time Powys allowed himself to be filmed or his voice recorded, and many years later, when Louis asked him why, he replied, "my fear of having my voice recorded is really and truly exactly a Savage's terror of being photo'd. I think it must come from my mania for following a certain special imaginary reaction to life of my own invention which I am scared of finding broken or shattered if I am caught off-guard by such a realistic thing as a mirror or a phonograph."133 Wolf's "mythology" may have been smashed, but at the start of 1930, John Cowper's was still firmly in place.

"For all these four years, I wrote with a board propped against my knees and my paper on the board."
—*Autobiography*.

"I had a most serious quarrel with Peter before breakfast. He thought it was an amusing game to tease his uncle by spying on him."   —JCP Diary, 4 June, 1930.

No wonder I followed the old boy (literally!) up the hill, attempting to emulate and take into myself some of his magic. And in a sense he was therefore justified in reacting so violently to such unsought-for expropriation."
—Peter Powys Grey, Diary, 25 February, 1986.

"They persuaded me with flattery to let them take the whole book and to publish it in two parts instead of 3 parts."
—JCP Diary, 15 May, 1931.

"Her garden has now become
a <u>Passion</u> with her."
　　　—JCP Diary, 17 May, 1933.

"I am profoundly happy this Spring
for it is such a relief to see the
countenance of the T.T. relaxeed
& easy . . . like a real young girl again."
　　　—JCP Diary, 26 April, 1931.

"These four years of country life in
America, years in which I have had a
greater chance to realize my identity
than I have ever had before in my life."
　　　—*Autobiography*

PHUDD BOTTOM

1930-1931

T HE STOCK MARKET CRASH IN OCTOBER 1929 MARKED THE BEGINNING of the Great Depression in the United States. Powys was fearful that "this ruin by so many by the Stock Exchange fall will mean few will have money to buy anything," much less his *Wolf Solent* and *The Meaning of Culture*, but he was sincerely troubled by the misery and poverty he saw everywhere. He felt he should write something for "bums and derelicts and imbeciles, as well as patient, respectable workers" that they could use "to steer their lives and get certain thrills of happiness—else perhaps quite unknown to them."[1] He began the book in November and called it *In Defence of Sensuality*. At first he was not sure that the rambling essay was worthy to be called philosophy,[2] but by April 1930 he had convinced himself that it was nothing less than "a new emotional psychology," the beginning of "a new Culture," even a new religion. "Our Western civilization at the present moment requires nothing so much as a John the Baptist of sensuousness, a Prophet of simple, primeval, innocent sensuality."[3] Needless to say, Powys saw himself as that prophet.

Stripped to its essentials, his thesis is that happiness is "the secret of life and the purpose of life,"[4] and the clue to an individual's happiness lies "not in expressing himself or in realising himself, but in losing himself in sensation,"[5] of giving oneself up to "a deep physical-psychic enjoyment of the thought of air, sun, earth, water, sky, warmth, food, amorous pleasure."[6] Attaining this happiness is a deliberate, self-conscious, willed act. To enjoy life in a certain way, indeed, to enjoy it at all, necessitates a "philosophy of selective experience."[7] The individual must, by an act of will, remember and relive only the happy memories and repress or "forget" the horrifying ones. Powys admits that this is difficult to do when a person is seeing "the long bread-lines of hungry unemployed men" or thinking of a friend "whose wife and children are sick with undernourishment,"[8] but he concludes: "We have to force ourselves to forget the extreme pain of other entities in the world. The power of forgetting is the grand healing, drugging, numbing anaesthetic that makes happiness possible for anyone."[9]

He wrote *Defence* as much for himself as for others. In 1917, Theodore had written him, "The reason is that you are ill, and that you cannot forget, like Father does. Father's one desire is only to go on living, only just that. Why can't you do the same."[10] That would have struck a chord with John even then, but he had struggled on. Now, emotionally and physically drained as he was, he knew that either he would drown with his brother in a pond of despair or he would find a way to release himself. Forgetting—the delicate art of forgetting—was the way of salvation. Forgetting was "that magical reservoir of Lethe which we all cherish in our Being at a deeper level even than our torment. If anyone asked me what is the most precious gift that Nature has given us, I—worshipper of Memory—would reply: 'the art of forgetting!'"[11] The tension between the art of remembering, which was the foundation of his creative life, and the art of forgetting, which kept him sane, was the driving force of his future novels.

He was still writing *In Defence* as he began a forty-four-day lecture tour in early 1930. This was one of the worst tours he had yet endured, traipsing from one grimy industrial town to the next—Pittsburgh, Chicago, Detroit, Milwaukee—always aware of the groups of unemployed men hanging about in parks and under bridges, with their "ravaged faces," and "impotent rage." Besides the interminable travel and often two lectures a day, he was expected always to be "on show" at lunches, dinners, receptions, book signings, even as a new ulcer kept him in constant pain.[12] He noted in his diary that he "shook hands with 50 young ladies, swaying & crouching like a sick Poke Weed in a shower."[13] His only relief was his daily letter to Phyllis, who was staying with her sick parents. These letters were divided into two parts: details of his lectures, his troubles with hotel clerks and train schedules, went "à trois"; privately to "Missy" went the endless messages of love, desire, dependency, and the recounting of the "good" memories—the different expressions on her face, the way she stretched herself before beginning to pack his things, the way she read "standing up between Bed and Table, while the ship's rudder bumps and thuds against the bulkheads."[14]

Despite his weariness with it, Powys was well aware of the advantages of the peripatetic life. Spending most of his time in hotels or on trains allowed him to "escape all real contact with my fellow-creatures . . . but whenever I did come into contact with the human race it was always as my *audience* or as *my attendants!*"[15] In those days of long-distance overnight train rides, the passengers' comfort depended on the coach attendants, who were almost exclusively Negroes. The porters looked after him as he was looked after by nursemaids as a child, making up his sleeper, serving him at his meals, talking to him in a soothing way. He could give a lecture, get on a train, be laved with good humor and attentiveness by his "attendants," and go on to the next stop. There is no doubt that two and a half decades of travel in the U.S. further reinforced his essential solitariness. That was all about to change.

The conflict with Lee Keedick had dragged on for months—with Simon and Schuster, Marian, and Llewelyn all offering advice. Keedick tried every trick in the trade to bully Powys into another five-year contract, going so far as to threaten that he would take all his royalties "as compensation if I announced that I wished to give up lecturing!"[16] He had almost resigned himself to lecturing under Keedick management for at least five months of the year, but his ulcer was so troublesome that when he returned to New York he saw a specialist who advised a major operation. Although Powys did not take this advice, the outcome was that the manager agreed to allow him a year's rest from lecturing. It may be that Keedick was relieved by this way out of their contractual disagreement. Powys's reaction to his audience was always mercurial, but it had now become so erratic that the agency was finding it increasingly difficult to find him work. With a sympathetic audience he could play the role of an inspired magician-savior, but equally he might use a less compatible audience to vent the accumulated rage in him that had no other outlet acceptable to him. "Some accidental concatenation of place and people, some situation where my nerves had been outraged, would pile up the black bile within me, until, safe on my platform, I would revenge myself upon every aspect of our mismanaged human life."[17] Phyllis described one such occasion.

> 27 February 1930: J. gave a very good lecture on Homer at the Town Hall this morning. In the middle of it he spoke of his relative Cowper, who went mad but delayed his going mad by reading Homer, and there was a ripple of laughter—J. paced up and down in silence and stroked his right eyebrow with a convulsive movement—I felt very scared. In the end he said in a quivering voice that in the Iliad, such a reference to anyone's going mad would not have evoked laughter—but of course in modern New York it was a different matter. The audience seemed rebuked—and afterwards when he said anything on the edge of amusing—they never dared the faintest ripple of relaxeation. J. hates that audience, and it is a trying one but there are a great many old ladies in it and most of them are very nice. I cried at the description of Achilles returning from the dead and so did the old lady in front of me.

This occurred a few days after he had seen the specialist and had it out with Keedick. His ulcer had kept him in constant pain for weeks, but Phyllis ends this account with: "He is better—why—no one knows."

To their delight and immense relief both *Wolf Solent* and *The Meaning of Culture* were bestsellers.[18] His letters to Phyllis during this time were buoyant; finally he could give her the "extras" she had for so long gone without. A new dress, their first piece of furniture, violets from the street seller, a pot of chives for the windowsill. She must have felt like Frances Hodgson Burnett's little princess in the garret to whom is brought each night by mysterious means some new comfort. But there was another reason for his exultant mood. He was moving out of New York City and into the country. When they first began living together, Powys was convinced that their secret liaison was only safe in the anonymity of a big city, but as the years passed he became less alarmed. By 1926 he was longing for a place in the country "to write book after book and to note every least change of the seasons in certain roads & lanes & fields and trees."[19]

In early 1927 he was tempting Phyllis by suggesting the possibility of their moving to France, where she had been so happy as a young girl. His visit with Arthur Ficke in Sante Fe that summer decided him on a very different location, although she may not have realized it at the time. He had simply mentioned to her that the Fickes had bought a farm of three hundred acres about thirty miles from Albany "in our very favourite country." Prophetically, he had added, "Ficke is a bit nervous as to whether he'll like the complete isolation & long snow-covered winters, but his wife is fixed & resolute to do it."[20] So was John Cowper. He knew how much Phyllis by now loved New York and that the Room had become her "own invented world,"[21] but at intervals thereafter he would mention his hope that *Wolf Solent* would sell well enough "to get us into the country." By December 1928 he was complaining that living in New York seriously interfered with his writing. Powys had accumulated young disciples, as he was to do his whole life, "mystic-headed doddipole-supernumaries . . . discuss[ing] works they've never written and causes they've never defended and ladies they've never kissed." Writing a philosophy for them was not sufficient to stave off a constant stream of visitors who sat "like frozen penguins" in the Room for hours "telling us with sleety grey tears of lives of troubles."[22]

Once John determined on a course, he followed it. Remembering how "competent & sagacious & benevolent" Arthur Ficke was, he wrote to him in January 1929, asking about the possibility of finding "a very small little house in your district."[23] In April he wrote Lulu that they were "still vaguely and rather helplessly looking and looking,"[24] but, in fact, as he wrote that he was in the very process of signing a purchase agreement. On April 25, 1929, they bought for $2,300 a farmhouse and small acreage in the Berkshire foothills, upstate New York, but he asked Ficke not to mention this to anyone. On the tenth of May, John wrote to Lulu with "a mingled excitement, numbness, satisfaction, dismay, agitation, bewilderment," as if this "recent occurrence in our life" were a total surprise to him, that Arthur Ficke had lent him two thousand dollars and "with this has purchased for us, to be paid for during the next couple of years at our convenience, a clean tidy oldish little Dutch or New England cottage."[25]

The postal address would become familiar to recipients of his letters over the next few years: "Route 2, Hillsdale." A mile from the tiny settlement of Harlemville, and four miles from the hamlet of Philmont, the white-painted clapboard house consisted of four rooms downstairs with an attic bedroom extending the length of the house upstairs. There was a hill immediately behind the house and a small stream and a miniature orchard on the adjoining six acres. The house fronted a dirt road, and immediately across was the chicken farm owned by their closest neighbour Albert Krick and his wife. Across the meadow on a knoll was "Hardhack," the home of the Fickes. He gave the name "Mt. Phudd" to the hill; the cottage became "Phudd Bottom."

Now that Phyllis's 1930 diary has been discovered, it is clear how she felt about the move. From the beginning she thought it would be a mistake to live there, requiring "too great efforts in an undefended exposure."[26] More ominously, she felt that her "five years in a city" had turned her against the "planetary absolutism of nature." She loved drifting about Greenwich Village, looking in the shop windows, buying flowers at the corner stalls. When John was on tour she went often to Carnegie Hall to hear the Philharmonic, to the circus, to the theatre, to art exhibitions. She wrote John that what she wanted above all was to live for a while in a large city in Europe, to which he responded by quoting Horace. "J. says the Latin sentence from Horace means 'They change the sky and not their soul, who across the sea run.'"[27] He asked her not to get it lodged in her head "that you're *never* going to Europe or that you're going to be landed in hardship at Hillsdale with Arthur's ribbed trousers waving i' the wind & Mr Krick's chickens dotting the view."[28] However, that is what happened.

It was not only her love for the cultivated life of a city that made her hesitate. Given her father's history of riches to rags, she was very worried that the "riches" brought with the success of *Wolf*—which John, in his characteristic way, was convinced would continue—would soon evaporate in the deepening gloom of the depression. His silliness with money constantly frightened her. At the end of 1929, Arnold needed an operation and once again called on his assistance. Powys paid the hospital fees, and possibly in the vain hope that the problem would then go away, proposed to pay the fare for the whole Shaw family to move to England. Arnold took the money instead to pay his back rent. Phyllis decided, "Henceforth I shall not take any part in whatever J. does and I shall *not* worry about the money being gone at the end of the year."[29] But she did continue to worry. The move to Hillsdale would mean they could not fall back on his lecture fees which had so often saved them from total hardship in the past: "It seems a little like having definitely cut some root—which drew on the Earth—to deliberately cut off *all income*. The Royalties are like a flower-pot—to grow in—so much—and *no more*."[30]

She also believed that when he stopped lecturing, something remarkable would be lost.[31] She wrote in her diary:

> 27 January 1930: At seven we went to Brooklyn for the lecture on Victor Hugo. . . . He had more material than he could possibly get in from all those 6 books he has been reading. He is a great actor. No one has ever done what he does in these lectures. Long lines of this generation should be waiting in the rain—outside London—Paris—Berlin—Moscow—Tokio and Melbourne for what, when he dies, will never be done again.

She noted that in this lecture John had said, "We can make our own worlds and the sun by god can rise in the west and set in the east if we so desire." She knew that Powys actually believed what he wrote and preached. He would point out to her gas tanks in the distance and visualize them as the lofty spires in a German city. He had the life-enhancing romantic imagination, which she did not share—or rather, having seen the practical results of it, distrusted. She thought that seeing a gas tank as a representation of Europe was simply "the final pathetic rise of consolation."[32] She tried, albeit with little success, to follow his advice and take solace in observing nature, but "in the midst of looking at the grass—it suddenly occurred to me that I had to buy toilet paper and cold cream and J's soap at Bigelow's before I came in." A flare of anger at his philosophy of forgetting the unpleasant is obvious as she goes on, "to forget these preoccupations with necessities is only like a game—it is only playing—my life is full of these and how can I get out of it?"[33]

Despite all evidence to the contrary, he convinced himself that she loved nature and the countryside. After all, she was his Elemental—the very personification of nature. In an astonishing feat of illogic he once wrote to her: "Sometimes a selfish person who never gives another person a pleasure they know they'd like is the one who can love very very much—just for that reason because their love is so selfish as to [be] natural. . . . It's like a person's happiness with Nature & indeed my Thin is like Nature itself to me & I love her like I love the earth and ferns and moon & tree-trunks and grass and this is what other feminines won't stand for—but that's because they aren't elementals! Aye I have to have an elemental."[34]

She finally gave in. Powys did his usual self-flagellation act: "To make you happy. It is what I do want & yet in my fierce impulsive selfishness what have I done but go & buy with my Wolf's gold a little house by a road."[35] He clutched on to every hint, however faint, that she might come to come to like it, but in any case, the deed was done. "How I did snatch at that place! How I do turn to what I want, in spite of my stern conscience."[36]

They left New York City for the small Pennsylvania Dutch settlement in Columbia County, on April 12, 1930. At first all seemed well. She was amused because "J. was so happy—all the time. . . . It is such a simple and profound well-being—like a child's or a dog's or a horse's or a cow's. . . . I was very happy too." On Easter Sunday she recorded,

> As I was finishing the dishes I caught such a beautiful light on the hills. . . .
> I snatched my cape and went half way up the hill and sat down for a long
> time and saw the dusk fall. . . . Our house looked like the ballad house—the
> perfect house we ever told ourselves stories about with the smoke coming
> from the chimneys. It seemed monstrous and incredible to me that I had
> ever hung back so and diatribed against it. Think if this had not happened.
> When I looked at that enormous hickory tree it seemed so strange that for
> a mere 2000 dollars anyone could be said to possess such a thing as that! . . .
> On my way later to the farm for a surreptitious load of wood to fill the bas-
> ket so Jack would not have to go so many times when he got back and
> would be surprised that it should be so full—my inner eye told me he was
> crossing the meadow where the trees are by the brook. . . . I dropped the
> basket and went under the fence and ran to meet him.[37]

Her love and admiration for him is always present in these early pages of her 1930 diary: "He recited poetry to me after tea and as always this fills me with happiness and adoration—and I sit feeling like an untutored savage maiden—to whom some god-like wanderer appears."[38] So too are present the all-too-evident sources of future grief. It is enlightening to compare their two diaries for a particular day. On the first of May he wrote in his: "I took her to the river. . . . But with my Pharisee fuss, a priggish, finicky, unease of conscience, I must needs make the T. T. cry over the Water Mint down there; by implying that she couldn't transplant it so 'twould be as happy—of course she could. She is herself a Water Mint and I have transplanted her." She wrote in hers:

> We went to the brook and he showed me mint growing there and said it was a marsh plant—that couldn't grow anywhere but in water—hastily—for fear I would want to transplant some of it—And so I did! There was almost a meadow of it. . . . I cried. I felt I could not bear J's sensitiveness in this way—out of all measure. . . . I am touchy—because of the conflict in myself— which I cannot reduce or straighten out satisfactorily and never will.

Visitors, almost always *his* friends or relatives, soon became another source of tears. It was Phyllis's tears that invariably are remarked upon, but John could be as childish as she, especially when his manias and phobias were not made allowance for. The first visitors were Marian and her young son Peter. From his birth, the boy had been a shared myth between Marian and John. Marian adored her son, as she adored her brother, and taught Peter to call John "Daddy Jack." Powys in turn referred to Peter as "my rival, my ouster, my young intruding lord."[39] Peter was only seven when, during this visit, an incident occurred which John Cowper reported in full in his diary. Following the Powys brothers' custom, whenever possible John urinated—"pumped-ship" as he called it—out of doors.

> Wednesday 4th June: I had a most serious quarrel with Peter before breakfast. He thought it was an amusing game to tease his uncle by spying on him while he went distracted to and fro hunting for a hiding-place wherein to pump-ship. At last I was seized with fury welling up from the very bottom of my soul (shall I ever recover from the shock of this feeling?) and I bore him kicking, hitting out savagely and even biting into his mother's room where I denounced his conduct (myself weeping and trembling with agitation). "He spied on me! He spied on me! When I was pump-shipping!" I kept crying out in a sobbing voice. "I hate him! I hate him!" screamed my antagonist with still louder sobs. It was a disturbing scene. The T. T. came flying from the kitchen and kissed away her angry mate's fiery tears while Marian soothed her outraged son. I went alone then (as ever is my wont when grievously upset) to a certain Hickory Tree in the field by the wood going to the village and kissed the soul of this tree and trembling still I cried to it, "O help me to forgive Peter! O help me to forgive Peter!" And I got just enough magic from this tree (the tree of knowledge of Good and Evil)

to forgive him but only if I did not see a certain expression in his face like that of a demonic Puck. This event has caused Pricking in my side.

The event was equally devastating for Peter—something John never knew. Years later, in an agony of spirit, Peter wrote in his own diary,

> February 25th 1986: And again I am faced with the old questions concerning this powerful, egomaniacal man: is he a white or black magician or, perhaps more accurately, is he a magician at all? <u>Wherever lies the truth</u> it is sure that my perfervidly jealous, skewed, view of this miserly possessor of my mother's heart finally crippled my own heart's growth. The flat truth is that Marian had some sort of idea that I would turn into a JCP clone and managed to vividly communicate this to me very early on as ineluctable doctrine. No wonder I followed the old boy (literally!) up the hill, attempting to emulate and take into myself some of his magic. And in a sense he was therefore justified in reacting so violently to such unsought-for expropriation. But only in a limited sense. His crazy over-reacting rejection was actually a rejection against anyone, whoever dear or close, who would enter his "demonic Puck" inner temple of self-adoration.[40]

John continued to "secretly struggle" with his anger against little Peter, reminding himself that he "ought to remember what a wickedly malicious child I was myself," but it seemed never to have occurred to him that it was jealousy—on both sides—that had created this traumatic scene. He could only conclude that "Marian's devotion to Peter is an infatuation. It always makes me tremble and shiver with dread. These desperate and passionate loves of mothers for only sons. One feels that if a mother & son are absorbed in each other like two lovers it doesn't matter what the outside world feels."[41]

Marian was an inspired gardener, a "Sorceress with Plants," and brought bulbs and cuttings from Snedon's Landing for Phyllis to begin her own garden. Gardening was to become for Phyllis an escape and a consolation, but for now it was just one more drain on her limited resources. Powys, who had lived with this woman for eight years, must have known that her upbringing in a rich and protected environment and her cultivated and sensitive personality made the move to a primitive cottage in a rural community a preposterous one. It would have taxeed the strength and skill of the most experienced housewife; Phyllis had neither the aptitude, vitality, or knowledge to deal with this totally alien life. John was equally ill-equipped. Almost any physical labor strained his ulcer, but in any case he was, as he often complained, congenitally clumsy. Carrying out ashes he could usually manage, but lighting a fire could take him up to two hours, and he never did master the art of opening a window or pulling up a blind. Two months after they moved in, Phyllis told him frankly that "she had not yet been happy here (save at rare moments) but had been shocked by moods of irritable misery and sudden angers. Something very deep she thought, some bruise, some hurt, some disappointment caused this and is yet causing it. My having snatched at this little house and spent two thousand when that two thousand might easily have kept us both for a whole year in Europe. . . . Thus we learn that it may be only a Servant is the alternative to staying in beautiful places in Henry James Pensions or Balzacian Inns."[42]

Most unluckily Powys decided that his cousin Warwick could be that very servant. He had not seen Warwick since 1928 when he returned to Las Vegas for a second summer. Then he had spent four days with this "Walter Scott character" on the lonely ranch, and thought he was "quite a good cook after his fashion and scrupulously tidy."[43] He sent Warwick $300 to travel from Las Vegas but found within a matter of days that Warwick was "really rather queer in the head." Phyllis, no doubt aware that Jack's kindness to the underdog had once again led him into a muddle, went home to her parents for three weeks and, for the first time, left him to deal with a situation he had himself created. The romantic myth of Warwick soon crumbled. John thought him a heartbreaking person, but "when he sings and sings and shouts and curses and talks drivel, it is very hard to be nice."[44] He took refuge in watering Phyllis's plants for long hours and writing for her a short story about their toy animals and dolls.

"The Owl, the Duck, and—Miss Rowe! Miss Rowe!" is a tender, charming little bagatelle, meant to remind her of the secret kingdom they had inhabited in the Room with their inanimate "children." It is the story of two "aged circus people"; the man had been a clown and the woman the ex-dancer of "the Cimmerian Troupe." They share the "Top Floor Front, Number Four" of Patchin Place with "a group of Persons, two of whom were human, two Divine, one an apparition, several inanimate, and two again only half-created." These latter are "wraiths from another world who had been created by a writer and left to grievance because the author had died before she could give a happy solution to their love." The divine ones are a tiny statue of the "great Chinese sage Kwang-tze, a headless image of Lao-tze (the old woman had knocked off his head in one of her rages) and a ten-cent statue of the Mother of God." The inanimates are a "fatalistic" glass fish, an "amorous" white china duck who has "a passion, a craving, a vice, an obsession" to touch "the polished and provocative flesh of young-lady dolls"; a doll called Olwen who is "a Princess" with slender legs, long graceful arms, blue eyes, a dainty nose, and an exquisite chin; a "metaphysical" owl; and Falada, "a noble, melancholy, wooden white horse" with only two legs, found by the old man in a garbage can. The old couple would be visited periodically by "The Authorities" who threatened to put them in a home which was "the one fate they both dreaded worse than death." When the Authorities threaten again, the woman gives the old man his bath in the tin tub, the gas oven is turned on, and they "laid them down together side by side under the covers of their bed." The others escape on Falada who "uttered only one word; and it was a word never heard before in the Known World. *Esplumeoir*."[45]

What makes this story so poignant to those who know its history is that just as "the Room" had been their enclosed world, this "group of persons" were, in every sense, their children. Olwen, Falada, and the little god Kwang remained always part of their lives, and indeed, they are now part of mine, living in my upstairs bedroom. But it is an aspect of, and a clue to, his genius that even those readers who know nothing of the background, will *sense* that all these wraiths and inanimates have their own rich and mysterious story. The stuffed owl belonged to the hunchback clerk, Archie Spring, whom Powys once described in a letter as "Arnold's typewriter, who always wore a black eye-glass and had a stuffed owl in his bedroom and was always lonely at Christmas."[46] After Spring's death, he and Phyllis took the owl to Patchin Place, and it is described in his story as having been "shot in the wilds of Virginia by a hump-back, who, in this way, both asserted his mutilated humanity and obtained for his lonely life a soft, silent, and watchful companion." This is exquisite prose—a laconic encomium for all the solitary ones of the world.

As Powys tried to cope with Warwick and the house and the plants, he received a cable from Llewelyn and Alyse saying they would be arriving from England in the next few days. This was a surprise to John but provided the impetus to get rid of Warwick. He sent the luckless cousin back to New Mexico, met Phyllis in New York, and both traveled back to Hillsdale to face Llewelyn's latest crisis. Gamel Woolsey had returned to Chaldon after her abortion in August 1929, and she and Llewelyn resumed their lovemaking. Astonishingly, Alyse accepted the situation but felt that Gamel was "a burden that will never lift."[47] However, a solution occurred in the form of the writer Gerald Brenan, who came to East Chaldon in the summer of 1930 with an introduction to Theodore from his friend "Tommy" Tomlin. On the tenth of July Brenan met Gamel at Theodore's. Less than a month later, Gerald asked her to marry him and she agreed. Both were escaping from sexual relationships that had become unresolvable. Brenan was running away from a hopeless love for Dora Carrington, the wife of his friend Ralph Partridge, and by this time Gamel loved Alyse almost as much as she loved Llewelyn and was fully aware of the pain she was causing her. Llewelyn was unable to change Gamel's mind, and in a "desperate passion" he left abruptly for America and John's solace, leaving Alyse to pack and follow.

From Phudd Bottom, Llewelyn wrote frantic love letters to Gamel and talked wildly of suicide. Phyllis rather tartly told him what suicide was *really* like. He acquired morphia tablets, but he still had them when he died a natural death in 1939. It was Alyse who used them lethally many years later. It was a difficult time for all four. John wrote in his diary, "He goes like a wounded Centaur or a wounded lion or an injured and outraged child of the gods—or just like Lulu <u>not having</u> what <u>Lulu</u> <u>wants!</u> . . . As for myself I am on Alyse's side but that is because I am for some mysterious and to me quite inexplicable reason, queerly prejudiced against this gentle, passive, dreamy, mediaeval, lovely incalculable young girl."[48] "The T. T. takes G.'s side and finds my simple prejudice hard to understand. I think it pure 'anti-feminine' inherited from my father & rage that a male animal should be so rattled. . . ."[49] Llewelyn proposed several unrealistic schemes—living *à quatre* or living alternately with Alyse and Gamel. Understandably, this suited no one except Llewelyn. John gave him the sympathy Lulu required, but while he saw the "real sorrow" in this forty-six-year-old brother, he felt privately that Llewelyn "wants to be the lamb suckled by both cow and sheep."[50] During this period, Gamel and Phyllis exchanged letters frequently, and Phyllis decided that Gamel's relationship with Brenan was not a "pis-aller but a happy ending." At Phyllis's urging, Gamel wrote directly to Alyse indicating that she had no intention of leaving Brenan. When Alyse broke this news to Lulu, he had cried, "But she belongs to me! She is mine. He is taking mine!"[51] Unable to bear it any longer Alyse went off for a week to visit her parents in Norwalk.

Without his wife to take out his frustration and hurt upon, and possibly feeling that his beloved brother was not being sufficiently sympathetic, Llewelyn turned to Phyllis and it was she who let him talk *sans cesse*. She wrote of one episode:

> 4 January 1931: I got so terribly tired before lunch washing dishes in the kitchen and feeling as if a <u>cold</u> were settling down upon me—that when Lulu in the green chair by my side in the midst of his perpetual and intricate elaborations of Mr B and G—talked about "grand Hotels in Rome" and appealed to me to agree with him that he couldn't care for them much, I had a bitter wave of reaction and said—"well I only know that there is nothing in the world I should like so well myself at this moment!" . . . When they had gone for their walk and I hurriedly tried to straighten up the room—deal with the stoves one of which I barely saved from going out again owing to neglect beforehand—filling the oil stove making my bed— and everywhere boots—cigarette ash—papers—confusion due to two men—I actually sulked for one moment and felt a victim.

Her mood did not lighten, when, instead of returning to New York for the winter as planned, "we" decided to stay at Phudd Bottom for the winter. Powys wrote, "The T. T. was so tired by scrubbing the kitchen linoleum floor that she was nearly dead. But O how she revived under this great decision! No, she didn't revive."[52] His nickname for her in the diary was by now "the T. T." The initials stood for the "Tiny Thin," the "Tylwyth Teg." She was his slender Welsh fairy sylph, his elemental, but elementals are designed for dancing in the midnight air, not for washing floors. Phudd Bottom had no electricity, no heating, no indoor plumbing. To make it habitable in winter required a considerable financial outlay, and the local tradesmen knew they were on to a good thing. Phyllis wrote bitterly in her diary, "We are a feathered fowl to be plucked by everyone."[53] She was constantly worried that their money would not last, and even more worried where to put for safekeeping what they did receive, because all the banks were "tottering" and beginning to close.[54] Not unexpectedly, John's ulcer now "spat out a froth of fury like an angry sea-anemone." The only alleviation appeared to be complete bed rest and this necessarily put the strain of running the house totally on a woman who was temperamentally undomestic and physically frail. Powys continued to feel guilty about the decision to stay the winter in the country and wondered "what I would do if the little T. T. had a great serious Nervous Collapse. . . . If we did go away all might be well. But where to go? As we are not married. . . . But I keep asking myself, 'is all this only rationalisation? Am I pretending this while really all the time I have my heart set on staying here?' I cannot believe this."[55] Nevertheless, stay they did, and Powys bought her a dog as recompense. They named the cocker spaniel "Peter" and then "the Black." Accident prone, nervous, untrained, the dog became their well-beloved, another one of their children.

The first months of 1931 were bitterly cold and the chores unending—fires had to be kept going, coal brought in, cinders and garbage taken out, the dog walked and fed, groceries ordered, periodic rat infestations dealt with, inevitable domestic crises handled—this as well as cooking, cleaning, dealing with guests and Jack's invalid needs. Phyllis hated and feared the cold, as he had always known. He compared her to a "huddled little wren" in her "shrinking from the Snow & Nature,"[56] but her response to the Phudd winter was not wrenlike: "14 February 1931: I took Peter down the road and faced such an annihilating North Wind I could only moan and cry and stagger on—rejecting my whole life ever being born—having to endure anything further except death."

From childhood, Phyllis's reactions to frustration or fear had always been extreme. She would have hysterics or, more seriously, hurt herself physically—biting her arm or hitting her head. Powys treated this behavior in a tolerant semi-humorous fashion as an aspect of her childlikeness. ("You hit the nice cat?") To make matters worse, Phyllis suffered from severe menstrual pain. She would have twenty-four hours of vomiting, which left her totally exhausted. Understandably, it was accompanied by extreme tension, both before and after her period, but this only partially accounted for her increasingly violent behavior. She was now lashing out at him, to her infinite self-disgust.

> 21 February 1931: The first day of my recovery—and return to my world—which began with seeing three enormous burned holes in the carpet and a pall of deep white ashes over everything. The room looked revolting. . . . An insane fury gripped me that he could be so absolutely without will or logic in relation to Matter. I felt I almost choked with the consciousness of it—and seized his hair at one point and made his spectacles fall off—and felt appalled at my conduct to the deepest nethermost fathom within me. . . . He was not annoyed—he was not insulted—his pride and dignity did not seem to be even so much as crossed by the shadow of a dragon fly. Neither was there a flicker of contempt, scorn, disgust, or righteous superiority. He picked up his spectacles like Pythagorus might have who had had them jostled off by a boor and a bully—with matter of fact—philosophical going on as if nothing had happened and without the tenor of his thought or feeling being in the least deflected. I felt as if I had never before experienced real

human dignity as I did when I looked at him at that moment. Somehow it even made my awfulness—nothing—it made the incident that had just happened no scar on the surface of time—even quite decent natural and humanly honourable. I deserve to be a bent sharp stick stuck forever in a muddy and uncomfortable crevice in Lethe forever. While Jack and Spinoza and Leibnitz and Bishop Berkley walk backwards and forwards on the Elysian fields pursuing the discussion of Monads and looking at the Fra Angelico flowers close to the earth. And I probably shall be. And not even able to know that J is ever passing on the margin.

It was obvious that something had to be done, and Marian found them a live-in housekeeper. An elderly German woman, Magda Hagen, arrived on January 22, 1931. Again, all went well at first. Powys was thrilled and relieved to see Phyllis "radiate a delicious vibration of a little girl being very happy."[57] As an added bonus, she was able to concentrate on typing his latest novel for, despite the agitations of the past year, Powys had been working steadily at another story. The pressure on him to produce a novel at least as successful as Wolf Solent was intense: their financial future and his reputation as a writer depended on it.

Powys began A Glastonbury Romance a week after they moved to Phudd, and he finished it a day after his fifty-ninth birthday, a year and a half later—a tumultuous masterpiece written during a turbulent time. Twenty years later, when he was asked by his publishers to write a preface to a new edition, he explained that this long book attempted to describe "the effect of a particular legend, a special myth, a unique tradition, from the remotest past in human history, upon a particular spot on the surface of this planet together with its crowd of inhabitants of every age and of every type of character."[58] The "particular legend" is the Grail Quest; the "particular spot" is Glastonbury, Somerset, in the late 1920s. The choice of Glastonbury was inevitable; Joseph of Arimathea was supposed to have brought the Grail to Glastonbury, and it was known as the Isle of Avalon, the place where, tradition has it, Arthur was carried after his death. Powys describes the town and the surrounding Somerset levels in such detail that the reader can trace, even today, almost every street, every house, every hill and river. At the same time he makes this ancient Isle of Avalon a "symbolic centre" for "visions that hint at strange degrees of consciousness in a world which, though as material as you please, remains . . . as insubstantial as the stuff of dreams."[59] His "crowd of inhabitants" include a sadist, a madwoman, a vicar, a procuress, eccentric servants, spinster ladies, lovelorn maidens, lesbians, not to mention anarchists, communists, romantic lovers, old men, and young children.

Although most of the action takes place in Somerset, the "sentimental journey" he had made with Littleton to Norfolk in 1929 provides the material for the opening chapter, a richly sensuous memorial to his childhood holidays at his grandparent's vicarage in Northwold, and an éloge to this brother. "He is my faithful, he is my constant . . . he dominates this early part of my book."[60] It is not so much Littleton that dominates as the vivid memory of their shared past. The novel begins with the funeral and the reading of the will of Canon Crow, a rich, eccentric clergyman. Of the many hopeful relatives who have gathered, most of whom now live in Somerset, there is the industrialist Philip Crow, who intends to use the money to further his ambition to turn Glastonbury into a prosperous industrial centre; the impecunious John Crow, newly returned from France, hoping to get a job with his cousin Philip; Mary, another cousin, with whom John immediately falls in lust. To the consternation of these relatives, Canon Crow has left his fortune to John ("Bloody Johnny") Geard, an itinerant evangelical preacher. Geard is determined to use this inheritance to establish in Glastonbury, "a new age of faith." He promptly hires John Crow, and together they plan a midsummer pageant as the first step to a "religious revival." This pageant, a wild combination of Christian and pagan elements, succeeds in drawing the eyes of the world once again to King Arthur's Avalon. After the pageant, in a burst of religious exaltation and magical power, Geard cures an old woman of cancer and raises a child from the dead. The novel ends with a spring flood which deluges the town and sweeps everything before it. Not only Philip's bridges, roads, industries, but also Geard himself, disappear into the muddy waters. Around this central narrative revolve at least two other semi-detached stories. One involves Owen Evans, an antiquarian bookseller and sadistic voyeur, who is writing a book about Merlin. Another concerns the son of the local vicar, Sam Dekker, and Nell Zoyland. Sam is deeply in love with Nell, but he "gets religion," renounces her, and finally has a vision of the Grail.

The older Powys thought he sensed in his *Glastonbury Romance* "psychological secrets deep almost as life"[61] but suspected that the intuitions of which he was conscious at the age of eighty were then "the more spontaneous and more instinctive workings of his mind." This is doubtful. As he says himself, he was a "born book-worm turned novelist or fabulist." Some of Powys's earliest lectures were on the medieval romances of Arthur and his knights, and what he called his "mania for the Arthurian legend," and particularly the legend of the Grail quest, continued thereafter. In 1929, on the ship returning from England, he read John Rhys's *Studies in the Arthurian Legend*,[62] an astonishing nine times and felt he was now "on the track of the mythological Graal far older than the Holy Graal."[63] It was the mythological origins of the quest that he wanted to base his story on. To this end he immersed himself in the groundbreaking theories of the Cambridge classical scholars Jane Harrison,[64] Francis Cornford,[65] and Gilbert Murray.[66] During the period between 1900 and 1915, they were persuasively arguing that Greek religion grew out of a primitive ritualism which, in the manifold variations of the dying and resurrected fertility god, celebrated or acted out the victory of the force of life over that of death. Other disciplines began to compare the rites of the Hellenistic mystery religions with the myths of wandering heroes who make the initiatory descent into the other-world or the "Realm of the Mothers," in order to find renewed life. On the lecture tour in early 1930, Powys borrowed more books to read on the long train journeys. He read Roger Loomis on the Fisher King,[67] W. E. Mead on Merlin,[68] and Alfred Nutt on the Celtic version of the legend.[69] But it was Jessie Weston's controversial theories of the Grail's origins,"the unholy elements in both its history and its mystery,"[70] that particularly absorbed him.[71] She saw in the events and symbols of the Christian legend—the waste land, the freeing of the waters, the fisher king, the medicine man, the hidden castle, the bleeding lance and cup—transformations of ancient fertility rites, and she argued that ritual had as its ultimate object the initiation into the secret of life, physical and spiritual. He wrote to Phyllis, "I am absorbed in it. Weston seems to have got hold of every scrape of neglected information in every tongue about the Graal; & incidentally many most exciting occult secrets about Merlin & Taliesin."[72] He felt, however, that there was not enough "real Grimm-fairy-story un-mystical simple magic power" in her interpretation. A Grimm story is what he proceeded to write.

He hit upon the idea of having two questers in his story—one searching for the Holy Grail, the other in search of the mythological Graal. In the medieval myths, the guardian of the Grail, called the fisher king, is wounded by a "dolorous blow," and his infirmity unaccountably makes the land wasted by drought. The king can only be cured if a naive, chaste, young knight asks a key question. Sam Dekker is a modern Grail knight. Johnny Geard, on the other hand, is intent on performing the mystery rites of the mother goddess, Cybele. Powys could (and did) model Sam's adventures closely on medieval myth, but Geard's pagan quest gave him more difficulty. Although he had to give up "all attempt to do any work while Lulu is here," all that autumn of 1930 he was thinking how to handle the Geard character. By the New Year he had decided that "Mr. Geard must think of the secret of real life beyond this spectacular world. He must think of the Graal as a symbol of this secret life beyond life."[73] The writing of *Glastonbury* now went quickly and both Powys and Phyllis were excited by what was evolving. Phyllis wrote in her diary: "Jack read me his XVI chapter—the most extraordinary and powerful chapter. I don't know what to make of it—nor will many else I think—but I am deeply impressed by it."[74]

In February, Llewelyn decided the winter in upstate New York was too cold for him, and John and Phyllis were suddenly told that he and Alyse were off to the West Indies. They were astonished, but as Phyllis remarked, "Lulu is as surprising in his power of sudden giving up what is on his mind as he is in dwelling on it sans cesse and sans fin."[75] After this trip, Llewelyn and Alyse returned to England, leaving John and Phyllis to re-establish their equilibrium. Then in March, Phyllis went to Joplin for six weeks to assist her ailing parents, entrusting John to the housekeeper. He wrote her twice, sometimes three times, a day singing his woes: he couldn't write very much, Mrs. Hagen's Germanic ways got on his nerves, coping with household decisions was too difficult. "When you are here—you do take all the responsibility away."[76] When she returned in April, it was to a calmer period, and May of 1931 was an especially felicitous time for them both. John noted that he "woke up to enchantment; as I do always these heavenly spring days,"[77] and the ulcer pain temporarily receded. As for Phyllis, she wondered if the depression that had struck her down as a teenager might finally have lifted and her childhood gaiety and promise returned. She gave all the credit for this to John. "No genii could have done to my life what he has done."[78]

> 24 May 1931: I live in a Valley—of the mind as well as of the body and I suddenly felt the absence of my unused and perished wings. When I looked at the Mountains I thought someday I shall return to this—my other self— my old self—will it then be too late? . . . I am obsessed by this garden. It is like some of those manias I had as a child. But I wake with the old intense happiness and intensity I used to have with my doll house.

Powys would watch with wonder this frail being in her garden and inevitably she became part of the pagan myth he worked through in *Glastonbury*. She "looked like a living fragment of earth; the youngest daughter of Demeter kneeling and digging in the rainy wind."[79] Sadly, it took little to send this Persephone back into the depths. More often than not she felt "miserably inadequate." Mornings were always her worst time. While she struggled to wake up, he would go for a walk, call her again, then do what he called his "yoga" lying on the sofa. She recorded despairingly, "I felt I could not get breakfast and said he looked 'smug' on sofa—only because I was inevitably and without any possibility of righting it irretrievably and forever—in the wrong."[80]

They were by now so short of money that they had to give up Patchin Place permanently. It was Phyllis who went to New York to make the arrangements. Despite her conviction that "I have nothing to meet the world with of myself,"[81] she got everything sorted, packed, and dispatched—"the resource of F. P. though inherited by me in such a feeble and diluted strain made me know what to do." This was the first time she mentioned inheriting her father's resourcefulness, but she had it, and it grew over the years. It was at this period that Powys began to remark upon, and to rely on, her "executive" qualities. In July they decided that Phyllis could manage without Mrs. Hagen, although John admitted that it was he who had deliberately engineered the departure by that "deep Meanness which lies in my Coward Nature; . . . steering things without any overt gesture . . . and getting what I want without striving direct for it—which must be a trick inherited from my Powys ancestors. . . . It is my cold Stonelike heart that is really sending the Old Lady away using the T. T.'s passionate nerves as my Weapon & Shield."[82]

By this time, his publishers were eager to read what they hoped was going to be their next bestseller. Maxe Schuster and his associates, Clifton Fadiman and Melrich von Rosenberg, visited Phudd and took back with them the partially completed *Glastonbury*. A month later they wrote disappointedly that it was far too long and had too many characters in it. Schuster and his editors were amongst John's greatest admirers, but they were disconcerted by the apparent formlessness of the action and the seemingly unconnected stories, of which there were many. There were, for example, a number of love stories, both homosexual and heterosexual, which end unhappily. Tossie Stickles and Tom Barter fall in love and are very happy until Tom is killed by a maniac wielding an iron bar. Angela Beere's love for Persephone Spear goes unfulfilled. There is the completely separate story about "Black Morgan" who suffers from some unexplained disillusionment and sadness. She finally drowns herself and leaves her little girl, Nelly, an orphan. Powys's detailed knowledge of the most esoteric aspects of both the pagan and medieval strands was prodigious and, like most authors, he wanted to use it all. *He* knew, even if the publishers and editors did not, that all these stories grew out of one short passage in Chrétien de Troyes's *Perceval*: "Ladies sad will lose their mates / The land in desolation lie/ Damsels unconsoled will sigh / Widows and orphans, mournful all / And many a knight in death will fall." Creating a fictional world out of a few lines of poetry always gave Powys great delight but it often left his publishers and editors baffled and vexed.

> 28 June 1931: Meditated long and long on the Schuster Fadiman letter about de emphasizing Crummie & Cordy & cutting Number One and Number Two and Red Robinson & Morgan Nelly. . . . I don't know that I mind very <u>very</u> much cutting out Red; but I don't like cutting out Lily & Louie and "de-emphasizing" as Mr. F. calls it, Emma & Tilly Crow. We shall see! I wonder what the T. T. will say! Not a little I wouldn't wonder!

Despite his protests (and hers), Powys knew he had no choice but to agree with the publishers' demands. Astonishingly, while he was cutting the first part of the novel by a third, he decided to begin writing the last chapter of the book and then work his way back, chapter by chapter, to the middle. No one could do that without knowing where he was going and precisely what he wanted to achieve. The strength as well as the complexity of *A Glastonbury Romance* lies in its underlying structure of myth, or rather in the interweaving of myths, but this does make huge demands on the reader, whom Powys forces into the role of an initiate searching for the "secret." Many years later, he admitted to a young disciple, Kenneth Hopkins, that,

> There is all the way through the book a constant undercurrent of secret reference to the Grail legends, various incidents and characters playing roles parallel to those in the old romances of the Grail, not without furtive dips into that world of weird ritual and mythology made so much of in T. S. Eliot's "Wasteland." It does not go to work with the pedantry of Joyce using the Odyssey in "Ulysses," but there is a vague sort of parallel to all that.[83]

There is indeed. In all the myths of the wandering hero, for example, there is a female "messenger" whose function is to start him on his quest. In the *Romance* this role is played by "Mad Bet" Chinnock, who suddenly appears before Sam Dekker and his companions and dances her mad dance.

"Here we go round the Mulberry Bush!" chanted the old woman, skipping up
and down with an expression of childish gravity, while the loose, beaded tassels
hanging from her hat bobbed this way and that over her ghastly white skull.[84]

With Mad Bet, Powys makes the interconnections between pagan custom
and later myth. Only in one medieval legend, the *Perlesvaus*, does the curious
detail of the maiden who has lost her hair occur, but in the pagan Adonis cults,
the women who took part in the rites had to shave off their hair. However
grotesque, his characters are never lifeless; the erudition is underpinned by his
own personal myths. Mad Bet is an amalgam of Emily, the beloved nurse of the
Powys family, who, by the time he was writing this was both insane and bald, and
the old tramp Happy Mary who would keep Christmas at Court House by lifting
her skirts and dancing the heathen candlestick dance.

Sam is the virtuous Perceval of medieval myth; the Fisher King is, in this
story, Christ himself. Sam accepts that in his encounter with Mad Bet something
critical has happened and that he has made a "final inward decision."[85] Previous
to this, he has fallen passionately in love with Nell Zoyland and they have consummated their love. Now he breaks off this relationship to devote himself to the
suffering Christ through a life of humility and asceticism. He goes to work in a
brickyard, and in order to make his self-imposed humiliation more savior-like, he
spends his evenings with the outcasts of the community. Sam's reward for
attempting to heal the Christ King is, as it was for Perceval and Gawain, a vision
of the Grail symbols—the Bleeding Lance and the Grail Chalice.

The man's abrupt progress from chastity to sexual passion to asceticism to
Grail vision is another example of Powys's knowledge, not only of orthodox
Christian beliefs and the mystery religions, but the syncretistic gnostic heresies
which he said he was "forever preaching at Corpus."[86] In most of the medieval
romances celibacy was the indispensable condition of achieving the quest. This
stipulation is, of course, in direct contradiction to the ancient fertility rites,
which required of the male participant something other than chastity. But a basic
doctrine of the gnostic religion was that certain select believers could be initiated into the "secret of life, physical and spiritual" by a twofold process: the "Little
Mysteries" required "fleshly generation," but after men have been initiated into
them, "they should cease for a little and become initiated in the Great, Heavenly
Mysteries . . . into which [House] no impure man shall come."[87] Powys has Sam
leave Nell so suddenly after their night of love because the first part of the initiation being complete, the second must begin. This may be a satisfying course of
action to a reader with a knowledge of early religious sects, but it leaves Sam's
motivation obscure to others. Phyllis, for example, thought Sam should go back
to Nell and *then* see the Grail, but Powys was not interested in what might be
considered the human response. He did, however, find the Grail vision a particularly difficult chapter to write. An entry in Phyllis's diary is an astute comment
on his writing in general, her role as critic, and, incidentally, on the associations
she makes with his writings and those of Theodore and Llewelyn.

Jack read me the rest of his chapter after breakfast this morning, and for some reason it seemed to have run completely off the track. It was as if inspired under malevolent astral conditions—as if he had got started in this way—and with his volatility and power of being a chameleon—he had given himself up to it to the limit—until everything that happened and the way in which he related it was all in this tepid thin vein of imagination with all the peculiar aspects of his writing washing backwards and forwards—as though in a wooden tub of some kind—and seeming like—Faults. Like Theodore's in their eternal repetition—whereas of course these same things become the strength of his genius when he is writing well—and they are carried on by Lulu's golden stream. It was a very strange thing. But J. was undaunted and without any gathering himself together even—immediately prepared to re-write the whole 100 pages—even starting out quite fresh— without using the old ones and filling in. . . . I wondered how it was I could so ruthlessly tear his chapter to pieces for the sake of the Abstract value of a book when I know that the writing of it makes his ulcer worse. To deliberately set him to work anew seems incredible—what should I care about his book compared to him?[88]

Powys liked to portray himself as a novelist who seldom revised his work; a writer driven by inspiration alone. This romantic vision of himself is belied, not only by his private diaries and now hers, but by his manuscripts which reveal multiple re-writings. In the case of the Grail scene, the end result is an inspired *and* controlled piece of work. As Sam trails along the bank of the ancient Brue, the river into which Arthur had once thrown his sword, he becomes aware that "the soul of the inanimate, the indwelling breath of life in all these ancient lifeless things, whereof the town was so full, was really moving towards him."[89] Then suddenly, "without a second's warning—the earth and the water and the darkness *cracked*."

What he saw was at first accompanied by a crashing pain. . . . The pain was so overwhelming that it was as if the whole of Sam's consciousness became the hidden darkness of his inmost organism; and when this darkness was split, and the whole atmosphere split . . . what he felt to be a gigantic spear was struck into his bowels and struck *from below*. . . .

But when the vision appeared, and it came sailing into the midst of this bleeding darkness that was Sam's consciousness, healing everything, changing everything, each detail of what he saw he saw with a clearness that branded it forever upon his brain. He saw a globular chalice that had two circular handles. The substance it was made of was clearer than crystal; and within it there was dark water streaked with blood, and within the water was a shining fish. . . .

Sam actually struggled up to his feet and cried the question aloud— "Christ!" he groaned in a harsh, queer voice that resembled the voice of a priest speaking from a scaffold. "Is it a Tench?"[90]

In order to identify himself with the suffering Christ, the Fisher King, Sam must himself be speared "from below" and go through the "bleeding darkness." Similarly, in the pagan myth, in order to find Persephone, the initiate must go with the mother-goddess by way of darkness, death, and the "abysses of the earth." As so often, the imagery in this powerful scene arose from a combination of personal memories and omnivorous reading. When they were together in Norfolk in 1929, John spent many hours watching Littleton fishing the river. One day they also visited a mill pond. These events coalesced in his mind and the two central informing images of the novel—the pagan waters of Cybele and the Fish of Christ—came into existence.

> Tried to work and adjust the engines of my mind to find some sort of a secondary place in my secret mythology for the God of my parents' grand-parents but found it rather difficult but in a certain way easier and less of a committal, than that crucified God of my son. . . . Then went to Harrod's Mill Pool dark and deep with enormous fish swimming in it great dace and chub & trout—a mystic sight—the pool of Cybele.[91]

Powys's mind was as retentive as his constipated gut, and he had the remarkable ability to use pieces of information and ideas in a way uniquely his own. The tench, like the chub, is a species of carp, a sacred fish in antiquity, which had a reputation for curing people with its touch. Sam's bizarre question, "Christ! Is it a Tench?"—is the magic question that cures the wounded king who is Christ and also heals the knight.

The morning after his vision, Sam sets out to give an enema to Abel Twig, who has severe constipation and piles. Only Powys, like old Abel, "turble weak in me stummick and turble sore in me backside," who knew well the intricacies of enema-giving and receiving, could create this funny and tender scene. Only Powys, who lived in a double world, could juxtapose the real and the symbolic in quite so convincing a way. As Sam bends over his task, the act of shoving the rubber tube up the old man's bleeding anus, and his own buggering by the "shaft of an Absolute" the day before, "mingled and fused together in his consciousness." The old man is purged and Sam has been purified.

During this time he was reading Gustav Fechner, a psychophysicist with philosophical leanings, and Fechner's theories on the nature of the relation between the spiritual and material worlds may have influenced the *Romance*.[92] However, it was Fechner's conviction of the interdependency of the body and the mind that served to reinforce Powys's awareness that a complex dialogue went on between his ulcer-afflicted body, his conscience-harried mind, and his characters,

> I got on well with my difficult chapter . . . for I come to Tossie Staples & the second I reach Tossie—all my mind becomes easy and relaxeed & my style flowed like fresh milk! It looks as if my mood for the day depended on some psychic influence emanating from the particular character in my book who then dominates. Poor Mr Evans 'twas & his tormented mind, like one in Hell, that gave me that severe dyspepsia.[93]

In November 1929, a certain Mr. Evans, a "Welshman on both sides," mysteriously turned up to tea in Patchin Place, and they had a "thrilling" conversation. Powys described him as a cruel mystic who "smells of prison life." Possibly it is this man he had in mind when he created Owen Evans. Equally he had himself in mind; he continued to be tormented by his sadistic imaginings.

> The T. T. came up at 2.15 a.m. & I held her tight trying . . . to sublimate that shivering, that scoria shiver rising up from depths below depths of my inmost being caused by the "ad" of that terrible book. . . . Most of it would have been far too violent and bloody for my taste . . . but little side touches in it simply over powered me swept me away like a Sirocco wind bringing back all those books. . . . It must be that the idea of "voyeurs" getting such wicked pleasures in itself stirs up my evil being even though the violence itself is totally out of my sphere! Certainly it shows that my sadistic tendency is actually after all these years of austere and rigid control . . . still exactly the same. I suppose nothing but my Death will end it. Or did Mr. Evans grey headed & reading Malory . . . find some mystical "Esplumeoia" of escape from Sadism ere he died up there in his little home in Glastonbury? I cannot understand it. But there are terrible things in the world. How can it be that the sensual nerve can work these madnesses?[94]

His Owen Evans keeps "scenes of sadistic cruelty" in the back chambers of his mind, glimpses of which produce in him "an inebriation of erotic excitement" so overpowering that it reduces all the rest of life to "tedious occurrences." One such scene is of a man being murdered by "a killing blow delivered by an iron bar." Only Owen (and his author) knew "how many of these abominations had actually been practised, how many described in forbidden books, or how many simply invented by a perverted imagination," but he has come to blame himself "for the innumerable forms of suffering in the world, of which he was entirely innocent." Barred from committing the sadistic act in real life, Evans turns the sadism on himself. Suffering from a "fever of remorse," Evans searches for a way to give himself "as much suffering as he would like to inflict on others."[95]

Powys knew from conversations with cousin Ralph that his astrological sun sign, Libra, was considered to be the driving force behind the mechanism of sacrifice, and that sacrifice could be displayed outwardly as a bodily wound or as an inner infliction of self-chastisement. His dreams told him the same story. In November 1930 he dreamt that "white excrement" ran out of his feet. "For this I was disgraced & a Scaffold . . . was set up to execute me with the word PUNISHMENT writ on it in vast letters."[96] In March 1931, he dreamt he was to act in a Pageant. He could now approach the mystery of ritual killing from a different direction with a different character. Through Evans, this antiquarian bookseller learned in the ways of myth and erotic aberration, Powys explored further the complex mechanisms of sacrifice, sadism, and maniacal self-punishment, far beyond anything that a Christian knight could comprehend.

Evans jumps at the chance to play the crucified Christ at Johnny Geard's pageant in the hope that this might be a way of atonement. At his request, he is bound on a cross with ropes, and before losing consciousness from the pain, he assumes the accumulated guilt of all the perpetrators of cruelty and victims of cruelty who have ever lived in Glastonbury. Evans, hanging on his self-imposed cross, is a dubious sin-eater and an even more dubious Christ. Just before he loses consciousness, "'We are alone,' his soul whispered to his body and to the pain that he was inflicting on his body."[97] The sacrificial pain is for himself—it gives him an orgasm. He triumphs in "the savage rapture of his self-immolation"; he exalts in his agony, "extreme pain and ecstatic triumph embracing each other in dark mystic copulation."[98] This is an immensely powerful scene of auto-erotic flagellation. Only Louis Wilkinson could draw a jeering parallel.

> Golly, what a man of sorrows, how acquainted with grief. And how insanely far he carries all that. I met his train at Chicago once. He walked along the platform, head bowed, shoulders bent, carrying a suitcase in one hand, bearing his Cross. . . . He couldn't get a porter when he was being Jesus Christ. The awful thing about that time was that he didn't know I was meeting the train. It was just his daily crucified posture that he wanted everyone to see. Every place a stage, every passerby one of the audience. . . . Does it on purpose, because he can't do without "sin" to whip him up. The "divine" and the "devilish"—you know—all that ridiculous tedious rubbish.[99]

Louis's clever mockery would have passed over Powys much as Phyllis's rages did. By now the book had taken on life of its own: "It is writing me. I am not writing it." However, he was conscious that a synchronic correspondence was operating between external events and his creative self. Phudd Bottom in the drought-stricken summer of 1931 was its own small wasteland, and Powys began an obsessive ritual of transferring fish from shallow ponds to deep pools—an expiating reversal of his childhood mania for killing tadpoles by taking them from ponds to drying puddles. His ulcer flared up, and he had a terrible struggle with constipation and an enema that didn't work: "Was it not odd that for the last few days in my book I have been writing of an enema & today this happened to me." Then, as if freed mentally as well as physically of "a cannon-ball stuck in my arse," he wrote eagerly the scene where Sam has his vision of the mystic fish.

> 26 September: After breakfast I rescued a lot of fish. . . . It was a curious coincidence that while I was at this job out of doors, on my couch I was writing about Ichthus the World-Fish.
> 27 September: I wish it would rain. O I do so long for it to rain.
> 30 September: I have finished my chapter. . . . And it is strange that this fish-catching should answer so well to Sam's vision of the Sangreal.

He wrote: "My Glastonbury Book is the expression of my natural & Normal life at Phudd Bottom." In a curious and profound way it was. When it finally rained at Phudd Bottom, it rained in Glastonbury. In the Grail myth, when the king is cured, the waste land becomes fertile again. The original ritual can be found in the Rig-Veda. In a country where the fertility of the earth depends upon sufficient water, the god Indra is worshipped. In one of the hymns, Indra boasts, "For all mankind I set the rivers free." In the *Romance*, the Atlantic Ocean itself floods the countryside and Powys's description of this inundation of the Somerset levels (almost four pages long for Powys never freed waters by half) is one of the most astonishing passages he ever wrote.

> The great waves of the far Atlantic, rising from the surface of unusual spring tides, were drawn, during the first two weeks of that particular March, by a moon more magnetic and potent as she approached her luminous rondure than any moon that had been seen on that coast for many a long year. Up the sands and shoals and mudflats, up the inlets and estuaries and backwaters of that channel-shore raced steadily, higher and higher as day followed day, these irresistible hosts of invading waters. . . . There was a strange colour upon them, too, these far-travelled deep-sea waves, and a strange smell rose up from them, a smell that came from the far off mid-Atlantic for many days. They were like the death mounds of some huge wasteful battlefield carried along by an earthquake and tossed up into millions of hill summits and dragged down into millions of valley hollows as the whole earth heaved. . . . Many of these incoming deep-sea waves had curving crestheads that were smooth and slippery as the purest marble, heads that seemed to grow steadily darker and darker, as they gathered toward the land, till they added something menacing to every dawn and to every twilight.
>
> And as these tides came in, over the brown desolate mudflats, they awoke strange legends and wild half forgotten memories along that coast. Ancient prophecies seemed to awake and flicker again, prophecies that had perished long ago, like blown out candles in gusty windows, cold as the torch flames by which they were chanted and the extinct fires by which they were conceived.

The passage ends:

> Of all mortal senses the sense of smell carries the human soul the farthest back in its long psychic pilgrimage; and by these far drawn channel airs and remote sea odours the inmost souls of many dwellers in northwest Somerset must have been roused, during those weeks in March. . . . That hidden wanderer, incarnated in our temporary flesh and blood, that so many times before—centuries and aeons before—has smelt deep sea seaweed and sunbleached driftwood and the ice cold chills of Arctic seas, sinks down upon such far off memories, as upon the stern of a voyaging ship, and sees, as if in a dream, the harbours and the islands of its old experience.[100]

Perhaps it hardly matters in the final analysis what individual events, what memories, or what reading have gone into the making of the novel. Powys's

greatness as a novelist ultimately resides in his ability to create images that reverberate at all levels of a reader's consciousness and unconscious mind.

When the flood comes, Sam and his vicar father find a raft and, with great
joy and zest, rescue stranded old folk. The waters are freed, and the Christian
knight returns to life. The waters are freed, and the other quester, Geard, returns
to the Mother-Goddess, Cybele.

> Such was the Mr. Geard who was now drowning in the exact space of water
> that covered the spot where the ancient Lake Villagers had their temple to
> the neolithic goddess of fertility. . . .
>
> What was he thinking about now? Not of Glastonbury; nor of Death.
> He was lying in the green spring grass of the Park at Montacute; and an
> incarnate Sweetness that was his daughter and yet not his daughter was run-
> ning to meet him with outstretched arms. . . .
>
> For the great Goddess Cybele . . . moves through the generations from
> one twilight to another. . . . About her turreted head blows the breath of
> what is beyond life and beyond death; and none, but such as are covenant-
> ed and sealed as her own, discern her goings and her comings.[101]

A *Glastonbury Romance* is an enormous book, not just in size but in scope.
Powys intended to "convey a jumbled-up and squeezed together epitome of life's
various dimensions"[102] and that he has certainly accomplished. There are forty-
seven "principal characters" in this extraordinary book and almost as many subplots. The characters, in their infinite variety, range from the larger-than-life
Geard, the unfastidious man who gets pleasure "from making water in his wife's
garden, from snuffing up the sweet sweat of those he loved"; to the vicar, admon-
ishing his son Sam to resist the temptation of Nell, "while his erotic nerve kept
repeating 'I'd like to, I'd like to!'"; to Mrs. Legge, the procuress, a "double-
chinned mountain of a woman, with astute, little grey eyes . . . that seemed
rather to aim at *not* seeing what she wanted to avoid"; to Paul Trent, the anar-
chist who "found that he was gesticulating furiously with his free hand right in
front of Miss Crow's face, and that Miss Crow had shut her eyes tight, as if she
were in the process of being shampooed"; to Bert, one of the "Robber Band" of
children who is "an infant of five, who in placidity and appearance resembled a
giant mushroom." The writing is often unfashionably extravagant, the narrative
slow, the dialogue sometimes inept. There are readers who have never got past
the metaphysically overloaded first page, which one critic labeled "The Beecher's
Brook of English Fiction."[103] For those who do, the novel is an exhausting but
enthralling experience.

On March 6, 1932, the first copies of *Glastonbury* arrived. In early April
Powys went to New York to give three lectures but turned down an offer to speak
on the radio about it—he told Marian that he thought that it would be inconsistent with his role as a solitary who had retired from society. In his secret heart
he hoped "for I know not what terrific Kudos including the Noble Prize & being

knighted by my Sovereign & receiving the acclamation of Europe & seeing the book translated into all languages—& best of all sold at the entrance to the Ruins in Glastonbury itself!"[104] But he was not prepared to give up his role-playing mask to forward this desire. The reviews were mixed, but over the years the consensus amongst critics is that the *Romance* is one of his greatest achievements. In a letter to Lawrence Durrell in April 1957, Henry Miller wrote, "The other day I began reading *A Glastonbury Romance* by John Cowper Powys. My head began bursting as I read. No, I said to myself, it is impossible that any man can put all this—so much—down on paper. It is super-human. . . . Old John had caught the world by the throat. And lovingly and surely he squeezed every bit of beauty, of meaning, of purposeless purpose out of it."[105] Such praise from a fellow writer would have meant a great deal to Powys, but that came many years later. Six months after it was published, it was obvious that the book which had taken him a year and a half to write was a financial failure. It sold only four thousand copies; while he and Phylllis were hoping to make $3,000 on it, they received only $750 and out of that they had to pay $500 for its typing.

Simon & Schuster also lost heavily on it, and when they asked Powys to write quickly a more saleable short book of "Ideas on Living," like the successful *In Defence of Sensuality*, he felt he "owed it to them" and agreed to do so. Phyllis was furious, insisting that "these hurried little Tracts for the Times," were nothing but "Pigeon Roost sermons," and "little Cults for funny ones."[106] She suspected that all S&S wanted was pop psychology of the happy-clappy school for all the lonely misfits in the world. In a sense, that is what they got. Even Powys privately subsumed these essays under the title "Be Happy Damn It!"

A Philosophy of Solitude was highly influenced by Rousseau's *Rêveries du promeneur solitaire*, which he was reading in the autumn of 1932, but equally it arose out of his own character traits, out of the years of enforced sociability on the lecture circuit, out of his increasing hatred of all aspects of modern civilization, out of his defiant rejection of society's emphasis on interpersonal relations as the source of happiness. *The Philosophy of Solitude* begins with the premise, "Every human being is alone in the core of the mind. When we are born we cry; and that cry is the cry of loneliness. . . . And the older we grow the lonelier we grow."[107] We can deny this "metaphysical horror" by indulging in "drifting, brainless gregariousness," but this is simply another "attempt to escape from this inherent loneliness of self."[108] A better alternative, he suggests, is not only to accept the solitude but to cultivate it. His argument here and *In Defence of Sensuality* is that, above all, the lonely self must create "a clear-cut, hard, resistant, nucleus of consciousness."[109] The Powys-heroes of *Wolf Solent* and *A Glastonbury Romance* celebrate the power and the joy that comes from the creation of a solitary, self-contained consciousness. John Crow thinks of himself as "a hard, round stone defying the whole universe" and exults "I am myself alone."[110]

Believing that there is no possibility of relation with other human beings, or indeed, any desire for relation, what Powys proposes instead is a solitary close communication with the elemental world. This, he argues, can bring comfort, sometimes happiness, and in rare moments, ecstasy. Once the inmost self has been made a hard crystal "immune to all invasion," the self chooses a piece of the inanimate universe, the "not-self," and embraces it. In this "erotic" embrace, the self achieves a "premeditated ecstasy," which "if it is not the Absolute it is as near to that mystery as we are ever likely to come." Although *Solitude* is a variant of his earlier philosophy tract, there is a bleak difference between the two books. In *In Defence of Sensuality*, he wrote: "In loneliness a human being feels himself backward, down the long series of his avatars, into the earlier planetary life of animals, birds and reptiles, and even into the cosmogonic life of rocks and stones."[111] By the time he was writing *Solitude*, he had eliminated the animate from his embrace. "The Inanimate—such as earth, stone, rock, water, air, vapour—is a better refuge for the self at bay than what is loosely called Nature. For Nature, even where free from humanity, is full of struggling, contending, teeming lives. . . . It is from our lonely communings with whatever fragments of far-drawn planetary chemistry we can reach . . . as we avoid the crowd, that the feelings come to us."[112]

Considering that Phyllis was now irrevocably a part of his life, Powys's insistence on loneliness as a condition of happiness could have proved sticky. However, as Alyse Gregory once wryly noted, he was a master at getting his loads around awkward corners,[113] and he explains "the soul that has made a habit of interior solitude can withdraw, even in the presence of those it cares for most, into its secret communication with the Inanimate; and instead of this withdrawal weakening its feeling for this other one, or for these others, it increases it."[114] Phyllis let this pass but pointed out "You are not really a Hermit—why then?"[115] She also objected to the "Pangloss doctrines" of these essays, pointing out that "hardworking women with lots of children who scrub for a living" have no opportunity for solitude nor have they time to indulge in "nervous or emotional unhappiness."[116] In effect, she was accusing him of writing out of his "Victorian Security of 2 or 3 generations" and metaphorically "doling out shillings to the starving children," with no "shiver of understanding of privation."[117]

Nonetheless, these tracts "for forlorn spirits to be helped by"[118] cannot be dismissed, for despite their sometimes insultingly simplistic message, they contain the seeds of his own complex life view. Powys stated clearly on any number of occasions that his writings—novels and all—were "simply so much propaganda for my philosophy of life."[119] His "philosophy" changed as he himself changed; new complexities and subtleties were introduced, but it began and ended with one fundamental question: is the individual unconnected/disconnected from everything and everyone else, or is it possible that there is behind or beneath the visible world, a pre-existing reality, a world of gods or patterns which binds all living souls together? Whether there is or there isn't "something behind" was the question he explored again and again, for "all living men and women—philosophers included—come, at moments, to a pitiless and adamantine 'impasse' where the eternal 'two ways' branch off in unfathomable perspective."[120] The "two ways" correspond to two permanent needs of human nature, characterize two familiar types of human temperament, and, for Powys, represent two conflicting impulses within the same temperament. He approached the conundrum from every conceivable direction. By the 1930s, his reading in mythology, psychology, anthropology, comparative religion, philosophy, and cultural history was enormous. He could see that many of the speculations being published in such diverse fields as cultural evolution, childhood development, and the unfolding of the individual psyche all pointed to a similar ontogeny and all had implications for his own dilemma. He was particularly intrigued by the theories that the young child and the earliest man have in common a lack of any sense of personal identity; they are, with plants and animals, an undifferentiated part of the whole. He read the theories which speculate that the individual takes the first step towards consciousness by creating a physical and emotional boundary between the nascent self and nature; then the further step toward self-consciousness—the state that Powys called the "I am I," the "crystal core of inviolability." In other words, civilization begins when man becomes a John Crow spectator instead of a participant, "watching everything from the outside."

Nietzsche called the "eternal two ways" Apollonian and Dionysian. "Apollo embodies the transcendent genius of the *principium individuationis*. . . . The mystical jubilation of Dionysos, on the other hand, breaks the spell of individuation and opens a path to the maternal womb of being."[121] What Nietzsche called the Apollonian and the Dionysian, Francis Cornford, one of the Cambridge Ritualists, called the "two traditions" and labeled "scientific" and "mystical." Much of what John Cowper did, thought, and wrote over a long lifetime represented a revulsion, which at times amounted to a mania, against a world controlled by science and the machine. In *Defence of Sensuality*, Powys called for "a return to a remote past whose magical secrets have been almost lost amid the vulgarities of civilization."[122] He was not the only one making such a call at this time. Herman Hesse in his *In Sight of Chaos* was demanding a return to the unordered, to the unconscious, to the formless, and still further back to all beginnings. D. H. Lawrence's *Apocalypse*, which was published as Powys was writing his *Philosophy of Solitude*, called for a re-establishment of the primitive bond between all living things.[123]

Ironically, Powys was attracted again and again to the camp of the enemy. The primitive and the mystic believe that there is only one cosmos, one interpenetrating unity, whereas, as Cornford pointed out, "the final achievement of science [is] the representation of a world of individual atoms, governed by Necessity or Chance." Pluralism, not unity, is the only reality.[124] As it was, apparently, to Powys: "To be a Pluralist rather than a Monist, is as much of an instinct to me as it is to every East Indian to be obsessed by Unity."[125] William James, whose philosophy was a "startling delight" to John Cowper, defined pluralism and monism in such a way as to make quite obvious the crux of Powys's surprising renunciation of one of the major tenets of mysticism. Monism insists,

wrote James, that "everything is present to everything else in one vast instantaneous co-implicated completeness," whereas pluralism means that the sundry
parts of reality may be externally related, but "nothing includes everything, or
dominates over everything. . . . Something always escapes."[126] Powys swung
wildly and sometimes despairingly from one world view to another. In
Confessions of Two Brothers, initially he insists that while he considers James's
pluralism "a pleasant theory to play with," he "must confess that the indissolu-
ble unity of the world of which we form a part is borne in upon me as an
axeiomatic necessity. . . . To call it a 'multiverse' is to use language which makes
language impossible."[127] A hundred pages later he says that he does not believe
that "hidden spiritual forces" are the true reality. "I do not believe in such
forces. I do not believe in such a reality."[128]

Isolating the self from the "herd" by the development of a "crystal core of
inviolability," the "I am I" that nothing and no one can touch, and therefore cannot hurt, is as far from mystic or primitive union as it is possible to get. And yet,
in these same books of philosophy, Powys called for a breaking down of the
boundaries between the real and the imaginary, between the civilized "self" and
the "other." His *In Defence of Sensuality* was a first attempt to resolve these radically opposite life visions. Here he demanded the development of a new kind of
ego—one that would reject its narrow concern with consciousness, one that
"steps sideways out of the human-consciousness groove into the backward consciousness of animal-vegetable life."[129] He called it an "ichthyosaurus ego," a term
he probably filched from Llewelyn's *Impassioned Clay*, in which Llewelyn refers
to the "ichthyosaurus" which "looked out at the world with its cold, self-enwrapt
lizard's eye."[130] There can be no better description of John Crow's ego, but John
Powys was attempting to push the idea further. "Ichthyosaurus ego" is a clever
term, an attempt to hold in creative suspension two opposing ideas: the solitary
apartness of the reptile, at the same time, the immersion in the natural world
that characterizes primitive beings. His "ichthyosaurus ego" would retain its indi-
viduality while being part of the magical world of the unconscious. In a moment
of self-awareness and self-loathing, he told Llewelyn once, "I am one for having
it both ways. I ought to have it engraved on my tomb, 'He had it both ways.'"[131]

In a sense the idea of the "ichthyosaurus ego" grew out of his reverence for
memories—memories of childhood, memories of pleasant, solitary walks. The
efficacy of memory, he wrote, was its ability to winnow and purge reality "of its
grossness, of its dullness, of its poisonous hurtings."[132] This is part of his happiness ethic, but with the ichthyosaurus ego, he was embarked on a much more
radical concept of memory and its purpose. Powys speculated that this
"ichthyosaurus ego," unlike the ego that has created a paling between its civilized consciousness and the lower levels, can touch these memories that reside
at a much deeper, prenatal level. It is contemplation of these "images" that
brings ecstatic happiness. Implicit in this theory is the metaphysical idea that
all matter—animate and inanimate—has a kind of memory, but he goes further

than this. Powys is stating that the individual's memory contains all memory. He wrote in A *Philosophy of Solitude*,

> There is more in the memory of each one of us than mere personal recollections. There is a dark-hidden store of race-memories hidden there, buried beneath our own life's casual impressions. Images, scenes, subtle and indescribable feelings, are stirred up from these sacred urns and vases at the bottom of the mind as the wind blows upon our face.[133]

The idea bears a remarkable resemblance to Jung's "collective unconscious." Jung discovered his "pagan spiritual roots and identity" as he was writing the second part of his *Wandlungen und Symbole der Libido*. What Jung was claiming in this seminal book was that through a return to the realm of the mothers or the deepest strata of the unconscious mind, we are reborn. The first step to this new life is through "introversion," when one's "libido sinks into its own depths," into what Jung refers to as "the world of memories" or the "collective unconscious."[134] This he defined as a second psychic system, distinct from the personal psyche, consisting of pre-existent forms, the archetypes, and which constitutes a common psychic substrate of a suprapersonal nature present and identical in all individuals. When Powys began to turn away from Freudian theories and interest himself in Jungian ideas is unknown, but it is possible that his old friend Mabel Hattersley may have been partly responsible. They had known each other since his early days of extension lecturing in the Midlands, and when they met again in Philadelphia in 1908 she became his "Ann Veronica tart." A quarrel interrupted the friendship, but they met again in 1916 at the home of Dr. Thomas, where he had taken refuge during his serious depression. By then this Wellsian "New Woman" had her medical degree and sometime later began her analyst training in Zurich under Carl Jung. Just before John Cowper and Phyllis left for Phudd Bottom in 1929, Mabel Hattersley suddenly turned up at Patchin Place. She was immediately helpful in a practical way to John by prescribing "powders of peace" which helped to control his ulcer pain. She came again to visit them in August 1932, just as he was finishing his *Solitude* essay. During their walks he questioned her a good deal about Jung's theories, which John decided, "I like very well."[135]

Jung would have attracted Powys because they not only shared similar ideas, but much the same family and cultural background. They were of an age; both came from upper-middle-class families, with an abundance of Protestant ministers on the paternal side; both had similar educational backgrounds dominated by classical Greco-Roman language, culture, and mythology. Even their personality traits had some interesting correspondences. Both felt from an early age that they had been marked out to do and be something special; the two were temperamentally introverted and solitary; both went through a period of intense depression and personal tumult during the years of the Great War; both embarked on a long search for a personal religion when the Christian beliefs of their fathers no longer satisfied them. Possibly most significant of all, the two of them came to intellectual maturity at the turn of the century.

The fin de siècle appeared to be dominated by a sense of an ending, of degeneration and decadence, but there was always a strong countermovement which manifested itself as a personal quest for renewal. The paths to cultural, political, physical, and especially spiritual rebirth were many: the ancient mystery religions, spiritualism, neopaganism, theosophy, nature worship, psychical research, psychoanalysis, occultism. The occultist movement in particular was immensely popular. Powys's cousin, Ralph Shirley, editor of the *Occult Review*, was a prominent member and introduced Powys to its main tenets at an early period.[136] Given their immersion in the same philosophic and religious/spiritual currents of the age, it is not surprising that Jung and Powys came up with strikingly similar ideas. Jung never denied the influence of the neo-Platonists, Goethe, Nietzsche, the Romantics, and the theosophists on his theories of the collective unconscious and the way of renewal, which he called "individuation." These same influences were operating in Powys, although he did not always give specific attributions to his most dearly held beliefs. It is always possible that he had little idea himself where the various strands of his philosophy came from. However, the result has been that his disciples, and perhaps Powys himself, have credited them with an originality that they do not possess. Taking Powys out of a cult status and putting him into an historical and cultural context does not lessen the significance of his rich and complex philosophy nor his syncretic genius in putting his ideas into new bottles.

For Powys, as for Jung, the relationship between the self and the not-self was not an abstract philosophical question; it was a personal Grail quest. This quest always begins with a sense of desolating separation from something beyond the self; the goal is reunion of the dualities of self and other. But neither man wanted to merge his individual identity in this All. They wanted the power and energy that they believed came from this re-connection with the larger Self, without a loss of self. The difficulty for Powys was that he could not convince himself this was possible. In the *Complex Vision*, even as Powys is reaching an ecstatic affirmation of the existence of "living gods," a second voice is saying, "there are certain human temperaments, and my own is one of them, for whom the very admission of a need for the invisible companions" means being "shut up in an unescapable prison." Powys ascribed this aspect of his personality to the presence within him of "malice" which expresses itself "in the desire to have as little as possible in common and as much as possible for ourselves alone." It is "love," he writes in the *Complex Vision*, that allows us to perceive the "eternal vision"; it is malice that causes the "desolating separation between humanity and Nature" and makes man feel himself "an exile in the dark."

It is curious that Powys chose the Empedoclean cosmology as the basis of his explanation for the conflicting philosophies present in his own thinking. For Empedocles, "love" is the primary state of the world and is the age of bliss. In the next stage of the cycle, love streams out of the circle and strife rushes in. From the mixing and meeting of these two arise all the individual things in the universe. Hereafter, the individual soul has two conflicting elements: Love which drives the soul toward the centre and unity; and malice or strife which drive it toward the circumference and multiplicity. The cycle continues until strife is in absolute control, at which point there is a complete separation. In the next phase, love again begins to prevail and draws the elements back into fusion, with the cycle ending in the state of original chaos. This is a radically different interpretation from many cosmologies, in which the original whole falls into two opposites—yin and yang, light and dark, heaven and earth, male and female. The hero goes on a quest to the underworld to unite himself with his lost half. For Empedocles, on the contrary, there is no possibility of a reunion of opposites; there is either complete separation or there is a return to the original chaos. The return to the golden age of Aphrodite/Cybele is death to the individual.

While Powys's philosophical conundrums seem light years away from the vitality of his novels; in fact, they provided him with an essential pattern which, far from inhibiting, gave mythological "permission" for the emergence of his characters, plots, and imagery in all their variety and complexity. In *Glastonbury Romance*, for example, Powys created two different characters to represent the two different cosmologies—Sam Dekker and John Geard. In several French versions of the Grail saga, Perceval, in his search for the vessel, frequently encounters the tracks of a mysterious being who is finally revealed as "the real secret of the Grail." Like Perceval, who meets Merlin simply as an "ombre" across his path, Sam has little awareness of the possibility that, side by side with his quest, a very different Grail hunt is being conducted. Geard's Quest is more than the pagan counterpart of Sam's heroic deed; it is in fact alien to the heroic quest. Geard is a new figure in Powys's novels, and Geard's successors, who become more and more identified as magicians, will allow Powys to explore with greater intensity and clarity the contradictions implicit in his philosophy. Which is the "real secret"—completeness attained by the heroic union of the self, the individual, with the Not-Self, or the magician's ecstatic merging of the self with the Not-Self?

In the *Romance*, the Powys-hero, John Crow, makes a third choice. He leaves town before the flood came. Powys did not let himself off so easily. He was attracted again and again to the magician's way. From earliest childhood, Powys's "dominant life-illusion was that I was, or at least eventually would be, a magician."[137] His desire to be a magician had gone beyond the helpless child's desire to have some control over his world. To be a magician was to wield power for good—to appease his conscience. Above all, to become a magician would be to have power over a fictive world, for a magician acquires the power that comes from "an actual tapping of some great reservoir of planetary, if not of cosmic, experience."[138] It was at Phudd that he began to see himself, not as a writer or a modern writer, but a visionary writer. The role of the visionary artist is not merely

to record an individual's stream of consciousness but to dive into this most primitive level of the mind to retrieve memories that are part of one great Memory,
to give a local habitation and a name to the archetypes in the deepest levels of
the mind.

But visionaries and shaman-magicians traditionally and mythically must go
through an initiation to acquire that power. It is said that to become a shaman,
the chosen one must have an initiatory dream, in which he sees himself drawn
into a forge of fire or torn to pieces, dismembered. His bones are reassembled and
joined with iron; thereafter he can see spirits, heal sick souls, and fly through the
air or journey to the underworld in ecstatic trance. Pain or suffering for the
shaman is the necessary vehicle to attain wholeness, to re-unite that which has
been divided and fragmented. The purpose of the suffering is the spiritual transmutation of the victim—whether shaman, magician, god, or novel writer. When
does self-inflicted misery become an art form? Powys said that it was Dostoevsky
who taught him "how weakness and disease and suffering can become organs of
vision," and he believed that the "vicious hurting" of his ulcers generated a "sensitized and electrified *fluid*," which acted as an "intensifying medium," through
which poured "thrilling waves of magnetic vitality, coming from what seemed
like some underlying planetary reservoir."[139] Pain was the "conducting element"
by which he reached the archetypal images in the mind. By sacrificing himself to
himself, the Norse God Odin is given the power of words—the magic runes.
Odin is a "forger of words"—a wordsmith, a seer, a magician. Powys wanted to be
that magician, and he knew that through language he could exercise that
power—whatever else he lost by having gained it.

At Phudd Bottom he embarked on his own initiation rite. At the summit of
the hill behind the cottage he found what he believed were the tombs of dead
Indians. He gave the name Avenue of the Dead to a line of stones leading to one
great stone which he called the Altar of the God of Phudd. At first, it was a play-
ful ritual of tapping his head on the stones for good luck, but he soon began to
hear these "dead spirits talk" and felt "their power and magic."[140] He knew that
the ancients thought that stones were the containers of divine powers, the
dwelling places of spirits or gods, and felt that they were calling him to join
them. Powys mocked himself for having "fancy quarrels with dead Indians" when
"sad is the great World-Novel in these woeful times," but for perhaps six months
it became an obsessive psychic and physical struggle. To be "one with the stone"
is to become a shaman, a magician, but it is death to the individual self.

> I prayed to the dead Indians. . . . But as I went away three more ghosts of
> dead Indians—dark swaying slender bodies cried come to me . . . come to
> us! come to us! But I would not . . . . But I was nervously agitated by those
> Ghosts of Indians calling to me & I talked to the tree saying unto it "Self
> first—self first—self first—Dead Indians second!" but the tree answered me
> not a word.[141]

They keep calling him to submit to them, in effect, to merge with them, and when he continues to refuse, they punish him.

> 27 January 1932: The Indians of Hill & the God of Phudd commanded me to come to the Phudd Stone & tap my head. But I refused. I too am a Magician! I said. So they set themselves to show their Power & I set myself to show my Power. Today has been a struggled day. . . . I gave myself a good Enema after my fashion with the squeezing tube and I squeezed it <u>sixty</u> times. The spirits of the Indians were making a grand coup, a great rally against me however & <u>all</u> <u>went</u> <u>Wrong</u>. It would not work!! . . . 10 times I tried again hurrying backwards & forwards & getting more hot water. Then I gave up the struggle & sitting on the Close-Stool in the Bathroom resigned myself to awaiting events. . . . Finally the T. T. was asked by me to get the Doctor.

He knew that for now at least he had failed the call, failed the initiation. But he continued, so to speak, in training. His daily life at Phudd Bottom became an arduous, tortured, often humiliating apprenticeship. He developed rituals which took up many hours of his day. There were "long drawn out morning head dippings combined with long winded incantations and conjurations," trees were kissed, stones were bowed before and head-tapped. An important part of his "magicking" was to perform Adam's task of naming. Gradually, on his daily walks in their small acreage, every stone, tree, pond he encountered was given a name. There was the Prometheus stone, the Skaian gates, the Mabinogion swamp, Ashgard hill, the Rhea tree. As he has one of his characters in a novel say, "we give things names to get power over them." But for Powys, the naming was not just a method of control. It was an invocation; each name gave the inanimate a connection and an expansion. The name became both an acknowledgment and a command: "this Stone of Fal . . . this stone I myself have made into a Stone of Power." As eccentric as they may have seemed to the "well-constituted," these rituals were an essential part of his personality, his philosophy, and his belief in his imaginative powers. It was through ritual, he said, that inspiration flowed through him.

The rituals were conducted, not only for his own creative gain, but for the pariahs and misfits of the world. He believed that his prayers had power, however nebulous, for good, and he had a long list of worthy recipients. The prayers were "compelled by my conscience"[142]; they were also at times a further way of punishing himself. "My errant thoughts passed to those French Sadistic Books which in my time have transported me beyond all other feelings I have known. . . . On my return I found my prayers on Negroes in the South un-said so I made myself stand erect in Bath Room and say them, clean to the Bitter End."[143] He could still laugh at himself.

> I did the chores & took the Black to the lower Bull Rush Bed over the rough Battlefield & held my serpent stick given by Lulu & heard the water-

fall of the Grotto & called out to the Nymph "Guard Lulu & Alyse & Gamel!"—leaving to this Naiad the problem as to how to work this out.[144]

His obsessive letter-writing was driven by this same conscience. When he was still lecturing, he often felt that he could "get in the precise fated word in a young Gaston de Latour's existence"[145] and had decided "my conscience will have to find a substitute whenever I settle down 'in the country.'" Responding to letters from these young men became the burdensome alternative. He regarded it "the price, one of 'em! that I have to pay for my happiness here."[146]

He was truly happy in this place, and he gave Phyllis the credit for it.

> 14 January 1932: Yesterday when I lay with my back to a stone fence on the top of One-Tree Hill above the Fir Tree House I had an ecstasy of pleasure at the deep deep deep beautiful lonely wildness of Columbia County. Oh how I do like my life here how I do like it. And it is given to me by the T. T. who sacrifices her Watteau sophistication in the City & her Theatres, Concerts & shops.

In a graceful if ambiguous compliment to Phyllis he had written in his *In Defence of Sensuality*: "The happy person in this world is therefore the person who has found his mate, or who with the creative energy of the true magician—and this can be done far more completely than most people realise—has managed, by psychic sorcery, to hypnotise his companion . . .—contrary to all expectation—into such a mate."[147] What had drawn John and Phyllis together originally was their individual unhappinesses. Or rather, that they fed and sustained themselves on each other's unhappiness. However, gradually he became happy and fulfilled and she remained unhappy. He may have "magicked" her into becoming a real-life companion, like the Welsh magician who created a beautiful girl out of flowers, but he knew the outcome of that. She was his "pet hare"; making her a happy bunny was another question.

CHAPTER TEN

MYTHIC MEMORIES

1932-1934

⌒

THE AUTHENTIC JOY POWYS FELT AT PHUDD MERGED WITH THE ONLY OTHER unalloyed happiness he had ever known—the childhood felicity at Weymouth. He would look at the gray posts of the fence rails on a cloudy day and think how "all was pearl-touched, all was fresh and shimmering and yet cool and clear like shells on Weymouth beach."[1] The tracks of Albert Krick's skis became "a child's goat carriage marks on the donkey sands at Weymouth."[2] The pebbles and shingle by his little river gave him "the old feeling of the Beach at Weymouth" where he was "rapturously happy with my mother & the little ones."[3] When Powys and Phyllis finished correcting the page proofs of *Glastonbury*, he began a new novel on his father's birthday, February 2, using his father's quill pen. He wrote Llewelyn asking for "all the guides, maps and town-plans naming streets alleys churches grave-yards bridges and back-water slums about Weymouth, Melcombe Regis, Wyke and Portland."[4] He studied the guide books "letting 'em sink into my mind"; he examined the maps carefully and wished he had "a vast number of photographs of many streets!"[5] They hung sheets of foolscap in the bathroom and wrote possible names of characters on them. As always for Powys, the act of naming was an act of creation: "characters that emerge out of Limbo, out of airy nothing, to receive these names and lo & behold! as I name them and name their houses they begin to gather to themselves a faint reality!"[6]

Despite the preparation, initially the writing did not go well. He made a second start, then a third start, but when he read the fourth chapter to Phyllis in July, she "condemned it as hopelessly old-fashioned sentimental and writ with the mere top & surface of my skull."[7] He re-wrote the chapters "in a different style altogether," but when this went no better, Phyllis proposed he introduce a new character, Magnus Muir, who would be "really more like myself than Wolf or John . . . & seeking for an ideal 'El Greco' Weymouth."[8] In November, she told him that his new first chapter about Muir was "not really good." This left them "both non-plussed as to what I should do." Phyllis then suggested he add a "Tempest-like" love story, and this became the story of Perdita Wane and Jobber

Skald.[9] He was by this time rather discouraged by his difficulties with the novel, especially when Arthur Ficke implored him "to stop bringing in my Mythology into my novels" as it was "poppycock" and "an insult to readers." He ignored this advice, but wrote gloomily in his diary,

> I have been trying to think about my Weymouth Book—but I find it nigh impossible to think in the void. . . . I am not a thinker, I am a Reed through which thoughts come! . . . She however—thank the Lord!—is able to think. She thinks all the time: Sans Cesse. And now she has thought out a wonderful idea for my book—about making Sylvanus Cobbold into a revivalistic preacher with a little idiot or sub-normal girl-friend & he to be Put away & I thought as I talked to her—about a Punch & Judy group too![10]

Now everything began to come together, and he noted that "once the characters assert themselves they do all with a sort of rush of their own." Phyllis advised that the Magnus character should be "very detached from events and involved against his will," and that is how he developed. The Powys-hero is a forty-six-year-old "hypochondriacal tutor"[11] for whom the study and teaching of the classics, and his preoccupation with communing with his dead father, has formed "a sort of invisible barrier for him between his interior world and the world of outer reality."[12] As the story begins, Muir foresees that his past is about to be "ripped up" and a new "reality" to begin. He has fallen in love with a young shopgirl, Curley Wix, an "incident" that he regards as "something frightening, disturbing, and out of control."[13] As time goes on, Muir spends more and more time thinking about and talking to Sylvanus Cobbold, the preacher with a "cadaverous face" and "wild gleaming eyes" who spends his day on the Weymouth sands expounding his gospel to the holiday makers. Although Magnus is convinced that Cobbold is a "born prophet" and even "the eternal recurrence of some undying 'gleichnis,'" he is irritated by him because "the mad mystic," although "heading for serious trouble," won't defend himself.[14] Muir is also frightened as he becomes aware that Sylvanus's involvement with young girls (the narrator refers to them sometimes as children, sometimes as girls) and his apparent insanity are like magnified mirror images of his own obsessions. "He began to feel how easily he, like poor Sylvanus Cobbold, might develop some anti-social mania that would bring him into trouble with the authorities. . . . This irrational dread of being handed over . . . began to mingle with his nervousness about marrying Curley." He has "one of those icy, dark, wedge-like panic-terrors" that he will be put into the county asylum under the power of evil psychiatrist and vivisector Dr. Daniel Brush.[15]

Sylvanus is engaged in a "desperate struggle to reach the secret of life," and in his ecstasies, he feels as if "life were returning to some mysterious Beyond life."[16] His brother Jerry mocks this: "Behind, behind, behind—that's where you tricky mystics always put the secret. . . . And I . . . have peeped behind that Curtain, when brother was playing his scrannel pipe and there's nothing there!"[17]

Sylvanus, "always a rebel, always dwelling in a mystical borderland of his own,"[18] pays no attention. Like Geard, he is wholly occupied in a dialogue with his absolute, which, for him, "was not the First Cause, or the Last Cause, or any other Cause! It simply was Everything, and there was no room in Everything for the idea of Cause. There was only All there was."[19] Sylvanus is an adept in Taoist mysticism, although how he acquired this esoteric knowledge is left unclear. Powys himself had long been fascinated by Tibetan yoga and during the writing of the novel he and Phyllis were reading Alexandra David-Neel's *With Mystics and Magicians in Tibet*.[20] He was also reading the ubiquitous theosophical publications which distilled and marketed the great philosophies of the East to Western civilization. More immediately, in April 1932 in the Simon & Schuster office, he had a long talk with one of their authors called Dr. Potter, who told him about "an astonishing Magician of that Thaktrad Yogi Cult a Secret Phallic Order under ambiguous Repute, with the best Oriental Phallic Library anywhere in the Land. . . . His name is Doctor Bernard. Dr. Potter is his disciple and says he is like Mr. Geard!"[21] Bernard, also known as "Oom the Omipotent," was a student of hatha yoga and tantra. He married a young oriental belly dancer (albeit with high social connections), and she introduced him to the wife of William Vanderbilt, who became another of Bernard's disciples. In 1924, with Vanderbilt money he founded the Secret Order of Tantricks on a seventy-eight-acre estate in Nyack, upstate New York, and this became a gathering place not only for the rich seeking enlightenment, but for visiting gurus and writers. The townspeople were convinced that Potter was also an abortionist and kept a private asylum for the wealthy insane. Powys must have listened very carefully indeed to Potter because he introduced into the novel a number of not totally convincing characters, including the "notorious quack and abortion-procurer," Dr. Lucius Girondel, whose house, Sark House, is a "rendevous for all erotic eccentrics"[22]; a psychiatrist, Dr. Daniel Bush, who operates the Asylum; and not one but two young exotic dancers called Tissty and Tossty.

It was, however, the postures and beliefs of tantric yoga that interested Powys most. According to tantric principles, the whole body, with its biological and psychological processes, becomes an instrument through which the cosmic power of the universe reveals itself. The goal for the adept is to immobilize bodily and mental functions—breath, thought, semen—through techniques which combine physiology with meditation. If properly performed, this leads to the abolition of all experience of duality and to perfect harmony with the cosmos. In Yogic texts, it is stated that the one who achieves this "instantly becomes a magician." The object is the reconciliation of opposites—man reunited with his female nature—through the arousal of "kundalini." This "coiled feminine energy" is a microcosmic version of the vast potential of psychic-sexual energy existing in latent form not only in every human being, but in every atom of the universe.

Ritual union with a young naked virgin, who is seen as the reflection of Sakti, the dynamic female principle of the universe, is one technique whereby this energy can be transformed and freed. If this sexual union does not terminate in an emission of semen, it may lead the adept to experience the "white light" of cosmic consciousness. Sexuality and spirituality become two ends of one energy. Something like this, presumably, was what Powys was alluding to when he wrote, "what has always interested me more than any other subject [is] the relation between sex sensuality, in all its confused aberrations, and religious ritual."[23] He has Sylvanus discover that "his masculine reason" is "a hindrance in his struggle to attain . . . the Absolute," and through certain rituals with young girls who have "a certain indefinable quality that might perhaps be indicated as erotic virginity," he can find "some secret entrance to the Deathless and the Immortal." It was as if "some half-crazed Faust had found the magic oracles of those Beings he called 'the Mothers' in the nerves and sensibilities of every ordinary young Gretchen he encountered."[24] He takes into his bed the child Marret, who "resembled the little Virgin."[25] Marret is not worried by any of Sylvanus's actions. Her father runs the Punch and Judy show on the sands, and she is accustomed to "the spasmodic movements" of "grotesque puppets."[26] In any case, as she confides to her friend Peg, "he presses me to him, but . . . he *never does anything*."[27] She is safe enough; the child is simply part of a rite in which the real goal is to remain in perpetual and ecstatic intercourse with oneself.

Unfortunately, the good people of Weymouth do not make the distinction between physical lust and "cerebral" lust. Sylvanus has "played the platonic nympholept a bit too far"[28]; he is convicted of having "corrupted children"[29] and is incarcerated. The magician now takes the obligatory trip into the underworld, which, in Sylvanus's case, is Dr. Brush's Sanatorium, "Hell's Museum," where he is like some "wandering Teiresias into the purlieus of Dis."[30] The psychiatrist analyzes Sylvanus and as a result formulates a "completely new set of pathological hypotheses," one of which is that "not only from the surface of that sea within us *but from all levels and depths of it* we have the power of coming into contact with one another." Sylvanus decides the psychiatrist has "a personality that was feminine," and that all this theory means is that Dr. Brush wants to "tart" his mind. Thereupon, "an extraordinary duel began which was fought at one and the same time on the rational, the imaginative and the occult level. It was also fought—strange as it may sound—on the sexual plane."[31] Powys appears to be setting up here what he considers a psychoanalytic version of the tantric ritual, and Sylvanus, happy enough to practice maithuna with himself as a young girl, refuses to play the game with Brush. This is a stylistically unsatisfactory interlude but indicative as an expression of Powys's philosophical ambivalence toward union or connection with other humans in whatever form it may take.

Powys never totally believed anything he passionately espoused and tantric yoga was no exception. He certainly had studied his texts carefully and Sylvanus practices all the techniques religiously, so to speak. A method of breath control, for example, is used to direct the flow of vital energy through the body, part of the purpose being to imitate the respiration in animals—the spontaneity of animal life the preeminent example of an existence in perfect harmony with the cosmos. Sylvanus, when in bed with his girl, would "hitch himself up a little and crane his head forward, while his long neck . . . would assume a striking resemblance to the head of a tortoise," which the narrator suggests "perhaps also was a trick known in Thibet."[32] Presumably he saw similarities between Sylvanus-as-turtle and his own philosophy of the "ichthyosaurus ego," for the magician's outstretched neck reminds Gipsy May "of what those other . . . non-human necks must have looked like . . . hundreds of millions of years ago."[33] While Sylvanus struggling to achieve harmony with the natural world intentionally or unintentionally borders on the ludicrous, much of the undeniable glory of *Weymouth Sands* arises out of Powys's attempts to make fictional sense out of his philosophical and psychological preoccupations at the time. It is no coincidence that he was writing *A Philosophy of Solitude* in tandem with *Weymouth Sands*, or that his encounter with the Indian spirits of Phudd was still fresh in his memory. He wrote that he was "so made that my imagination inevitably converts every mental process which is at all important to me into a ritualistic symbol."[34] The very first sentence in the novel reflects the conundrum of retaining individual identity while still being part of the all, and the peril implicit in the attempt: "The Sea lost nothing of the swallowing identity of its great outer mass of waters in the emphatic, individual character of each particular wave." The sea is omnipresent in the novel, as are the stones of Portland. *Weymouth Sands* is as much about the inanimate world as it is about human beings.

It was in 1929, when John Cowper visited Stonehenge on his way to Norfolk with Littleton, that the primitive worship of inanimate matter began to fascinate him. He wrote Phyllis that "these vast monstrous blocks" symbolized "the cosmogonic original material (or dream-conscious stuff) out of which, torn from the Sun, the earth rounded itself off in its first separation as a planet," and that the stones "seemed to retain some of the super-human and sub-human consciousness that Fechner said the sun and the moon and the earth possess different from man's." He concluded triumphantly, "And thus the worship of the *Inanimate* in its primal form, *Idolatry*, is strangely justified!"[35] In *Weymouth Sands*, the stones of Portland become the equivalent of Stonehenge, bearing "the weight of all the in-breathings and out-breathings of the orbic motion of the world, of the systole and diastole of space and time." Wayfarers are allowed "to listen to a speech too deep for sound; and they become eavesdroppers of the ancient litany of aboriginal matter and grow confederate with the long piety of the cosmos."[36] Stonehenge, Portland, and the Stones of Phudd combine in a sublime meditation on the mystery of the Spirit in the Stone.

As well as studying Gustav Fechner, Powys was reading R. R. Marett, who, in his book *The Threshold of Religion*,[37] speculated that earliest man regarded certain inanimate objects as sacred, full of special potency, and that this potency or aliveness was not a soul or a spirit but a kind of communicable energy. The warrior has power, not because of any prowess he may possess, but because of the

mana-containing stone amulet he wears. Around these two ideas of the sacred-
ness of stone and its communicable power, Powys wove the story of Jobber Skald.
Jobber Skald is intent on killing Dog Cattistock, not so much because the capi-
talist has taken over the small stone quarries owned by the old hereditary quar-
rymen of the island and driven them into misery and poverty, but because of "the
outrage done to the actual *stone* itself." The Portland stone had always been
"something to be handled reverently, piously, and *in fear of the gods*."[38] The Jobber
intends to kill Cattistock with a stone he carries in his pocket, thus becoming
the warrior with the mana stone defending the Stone.

Powys skillfully weaves the concept of the power of the inanimate with another of his beliefs. Both the "contemplation of the Inanimate" and memory itself are
"the natural nepenthe for human unhappiness."[39] The unhappy Perdita Wane is
"soothed a little" by the dark-flowing waters, "for there is almost always, for the
troubled human mind, a degree of comfort in the presence of the inanimate, even
when it is attended by the sort of shivering forlornness that the look of a dark tide
at night-fall necessarily brings."[40] Magnus Muir, who becomes obsessed by the
notion that the lunatic asylum doubles as a laboratory that experiments on dogs,
"could easily imagine that a sensitive person, who brooded night and day upon
vivisection, going mad from the horror of it."[41] The only release from his tormented imagination that Magnus can find is some childhood memory associated with
his beloved father, and the memory is always connected with an inanimate object.
No sooner does he catch sight of a large derelict piece of cork half-embedded in
the sand on the beach, "than a rush of happiness, so intense, so overwhelming,
took possession of him that he was as one transported out of himself. . . . That piece
of cork became all the summer afternoons when he and the elder Muir had set out
from Penn House to walk to Redcliff Bay. That piece of cork became the splash of
the waves into all the rock-pools from the Coast-Guards to Preston Brook."[42]
Memory is the brief epiphany in a world suffused with pain.

In the intricately drawn relationship between Magnus and the spirit of his
dead father, Powys rehearses his double-minded love for his own father. Magnus
is inseparable from his stick, which was his father's, and upon which he "loved to
lean his full weight till he felt he was leaning upon the undying strength of the
formidable old man."[43] The stick represents "the protection of his father, the
security of his father . . . the indescribable safety, like the feeling anyone has who
hugs himself in bed on a freezing night."[44] On the other hand, Magnus hopes that
his love for Curley will finally allow him to "treat his Father's majestic ghost as
an equal, not as a cringing dependent" and that he will begin to "rise above all
those timidities that had so fettered his spirit."[45] But in his heart he accepts that
if he *does* lose Curley, he will "just go on, taking my walks, teaching Latin, reading Greek, talking to my Father's spirit."[46] In the end, although he cannot break
free from this father, Magnus knows that in one respect they are different. His
father "had lived to eighty without really encountering the underlying chaos and
violence and shame that exist in life"[47] and was "happy by nature." Magnus *has*

seen what lies beneath, and it is to avoid being driven mad by the vision that he makes his soul take his body "as though by a leash, like an animal, and forces it to go through the motions of happiness."[48]

Powys's philosophical tracts are propaganda, deliberately upbeat; his novels seem to come out of some other, deeper, part of him. As a storyteller Powys often starkly subverts his philosophic ideas of willed happiness in solitude, of the solace that communion with the inanimate brings. In this novel, not only Magnus, but almost every character in the book is desperately unhappy, weighed down by an awareness of the cruelty and loneliness of the universe. With the exception of Larry Zed, protected by his half-wittedness, the dwellers in Weymouth are like animals being tortured by some unseen power. Even the lovers, Jobber Skald and Perdita Wane, are transformed utterly by pain. In attempting to redress the evil done by Cattistock, Skald succeeds only in almost destroying himself and Perdita by his obsession. Although they are finally reunited (the only two people, by the end of the novel, not completely alone) the lovers' union is hardly the customary symbol of joy, renewal, and new life:

> It was as if they were animals, old, weak, long hunted animals, whose love was literally the love of bone for bone, skeleton for skeleton, not any mere spiritual affinity, not any mere sexual passion.[49]

The novel is not unremittingly dark. Powys reached into his past and came up with the retarded son of his first landlord in Sussex. Larry Zed's unforced, unthinking connection with the natural world gives him a contentedness and a connection the other characters lack. Larry asks Blotchy the cow, "Don't 'ee let the Nothing-Girl take 'ee on lap and give 'ee her titties to suck? Don't 'ee ever let the Nothing-Girl love 'ee, like her do love I o' nights?"[50] Powys is at his best in portraying half-wits and children, and there is a captivating scene on the sands with an "enormously fat old grandmother . . . reading the Melcombe Regis Circular" and an infant "armed with a brilliantly coloured bucket," who "like the Israelites without straw, struggling to make mud-pies without water" solves the problem by producing "water from his own body."[51]

Nor is the novel as weighed down by philosophical and abstract ideas as it might well have been. It is above all about real people in a real landscape sieved through the memories of its author. In *Suspended Judgements* Powys wrote that characters in a romance "must be penetrated through and through by the scenery which surrounds them."[52] In all his novels this is true, but never more so than in *Weymouth Sands*. For Magnus, the landscape *is* his father. "The White Horse, Hardy's Monument, the White Nose, the Nothe, the Breakwater, Sandsfoot Castle, and above all this great pebble-bank where he now stood was seen by Magnus in a different way from the way others saw it. *It was a piece of his father's life*."[53] The Weymouth Esplanade is similarly a part of himself and his past. As he passes the Jubilee Clock, the old King's Statue, the donkeys and the goat-carriages, sweet-sellers, the bathing machines, the Punch and Judy Show, Mr.

Jones' Refreshment Tent, "the smell of tar, of fish, of shag-tobacco, of ancient seaweed, of human sweat, of stale cake, of girl's cosmetics, of children's wet clothes, of men's new clothes" are caught up "in the larger smell of the hot sunshine itself pouring down upon the sand and pebbles." And suddenly, "all the old sensations of hot summers on Weymouth beach hit him to the heart."[54]

Powys is most inspired when he is describing a landscape, particularly a landscape of memory, but even here there is a note of desolation.

> The after-glow of the sunset gave the sands an incredible look of enchantment. Some of the pools and canals in the wet sand that the children had made gleamed as though, ere they were deserted, buckets of liquid gold had been poured into them. . . . But by degrees the golden reflections died away and a curious chilliness, that gave to the dark blue water a cold, untouchable marbly look, and to the sands themselves something unfriendly and remote, established itself there, a chilliness that was the chilliness of a cemetery across which a gay procession of intruders has come and gone. . . . It was as if with the approaching darkness, and the chilly rising of the tide, and the near departure of the familiar seven o'clock train, the magic enchantment of those shores vanished away.[55]

Despite some exquisite writing, *Weymouth Sands* is a strangely scattered novel. Powys alleged that "I divide myself into at least three characters if not more!"[56] but if Sylvanus, Magnus, and Jobber are aspects of his own personality, he was content to display them as *disiecta membra poetae*, limbs of a dismembered poet. The numerous subplots are allowed to fly off and float into extinction like sparks from an untended fire. He admitted to Lulu in May 1933 that the plot was "weak and unconvincing" but added, "the mere word 'Plot' suggests something un-natural, un-poetical, un-psychological, un-philosophical." He was not quite sure why, but decided that "it is a curious book, this Weymouth book."[57]

It may be that in some "curious" way, setting the novel in Weymouth was disruptive. He wrote to Marian at this same time, "How things in the past seem like chapters in a book that you know is there, on the shelf!—but now you are reading the sequel and it is all so different."[58] Powys probably intended initially simply to write a nostalgic novel about the town in which he had known "ravishing transports of happiness."[59] However, the child is now a sixty-year-old man, burdened with pain and poverty, who creates instead "a strange phantasmal Weymouth, a mystical town made of a solemn sadness . . . a town built out of the smell of dead seaweed, a town whose very walls and roofs were composed of flying spindrift and tossing rain."[60] Superimposed on that world of glinting summer sunlight are the perceptions of a neurosis-blighted, winter-ridden adult. The two voices are gloriously caught in the final chapter entitled "Lost and Found." Magnus, who has lost his girl to another man, walks out to the sea rocks at the base of the cliffs at Portland.

> He sank down on a rough lime-stone slab, overgrown with sharp indented rock-shells and gazed into a rock pool. . . . Here in this enchanted fissure,

he could see purple and amber-coloured sea-anemones, their living, waving antennae-like tendrils swaying gently, as the tide swell took them. And tiny, greenish fish with sharply extended dorsal fins darted to and fro across the waving petals of those plants that were more than plants! But it was the motionless shells at the bottom that he now gazed with his strongest sense of the past. . . . He could see one involved mother-of-pearl shell, with a tiny seaweed actually growing from its surface. . . .

Suddenly . . . against his will the shell-like radiance of his lost girl's flesh and blood, that incredible transparency her face used sometimes to assume, shot through his senses like an arrow, an arrow of sea-pearl!

Up he sprang and fleeing desperately from those rocks, as a lost soul might fly from an oasis in its perdition where the memories cut its feet, he made his way across Chesil, across the road, across the railway, till he came to the shallow mud-flats of the Fleet Backwater. . . . Across this Waste Land drifted the stricken man.[61]

The juxtaposition of the two Weymouths does not rouse in the reader a simple vision of experience defeating innocence. Still less does it make the comforting intimation that the memory of the bright world of childhood helps to make bearable the darker world of the adult. The discomfort arises from the way in which the memories of the past, *while remaining the only balm*, become transformed into cutting instruments to make the present event more hurtful. As a result of such long reading of so many diaries perhaps I have an inkling of what the memories were, but what is important is the way in which in his novels he can transform a memory into a sustained image of great beauty and menace. Nothing in any of John Cowper's philosophical essays, however insistent the message that happiness can be found in memory, however bleak the decree of solitude, can approach the quality of inevitability that is found in his finest stories.

After many revisions, with Phyllis working alongside him, he sent off the novel to Simon & Schuster on July 22, 1933. As the years passed, the "T. T." was giving him more and more assistance. Her experience as an editor with Haldeman-Julius came in handy, and she did the proof-reading for all his writings. She typed and made suggestions for *Wolf Solent*, and he noted that with *Glastonbury Romance*, "she composed whole passages."[62] Just before the *Glastonbury* typescript was sent off to the publishers in November 1931, she insisted he change the last chapter and bring in Cybele with her turreted crown, and he wrote those last powerful and mysterious pages about the Phrygian earth-mother at her direction. Her involvement increased over the years, and by the time *Weymouth* was finished, he admitted that "she ought to have her name on this book but I am far too selfish to let her have it there!"[63] From the uncertain woman in the 1920s and in the earliest years at Phudd Bottom, she was developing into an incisive and at times impatient critic, at one point telling him "your fault is not a cold heart but facile writing."[64]

Phyllis was changing in other ways that were disconcerting to Powys. Her father died on January 12, 1933, and when she returned from Franklin Playter's deathbed, John detected that something had occurred "in her deepest Nature." Phyllis had the same close, reverent relationship with her father that John Cowper had had with his, and equally, Playter's death in some way freed her. Perdita in *Weymouth* is modeled closely after Phyllis, or rather, as Phyllis had described herself at twenty-five in her unpublished writings. "Perdita's few friends were older people . . . who petted her and encouraged her and wondered at her, as an intellectual prodigy, but made no attempt to understand her, and indeed saw nothing of her real nature. Thus she had been very happy as a child, but very unhappy and very lonely as a young woman." However, Phyllis was now thirty-eight and when he read her "the Perdita & Jobber part of this chapter X . . . she burst out in wrath— very eloquent sarcasm because I let Perdita be too passive and docile to the Jobber."[65]

Phyllis's increasing independence may have been, in part, the result of her growing friendship with Marian. Powys was uncertain what to make of this. When Marian said she might "rush over" to Phudd after a big sale of lace in New York, which included Napoleon's marriage coverlet for $15,000, John wrote in his diary: "To this I said nothing; for well do I know the danger when your third Hareem meets your Last Hareem when one has her head full of Napoleon's Marriage-Bed."[66] How much Powys had told Phyllis of his former relationship, real or imagined, with Marian is unknown, but Phyllis felt "respect and awe" for Marian's determined self-governance. When John made the mistake of praising Alyse for "being so good at looking after Lulu's health, the T. T. with more than usual intensity launched into a scornful attack on the Powys Family for making so much of the quiet virtues of devotion of a neutral kind and always saying 'Out you go!' to any person of spirit and of independent original character." John decided there might be something in this, "for I recall well what my father was in this very peculiarity."[67] Phyllis was taking the first tentative steps toward being a Marian rather than an Alyse. But Jack, like the Jobber, needed a Perdita, and like Lulu, he especially needed someone to look after his own shaky health.

Another result of the death of Franklin Playter proved equally unsettling to John. Over the years together John Cowper and Phyllis had accumulated a toy child—the doll Olwen—and a fantasy child, Glauk. At Phudd, Powys named two stones Perdita and Tony, calling them his "stone children." Only now, seeing her father die had made Phyllis "feel deeply as if nothing were important save life itself,"[68] and she wanted a real child, a living Perdita.

> Last night the T. T. spoke about Perdita by the shores of Lethe. . . . But I will not ever consider—in this point [my] deepest Selfishness or Egoism is Adamantine—even so much as a thought of a little Perdita! My only daughter is a Stone—the daughter of a stone—& my only little girl is the T. T.![69]

Perhaps to comfort her, he wrote into *Weymouth Sands* a passage about a young girl's beloved doll: "It is perhaps hardly strange that human beings in their abysmal craving for some over-consciousness that shall record and retain in memory events and occurrences and words and deeds and groupings . . . should have been tempted to attribute a consciousness like this to those symbolic Inanimates. . . . *When*, in the life of an object adored by a fetish-worshipper, [does] this sacrosanct Inanimate become animate?"[70] Whether this piece of compassionate abstraction consoled Phyllis we do not know. She was never to have a child, contenting herself with the doll Olwen (who, with her bed, her chest of drawers, her chair, her hand-made clothes, still, ironically, exists) and with the stone children who may, for all we know, still lie "at the opposite end of the great field near the rails where you cross into that rough field that extends to the old Bullrush bed near the Grotto Plane-tree."[71]

By this time, 1933, Powys being Powys, "Jack's pain" had assumed an intricate web of meaning. The ulcers were undoubtedly painful, but he continued to do things, such as taking long walks, which, as he says again and again in the diary, he knew would make them worse. He refused to have the operation at Johns Hopkins that Phyllis urged and the specialists advised, relying solely on the powders Dr. Mabel supplied and a diet of bread, milk, tea, and raw eggs. The fact is, Powys *used* his ulcers. He used them to escape tiresome social responsibilities in the local community and left it to Phyllis to do the neighborhood visiting, attend the village socials, and deal with the tradesmen. He used his ulcers to give himself time and space for his writing, for the only answer to their alleviation appeared to be long hours in bed with a writing board. He used them to punish himself and others, fully aware of the interconnection between ulcers, masochism, retaliation, and his fantastic experiments in diet. In *After My Fashion*, Richard Storm is angry with his pregnant wife,

> To revenge himself on her he deliberately reduced his own diet to an absurd minimum . . . and living almost entirely upon bread and tea. The result of this was that he began to suffer from acute dyspepsia. . . .
>
> He did not attempt to conceal from himself that this ill-balanced economy was not really undertaken for his wife's sake. For her sake—if that was what he was about—he ought obviously to take every care of his health. The real motive that prompted him was a kind of voluptuous self-cruelty.[72]

There is another revealing, perhaps deliberately revealing, passage in *Weymouth Sands*, where the domineering old man, James Loder, uses his ulcers to keep his daughter and everyone else in check with his "pain antics."

> He really *did* suffer! . . . But the very fact that it was a shock to people to see him twist about made it the greater relief. He derived an almost sensual pleasure from doing it. He experienced a satisfaction in bringing down the high spirits of others by flinging over them, so to speak, the mantle of his leprosy. There were doubtless subtler aspects still.[73]

The "subtler aspects" were that for Powys, the hurting actually increased "the devouring intensity of my peculiar vice," the pain "transforming itself into lust."[74] Old Loder, in an elaborate psychic-sexual game, would strip himself naked when he was in pain, knowing that his daughter was perfectly aware that he did not do so "until she had begun to ascend the stairs."[75] Pain, sexual desire, and emotional control became a complicated equation that operated not only in his fiction, but in his life with Phyllis. The diary entries make the pattern apparent. Phyllis's absence, part of her increasing independence, causes him distress, which brings on an ulcer attack. He goes to her for help and her solace excites him sexually—"imparadises" him.

> 11 December 1931: Something in her going must have left me in my nerves completely deserted for I got very nasty suffering in Pit of Stomach. She came [home] when I had been to bed but I came down in my hurting and begged for help & comfort. . . . She came to bed then & it was like sleeping with the loveliest Nymph that has ever been made—a little Elf-child of incredible slenderness & exquisite docility.

When Powys limited his diet to nursery food, Phyllis lost interest in cooking a proper meal for herself, and she became dangerously thin. This worried him and yet her fragility invariably roused his sexual desire. Her thinness was vital to two inter-related myths that they were enacting, the sylph and the child. Sylphs are by definition slender. Phyllis now weighed only ninety pounds—six and a half stones. Someone that thin not only looks like an otherworldly creature, like "one of those Fairies dancing in the old editions of Punch," such as Powys used "to hunt so feverishly for" in the Sherborne library, but may act like one, as physiological and mental changes occur in a body that fragile.[76] And of course, what Jacques Lacan calls "lines of fragilization" are those places where a body part is so delicate that it can be snapped off, bitten off, cut off: the child's fantasy of dismemberment. That was the other myth. She had to be thin because she was a child.

> 15 February 1932: The little T. T. . . . lifted up voice & said for these last two years I have not had enough to eat. O I feel (she wept) like a child left without its mother!
>
> 23 November 1931: She brought my beautiful pyjamas which I hope to wear when I seduce my Cimmerian Elemental. I seduce her all over again very often! That is because she is always a little girl & needs to be seduced again & again.

In these entries, Powys uses his favourite names for Phyllis—the T. T., his Elemental, his Nymph, his Elf-child. They signify her meaning to him. In medieval philosophy and alchemy, elementals were sometimes thought of as imaginary beings, personifications of the powers of physical nature, but Paracelsus insisted that elementals were "flesh, blood, and bones." Blake's elementals nearly always had an erotic significance, connected with the awakening of male desire. Verbal intercourse was considered to be "the highest aim of the philosopher," but a fantasy of the other kind was not unknown. Powys was well aware of all the connotations of nymphidic lore and they played a large part in his creation of the T. T. She conjoined in one frail desirable body the two worlds that he sought: the material world—nature manifested—

and the magical otherworld.[77] Intercourse with a child is yet another aspect of the myth. Phyllis, apparently willingly, entered into the sexual fantasy.

> 29th April 1939: Up at 7.45 after enjoying the feeling of sunshine and the little T. T. with little girl scrabblement, cuddling up against my iron spine! It is like sleeping with a child of twelve to sleep with this girl.

As a child, Phyllis was also incorporated into the myth of the earth mother, Demeter, whom Powys worshipped. He was, he wrote, "enamoured of my great planetary dead Mother," and the "dead winter earth" gave him a greater thrill "than from anything in Nature save the coming back of Proserpine." Demeter, the earth goddess, is raped by Zeus in the form of a bull and brings forth Proserpine/Persephone. Persephone is the budlike primordial child, the unfolding leaf—the *phyllis*—but one day, while gathering flowers in a meadow, she is dragged by Hades, brother of Zeus, into the ground and becomes the wife-goddess of the underworld. Demeter, hearing her daughter's despairing cry, hunts everywhere for her. When the goddess threatens to make the earth barren, Zeus arranges for her daughter to be returned to earth for two-thirds of the year. In Greece, the return of Persephone was celebrated in the *Lesser Elusinia*, which took place in the month of February. At Phudd, the mythic doubling is re-enacted: Phyllis becomes both mother and child and John becomes the bull god and the lord of the underworld.

> 6 February 1934: She came about 3 a.m. . . . I had prepared for this so I made love to her. . . . And I woke up too at dawn & made love to her. And she called out, "Mother, Mother, come!" like a little girl on her bridal night!
> My will is . . . the will of a great old Bull or Ox with a little girl who pulls and tugs at the rope tied to a ring in its nose. She stops to pick flowers in the ditch & jerks the rope without remembering that there is an Old Bull at the end of it and the animal waits till she has picked what she wants with its fiery breath against her pinafore.[78]

Their life together at Phudd Bottom was a constant shifting from myth to reality and back again. The reality was pain—his ulcers, her menstrual period. Every twenty-eight days Phyllis would disappear into the bedroom to suffer twenty-four to forty-eight hours of vomiting and hemorrhaging. There is a certain irony in the fact that a man who in his earlier days had such a revulsion against female blood now lived with a woman for whom the bloodletting assumed tremendous physical and psychological significance for them both. "O woe is me—she is gone away when she is so sick & I be left alone. . . . Tis like her having temporarily & pro-tem died on me."[79] When the worst was over, a solicitous Jack would administer a variety of remedies—malted milk, ice-cream, ginger beer, and cigarettes, but only when she came down did life begin again for him and the animals. Inevitably the process assumed an abstract mythic pattern, an aborted Persephone myth: the tense approach, two days of total domestic disorder, then the return to a semblance of normality—all within the ordered cycle of the moon. The meaning of their pain was mythic and sexual, but it was not abstract. His ulcers and her menses were not words but body language. They were, so to speak, cries from the underworld: look at me, see me, recognize me as real.

There were other realities. In *Glastonbury Romance*, the narrator says that compared to the "delirious ecstasy" of consummated love felt by Nell and Sam, "the neurotic intensity of the attraction between John and Mary Crow was "something as sad as it was sterile."[80] Again, in *Weymouth Sands*, the sexual union of Jobber and Perdita has no element of Sylvanus-like Tibetan mysticism or Powys-hero "vicious lust." For whatever reason, these scenes of "normal" love-making are some of the most movingly written in both novels. It was at Phudd that Powys first introduced the code phrase "à la Lulu," to indicate penetrative intercourse.[81] Although more often the lovemaking was "in my own Tibetan manner,"[82] he laughingly admitted that he sometimes got carried away.

> 20 December 1933: The T. T. came at <u>3.30</u> Aye! but I was reckless! I was so thrilled to see her that my pleasure passed the limit practised by the Late Dalai Lama, whose death we read, & attained the level always spoken of by Lulu when he writes "I was Happy."

Another reality which was intensely sexual was his use of enemas. One of the "subtler aspects" of Powys's ulcer was that he knew the fiberless diet he insisted upon was "hopelessly constipating,"[83] so constipating that he had long resorted to enemas. He frankly admitted that he had "come greatly to prefer this artificial method to the natural one!"[84] Enemas brought back memories of the nursery when the Powys children were routinely given enemas to "keep the bowels open," and John had been using them since at least 1910. For some years he gave them to himself with a handheld clyster. However, after the Indian episode in 1932, he asked Phyllis to "help" him with them. Neither of them could avoid being aware that the anal sphincter has sensitive nerve endings, and the introduction of an enema nozzle could be experienced as sexually pleasurable—in effect a buggering.[85] At the same time, perversely, there were strong sadomasochistic elements for both of them in the procedure itself. A favourite subject in the pornographic literature he was familiar with involved the forced administration of an enema and the attendant humiliation of the victim. Possibly for Powys it became another masochistic turn-on. Whether it was or not, the regime was a strict one; he insisted on an enema every third day. Even when she was prostrate with her period, he had her come down from the bedroom to administer it, although he hated to see her look "so white, so tired, so pinched, so haggard."[86] Once he began relying totally on enemas, he had another valid reason for never lecturing again, indeed for not leaving Phudd at all for more than two days. Once she began delivering the enema, it was also impossible for her to get away. When he un-learned how to give himself an enema, he learned how not to be abandoned.

Although Powys found the final revisions of *Weymouth* "a struggle,"[87] in the end he was, quite properly, "rather proud of my skill in gathering up the Various Puppets of this Planetary Book between Sea & Land. This book on the <u>Beach</u>."[88] He dedicated it "to Gertrude in memory of her days at Greenhill Terrace with Father." A few months later he heard from the publishers. Their reader, Clifford Fadiman, did not like it at all, and Maxe Schuster did not like most of the characters, least of all Sylvanus. Simon & Schuster finally agreed to accept it with revisions but decided not to publish it before spring of 1934. They also strongly suggested he write his next novel about small-town America. The story was all there in his diary—the landscape, the people and the animals of Columbia County all described in affectionate detail. There were their nearest neighbors, Mr. and Mrs. Krick and their nephew young Albert and his wife Dora, who were "the nicest and best Four Persons in the world." Mr. Krick, especially, became "our Guardian Angel." There was Daddy Scutt, the "unctious, vicious, amorous, hypocritical, kind, sly, lame" carpenter who called him "Pop" and Phyllis "dearie." There was Rummery the slap-dash plumber; Shaver "the Perfect Gardner"; Mr. Johnson, the "heroic postman"; Miss McNeill, their cleaning lady, who came faithfully—"gallantly marching on foot covered with snow like a robust virgin Cow"; Mr. Steuerwald, the storekeeper "of Herculean proportions," who was such a nice man but could not cope with business; old Mrs. MacNeil with "her face half-paralyzed"; Mr. Curtis, whose father was "dotty in mind"; Dr. Baldwin, "delicatest of all Dentists," who killed himself in his office "with some kind of knife." There was Maggie the Heifer, Mees and Toby the cats, Belle the blind horse, "wild sad disconsolate Racoons crying out at dawn"; their nervous dog, "the Black," who went at "strangle-hold pace" on their walks but who sometimes "like a little Elephant with great ears flapping . . . caracoled for joy." For a few months in the autumn of 1933, he referred occasionally to "when I write my Columbia County Romance,"[89] but he never did write a Phudd Bottom story, perhaps because he intended one day to publish his diary. In the meantime, he had something else in mind.

February 2, 1933, again his father's birthday, was an early spring day. He sat by the open window "in a trance of delight recalling a thousand 'essences' of old days." He watched Phyllis and their dog jumping the stream from stone to stone and noted that "I have hesitated at that rushing stream just as I used to do at Preston Brook beyond Redcliff Bay where Littleton always jumped and I used always to draw back." When she got back, she told him she "had the idea of writing an autobiography not to be published till after death. It awes me to think of such a work. Will she really do it?" She didn't, but a week later Powys wrote Llewelyn, "Do you know what my next book is going to be . . . ? My Autobiography!"[90]

In a sense, it was inevitable. *Weymouth Sands* started as a story about characters in a seaside resort and became an extended reverie on the landscape of childhood. Memory is, in its structures, highly spatial; the recapturing of lost time is possible through the rediscovery of lost places. As he was struggling with the writing of *Weymouth*, Powys was also re-reading Joyce and Proust for an article on the modern novel and puzzling on the personality of the exiled writer. It has been said that exile is a medium through which to re-imagine one's beginnings,[91] and that was the role that Phudd played. "One's beginnings" is both a place and a time—what another exilic writer, Vladimir Nabokov, called "the whereabouts and whenabouts of memorial space."[92] The long daily walks recorded in his diary exposed John Cowper to sights, sounds, weather conditions, and smells which would trigger in his mind sudden upsurges of childhood memories. The landscape of upstate New York became the necessary medium for the West Country of England; the fact that they were totally dissimilar in reality was irrelevant. Phudd Bottom became a kind of Calypso's isle, a zone of intermediacy in which he could recreate his Ithacan home. "In this place," he wrote, "all my past began to be Retrouvé—Le Temps Retrouvé."[93]

A more commonplace reason may have been that a number of his friends were writing autobiographies. Helen Dreiser told them she was working on *My Life with Dreiser*; Floyd Dell, whom Powys had known since Chicago days, told them he too was writing his lifestory. Phyllis and John Cowper read all the modern autobiographies they could get their hands on. Dr. Frink, their psychiatrist friend, gave them a copy of Lincoln Steffen's autobiography, which had come out the year before, and that autumn they read aloud to each other Gide's *If It Die*.[94] A few years earlier Powys had also read with great interest Yeats's *Reveries over Childhood and Youth*[95] and wrote several letters to Phyllis about it: "This book of Yeats brings so many things back to my mind. I keep reading passages of it again and again." He noted that Yeats was "over 60"—as he was—when he began his autobiography. Powys felt an affinity with Yeats from a very early period. He addressed one of the verses in his first book of poems to Yeats, who had responded with "a lengthy and most exciting letter in acknowledgement." Cousin Ralph had done both their horoscopes, and Powys was flattered when Yeats told him "that my moon was exactly & most astonishingly identical with his."[96] Almost certainly Powys would have met him, probably through Ezra Pound and Frances Gregg, when Yeats was on an American tour in the spring of 1914 and both were lecturing in Philadelphia, Chicago, and New York. Yeats is reported by Strand American Tours to have said, "If poetry is to be a personal utterance, there must be personality, and personality needs a disturbed life for its development"—a sentiment which would have rung bells with Powys.[97] When Yeats returned to England, he began writing his "Reveries over Childhood and Youth," which he told his friend Quinn, in a letter dated July 9, 1914, was "the history of my mind." What would have struck John Cowper strongly were the similarities in their family backgrounds and upbringing. Yeats's father Jack remarked that the paternal side of the family was "dyed in a sort of well-mannered evangelicalism" whereas the maternal side of the family were drawn to "mysticism and morbidity." Yeats's mother, like Mary Cowper, was sensitive but undemonstrative. Jack Yeats said sadly of her that she "put up barriers," longing for affection and the "longing was like a deep unsunned well."[98] In both families the relations between the children were intense, close, and often quarrelsome. They both spent their childhood summers with grandparents by the sea. Sligo for Yeats and Weymouth for Powys were for years the centre of their world. Despite this, both insisted that their childhood was unhappy. The first chapters of Powys's *Autobiography* echo Yeats's sentiments in his *Reveries* that "I remember little of childhood but its pain," noting that the misery was "not made by others, but a part of my mind." In early adulthood, both were attracted to theosophical beliefs. Yeats's particular blend was Rosicruciansim, spiritualism, Irish mythology, whereas Powys was attracted to Welsh myth and eastern philosophies. The routes to esoteric wisdom differed, but both, from an early period, had a similar aim. Both artists sought to be magicians, and as Yeats wrote, "for men to attain to the supreme wisdom" meant "a loneliness that is like the loneliness of death."[99] This is the *Philosophy of Solitude* in a nutshell.

If he saw similarities between himself and Yeats, Powys saw an even greater likeness between himself and Rousseau. Rousseau's happiness in country life and the natural world; his need for solitude; his idealized image of his father as a link between himself and his lost paradise of childhood; his love of simple "childish" food; his masochism; the strongly erotic element in his fantasizing which he specifically links with his "disastrous" habit of masturbation; his many illnesses; his "madness" (which the unsympathetic Scottish philosopher, David Hume—playing a Louis Wilkinson role—suspected was simply acting a part).[100] All these traits have echoes in Powys's personality and life, or at least, as Powys chose to portray them in his *Autobiography*. Rousseau, of course, traced the personality characteristics of his adulthood back to incidents in his childhood, as did Goethe[101] and Wordsworth, who followed his lead. Wordsworth's *Prelude*, which Powys said he knew by heart, is not only autobiography which relies heavily on introspection and recollection, it also lays stress on the psychological significance of childhood experience. These ideas were not exclusively romantic; they were part of an ancient system of beliefs, and they continue to this day in the theories and research of childhood development. Powys was perfectly aware of all these ideas and utilized them when he was writing his own autobiography.

John Cowper had written a long essay on Rousseau as early as 1916, praising him as a "scandalous individualist" and an "ingrained pursuer of his own path." His interest was renewed when, in December 1932, Llewelyn sent him the edition of Rousseau's *Confessions* which John had given his mother twenty years before. His enthusiasm for Rousseau extended to buying a bust of him for the newly redecorated dining room at Phudd which the dog insisted on barking at hysterically. What intrigued Powys most were the extremes to which Rousseau took his introspective narrative. He was by no means the first in the field, but conventional confessions up to that point were to God in order to gain forgiveness; Rousseau's confessions were to his readers and the end was not so much to gain forgiveness but to gain relief. Powys admired Rousseau's "voluptuous desire . . . to lay bare all his basest and meanest lusts," his "mania for self-exposure," his "passion for self-humiliation."[102] The reader can be forgiven for thinking that Powys is describing his own *Autobiography*. Another favourite author, Goethe, was also in his mind and he wrote Marian that he wanted to "catch the salient & curious points in my own mental & moral & spiritual pilgrimage up to Date" and thought that his "experiences, sensations, ideas, feelings, overtones, sins, vices, weaknesses, manias, recoveries, books, places, pictures, scenes, surroundings, lend themselves to a sort of Faustian Pilgrimage of the Soul, or a sort of Goethean Pilgrim's Progress."[103]

John Cowper now had a method (confessional); a focus (the influence of childhood events on his adult personality) and a technique (dramatic self-exposure). However, he knew that to sell yet another autobiography, it would have to have a unique slant. He wrote Llewelyn on July 24, 1933:

> I have been planning all sorts of original devices certainly never used in any Autobiography before. . . . Once (oh what will Alyse say) I even decided to leave out all mention of all feminine persons, but since such Beings have played such a role in my existence, I don't think this exclusion wd. exactly be conducive to that Spiritual Sincerity which you . . . have, ere now, so strongly insisted upon.

Nonetheless, that is precisely what he did. Two and a half weeks later he told Littleton that "the main portion of it will be the history of the growth and development of a solitary human consciousness," but that he was "going to make it the most original of all autobiographies by deliberately omitting all feminines in it."[104] Initially this was obviously a marketing ploy to make the book more saleable, although interestingly, he did not mention this omission in the synopsis for his publishers. Still, there were five women who held places of the greatest importance in his life—his companion Phyllis; his wife Margaret; his first love, Frances Gregg; his sister Marian; and his mother—and to leave them out raises many questions. Possibly the reason he would have found most plausible was that he did not want to upset his wife and son. One of his stated aims was to avoid hurting people, but his accounts of lusting after girls on beaches near their Burpham home and his encounters with Tom Jones's "sweet-natured women" (lower-class women were exempt from his definition of "feminines") must have wounded Margaret terribly when the book was published. However, Margaret and Littleton Alfred *still* did not know how deeply in love with Frances Gregg he had been, and they most certainly did not know about Phyllis, with whom he had been living for almost ten years by the time he wrote *Autobiography*. Arguably he could have simply omitted to mention Phyllis and Frances, in much the same way that Llewelyn's biographer left out all his sundry mistresses, including Gamel Woolsey. John Cowper could have said something evasive about his marriage with Margaret and something anodyne about his five sisters and included all of them.

It is the omission of his mother that is the real mystery. Since both his parents were long dead, he could not possibly have hurt either of them by anything he said about them. Llewelyn had already published some very cogent and critical remarks about both parents, and Louis Wilkinson, who was writing his own autobiography, *Swan's Milk*, at the same time, had referred to the "mental masochism" of Mary Cowper and the "repressed ferocity" of Charles Francis.[105] John defended Wilkinson against the ire of Old Littleton about this description and yet, even in a late correspondence, he stated bluntly that he would discuss absolutely anything *except* his mother. With all the eloquence he could so easily call up, John might have drawn a series of portraits of his mother: Mary Cowper as a cultivated, literary, albeit rather un-self-confident young woman; Mary as a constantly pregnant wife, giving birth on average every fifteen to twenty-four months; Mary as the prematurely old woman longing for death but "afraid of the spirits." He didn't or felt he couldn't. But why not, since he was prepared to say things about himself that even in 1934 were rather outré? He describes in great detail his blood and breast phobias, his fears of "going in," and admits that "femininity . . . made me shudder with a singular revulsion," but he does not attempt to explain the genesis of this. It cannot be argued that he was psychologically naive and would not make the connection between his own personality problems and his mother. He could have discussed this with great perception, for as early as 1923 he was insisting in his book, *Psychoanalysis and Morality*, that "psychoanalysis throws the influence of woman as mother into a very searching light."[106] Then says no more. In *Weymouth Sands*, Magnus's mother had died in his early childhood. Powys could not erase his own mother so easily from his life, but he could eliminate her from his story of self.

Instead, it is his father who dominates *Autobiography* in the same way as Magnus's father, even in death, held sway over his life. John Cowper's memories of his father must have been flooding him as he wrote *Weymouth*—that ghostly father who influenced his reactions, his thoughts, his relationships "with the unwitting power of some dim pre-historic god."[107] The most intriguing comment John Cowper made about the writing of *Autobiography* was to a relative stranger: "In this ticklish business of writing an autobiography I am going to play safe—so fantastically & exaggeratedly safe indeed that from this 'safety' itself will emerge a quite special sort of irony . . . of a kind for which at present there is no name."[108] He could have meant that by doing away with half of the people who were most important to him he was playing it "exaggeratedly safe." That indeed could be considered, in an autobiography, "ironic." Or does the clue lie in the portrait of his father? Is the affectionate, almost slavishly admiring picture of his father that he presents in the autobiography intended to be ironic? Or was the depiction a case of misremembering? Or was the portrait intended to be part of a larger myth of the omnipotent Powys patriarch, a myth shared by at least some of the other family members?[109]

There is another possibility. In the first chapters of *Autobiography*, what John Cowper says about Charles Francis, and the images he uses in describing him, are often two different things. Was he, in his portrait of his father, once again trying to have it both ways—falling in with (and even creating) the Powys family myth and at the same time employing a rather subtle and difficult ironic reversal, using the memories and the images to play against each other? By using the indirectness of irony Powys would have been able to maintain the advantage of self control and detachment and leave it to the images to convert the compliments into insults. As Dryden said, "There is still a vast difference betwixt the slovenly Butchering of a Man, and the fineness of a stroak that separates the Head from the Body, and leaves it standing in its place."[110]

What we do know is that both parents were omnipresent as he wrote *Autobiography*. He wrote in his diary: "I sat down on a fallen tree & looked at Phudd through the trees & thought it looked like Montacute Hill & I thought of my father & mother there buried and in their graves and I thought how their characters abide in my mind—their power & individualism last still."[111] The sights and smells and sounds of the present merge with those of childhood in a magical re-creation of lost time. Re-reading Rousseau, Powys remarked how "Madame de Warens when he was so happy showed him some periwinkles when he was absorbed in amorousness & too shorted sighted to see them properly but long afterwards—20 years afterwards—he saw periwinkles again & this time undistracted did he look so closely at them—'Mama' either lost or dead! Hush!"[112] Does the irony of *Autobiography* consist in the "Hush!" or in "Mama" being both dead and lost? The voyeur-exile re-creates the lost paradise of childhood and then insists on identifying it with the mother—with Demeter. The mother is in the underworld, that place of vision and menace. Does the irony, then, lie in making his childhood a paradise that is nonetheless mysteriously filled with fear?

It is not easy to grasp the sequence or significance of the events Powys relates, because, as I have said, he inserts into the story the immense sophistication of his own psychological knowledge, as well as his familiarity with psychoanalytical literature and its concepts of psychic development. This familiarity is never overt—it is almost a counter-tune or rhythm, at once expanding upon, and negating, what he is saying. It is easily argued that the first chapters of *Autobiography* read, almost sentence by sentence, like a classic Freudian case history. But is that not exactly what Powys intended? Did he really have the manias and fetishes he describes? For that matter, how genuine is the story of his childhood sexuality and his psychic development? Are those first six chapters, which read like a textbook case of anxiety neurosis with associated phobias and obsessive disorders, an immense conjuring trick? Let me give just one example. Throughout *Autobiography*, Powys refers again and again to his Fear (which he always capitalizes), which he says persisted all his life. He is unable or refuses to name this "fantastical Fear" although he is able to discuss various other "neurotic fears," none of which seem, on the surface, to be connected to the Fear. Powys was familiar with Freud's *The Psychopathology of Everyday Life*[113] in which the analyst discusses different types of repression. In it, Freud tells the story of when he, barely three years old, heard the word "confinement" used in two ways. A nursemaid was arrested for stealing things from the house and confined at the police station at about the same time that his brother was born. During her confinement, Freud was excluded from his mother's presence, and he remembers insisting on seeing inside a chest, weeping because he is afraid that his mother has been shut up in it. Forty years after the event, he knew that there had been no rational grounds for this fear but recognized that something had taken her away from him which he felt forbidden to understand. This piece of analysis on Freud's part is a perfect example of screen memory: he remembers only the event which covered the cause of his anxiety; not the real nature of the anxiety itself—that is, the role of the father in the confinement.

A surprisingly similar "case history" is related by Powys—the episode of the stick in the water and Johnny's subsequent terror of being imprisoned. Although he is deliberately vague about dates in *Autobiography*, this happened at Osmaston Park when John was six and a half. It was a picnic, possibly held in recognition of his father's departure from Shirley, which was announced August 9, 1879. His mother would not have been present because she gave birth to Nellie on the twentieth of August. In other words, she was "confined," at the same time that the little boy was threatened with confinement for throwing the stick in the water. Powys was by nature what he called "self-analytical" and he even referred to himself in his lectures as a "psychologist." In 1923 he was both excited and frightened by the possibilities of Freudian analysis, writing, "Psychoanalytical research sets free such creative and destructive powers in the abysses of our own souls that we pause on the precipice-edge of the gulfs which are ourselves."[114] By 1934 he was dubious. In *Autobiography*, immediately after relating the stick episode he goes on to say,

> Few of us but have, hidden away deep down in our nerves, some secret Fear which we are not "allowed" to speak of, even to our dearest. I suppose there have been cures by these ambiguous and dangerous psychoanalytical methods, but for myself I am inclined to think that it is better "to leave well" though it is not exactly well, "alone." It is certainly alone we are, and must ever be in the last resort; and it seems to me that it is the wisest and safest course to carry our "madness," our hidden Fear, about with us, and allow it to change, as it will, its outward form according to the age we have reached.[115]

That is what he did do, the Fear taking increasingly grotesque forms the older he became. But the question must again be asked: is Powys, in the first half of *Autobiography*, saying to himself: I can do a detailed analysis as well as that scientist Freud; I will simply interpret the details of my life according to psychoanalytic dogma, but screen out Freud's main thesis—the Oedipus complex? Instead of love of Mother and hatred toward Father, I will eliminate the Mother and adulate the Father. It will be like drawing a maze with no essential key.

He was to write in a later book of criticism, "We must go about collecting magic words and symbols! Every critic who is worth his salt makes use of some particular clue-word of his own, some invoking symbolical keyword which serves him as his particular *Open Sesame*. I don't say he invents the word himself. As a rule he steals it. But he makes it his own and often makes more of it than its inventor did. My own favourite passwords of this sort are the word 'secret,' invented by Matthew Arnold; the word 'life-illusion,' invented by Ibsen; and finally the phrase 'stupid being' invented by Gertrude Stein."[116]

Powys probably should have added another "clue-word": maze. It has been said that a story answers "what happened next," but that the plot tells us why it happened. Is it possible that Powys deliberately concealed the "why" both in his own story and in his fiction? In *Wolf Solent*, for example, the "why did it happen" is answered: because the hero remembered a nursery rhyme. However, this motivation is so obscure, or so disguised, that few readers follow the trail to the inner "secret." The original Greek for "plot" in Aristotle's *Poetics* is *mythos*. One of Powys's greatest strengths as a novelist was to use myth as plot; the answers to "why" in his stories are to be discovered in the myth. A *Glastonbury Romance* finds its coherence in the myth of the journey to the underworld, but at the same time its incoherence resides in the fact that few but the author know the intricacies of the myth. He leads the reader into the maze but gives him few or misleading clues how to get to the centre.

It is possible that *Autobiography* is a similar paper-maze. Equally possible, it is an inspired case history. A case history is a mode of imagining, however "outer" its style. If it is presented as factual history, as an account of what happened, it is a fabrication. But Powys never claimed his autobiography was history. He set out his intention early on in *Autobiography*:

> What excites our more intelligent interest *is a story*, that is to say the strug-
> gle of a soul, conscious or half conscious, with the obstacles that hinder its
> living growth, that obstruct the lilt of its pulse and joggle to left or right its
> integral continuity. The only interest in events, devoid of the negative sig-
> nificance of being obstacles in our path, is a symbolic one.[117]

A simple narrative is not enough to grow a soul. An event must become a sym-
bolic experience, moving from outer to inner. The events that he describes in the first chapter of the autobiography—the tadpole incident, the loss of the laurel axe, the hanging of his brother, the infantile eroticism and its punishment, the Lord of Hosts incident, the stick in the water—are the *significant* events in his early childhood that he remembers. In the process of remembering, the events are reconstructed, turned into that secret myth by which one knows one's self, one's soul. The "bio" in the autobiography is the story of outer events; the "auto" is the story of the growth of the soul. They are not the same stories; often they are not even similar stories. Nor can it be forgotten that a third factor enters into the complot: the "graph," the writer of the two stories. It was Powys who was writing his own case history and he understood as well as Freud that the narrative of a human life is structured by the *selective* logic of the *mythos* in the psyche; that there is history not remembered and there is memory that is not historical. This remembering-what-
never-happened must rightly be called imagining. A biography of soul assumes a poetic basis of mind. Any case history of that mind will have to be an imaginative expression of this poetic basis, an imaginative making, possibly a healing fiction.

There is, of course, a fourth factor: the biographer, who can only watch intently this Yeatsian "Mirror on mirror mirrored,"[118] and patiently sort through the constructions, reconstructions, and deconstructions. But whether in his autobiography and his novels Powys was playing maze games with an innocent reader or whether part of the game was involving the reader in a double-natured complicity is something that, after twenty years of close familiarity with Powys, I remain unsure. However, as Phyllis told him, "keep it a story, a story, a story & let readers do their own bloody interpretations of it."[119]

"The T.T. & I started off to East Chaldon and visited Theodore to whose little Sue we presented the dress and bonnet."
—JCP Diary, 10 July, 1934.

"Her large calmness like the touch of a healing 'goddess of the infant world'í extends itself to everyone she approaches."
—JCP letter to Phyllis, 11 September, 1924.

"Worked hard at my book till after lunch and then walked over to the White Nore to meet them all coming here to tea. But there was a lot of photography first." —JCP Diary, 23 June, 1929.

"This best of well-balanced worlds is so constructed that at every turn it thwarts the wishes of one born of the spirit and of earth."
—JCP letter to Frances, 27 August, 1912.

"How lost to everything the brothers were at this moment. Whatever it was they were whispering they were completely oblivious of every other living soul. Names, places, events, occasions, passed like bubbles between them, forming and reforming on the tide of their memories." —*Porius*.

"The wind howls round the house rattling the casements and wailing in the chimney. . . . The view from this window stretches away down the steep valleys with a winding grassy road (no other approach except across the down-turf) disappearing & re-appearing over one crest of a ridge & then over another & right above them all (over the very top of the Five Maries) you can see the expanse of Egdon Heath."
—JCP letter to Phyllis, 10 September, 1924.

"Penn House, Brunswick Terrace, brings back to me many sensations. . . . The bow windows of the drawing-room opened straight on the Esplanade—which was very narrow just there—and on the pebbled bank of the sea." —Autobiography.

CHAPTER ELEVEN

THE DORSET YEAR

1934-1935

⁓

I T WAS WHILE HE WAS WRITING AUTOBIOGRAPHY THAT POWYS DECIDED TO leave America. This apparently sudden decision was something of a puzzle because Phudd Bottom gave him that wonderful combination of physical and psychic freedom that writers long for and seldom have. He wrote that his four years in Hillsdale were "years in which I have had a greater chance to realize my identity than I have ever before had in my life."[1] It was here that he began to learn the language of what he called his "magicianship." Here too he could let his "inmost impulses have their free swing."[2] Powys's tolerant farmer-neighbors allowed him to walk where he would in their fields and gave him the privacy to indulge in his rituals, his prayers, his head-tappings on ground that (he was convinced) was thereby made sacred. While he may have failed the Indian's initiation, here, in this place, he made his own initiation. After so many years of struggle, John Cowper finally made the connection between his love of nature and his creativity. He learned not only to mythologize the processes of nature; he learned that these processes were symbolic expressions of the inner drama of his own psyche. The magical power of his landscape descriptions in his mature writings arose out of this knowledge.

More prosaically, in their four years there, he and Phyllis had built what are now called "support systems"—very necessary for two people totally incapable of coping with the trials of everyday life. When they could afford it, they could count on the handyman, the gardener, the cleaning lady. Above all, they had the friendship and aid of the Kricks, for whom they had come to feel "such deep deep affection." What part Phyllis played in the decision to leave is unclear; once she stopped writing a journal, we see and hear her only through Powys's eyes and pen. However, from his diary it is obvious that while she still hated the cold winters, visitors, and housekeeping, by now Phudd had become her home. She particularly loved her garden, willing to give up buying fuel when they ran out in early spring in order to buy mulberry hedging plants and a ginko tree which would only come to maturity in the distant future. She had become part of the community; in her "lovely black short-skirted dress that is up to her pretty knees" she went to the Ladies' Social, the Philmont Minstrel show, and various local plays and musical events. The Kricks would take her to see a movie in a nearby town; Dr. Frink, who shared her love for poking about in antique shops, would take her for a day's drive. She still raged when Jack dropped hot coals on her new rug or put his feet on the couch in his wet boots; she still had hysterics when he let the dog piss in the kitchen, or he "accidentally" lit the fire with the theatre page of the Sunday paper—her one remaining link with city life—but he recognized that she was "deeply and authentically happy these days."[3]

Why then was he intent upon leaving? There were valid arguments for finding somewhere cheaper to live. By the time *Weymouth* was sent to the publishers in mid-1933, their financial situation was dire. For the entire year of 1933, his four books with Simon & Schuster brought only $1,525 in royalties while they needed a minimum of $2,400 to live on. He wrote Alyse that he sometimes thought that "it would be a good idea for a nincompoop of my calibre to say to Schuster, 'Give me a regular sum of . . . $200 a month for life, and then take all! English Rights, Foreign Rights (if there be any at all!), all, all, all, only give me Peace of Mind and Security'!"[4] Had he made this proposal, their subsequent history would have been very different, but he did not. Instead he demanded and got a five percent increase in royalties (from ten to fifteen percent) but in return he unwisely signed a contract for *Weymouth Sands* which gave Simon & Schuster options on two further books, which later included *Autobiography*. Schuster also suggested a broadcast series on the topic of "Romance," a promotional tour, and the very tempting offer to sell *Glastonbury* "to the Movies," all of which Powys declined. When Arthur Ficke heard that he turned down the latter, he was aghast and a "great argument" ensued. Powys told Ficke that "it was a deep but noble malice to say no" to "these unspeakable Hollywood Vulgarians."[5] Powys never let money get in the way of his principles—or his malice.

He was still sending his wife and son (now thirty-one) a generous allowance; however, he had to write Margaret apologetically in April 1933 that he could only send her half her usual money because he now had to live on the other half. Despite their financial straits, when a relative stranger, James Hanley, wrote in March and asked if he could have $250 "for the birth of his wife's child," Powys immediately sent the money, but it wiped out "all my New York current account."[6] His cousin, Father Hamilton, was "fussed-up over my doctrines of giving money to all who ask,"[7] but he continued all his life to do so. Worse was to come. Despite Franklin Playter's warning as early as 1930 that there would be bank failures during the Depression, and his advice to put their money into a postal savings, John continued to put whatever money he received into the local bank, although he worried "where would we be if this really occurred?"[8] In April 1933 the Philmont Bank closed, with all the rest of their remaining funds—$300—in it. Mr. Krick lent them money until it reopened.

Phyllis explored the possibility of their living more economically in lodgings in Chatham or Philmont, the nearest towns, or if worse came to worst, with her mother in Kansas. Friends made other suggestions, and in October 1933 Mabel

Pearson found a cheap house with a maid in Cannes for them. Although they both agreed that "Cannes would be ridiculous" for Powys, he felt "a sort of shame not to carry her to some warm place," or to "a foreign inn in some old town," where he knew she would be happy.[9] He knew very well that "I have been very stupid if not very selfish,"[10] but it made not a whit of difference. He had a different destination in mind. In May 1933 he felt "a strong nostalgia for England—a longing for more austere weather & more wind."[11] However, it was to Wales that Powys was determined to go. He had never forgotten his father's stories about their descent from the ancient princes of Wales. In their different ways, all the Powyses were snobs, inverted or reverted. From early in his marriage, he had a longing to live in Wales, but he must have realized fairly quickly that Margaret was not wild Wales material. He hoped that Phyllis might prove more tractable. He explained to her that if they lived in Wales he would be able to "write the greatest Romance of Modern Times, with the Welsh Legends & Myths to back me up." Her response was not encouraging: "The T. T. has many reactions now— O so many! in favour of this House—in favour of the ease, the comfort, the calm, the convenience, the familiarity of our life here. . . . But I answer to it all—'I must and will write that masterpiece about Wales in Wales.'"[12]

Phyllis said flatly that "the stars are not lucky in her horoscope for any move just now!"[13] and set about digging in. She arranged to have a midday meal with some neighbors and John could see that as a result her health and spirits perceptibly picked up. She then proceeded to have the parlor redecorated. He was dubious about the changes but "she says that the effect of this Carpet with the gold Pears on the green ethereal sunset wall paper & the salmon coloured Cushion on the velvet couch gives her for the 1st time in life the Watteau essences she has so pathetically & desperately struggled for."[14] However, as the winter progressed the old problems surfaced. A recurrence of his ulcer in December meant that once again Phyllis, "weeping & collapsing," had to manage alone. He gave her full marks for her "executive skill."

> Even while we were still at breakfast Mr. Decker the Coal Man appeared— & while Rodgers [a visitor] & I continued our meal—the heroic little T. T. rushed out just as she was in the falling Snow & put bricks under his truck so he could shovel thro' the aperture & came back with her head covered with snow & her hands black with Coal. It is so strange that so fragile a being can cope with a sudden practical crisis like this![15]

The crunch came in early February 1934, when a letter arrived to say that they would receive only $600 in royalties in May, when they had been told in the autumn that they could expect $1,000. Powys began to see himself "exploited for ever & ever . . . my Books (as I write them) entirely in the power of S. & S."[16] Marian wanted him to deal with Schuster "in a very drastic manner" and "issue ultimatums," but he replied that he had not "yet reached the point of feeling escaped from a double obligation to these 'boys.'"[17] He had reason to be grateful to Maxe Schuster and John Simon. They took a personal interest in Powys over the years, they accepted his vast novels, and publicized them well. They arranged to find English publishers for his books, and in return they received a whopping 50% of those royalties, but this was a contractual point that Powys never protested against, despite repeated urgings from relatives and writer friends. Indeed, he had been thrilled by the news that in July 1933, John Lane the Bodley Head had signed a contract with Simon & Schuster for *A Glastonbury Romance* to be published in England. He advised Theodore Dreiser, who was visiting at the time, to "stick to Jewish Publishers" and "avoid Gentile publishers—for in business they are like Gangsters" to which Dreiser had muttered, as it turned out, prophetically, "lest you pay to the uttermost farthing!"[18]

In the midst of all this, brother Will and his new wife Elizabeth arrived for a visit. Will was by now a very successful farmer-landowner in Kenya, and they suggested that John and Phyllis come to live with them. Powys knew this would mean that Phyllis would escape the cold and the housework and that she would "really & truly like it";[19] however, the next day he told Will that he did not want to live in Africa. In the meantime, Arthur Ficke was busy on his behalf. In March 1934, the naturalist writer Alan Devoe, a friend of Ficke, offered them $3,000 for the house and property. Powys tapped his head with gratitude to the spirit of his mother and accepted. He could not understand why Phyllis was "very very nervous just now very easily upset" but concluded the reason must be "the effort to be mistress of a house," adding, "You wait until we are safe off & then I will see to it that never again will she have this kind of responsibility and all this effort & tension which so upsets her nerves. I must get this absolutely lodged in my mind. I must not forget as I tend to do. I must see to it that her life is happier & much much easier when once I get her safe the other side of the sea!"[20]

"The other side" was now where Powys wanted to be. America had served its purpose as a place of exile. Powys knew his *Odyssey* at least as well as James Joyce did; he once wrote that he read it daily as a breviary. So he understood the spatial frame of an exile's story, which is from centre to periphery and return. The myth of exile is in fact the myth of exile *and* return. In Samuel Beckett's novel *Molloy*, the eponymous hero, in his search for his lost mother, moves away from his mother's room. He finds himself in a forest (or more precisely, like Powys, on the edge of the forest). He is in exile but he is free. However, he cannot stay there. Indeed he feels he is not "free" to do so; that to stay is to go "against an imperative."[21] Interestingly, Powys also uses the word "imperative" in a diary entry for January 16, 1934, as he argues with himself about leaving America.

> As I stood down by the Alders River beyond Spinney on which the sun shone so strong as it rushed so black and glittering between its snow-banks there came over me another Inspiration or rather a powerful Impulse a Magnetic Imperative towards my Book about Merlin and Taliessin & Ceridwen & Welsh Mythology.

Phudd was the place where learning through, or in spite of, pain occurred. It was here that he discovered his own special myth—the myth of the incurable wound. He is Philoctetes, the Greek hero who, while making a sacrifice to the mother-goddess, is bitten on the heel by a snake, and who becomes thereby an exiled non-hero with a wound that never heals. Philoctetes had an ulcerous heel; Powys had an ulcerated gut. In André Gide's version of the story, Philoctetes becomes convinced that his exile, while full of pain, has allowed him to "come to know more of the secrets of life than my masters ever revealed to me. And I took to telling the story of my sufferings, and if a phrase was very beautiful, I was by it so much consoled; I even sometimes forgot my sadness by uttering it. . . . And I gradually got the habit of crying the distress of things. . . . Their distress and mine were the same and I was comforted. "[22] Powys was equally sure he knew now "the secrets of life" and that these magical powers gave him the sovereignty of words and sovereignty of self. Phudd was no longer necessary and he left as abruptly as he had come.

Powys's decision had immediate consequences. He first had to break the news to his wife and son, and to tell them about the existence of Phyllis. The only other member of the family who did not know about Phyllis was his beloved brother Littleton. He now wrote them on March 7th "about the whole business." It was hardly a frank letter. He wrote Gertrude on the tenth describing the missive as "after my Lord Chesterfield manner" and that he had described his "Hareem" as a "proposition more closely connected with my being in health and with good care and nursing than with any flaunted immorality."[23] On the twenty-seventh he received a letter from his son wanting a "Secular Confession." Experienced in the way of confessions, John wrote one—"four pages long!"—but he also had to "confess" another piece of news. On February 22, 1934, he had been informed that he was being sued for libel. At first he was more amused than concerned.

> 29 April 1934: Guess what, Frances? A law-suit for Libel!—yes a libel action! Unwitting, I made in *Glastonbury* my Bete Noir & Antagonist of the Grail an air-man who owned Wookey Hole & the factory at its mouth. Now I am to receive a Writ from the Owner of Wookey Hole who is an air-man & incidentally a war-hero—Captain Hodgkinson M.C., who says that I have libelled and injured him in the person of Philip Crow!

Powys could not have been unaware of the dangers. He knew that he was almost "psychic" in the way in which he modeled, in all innocence, his characters after real people. Indeed a year later, he was to write Dorothy Richardson, "It does tickle my fancy to think that I appear to have unwittingly hit upon the truth a second time for my young town-clerk in *Weymouth Sands* seems exactly to resemble the real young Town Clerk there."[24] Furthermore, it was a notorious period for libel actions against writers. D. H. Lawrence, James Hanley, Havelock Ellis, Compton Mackenzie, Gamel Woolsey were only five writers known to

Powys who, in preceding years, had been involved in libel cases or charges of obscenity. His businesslike wife, however, immediately saw the writing on the wall and took the first steps to insure that she and her son would not lose anything if the case went against him. She demanded that John write a new will giving everything to Littleton Alfred and asked him to sign over the deeds to the Burpham house which she immediately put up for sale. She already had all his other English possessions, including the proceeds from his father's estate. Marian, bitterly angry with Margaret and by now devoted to Phyllis, "talked very strongly about my doing justice to the T. T. both psychologically over calling her 'Mrs. Powys' in our lodgings & so on & also that I must make a new Will telling my son clearly what I am going to do & leaving her certain definite things." Marian's words made him feel "weak and cowardly over defending the T. T. at all points."[25] Llewelyn also thought he had handled the whole business extraordinarily badly, accusing him of "a Powys obstinacy and a Powys stupidity and a Powys Pride inordinate—like Father's, like Theodore, a rustic bigotry."[26]

During this time Powys received a number of worrisome letters from the solicitors of the owner of Wookey Hole. Phyllis wanted to go herself to see the Simon & Schuster lawyer, Leon Shimkin, not only about the libel, but also about the English royalties and the business about "options" which Powys had once again ensnared himself in, but "of course I shall not let her do that."[27] He did ask brother Littleton to go to Glastonbury to see if the libel threat could be settled out of court,[28] but on May 24, John Cowper was served a writ naming him and the English publisher, John Lane the Bodley Head, as co-defendants. Leon Shimkin advised him to try for an "amicable adjustment" and followed this advice with the ominous words (the implications of which apparently JCP did not grasp): "However, since under the terms of Lane's contract they may hold you responsible for any moneys paid by them, it would seem to be to be only fitting for you to be given the opportunity to present your case."

Saying good-by to the neighbors and friends, to the house and garden, to the familiar landscape was difficult for Phyllis. Possibly there was another reason for John's decision to leave Hillsdale, albeit an unconscious one. When he moved Phyllis to Phudd, he had told her that he wanted to "hold on long enough to our little house for you to feel at home & 'racinated' there. I think that Lulu's famous epochs or 'Lustrae' of five years . . . must in some sense be the minimum."[29] In fact, they lived at Hillsdale for precisely five years. As he had done with Patchin Place, he moved her on when she began to feel "at home."

> Poor little T. T. she was piteously upset again and cried & cried. She leaned against the open china cupboard with big tears streaming down her face & pitiful words issuing from the barrier of her teeth—a barrier that these days is like a dam that is drawn up! I much prefer her to be very angry & to scold than to cry like this. Is it not strange—that I the suppressed Sadist—feel so very sorry for this sad little Abject when her whole slight being melts as if it would melt away in these flowing tears. The snow melts these waters are

released and the tears of this Elemental are released. I shall never forget
these wild disturbed days.[30]

However, despite the tears and collapses, it was the Abject who packed and
made all the arrangements for transporting their goods to England, while Powys
worked steadily on finishing *Autobiography*. Waved off by Marian, Peter, and
Arnold Shaw in New York, they arrived in Southampton on the June 5. They
put the dog into quarantine and traveled to Dorset, where for the first time
Phyllis met "the Powys Clan" en masse.

The clan may have appeared formidable to her, but to John they seemed
strangely diminished. He had not seen Theodore for five years, and much had
happened to this brother in the interval. In December 1923 Theodore had sent
his first son, Dicky, to Will in the hope that he would have a better chance in
Africa than in England. In October 1931 the boy was found dead. At first it was
believed that he had been killed by lions, but it turned out that Dicky had suffered
a peculiarly unpleasant death—he was torn apart by disaffected natives. The second son, Francis, was working in London as a bookseller. He met his future wife,
Sally Upfield, in dramatic fashion when he saved her from jumping off Waterloo
Bridge. The romantic and tender-hearted Francis fell in love and they married,
despite the fact that Sally was pregnant by the notorious Count Potoki. In a series
of events which to this day remain shrouded in mystery, Theodore and Violet
adopted the baby whom they named Theodora. "Susie," as she was quickly nicknamed, had the unenviable task of taking the place of their beloved dead son.[31]

Llewelyn and Alyse gave up their coastguard cottage in the autumn of 1931
and moved inland into the smaller of the two attached houses that made up
"Chydyok." Gertrude and Katie were pleased to have this adored brother next
door, and Alyse, being near to Gertrude with her "compassionate heart and her
cool wisdom,"[32] found the continuing tension between Llewelyn and Gamel (now
Gamel Brenan) easier to endure. In August 1933 Llewelyn had suffered another
severe hemorrhage, and although by now convalescent he was forced to spend
much of his time lying in bed in his outdoor shelter.

The family was eager to see their eldest brother again and to meet Phyllis.
John wanted to see for himself how Lulu was but had no intention of staying in the
area for long. His pleas to his brothers and sisters to leave him "absolutely free to
decide for himself where he lives"[33] were ignored and it was arranged that they
would live at Rat's Barn, an isolated farmhouse in a deep fold of the downs.
Reached by a long flint track, the place was one mile across the valley from
Chydyok and about the same distance from Chaldon, where Theodore lived at
Beth Car with his wife Violet and Susie, now two. Although Powys always carefully referred to it by its alternate name of "Down Barn," according to his nephew,
Francis, who remembered playing there as a child, Rat's Barn was aptly named—it
was overrun by rats. The cottage itself was more or less habitable, but the attached
barton was in semi-ruin. There was no electricity; the water, when there was water,
came from a pump outside the door; the only heat was from a large fireplace.

Henry James was one of John and Phyllis favourite authors and it was probably not a coincidence that they read him almost constantly during their four
month stay at Rat's Barn. James was another exile who returned "home." There
are some interesting parallels in their experience of return. James was nostalgic
for his homeland of America and in 1904 left England to spend a year there.
Initially he was happily reunited with his brother's family, and a trip to Boston
revived old memories, but he finally realized that he now belonged in neither
country: "I saw, moreover," he wrote, "that I should be an eternal outsider."[34]
Powys too had gradually to accept that he was an eternal outsider. In a letter to
Dorothy Richardson he refers to himself as "a Returned Native" and to "alien
encounter after encounter."[35] And these aliens could not be ditched by taking the
next train, as he had done so often in his land of exile. Nor could Phyllis protect
him from these encounters as she had at Phudd, for now she too was an alien.
Exhausted by the move, worried about the libel, and trying to come to terms with
a land and a culture totally strange to her, Phyllis became more and more upset
by the situation in which they found themselves.

Only recently, with the accidental discovery of the entire correspondence in
the proverbial green garbage bag, have the details of the *Glastonbury* libel case
become known.[36] It profoundly affected Powys's creative and personal life, but he
handled the affair with an ineptitude bordering on the self-destructive. A week
after arriving in Dorset, Powys traveled to London alone. He saw his son first,
and it is clear that a deal was done. Marian's criticism that John was being unfair
to Phyllis had obviously rankled. He reported happily the outcome of the meeting with Littleton Alfred to Marian.

> He was sweet to me and agreed that I could change my will leaving all my
> MSS and all my Royalties both English & American to Phyllis. Then next
> day he & I went to Blundell & Baker, Margaret's lawyers, and I gave the
> Libel Suit into their hands and they think they can arrange to keep my son
> & his mother's money out of the clutches of the Captain.[37]

John seems not to have realized it, but in effect, since royalties were their
only income, the son had transferred any liabilities that might arise out of the
court case on to Phyllis, while safeguarding his own financial future and that of
his mother. Powys should have found a libel expert instead of putting himself in
the hands of "such genial Sir Walter Scott kind of persons." The outcome may
not have been much different—it was not until 1952 that the defence of unintentional defamation was introduced, so John was guilty according to the laws of
that time, and the court would have found him so—but some of the ensuing
muddle may have been avoided. On the second trip into London, Phyllis went
with him. To make sure that Margaret would not be liable if the court made him
a bankrupt, Blundell and Baker had John sign a long document concerning the
money from his father's estate which he had made over to his wife in 1923.[38]
They then advised JCP to settle out of court, and he turned over to them £200—

at that date $1,000—although he was "in complete obscurity as to just why."[39]
The £200 was a large portion of the £600 they had from the sale of Phudd.
Having given everything else over to his wife and son, the Phudd money had
gone into a savings account for Phyllis "as a preparation for my death."[40] Needless
to say, Phyllis had "a violent Independence Day reaction" against English law,
English ways, and English men. Powys wrote ruefully, "The libel and the will &
the £200 all were the cause of volcanic agitation from the pit of her stomach."[41]
Another cause for agitation was their uncertainty whether Phyllis, an American
citizen and not married to Powys, would be allowed to stay after her three-month
visiting permit expired. Powys wrote sadly in his diary on the fifth of July,

> It seems as if a fatality were possessing everything I do & say so as to drive
> my little T. T. to the breaking-point. It is a state of things that has driven my
> own soul to its final & ultimate resources! I am her <u>lover</u> & <u>her</u> <u>adherent</u> &
> I would give up almost all to make her happy but I fail & fail & *fail*. . . . All
> I can do is to hold on to her tight & pray that I can do wiser in the future or
> feel more clairvoyant in the future or change my nature in the future.

The trip to London ended on a happier note with a visit to Dorothy
Richardson and her husband, Alan Odle. Although this was a brief first meeting
with Phyllis, Richardson realized fully the pressures on her. She subsequently
wrote to John, "If I were she, I should wish to remain numb, & entirely silent &
withdrawn, living quite automatically, for about a year. Anyone who rallied, or
attempted to rally me, would be promptly shot."[42] Powys responded, "She's off for
the day to Weymouth with my American sister-in-law Llewelyn's wife so they'll
be able together to feel like easy tourists & forget their burden of heavy Powysian
cults for twenty-four hours! . . . She likes to be taken, as your words now prove—
not as if she were pilgrim swallowed by Gargantua with his lettuce, but like a girl
with her own thoughts as she rides on the Centaur's back!"[43]

On the July 27 he heard from Blundell and Baker that the captain had
accepted a settlement. John felt "very grateful" to them and was "astonished and
pleased" that his lawyers' bill was only £27. He seems to have thought that his
own total costs might be, after all, £227 and some deletions to the text. However,
although Blundell's next letter of July 30 was ambiguously phrased, with it he
enclosed "herewith copies of the Terms"—and the terms of the settlement were
in total £1,100 (approximately £66,000 in today's currency).

Schuster had suggested that they contact Laurence Pollinger, who at this
period was employed by Curtis Brown. This was the company that represented
the American publishers as agents in the contract with the Bodley Head. Both
John and Phyllis went to see Pollinger and so delighted were they with his common sense that they asked him to represent them independently. After the initial meeting, it was to Phyllis that Pollinger wrote, and in August he suggested
that she come up to town to discuss the further complications of the *Glastonbury*
libel suit. At first, Pollinger could not understand why Powys had had to pay

even £200 toward the settlement. The normal procedure in the case of libel was for the publisher to pay; for that they carry insurance. John Lane's insurance policy made him liable for twenty percent of any claim. In effect, Lane had got Powys to pay his deductible. This was fair enough; Powys's contract with Lane had a clause in it making Powys "responsible for any moneys paid by them"—as the letter from Simon and Schuster had already pointed out in April. However, the insurers were most unhappy with the large settlement, and to his indignation, Pollinger found that they had decided that the clause in the Bodley Head contract meant they had no responsibility at all as insurers. Undaunted, Pollinger took the problem to the Society of Authors. The lawyers for the Society of Authors were of the opinion that "it is not reasonable or reputable for a firm of Underwriters to accept a full premium and then seek to take advantage of an indemnity to which they were originally no party."

In the middle of August, Phyllis again went to London to see Pollinger and Allen Lane, the owner of the Bodley Head, as well as to consult a specialist about her lungs. Her physical health was breaking down; furthermore, despite John's sanguine reply to Richardson, Phyllis *did* feel increasingly "swallowed" by "Powysland," as she called it. Llewelyn had another near-fatal hemorrhage in early August, and Chydyok was "a whirl of nerves." John wrote Marian that "there are too many Cooks over Lulu's Broth. Too many people about him, too many opinions, too much advice, too many visitors. He holds a sort of continual court—and there are too many who attend it." He wasn't sure how it would end, with the nerves of both Llewelyn and Alyse, "more jumpy and tense than any outsider can possibly conceive," and Katie swinging "as ever from pole to pole of extreme emotion." Only Gertrude retained a "wondrous calm."[44] Both for Phyllis's sake and his own, Powys realized they must get away from Rat's Barn. The daily visit to Chydyok to read to Llewelyn, the constant dropping in by his other relatives, friends, and locals, the long walks to stores and post office, were preventing him from writing. But where to go, how to get away, and what to write that would make some money were practical problems he was ill-suited to deal with. By this time they had been to Weymouth a number of times, and it seemed to Phyllis "like an Ideal Children's Paradise where she would be so happy to live always."[45] She searched for a flat there but the rents were too expensive. They began looking in Dorchester and finally found a tiny flat in the middle of the market town. Ever the optimist, John hoped it would make Phyllis think she was back on Patchin Place in New York City.

The libel case now took another bizarre twist. The verdict of the Society of Authors sent the insurers back to the fine print of the original *Glastonbury* contract between the Bodley Head and Simon and Schuster. They discovered that it made the *American* publishers responsible for any libel action arising out of the publication of the book. Simon and Schuster's response to this was to point out that if "they are bound by the libel clause in the contract with Lane, they are equally protected by a similar clause in their contract with Mr Powys." Pollinger had to convey this blow to Phyllis in a letter of August 22, 1934: "In the last analysis, therefore, Mr. Powys appears to be responsible for the entire amount, awarded to Capt. Hodgkinson."

It was the last straw for a "sad and bitter" Phyllis, who found her independence jeopardized on all sides, not only by their financial situation, but by "the ways of the Powys family," and she included John as a member of that "convoluted breed."[46] She threatened to return to America—a measure of her desperation, since with no money she would have to live in Joplin, and for Phyllis that would have been another kind of stifling. This period was perhaps the lowest point in their long relationship. Powys was well accustomed to her rages, but he found her newest defence—physical and psychic withdrawal—impossible to comprehend.

> 10 September: The T. T. did not come to bed last night till 2.30 a.m. . . . but what she spent her time upon from 10.30 when I went up till 2.30—four hours—I have not any notion! . . . She looked very white the next day—today—& when I said "you are dissipated," she said the fairy story princesses "wore their shoes out at the dance." But I heard no dance of elementals only the familiar wind of the downs and some rat saying to itself, "I must take shelter ere the weather breaks up." . . . I shall never know how she spent those four hours!

Some of the tension and despair of that time he wrote out in the first drafts of his new novel, started in late August. Initially he intended to set it in the countryside around Rat's Barn, and one version begins: "With heavy steps, as if his bones were made of lead, he slowly descended the cart-track leading over the hill to Nettle Hut. It was late in August . . ." The hero, "J," envisages a life alone. "Anyone watching his movements might have supposed him to be awaited by some sympathetic human welcome in that out-of-the-way spot. No such welcome did the man expect."

There is a paragraph which vividly describes a man in intense shock, for whom even nature cannot give solace.

> Keeping his eyes carefully on the rut before him, his mind visualized rather than articulated the syllables "Fever-Few" and, immediately afterwards, the syllables "Camomile." These words he permitted to linger for a few seconds in the surrounding nimbus of empty thought-space that moved as he moved. Here, in the margin between consciousness and unconsciousness, the two words, or rather the faint simulacra of the two words, hung suspended, like dimly-seen vessels in a region where sea and sky were indistinguishable.[47]

Their cries of woe—her "upsets" and his "ailinons"—continued to be heard frequently in September. There was every reason for them: the primitive conditions of Rat's Barn, Llewelyn's unceasing physical and emotional demands, the living costs in England which were much higher than John had expected, and, above all, the possibility of total penury hanging over them. The Lane brothers were now worried that *Weymouth Sands* might also prove libelous, and visited Rat's Barn to discuss how the novel could be made "suitable for this market." The alterations they suggested were draconian: the names of living people and identifiable places must be changed, and any text that might be considered even remotely libellous must be altered or deleted. Totally devastated by the *Glastonbury* experience, John agreed and set to work. By the September 18, he had finished. "All is changed now. No bloody Libelled Magnate could possibly recognize himself." The novel was finally published under the title of *Jobber Skald*. The original American text, with its title of *Weymouth Sands*, did not appear in England until 1963.

John and Phyllis moved to Dorchester on October 18, 1934, Powys's sixty-second birthday. Their flat above Mr. Davis, the grocer, had a "very old Attic bedroom," a kitchen on the landing, "a perfect front room with two fine wide windows looking over ancient roofs at ancient tree-tops" and a toilet and water-tap "down one flight." In spite of the worries, in their separate ways both took increasing pleasure in this "*Vita Nuova* in Durnovaria."[48] Remembering his childhood in Dorchester when, with his nurse "Little Emily," he explored the countryside, he now derived "deep joy from walking those old familiar meadows." As for Phyllis, she recognized that she was caught in an environment foreign in all ways to her, but the attic at 38 High East Street became a "best refuge." She searched the second-hand shops, took delight in going to the movies, and her health and spirits improved when she began getting her main meal at "The Wessex."

After four months of family and legal involvement, Powys began to "work again at last properly." Finding that "money seemed in England rather vaporous," John asked Pollinger for the advance owing him on *Autobiography*, and the new agent sent the £150—less his ten-percent commission. Powys also wrote Simon and Schuster asking for $500 to tide him over, and Maxe Schuster immediately cabled that they were sending $1,469: "Naturally, we are delighted to be able to exceed your figure and thus banish all economic concern from your mind." Powys kept that cable to the end of his life. In a letter assuring him that the money was on its way, Schuster also asked Powys "to write that little book less than 55,000 words on the old 'Art of Happiness' under some other title," offering "funds" to keep him going while he was writing it. Remarking that "this is the very first time in my days that I have received an offer of this sort!" John immediately put aside the first chapter of his novel and began another "Handbook of Psychological craft for people teased and fretted by the sort of obstacles of a mental kind that I understand best."[49] A month later he had two of the five chapters written, noting wryly that "the title has been carefully selected by Mr. Schuster. The contents will be hastily concocted by the author."[50] The first chapters rather tediously reiterate the theme of his previous essays: the right and even the "obligation" to be happy in spite of one's own miseries and the miseries of other entities. However, the middle two chapters suddenly take fire when he discusses how a couple can be happy together "when use & want have blunted the passion of love and turned it into affection & tenderness." These chapters verge at times on the pre-posterous, even the outrageous, but at other times show a remarkable insight into this perennial dilemma.

He tackles first the ways in which a woman can be happy with a man. He sug-gests, "the path to happiness for a woman lies in making her man comfortable in his background, and then leaving him alone there, while she enjoys herself in her own way . . . either in her own thoughts and feelings while she works and ponders on alterations in her room, or as she drifts down the street, past the shop-windows or through the booths of the Fair, pondering on alterations in the adornment of her own person."[51] He suggests that a woman has, however, two conflicting desires: "the first driving her on to escape into her own world" (of sensation and creation), and "the second driving her on to invade the life of her man, to cover her man's body with her body . . . as a glittering boa-constrictor wraps itself about the beast it swallows."[52] When this "cannibalistic, pythonish possessive 'love'" is expressed "unctuously, shamelessly, indecently" in a sudden kiss, the man "feels as if he were a final tit-bit on a plate flickered over by a well-satisfied tongue."[53] He ends the chapter "Woman with Man" by warning the woman that she must use her "duplicity" and never reveal "how deep you see through him, and how disil-lusioned you are with regard to his pathetic masculine conceit."[54]

He was relieved when Phyllis made no comment on this chapter and went cheerfully on to write the next. After living for thirteen years with the highly-strung and volatile T. T., only a determinedly "happy" Powys would think that the "easiest of all chapters" would be the one on "the way to be happy with a woman."[55] He begins this by saying that women are "reality-addicts, reality-ine-briates" who love "the dark chaotic swirl of Nature's life-stream" and who immerse themselves in the everyday world, the world of reality. Every man, on the other hand, "instinctively uses his theories, his purposes, his hobbies, his ideals, down to his inmost life-illusion, as wrappings against this reality terror which never quite leaves him."

> It is this that gives a woman such power over her man; for she quickly becomes aware not only of the cracks in his world-armour, but of the ragged places in his interior swaddling-bands; and when she wants to hurt him, as she does in her moments of nervous anger, she can turn on these weak spots not only her own devastating insight but a thin black jet out of the recesses of the cosmos.[56]

Her anger therefore is terrifying to an imaginative man ("and all men are more imaginative than women"[57]). This is the point at which a man's life-fear "so naturally turns into his woman-fear."[58] He then goes on to give some advice to men on how to be happy and to keep one's self-respect in the presence of all this: always keep your stoical reserve, never argue with her "unless in the spirit of a chess champion playing with a beautiful savage," and "sink deeper and deeper into [your] own secret world."[59]

On December 20, he read this chapter to Phyllis. "She <u>was</u> indignant. Last night she hardly wd listen. In fact I had to stop reading & skip a lot!" What upset her most was his drawing on their own personalities and private habits to support his generalizations about the differences between men and women. The distressed Phyllis would not have been made more cheerful by hearing that "women, for causes obscure to the intelligence of man, seem often to cherish and foster their unhappiness as if it were a suckling babe."[60] However, he did his "revising to please her," making the chapters "free altogether from mischief and all trace of Strindberg."[61] Since the above quotes are from the revised version, it is difficult to imagine what the unrevised version was like. Powys was of course aware of his "anti-feminine prejudice" and was convinced he had "inherited" it from his father. This admission was made to Marian in 1919, when he assured her that not to "stamp it out . . . would not only be wicked but quite mad." He still had not quite eliminated it by 1934.

Nonetheless, there are some deeply perceptive insights, often non sequiturs tucked into the text, which go far to make this essay more than simply a misogynistic rant. These passages, such as the following, show he knew exactly why Phyllis stayed with him, despite her unhappiness.

> What we must recognise is that this Being at his side has burnt her ships in committing herself to him in a more tragic sense than he has any conception of. He must realise that she has given herself to him—below all their quarrels—to an extent that has a terrible finality, a finality far beyond the implication of anything she says or does.[62]

He added another very endearing, if revealing, insert.

> In this whole matter of a man's happiness à deux when the state of "being-in-love" is over, the strangest thing is the obscure and unconscious depth of his hidden dependence upon her. . . .
> Against this background his happiness grows and flourishes, but the tragedy is that his awareness of it so often does not come *till he loses her.* To be fully happy with her, then, he had better constantly imagine what life would be like without her. . . . A man is strangely detached from Nature; and deep in his heart lies a fear of Life beyond the comprehension of any woman. But holding a woman by night and by day *between him and Life,* he is protected from this underlying fear. He is like a frightened infant who has got back into the snug "cowry-shell" of inviolable safety from which he was driven forth at the cutting of his navel-string.[63]

Despite the re-writes, Phyllis was "heartbroken" and said that his philosophy was a reaction from living with her. He denied this and said it was his "Protection against Reality & Responsibility." But what he *felt,* he wrote in his diary, "was simply fear of my Ancient Terrors, Manias & Imaginative Morbidities" if he gave up his philosophy.[64]

The dog, now called "the Very Old," came out of quarantine in December. With him, Powys resumed his two long walks a day. Poundbury and Maiden Castle were his favourite destinations, but his customary "round" was in the countryside immediately to the north of their flat and around the edges of the Frome valley. It was a sign that Powys was beginning to feel settled in Dorchester that he decided in January which of the trees that he encountered he would designate "The Saviour Tree." The custom began at Hillsdale where he chose an "old noble Willow" near the Agawamuk River which flowed near his house. This Tree he named Demeter—she is "the great God-mother Saviour Bearer of all Troubles" and "she has the power of receiving any worry you have and turning it into sap." He needed all the help he could get. The settlement of his libel case dragged on, with the financial implications getting more and more serious as the months passed. He was also anxious about the mental and physical states of Llewelyn and Alyse. Twice a week he would take the train and bus to visit Lulu, who was still trying to cure himself with a diet of nuts, seeds, and "damned fruit-juices" devised by Alyse, and by lying still, hour after hour, in his garden shelter. He refused to have a doctor, relying instead on being nursed day and night by Gertrude and Alyse. John wrote Marian, "You can't realize unless you've been there how isolated & obstinate in their groove out there at Chydyok they are and what a narrow curious and tragic little world it is on the top of that hill."[65]

To add to the anxiety, Llewelyn was also involved in a lawsuit. Early in 1934, Llewelyn and the writer Sylvia Townsend Warner, along with her companion, Valentine Ackland, became concerned about the running of a home for retarded girls in Chaldon. They took a petition around the village which expressed the opinion that the two owners were not suitable persons to have the care of such girls, then sent it to the County Council, urging that the case be investigated. The owners of the home sued them for libel. Given the *Glastonbury* fiasco, it was astonishing that as soon as John Cowper arrived in England Llewelyn dispatched this elder brother to Dorchester to find a solicitor for him. John found them a "poor nice old half paralysed Dribbler—very honest & decent & a young Smart Alec of a 'Help.'"[66] Although he did not mention this to Llewelyn, one of John's first objects was to try to persuade the lawyers not to call Theodore as witness. Theodore's heart problems were authentic, and relatives and friends knew that in any case to appear before a court would have been virtually impossible for this reclusive man. Theodore was also terrified that, having signed the original petition, he might also be liable if the case went against them. Once again, Powys was caught in the middle. Although understanding this brother's sensitivities, John knew that Theodore's renegation would hurt Llewelyn and cause more family upsets, and so it proved. The case was heard at the Dorset Assizes on January 21, 1935, and Lulu was determined to attend on a stretcher. John, who was during this time writing Marian once a week, reported: "He wants to do this really I think as what you wd call a Bit of Sport—but the official reason is a Point of Honour." The media was thrilled by the drama. "Dying Author in Witness Box"

was the headline in the *Daily Telegraph* for January 21. The jury found all the
defendants guilty of "malice." Fortunately, a well-to-do friend of Llewelyn's,
Rivers Pollock, paid his damages, but Sylvia and Valentine were paying off their
debts for years afterwards.

John's own long-drawn-out libel suit finally ended a few months later in
March 1935. He had to give the underwriter all the English royalties from
Glastonbury Romance as well as the £200 he had already paid. He also had his
solicitor's fees and those of Hodgkinson to pay. The final affront was that the
Bodley Head's solicitors demanded that he pay the fifty-guinea cost of *their* legal
expenses! In all, the case must have cost Powys between £650 and £700. If
Simon and Schuster had not employed (and paid for) their own more sophisticated lawyers finally to settle with the insurers, almost certainly he would have
been coerced into paying the entire £1,100. Although the English solicitors later
admitted that their client had been "fleeced," Powys had only himself to blame.
In the end he and Phyllis lost all the capital they possessed—the $3,000 from the
sale of Phudd Bottom—and were in debt. Neither Phyllis nor John ever quite
recovered, financially or emotionally, from the blow.

The Art of Happiness was posted to Simon and Schuster on January 15, and
a few days later John made a fresh start on the novel begun at Rat's Barn. He now
decided to set it in Dorchester in "the present."[67] He called it *Maiden Castle* and
intended it to be "a Rival of the *Mayor of Casterbridge*."[68] The hero of the story,
the solitary Dud No-man, is a financially unsuccessful writer of historical novels
who has returned to Dorchester to write about the burning of Mary Channing in
Maumbury Rings in 1705. Ten years before the forty-year-old lost his mother and
his wife Mona in a flu epidemic. In the intervening years he has built a wall
around himself of mythological imaginings about his parental origins and erotic
fantasies about his dead wife.

No-man is vaguely aware that by returning to the place where they are
buried the "old meticulous continuity of his existence" will be shattered.[69] The
discontinuity begins almost immediately: he impulsively buys an orphaned circus
girl, Wizzie Ravelston, and he meets a strange, magician-like figure—Uryen
Quirm. Although there are many other characters and sub-stories, the novel
concentrates on Dud's relationship, or lack of it, with Uryen and Wizzie. Wizzie's
"lurin figure" arouses Dud "to give his sensual fancy full range." He sets her up in
a room in town, where he spends the nights with her after he has finished his
day's writing in his own attic flat. She becomes increasingly angered by his ways,
and the novel ends with her departure for America to resume her career as a talented circus rider. Uryen Quirm spends much of his time on Maiden Castle, the
nearby neolithic earthwork. He believes that "Mai-Dun" is a centre of enormous
chthonic power and that he is the reincarnation of this power. Poverty forces
Quirm to write newspaper articles about his "life-illusion" and this causes some
"hurt to his inner self." Uryen dies insane, and by the end of the novel, the hero
is once again alone, holding "fiercely to all those 'sensations' of his."

Aware that his new novel contained "fantastic situations & weird persons," Powys saw "the necessity of thickening it all out with as many touches of reality & of verisimilitude as I can gather in."[70] The opening of the novel is a meticulous description of his and Phyllis's own flat at 38 High East Street, and the sights and sounds that greeted him every morning. His daily walks with the dog often took Powys in the direction of Maiden Castle and his descriptions of that site contain hundreds of carefully observed details: the different sorts of butterflies, the "almond-like fragrance of the gorse bushes on the turfy slope," the "long-drawn whistle from one of the trains between Dorchester and Weymouth." A large-scale archaeological dig, directed by the famous Sir Mortimer Wheeler, began on Maiden Castle the summer Powys returned to England. On March 22, 1935, he toured the site with Phyllis and his brother Littleton, and attended a lecture by Wheeler that evening. The excavations and discoveries at Maiden Castle play an important part in the story; most of his characters are excited by the finds and endlessly discuss the significance of them. However, as always, Powys interpreted the facts and theories to suit his own fictive world.

Despite his attempts at "verisimilitude," this fifth novel to be set in the West Country has been described as "the most Powysian" of all of them. Less kind critics have described it as "a parodist's dream." The plot is absurd, the characters over-the-top, the dialogue often unintentionally comical, but *Maiden Castle* sticks in the mind. Written by a man who insisted that he could not get angry, what makes this novel unusual in the Powys oeuvre is its overpowering anger—anger in the form of seething frustration, which, to a greater or lesser extent, all the characters feel; anger in the form of malice which is the Powys-hero's only sure defence against "reality." Dud No-man's misanthropy begins when, in early manhood, his mother abruptly tells him that he is a bastard. Thereafter Dud is "led by his malicious pride to detach himself from the human race by becoming No-man." It was his dead wife who gave him his other name—Dud. He is a "dud" because he was "nervously incapable of consummating his marriage,"[71] and is still a "dud" as a writer. Dud's anger is directed at his failed self but it is also directed at women. Although the man has spent the last ten years obsessively thinking of his wife and mother, Powys does not say *what* he has been thinking, except to slip in the telling clause "when his mother and his wife first deserted him."[72]—they deserted him by dying. Wizzie will desert him by going to America.

The anger which Powys projected on to the characters in the novel, and specifically on to "our friend," as he insists on referring to Dud, almost certainly arose directly out of his own situation. The draft of the first chapter, in which Powys works out Dud's namelessness and his inability to consummate his marriage, was written in August and September of 1934, immediately after receiving the letter informing him he was going to be responsible for the entire court settlement.[73] It was written out of his first undefended awareness that he was also a "dud" in handling his business affairs; that bankruptcy had quite literally made him a "no man"; that Phyllis, by taking over the handling of both

Pollinger and the publishers in an attempt to rescue the situation had, in effect, taken away his manhood.

Another cause of his anger was the reaction of Llewelyn and Frances Gregg to his *Art of Happiness*. Llewelyn denounced it as "insincere." Powys protested, quite justifiedly, that "if ever a book was written from my inmost personal life—this is the one."[74] But it was Frances's comments that upset him most. In November 1934 Powys had gone to visit Frances, who was now living on the north coast of Norfolk with her mother and children. Oliver, her son, said most truly that they always "lived on the rim of existence," and he meant more than geographically. Not long after John's visit, their bungalow burnt down. Everything they owned, including her manuscripts, was destroyed, and even their dogs burnt. Jack subsequently sent his *Happiness* book for her birthday. She wrote to thank him for it and then to flay him. She did not agree with Lulu's verdict of insincerity. On the contrary, she thought that "this book is written with your great gift of sincerity that is like a strange and magical reverse to your treachery." Her letter went on:

> What I call your "infantile fixation" is responsible for much. . . . You and others of your sad ilk have *remained* as little children, spying into the domain of maturity and stealing such sweets as your impotence could cope with . . . but blind, blind, blind to their true meaning and to their true intent. You, with these god-like gifts, and with your deep child-like cunning, and with that something that is so sweet and pure and beguiling as to be almost heaven-like in your nature, become so plausible in your writings that I could tremble.

The scourging ends,

> I note that you say that "happiness" releases magnetic currents of good. Do you know that I . . . believe that the terrible malice that you have directed towards Llewelyn and towards me, in your moments, accounts for our ailing lives and broken wings. We have, each in our way, *raged* at you—as you would never rage openly at anything, but never never never have we felt anything but love for you, and that love goes far to sustain you through your healthy maladies. Do you know that when I saw the house burned and they said, "Why should it happen to us?" that I said, "It does not surprise me, Jack has been here." That need not trouble you. You could not help it, but you have gathered just those forces about you.[75]

Frances's love for Powys was, in H. D.'s evocative phrase, "terrible with banners."[76] Frances's son, Oliver, knew better than most the violence of her love, but he said that "there is violence too, in Jack, but it is disguised as concern or banter or apology. Jack's propitiations are often murderous."[77]

Although Powys usually noted in his diary letters to or from Frances, he does *not* mention this letter. He only wrote, on April 18, that he and Phyllis "discussed at breakfast the tendency of Frances & Lulu (in their different ways) to

rage against me & my refusal to rage back." The subject was not referred to again.
Frances's accusations struck hard at his life-illusion as a good, if suffering, magician and he did not care to confront or absorb her accusation. Or, at least, he did
not want it to confuse his carefully built-up self-portrait. Months later, Phyllis
asked him how he could relegate Frances "so coolly to a place on the remote
horizon." His response was, "Because the deepest instinct in all men is their
secret Life Illusion of themselves. . . . Frances attacked this inner self, this deep
inner self or life-illusion habitually."[78]

    There was a third possible reason for his rage, however covert. When
Autobiography was published, many reviewers remarked unkindly upon the curious
omission of any women in a life story. If *Autobiography* is almost solely about men,
Maiden Castle is a book dominated by women. It is as if Powys had said to himself:
"Well then, damn you, I'll give you the *other* half—as I see them." Not for the first
time, a Powys novel has arisen out of preoccupations expressed first in essay form;
it might be said that *Maiden Castle* is a fictionalizing of *The Art of Happiness*.
Neither book makes comfortable reading in our politically correct times.

    The first half of *Maiden Castle* is "strained through the consciousness of Dud,"
and Dud makes it very clear what he thinks of women. He is convinced that the
wives, mistresses, and daughters that he encounters feel only contempt for the
male characters. Thuella Wye supports herself and her father by painting modern
pictures. Dud considers that she keeps her father, an ineffectual Greek scholar,
totally subjected: "Dud saw Thuella . . . give her father the sort of look that an
animal trainer gives a dog when, at the wrong moment, it stands up on its hind
legs."[79] Jennie Dearth, whom Dud nicknames "Horse-Head," loves Claudius Cask,
but she is furious when Claudius's commitment to communism leads him take on
physical labor that ruins his health. Dud thinks bitterly to himself, "He has committed the unpardonable sin from a woman's point of view. He has obeyed his
conscience and not her. What they want is to possess a man's whole identity."[80]
Even Nancy Quirm, whom Dud likes, gives proof of her possessive contempt
when she "bending down, kissed her husband lightly on the top of his head." Dud
thinks "there's something indecent about it."[81] Dud is not only enamored of the
circus girl, Wizzie; he is also sensually attracted to Thuella who is "so thin as to
resemble the fancy of some perverse sculptor who had turned in fastidious
loathing from every normal curve in a woman's body."[82] He soon becomes convinced that Thuella is a "Lamia" attempting to seduce his Wizzie, but the main
source of his chagrin appears to be that the two girls refuse to remain fixed in his
fantasy world. They are what Powys called in his happiness essay "reality addicts."
Dud is distressed when he sees the two girls "enjoying a party": "In place of two
mysterious worlds of evasive attraction through which he could move like a magician among spirits of the deep . . . all he saw now were two lively, young people,
using a language totally alien to everything that appealed to him."[83]

    It is not just the women who break up his fantasies. Not knowing who his
father was, Dud had told himself "a childish story about his father being some

great Welsh nobleman, who claimed to be descended from Sir Pellinore."[84]
Reality abruptly breaks up his storytelling when Uryen Quirm tells Dud that *he*
is his father. Before he broke this news of his paternity to No-man, Dud has been
telling himself other romantic stories, such as Uryen being a reincarnation of the
Welsh corpse-god, Bran the Blessed, and that Uryen's soul is "sodden with some
abominable suffering" and "hangs suspended on some colossal cross."[85] But when
Uryen drags Dud up to Maiden Castle and tells him that he *is* Bendegeit Bran,
and that he *does* feel that in order to "break through" to "the secret" he must suffer intensely, Uryen's confession is met with "sullen incredulity."[86]

Powys never let a preoccupation go; it simply became more complex. His
encounter with the Indians of Phudd led him to explore the ambivalent relationship of the magician and the initiate. In *A Glastonbury Romance*, John Crow stands
aloof from the quest of Johnny Geard. In *Weymouth Sands*, Magnus Muir, although
attracted to Sylvanus Cobbold, refuses to follow him into the underworld (in this
case the mad-house). He sees Cobbold's immurement as some Christlike sacrifice
that somehow saves him, Muir, from madness, not as the action of a hierophant
whom the initiate, to become a god, must imitate. In *Maiden Castle*, the hero, No-
man, comes one step closer to identifying with the magician figure. Powys knew
his Homer. In the ninth book of *The Odyssey*, the hero enters the cave of the man-
eating Cyclops. The one-eyed monster asks his name and Odysseus, the wanderer,
instead of saying "I am Odysseus" [Ὀδυσεὺς] says, "No-man [Οὗτις] is my name".[87]
Just as the naming of names is a mechanism of sovereignty and consciousness,
divesting oneself of name, fame, and identity is necessary in the approach to the
boundary between self and non-self. By calling himself Nobody, Odysseus is
allowed past the threshold guardian and crosses the boundary into No-man's land.

As does Homer, Powys sets the scene at the junction of the human and the
monstrous—the earthwork Maiden Castle. Like the cave of the Cyclops, it both
attracts and repels the wanderer. Maiden Castle is a metaphor both for a return to
that magic centre which Powys has longed for, and the entrance to the other-
world which he fears. In one scene No-man and Uryen are walking on the earthwork, and Uryen articulates the basic premise on which a lost paradise is regained:

> Everything's in the mind. Everything's created and destroyed by the mind.
> . . . Don't you feel this whole great fortress ready to shake, shiver, melt, dis-
> solve? Don't you feel that you and I are behind it, making it what it is by
> the power of our minds? Don't you feel it floating, with all its bright grass,
> on the dark sea of our terrible ——[88]

The human crosses the border of bright grass into the monstrous dark sea.
Uryen says of the image that has just been dug up in the excavations—a bull with
two human torsos impaled on its horns—"*You've* had, Mr. No-man, haven't you
. . . visions of life that suggest our being impaled on the horns . . . of darkness?"[89]
and discusses the necessity of impalement as a prelude to "breaking through" to
"take by storm" the secret that is life beyond death.

In the end No-man cannot follow his magician-father, even though he has the "appalling sense that . . . he was his father, arguing with his father."[90] He walks away, just as Odysseus escapes the cave of the Cyclops clinging to the underbelly of a ram, and as Powys rejected the Indian initiation. Uryen is portrayed as a grotesque, mad fantasist whom no one, not even a dud, can take seriously. It is said that when an initiate encounters his "guardian spirit," he must identify with him. If he fails, he is regarded as a "nobody," a no-man.

With Dud and Uryen, Powys brings together several of the themes in this novel—the hero's fundamental lack of relationship and his aversion to generative sexuality. Dud does not want a father; he does not want connection. The "singular reluctance of his, the reluctance to have a name!"[91] is the reluctance to admit that his was not an immaculate conception. "For a moment he struggled desperately to find a rational defence for his loathing of the process of generation. *Parthenogenesis* is the natural thing! That's why the act of love is monstrous and ridiculous." Dud agonizes, "How *could* Mother . . . have been seduced by such a person." Then "the impulse to go further in his thoughts, to go *the one step further*, had become to him like a menace that *had* to be obliterated, suppressed, reduced to nothing." Powys leaves it to the reader to visualize what "the one step further" is. If it is not seduction of the mother by the father, it is seduction of the mother by the son. "I" and the father are one. However, "the second it heaved up, pushing him forward, he retorted by a quick mental act of deliberate negation."[92]

Dud's reverie on copulation leads him inexorably to his own "unmanliness," thence to his relationship with his virgin wife, thus intertwining his lack of identity with his lack of potence. Dud never loved his wife "with a normal love," but in the ten "half-insane" years since her death he has used the "Mona wraith" to give himself sexual gratification. His love for Mona No-man was onanistic in life and in death. This information is conveyed rather blandly in the published version, and it is often only in his discarded drafts that it becomes clear where Powys is coming from. In them Dud gives various reasons why Mona died a virgin: he had "respected her too much while she was alive to feel ordinary passion for her"; he had not "meddled with her virginity" because "how could he have coped with a child?"[93] In this latter draft, he gives another reason, describing his wife as "a being from a diviner air," and himself as "her apologetic Tithonus."[94]

> [Dud] was an ardent though not very scholarly reader of the ancient classics, always giving them a twist in the direction of his own case, and he never touched the stories of Tithonus but an odd sensation, at once queasy and exalted, stirred in the pit of his stomach. "Why did I let her die a virgin?" was in fact a sentence that had for many years been hovering about the threshold of his consciousness. This daring cry met with too great a psychic barrier in his deeper being ever to be articulated.[95]

Articulated or not, No-man has already answered his own question, or Powys has answered it for him. The beautiful young Tithonus is loved by Eos, the Dawn

Goddess, but being mortal, he grows old and shriveled until finally only his voice remains "active." The goddess puts him into a chamber and locks the door. Like some nightmare any writer might have, Tithonus in the myth ends up imprisoned and impotent, endlessly babbling meaningless words. Dud may have given the ancient classics "a twist in the direction of his own case," but the moral is clear. It is the woman-goddess who is in control. Consummation means imprisonment—powerlessness—for the man. Only if a man refuses consummation, that is, if his wife remains a "virgin," can the man retain his creative potence, his power.

In Uryen Quirm, Powys approaches this in yet another way. After Uryen's death, Dud explains to a somewhat bemused Nance that her husband and "my father" believed that he had inherited the supernatural power that had resided in the Uryen of Welsh mythology, and that "this Power was attended by some sort of beast—the whole thing's mixed up with sex and death and good and evil . . . and as far as I can make out it's with this beast, or *through* this beast—and that's where the sex part of it comes in—that we touch some great secret!"[96] Dud goes on to explain to Nance that Uryen believed that the key to breaking through "into the underworld, or the overworld . . . to reach the secret—'the Mothers'" was "frustrated love"; and "for some reason he got it into his head that Thel's love for Wizz was like that!"[97] Lesbian love had a powerful hold, not only over Uryen, but Powys. As perplexing as the idea of the connection between death and "sterile love" is in *Maiden Castle*, it was one of his most persistent fantasies, and one which he professed not to understand himself. Some years later he confided to his diary, that whenever he washed his hands,

> It is my fixed custom to imagine myself Dead in Cemetery & other entities bustling about & making love to each other & isn't that a queer thing that . . . it is my natural and instinctive habit to think of those young persons who are making love as two girls. Isn't that a queer thing that second to my chief vice nothing excites my amorous nerves more than the sight of two young girls twining & twisting round each other in excited desire. . . . But why should I myself have to be Dead & in Cemetery when this engaging and bewitching scene is to be seen?[98]

Powys continued to explore the implications of "sterile love" in Dud's relationship with Wizzie. Dud feels that his return to Dorchester is "like a new birth, the birth of a middle-aged man over forty into normal human life." He realizes that "in his cerebral love-making during all these later years, he had furtively turned [his dead wife] *into a different girl*, a girl with erotic vice in her."[99] It took Powys several manuscript pages, later discarded, to come up with this version. It began differently: "All these years," he thought, "*It has not been Mona at all* to whom I've been making love. The 'she' of my fevers has been a phantom Fata Morgana, a sylph of my imagination. . . . But now that it's gone what I want—and what I must have—is a real living body to make love to." In another discarded page he makes it his wife's fault for his situation: "In her complete docility to his perversity she had for all these years stood between him and all natural satisfaction."[100]

This is why he buys the lively young Wizzie—she is a "real living body." But Wizzie soon learns that "the actual touch of her flesh was not in itself enough to stimulate his senses"; he "had to whisper, 'I bought you, I *bought* you!' to turn her into what he called his 'Bronze-Age girl.'"[101] The "normality" he thinks he embarked on with the buying of the rider does not materialize. He simply has substituted one sexual fantasy for another. Dud ponders on Wizzie's "growing irritableness," and wonders if the cause might be his "sterile viciousness": "Am I tantalizing her . . . in the same way I did Mona?"[102] He even wonders if he is "taking from Wizzie both her chance of a child and her chance of a career"[103] Dud thinks "it was a weird thing that he, D. No-man, should have the power, by yielding to his nervous manias, of actually preventing a woman from bringing to birth a living, conscious soul!"[104]

For both Uryen and Dud, "power" resides in sterile love. But power is approached from many directions in this novel. In another discarded scene, No-man has an "extremely distasteful" encounter with a carter on a "heavily built horse"—something that happened to Powys himself while he was at Rat's Barn.[105] There are four different versions of the meeting between Dud and the laborer, but in the final version, all that is left of the carter episode is a vague allusion to "Derfel's Horse"—that potent symbol of death and sexuality. There is another horse in Maiden Castle, the one that Wizzie rides so superbly in the circus. Presumably the author is playing with his dense hero. Dud in his unawareness thinks he is "rescuing" a waif; Powys would be perfectly aware that a woman who rides a powerful animal is a woman in control. Wizzie's power resides in her past. No-man's fantasy that Wizzie is "a virgin" like Mona is shattered when he finds out that she was raped by the circus owner and has a child. After three years, Wizzie remembers this rape by the man who taught her to ride "no longer as a brutal violation," but as something in which "she could even exult!": "You taught me my job. You taught me my power. You taught me my life. You re-created my body!"[106] "At least," her body had cried, "You didn't play doll with me."[107]

The relationship between Wizzie and Dud continues its downward spiral. No-man's other enduring fantasy is that with his great oak cudgel, his "awkward figure with its long arms, bony countenance" he might be "some necrophilistic Cerne Giant . . . rather than an innocent antiquarian recluse."[108] This stick particularly irritates Wizzie, and one day she kicks this symbol of stone-age virility under the bed. To Dud, "this deliberate kicking of his stick assumed . . . the proportions of an unpardonable crime."[109] Wizzie's anger and frustration reaches a climaxe on Midsummer Eve. They have gone with their little group of "enemy-friends"[110] to Maiden Castle to see the startling archaeological finds recently unearthed and afterwards Dud lights a bonfire in a dewpond. As the group gathers around, Thuella begins "screaming in hysterical shrillness" that no one appreciates her paintings. Dud tells her to "concentrate on your own mind instead of on your work." To his "babyish bewilderment" his fatuous advice is badly received.[111] Wizzie sees that this "half-circle of highly strung men and women . . . were swept by some sudden psychic wave of irrational hostility toward their lonely bonfire maker"; moreover that there was something in Dud himself that was "drawing towards him this psychic wave of hostility."[112] Wizzie thinks,

> Other people, men who were men, hit back openly and honestly when they were attacked. D. never did. . . . He seemed to like looking a fool with you. . . . And now at this moment the man looked as if nothing would please him more than for them all to leap on him and throw him into those red embers.
>
>   "He's like a malicious scapegoat!" she thought.[113]

The bonfire chapter is one of the most vividly written, and the most psychologically complex. Wizzie has articulated what others have already noticed in Dud—his "air of martyred helplessness that seemed to be murmuring, 'Hit me! Hit me!'"[114] This biographer of Mary Channing appears to have made the midsummer fire as a kind of obscure expiation for his heroine's burning, inviting for himself the proverbial roasting. But with the hit-me personality goes a profound malice. Wizzie exclaims, "I can't understand how anyone like you, who's writing books about people . . . can hate everyone like you do."[115] The final quarrel comes a few days later. When Dud asks, "What do you mean about 'something wrong with our life'?" She answers, "I mean you're *not a man*, D." He responds to this with "overpowering astonishment."[116] Wizzie goes off with Thuella to America. It is not until he is once again alone with his sensations, that No-man finally realizes "what he had really done—and the girl had known it—was to use the living Wizzie as he had used the dead Mona." He feels ill-used that "it meant nothing to her that there was in this a proof of the intensity of his feeling."[117]

Dud is so totally without self-awareness that when he refers to his "new mania for dissecting women's souls," the reader must assume that Powys is poking fun at this neurotic creature—failed novelist, failed man. Part of the difficulty in deciding whether he is treating his non-hero with heavy irony is that the main character is so patently the author and so much of *Maiden Castle* is an echo of the events taking place in Powys's own life at this time. He even brings the libel case in by the side door. At the very end of the novel, Dud is presented by an old woman with a lawyer's "dockyment." The phrases in it so alarm him that he gives her all his savings, but "his loathing of the preposterous woman mingled with his almost malicious eagerness to be robbed."[118] Powys uses the word "malice" often in his diary, his letters, and novels. He professed not to be sure what it was, although he did not think it was the same as sadism. He wished he could analyze it: "I *ought* to be able to; for I believe there has never lived a human being so addicted to it as I am."[119] He admitted to Llewelyn that "the depth of malice in me goes beyond what Theodore so often confesses to—with me it is worse; because with habitual dissimulation I conceal it."[120] If his malice was often self-inflicted, it was also turned against everyone he thought had hurt him.

Phyllis was in no doubt that his malice was a "detached self-righteousness that refuses to quarrel but conceals a deep grudge & brings it out in Books which is . . . much worse than any personal immediate anger or even a blow." She hated *Maiden Castle* for much the same reason she had disliked *The Art of Happiness*. She considered it a "mean base and profoundly revengeful Hit-Back at the Feminine."[121] After writing six chapters "strained through the consciousness" of No-man, he decided to "make Wizzie my mouthpiece . . . in order that Dud-Dud's attitude to women shall no longer dominate the book."[122] This only made matters worse. He was shocked to find that "people think that the T. T. is like Wizzie,"[123] but to anyone reading the diary (which he constantly invited friends and relatives to do) it is clear that he put many of Phyllis's activities, moods, and ideas into Wizzie. It was a kind of double malice, not simply because Dud thinks of her as "my selfish, touchy, spoilt, wayward Wizz." In having Wizzie, for example, think to herself, "I *hate* you. Put *that* among your sensations! I hate you; and I hate your book and both your dead bitches!"[124] he is making Phyllis say, "I hate you and your book and your two bitches—your mother and your wife." Whether Phyllis actually said anything of the sort in her anger is irrelevant. He was using the device of making Wizzie "my mouthpiece" to be "fair" to Wizzie, and to allow her to hit at him. At the same time Dud/John was hitting back at Wizzie/Phyllis.

Although Powys may have thought that having all of Dorchester and Dorset on his doorstep would make the writing go faster, in fact *Maiden Castle* gave him great difficulty. He had written his brother Littleton as early as 1927, when he was writing *Wolf Solent*, the prophetic words: "I am pouring forth in this long novel about Sherborne & Yeovil & Bradford Abbas all my feelings about the west country & I expect if I were in it instead of being where I am I couldn't do that—I shouldn't have to need to."[125] That was the significance of Powys's self-imposed exile to America. It allowed him to recreate a place from which time had barred him, but into which the unconfined imagination could force re-entry. For some artists, and Powys was one, exile frees the imagination: time and distance are necessary to actuate it. Joyce, Nabokov, and Dante, Proust were more at home in the remembered spaces of their works than in their homelands. Powys was now back in the landscape of his real childhood rather than his imagined childhood, and he could not finish the novel until he had once again exiled himself.

He had only reached chapter four when a visit to Dorchester by his friend James Hanley with his wife Tim resulted in the Hanleys finding John and Phyllis a rental cottage near where the Hanleys lived in the village of Cynwyd, near Corwen, North Wales. They went for a month in May, stopping on the way at Ludlow and Bitterley Court "to see the grave and Monuments of our Powys ancestors." Although Phyllis was beginning to find Dorchester to be a "thrilling and a very romantic place," John was determined to carry out his plan to move to Wales. The young Hanleys helped them to look at various houses in the vicinity and they looked in Bala and Dolgellau. They finally found "a just built, in fact being finished, workman's cottage with all modern improvements—bath, electricity, etc—on the slope of the Berwyn range of mountains, on the outskirts of the little market town of Corwen."[126] Both were "simply thrilled" by 7 Cae Coed and they promptly signed a year's lease. If the young Hanleys hoped that a close friendship would develop, like the Fickes before them, they were to be disappointed. Powys wrote, almost in panic, that he feared that the "so sociable & genial & good-natured" Hanley "has not the least notion of my mania for loneliness . . . which I hide up under my indulgent & even obsequious manner!"[127] Corwen was a perfect compromise—not so far away to constitute an insult to the Hanleys, but sufficiently far to prevent any intrusion on his solitariness.

Despite finding the house in the land of his dreams, John had an ulcer flare-up during this holiday. Possibly he was anxious about abandoning his brothers and sisters, for abandonment was what they accused him of. He also may have been apprehensive that this total break with the past was a leap into the unknown, or rather, it was a leap into a long-held fantasy, and he knew better than most that fantasies are not always meant to be translated into reality. Wales was an "elsewhere," but as someone has said, an elsewhere is no more possible than a formerly. However, it was no coincidence that Powys mentioned in his diary that he was now reading Book XI of The Odyssey. This is "The Book of the Dead," where all those whom the hero has loved "like a shadow or a dream . . . slipped through my arms." There is no doubt that the family wanted him to settle permanently in Dorset, preferably near Chaldon. He was the head of the Volentiä army of their childhood: their shield-wall against the outside world. John had collaborated with the myth of "The Powys," possibly even created it. But it was now 1935, and while Phyllis would protest against "the arrogant & Devouring Clannishness & Anti-Social Savagery of Solidarity & to Hell with all who are not Powyses so underlying my Family!"[128] John Cowper himself saw that the idyllic world of intimacy and solidarity that was the Powys family romance no longer existed. This would not have come as any surprise to him. As early as 1923 he had written, "What a veritable mad-house of invisible desires; desires to escape; desires to prevent escape; desires to destroy; desires to liberate; every family, every household, must present to the discerning eye!"[129]

Powys used Magnus Muir in Weymouth Sands to forecast that his past was about to be "ripped up," and a new "reality" begun. While the "reality of the phenomenal world," with its libel suits, its illnesses, helped to break up the old clannishness, ironically, it was Autobiography, that apparent pæan to a lost golden world, that was the agent of dissolution of that world. The timing of its publication—October 8, 1934—was unfortunate. There was a spate of autobiographical writings published that autumn, including My Confessions by Havelock Ellis, the friend of Faith Oliver—Bertie's new wife. Louis Wilkinson's own autobiographical book, Swan's Milk, was also published in 1934. H. G. Wells's Experiment in Autobiography was advertised in the papers only a week later than Powys's autobiography; inevitably, Wells was reviewed by such luminaries as his friend

George Bernard Shaw, and received much more publicity. *Autobiography* had mixed reviews: its very nature demanded extreme responses. In a fairly representative article by R. Ellis Roberts, a well-known literary reviewer, appeared in the *Sunday Times* on October 14, 1934, in which Powys was called a "self-tormented neurotic" whose "world is that of the solitary to whom solitude is a vicious habit." Roberts ended with, "It is evident that to JCP the world is divided into the Powys clan and others." There was a "family storm in a tea-cup" when brother Bertie praised as "just" the reviewer's derision.[130] In a letter dated "Autumn, 1934," Llewelyn attempted to reassure Bertie that "the prestige of our family will be in no way reduced" and that John's autobiography would be read when the life of H. G. Wells would seem "hopelessly out of date." Lulu concluded with a perceptive comment that could apply to all John Cowper's writings: "John's net is very wide and its mesh carelessly woven but amongst the weeds and silt and dead matter— see what baskets full of shining silver fish!" He made another interesting remark about it to John himself: "You made Father into an image of yourself at the last."[131] Although the response of "The Clan" to *Autobiography* was itself mixed, it is possible that they all detected that beneath its glittering surface it was a farewell to the magical bond of childhood, to "those little wraiths of the past." As he wrote in *Autobiography*, "The persons we have been are lost rather than fulfilled in what we become."[132]

Bertie's "fixed idea" from early manhood, secretly shared by most of them, was to build a "Powys Castle"[133] where the brothers and sisters could once again congregate and shut themselves in. The fortress would be a kind of "Maberlulu," the little hut the children had built against the Montacute kitchen/garden wall, and where they had spent their happiest hours. Marian was to write, "Bertie in one letter to me in America said surely it will come back again to us one day."[134] John's "fixed idea," on the contrary, was a longing to escape to "a private, secret domain of my own, where no one could intrude, where it was indeed almost impossible for anyone to intrude!"[135] That secret domain was Wales. He escaped to "the very heart of Powysland," as he taunted his beloved Lulu. Not Chaldon of the Clan, but Wales, is now the heart. Some years later, when he was writing *Porius*, that novel of ultimate solitude, he has the hero slip in the following:

> The inherited landscape . . . over which his soul like a swift winged bird had to fly, contained a number of camps of opposed reactions, contrarious enclosures, hostile climates, all of which, in the blurred and scrawled-over map of his psychological inheritance, were perpetually trying to lure his light-flitting uncommitted psyche to descend and be caught in some fowler's net."[136]

After a brief return to Dorchester to say good-bye to family and friends, on the second of July, 1935, John Cowper Powys and Phyllis Playter escaped to Corwen and, except for a few brief summer holidays in Dorset, spent the rest of their lives in Wales.

CHAPTER TWELVE

WALES

1935-1943

I N A LETTER WRITTEN SHORTLY AFTER THEIR DEPARTURE, BERTIE INDICATED
that he knew what the move to Wales symbolized.

> I don't think I feel any desertion because you have gone to Wales. I'm sure
> I don't—but I have a sense of your having gone for two reasons, both
> good—but one weakening the sense of security I have in the world . . . on
> w^h I find I have much relied, namely the reliance on the presence of my
> brothers & sisters in the old Montacute way w^h somehow has lived in me
> strongly as a background. That's what I feel you are almost deliberately
> breaking, probably for good reasons as an illusion dropped, worn thro. It's
> that individual isolation that . . . has in this particular sense carried you
> apart & as a symbol of it you've gone to Wales. . . .
>
> I thought I detected a real anger in your letter, almost as though you
> feared I was right & would like to destroy me before I convinced you I was.[1]

His brother's accusation stung and, characteristically, John used a published
essay to respond to it. "Why did I thus isolate myself, so far from my brothers and
sisters? Not, I think, from my mania for solitude and independence, but as the
fulfilment of an early and youthful longing—'hiraeth' is the Welsh word for this
obscure stirring of some secret destiny—to return to the land of my remote
ancestors."[2] Bertie was irritated by Jack's insistence on the "Welshness" of the
Powyses, for the blood connection was remote. But literal truth never gets one
very far with John Cowper's motivations. There were two worlds that constituted his universe of meaning: the world of childhood memories and the world of
ancestral memories. The childhood illusion demolished, he entered into an even
older world, less susceptible to destructive reality. As the poet, R. S. Thomas says,
"You cannot live in the present, / At least not in Wales."[3] That suited Powys fine.

They settled into the little house on the slope of the Berwyns, and John
began to explore delightedly "my Welsh Home." How Phyllis felt about this latest move was less clear. Her actions, reactions, moods, and thoughts are obsessively recorded in his diary, but her own voice is absent. However, a rare surviving letter written to American friends in October 1935 suggests a certain initial

happiness: "We have a lovely view of mountains which remind me of the Far West . . . but I am afraid this is largely wish fulfilment for other American visitors who have been here have not at all been reminded of it. . . . I can't tell you how absolutely overjoyed we are to have this ugly little house . . . with electricity and <u>sunny</u> windows—when there <u>is</u> any sun!"[4] When the house next to them became vacant, Phyllis immediately rented it and invited her mother, "The Mistress," and her mother's sister, "Aunt Harriet," to join them.[5] Phyllis's perception of her mother as a strong emotional support and a person who could deal, as she could not, with everyday practicalities, was soon shattered. Although her mother cooked for her the one good meal a day necessary for her health, Phyllis quickly discovered that the two homesick and disoriented Americans were otherwise totally dependent on her. Phyllis, now 41, found she had three elderly people to cater for. John was 64, her mother 70, and Aunt Harriet 74. Fortunately, they found a young girl, Betty Evans, to help with the heavy work and to light the fires in both houses. It was Betty and her extended family who in future years were to solve the domestic problems of the "frail shaky poor upper-middle-class waifs like us."[6]

John once again took up *Maiden Castle*, which he finally finished in February 1936. Phyllis disliked the novel to the end, condemning it as "frivolous and unreal."[7] Schuster wrote him a perceptive letter about it: "I felt that I was back in the land of *Wolf Solent*, *Weymouth Sands* and *A Glastonbury Romance*. With some crucial differences, and a number of endlessly interesting variations, all these books are of course, your own story. Every poet's novel is his autobiography, but especially so in your case."[8] After long deliberation, Simon & Schuster decided to publish it, but only after it had been severely cut. Pollinger sent it around to six different English publishers before they heard, in September, the "comforting & relief-causing & happiness-bringing piece of News" that Cassell had taken his "ragged Maiden."[9] As he struggled to finish *Maiden* in the autumn of 1935, Phyllis was reading aloud to him L. H. Myers's trilogy, and it gave her an idea. "She did speak with great eloquence on the subject of my future writings—how—as in this Indian book, *The Root & the Flower*, I ought to bring in <u>Reality</u> in the more stirring & historic form of large national movements, both political & religious—& no longer be content with vaporous summer-lightning but by getting historic reality have some <u>real</u> thunder & some dominant subject."[10] With Myers in mind, she suggested that he abandon his traditional romance novel and write a historical novel about Owen Glendower. This idea suited him well since from a very early age he had been fascinated by this Welsh hero. The move to North Wales, the physical and psychological centre of Glendower country, was not therefore altogether the mystery that his family and friends considered it.

As soon as he got to Corwen he began his mental mapping for the novel. An almost daily walk was to the top of Pen-y-Pigyn wood where he got "a wondrous view in the rich rain-soaked colours—browns & greens & purples—of the valley of Glyndyfrdwy & Carrog." In the Corwen churchyard he found an old pillar

which he decided must be "the cross of Glyn Dŵr's angry dagger." He and Phyllis
took short bus rides to the Pillar of King Eliseg, to Valle Crucis Abbey ("here was
buried the famous family-bard of Owen Glendower, Iolo Goch"), to Llangollen,
from where they could see the ruins of Dinas Bran, the fortress of Bran the
Blessed. He explored the banks of "the sacred river Dee" and the "pre-historic
hill-city of unknown antiquity, whose fallen walls make a massive stone-coronet,"
across the river valley. This was Caer Drewyn which Powys renamed Mynydd-y-
Gaer. Eventually, all these places were woven closely into the tapestry of his story
of Owen Glendower. He was also recording and storing images: the sweet smell
of rain-soaked hedges; the way Welsh farmers dress—"their huge inner life-illusion of a dramatic appearance"; "the sun and the mist wrestling with each other,
losing, winning, losing, winning over the Berwyns," the column of smoke "rising
straight up like an enchanted lily-stalk"; "the very dead large Mountain Ash with
new leaves out of its death."

Although at first he felt he was living in "some story in the *Mabinogion*," they
were soon plunged into village life and having to deal with very real people and
situations. At first this disconcerted Powys, but by the end of the year he began
to move more easily between the interpenetrating real and mythical worlds of
Wales. The Diary suddenly teems with new characters: Eben Jones "of the one
arm" and his "'ooman" Hannah; Llew Williams, the shopkeeper; Jones, the signal-
man; Thomas, the Nationalist whom John called privately Llywarch Hen because
of his interest in this famous Bard; the unfortunate Mrs. Morgan and baby Fenna;
Ellis Evans, the chemist; Admiral and Mrs. Cotton, owners of the Cae Coed cot-
tages; old Annie Davies from the almshouses; Mrs. Peake, the fortune-teller; John
"Goch," the town crier; the Reverend Mr. Simon "with black hat and cow-slip
yellow teeth." Eventually, they too found their way into *Owen Glendower*.

While Owen's story remained omnipresent in his mind, it was not to be
started for another two years. His only income was from his books and that
income was shrinking year by year, so he accepted a commission from Simon &
Schuster to write a book on reading, a "Book on Books." At the same time he
decided to write "a Dog Story." Both he and Phyllis had been members of an
anti-vivisection society in America, and as early as 1933 he was composing a
piece on vivisection, which he variously called an article and a book, intending
it to be "an attack on all the ways & hasty dogmas of Modern Science."[11] This
was never published but parts of it were incorporated into *Weymouth Sands* with
the business of Dr. Brush & Hell's Museum. When they got to Wales, they joined
the British Society and met Leo Rodenhurst, editor of *The Abolitionist*. The stories of tortured dogs in the magazine so troubled Powys that he felt he "ought to
go out on a speaking Crusade against it."[12] Instead he wrote a novel, although it
is questionable whether *Morwyn* is a story or a long sermon. Certainly it is
Powys's fullest indictment of vivisection as man's "most vicious cruelty," in which
he brands as vivisectors all those who torture in the pursuit of science or of religion. Powys's hostility to science in general and to vivisection in particular led

him down extreme paths, but he was brought up short when Mabel Pearson told him that his anti-vivisectionist mania sprang from his own "hidden sadism."[13] Denial of guilt comes first; projection of destructive impulses onto someone or something else comes next. He was quite sure that vivisection was a sadistic impulse, and he admitted how "beautifully complicated" sadism was, with its "delicate feelers and its subtle arts of self-protective concealment,"[14] but he found it more difficult to accept that his revulsion against vivisection originated from the same source.

He took up Phyllis's suggestion to "make it imaginative like Dante's Inferno"[15] and set the main adventures in hell. In September 1936 they made a visit to World's End, near Llangollen, where he thought the Elwyseg Rocks there were "a retreat for the old gods." He noticed that the Gorge above was "full of Caves & one terrifying Hole, probably bottomless whose peculiarity is 'Hynoddrwyd' & that it goes down to Hell." Presto! he had his dramatic opening scene. The narrator, who is not named, his dog Black Peter, his new-found love Morwyn, and Morwyn's vivisector father, Mr. —, walk to the top of the mountain and there a cataclysm occurs that transports them to the centre of the earth—a "cosmogonic fall." The little group find themselves in hell, and after long conversations with, and escapes from, the most famous sadists in history, they are rescued by Taliesin, the fifth-century Welsh bard who has spent the centuries in hell in his "Quest" for "the great enchanter Merlin." Pursued, they sink *below* hell and reach the shore of "a vast subterranean sea," only to behold "the twin-gods of Religion and Science" "locked together in a loathsome embrace" in the process of becoming one. Beneath these "sea-krakens" they find a tunnel into a cavern. They discover that the first room is the lost Merlin's "esplumeoir." The room beyond is Caer Sidi—"the resting place of the age of Gold"—and in it sleep Ceridwen and Cronos, with the Cauldron of the Mothers resting between them. "This is the navel of the Universe, this is the lap of the Great Mother, this is the Centre of the Circle."[16] This is where it all begins: the centre, symbolizing the early oneness with the mother, the bliss of the amniotic fluid before the first awareness of a separate, a separated, identity. In a sense, the narrator's journey to the centre of the maze is the one Powys as a novelist-magician made again and again: the impossible journey toward the unattainable first unity with the concomitant sense of irrecoverable loss.[17]

In *Morwyn*, Powys introduces a new twist to the archetypal tale. A monkey from hell has followed them unnoticed into this inner sanctum. He now falls into the Grail Cauldron and emerges as a young vivisector who kisses Morwyn three times. When the narrator objects, the young man uses the jagged end of Rhadamanthus's staff "like a broken spear-head" to wound the older "I" in the groin. Until this moment, the narrator has looked on the magical events with the "curious eye of my detached self," but the wound, as Taliesin tries to make clear to him, absorbs him into the myth. The narrator has become the supplanted king of the fertility myth. One day, from yet another room, the figure of Socrates emerges. In this room is Tityos, still being "vivisected by these birds at the command of Zeus." The case for the defence is conducted by Kwang Tze and Socrates, who argue that "the old animal crime of struggle and violence and rape [is] less wicked than the cold-blooded, deliberate, *rational* crime of the vivisector," and Tityos is absolved. The little group is returned to earth, and Morwyn, her dubiously reformed father, Black Peter, Tityos, and Taliesin go off to America to preach the gospel of anti-vivisection. The uncured narrator returns to his home and writes this book about "the extraordinary day that ended in the devastating experience that left me . . . an old battered figure-head washed up by the sea."[18]

Despite Powys's astonishing depth of knowledge of mythical underworld journeys, the imagery and the symbolism of this inferno story is lifeless. One of the purposes of the mythic quest is to reach the "Centre of the Circle" to bring renewed life and although the storyteller insists that the journey has changed his life, his retelling of it, unlike the Ancient Mariner's, does not hold the guest enthralled. It is almost as if the trip, instead of giving new life and inspiration to the narrator, has given him instead death and dryness. Not only is the hero left alone in his detachment, he is left wounded. In a sense, he has slipped away from the nebulous achievements of the previous heroes in Powys's novels. They at least come to some bewildered acknowledgement of their complicity in evil, but the narrator in *Morwyn* remains content in his strident denunciation of cruelty, and his total unawareness of his own guilt. Perhaps that is what Powys intended. *Morwyn* is not a narrative in the genre of the hero archetype, not even the story of his usual anti-hero. There is neither a tragic battle for deliverance nor a comic resolution and acceptance. Instead he has written a picaresque parody of the individuation epic. The unnamed narrator-character suffers defeat, depression, suffering, but he does *not* progress by means of suffering into the light. Perhaps the author has concluded that there is no hero myth; there is only a life led as a picaresque fantasy.

As so often, what rescues Powys's less successful novels from the long philosophical discourses, the often careless writing, and his own personal manias, are the sudden aperçus. Just when the reader (at least the female reader) becomes tired of being told, once again, about the "maddening sweetness" of looking at young girls' legs, he will suddenly come out with a statement which every woman, however much she may resist it, knows to be deeply perceptive.

> Until I walked up that hill . . . I never knew what a thunderclap of finality a woman's love could be! I supposed that all of them chopped and changed in these motions of the blood even as we ourselves. . . . When a woman . . . once loves, her whole nature is affected. She may come to hate later, with that peculiar hatred of the heart for the being to whom once and for all it has been given, which is the most merciless of all hatreds, but hate as she may, to the end of her life she will bear that particular signature carved on her vitals.[19]

On March 10, 1936, Powys had a cable saying that Bertie was very ill. John hurriedly traveled to the nursing home at Hindhead, Surrey, feeling that it was "the thing to do," since "Bertie got into his old head the erroneous idea that I wanted to isolate myself from all the family! So this will show the old Bugger if he is conscious!"[20] When Powys got there he found that his brother had already died.

Albert Reginald Powys had been secretary of the Society for the Protection of Ancient Buildings since 1911. He was a formidable and influential administrator, highly respected for his authoritative views on planning and architectural matters, and for his persistence and competence in carrying these convictions through. He was elected a Fellow of the Society of Antiquaries in 1931, in recognition of his knowledge of ancient buildings and their restoration, and awarded the C.B.E. in 1934. Although he adored his daughter Isobel, his marriage to Dorothy had been unhappy for many years, and in 1930 they divorced and he married Faith Oliver. The twins born to them in the following year delighted him, but financial support for two families meant that he carried on a grueling schedule of work despite being warned by a doctor in December 1935 that he was endangering his heath. The nursing home doctor who signed his death certificate listed the cause of death as duodenal ulcer, and a request for an inquest was refused, but the cause of death was probably peritonitis. This condition, caused by a perforation of the stomach or intestines which allows bacteria to escape from the digestive tract into the abdominal cavity, demands immediate surgery, which Bertie did not get. The family afterwards discussed endlessly why he did not go into a proper hospital and have x-rays. Whatever the reason, it was a terrible and probably unnecessary death. John himself became convinced his brother had died of constipation. He explained to Frances, "They made him have enemas and there disturbed some old hard rocky lump of I don't know how old excrement near his colon & this gave him a terrible haemorrhage & he really died of that."[21]

The death of this brother hit Marian and Llewelyn particularly hard. The three of them had been the closest of companions in childhood, spending much of their time together in the little lean-to shed against the Montacute garden wall they called the "May-Ber-Lulu Castle." Llewelyn subsequently wrote a loving essay which was less about the successful man that his brother became than about the persistence and poignancy of memory.

> I would see my sister in her red overall stirring a mess of Quaker oats for my birthday feast on a wood fire in the little yard, Bertie kneeling at her side selecting the exact, right-shaped sticks to put under the pot. The smoke would be mingled with the smell of flowers lying upon the air in that sheltered spot. . . . In after years whenever I have smelt burning wood . . . in a single instant my spirits would be freed from ordinary time and space restrictions to be transported, swift as any Ariel, back to the Maberlulu.[22]

Marian was in America and Lulu too ill to do so, but John attended his brother's funeral at Winterborne Tomson in Dorset, the tiny Norman church the restoration of which Bertie had overseen five years before. At the time, John did not register any particular upset except shock but from then on, and increasingly as he got older, he became more than ever obsessed with his own bowel functions and convinced that he would die as Bertie had.

Sister Katie was the first to visit their new Welsh home, and while she was there in May 1936, John was installed as a Bard at the Corwen Gorsedd. It was a propitious beginning for his new life. The *Gorsedd-Cadair*, at which he was given the name Ioan, was "an extraordinarily thrilling event in our life." Always a poet-bard in his own imagination, "it was as if some <u>Secret Glory</u> had been obtained for us, like one who has blundered into a magic circle of fairies & has by chance rescued the Queen's child by uttering, without knowing, some occult word!"[23] Oddly enough, he does not mention in his diary that his young friend Hanley was also created a Bard on the same occasion.[24]

He finished his anti-vivisection novel in January 1937. He wanted to call it *Hell* but decided that was "a little crude" and accepted Phyllis's suggestion that it should be called *Morwyn* "so as to mislead buyers of it." He also hoped he had finished his "Book on Books," tentatively called *Read to Live*, but in December 1936 he received a letter from the Simon & Schuster editor saying that he wanted the book to be "simply essays on famous writers." He began again, and Phyllis sent off both typescripts to New York on the sixth May of 1937. Littleton and his wife Mabel arrived for a holiday shortly afterwards. While they were there, Littleton insisted that John confront several financial and legal problems, namely his income taxe, the generous allowance which, despite their own poverty, he was still sending his son (now aged thirty-five and a curate), and his will. With Littleton pushing, John arranged to get his income taxe reduced by claiming Phyllis as his secretary. Littleton then turned his attention to revising John's will, pointing out that the 1934 will John had signed meant that the son would get everything, even the contents of the Corwen house. John agreed that "this of course is an unthinkable proposition! And I am glad old Littleton in the T. T.'s interests has made me rake it up & face the matter."[25]

Ever resourceful, Littleton next suggested that John Cowper write the University Library at Bangor to see if he could get the necessary books to research his next novel, tentatively begun. In the next year and a half he borrowed many books on Welsh history, culture, and mythology, including R. E. M. Wheeler's *Prehistoric and Roman Wales*, J. E. Lloyd's *Owen Glyn Dŵr*, Rhys's Hibbert Lectures, and the four-volume *History of England under Henry IV* by J. H. Wylie. On a beautiful June day, Littleton drove them to Meifod and Mathrafal—places which play an important part in the novel as well as in Powys's personal mythology.

> Old Littleton drove us on Highway 5A past the Viaduct & past my imaginary Tassel Inn & past the route taken by young Rhisiart ap Owen from Chirk towards Valle Crucis—through Gobowen & thro' Oswestry to Meifod. . . . The Sexton had told us there were three Maen y Meifods one of which we believed was our ancestors' abode. . . . We finally arrived at the grand & supreme point of our Journey. This culmination of our pilgrimage

was MATHRAFAL the palace of the Princes, built by none other than King ELISEG. I cannot describe to you the romance of this place. It was more than magic, more than mystery—like a thousand years of high reveries of an intense imagination, of lonely thoughts separated from everything—alone—an airy castle above tree-tops.[26]

John was immensely happy. He was recognized in Wales as a bard, and in Wales he recognized that he was finally in a place in which he felt grounded, at home. "Certainly," he wrote, "no lover of the historical, no lover of the mythological, could find a spot more suited to his taste." Writing an historical novel rather than his usual romance was a daunting prospect, but he could not put it off any longer. The subject was chosen—the rise and fall of the Welsh Prince, Owain Glyn Dŵr. He was living in the very landscape in which Owen Glendower had lived, fought in, and eventually died in. He now had access to books which gave him details of how court and commoner lived in the fifteenth century. He had his own immense background of knowledge in the philosophy, religion, and magic beliefs of that period, all of which he could bring into the story. He began to write Owen but got no further than the first chapter when they received bad news from the American publishers. The new editor, Quincey Howe, rejected Morwyn "very viciously and contemptuously."[27] Cassell did publish it in England, but the book he considered "the best thing" he had written got unfavourable reviews. Even Llewelyn, who called it "a volume full of divine imagination" had to point out that "you have not learnt yet that restraint is power, and I think it would have been more effective if you had been less excitable and extravagant."[28]

Quincey Howe indicated that he also intended to reject his book of essays, now called Pleasures of Reading, unless JCP cut out the long St. Paul essay. Leaving America had profound implications for Powys's publishing life there. He began with Simon & Schuster when they were an adventurous small firm just starting out, and both Simon and Schuster had become friends. But they were a large firm now, and dealing with Powys became the job of a young, unsympathetic editor. Nor were his books selling in England. John knew that his books were "not doing nearly as well as they used to."[29] In fact, they never did well from then onward.

The only light in the dark of deepening poverty was a cable from Maxe Schuster ("my benefactor") in the New Year. Schuster had finally read the manuscript of "Pleasures" himself and decided it could become a bestseller like Durant's Story of Philosophy. John copied the telegram into his diary: "Redoubled Congratulations magnificent pleasures reading profound thanks dedication book so important suggest additional chapters Shakespeare Cervantes Melville and few others to make it comprehensive & basic potential enormous appeal will provide additional advance royalties to enable you to write new material earliest convenience writing full details also suggest changing title to the Enjoyment of Literature if agreeable in principle please cable two words 'Agreeable Enjoyment.'"[30]

Having already re-written the book once, Powys had to begin again, adding eight more essays. Meanwhile, Cassell, the co-publishers, who already had the book in galley proof, objected to the change of plans and refused to pay any more advance. They wanted the St. Paul essay included and the proposed Joyce essay deleted. Throughout the first six months of 1938, letters kept arriving from the Simon & Schuster editor, Quincey Howe, suggesting more changes. Powys found that what had come so easily to him in the past was now much harder, and that he could not count on his "old dythyrambic criticism," which he now saw was "thrilling in conversation or lecturing—but rather irrelevant when written down."[31] Nevertheless, he finally finished the book at the end of June 1938, and eventually Pollinger managed to convince Cassell to take it as well. The involved story of publishers' conflicting demands and the demands of editors reveals Powys as not only a tremendously versatile writer but a persevering and patient professional. The book came out in America in October as *Enjoyment of Literature* and in November the Cassell edition, slightly different, came out as *The Pleasures of Literature*. It did fairly well in England but was not "the spectacular success which old Schuster gambled on" in America. It was the last non-fiction of his that Simon & Schuster ever published.

Inevitably, Phyllis had a reaction against Wales, deciding that there was a "Demon under all the ideal spiritual mists," that "any good honest material Success in Wales is impossible," and that the only answer was to leave.[32] Phyllis's reactions were always extreme, and he would "get wild notions into my brain & imagine her rushing down to the Dee to drown herself."[33] He knew he must not "let her temperament murder my temperament and her 'unhappy' glands kill my 'happy' glands and her pessimism sap the fount of my moralizing & philosophy." When he became "too disturbed by her sad voice" he would walk and try to "get pleasure from the rocks & stones & trees. I <u>have</u> to get something from these things—I <u>have</u> to! in order to feed my spirit!"[34] On the other hand, his attempts to lift *her* spirits by having the sophisticated conversations she craved all too often ended disastrously.

> Just as we were sitting down to breakfast I must needs try & put on a big lump of coal with the tongs O such a huge black <u>Coal</u> & lo! & behold this piece of coal was dropt by me out of the tongs. . . . I have like President Wilson a one-track mind—I find it hard to cope with the League of Nations & with Communism at the same moment—out of the tongs, I say, <u>into her saucepan</u> of <u>Coffee</u>!!!! . . . I keep pondering on why it was that I failed to keep up the T. T.'s spirit![35]

His inveterate clumsiness, or what he called "this mysterious anti-mechanic magic in my hands,"[36] must at times have driven her to distraction. He had abandoned his attempts to light the fires, but his lack of coordination got him into endless difficulties. He would make sporadic attempts to get Phyllis her breakfast, but "I can see my grand difficulty would be to get the fried egg out of its pan and on to the plate!"[37] Once, in trying to clap his hands in pleasure, he "ran the nail of my left thumb into the base of my right thumb & made the hell of a fuss till

the T. T. tied it up."[38] This incident reminded him once again of the humiliations he suffered in childhood when he would try to hit cole-tits in the orchard
at Montacute with his catapult and "the shot always hit the side of the catapult
instead of the softer side of the little tit."[39] It was by no means all gloominess. He
could and did laugh at his mishaps, his absentmindedness, his maladroitness. He
also saw the amusing side of his encounters with his neighbors and recounts these
with gentle slyness: "I met that old Stone-Deaf Ex-Postman with his plump black
dog who said the said Dog had nearly killed a Pheasant. God! it must have been
a stone-deaf pheasant."[40]

Equally often his malice was less amusing. Aunt Harriet treated Phyllis to a
much-needed holiday of five days in London in June 1938, when they saw Noel
Coward's _Operette_. Phyllis told him excitedly about it when she returned: "And
the T. T., speaking of _Operette_, _Became_ _a_ _Dancer_: yes the T. T. _saw_ _Herself_ as a
mysterious _Grotesque_ _Dancer_!" The next day he reported that "She was _shy_
about having told me she was like a great Dancer. . . . I do so enjoy it when she
feels _embarrassed_. The great thing is to tease her in some subtle sideways manner & make her feel shy all suddenly—I can make her even put her fingers
against her cheek! I do so like it when she does this. I like playing on a girl's self-
consciousness, like you would play on a piano—tra-la-la-la-la! A girl is a harp—
and you can flick the strings without striking them."[41]

The truth was he hated her to go away, which she seldom had a chance to
do. Even a day in Chester with Tim Hanley was "a sad day for me."[42] He was
always convinced that she would come back "a different person, from what she
set out" and that "the two chief pillars, bases, props, _foundations_ of my life—_tea_
and _enemas_"[43] would tremble under the feet of this new T. T. When she went to
London with her aunt, she had suggested he give himself an enema on the usual
third day but he did not. The result was a more than adequate punishment for
her going away.

> Met the T. T.'s train last night. . . . But directly we got in I asked for the
> ENEMA & aye! if it hadn't been for the T. T.'s skill & competence & keep-
> ing her head & her heroic lack of any disgust, repulsion we would have had
> to have got the Doctor or the Nurse. How could I have been so foolish not
> to have done as she said? The whole bathroom was my privy.[44]

Despite the subtle and not-so-subtle games that all couples play, another
entry in the diary bespeaks a relationship that was by now deep and enduring.

> 3 June 1936: When the T. T. woke up she was only silent from the teasing
> worry of her eyes. . . . But after a while she was seized with an Inspiration .
> . . & after an unlucky interval—when I foolishly tried to relieve her of her
> tray—which she said I did as if I were docking the _Queen_ _Mary_ yes the
> _Queen_ _Mary_—she began after some coaxeing on my part to talk of it. . . .
> And she said—The New Intellectuals—the new young Einsteins—will give
> the _Mind_ a holiday, or a time in gaol, or let it go & play as it likes. And then

they will use what hitherto has hardly been explored at all—our sources of Knowledge <u>independent</u> <u>of</u> <u>the</u> <u>mind</u>—not necessarily the ordinary <u>senses</u>, but the impressions derived <u>about</u> the senses from our continuous stream of <u>sub-conscious</u> <u>life</u>. . . . The thought came into her head from thinking how she & I knew each other so well that mental knowledge had come to an end. We began with mental knowledge & then came a point when she used to cry unhappily—"We don't know each other any more!" but now she realizes that that was because of the beginning of this deep knowledge—outside ordinary mental processes—which takes the place of the other.

Powys thought that their "emotional imaginations" were identical because "I always <u>feel</u> <u>like</u> all the deep and strange identities I encounter & for the time I <u>am</u> like them while I follow their thoughts." In an addendum that recognized the limits of his magical identification, he admitted, "But she sees round me, as I don't have the power to see round her."[45]

It was family illnesses that dominated their lives in 1938. Will had been in England with his wife Elizabeth since March to consult specialists about *his* ulcer. He was at Rat's Barn when, in April, Theodore had a stroke, and was of great assistance to Violet during the crisis. Indeed, with his big American car and frenetic energy, Will, in his way, was now looking after all his older brothers and sisters. He sent Phyllis and John a cheque which John accepted but felt a shock that this much younger brother was "tipping him." Will then offered to drive up to Corwen in July and take them back to East Chaldon to see Theodore, Gertrude, and Katie. Theodore's stroke caused John to think a good deal about this brother and his reclusive personality. He decided that Theodore had "always been subject to Interior <u>Withdrawings</u> from all outer contact—especially from his brothers & sisters—& I think he has now allowed this withdrawing inwards its full scope & indulgence."[46] During this visit, however, JCP concluded: "What I had fancied was that Theodore was <u>using</u> his illness—as I can conceive in my anti-social heart a person very well doing as an excuse to avoid everyone . . . but now I have changed my mind. I think now that Theodore is fighting for his life." Theodore was afraid that "he had the same disease as Swift," who in his last years was paralyzed and declared unsound of mind.[47]

The next brother to cause concern was Llewelyn. After another serious hemorrhage in September 1936, Llewelyn decided to return to Clavadel, Switzerland, where once before he had been cured of his tuberculosis. He had gradually gained a little strength there and, at Alyse's suggestion, began working again on his "imaginary autobiography," *Love and Death*, which he had laid aside after his first crisis in 1933. He was well all the summer of 1937 but had another severe hemorrhage in December. In the first four months of 1938, he was so weak that Alyse had to attend to every bodily function as well as read aloud all day to him. It was at this time that he wrote John and Phyllis asking them to come. He had other friends and relatives visit—the faithful Louis Wilkinson, Rivers Pollock, Reginald Marsh, Edna St. Vincent Millay, Gamel, Will—but it was his brother

Jack that he wanted. Llewelyn was always convinced that John held "my mind and body up with the power of his mighty Merlin's spirit."[48] He sent forty pounds and asked them to come in September.

In August 1938 Marian and her son Peter came over, going first to see Llewelyn in Switzerland. Llewelyn felt very drawn to this boy, writing a friend, "He attracts me very much, very exciting to look at and madder than my brother John. I only hope he will not be destroyed by the crabbed world. To see him is to long to protect him. He looks so beautiful, so imaginative, and so vulnerable."[49] Unfortunately, these were prophetic words. Marian and Peter went on to Corwen for a week. The close relationship between Marian and John still existed, and Marian could say to him things no one else dared. For two years John had put off having his rotten teeth extracted but by now had had them all removed. Marian gave him a hundred dollars to buy new teeth, telling him he looked like the person in "The Waste Land," but he refused and went toothless for the rest of his life. More troublesome were conversations with Peter, now seventeen, who asked him "about the circumstances of his birth & parentage & about his mysterious & evasive progenitor. . . . Aye! but I cannot help wishing that his origin was yet <u>more</u> mysterious than it was! I will say no more."[50] The myth shared by John and Marian became more destructive with time. She refused to tell Peter who his father was, and Peter was by now convinced it was John himself. Peter was twenty, attending Harvard, before Marian finally told him he was actually the son of Ernst Angell, an eminent New York lawyer who was a married neighbor of Marian's at Sneden's Landing.

Marian gave them a further ten pounds so that he and Phyllis could stop off in Paris for 3 days—she to visit the Louvre and Chartres and John Cowper to see "whether 'those books' are still there."[51] Excited letters flitted back and forth and Alyse sent a further twenty pounds. They went to Liverpool to renew their passports and book tickets on the Cunard line.[52] However, Phyllis was very worried by the extras costs incurred by the visitors, however welcome, and the cost of the trip to Switzerland: "She says we are so poor that we are best quietly <u>plodding on</u> & not having shoes or underclothes or overcoats but if we go to Lulu we shall have to buy some of these things & she says we simply can't afford it."[53] Will, Elizabeth, and their two girls arrived in Corwen again in September, but Will went directly to Ruthin and booked himself into the Castle Hospital, suspecting that his gastric ulcer was causing a fever. A few days later the ulcer perforated and he too was in danger of peritonitis. Unlike Bertie, Will immediately called for a surgeon to operate, and he survived. Elizabeth stayed with John and Phyllis while Will was in hospital, and John wrote Lulu to postpone their trip. When Will came out of hospital on October 12, they stayed with them a further week and then returned to Africa.

"Plodding on" was about all Phyllis could do, worn out by visitors, money, and domestic worries. Brief forays to neighbors lifted her spirits, but as Powys remarked, her "childish excitement and high spirits <u>was soon brought</u> [down] a Peg or two, by her 3 elderly Teachers."⁵⁴ A Playter relative visited them in November and wrote to a friend of her sadness at what she had found. She remembered a young Phyllis "always ready for new experiences," who in New York "drew around her a choice circle of interesting minds." Now she saw "a quiet subdued woman who lives in a far-away village at the end of No Where and whose only companions are an old mother, an old aunt, an old lover and an old, old dog!"⁵⁵

Something happened in early December 1938 that temporarily took their minds off the impending war and their financial straits. It began when a young Irishman living in Bridgend, South Wales, called Gerard Casey, wrote in *John O'London's* weekly, championing the neglected genius of the novelist. Casey subsequently began a correspondence with Powys and then visited them. He reminded John of "poor Dicky," Theodore's dead son, and any connection with "family," however faint, always spurred Powys to extraordinary helpfulness. When Will was there in October, John talked him into offering Gerard a job. Gerard was in Africa by the end of January 1939, as Powys put it, "on his quest for the magic cauldron." Unlike "poor Dicky," Casey did indeed find his pot of gold in Kenya, including marriage to Lucy's only daughter, Mary, in November 1945. Before he left, Casey arranged for John to give a lecture in Bridgend in December. Preparations for this first lecture "in the land of my fathers" began in November. Perhaps slightly apprehensive—for he had not lectured for nine years and had no teeth—John told the organizer, Benson Roberts, that he was "a permanent invalid" and "dependent entirely on a particular sort of American enema which I can only get here at home."⁵⁶ (That was certainly one way of describing Phyllis to a stranger.) At first he was very nonchalant about the coming lecture, referring to his putative audience as "these great musical Rugger-lads," but he soon realized he was in the presence of literate and appreciative people. Feeling like an "old Circus Clown smelling the saw-dust of the arena again,"⁵⁷ he lectured on the *Mabinogion*—for two hours. It was at this lecture that John met the poet Huw Menai. His friendship with Menai was an unusual one, but there was no doubt of the attraction. He felt like Panurge meeting Pantagruel, "and they loved each other at first sight." Possibly in part it was because he saw Menai as an example of the "Helpless and yet Original type of Welshman,"⁵⁸ and he could play his favourite role as helper. They were to write each other faithfully once a week for almost twenty years.

All this while, his *Owen* went in and out of the manuscript drawer, the writing of it constantly disrupted by publishers, domestic contretemps, and sibling crises and visits. Despite this, he had finished thirteen chapters by the end of 1938. Their finances were now desperate. He contemplated writing short stories or articles for the papers, but decided the only answer was to finish *Owen* as quickly as possible. Phyllis had the idea of privately printing the book and selling it in instalments on the bookstalls at railway stations. He wrote Lulu in November that he would have to use the journey money he had sent to tide them over until May when he hoped there might be some royalties due. Llewelyn immediately sent him a further fiftly pounds. Unbelievably, John Cowper sent this money to his wife and son. With no apparent sarcasm, on January 7, 1939 he noted in his diary: "Letters from my wife and son happily in Bath where the waters seem so to cure them both."

Although "our heads the moment we are silent together turn like compass needles to the Cold North of our coming <u>Penury</u> & <u>what</u> we shall do???" it was on "the Old," their dog, that all their thoughts concentrated that cold winter. He died on March 28, and Powys blamed himself: "Well I was destined to kill the Old with my peculiarities. . . . With 'Peculiarities' we save and with peculiarities we destroy. . . . If I hadn't killed the Old that snowy day sooner or later I'd have done it by taking him—deliberately—<u>too far</u>."[59] They buried this well-loved pet in their garden. Phyllis felt that her life was "cracked & rent in some way" and cried so much that John thought that to the end of his days her face, distorted with grief—"an Intaglio of Grief"—would be imprinted on his mind. He visited the grave every day, rehearsing obsessively in his mind the Old's final walk and his death, and protecting himself by "the idea of living things that can cease & yet <u>cannot</u> cease."[60] Despite his personal sorrow he struggled on with his *Owen* and in it described the ruined castle of Dinas Bran: "Its foundations are sunk in that mysterious underworld of beyond reality whence rise the eternal archetypes of all the refuges and all the sanctuaries of the spirit, untouched by time."[61] Writing out grief was something he had become an adept in. Knowing that war was now at hand, they went to Chaldon in July for a brief visit with his family and Bernie O'Neill. The diary while he was there becomes a reverie on memory and death.

18th July 1939: I heard the Reef bell of the Light ship on the Shambles so loved by Lulu. Looked out of window at the weeds in Lulu's garden—at the weeds in Lulu's garden—the weeds the weeds the weeds in Lulu's garden! the weeds!

19th July 1939: Didn't go to bed till 12 . . . but was recalling with violent outbursts loud & Rabelaisian those ancient wayside episodes & characters & above all sayings—logos of queer ones & of naughty ones of reckless ones of the remote past—<u>all</u> <u>dead</u>. Thus do I live again the Past; <u>our</u> <u>Past</u>, which was Imaginative then & is Imaginative still—with Bernie. . . . Gertrude doing it all as she does all for Katie all for Theodore—and used to do all for Lulu; <u>and</u> <u>did</u> <u>all</u> <u>for</u> <u>my</u> <u>Father</u>. . . . I had a lovely walk along the dangerous grassy cliff—down toward the White Nose. Gazed at Portland and at Chesil Beach and at the Nothe or rather Wyke Hill. Saw a Marble white butterfly—a Marble white—these butterflies remind me of old Littleton of my Father of Maiden Castle of Redcliff Bay. They carry my memories on their wings. Those black dots are my memories. Black dots of Marble Whites. The memories of a Maniac.

20th July 1939: I visited Theodore & tho' Violet tried to hush him for fear of it exciting his wounded head, where a blood clot goes pulse! pulse! throb! throb! tick! tick! all the time, yes where a blood clot a Blood Clot! dances a devilish dance in his great head!—he talked very very freely to me of his feelings in this illness; he exposed himself and his feelings & his self contempt and his unequalled Originality. . . . I listened to his fears his terrors his fancies his extraordinary remarks, <u>with</u> awe and <u>reverence</u>. . . . Then we drove to Bertie's Grave. Weeds were growing on it—grass uncut round it—Gertrude's <u>Lavender</u> with its fragrant roots in it.

They stopped off in London so that he could join the London Library. While there they saw Stravinsky's ballet *Petrushka*, in which the Magician-Showman brings to life three puppets—the sad clown Petrushka, the Moor, and the Ballerina. John decided that in watching the puppet with a head of wood and a body stuffed with straw, he was seeing "his double." Thenceforth he often referred to himself as "Petrushka" and Phyllis as "the Dancer." They returned to Corwen to await the war. Despite their isolation, they avidly read the papers and listened to Aunt Harriet's radio, attempting to understand the tumultuous events and their own responses to them. They "talked of the war from every possible point of view of the fact of the ordinary quiet Germans (so exactly like ours) & so much easier to understand than French or Russian—all sitting just as the T. T. & I are <u>over</u> <u>our</u> <u>kitchen</u> <u>stove</u> & not wanting war at all . . . feeling it <u>inevitably rolling up</u>. What is the mistake we are all making? Here we all are heading for a ghastly world catastrophe—& even yet at the bottom of our hearts we common people are <u>not</u> . . . convinced Pacifists. Why aren't we? . . . The old clown (safe in his arm chair) sees it through!"[62] In the months that followed, he continued to "analyse and dissect" his feelings about the war.

> I find desire to stop the physical pain that the war will cause to so many. I find a deep animal-like annoyance that Hitler & Mussolini (and above all Franco) shall not be forced to say the words "We are beaten." . . . I find a love of the pure dramatic excitement—as Homer says—a situation & a world crash—that there may be a "subject for Song" for the men to come on the earth. But I also with all my reason & soul & body feel it may gratify various monstrous & outrageous instincts in me.[63]

Theodore's grandson, John Francis Cowper Powys, was born on August 26. With his mind still on Homer, John Cowper called his birth "nature's retort to the prospective slaughter of the human race—another Head appears & forces its way into the world to off-set the 'powerless Heads of the dead'." World War II began on the first day of September. The Mistress, over seventy, and Aunt Harriet, seventy-five, were "elevated & exalted & thrilled & excited—think of that!" Phyllis immediately signed up to take an evacuee child but ended up sewing Red Cross bandages, at which she was very bad. Powys "meticulously and minutely" answered the questionnaire for the Ministry of Information and told them, "I would be an absolutely perfect War Propagandist for them now (save for my living on liquids (& of course (really) my 'enemas' are given me by the T. T. alone)."[64] The Ministry did not take up his offer.

Gamel Woolsey was with them for a brief visit when they received the news that Llewelyn had died on the second of December. The autopsy gave as the cause of death, not his old enemy tuberculosis, but "a hemorrhage from the ulcer flooding the intestines."[65] John recounted that "one of them—was it Gamel or the T. T.—uttered the words 'There it is!' with true bone rock red Indian American stark stoicism—but I bent this way and that very slowly in the wind— an old stump with a shoot & a stone beneath it and a stone caught up in its substance."[66] On December 4, they went up the mountain near the Grouse Gate where there was a clear space and there, in sight of the other Carnedd Llewelyn of Eryri, they made a small cairn of rocks, a "Carnedd Llewelyn Mhowys."

> We carried milk and honey mixed exactly as Circe directs—the daughter of Lulu's Sun—& sweet wine and meal & we got water from that deep rut in the way & John played the part, "the Man" played the part of the Priest of Dis & did kneel and say πολλὰ δὲ γ ουνούμην [Pray long prayers] & the two girls did answer νεκύων ἀμενηνὰ κὰρηνα [for the powerless heads of the dead]. And the silver light on all the floods of the Dee & on all the pools in the path did light us down.

Under normal circumstances, when Powys was "mentally or nervously attacked by one of my HORRORS," he would "deal with him or with it according to an elaborate psycho-analytical psychi-psychiatry of my own invention."[67] But after 1939, worry about money, the menace of war, Llewelyn's death, the illness of his brothers (for Littleton was also now in bed with a duodenal ulcer), left him unable to forestall "these perpetual forms of madness" from finding their way into consciousness. He had written in his autobiography that we carry our "madness," our "hidden Fear," always with us, watching it change its shape with the years. He was now sixty-seven. Some of his hidden fears, horrors, and manias had changed form; others were added. He described them all in his diaries, which by now had become, as he admitted to Littleton, "an enormously long autobiographical book."[68] Each year these journals had become more detailed; the content more explicit; the style more idiosyncratic; the slippage between the conscious mind and the unconscious psyche ever more complex. And sometimes breathtaking for the conventional reader.

One of his "morbid horrors" was of spiders, which he thought had originated when, as a tiny boy, a nursemaid had chased him with a spider.[69] By now, the phobia had broadened to incorporate other areas of psychic danger, linked with his "peculiar brand of sadism" and with "the war in my members or the inner war of my life." He identifies himself with Dostoevsky, who, he says, "speaks of lust as The Insect in us."[70] Another source of dread was his dreams. Powys declared himself a "sworn hater & destroyer & opponent & persecutor & deadly enemy of Dreams." In part he feared them because the terrors he could usually keep in check would emerge uncontrolled in nightmares. But he also hated his dreams because they insisted on making "thrice accursed associations" between his sadism, his sexuality, and his anal preoccupations. He now became terrified that, like Bertie, his insides would become filled with putrefying waste, of "decomposition."

> Had <u>loathsome</u> Dreams. It is my inside, with a touch of dyspepsia & also my memories of the times when I had <u>not</u> saved myself by enemas being still dominant in my dreams! Yes that is what it is—the heavenly Salvation & Redemption of the <u>enema</u> has not yet arrived into the land of dreams! . . . As I heard that divine Medieval Bell strike <u>Nine</u> I <u>stood</u> <u>like</u> <u>Aaron</u> between the horrors of Decomposition—my <u>Dreams</u>—and the intense absorption of my soul in all the fronds, & ferns, & <u>new</u> <u>leaves</u>.[71]

Theodore had told Alyse, "John escapes by way of madness," to which John had replied that "it would be still truer to say, 'John has so much madness to escape from that he runs too blindly to see the other things.'"[72] He thought he had learned to "<u>balance</u> <u>my</u> <u>mind</u> . . . between going too far in facing Horror—which is a bad thing to do—& running away too quick & too universally <u>from</u> Horror."[73] Running away from the horrors within himself, he called his "anti-narcissistic mania." *Not* running away, which his "diseased conscience" demanded, courted disaster. It was indeed a constant balancing act, and it did not always work.

> I went to Grouse Gate. . . . Here I <u>forced</u> myself to contemplate Nature; that pretty little path, those larches, that chicken wire fence & far away, Moel Morwydd in thin clouds. And coming home I <u>forced</u> myself to enjoy the sun in my bones & with my knees and hands and skull like a gorilla. And I forced myself to enjoy my own <u>Shadow</u>. This forcing myself to enjoy my own shadow and to <u>lean</u> <u>motionless</u> on gate meant of course that I was flouting and defying my Anti Narcissistic Mania according to which I ran away oh so quick & always <u>from</u> <u>myself</u>. Thus as I knew would happen— tho' I <u>foxed</u> <u>the</u> <u>black-out</u>—yet there remained even <u>in</u> the <u>black-out</u> those queer nervous and quite <u>mad</u> physical psychic feelings of all my pulses beating and a sort of swelling of interior Breasts![74]

Somehow, despite the "manias" and the energy it took to keep them under some kind of control, despite all that had happened to them since they first conceived of it in 1935, on the twenty-fourth of December 1939 he took his *Owen* to the top of Mynydd-y-Gaer and wrote the last lines. As uncharacteristic as it is in the Powys oeuvre, *Owen Glendower* is a consummate achievement.[75] The summary "Argument" at the beginning of the novel is itself a tour de force. The rebellion of an obscure Welsh prince is put into the context of world events occurring in the fifteenth century, an age of emerging nationalism, revolutionary religious doctrines, and chaotic social, economic, and political change. While Powys makes no reference to the battles once again raging in Europe, they were in attendance in his mind.[76] So too was his vivid memory of his father reading him as a child Aytoun's *Lays of the Scottish Cavaliers*. During the war, Margaret had returned to him the book that "has influenced my Deepest Life more than any other book," and he spent many hours "showing the T. T. certain illustrations of swords & bucklers & Helmets & graves on lonely moors & ruined Castles above swollen rivers & crescent Moons above lost battles and broadswords brandished in Victory."[77]

From 1400 to 1412, under the leadership of Owain Glyn Dŵr, the people of Wales made an attempt to rid themselves of English rule. With the aid of his allies, Scotland, and France and the commitment of the ordinary people who flocked to his standard, Glyn Dŵr at first enjoyed huge success. He held two Welsh Parliaments and was declared by the men of Gwynedd and Powys to be Prince of Wales. However, his redoubtable commanders were gradually killed in the endless taking and re-taking of castles and fortresses; the burned countryside could not support his huge army; his allies lost interest; his family and friends were killed or captured. In 1413, with the remnants of his once great army scattered, Owain vanished.

The novel begins with the meditations of Rhisiart, a young scholar fresh out of Oxford, who has come to fulfill his dream of serving Wales. Feeling like "Kilwch at the gate of Arthur," he presents himself to Owen Glendower and is taken on as Owen's secretary. As the tumultuous events unfold, a close relationship develops, and Owen acknowledges Rhisiart as the "son of my secret soul." Since Owen is portrayed as a magician, and Rhisiart, in the beginning at least, is the usual self-absorbed Powys-hero, the novel might seem to be yet another magical quest for a home and a father. But with Phyllis constantly reminding him that this novel must "touch Reality," and with "reality" in its various guises constantly jostling him over the years that he took to write it, *Owen Glendower* is quite unlike anything he had written before or would write again.

However, Powys being Powys, it is a historical novel with a difference. Despite all the reading he did for it, he decided that in the end "exact scholarship" would greatly handicap him and that instead he would trust to "dear John's power of telling stories." He told Marian he thought his best line was to "follow humbly the method of Sir Walter Scott & write fast & bold & free & in large strokes, staking all on the humour & naturalness of the characters & on the descriptions of nature & on the exciting adventures & on the clash between monks and bards and orthodox churchmen & Lollards and Welsh & English."[78] That he most certainly did.

Almost immediately the novel explodes into the first of innumerable vivid, boisterous, often rowdy scenes. Against the backdrop of the battered Dinas Bran, "lifting its majestic battlements" and "the sacred river winding through its sun-illumined valley," a market fair is going on, thronged with peasants, earls, stewards, monks, friars, bards, cooks, cutthroats, prophets, poets, herdsmen, heretics, soldiers, wandering scholars, and even the Lord Abbot of Caerleon himself. This brilliant opening allows Powys to give a local habitation and a name to a large number of his forty-four characters "mentioned in history" and twenty-three "unmentioned in history." Events turn ugly and the fair suddenly becomes "a place of execution." Rhisiart, on his old piebald horse, brandishing his old-fashioned crusader's sword "in the face of the best archers in England," accidentally manages to save a mad friar and a beautiful girl from being burned at the stake. Powys has established in a few short chapters two of the main themes of his story: that all men are "at the mercy of uncontrollable events," and that "all the events in the great world are so different from what the historians say."

There are numerous scenes equally dramatic: there is the sumptuous banquet at Glyndyfrdwy when the death of his bard, Iolo Goch, precipitates the declaration of Owen as Prince of Wales; Glendower's theatrical rescue of Rhisiart, who has been taken hostage by the English in Castell Dinas Bran; the great victory of Bryn Glas and the grisly scene in the battlefield afterwards when the Welsh women desecrate the English corpses. The stories of the mean lives and private worries of the maids, the retainers, the children, nurses, and pages are almost as fully detailed as those who are changing history, with thousands of small touches of domesticity that Powys insisted are as much a part of the history as the larger happenings. He believed deeply in the force and influence of "passed-by things of no importance." Powys also makes sure that the stage is full of authentic props; this is more Sir Henry Irving theatrics after his own heart than a minimalist Maurice Browne play.

There are vignettes of the absurd: Broch at Harlech wading into the sea like Bran the Blessed to rescue a swimmer "nigh to the limit of his endurance," and Prince Owen jumping in stark naked to rescue his friend with both ending up rescuing a chimpanzee. There is the bizarre scene of King Henry, the dwarf, the dog, and Mad Huw; the melodrama of Broch's wife setting the mill-wheel going and predicting Owen's downfall; the scenes of erotic maso-sadism in which Powys once again explores the mystery of cruelty embedded in creation itself. There is the infinitely compassionate interlude when Rhisiart, wounded and imprisoned at Worcester, accepts his wife's dishonor in return for his life. Often Powys's most engaging images are those which unite the human with the natural world—Owen's wife and her maids are "like a flock of starlings around a stately ewe"; Elliw is "a queer looking creature, her long hair floating around her frail form like the dusky smoke about a bonfire of weeds." This master of the image can create in a few sentences the sense of the horror of life that needs no battle to prove. Prince Owen, waking into reality in his "night of accumulated disasters" and recognizing to what destruction his dream has brought his people, "gazed at the monk with the expression of a child who has turned a page of a lesson book and found a picture of a boar-hunt."[79]

A reviewer was to say of this novel: "It sweeps the reader on and on at an ever increasing pace until, like a great wave, it deposits him safely on the strand, bruised, bumped, surprised and shaken with emotion. . . . It is not, however, a book for little people."[80] The novel is not, indeed, a book for little people; it gives much and asks much in return. There are so many characters with weird names, so many skirmishes, assignations, and journeys that the reader can be forgiven for feeling at times that if he has not been drowned, he is at least waterlogged. Nor is his *Owen* for readers seeking textbook accuracy. John told Marian that the fear of "making historical or antiquarian blunders" would "fuss him up" as much as the fear of libel, but that did not stop him from giving his own characteristic interpretation of the man and the movement. For example, there has been much speculation about where the historic Glyn Dŵr spent his last years or where he was buried. Most unorthodoxly, Powys has Owen disappear into the secret chambers of Mynydd-y-Gaer—the prehistoric camp above Corwen that he had looked at from his bedroom window every morning since he arrived in Wales four years before. With his predilection for seeing history through landscape, it is possible that when he saw in those first early days at Corwen that "the stone wall of Caer Drewyn with the red bracken when the Sun struck it was like an iron crown with a circle of Blood" he already knew where *his* Prince would disappear.

The last chapter of Powys's novel begins five years after Owen's vanishing. Rhisiart, now an English judge, and Meredith, Owen's son, have come to Corwen to deliver a pardon to Glendower from the King. He has been living in a cave, "the mound-dwellers' hiding-place beneath the mystic walls of Mynydd-y-Gaer," looked after by his friend Broch. Now, with an audience, there is only just enough strength left in him, as Broch says, "to play the dying actor." He dies crying "Prince of Powys—Prince of Gwynedd—Prince of Wales—Prince of Annwn!"[81] Broch and Owen together burn his body on a vast funeral pyre. Given his knowledge of religious beliefs and customs, Powys would have known that cremation would not have been countenanced in any Christian society of that period. To speculate on the process by which he decided to have Owen disappear into the flames is to ponder on the mystery of the creating mind. Was he thinking of the funeral rites in his beloved *Odyssey*? Or was he remembering a chance phrase by Lloyd, his favourite Welsh historian, who begins the final paragraph of his life of Glendower with, "At last the flame had flickered out which had once blazed fiercely and wildly throughout the length and breadth of Wales." It is exactly the kind of vivid phrasing that would sink into a mind like John's to re-emerge much later totally transformed into something else. An equally likely spark was a chance visit by one of his young disciples, Nicholas Ross, at this time. He noted in his diary,

> He sent up Cecil—whose head he has turned just as he has turned mine—last night with a letter threatening to disappear. . . . He had been up the Mynydd y Gaer last night & had lit a fire in that hollow in the stones and seen the sun set & the Full Moon rise. He lit the fire at 10 p.m. so I could have seen it.[82]

Perhaps all these played some small part in his decision to burn rather than bury Owen. However, on the second of December, as Powys was beginning his final chapter "Difancoll," Llewelyn died. Llewelyn had given instructions that he was to be buried in a foetal position in a grave on the Dorset cliffs, but wartime regulations intervened. He was cremated.

The chapter became John's inspired requiem for his lost brother, and on December 18, he read it to Phyllis. She found it powerful, but "too crowded with action," and suggested he make the ending a quiet one. And so he did. Perhaps remembering Lulu's admonition that "restraint is power," instead of finishing with the dramatic and wrenching death scene of Owen, whose sometimes-incoherent words were "like the falling of winged creatures," the novel concludes with Owen's son, Meredith, starting down the bracken-covered slopes of Mynydd-y-Gaer to Carrog in the gray dawn, after the night of burning. He sees "the oldest winged creature in Edeyrnion, the croaking raven of Llangar," with his mate, and he watches "as the pair rose on their heavy-flapping wings and sailed away eastward, mounting up in huge spiral circles higher and higher as they followed the river's flow."[83] Powys knew that the word *difancoll* meant "disappearance," but that it could also mean "utter extinction," "complete loss." The cumulative events of 1939 could easily have left him lost for words. Instead he went on to write *Porius*, one of the most beautifully sustained threnodies for a lost world ever written. The war prevented publication of *Owen Glendower* for a further two years. By then the whole world was focused on the conflagration before them and had little time to contemplate the rise and fall of the fifteenth-century Prince of Wales.

The winter of 1940 was the coldest Powys could ever recall. Phyllis struggled to unfreeze blocked pipes; he struggled to feed the birds. The latter was more often than not a cause for upset between them—how much to give, which birds to give the food. He would mistakenly give them the cake she had bought for visitors, then blurt out the bad news before her morning coffee when he knew she was least able to deal with it. It was in such small matters that Phyllis was able to confront him with a charge of "malice," which she seemed unable to do in more fundamental matters. He was unfailingly amazed, both by her agitation, and by her accusation.

> It is very odd that such a self-analyst as I am with my whole life-illusion opposed to self-deception should be wrong over my own motives. Is it possible that a person's body or lungs or lips can be malicious without the person knowing anything about it in his mind no not to the very depth of his mind? I begin to fear it must be possible—a sort of marrow of malice.[84]

It was hungry tramps, even more than starving birds, that became the focus of his concern. From the earliest days in America to the late years in Wales, a large amount of space in Powys's diaries was devoted to descriptions of, comments on, sympathy with, guilt about tramps, down-and-outs, and men on the dole. There was something about what he called their "endurance"—a quality he also admired in animals—that chimed deeply with his philosophy of "in spite of": his struggle to be happy in spite of the pain, the poverty, the unhappiness he saw within and around him. If their own worries were perhaps too close and the world's woe too remote, the plight of the tramps he saw every day on his walks could and did become a symbol of a life of quiet desperation, against which all his magician's arts were directed. There were tramps enough around Corwen.

> Yesterday on the road by Ty-n-Cefn I met the miserablest ragged young tramp (about 28 to 30) I have ever seen. His coat and trousers were in Rags & he had no over-coat, nor had he even a shirt or a hand kerchief—as they all have—round his neck and last night, tho' a tiny bit warmer than in early morning, was bitter cold. My own enormous Black Coat was supplemented by Aunt Harriet's Black Scarf. . . . I gave him Aunt Harriet's scarf. . . . But when I said, pinching this ragged coat gingerly with finger and thumb, "how cold, how icy, you must be!" he said—speaking King's English—with an indifferent and detached air, like Meredith ab Owen; son of Glyn Dŵr, "I have a very warm singlet on."[85]

When Marian's Peter protested that he gave money to tramps only to satisfy his own ego, Powys explained that if it gave him pleasure and the tramp pleasure, it was unnecessary "to analyse the kind of pleasure (whether moral or immoral) that both of us get."[86] Privately, he felt only self-loathing when he contemplated his own lineage: coming from "5 generations of rich clergy doling out sixpences and used tea-leaves at their back doors."[87]

It was not just tramps and rooks that roused his pity. As the war went on, every day Betty, the little maid, brought them more news of its terrible effects on the people of Corwen they knew. "How the war spreads and spreads—its ripples, as from a great rock heaved into water, break into the most distant lives & down they go—down they go."[88] His "acid-drops" began to "peck, peck, peck, like baby vultures at my waist";[89] as always, he sought assuagement in writing. He began a "New Book of war thoughts" which he intended to be a "War Diary," but it did not go well. He forced himself to go on writing despite a "whoreson lethargy," but increasingly he felt that "my patriotism is simply old-fashioned romantic poetic History-Tripos."[90] Phyllis pointed out that he knew nothing about economics and that he had better stick to a position "which makes the war almost entirely Personal." He proceeded to do so and connects the war with the battle of everyman to practice "a philosophy of our own that helps us in the struggle of life."[91] Whatever the subject, he seemed to apply the same familiar panacea, but he sincerely believed that he had found a philosophical/quasi-religious support system for the dispossessed and the lonely, and his "Kantian conscience" beat the drum for it whenever there was an opportunity. His books of philosophy were in some sense the equivalent of his giving money to tramps—verbal manna from heaven. In fairness, this philosophy was dearly won. He knew his own "too many manias" prevented him from "just enjoying a little nice happiness" so he "forces" himself—not to enjoy, but to "make the gesture of enjoying," something in nature. "When I've enjoyed it . . . I hurl it through the air to the most unhappy person in England, Wales & Scotland whoever he or she may be & conjure and magick & compel & force—how all my healthy spiritual life is 'force' 'force' 'force' (like that Devil Hitler in a way!)—this unhappy unknown to enjoy this electric thrill which I hurl at him."[92] When the time came to give the book a title, Pollinger misread his handwriting and called it *Mortal Strife*. Powys's intended name, "Mental Strife"—after Blake's "I will not cease from mental strife / Nor shall my sword sleep in my hand"—would have been more accurate. The war was forcing him to question his life-illusion that he was a "helper": "We have just looked up Charlatan, Saltimbanque, Mountebank & find they all are what I, Petrushka, am . . . i.e. a Lecturer on sham cures—Quack Cures, for the Soul."[93]

Understandably, he wanted to help those closest to him. Alyse returned to England after Llewelyn's death, and by February 1940 she was back in her old home at Chydyok to face the war and her own ghosts. She wrote in her journal: "A more tranquil landscape could not be imagined. A cuckoo was calling and the larks were singing. It is difficult to believe that the country is at war, and yet I could see battleships at anchor in Weymouth. . . . I see Katie . . . in the garden, her figure both enduring and defenceless; and Gertrude chopping sticks . . . so grave and beautiful."[94] She visited John and Phyllis for a few days in April and thought Phyllis looked "as rare and beautiful as I had remembered her" and John "full of a goodness that seems to have no reserves." While there, Alyse discussed with them her intention to follow up Llewelyn's imaginary autobiography, *Love and Death*, which had been published a few months before his death, with a collection of his letters to friends and relatives. She was "agitated" when Powys suggested she was not the appropriate one to edit his letters but he decided "it is inevitable that Alyse should feel super-sensitive & on the 'qui vive' over me, about Lulu," and that he must respond "quietly, affectionately and without a grain of even hidden hit-back."[95] Phyllis and John wanted the letters to show a Llewelyn "radiant & alive" and feared that Alyse now saw herself as "a Priest of a Dead God."[96] Alyse subsequently asked Louis Wilkinson to edit the letters, but she did keep firm control over what was included and excluded.[97] Whether she deified Llewelyn is open to question. In the immediate emotional aftermath of his death, she strove to present him, both as a writer and as an individual, in the best possible light. In that sense, John was right. But she was always more than the "gallant little Simple Intellectual"[98] Powys thought her. In November 1942, Alyse sent Phyllis her journal and Phyllis found it "powerful & terrible & tragic." Her portrayal of Llewelyn in her earlier novels was unflattering but honest, and her massive ambivalence toward Llewelyn and her life with him is on every page of her journal, the following only one of many similar entries: "16 April 1941: Llewelyn was in my heart's deep core, my *only* life, my only reality, a love that has despoiled my life and even in death pursues and destroys me." It was Llewelyn's romantic vision of love as he portrays it in *Love and Death* that was "simple" when compared to this.

1941 proved to be another appalling winter. They could only afford to keep one fire going, the pipes froze frequently, and the electricity was more often off than on. In between chores, Phyllis was reading the Muirs' translation of Kafka's diary. Kafka was one of her favourite authors, along with Radiguet and Gogol. Powys opined that she and Kafka were alike in their unhappiness "in that they could have avoided it." He felt that her unhappiness as a young girl "was external (not like Theodore's). But she <u>couldn't</u> face it. The T. T. recognized that she <u>couldn't</u> <u>live</u> <u>save</u> <u>her</u> <u>sophisticated</u> <u>life</u>." There was no apparent irony lurking, either in this view or in his praise: "Yesterday after working all day sans cesse with boiling water soaked rags held to pipes . . . the T. T. has won a great American Victory & has got the hot water running."[99] Invariably, she would, in turn, lash out that he had always considered his manias more important than her happiness. It was, he thought, "a very very old dilemma a pitiful dilemma that in a large issue would be a tragic dilemma."[100] The edginess was due in part to sheer poverty. The faith they had placed in Pollinger to handle their publishing affairs had been diminishing ever since the *Maiden Castle* fiasco. When Dent turned down *Mortal Strife*, Pollinger tried Jonathan Cape, who offered £50 for it. When even Powys objected to this miserable advance for a year's work, Pollinger got a revised offer of £75 but only on condition that it be totally revised. Phyllis was "violently opposed" to the Cape offer. She felt the book had been written for "easier going people—not specialists" and thought it would do better as a Penguin book.[101] Powys went ahead and accepted the Cape offer. It was left to Louis Wilkinson to explain to his friend that he had, once again, signed a contract with an option offer and now owed this publisher another non-fiction. Their spirits were raised slightly when, in March 1941, the Simon & Schuster edition of *Owen* arrived, "beautifully published" in two volumes. Pollinger had not been able to find an English publisher, presumably partly because of the paper shortage during the war and partly because of the length. After eight publishers turned it down, Pollinger wrote to suggest a "gentleman's agreement" with the Bodley Head rather than a contract. This time Phyllis put her foot down and would not allow John to even consider such a thing. The agent did finally get a contract from the Bodley Head but the offer was a risible £20 for the English rights to *Owen Glendower*. After "an agitating argument between the T. T. & the man of iron (not of iron then!)"[102] John posted the signed contract.

Frances Gregg had continued to move her mother and daughter from place to place, despite breast cancer and a weak heart valiantly striving to make enough money to keep them all going. In February 1941, she got a job with NAAFI (the Navy, Army & Air Force Institutes) and moved them to Plymouth and into the eye of the storm. Her son Oliver wrote John to say all three had been killed on April 21, 1941 during a bombing raid. Powys recorded the event in a kind of numbed confusion. The day after he heard of her death, a new fetish started. He began to record in his diary which walking stick he took on his daily walk, the characteristic of that stick, and its associations, "so I shall always link up the Spirit of Frances with my Fourteen (or Fortnight) STICKS."[103] At this same time he also began to "record the colour of my Ties as well as the nature of my Sticks," not, he wrote, out of narcissism, but "out of pure <u>Animism</u> for my <u>sticks</u> are my <u>Idols</u>; and my ties are living sans-doll-Rags."[104]

With Frances's death, the reality of the war became ever more present to him. He worried about his brothers—the fall of France in June 1940 meant that the Germans were only seventy miles away from the Dorset coast. Weymouth and Portland became military controlled zones in 1940, and hundreds of battleships arrived in Portland Harbour. As a prelude to a planned invasion of England, Germany attacked British coastal defences, radar stations, and shipping. Sherborne, where Littleton still lived, suffered badly during the Battle of Britain, but the coastal towns were also bombed. Following its defeat in the daylight skies, the Luftwaffe bombed at night, guided by their incendiary bombs. Chaldon and Chydyok were literally surrounded by air, army, and navy bases, munition factories, and radar installations, all attracting German attacks.[105]

Despite his perception of himself as ever "waiting for death," when war broke out Theodore decided to move inland to Mappowder, out of the danger-zone. As if to punish himself for his cowardice, he chose a small dilapidated cottage by the church which was, according to John, "the very house where his <u>Father</u> & <u>mine</u> went to school & was <u>miserable</u>."[106] The three women—Gertrude, Katie, and Alyse—were left to their own devices in the isolated cottage on the downs. Their own constant battle was to grow enough food in their garden and to find enough fuel for minimal warmth during the war. Through the long terrifying nights in early 1941 the air raid sirens sounded almost continuously, and on May 22, 1941; a German plane came down in the field adjoining the house, killing two men. Not only was this area in a direct bomb path, but they need only walk a quarter of a mile to the coast to see the military activity at Weymouth. In her dispassionate fashion, Alyse recorded the heavy bombing.

> Last night the Germans came over dropping their bombs all about us. We saw a chain of fires on the heath. The sky was filled with searchlights converging from all directions. Gertrude and I walked into the corn ricks. They stood up majestic in the velvety darkness of the night, as large as the monoliths of Stonehenge, and of a monumental beauty—the corn of man against the destruction of man; and all about us, like shafts of hell fire, restless and inexorable, the lights plied their way through the eternal heavens.[107]

The letters from Gertrude and Katie to Jack during the war illustrate well their different personalities. Gertrude's were full of warm calmness, usually speaking of her bees and her breadmaking. Even the bombs are approached domestically. When over 100 incendiary bombs were dropped in the next field, she can only say "What a mercy these little dangerous tubes were not dropped on the house and the barn," and thinks she should have the old Montacute watering can filled and ready for such an event.[108] Katie's letters were much more dramatic: "Weymouth had an awful attack . . . so many people killed & injured. . . . Two bombs fell at the bottom of the White Nose & it all became so bad . . . that we went out to our Dug Out."[109] Although Powys admitted that he was scared of "meeting Parachutists on my lonely walks with Nature,"[110] when Katie wrote to her brother describing how she "hid under that familiar Sea Wall at Lodmoor from an air battle," he was perturbed by her reaction. "I felt I could not believe that she didn't feel the sort of pride we as a family inherit from my father in any sort of warlike adventure."[111] No bombs or passing parachutists fell on Corwen, and the former leader of the Volentiā Army wrote thankfully to a friend, "Here I am in this safe place, knowing nothing of the war."[112] Without a hint of mockery, Gertrude wrote to him in November 1942, "What a lovely walk you must have had in that calm morning. Alyse & I went to Bat's Head when we got there all the sirens at Weymouth & Portland went off. And our planes went out to drive the Germans from a convoy that was coming round Portland. We tried to count the ships in the convoy each with a balloon tied to it."[113]

Despite the war, visitors, almost always young men, would cast up at their Corwen door. Some they found stimulating, some pathetic, others simply a drain on their physical and emotional resources. These admirers were more often than not unemployed, and Powys would subsequently write to friends asking if they could help to find them work. He was well aware that he was "the Cult of certain young men" who treated him "almost as Charmides treated Socrates,"[114] but he always vehemently denied that he had himself any homosexual tendencies. However, late in life he wondered to Louis "in some very subtle psychic or . . . cerebral or mental, or what the Xtians call in a 'spiritual' sense—how far am I homo-sexual????"[115] Since it was usually his essays, written to help unhappy individuals to cope with their circumstances, that attracted them, he felt he must spend precious time responding to these nonentities and encouraging them. John described this in one of his novels as a "super-imposed destiny"—to be "a formidable protector of the imaginatively eccentric, the emotionally weak, the mentally disturbed, the nervously deranged. And the curious thing was that all his life such abnormal persons had felt this, and had instinctively clung to him for protection."[116] One such visitor was a seventeen-year-old boy with "devilish brain-sick trouble" who turned up on July 2, 1941.

> He feels weak and languid and can only eat and drink and smoke & sleep & talk sans cesse about books and bookish ideas & writers. . . . He adores milk & laps it up—also tea with all the sugar I give him and the sweeter it is the better. . . . In all these ways he is exactly like myself & therefore a Rival in the House. . . . Thro' wall I heard him pacing the room & standing and then listening. O I hoped the T. T. would come back. Presently I heard him whispering "John! John!" At this I lost all control idiotic weakling that I am!—without any of the excuses of this boy, who is mentally sick; whereas I am only uncontrolled & a doddering old fool! But all I did was to shout & I doubt if he had any knowledge of or interest in what I did! Anyway the T. T. took him off then. . . . When they had gone I had a stab of one of the Worst Terrors I've ever had, a Nervous Panic Terror.[117]

As usual, the experience, which offended his sense of himself as the magi-cian-helper, occasioned an outburst of self-accusation: "The SERIOUS thing in our life at present is that the T. T. can't get enough to eat, . . . no! no! do you hear the T. T. can't get enough food. . . . But meanwhile the selfish man has 3 eggs every day and five bottles of milk & as much white bread as I require and as much sugar."[118] A neighbor kept the chickens that provided the eggs, and this provoked another scene. Another "rival in the house"—the little boy from next door—roused all the old childhood fury of being one of "too many": "I disgraced myself by my weak lack of Self Control when I howl yes! yes, when I set up a howl because DAVID wanted to feed the chickens with me!" The child and the child's impulses live on. Belatedly remembering that he was almost seventy, the next day when David, aged four, turned up again, "I had to behave as the eldest of eleven."[119]

Some visitors became good friends. Gilbert Turner arrived with a friend in May 1942. By 1943 they "adored him." The thirty-year-old librarian had the delightful tact to come for brief periods only. More importantly, he gave rather than received. He offered to do some typing for Powys, an offer which was grate-fully accepted, as otherwise Phyllis had to do it. As chief librarian at Richmond, Gilbert was of inestimable help in getting him the necessary books and informa-tion during the war when other resources became inaccessible. Powys worried sometimes that he might be "taking advantage," but the friendship was as impor-tant to Turner as it was to them. The warmth of it is evident in the some 450 letters John Cowpy wrote this friend between 1942 and 1962, and after his death, Gilbert remained Phyllis's champion and confidant.

An older waif and stray was the fifty-year-old Jewish bookseller George Lionel Lewin, escaping the London Blitz. Lewin turned up at Cae Coed in the autumn of 1940, and Powys promptly made him the unhappy hero of a new novel, tentatively called "Edeyrnion." Presumably this idea arose out of his continuing "mental strife" over the war and its atrocities. References to the conflict—from the campaign in Crete to the burning of books in Nazi-occupied Europe to the bombing of Birkenhead, sit uneasily beside the story of "the bombed-out for-eigner" and his lost love, "Nesta-Fair," now married to a man of "seventy, if he was a day." Powys dropped the book after writing "a very very long & a very com-plicated First Chapter."[120] Phyllis suggested that he write instead a book about "myself as I am now exactly." Two months later, he had written only two chap-ters, and when Phyllis told him that "the Dangerous Mixture of Ballad Romance and Philosophical Analysis & Irony & Poignancy Must be stopped,"[121] he abandoned this second attempt at "modern realism"[122] even more quickly. The extant man-uscript suggests this was a wise decision. In any case, Powys had no need of a modern novel to describe himself as he was "now exactly"; it was all in his diary.

In the meantime, he had another project in mind. It is marvelous to watch how, in the secretive and sexual ways of the imagination, a fictional idea is first conceived. In August 1941, he suddenly began to report that when he put his head in water with his eyes open—something he thinks will cure his failing eyes—he sees a short twig "with sometimes blossom or bud, like what sprouted from Aaron's Rod, at its top, coming out of it."[123] Out of the rod of magical potency came this "thin tremulous offspring" eventually to grow into his novel *Porius*. Initially he intended to write another "great long heavy massive deep Historical Novel,"[124] this time about the epoch from 475 to 525 and centreing around the figure of Boethius. During the remainder of 1941, he read an astonishing amount about this philosopher, as well as about the Dark Ages of Britain, and Wales in particular. Although he soon discovered "romantic modern and Magical Wordsworthian and original personal elements in Boethius,"[125] in the novel as it was finally written there are only eight specific references to the neoplatonist in the entire thirty-three chapters. Phyllis "twigged" to what was happening: "She has divined by instinct what a Prophetess the T. T. is! that I want a Welsh hero for my Boethius Romance & would, yes, like a son of ELISEG."[126] It was inevitable that the story would take place in and around Corwen so once again he had a hero, a period, and a location. However, the novel, begun in January 1942, was to take the seventy-year-old seven years to write. Given the financial, physical, and emotional struggles of the next years, it is astonishing that it was ever written at all. But it could not *not* have been written, for this novel was what his whole life had been steering toward. Into it he decanted not only a half-century of reading and thought, but "my soul & psyche & inner essence."[127]

The constant visitors and letter-writing meant that at this period he had, on average, no more than two hours of writing time a day. His "acid-drops" were always troublesome and his eyes were inclined to "rebel and go on strike," with the right eye particularly "all bleary and funny." Phyllis decided that the only cure for both troubles was to turn away visitors and answer all his letters herself. This "Grand Regime" did not last long—both activities were in some way necessary to him—but it resulted in their both now accepting that she was the "dominant ruler of the House & defender of its Inmates."[128] This was no easy task, as the effects of war became ever more severe. By 1942 there was drastic rationing of clothes, coal, gas, electricity. They were a mile and a half from the town and running errands and carrying heavy baskets up the steep hill for both households drained her frail strength. She seemed to have a constant bad cold or neuralgia throughout the war and her mother and aunt were frequently ill. She often felt, she said, "like a dying Bumble Bee on the last of the Ragworts swaying in the wind & rain!"[129] This was a rather poetic description of an exhaustion that would frequently erupt into a more vocal "Fit of Screaming Hysterics." This release of frustration would leave her "all relaxeed and well & happy," something Powys found a "mystery."[130] He usually took her explosions fairly calmly and with a certain humor: "Last Night the T. T. had Hysterics over Addyer Scott the Rich Book collector. . . . The T. T. flung 3 of his precious Bibliophilic Treasures <u>like</u> <u>balls</u> about the walls & floor of our room! Aye! I had such a hunt for them when she had gone to bed!"[131] Despite the hysterics and the rages, she was, in her own way, a wonderful storyteller. After seven years, they knew everyone in Corwen, and she would come back in a merry mood with some "amusing mockingly pessimistic tale" or an "inspired description of objects such as iron spikes & dusty mats & floors everywhere." This little Welsh town would suddenly become "a regular Balzacian town! full of smoulderingly rich & fathom-deep involved recedings and withdrawings."[132] Powys paid her the compliment of saying that it was like listening to "the Henog," the official court storyteller, "in my own story."[133]

He had hardly begun this story when he had "MONEY PANIC." He blamed himself for having "always dodged, evaded, shirked, & avoided such responsibility," and "leaving all our money-affairs entirely to the T. T. & others; leaving it to everybody—except myself!"[134] He once again wrote Max Schuster, "the only one of all my Publishers who is consistently friendly & who recalls our existence."[135] Schuster promptly commissioned a book about old age, and sent them "250 dollars for advance royalty on any of your books past, present, & future."[136] Powys also wrote Pollinger, urging him to "get me one of these paperbacked series to write for any publisher he can interest and on any subject under the sun!"[137] Their friend James Hanley, who lent them money whenever he could afford it, strongly advised Powys to leave Pollinger for an agent who would be livelier about getting more contracts and better money for his books. Hanley was not the first to urge this, or the last, but "I shall of course stick to Pollinger."[138] This was not altogether a sense of loyalty. Whether it was tramps or Pollinger, what motivated him, he confessed to Louis, was "my fear of people (of everybody)," and "my propitiation of them (of Mister Everybody)."[139] Although he berated himself for being "so scared of Publishers & Agents,"[140] he had no illusions about them. He told his friend Ben Roberts that they were only interested in best-selling novelists. "I know these publishers . . . and they are *all*—I say *all*—the same."[141]

Aware that he was getting into a state both about the war and about money, Phyllis proposed that they start a paper. They were to call it "*Tempus* or *The North Wales Malignant.*" This was one of her more bizarre ideas, but it did serve to steady his "weak fussy nervous complaints & groans and disintegrated all-to-bits soul."[142] He wrote several pieces for it and further calmed his nerves by copying all the war news from the newspapers into his diary in prodigious detail. There were some brief respites in their worries about money. In February, they took a rare day trip to Rhyll and were "entranced" to be by the sea again. He wrote in his diary, "The T. T. & the 'Man of Iron' enjoy a HONEYMOON."[143] "Honeymoon" was perhaps not *le mot juste*. Four days later he noted that "for the 1st Valentine's Day since San Francisco I did NOT make love to the T. T." He told Phyllis that "EROS had left my PRICK and gone into my BONES."[144] He does not record her reaction to this announcement.

All this while, it was Littleton who kept them going financially. In October 1942 they had an opportunity to repay his generosity with their sympathy. His wife Mabel had died from cancer a month before, and he arrived for a visit of two weeks. Marian wrote, with compassionate understanding, "That old love you have for one another will stand by him now more than ever."[145] While Littleton was with them, a birthday parcel for John from Elizabeth Myers arrived—a Latin Virgil and her photograph. Littleton already knew about this woman. In the previous January John wrote his brother that a "very brilliant young writer"[146] was going to review *Owen Glendower* for John Middleton Murry's *Adelphi*, and John began corresponding with Myers shortly after that. He also showed Littleton one of her letters in which she praised both John Cowper and Arthur Waugh— something John knew well would endear Elizabeth to his brother, as Waugh was a former student and friend of Littleton. Elizabeth Myers had made her way in the world through determination and a sharp intelligence, and by this period she was an accomplished reviewer, publisher's reader, and writer of short stories. Waugh, by then chairman of Chapman & Hall, was about to publish her first novel, *A Well Full of Leaves*. Powys was later to refer to her "strange power over people"; certainly she had an ability to contrive an intimacy almost immediately. She was learning Greek, and as soon as she discovered Powys's love for Homer, she pressed him to criticize her translations. She reckoned that this appeal to his scholarship would do the trick—and it did. Most of Powys's correspondence at this time was written on automatic pilot but his letters to Elizabeth were quite different. She stimulated him intellectually without threatening him with her cleverness (a word of disapprobation in the Powys family) and he returned the favour with letters of unusual candor. He was also extremely grateful for her generosity in this period when they wanted for even the most basic things. She overwhelmed them with her thoughtfully chosen gifts—razor blades, writing paper, cigarettes, scarves, ration coupons, clothes for Phyllis, valuable and needed books, even nail scissors.[147]

It may have been Elizabeth's history of tuberculosis that first attracted Powys's interest, and he wrote her pages of detailed advice, much as he had once written to his Lulu. He urged her to go to New Mexico for a cure, telling her "if Llewelyn had gone there instead of to the Cold Storage of snow-cages-for-squirrels blood-tinged vomit-tinged manure-tinged of that tricky Death-Trap of a Switzerland (where no one ever is cured) he would be alive now."[148] Another frank letter was in response to her question whether there were any topics he preferred not to discuss. He replied that there were only two danger zones: "Anything to do with my Mother I am the devil of a Malicious & very Dangerous Withdrawer over. That is the really important Taboo. But also and Second— only far less dangerous—than that, I am still a bit touchy about My Son & His Mother." He admitted, "We are an EXTREMELY CLANNISH family—only we all are afraid of Theodore and treat him with more reverence & respect & consideration than we treat each other."[149]

After Littleton returned to Dorset, John began what he called his "pot boiling campaign." With only enough money left to last them a few more months and an awareness that it was "the hell of a job to get some more these war years,"[150] he decided the best plan of attack was to write reviews and short articles. Reluctantly, he shortened the time he devoted to writing letters and his diary, and to his "lessons" in Greek and Welsh. The two-hour-long walks remained a physical and mental necessity. Hanley got him a commission from Reginald Moore, editor of *Modern Reading*, to write an article on *Finnegans Wake*. It took him a month to write, and Phyllis had to point out that an essay of 5,000 words, for which he read not only *Finnegans Wake* but several books of criticism, had brought him only £6. In November he sent off his Old Age book to Schuster and began a short book on Dostoevsky which had also been asked for, and which took him a further four months to complete. Simon and Schuster did not take either the Old Age book or the Dostoevsky—an ominous sign of things to come.

Despite the seriousness of his own situation, Powys was always remarkably generous in giving his time to help other writers. Between 1937 and 1947, he wrote no less than thirteen introductions, forewords, and "blurbs," not only for relatives and friends, but for imploring strangers. ("I am now composing a Blurb of praise (extravagant but absolutely nice) on 'Cleanliness & Godliness' by Reginald Reynolds; which I like particularly, particularly! It is in Praise of Good Privies.")[151] More often than not, he made strenuous efforts to champion these aspiring poets and writers.[152] Huw Menai sent him "a heap of poems," and Powys chose fifty, wrote a preface, and set about seeing "what I can do" to find a publisher.[153] He reported to their mutual friend, Benson Roberts, that Elizabeth Myers was "helping me nobly . . . with getting our old Huw's New Book of Poems taken and Published as well!"[154] Another considerable drain on his time was the ex-schoolmaster-turned-poet, Redwood Anderson. Beginning with the usual adulatory letter, from 1938 onwards Anderson made long visits to see John Cowper and Phyllis, and in 1943 he came to live in Corwen. His various marital crises and his "erotic nerves" required much attention on their part; in addition, for several years every Sunday evening would be spent listening to Redwood reading aloud his long poems. Sometimes a long-suffering Powys would report that he was "absolutely done in by dear Redwood's 'Pome' which took from Nine to Twelve to read (reading steadily)." On occasion he would find himself "in the vexing & shame-faced situation of cursing a poem as physiological & Swinburnian which I had formerly—well! to confess truly—a week ago praised as—well! as very poetical."[155]

His attempts to concentrate exclusively on writing pot-boilers did not last long. By now he had acquired an excellent reading knowledge of the Welsh language and he soon resumed his reading and re-reading of the early texts that had preserved his beloved *Mabinogion*, as well as modern Welsh newspapers.[156] He always found some time to read Homer—his "breviary." He would write regularly from noon to one o'clock in his diary, adding bits as the day progressed, and, in addition, wrote up to fourteen letters a day. His eyes would pack up by evening and Phyllis would then read to him for an hour or two after she had had dinner

with her mother and aunt next door and had settled them for the night. His preference was always for the older classics, such as Dickens and Scott, although
Dostoevsky was his favourite novelist, followed by Henry James; hers was for
modern novels. She ordered library books from various book clubs—Smiths for
herself, the Times Library for the ladies next door. However, over the next few
years it was Gilbert Turner who provided many of the books they requested, varying from the novels of Carson McCullers, C. P. Snow, and Osbert Sitwell, war
diaries, science fiction, critical essays, philosophy, and religion. They ploughed
their way through Berdyaev, Maritain, Niebuhr and were "absorbed" by Sartre's
The Age of Reason, although he confessed to Turner, "I really cannot for my life
understand what Existentialism really is!"[157] C. S. Lewis excited his wrath and he
insisted on referring to *The Screwtape Letters* as "the Tape-worm Letters by
Torquemada." As the war progressed they sought distraction in lighter material
and especially enjoyed Simenon's Maigret detective novels ("God! we are
becoming Detective Fans. Think of that! ho! ho! ho!")[158] By the time the war
ended, they had resorted to reading aloud to each other any popular novel and
he admitted that "to tell you the truth I seem to prefer the Works of Mrs. Norah
Lofts to my own"[159]—something that must happen to all writers eventually. He
found intensely irritating Phyllis's habit of reading alone into the small hours of
the morning after he had gone to bed, and then falling asleep in her chair. After
her death, dozens of small notebooks were found containing lists of books that
she had read, or perhaps intended to read. Certainly his diary confirms that in
these years she did get through a great deal of the most recent fiction, as well as
books on politics, biology, philosophy, history. She also listened avidly to modern symphonic and ballet music on Aunt Harriet's radio, another practice the
tone-deaf John disapproved of.

They continued to follow war events closely, subscribing to three English
daily papers, as well as his Welsh newspapers. He read *Punch* every week, which,
he told Louis, gave "an elderly old-fashioned upper-middle-class gent like me the
best idea of this present epoch in history that could be got!"[160] Their views on the
war veered as widely and changed as often as those of most ordinary people.
Initially in favour of Chamberlain's position, later what he called his "patriotism
led Powys to support the war." Many of his young disciples were pacifists and
would have been astonished to read his view that they were "priggish pharasaic
selfish moralists," but he admitted to Ben Roberts that "I only talk like this to
people like yourself well over military age! To young Pacifists I offer sympathy."[161]
He decided that his reaction to Katie's fears and his disciples' pacifism were both
grounded in the early influence of Aytoun's *Lays of the Scottish Cavaliers*.[162] He
and Louis exchanged opinions about various "isms." His long friendship with
Emma Goldman and his own predilections made him sympathetic to the anar-
chist cause, but he considered that "they are too good to be true." He felt
"intense and emotional gratitude to the Russian people for having quite literally
& undisputedly saved our malleable Capitalistic Democracy from Hitler's cast-

iron 'master-race,'" but was worried about "this new Stalinian Communism." He decided that his gratitude to Stalin in this case was "the gratitude of a man who has been saved from a rhinoceros by a tiger."[163] It is difficult to know how serious-ly he meant such sentiments as "Aren't the dole men, aren't the tramps, aren't the old-age 10/- pensioners, aren't the dwellers in the suppressed, I mean dis-tressed areas, really and truly happier than [is] the common herd under Stalin and . . . Hitler?" He concludes that "the armies of the homeless and the unfed" are "happier under Imperialistic Capitalism" than under a Nazi or Communist regime.[164] He loathed Franco particularly and anyone who ventured to disagree was raged at. Nicholas Ross remembered that a careless remark caused "such a spasm of anger in Powys that he dropped his walking stick on the ground and ran across the bull-filled meadow cursing and shouting 'Bloody Franco.'" Ross added, "Apart from being terrified of bulls, I was even more terrified of Powys in his fit."[165] Temper tantrums were not part of Powys's life-illusion, and he usually kept them well-suppressed in public. In private, Powys's explosions were often as vio-lent as Phyllis's.

The pot-boiling campaign went on. Cape accepted his Old Age book and published it in January 1944 as *The Art of Growing Old*. Pollinger had managed to get a commission from the Bodley Head to write a book, *Introducing Rabelais*. Thinking he could finish the Rabelais by the end of the summer, John again took up his novel on the Dark Ages and worked on both of them on alternate days. In fact, the Rabelais proved much more onerous than he expected. It took him a year to do selected translations and a biographical sketch, and another year to write an "interpretation of his genius and his religion," so it was not finished until December 1944. With so little time to spend on its writing, much of his planning and thinking about his "Dark Age Romance" was done while on his walks. However, he read the first half of the first chapter to Phyllis on Easter Sunday of 1943, and he was delighted and relieved that she liked it.

Despite this happy beginning, the many phobias he was mostly successful in controlling came bubbling up once again. They were serious and took up much of his psychic energy. One of the worst at this time was what he called his "breathing terror" when he would become convinced he would stop breathing unless he took each breath consciously and deliberately. This first manifested itself in November 1937 and became steadily more frightening to him. "It was before Dawn that my attack began and it lasted for about an Hour. It is MEN-TAL: it is a definite form of INSANITY far the worst I have known in my life."[166] Remembering his long-ago treatment of Littleton, he called it his "strangle hor-ror." His worry about his eyes caused newer manias to surface, and his descrip-tions of them, complete with underlines and capitals, are always graphic.

> 10 June 1943: I strained my eyes & from the thought of Winking & Blinking eyes or eyelashes or eye-lids chiefly eye-lids going up & down up & down up & down up & down flicker clicker bicker wicker ticker sicker— one dam came open of all the Manias of Horror & Fear such as tape-worms

& spiders & centipedes & Masturbations & all self-conscious bodywarm lovingnesses & it needed all my art of forgetting & all my philosophy to cope with these DEVILS.

In July he was forced once again to appeal to Littleton, who sent him, by return post, a present of £100. That got them through to the end of October, when once again "the T. T. posted my Begging Letter to Old Littleton just married & returned from honeymoon imploring him to lend me a 4 per cent the sum of One Hundred Pounds for we have almost nothing left!"[167] This diary entry requires a bit of explanation.

When Littleton was at Corwen the year before, amongst Elizabeth Myers's letters to John was a note addressed to Littleton, commiserating with him on the death of his wife. Powys told her how much this had pleased Littleton but went on "I don't know whether old Littleton will or won't try to answer your noble letter. I hope you'll forgive him if he doesn't."[168] In fact, Littleton responded immediately, and two months later she wrote John that she intended to visit his brother, to which he answered, "the sooner the better." Elizabeth went to Sherborne to visit Littleton for six days in June 1943. When she left, Littleton gave her a copy of his autobiography. She not only came back with *The Joy of It*, she came back engaged to him. It seems to have taken John a few weeks to catch on to this, and his eventual congratulations to her were muted, with just the faintest touch of malice. "Well my dear Elizabeth, What a delight & joy to me is this great News! And think of it coming just on the news of the Invasion of Europe." The short note ends rather cryptically: "Words of great thundering omens & auspices & divinations (of luck and of ill-luck) are too mysterious & perilous, so let us say: 'Jack shall have Jill Naught shall go ill The Man shall have his mare again and all shall be well!' Yrs John."[169] Littleton, aged sixty-nine, and Elizabeth, aged thirty, were married in London on October 7, 1943, during one of the worst air-raids; Stevie Smith wrote a witty and tender poem about this May-December wedding night.[170]

Elizabeth was what John Cowper called "outspoken." Marian, more blunt, said that she was always "up in arms about everything." Even Elizabeth's admiring friend, Eleanor Farjeon, admitted "Her militant spirit was rampant."[171] She displayed this combativeness almost immediately after marriage. Louis Wilkinson's comments in *Swan's Milk* and in *Welsh Ambassadors* about the Powys brothers and sisters, and particularly about Mary Cowper and Charles Francis, had long rankled with Littleton, and Elizabeth now took up the cudgels for her husband. John was in a very difficult position. He did not agree with Littleton's ten-year anger with Louis; however, he owed this brother not only loyalty but a considerable amount of money. Furthermore, he was broke again. On December 15, he wrote an astonishing thirty-two-page letter to Elizabeth. It was, in effect, a begging letter—asking for her "most concentrated wise thoughtful powerful & MAGICAL help." In it he says (several times) that he is so obliged to Littleton for his gifts and loans, but he didn't want to come to feel "like Coleridge that dubious & damaged daemon dependent on Robert Southey." He goes on, "Since I write very fast that is when I am writing my semi-demi philosophical theological psychological moral immoral Tracts for the Times, I see no reason why if you live and P lives & I live I should [not] get on my own feet again." By extraordinary indirection, he asks her, in effect, to be his agent. However, he says, "I refuse to hurt Pollinger's feelings . . . or to break with him or even to contemplate leaving him & being really & truly 'run' by our little Auntie Liza-Lu!" After several more pages of divagation, he finally gets to the point: "But there's no scruple in me (naturally not!) about arranging all first & then after all is arranged tell my friend Laurence i.e. Mr. Pollinger . . . and letting him . . . finish the transaction & receive the cheque or cheques from the Publisher and forward the same to me minus (naturally) his ten per cent." He ends this letter, "32 pages! & my eyes have 'stood up' to it as I was by way of persuading my new little Auntie Liza-Lu to 'live for us.'"[172] Most unusually, there is no indication in his diary that he wrote this letter. Possibly he did not want Phyllis to know he had written it. She was already "terribly upset in her Red Indian Independence by my dependence on Charity."[173]

Elizabeth answered this extraordinary missive very quickly, saying that she would be happy to help and that "there will be no need for the feelings of that shark Pollinger to be hurt." She then went on to explain that she had been asked to write a review of *The Letters of Llewelyn Powys*, edited by Louis Wilkinson, which had come out on October 15. She warned John that the editor had told her she had written too favourable a review, so she had "re-written my review with criticism, but in pointing out Llewelyn's faults I have been careful not to take from the tree the leaves as well as the caterpillars. . . . I'm afraid Alyse is going to be upset but I can't help it if she is."[174]

To an outsider, Myers's review in the January 1944 issue of the *New English Weekly* appears balanced and objective. She wrote, "Llewelyn Powys is not well served by the inclusion of too many of his indifferent schoolday letters, those ventilating certain bovine indiscretions during his sojourn in Africa, and a careful editor would have pruned the too-frequent references to temperature readings." But she also wrote, "Taken as a whole, these letters release the bright torrents of felicity, naturalness, and faith in vitalism which so distinguished Llewelyn Powys's life."[175] By a most unfortunate coincidence, Alyse had been asked by the editor of the *Adelphi* to write a review of Elizabeth's highly acclaimed novel, *A Well Full of Leaves*, at the same time. Marianne Moore, who had followed Alyse as the managing editor of the *Dial*, once referred to Alyse's "delicately lethal honesty,"[176] and the punchline in this review was "She seems to look upon life through the shocked, wide awake, suffering eyes of a precocious, highly-strung child."[177]

Despite her warning, when John saw Myers's review, he was "very very very disturbed by Elizabeth's attack on Lulu & on Louis and on his letters." It made, he said, "a fatal impression on me."[178] The next day he wrote Elizabeth,[179] beginning with effusive thanks for their Christmas presents, then coolly taking back everything he had said in the December 15, letter: "nothing would induce me to—(it's a rigid puritanical very wise principle my dear Elizabeth with me) to have your publisher publish anything of mine while you are, so to say, one of its—whatever you are! . . . No no my dear Elizabeth you misunderstood me." Eventually he gets on to the second reason for writing—her review of *The Letters of Llewelyn Powys*. He writes that he is not himself "in the least touchy" about reviews, but that in any case he holds the opinion that reviews are unimportant ephemera and that he agrees with Tennyson: "'Irresponsible ignorant reviewers' is what old Tennyson called the whole lot of them." He then goes on to say that he thinks it is a great mistake for relatives to review each others' works.

Up to this point in the twenty-nine-page letter, he has not said what it is *about* her review that has disturbed him. Eventually he gets to the point: "I cannot help feeling what Llewelyn would feel if he read the words 'ventilating bovine indiscretions!'" The letter that caused all the trouble was one that Llewelyn wrote to John from Africa dated 6 February 1915, in which he mentions visiting a sick native and touching the thigh of the native's "Bibi" [Bebi].[180] It was the kind of jejune letter that Llewelyn and John regularly wrote each other at that time. Powys thought perhaps Elizabeth had misunderstood, and in another letter, tried to explain. "But do listen my dear Elizabeth. That girl on that page you talk of wasn't a child at all! You've got that quite wrong. 'Bebi' means the chap's wife not his daughter. The word 'Bebi' doesn't have anything to do with baby." He then went on, "But even if your interpretation at its worst were true it still remains according to my view that we ought in a person's letters to get the bad as well as the good side of him. Surely we want to get him as closely as possible as he was? But this will land me soon—indeed has already!—in my old argument with old Littleton about being presented to the world & to posterity at your best or at your best & worst!"[181]

Powys was really in a cleft stick. Neither Littleton *nor* Alyse, however bitterly they were now quarreling, shared his intrepid view of the desirability of presenting a person "as he was." With few exceptions, only the most unobjectionable of Llewelyn's letters to friends and relatives were chosen in the *Collected Letters*. Even those that were included have had indiscreet sentences firmly scribbled out in Alyse's hand. Given her attempts to present Llewelyn in the best possible light, it is astonishing that this particular letter slipped into the book in the first place. It turns out that it was Phyllis who selected "for Alyse Gregory various ones among the perfectly free shameless and aye! aye! so full of school-boy laughing-fits letters of Llewelyn to me."[182] Presumably Phyllis chose this one because they wanted Llewelyn to be seen as "radiant and alive." Only Alyse's high regard for Phyllis would have led her to accept her judgement in this case. Similarly, when Littleton edited a collection of Elizabeth Myers's letters after *her* death, any that did not contribute to her virtual sainthood were carefully omitted. It is an accident of fate that the Powys/Myers letters, although they remain unpublished, survived at all.

Alyse might not have taken it so badly if *The Letters of Llewelyn* had other-wise received good reviews, but as Powys mentioned to a correspondent a little later, "It is *extraordinary* how Llewelyn's personality has always *infuriated* the typ-ical journalistic and modern newspaper review mind! . . . [It] excites a curious & quite special hostility that is almost like *a physical desire to beat him up!*"[183] However, undeterred by the bad press, six months later Alyse asked Malcolm Elwin—a friend of Louis Wilkinson—to write Llewelyn's biography. John sensed more trouble ahead, "considering all that's involved of (thin ice nothing!) explo-sive ice, thick-ribbed regions of fiery ice!"[184] He was concerned that Elwin would idealize Llewelyn, "making him both more intelligent and wiser than he was," and confided to Gilbert Turner that "Llewelyn scholastically was a 4th form cul-ture. . . . I hope our Mr. Elwin takes that in."[185] He was even more aware that "the great question is to handle Llewelyn's amours with the right touch . . . and yet not depart from the real tragedy or the real comedy they have proved themselves to be!"[186] The rest of the family were circumspect, but when Elwin asked Marian about "the loves of Lulu's youth," she gave him a straight answer: "The only loves that mattered were his conjugal love for Alyse & his passionate love for Gamel Wolsey [sic]." Marian wrote Jack to tell him about this and went on about the Elwin biography: "I think it is a pity to have a Bowdlerised Victorian Life of Lulu. In fact I think it is an outrageous travesty of the truth. Your leaving the women out of your autobiography was bad enough, but characteristic, but for Lulu to have a womanless life except for his wife—seems to give the lie to all his writ-ings."[187] Elwin was faced with a decision every self-respecting biographer dreads: insist that the truth be told, lie, or walk away from the project. Elwin chose to leave Lulu "womanless" in his *Life of Llewelyn Powys.*

Unfortunately, the querelles de turterelles, as Phyllis wittily called them, did not end there. John wrote in his diary, whether sadly or excitedly, "The war extends to the Powys Family & Powys as a kingdom (as happened so often in the early centuries) is DIVIDED against ITSELF."[188] He reports that "Old Littleton himself comes to the Front to defend his Bride from his Brother," and even the pacific Gertrude was drawn into "the Battle of the LETTERS."[189] Alyse appears to have remonstrated with Elizabeth, and Elizabeth fired back: "I had to reduce those soiling little adventures to their right proportion in his life. This I did by using the adjective 'bovine,' not at all a bad word to describe any white man's nether encounters with the black female population of Africa."[190] This letter, which has lain hidden for years, indicates how destructive the row was. If John's disappearance into Wales began the dissolution of "The Powys" from the one into the many, his (presumably) unwitting introduction of Myers into the family certainly finished it.

"Betty arrived with those
wonderful pictures of
Petrushka like Paracelsus
calling up a ghostly T.T.
his Undine"
—JCP Diary, 5 November, 1939.

"a retreat for the old gods."
—JCP Diary, 17 September, 1936.

"I shall ever recall the look of the
beech branches & emerald leaves
against the grey rainy valley &
the look of her face with eyes
rather swollen & blurred & her
expression rather like the portrait
of her by Adrian"
JCP Diary, 3 June, 1936.

"Owen's Modern Biographer tries to reach him to tell him about the New War."

CHAPTER THIRTEEN

PORIUS

1944-1949

OWYS CONTINUED TO FUME OVER MYERS'S "SAVAGELY ABUSIVE"[1] LETTERS, and in the privacy of his diary compared her to Hitler, to Irish bullies (and hence to his *bête noire*, Deacon), until finally she became "one of these Daimoniai."[2] Still, Powys had the remarkable ability of transposing every experience and every person he encountered in real life into a *mabinogi* of his own. He knew that "the agitation over this Row with Elizabeth Myers" had actually helped him with his novel: "Quelle querelles des Femmes are great inspirations to people like me!"[3] In *Porius*, Elizabeth becomes Sibylla, the "ferocious Gwyddyl-Ffichti" woman who foments quarrels. Littleton is transformed into Porius's foster-brother, Rhun, who marries Sibylla. Llewelyn becomes the beautiful, woman-chasing, ultimately doomed Prince Einion.

The quarrel may have given him creative inspiration, but it was calamitous in other respects. He found himself caught between his commitment to the dead Lulu and his gratitude to Littleton for his financial support. Moreover, had Myers become his manager, her influence and energy might have made all the difference to his writing career in the next few years. He was now forced to confront the grimness of his situation—"at most twenty pounds is all I have in the world."[4] He had written in *Autobiography* "Independence! Independence! That is the secret of all philosophy." He was convinced that "the great battle of the future" would be "the struggle of the individual to be himself against the struggle of society to prevent him being himself."[5] Despite setbacks, Powys had always been "himself," writing books as he wanted to write them, living with whom and where he wished. Now he was face to face with an inescapable reality—he was totally dependent on others to keep himself and Phyllis alive.

James Hanley suggested a Civil List pension but John resisted this idea. To friends he gave a variety of different reasons: because Theodore had one and "you know the convolutions of all family & domestic affairs";[6] because "the publicity might be a worry to Mrs Powys and my son." However, he got a mere seventy-five pounds from Cape for *The Art of Growing Old*, and "hack-work pay of 30£" for *Rabelais* which was still not finished.[7] The Dark Ages novel was still in the early stages of writing. Hence, when Louis Wilkinson wrote in February 1944 offering to get him a Royal Literary Society grant if he were not "too proud," he agreed to consider it, although he was afraid that such a grant would diminish his reputation and possibly even lessen his royalties in the long term.[8] Needless to say, Littleton did not like the idea of his brother being in any way indebted to Louis.[9] When John responded that the only alternative was for him to move to London and find lecturing work, Littleton rightly pointed out that this was totally impractical. The Littleton/Louis difficulty was avoided when Jonathan Cape and two other publishers proposed to support the appeal, rather than Louis, and Powys was eventually awarded £100. At the same time, Pollinger finally bestirred himself and extracted a further advance of £90 from Cape on a second printing of *The Art of Growing Old*, and the £160 long owed Powys from the Bodley Head.[10] In June, he received a surprise £280 from "Anonymous Friends of Friends."[11] The grant, the advances, and the gift were "an Indescribable & Abysmal comfort & Relief."[12] Possibly the relief made him forget that his lust had "left my prick" or perhaps it was because his new reading spectacles had "the peculiarity or 'Cynneddf' as it says in the Mabinogion of seeing the T. T. as Perpetually Young." Whatever the reason, he once again found that the T. T. had "the Most Enchanting & the most maddeningly . . . lovely figure in the world," and resumed making love "à la Lulu."

There was, nevertheless, an intensely serious aspect to this naming. Once
Whatever the worry, or the relief, his stability depended on a rigid routine, an important part of which were his walks. He visited daily the Great Willow "that is my Mother-Confessor—my Psycho Analyst Practitioner & my Saviour Tree."[13] The naming of features in the landscape, so characteristic of the Hillsdale period, was now repeated in Wales: the Grouse Gate, the Rocks on the Right, the Homeric Fount, Eliseg's Tower. Soon after he arrived in Corwen, he began dedicating stones after family and friends, and thereafter each would be greeted by touching them with his "magic stick." Eventually, the rock identification assumed absurd proportions—he extended his dedications to the dead, thence to distance acquaintances, to people he wrote to, then to individuals he had not heard of for seventy years. In July 1944, he was delighted by his "newly Dedicated Stone (one of the best it is!) for old Celia Stephenson aged Ninety the first lady to whom taught by Cousin Alice I took off my hat!"

There was, nevertheless, an intensely serious aspect to this naming. Once named and baptized, the rocks become, so he said, "Stone-Souls." In some way they were also repositories of memory. He would be upset because he had difficulty remembering the names of all the characters in this latest novel,[14] but "then I remembered what a mystery is memory!!"[15] Even if the word is lacking, the thing is present: the name of Creiddylad may have escaped his mind, but it was still there in the stone. Naming was still for him a way of keeping control or, in this case, remote control. One of his heroes had read in a book somewhere that "the way to compel spirits to obey you was to know their names."[16] As the magician he now considered himself, he could call on powerful spirits to assist him in his helper role.

The rock naming and the long prayers that accompanied the rock touching were "forced on me by my conscience" "to help the people in Pain of Mind & Body." However he ruefully admitted that "my imagination & my manias and my realism & my love of fiction soon forgot the Main Purpose in the <u>expressions</u> of that purpose so that I have added a vast Accretion of superogatory unessentials to these Prayers; until the unessentials have driven out the essentials."[17]

Many of the rituals that always accompanied the prayers were deliberate self-humiliations. When he said he is not a masochist but an autosadist, technically he was perfectly correct. The hurt was not inflicted by anyone but himself. In many ways he was a "self-executioner hugging his drowning stone."[18] Even so, the autosadism was convoluted—a kind of exotic account keeping of rewards and punishments. He would decide to "resist my tendency to press my naked face against the jagged rock," lest this allow him to keep on his warm gloves. Somehow, even resisting the temptation to punish himself was cause for self-contempt. "I also decided to resist my auto-sadistic tendency to humiliate myself—down flat on my belly!—no! flat! I say flat on belly at the stream over the golden rock below the grey waterfall."[19] As always, his manias, invariably connecting the sexual with the excretory, accompanied him on these walks. "On this spot, as I stand & wait & <u>Contemplate</u> the <u>Cosmos</u>, two devils have bothered me—one a great big <u>Turd</u>, if you know what I mean, that the devil persists in suggesting ought to be popped into my toothless mouth—the other that curious old neurosis about my old flat chest growing into vast women's breasts!"[20] He would make sporadic attempts to deal with "my mad mind." He would vow to let the "Angels of Mercy" who carried his prayers go free. Like Prospero, he would resolve to break his sticks and abjure his rough magic—"to carry no more these little exorcist magic-wands but to let these rocks bide as they are whether named or un-named."[21] The prayers, the multi-colored angels, and the manias always crept back.

For many years, one of Powys's strongest defences in times of great stress was escaping into nature. It was far from a passive enjoyment. In *Mortal Strife* he called it "this trick of *having* the Cosmos." By 1944 he had discovered a curious, unwieldy word in a churchyard—"cavoseniargizing"—and this became the key word for a defensive strategy which he insisted was an incorporation into himself, an almost aggressive internalization, of the elements: "I did play my Cavoseniargizing game of eating drinking & fucking or rather shagging in joy against the sweet elements of that indifferent Nymph Natura Multifaria!"[22] His "cavoseniargizing" brought a sexual and emotional release, which would temporarily dissolve the "perpetual margin of agitating, frightening, hurting humiliating puzzling annoying and irritating things." He had need of every defence he could muster. For the next two years, what Phyllis described as "Random Bricks of Chance"[23] rained down on their heads. The last weeks of December were taken up by "the ladies," both of whom had begun to wander in the dark and only just avoided serious accidents. Then eighty-one-year-old Aunt Harriet fell ill. Phyllis spent two weeks sleeping next door in a deck chair, looking after her aunt and her increasingly infirm mother. He was worried to see the T. T. so worn and wondered if her lovely long brown hair that fell to her knees ("aye! aye!") would turn gray. He was also troubled that his dyspepsia was getting worse. As always, he turned to her for comfort: "Yesterday, when I was scared, the T. T. uttered the words 'I'll be there.'"[24]

In February 1945, Louis sent them Oliver's play about his mother Frances. For a few days they talked of little else. It moved Phyllis greatly, but for John it brought such painful memories to the surface that he could not bear to finish reading it. He was deeply impressed by its power, but "some psychic outward force, or more likely some inward inhibition suddenly interrupted my reading of it!"[25] The play, *Ark Without Noah*,[26] is indeed an extraordinarily revealing play about Frances Gregg, her mother, and her children Betty and Oliver, as they struggled to survive—without a Noah (not that Louis ever filled that role). As Oliver depicted her, Frances was neurotic, bitter, trapped, unfulfilled, and at times close to being psychotic. It was understandable that Powys was upset by the portrayal, possibly because he could not face that this was what Frances had become, or possibly because he was aware that, more than once, she had accused him of making her into the person she had become. However, the "psychic" force that stopped him was more likely that Oliver was documenting his deep love/hatred for his mother, and this re-aroused Powys's ambivalent feelings about his own mother. He told Louis that he identified so closely with his own mother that "I am she," inferring that this was equally true of Oliver. But in an implied criticism of Oliver, he insisted that he ferociously defended his mother's "manias and inhibitions and fantasies and prejudices and badnesses and darknesses beyond what I'd think . . . of doing for myself."[27] He said no more about the play, but it started him on the way to portraying the relationship between his hero, Porius, and Porius's mother—a portrayal at least as equivocal as Oliver's. He finally finished *Rabelais* and in March 1945 turned once again to his novel. In the three years that had passed since he began it, he had written, off and on, nine chapters. He now revised and "practically re-wrote" these, and by the time he had his annual few days' holiday with his son Littleton Alfred in August he had written a total of thirteen chapters.

The son was now in his forties. After training as an Anglican clergyman, Littleton had obtained a living as rector at Wiston in Sussex where he continued to live with his mother—as Old Littleton expressed it, "entirely possessed by Margaret."[28] They exchanged fond letters and once a year, beginning in 1935, Powys and his son met for a few days every summer at various locations. In September 1939 Littleton Alfred was "called to Aldershot as a Chaplin [sic]." Although Littleton initially thought of the war as a "crusade," some eight months later, in May1940, he abruptly gave up his commission in the army, returned to England from France, and resigned his living. Silence followed and John, wondering what had happened, decided "he is an unknown quantity to me—my son." A few months later, he was told that Littleton Alfred had converted to

Catholicism. John was initially upset but remembered that when he was young he had also been infatuated "by this honeyed logic & sadistic strawberries."[29] In the autumn of that year Littleton entered Beda Pontifical College at Wigan to train to become a Catholic priest. In 1941 they met in Wales for the first time, at nearby Valle Crucis. By 1943, Littleton was bringing with him a "semi-adopt-ed" six-year-old boy he called Francis; the pattern of Harry Lyon and Littleton was being repeated. These were generally happy interludes; they walked, Littleton fished, and John read. While they were at Valle Crucis this summer of 1945, Japan surrendered and Powys wrote hopefully, "It may well be after the Atom Bomb the LAST WAR of all the History of Humanity on this Planet."

There was always a certain secretiveness about these meetings in Wales, pre-sumably so that Margaret would not be hurt. Powys was not open about them even with friends, telling Iowerth Peate that "as per usual I really literally go into RELIGIOUS RETREAT."[30] Obviously Phyllis was in on the secret, if that was what it was, since it was she who did all the arranging and packing of supplies for their annual meetings. Despite this, the son had not yet met her. Marian was indignant about this, insisting that Littleton Alfred should " go and see you now at your own home" and meet "that saintly lady your common law wife." She pointed out, "Your boy is now I believe 44 and should have learned tolerance and charity and ordinary good manners." As a heavy hint, she enclosed a newspaper article to the effect that common law marriages were valid now in Pennsylvania.[31]

The excitement of being with his son unfailingly exacerbated John's dyspep-sia, but this time he knew that something more serious than "the old acid trou-ble" was causing his pain. On September 17, he vomited "a pail-ful (well! a big piss-pot full!) of Coal Black stuff as I did 40 years ago at Burpham before my first operation." He was taken to the Emergency Medical Hospital at Wrexham where he remained for almost a month. As always, he was grateful to Phyllis who made the six-hour journey every day to visit him in the hospital. The "great Ruthin Castle doctor" (the same one that successfully treated Will) decided it was better not to operate, and the bleeding ulcer was treated conservatively. Just before he was discharged, he had a gastroscopy to determine that there was no cancer. Will sent Phyllis a hundred pounds to pay the medical bills.

Powys remained in bed, recuperating, for six weeks. Phyllis had the front parlor, kitchen, and bath set up as an enclosed flat to save coal and to make it easier to cope with his invalid needs. He continued to love Wales, and despite all that had happened to him and in spite of their strangling poverty, he could say truly that "these ten years of my life have been my happiest."[32] He began tak-ing short walks in December and tried to do a little more work on his novel. However, in the New Year he started to suffer a different kind of indigestion which, at first, he thought was another ulcer. From the graphic description he gave to Gertrude, it suggests a hiatus hernia: "Burning horrid stuff (like what you see in pools in farm-yards only burning hot and of course coloured by the Bismuth I have taken in my Powders a lurid brown colour) coming up in my mouth all the time—and ending in vomit—vomit—vomit, which I try to hasten by putting my fingers down my throat."[33] The local doctor tried a variety of remedies, but nothing seemed to work. Powys chopped and changed his already minimal diet in an attempt to alleviate the hurting: tea only one day, the next day no tea but a little bread, the next, tea but no sugar and no bread. The pain, vomiting, and nausea continued. Moreover, John knew it was a diet which would make his severe constipation worse.

After the hospitalization in September, he had ceased the habit of decades of having an enema every third day—perhaps the specialist insisted upon it. By good fortune, the man in the next bed was a chemist, and he prescribed petrolagar and cascara (both laxatives). At first he rejoiced that "Mr. Owen has saved me from enemas for ever!" By the end of the year, this prescription was not working so well, and on top of the ulcer pain and the "Heart-Burn Acids boiling & singing inside me," he was in a panic about his "vent." He was not sure which of his troubles was the worst but decided it was "the old Anus the old Animus the old mania."[34] His "rocky turds" were "enemy No 1 and they are the boys who killed Brother Bert!"[35] In March, he reverted to the old enema routine.

> Yesterday to me was one of the most unpleasant days I've ever had in all my life & of course I made it awful too for the T. T. who was a MARVEL & a WONDER & a Heroine & in the end saved me. But the time we spent me half-naked on floor of BATHROOM & she giving me or trying in vain to give me on & on & on on on on a proper enema & my Anus bulging . . . & the floor was drenched with water.[36]

This struggle with constipation went on for months, and at times he was beside himself with fear: "Went at my Arse-Hole with my fingers. I ought to have cut my nails first. . . . I got it out."[37] Still in constant pain from the ulcer and the dyspepsia, and eating less and less, by mid-March, he felt "as if I might go to sleep from Weakness & never wake up."[38] Although they loved their local doctor "because he is so Welsh" Powys finally decided he must have a second opinion. The specialist who had treated him at Wrexham came and advised sugar and Benger's Food for energy, told him to eat more, prescribed sedatives and a variety of medicines and, what finally helped most, ordered him to drink neat pure olive oil. Although "my stomach clear round front & back so sore so tender! so touchy & hurty! as if there were ulceration & even 'adhesions' all across my front,"[39] gradually during April, the bowel became regular and he got stronger. He did not seem to connect the "elephantine actions" he now happily announced in his diary with the fact that he was actually eating properly.

Once again, he began writing his Dark Age Romance. With the extreme weakness, the tormenting ulcers, the constant dyspepsia, nausea, and constipation, it is astonishing that he could struggle on writing a vast and complicated novel. His need for a philosophy of "happiness," however forced, to get him through the unrelenting pain, becomes more understandable. So too does his emphasis on the excremental in his novels. It was at this period that he also, finally, concluded that he was what Freud called "an anal character": "I have both sexually & nervously a terrifically dominant Anal Complex!!"[40] Suddenly all the manias, phobias, neuroticisms that made up John Cowper Powys became clear to him.

> I live by the VENT on the VENT & through the VENT. I am an arse-hole maniac & bum-eroticist and an anal aesthete! That's why my viciousness my sadism my voyeurism, all gone now in Old Age & Other Joys.[41]

Someone has said that if you know what the purpose of a symptom is, you've robbed the symptom of its own peculiar intentions; Powys never made that error. Powys knew that his "anal soul"[42] was more than merely a stalled developmental stage in his character, which may have given rise to his rigidity, his obsessiveness, his sadism, his autoeroticism. It accounted for much, but not for everything. He had learned as a child that the devil chose the anus as his special location in the body. Violent medical purges were justified as cleaning out the bad stuff. Punishment too could be vindicated as an attack on the demonic in its bodily lair. If the anus was the erogenous zone that harbors bad spirits, then obsession with it not merely expressed toilet-training fixations but kept the demonic constantly present, giving its symbolic locus the ritual attention it demanded.

> We must cherish our mania, or our madness if you prefer that word, as we would cherish a second self; for our madness is our second self.[43]

During June he was still spitting acids but getting stronger and walking further each day, although it is not until July, after almost a year of illness, that the specialist pronounced him cured of this last ulcer. He began walking again and as happens in the convalescence stage, "had a gentle thrill of joy a mild & quiet ecstasy of joy or of enjoyment to see the rain splash on that stone & to see the clouds moving."[44] Gilbert Turner sent him a newfangled ballpoint pen to mark his recovery, and John's mounting spirits are evident in his thank-you letter: "I have clearly used this blighted Biro too vigorously." He adds that Phyllis is "at once laughing & crying to see the Ink-Pot back!"[45] His exultation was short-lived. Aware for some time that he was "seeing 2 horizons and 2 moons," an eye test revealed that he had a cataract and was virtually blind in the right eye.[46] 1946 ended on another cheerless note. Phyllis's physical and mental health was increasingly shaky under the burden of war-time shortages and the care of three elderly sick people, and from Powys descriptions it is likely that she was also going through menopause. A picture of her favourite Kafka would be enough to set her off: "The T. T. was very very very upset upset upset over her own nervous troubles and she wept & she cried and she & Kafka together cried Captive-Bound-LOST."[47] He noted sadly a few days after Christmas: "After her coffee & rolls she felt very peaceful—really at ease & quiet & actually happy—the little T. T.—she said however that she pondered on her preference for being DEAD over being alive & she decided that if by walking into the Kitchen she could be quite DEAD she would walk into the Kitchen!! So there we are." He understood her reasons for wanting either death or, as she put it, "kicking up starry leaves in empty space": "The Mistress & Aunt Harriet touch her to the quick with the pathos & poignancy of their second childhood nor am I (in my 75th year) much better but it's one thing to feel the poignancy and another thing to look after poignancy night & day sans cesse."[48]

Matters got no better in the New Year. Both the mother and the aunt were ill in bed, and in another bitterly cold winter, the government announced rationing of all sources of heat. Powys watched Phyllis "struggle to get coal for the Mistress & to manage Aunt Harriet & to keep our electric going & to weave in & out like a shuttle between the two houses—she has a cough & is very very very very anxious about the future."[49] He fantasized carrying them all off to a Latin country or some warmer place. Phyllis considered taking them back to America, but in the end, there was no practical escape. He wondered and worried "whether she will get through it." He was well aware of his total reliance on her now.

> 22 February 1947: I kicked over with my beautiful new shoes provided by the T. T. one of the two Bottles of MILK provided by the T. T. from the Co-op man & placed to warm by the T. T. by the Gas-Heater . . . wh. she had provided to keep me warm now electric is cut off. But & but & but & but she kissed me without any anger.

Marian arrived in February, flying the Atlantic for the first time. It was eight years since he had seen this sister who was "like my American Wife till I met the T. T." They could "talk of things in general & of our lives absolutely freely as with perhaps as certainly with O so few!"[50] Marian told him about the visit Littleton and Elizabeth Myers had made to her in New York on their way to Arizona where they hoped to improve Elizabeth's deteriorating health. Elizabeth's consumption was now in her throat, and John with his own breathing terror could well understand the victim of such a malady growing "funny, queer, wild, furious, savage!" Whatever Marian may have said to Elizabeth, Littleton's bride had made "a savage attack on Marian calling her 'Mrs. Hitler' & so on." Powys was "glad it's Marian not John!" but saddened to think "how uncomfortable it must make Old Littleton for his new wife to quarrel with us all."[51] The quarrels ended when Elizabeth died in May. Shortly after Marian left, John heard from his son on February 28, that Margaret had died that morning. He was glad that in the last months of his wife's life they had exchanged very affectionate letters, and in his last letter to her he had told her "how I remembered the Green Ribbon which she always tied to her Mandolin."[52] It is a gentle remark to end an unhappy marriage.

Five years had now passed since he began his novel, the name of which, *Porius*, he kept secret from everyone except Phyllis and his diary. During times of greatest financial and physical distress, he sometimes managed only a page a day. Despite this, by the spring of 1947 he had written twenty-two chapters. He wondered if he should stop there because, as the worshipper of the quaternity over the trinity explained to a correspondent, "2+2=4 & as you know 4 is the Circle Deific." By June of that year, he decided he would "have to continue my Romance for 3 or 4 more chapters in fact until Chapter 26 for 2 and 6 are 8 which is the 'Multiple' is it? of my favourite Pythagorean number 4 & the day of my Birth." In August, he was interrupted by a request by Keidrych Rhys, the editor of *Wales*, asking him to write another essay to add to other articles Powys had already written for the magazine so they could be published as a book. With the exception of an essay on his philosophy, Powys considered *Obstinate Cymric* a "rather tiresome & dull & superficial book I mean this rather popular & shallow & academic book." He was further delayed by a request from Malcolm Elwin, by now the general editor of Macdonald's new series of classics. No doubt aware of his precarious financial situation, Elwin commissioned Powys to write an introduction for a new edition of Sterne's *Sentimental Journey*. So impressed with this was the joint managing director of Macdonald, Eric Harvey, that he doubled the agreed fee of fifty pounds and suggested that John write a further introduction, which was finished in February 1948, to *Tristram Shandy*. He could now return to *Porius*, but it was another year before he completed it. The question was whether he *wanted* to finish. As he wrote to his sister Gertrude, by now he felt as if he were "Grandmother Patteson reading the Children of the New Forest to me at 6."[53] He added so many "insets" that Chapter 26 had to be divided into further chapters. Ironically, he ended with thirty-three chapters, his hated Christian "three" instead of the magic number four. He was "not a good compressor," he admitted to Gilbert Turner, "I am a born *enlarger*."[54] It was not until February 27, 1949, that he scrawled on page 2811 of the manuscript, "THE END."

It is almost impossible to summarize this huge "Dark Ages" novel of nine hundred typeset pages with its forty-nine characters and its chaotic events. Even more difficult to convey in a few pages is its multifarious levels of meaning. It is perhaps most easily read as a historical novel (his first intention), a novel of war written in the aftermath of a world war. The time is A.D. 499; the place North Wales. The principal character is Porius, son of Einion, the reigning Prince of Edeyrnion and descendant of the Brythonic chieftain Cunedda. Edeyrnion is one of the kingdoms which the Romans gave to the Celtic Brythons to rule over, provided that they gained control over the indigenous population and remained loyal to Rome. The aboriginal races, still living in the dense forests of Edeyrnion, have bided their time, waiting for an opportunity to restore their once all-powerful matriarchy. Word has come that the Saxeons under Colgrim are advancing on the kingdom and the forest people, ruled by "three ancient aunties" called the Modrybedd, and their Druid, see their chance and join the enemy. Porius gets word that Arthur, the Emperor of Britain, has begun a forced march to head the Saxeons off but in the meantime has sent ahead Merlin (or Myrddin Wyllt as he is called in the novel), Nineue, the sorcerer's mistress, and Medrawd, the emperor's nephew, to help beleaguered prince Einion. These latter only serve to crystallize into two armed camps all the submerged and frustrated hatred of the various "sys-

tems" swirling about the kingdom. Porius's father proves ineffectual, so it is left to
the thirty-year-old Porius and his foster brother, Rhun, to attempt to contain the
situation. After several skirmishes between the forest people and Arthur's horsemen, the Saxeons arrive and are temporarily defeated. In the meantime Porius
marries his cousin Morfydd, mates with Creiddylad, a Cewri giantess, hears the
prophecy of the magic child, Bleiddyn, and, in the final chapter, rescues Myrddin
from under the stone grave where the magician has been imprisoned by Nineue.

The introduction of a giantess and a magic child gives the hint that the
novel, which began as a an account of the clash of cultures, religions, and philosophies in a certain place, at a certain period, has shifted into a different plane.
Gertrude had sent them all her paintings for safekeeping during the bombings,
and he hung her portrait of their father in his study. He told Gertrude that it was
this picture that influenced him "to make it more about Caves and Precipices and
adventures and ouzels and giants and Avanca (unknown monsters!) than about
the learned and metaphysical and fortunate-unfortunate Boethius!!"[55] Ever desiring to be his father, he called himself "a born Inventor of Fairy Tales," and *Porius*
is John's version of his father's "interminable story about two mythic personages
called Giant Grumble and Fairy Sprightly," and a villain "whose sinister activities
required all the arts of both Giant and Fairy to circumvent and neutralize." Given
the mysteries of the imagination, he may not have been conscious of this at the
time he was writing, but by 1950 he was, referring to "that fons et origo of Porius
& of my 1st & 2nd childhood namely Fairy Sprightly & Giant Grumble."[56] In it,
John plays the part of Porius, who has in him "the blood of the aboriginal giants"[57];
Phyllis, as Morfydd, "has to play the part of Fairy Sprightly in my father's story."[58]
However, his fairy tales were infinitely more sophisticated than his father's, and
the battles against the "villain" in *Porius* are fought on every level—physical, psychical, sexual, emotional, and mythological.

Powys had a self-confessed "pedantic mythological mania for the past";[59] the
past in the case of *Porius* is both Wales in 499 and his own past, which was always
with him. It was at Shirley in his very earliest infancy that he "used to press my
knuckles against my closed eyelids and watch with intense delight the marvellous
kaleidoscope of colours which then formed and re-formed before me."[60] One of his
well-established rituals in the years during which he was writing the novel was
ducking his head into a basin of water and opening his eyes, while thinking "of all
the People of my Life." There is therefore yet another way in which the novel can
be read. Phyllis maintained, and Powys agreed, "that this Porius book of mine is a
true Picture of my Family!"[61] He already had himself as Porius and Phyllis as his
betrothed, Morfydd. He had Elizabeth Myers as Sibylla, Littleton as Rhun, Llewelyn
as Einion. The rest of the family were introduced as the novel progressed. Harry
Lyon became the homosexual Drom, the "Jesus-lad" who can finally be viciously
rejected. Even a tiny remembrance of Gertrude during the war was slipped in when
the Little Peacock is reminded of his mother who went on making bread when
"friends and enemies" were "slaughtering each other in the next hamlet."[62]

It *is* a "true picture" of his family, but not because each one of his characters is identifiably a member of the Powys clan. Indeed, to go down that route results in confusion because to a certain extent each character is like a kaleidoscopic image broken up by the action of water on eyes. For example, Porius's father, Prince Einion, has all the physical and personality characteristics of Llewelyn, but the "habitual clash of their souls" is more akin to the tension between John and his own father. The Powys father becomes Porius's old-fashioned, rather pathetic, grandfather for whom he has a loving and filial regard. Porius's mother, Euronwy, has the physical characteristics of Margaret, but in her religiosity, her control, her resignation, she is Mary Cowper, the Powys mother who "never shed a tear." While Rhun is obviously Old Littleton with all Littleton's conventionality, religious feelings, lack of sexuality, obtuseness, and loyalty, in the novel he is distanced as a "foster brother." More obviously identifiable are the memories and the feelings. Porius, smelling the scent of the giants, is reminded of "the smell of the tadpoles . . . which he had carried as a child to certain way-side puddles at the foot of the Gaer."[63] However, the memories too suffer a classic displacement. In the novel, he ascribes to Rhun/Littleton his own ancient resentment toward "this intruder at his mother's breasts." It is Rhun who, as a boy, "used to threaten to 'beat [Porius] like a dog,'" whereas it was John who made that threat to Littleton.[64] Porius is therefore less a portrait of a family than a portrait of the dynamics of relationship explored with fathomless hurt, abysmal honesty, and, yes, residual self-protection. It can be argued that *Porius* is the autobiography he couldn't write in 1934. All of Powys's novels were *romans à clef*, the real persons and events only minimally disguised. But by the time he wrote *Porius*, the tale had become almost wholly metaphorical and the characters, in a certain profound sense, figures in his psyche.

On certain days, as he held his head under water, Powys would "think of the shells & sea-anemones & sea-weed & pebbles. . . . Thus I daily go back to the Edge of the Sea out of which all life originally sprang."[65] His rituals were more often than not rehearsals of memory, and the memories were of beginnings. Initially he intended the novel to cover the forty-odd years between the birth and death of Boethius, 480 to 525.[66] Then he suddenly decided to narrow the time frame to one week, specifically from Thursday, October 18, to Thursday, October 25, 499. Why, he does not say, but the following entry is reason enough.

> 22 October 1943. Why do I enjoy this late October weather so??? I will tell you. Because I was after birth kept by my mother in Bed at her Side for Ten Days. So that's—so that these days from the 18th October to Oct. 30 are my First two weeks in this Dimension as an Independent Entity! I go once more by the PATH of Miracles.

For a writer like Powys, once such an intuition emerged into consciousness, it *had* to be expressed in some way, but how? You write a fairy tale about the birth of a hero and his escape from the domination of the maternal world into the independent dimension. Better still, you collapse those crucial "first two weeks" into seven days and disguise it as the seven stages of an alchemical opus. That way, through arcane images and symbols, and above all in a hermetic text that traditionally is "secret," you can safely express toward that mother-goddess and that real mother all the ambivalences and angers and longings of a lifetime. This is indeed the "path of miracles."

It is the writings of the alchemist Paracelsus, not the philosopher Boethius, that provide the framework of this novel. In one of his last essays, Llewelyn had written, "Never has a cabalistic soothsayer existed that has provided the fancies of my brother . . . with firmer foundations than did the old magician [Paracelsus]; nobody ever knew better than he how to underpin the unseen cellarage of such airy castles of the human mind."[67] Possibly Llewelyn's essay sparked the idea in the first place, but John had been interested in alchemy ever since he played with his chemistry set in the apple loft at Montacute. His mother had given him a "splendid Paracelsus"[68] as a wedding present, and Phyllis's father had given her the complete works of Paracelsus and his formulas. Phyllis as a Paracelsian "elemental" was his continuing myth. Throughout his life, he read and absorbed the ideas of Pythagoras, Boehme, Plotinus, Hermes Trismegistus, as well as Paracelsus, and these were the great alchemists.[69] Most importantly, his study of Goethe's *Faust* taught him the art of transposing alchemical processes into a creative work of myth.[70] By the 1940s he could call himself, unselfconsciously, "an industrious, patient, hard-working old Alchemist like that alchemist in Faust."[71]

Powys liked to project the illusion that he was a "charlatan"—someone who would become enthralled by "something exciting in life or nature or books or history or psychology" and work out the idea without bothering "to get the details correct." His best novels simply do not bear this out. He may interpret the details to suit his own needs, but the details themselves and the substructure on which he builds are scrupulously worked out. Just as *A Glastonbury Romance* grew out of the Grail myth, so *Porius* is grounded in the firm foundation of the alchemical transformation, each of the seven stages worked out methodically, every essential image and occult symbol in its proper place. Although the ostensible goal of alchemy was to transform base metals into gold, many of the texts make it clear that the often dangerous chemical procedures were but outer manifestations of the inner search for the "secret" or meaning of the whole material universe and on a personal level, an outer symbol of what was also an inner, psychic process; an allegory of the transformation of man. It was a quest, in fact, for something that was lost—lost both in the depths of matter and in the depths of the mind. Many of the stages and symbols of alchemy are reminiscent of stories of the Grail. Just as the aim of the Grail quest is to ask the right question that will heal the maimed fisher king, in alchemy the *werk* is often described as the redemption or release of the deity who is imprisoned in the stone or lost in matter. There are also many points of similarity with the stages of initiation in the ancient mystery religions in which, through a death and resurrection that imitated the sacrificial death of a god, the initiate and the god become one. Powys's hero, Porius, is at once an adept, a quester, and an initiate. The seven days of conflict in Edeyrnion, during which Porius is profoundly altered by his experiences, are modeled on the seven stages of alchemy. His "work," toward which the whole week (however filled with other events) moves, is to rescue Myrddin from his imprisonment beneath the stone so that another golden age can be initiated. But concomitant with this physical work is the psychic opus which involves Porius in a struggle to free himself from his own particular prison.

Somehow Powys manages to keep all the historical, familial, mythic, alchemic balls up in the heady air of esoteric speculation and chaotic action throughout thirty-three long chapters. What prevents the whole thing from collapsing into a *massa confusa* is that the story is at all times firmly anchored in the stable, identifiable world of his daily walks around Corwen. The animals he saw, the places he visited, the people he met—all found their way into his tale. Even if the reader does not know this, he senses a present reality underlies the dream world of giants, magicians, and impenetrable forests and is thereby obscurely reassured, like a child clutching his familiar security blanket, entranced by a fairy tale.

In the spring of 1943 Powys began sketch maps in his diary of trails in the Forestry Commission conifer plantation beyond their house. These tracks he called Trent Lanes—the lanes of his Sherborne youth—but they were to become the byways of the primeval wood in his novel. By 1944, he had worked out all the paths through the dense forest that Porius will travel in his *aventures du Graal* and had named them. He reminded Gertrude, "You recall that long narrow path under our great overhanging rock after another that leads towards the hill above Mr. Irvine's house. I call that path the Avenue of Death but its in the real landscape and not (for all I may have said!) in the invented landscape!"[72] Mynydd-y-Gaer, the hill fort across the river Dee standing high above the forest, now becomes the home of Porius and his parents, rulers of Edeyrnion. As Powys walked along the river Dee, the gray cow he passes becomes Eigr Mallt, the cow Merlin milks in Gwendydd's sumptuous tent; the "terrifying White-faced Horse" with "the huge prick" grows into the gigantic stallion that Nineue rides in the last chapter; the white owl that "flew close round & round my head" is transformed into Blodeuwedd, the owl maiden reincarnated by the magician. The indubitably real animals he encounters are at the same time *Mabinogion* animals—the gray cow is a "magic cow," the horse "a Fairy Stallion fed on fungus"; the owl is made of flowers. The inhabitants of Corwen are similarly transformed. Early in 1941, he and Phyllis had begun discussing the different racial characteristics of the people they saw around them. Eventually he peopled the novel with Celtic Brythons who are partly Romanized; with the "anarchical and peaceful" race of the forest people, descended from the Iberians of North Africa; with the even earlier, mysterious Ffichtiaid (Picts) and the savage Gwyddyliad (Scots); even with members of an ancient giant race, the Cewri. With the (possible) exception of the giants, he believed he could see these races still in the faces and actions of his neighbors and passersby. He hails the "rough wild fierce dark mad black-mustached Cymro on a bicycle" who responds with "that mysterious unequalled Mabinogi Welsh smile"—and lo! he is Afagddu, the old retainer of the Princes of the Gaer. The "Roman Brython" from nearby Cynwyd who has an accident to his tractor wheel, becomes "the Horse-Breeder in my Chapter 27";[73] the three sisters at Dee Bank turn into the three aged Princesses, the Modrybedd. The eldest (who in real life is a reporter on the *Daily Mail*) is "an Aboriginal Matriarchal Witch of the true <u>Iberians</u>."[74] Teleri, a young girl he sees in the village, becomes a half-witted girl who is raped by Medrawd; Mrs. Hughes next door has "the Temperament of a Pure-blooded Brython & I confess we as a family have inherited from my dad a few drops of this same blood! A troublesome blood a wilful blood a dangerous blood!"[75]

As the novel opens, Porius is standing on the watch-tower of Mynydd-y-Gaer, surveying his father's kingdom and pondering on two pieces of news, one religious and one to do with war. While he feels a "personal responsibility"[76] for dealing with these crises, what he really wants is freedom. He has a craving "to be free from an over-loving mother and a contemptuous father." He wants also to be free of the struggle between the two parents that "had gone on all his life."[77] His mother's loyalty to Mynydd-y-Gaer and to her cousin, the Emperor Arthur, constantly battles with his father's devotedness to the "Three Aunties" (the Modrybedd) and the aboriginals of the forest. Actually, his father plays a minor role in this conflict; his place taken by Porius's betrothed, Morfydd, who is a "child of the forest" and a pet of the Aunties.[78] Porius muses on his "complete submission" to his mother and his betrothed. What he really wishes freedom from is "all the femininity that had so long enslaved him." It is the magician, Merlin, who sets him on "the road of his own liberation."[79]

The first step in the alchemical process, the *nigredo*, is to dissolve the base metals, that is, all forms appearing in the world, back to their initial unformed state as the *prima materia*. Regarded as the basis of the whole opus, the alchemists gave it many names: ore, quicksilver, earth, river, dragon, mother, Cronos. In *Porius*, the *prima materia* is Merlin, identified as Cronos and the earth itself. Porius has been with his foster brother Rhun in the Cave of Mithras when, hearing unusual noises by the river, they go down to investigate and find Myrddin Wyllt, surrounded by animals. When the magician collapses and Porius has to take him into his arms to hold him up, Porius feels he is "tapping in some unknown way a great reservoir of magnetic ubiquity." Then it seems to Porius that "by degrees the figure he was holding grew less self-contained, less buttressed-in upon himself, and the man's very identity seemed slipping back into the elements."[80] This reservoir of power, this "prima materia" is always double- natured: it is both the mother and a dragon. In Paracelsus, the figure of Melusina is earth in its terrifying aspect—a succubus but at the same time the mother of all being. Powys calls her Nineue and signals her nature by giving her the patronymic "ferch Avallach" (daughter of Avallach, the Welsh god of the underworld). Porius is both attracted and repelled by the alluring Nineue when he first meets her in the emperor's tent early in the morning of Friday, October 19: "A weird fear assailed him lest this whole place with all its surroundings and with himself . . . should be carried down into some faintly lit greenish-black underworld." Powys gives Nineue the negative, dragon aspects of Merlin, and it is her "serpentine treacheries" that are presumably responsible for Merlin's final entombment.[81]

There follow several chapters of realistic writing which introduce the other main characters in the story and carry forward the outer events of the novel. Porius discusses with his "irresponsible" father, Prince Einion, how best to defend the kingdom against the invading Saeson under Colgrim. Porius's relationship with his father is at "a point that was both infanticidal and parricidal."[82] He hates his father for being unfaithful to his mother, but at the same time nothing is more painful to Porius than to think of the two of them in their bedchamber. Another chapter introduces Brochvael, Einion's brother and Morfydd's father. Brochvael, the toothless scholar who has many of Powys's own characteristics, makes a variety of fruitless efforts to calm the complicated and dangerous situation evolving in the kingdom. With a similar view in mind, Porius's mother, Euronwy, and Morfydd make an uneasy pact, although both are contending for Porius's love and loyalty.

Then comes one of the most curious episodes in a book full of wonders: Myrddin's agony in the boat. Chapter 15 ("my best & most important chapter entitled Myrddin Wyllt")[83] marks the second stage in the alchemical process— *calcinatio*—in which the *prima materia* is reduced to ashes. It is now October 20, "Saturn's Day or the Day of Cronos." Myrddin slips away from the Arthurian camp and goes to the sacred river Dee. He falls into one of his "fits of abstraction" in which he can journey through "huge spaces of time." He calls on his human mother "who gave me life only to loathe and despise me" and on his "enormous earth-mother" Gaia, to tell him who he is, and if his belief in a future golden age is a delusion.

The "hideous answer" the Mothers give is to show the magician "the actual countenance of Styx." Her eyes send him the message: "From death . . . all that exists has sprung; and to death all that exists will return." "'Give up,' those eyes said, 'striving so hard to give men and women and beasts and fishes and birds, and all that feels pain and draws breath, a Golden Age without the meddling of gods and rulers.'"

> Myrddin Wyllt . . . might have given the impression to a stranger come suddenly upon him of being some species of saviour-beast or animal-redeemer who had at that moment accepted on behalf of all the beasts in the world the sentence of the slaughter house, and was weighed down by the appalling weight of the burden he had undertaken. . . . "Death, death, death, death," he said to himself; and again the face of the eldest daughter of backward-flowing Ocean, as he had seen it through the ribs of that grey ruin of an ash-tree, returned upon him with a sense of inescapable doom.

Then Myrddin becomes aware that "curled up on the back of his hand, its hind feet steadying its cold, wet, plump body, was a bright-eyed water-rat, assiduously and with absorbed and intense concentration licking his knuckle," and Myrddin feels that although "the darkness that covered him now . . . was as it *were* death," the "licking of that tiny tongue" sufficed as an answer "from all the doomed creatures of earth to the eldest daughter of Oceanus."[84]

Other than for its strange beauty and imaginative power, there is no reason in the narrative for this very long scene; it has nothing to do with the outer action. But for the *opus alchymicum* it is essential. In the boat Myrddin-Mercurius-Cronos, the *prima materia,* dissolves back into his mother's death darkness. Most readers will recognize that Myrddin has "died" in order to bring back an "answer," but it is the imagery that sets up reverberations in the mind. The most precious material which the alchemist can produce at the beginning of the work is ash. The chapter opens with the image of the "burning white fire" of the rising sun, and then with images of ash or grayness—the color of ash. But Powys broadens the implications, connecting the *calcinatio* stage with the myth of the world tree and the hanged god. Merlin's agony is the equivalent of the god Odin hanging himself on the ash tree in order to learn the secret of the runes of wisdom. But neither the care with which Powys works out the esoteric details of the alchemical purification nor the inspired connection with mythological dying would give this episode the intensity and urgency that it has. That comes solely from his ability to permeate the abstract with his own experience. This chapter was begun after he returned from the hospital in October 1945, and he was writing it in those first months of 1946 when he too felt that death was the only answer to his suffering.

The death of the god prepares the way for the third stage, the *coniunctio oppositorum.* The alchemist portrayed this as a marriage of opposites: male-female, brother-sister, sun-moon, spirit-soul. Although Morfydd loves Rhun, she and Porius marry in the belief that "the power and peace of tribes and nations are cemented by marriages"[85] and that this marriage might prevent open conflict between the Romanized Brythons and the forest people. That the marriage is to be seen at another, more magical level is obvious from the lengths to which Powys goes to suggest that the couple are brother and sister. They are certainly cousins, but Porius fantasizes that his father and Morfydd's mother were lovers, and that Morfydd might therefore be "his half-sister." Powys's fascination with incest was a long-held one, but he could now distance it from personal preoccupation and put it into a mythic context. It is a common symbol in alchemy, standing as an allegory for the royal union of the masculine and feminine principles. Interestingly, the first conjunction, the *matrimonium corporale,* in alchemy is never successful. The consummation of the marriage of Morfydd and Porius is similarly only a partial union, a physical but not a psychological one: "If it suited *his* method of existence to take possession of her with no more than a tenth part of his personality, it suited *hers* to be so taken. It left her free."[86]

During their mating, close by the "age-old ritual" of the fisher king is enacted —a huge lance, "conveying the impression of a colossal and hideous phallus," is plunged into the water. Even while this rite is being enacted, "wild disturbance and angry fighting" between the druid's archers and the little band of horsemen of the emperor's mission breaks out.[87] It becomes a battle between the druid who has joined forces with the Christian priest, who represents "the Mystery of the Three," and the magician who represents "the Magic of Four."[88] There is total confusion, with a crazed riderless horse and a hound circling around in the midst of the mayhem. This scene is a wonderful mix of Volentiā Army fighting, mythological symbolism, and alchemical notation. Powys knew his alchemy down to the smallest detail. In what appears to be a charming domestic image, Merlin is "standing over there like a great tremulous black-feathered hen, guarding those lads and horses as if they were its chickens."[89] Well conducted heat is the essential key to alchemical change, and one alchemic analogy is the heat produced by a brooding hen. Unregulated heat produces death. Merlin saves his chicks but the Christian priest works himself up "into such an abnormal heat" that he dies.[90]

One of the most awe-inspiring aspects of Powys's ability as a storyteller is the way in which he handles abstract and unlikely material in a hauntingly believable way. The failure of the conjunction in alchemy means that the brother and sister are "overcome by death" in the hermetic vessel, to be reborn after further purifications. Obviously the hero and heroine cannot die in the marriage tent, halfway through the novel, so Powys has death go on around them. Powys signals the fourth alchemical stage—*putrefactio*—with a startling image. Porius leaves Morfydd sleeping in the tent, which is close by the water. As he creeps through the mud and reeds he stops to listen to something, then says to himself: "It's no good . . . this ridiculous standing on one leg in these reeds, till my flesh turns putrid for Gwydion's sow!"[91] Here Powys has united alchemy with his beloved *Mabinogion*. Llew Llaw Gyffes turned into an eagle when the lover of his wife Blodeuwedd smote him with a poisoned spear. Gwydion the magician finds Lieu by following a sow that goes every day to eat the putrefying flesh that falls from the wounded bird. Porius is wondering if Morfydd and Rhun are lovers, but the image is remote unless it is meant as a deliberate signal that the next stage, putrefaction, is beginning. In the next chapters, there is death all around. There is the drowning of the Cewri; the dying of Father John; the murdering of Princess Tonwen and her lover; the dying from incestuous passion of Auntie Erddud; the spearing of Auntie Esyllt, the druid, and all their followers; the slaughter of the hound and horse; the clubbing of twenty Saxeons by Porius; the mortal wounding of Porius's father and the death of his grandfather.

It is, however, the "deaths" of the royal pair that are the important ones in the alchemic opus. This phase corresponds to the many myths of the Night Sea Journey—Theseus in the Underworld, Hercules in the vessel of the sun, Arthur's journey to Annwn. The Welsh myth of the journey to Caer Sidi makes it clear that the purpose of the voyage or descent is always the same: only in the region of danger can the hero find "the treasure hard to attain." Instead of joining the battle, Porius begins a search for the Cewri, the aboriginal giants who have been seen eating the corpses of the slain. Porius follows the giant and his daughter up the mountain, Cader Idris, thinking he might catch them by surprise. One of Porius's ancestors married a giantess called Creiddylad, and the possibility of meeting a second Creiddylad has given a "rich, inchoate magic and nameless sweetness [to] the under-dreams of his entire life." Suddenly before him, having given her giant father the slip, is "the very Creiddylad of his secretest broodings." A goddesslike young girl "came forth from that thick chaos of autumnal vegetation and stood before him, with one finger pressing her lips in the immemorial gesture of feminine warning, and with the other loosening her belt of plaited reeds in the immemorial gesture of feminine complicity and consent." They mate, although "the rape of this last *cawres* of the Cader was rendered difficult by the goddess-like creature's own overpowering passion. But he was not a Hercules for nothing, and it was accomplished at last."

In myth, Creiddylad is the daughter of Ludd the sea god; in other words, Porius's giantess is Beya, the maternal sea. In the *Rosarium*, the death of the son is the result of his complete disappearance into the body of Beya during coitus, which the philosophical alchemists interpreted as the masculine, spiritual principle of light sinking into the embrace of physical nature. But if union with her is a kind of death, it is also for the hero life-releasing. If it was Creiddylad "who had drained him of his strength, it was now she who was restoring it to him." Porius's dread of and resistance to being swallowed up in the embrace of the feminine—whether it is maternal nature, the mother, or marriage—is, for a moment at least, forgotten in this sexual act. The giant father, like some Freudian ogre, now comes after him and Porius, weaponless, can only "skip and dance for his life." Creiddylad, seeing her lover's exhaustion, flings herself between him and the blow with the club, and the giant leaps with his dead daughter into a deep mountain tarn. The sight of her eyes "staring up at him through blood and hair and green water" and Porius's "eternally varying reactions to it would from henceforth be *his* voyage into another world, *his* visit to Caer Sidi."[92]

Rather belatedly, Porius feels shame that while he had been "absorbed, possessed, obsessed, angel-hunted, devil-ridden by the tragedy," the Saxeon invaders may have been "murdering his people."[93] On the fourth day of that eventful week, he goes to the camp of the emperor's soldiers to find that they have been doing just that. "Our Brythonic Hercules" manages to kill twenty Saxeons who are sleeping in a drunken stupor after their orgy of slaughter. He then has a long philosophic discussion with Medrawd, who tells him he has slept with Euronwy, Porius's mother. The killing continues on both sides and in the next scene, Porius, his uncle Brochvael, and his mother gather round the mortally wounded Prince Einion in the middle of the forest.

This chapter was a particularly difficult one to write, and in the end Powys cut half of it. During its writing in the spring of 1947, one of his closest and oldest friends, Bernie O'Neill, died. Whether it was this, or some unmentioned upset, he was "assailed by all my devils all the ones compounded of pulses & hearts & nipples & midriffs & diarrhea & vaccination & handkerchiefs & snot & blinking eyes & tape worms & my own self & its shadow."[94] It was a constant battle, but he came to the conclusion that it was "the physical things of life that we are supposed to get through unconsciously or if you like automatically!!" which were the worst. He could, he said, "walk about quite familiar and easy in what they call the 'unconscious' a world or region or Hades or Annwn that is as well-known to me as my ordinary mind is! I don't mind the atrocious things of the Unconscious one little bit—I am at home with them."[95] It was dealing with the "physical things" that was for him a constant misery. He struggled to ameliorate, if not sublimate, them by integrating them into his philosophy and, if possible, into his stories. His anal fears remained omnipresent. He continued to take huge doses of laxeative to stave off his obsession that he would die of constipation. This resulted in uncontrollable diarrhea. Sensitized to his own incontinence, he began to see excrement everywhere on his walks, including in all the places that were "sacred" to him.[96] In July, he moved with his stick a tramp's vest that he saw in the hedge and uncovered "a heap of diarrheaistic golden orange-red Shit." At this time he was writing the long unhappy conversation that Porius has with his mother at the sacred crossroads, waiting for the wounded Einon to be carried to them.

> Not far from where he was standing . . . was a large fresh deposit of human excrement. The man who had eased himself there . . . had partially concealed the shining red-brown heap, of which hosts of brilliant coloured flies were already aware, by throwing down a piece of rag upon it; but instead of concealing what he had done . . . this unhappy Manichean rag emphasized the sacrilege, neither discouraging the flies nor obliterating the disgust.[97]

It was because Powys found almost everything connected with the body loathsome that he has his hero Porius (and himself) "cavoseniargize": "I decided to cavoseniargize—to taste smell see touch hear & (sixth sense) embrace & ravish erotically—every external object & element such as earth air clouds sun trees . . . and forgetting things that I dislike so much & loathe with such disgust, yes forgetting forgetting forgetting these loathsome things."[98] Until his encounter with Creiddylad, Porius's own cavoseniargizing had been "narrow and defensive, a willed enjoyment of the general and particular aspects of the time and the place." But he thinks that "the shock of his rape of the [Giantess], and her death so quickly after, had roused forces within him which he felt were enlarging if not altering the whole nature of his consciousness."[99] Porius now feels he can "include in its scope . . . along with death, all those nervous manias and horrors and terrors and morbid fears that had ere now come near to causing him . . . to long to lose himself in that same blessed annihilation." Pain is part of this enlarged consciousness. He feels he can not only "force himself to enjoy both the outward world, with all its forms and colours, its splintered rocks, jagged spikes, dizzy peaks, slippery precipices" but also "the inward world with all its prickings and ticklings, its messings-up and missings-out, its throbbings and pulsings, its heavings and spasms, all that the mind whistled to him, all that the conscience clamped down upon within him."[100] Out of his own experience of pain and loath-someness, Powys invented some phrases in the Cewri giant's tongue: "Thumberol Gongquod," for "ravishing Mother Earth . . . with our feet," and "Tungerong larry Ong" for "enduring life till it ends."

But ravishing mother earth is for the Powys-hero like applying pain as an ointment to an open wound. Einon takes a long time to die, and as Porius looks on, in "sluggish self-absorption,"[101] it is on his mother, not his father, that his "thought-clouds" descend.[102] Porius has long known that all the "master-influ-ences of his interior life" take some material form or shape, not "an intelligibly symbolic shape" but rather "some accidental chance-bestowed pattern of form and colour that in itself was quite meaningless, and very often absurd."[103] So that now, as he stares at one of his mother's bare ankles exposed as she kneels before her dying husband, he sees that "this ankle happened to be both slightly swollen and slightly reddened, and without any remotely rational justification Porius both grossly and morbidly linked it with her seduction by Medrawd."[104] Whether this is an accidental or a symbolic shape, what Porius is seeing in his "self-tormenting soul"[105] is a swollen and reddened vagina—"one of the master influences of his interior life." A "strange and terrifying sex-horror" takes hold of him and he feels "as if women were not only of a different sex but of a different species." He feels that everything about his mother is false, that "she has no honesty in her." "He could see this grave, resolute, competent, spiritual face change its expression as Medrawd had his way with her."[106]

"Endurance" is not sufficient and "treading mother-earth" becomes a sexual terror. Never has Powys so magnificently summed up his own hard-won defences against an enlarged consciousness as he does while his hero waits for his father to die. Porius stares at a clump of white moss that he knew was used "in the staunching of blood and the binding up of wounds."

> His consciousness hovered now like a swift black butterfly, over the purple bruise whose surface was still liable to be speckled by minute out-jetting spurts of red blood when a certain idea brushed it with its wings. . . . Thus the self-created tendency to be pursued by the very association of ideas from which he shrank away was always forcing him to employ all manner of curi-ous devices; and he had, indeed, become a successful adept in a thousand self-healing tricks to help him escape his self-created devils. One of these tricks was the extremely simple one of forcing himself to forget what to himself he would call "the horror."[107]

Instead of attending his father's death feast and funeral, Porius goes off to bury his grandfather who has also died. He then goes to the hermitage of his teacher, Brother John. There he finds Myrddin asleep and "the perilous and lovely" Nineue nearby in another bed. Although he suspects that before he had appeared she had already begun to abandon herself to a "sensuous ecstasy, practically identical with his self-centred cavoseniargizing," the "distracting and maddening silkiness of her yielded body began to make dalliance predatory, and desire rapacious."[108] As he embraces "that Persephonean form," "he seemed to be ravishing . . . all the waters of the divine river itself and all the enchanted swamps and forests."[109]

While Porius has been making love to a giantess and a seductress, Morfydd has been dealing with the crises at the Gaer fortress. Exhausted after a day of bloodshed, she goes to sleep in a small room in the Gaer. She awakes in the night to find Teleri, a half-wit girl, dying outside her door. The girl has been raped and poisoned by Medrawd. The child dies in Morfydd's arms and her death becomes for Morfydd "a turning point in her life."[110] Morfydd's journey to the underworld is quite different from that of Porius, but it is perhaps more decisive than that of the hero. It transforms her into the "Gaer Princess" who feels "that she could rule, like any of the great queens of antiquity."[111]

Immediately after her night sea journey, on the twenty-third day of October, Morfydd and Porius meet and "pay their tribute to Eros" a second time. This second coming-together of the cousins is unnecessary so far as the story goes, but it *does* show how closely Powys was following the alchemical stages. In the fifth stage, after their emergence from the purifying fire, the new King and the new Queen (Morfydd and Porius are now referred to as "the new rulers of Edeyrnion")[112] must mate again. This is called the *matrimonium coeleste*, "the celestial marriage," because all the properties, all four elements—earth, air, fire, and water—of the purified couple mutually penetrate each other. Powys puts it thus:

> Their separate consciousnesses, impalpable, indefinable, without form or shape . . . exchanged those alternations of sex-excitement that with a quiver of sun-flames, air-clouds, sea-waves upon the sweet resistance of earth-furrows make a fusion of the sexes and press forward to the super-sexual.[113]

As always with Powys, one never knows whether his art reflected his reality or that he forced his life into echoing his art. However, on August 22, 1948, he noted in his diary: "LAST NIGHT I made love to the T. T. à la LULU. Was it perhaps for the last time?" According to evidence from the remaining diaries, it probably *was* the last time he made love to her, and it was while he was writing the beautiful passage about the second consummation of Porius and Morfydd.

Most of the alchemical processes, strange as they are, Powys has been able to conceal in his imagery, but an androgynous child, the symbol of the union of opposites, is more difficult to disguise. Nonetheless, into his description of the mysterious boy Powys has poured a distillation of more than a half century of reading in classical and Celtic mythology, religion, and philosophy. For many readers, Powys's interweaving of strands of arcane lore and esoteric myth is of no interest or significance. To those who are fascinated by complex visions, the richness of the patterns in his mind is a source of endless wonder.

Leaving Morfydd, Porius enters the now-deserted druid's cave and is astounded to find sitting crosslegged on a chest a redheaded boy of four or five called Bleiddyn, who is holding a terracotta image of a wolf cub with a "hairy penis."[114] Powys was probably thinking of a story in the *Mabinogion*. The magician Math punishes Gwydion and Gilfaethwy by changing them into wolves. Although both males, they are forced to mate. The offspring is a wolf-cub whom Math transforms into a child that he calls Bleiddyn. Powys's child has been incubated in the secret druid's cave, in a chest whose "whole appearance emanated an aura of occult alchemy."[115] Paracelsus believed that man's semen spilled by libidinous thinking was highly prized by creatures of the air, who would carry it away "to hatch it in some secret place." The boy's red hair is the easiest clue to his identity. The androgynous son of the alchemical union of stage five is sometimes called *heros rubens* as an indication that the red or red-gold final stage will soon be reached. Some time before he wrote this chapter, Powys had "a very very very very VIVID dream of Mrs. Powys & she was accompanied by a tall youth with <u>flaming</u> <u>red</u> <u>hair</u>. I must tell my son about this & see if he can explain it as he has been <u>studying</u> <u>Jung</u>."[116] Presumably Powys is having a private joke with himself, for he would have know very well Jung's theories of alchemy—and that his son Littleton might well be considered androgynous.

The child's presence in the cave and his votive image with its "rudely chipped male organ" also connects him with Hermes, the primordial child of Greek myth and god of revelation. Bleiddyn now proceeds to predict a future when there will be "no difference between Brython and Gwyddyl or between Ffichtiaid and Coranian. All will be equal. All will be one."[117] Gwion, a North Welsh cleric of the thirteenth century, wrote a romance about a miraculous child who possessed a secret doctrine which nobody could guess, but Porius now has the key to the secret and understands. His journey to the underworld has been his mating with the giantess and her subsequent brutal death. This is the main aim of alchemy—to understand that out of death, which dissolves or purifies the old one-sided hating, a new conjunction of opposites occurs that contains everything: male and female, good and evil, god and devil. The original hermaphroditic perfection will be regained.

After this revelation, Porius must make a decision: to take the responsibility of ruling his new kingdom or to follow Emperor Arthur. An even more fanatical Christian priest has taken over from the dead one and is attempting to gain control of Edeyrnion. Porius decides that for him to fight this priest would be impossible, and that the only hope of overcoming him "would be to use the feminine element in the heart of religion itself."[118] With this (as Powys would say) Porius "buggers off," leaving Morfydd to deal with his father's funeral and the resulting conflict between her group of followers and the priest's. In fact, Porius gives over the governance of the kingdom totally to Morfydd, who becomes "the acknowledged chief, the arbitrary leader."[119]

As darkness falls on the evening of October 23, a large crowd collects in two hostile groups around their leaders. Above the crowd an immense owl flutters. Myrddin and Nineue arrive on two gray horses. The whole scene is dominated by the moon, which, because it is hidden, gives the "effect of enchantment." This is the penultimate stage of the process—the *albedo*. The alchemists called it the silver or moon condition; it might well be called the "owl resurrection." The owl circles over the head of Myrddin Wyllt, brushing him with its wings. The magician reaches up, and, taking the bird into his hands, draws it under his cloak. The crowd falls silent.

> And the silence of that crowd deepened to a level that was like the silence at the bottom of the ocean, and as if through some planetary sluice at the bottom of the ocean the lives of men and animals and birds and fishes, yes, and of plants and trees also, drained away, and nothing was left within that river-curve of the Vale of Edeyrnion save the four elements, save the air filled with the mystery of moonlight . . . save the waving torch-fires full of the mystery of death, save the earth itself, mother of both the darkness of life and the darkness of death.[120]

Then "as if the counsellor's mantle had been a maternal womb," there emerges a girl with "long naked legs," "beyond all words beautiful, in that wild-tossed torchlight under that far-flung moonlight."[121]

The owl is Blodeuwedd, the maiden made of flowers by the evil magician Gwydion for his son. When she falls in love with Gronwy, Gwydion transforms her into an owl. As always Powys takes what he sees on his walks as a sign: "I went to the Bwythyn in complete ruin & Deserted just as in the beginning of the Dream of Rhonabwy. There I found a White Owl just as I am writing about the owl that turns back into Blodeuwedd."[122] For months before writing the chapter, he pondered "on various ways of defending Blodeuwedd & her Gronwy from Gwydion & his Christian Mob!" He does it gloriously by having Merlin turn her back into a girl.[123] Just as he once defied the power of the resident God of Phudd in Hillsdale, Powys, the "outsider," challenges the established Welsh magician Gwydion and this time succeeds. In his creation of this powerful scene, Powys becomes, finally, the good magician, who re-creates the blossom-bird-maiden— the "lost and condemned Blodeuwedd."[124]

The completion of the opus, the final step, is the transmutation of the base metal into gold, or into the "philosopher's stone." In philosophical alchemy this final stage is represented as the resurrection of "the world-creating spirit concealed and imprisoned in matter." After the re-creation of Blodeuwedd, Myrddin and Nineue go off on horses to y Wyddfa—"the Tomb" on the summit of Eryri. Porius follows them there, knowing since he had first met "this strange Being, at once so powerful and so weak, so god-like and so animal-like," that it was his fate to "break the bonds," that were now threatening to imprison him "under a stone."[125] The mystery of the rescue of Cronos, of the lost age of gold, of the grail, of the philosopher's stone, is that it must be done over and over again. The Gnostics could never decide whether the need for this eternally repeated act of redemption signified the mystery of evil constantly attempting to overcome good or whether it signified the mystery of life constantly drawn toward death: the Anthropos, the original man, is imprisoned *either* because he has been seduced by some evil power *or* because he has been drawn down by his own reflected image in the depths of the water.[126] Powys's old obsession of the stick in the pond proves to be an archetypal image of the mystery.

It seems to Porius that y Wyddfa is "crouching like a titanic dragon-foetus, its scaly tail twisted about it in a womb of rock."[127] He cannot decide whether Nineue is imprisoning the magician in a tomb or if Myrddin is using Nineue to bring about what he himself desires, his disappearance into the maternal womb. The simplest resolution is that Nineue is the evil power that has imprisoned the good. But even in myth there are hints that in some way good and evil, Nineue and Myrddin, are two halves of one whole. In the early Welsh *Dialogue of Gwenddydd and Merddin*, Nineue calls Merlin her "twin-brother."[128] Porius associates her with the "mother of Cronos"—that is, the mother that Myrddin-Cronos has been praying to.[129] Like Anthropos drawn down into matter by his own reflection in the depths, Myrddin has looked into the eyes of Styx and he wants to "return" to his stone grave, y Wyddfa. He *is* the *lapis*. This mystery is caught in a haunting image. Porius follows Nineue and Myrddin up the mountain in golden sunlight, but suddenly the sun disappears:

> Not only had the sun disappeared, but in its passing it had carried off the whole sky. It had wrapped the whole sky round itself like a shroud and dived into Space. Headfirst it had dived, like a self-executioner hugging his drowning-stone.[130]

Although Porius sees Nineue as the seducer and imprisoner, he suspects that she "couldn't really hurt her titanic lover against his own will."[131] What further confuses him is that while Nineue is "the creature from whom it was his fate to protect this man,"[132] there is a "queer strong link between them," a "psychic bond," that holds all three of them. He feels both of them are "completely in this mysterious Being's power"[133] and are bound in double-natured implication; her burial of the magician and his rescue of Myrddin are twin aspects of an alchemical opus.

Now, on the summit of the mountain, he sees Nineue alone on her gigantic horse—Epona, the mother goddess. Before his eyes *she*, not Merlin, turns into alchemical gold, the long-awaited and worked-for goal of the opus. The sorceress stretches herself out "at full length on that sun-flecked back, like a mermaid on a golden reef."

> With a rush Porius was at her side, one hand on the beast's rump and one on the woman's knee, and in that last flicker of the sunset his eyes met hers and up to those arrow-slits his whole soul climbed and peered into her soul and was on the edge of forcing itself through those slits into her soul and of plunging down. . . .

> And suddenly as if the sun were stretching out a last passionate pharos-ray
> in search of some invisible *stele*, or death-pillar, on the very summit of y Wyddfa,
> Nineue's figure under Porius's hand became transmuted into glowing gold.[134]

He is able to resist her only because she "now deliberately . . . exposed one
of her breasts" to the sun, and Porius does not like large nipples in small breasts,
because "owing to some obscure babyish association," he is attracted to large
breasts with small nipples.[135] This piece of business, which seems quintessential-
ly Powysian, needless to say has an alchemical background. In Paracelsus's *De
Vita Longa*, the following rather enigmatic direction to the adept occurs:

> But in order to become fixed, that is, brought to an end, they have to
> oppose *the acts of Melusina* . . . which of whatever kind they may be, he says,
> we dismiss. Returning to the nymphididic realm, in order that she may be
> conceived in our minds, and that in this way we may attain to the year
> Aniadin (the time of perfection) that is, to a long life by imagination.[136]

Porius rejects the *gesta Melosines* and Nineue disappears, to join him in his
mind and imagination. As part of him, she becomes a helper. She gives him the
one thing needed to rescue the buried magician: "She drew forth from between her
unequalled thighs a small, hard, heavy pear-shaped lump of iron-ore and handed it
to him. 'He gave it to me. . . . It has been in his body since the lightning struck him
on the day he fell.'"[137] The *materia prima* is often referred to as an "ore deposit," the
raw material from which the gold is taken. The piece of lodestone (the thunder-
bolt) gives Porius strength to lift the rock from Merlin's "four-square grave."

> He felt as if he stood on an earth-crust that covered a cosmogonic cavern
> wherein the bones and ashes and the mouldering dust of gods and men and
> beasts and birds and fishes and reptiles had been gathered into a multitudi-
> nous congregated compost, out of which by the creative energy of Time new
> life could be eternally spawned.[138]

With this final alchemical vision of the *prima materia* and the four-sided
stone, the beginning and the end, the opus is complete. Both Merlin and Nineue
return to the "nymphididic realm" and Porius finds himself next morning, quite
alone, "on a rock at Harlech above the sea."[139] He reminds himself that he has
"come round full-circle this eventful week"; he began last Thursday on the platform above the eastern gate of the Gaer intent on feeling the "wicked rapture of
being for the first time in his life absolutely and uncompromisingly himself
alone,"[140] and now he is. In the process of rebirth, the thirty-year-old hero appears
to have achieved his sought-after independence and freedom. But he will never
be sure whether he has released the magician from his imprisonment by or in the
feminine, or freed him to return to the watery realm of the mothers.

Powys's own fundamental ambivalence toward freedom and containment has
never been more magnificently captured than in this novel. In 1945, at the time he
was exploring the forest primeval/forestry commission, he found a cave. He explained

to a friend, "I went through a wood above the road rail & river by a forester's 'drove' ending in a sort of mossy rocky precipice with a cave I wanted to experiment with (I mean in!) in view of my Romance of Corwen in 499 A.D. into which I am now plunged . . . and in which I now float & swim & rest on its coral-reef and its isles in perilous seas."[141] The equivocal cave/grave of the mother's womb is both a place of sweet content and entrapment. "Yesterday was the Day when at nine o'clock exactly I First huddled & crouched with deep content O sweet Content! In a Real Cave were the Stone to FALL I should be caught & doomed to DEATH."[142]

Porius could be said to be the story, perilous to write, of a man freeing himself from the maternal womb, of becoming an independent entity. But it could also be said to be a story of endless desire to return to that sea "out of which all life original- ly sprang." Endlessly repeated, images of the sea and of sexuality interweave in this novel, connected always with birth and death. "These long, slow, tranquilly-rolling ripples of sex-satisfaction resembled those other drowsily curving time-waves . . . rocking so gently upon the brimming sea of contentment, such as every child born into the world may be imagined feeling, in its first independent falling asleep after its navel-string is cut."[143] This is the "narrow chink between sleep and wake,"[144] the gold- en October week of felicity, when his mother released him from her bed and Powys became an "Independent Entity."[145] Then "the November cold winds" began.[146]

Porius is the culmination of a lifetime of learning and hurting. Into its long gestation Powys poured his manias, his memories, his magicianship, his most secret fears. Years before, Phyllis wanted him to write a book that would be "full of echos, tags, fragments, breaking it up—queer parodies of ancient very old things—inspired parody—giving indirectly the subtle values of thought without the weight of actual dullness of thought—using the strange old Mythology of the Mabinogion—why not?" He wondered then, in 1932, "Will I really ever be able to try what the T. T. thus suggests? We shall see." We *have* seen, for that is pre- cisely what he has done in this, his greatest masterpiece.

The indomitable Mrs. Meech had transformed the 2,811 pages of longhand, not one without its innumerable crossings-out, dislocated sentences, and paragraphs adrift, into 1,589 pages of typescript by the middle of June 1949, after which Powys began correcting it. On September 15, Phyllis posted one copy to the Bodley Head; the second copy went to Pollinger's office, to be sent to Simon & Schuster. John was anxious that they would find it too long and was cross because the Bodley Head had just reprinted "my confounded Autobiography" instead of using "all their boldness & imaginative spending of capital to go into publishing PORIUS!" Another worry, he confided to Louis, was that they would delay publication until after he died on the assumption that "when this old sod dies his price will go up."[147] It did not occur to him that novel would be rejected altogether, but that is what Simon & Schuster did in November, calling it "indecipherable" and "over-written." Powys became very agi- tated, imagining snakes popping out of his breasts and a devil in their houses. Phyllis could not give him her customary support, as she was spending all her time next door caring for her two infirm relatives. Aunt Harriet had always been "Capricious &

Despotic," but by now she was "a bit funny in head." He reports her impatiently opening a tin of milk "with a strong and a heavy Hammer," and throwing her false teeth out the window, which Powys considered showed "her absolute contempt for her neighbours, for the T. T.'s garden & for Wales!!" On November 28, he was called over in the middle of the night to find Phyllis's mother "half-naked taking off her night things & trying to put on her day things," and Aunt Harriet "in a crazy state . . . you might say RAMPANT." Phyllis managed to calm her aunt down while John "tried to help the poor dear Mistress disentangle her clothes." Powys would have made a wonderful comic script writer; he had great admiration for Danny Kaye and Charlie Chaplin, and the diary often has a strong streak of the zany. However, it was an "unspeakable Relief & Release" when Aunt Harriet died the next day.

In early December, they had more bad news about *Porius*, this time from Norman Denny, the Bodley Head's reader/editor. Although Denny at that point had not finished reading the typescript, he felt he should tell Powys his misgivings. He liked the opening but felt the book from then on "began to go downhill." He said that it was the Cewri episode that "stuck so badly in my gullet": "If you had presented it as a kind of erotic vision—a wild wet dream!—I might have been able to accept it. But being offered it on the same level of reality as the rest of the book, I jibbed badly." Denny ended his letter by suggesting that Powys "regard the book as unfinished—simply as a first draft" and to "remorselessly cut it down to round about 1,000 pages of typescript."[148]

It was, Powys wrote, "one of the very SADDEST DAYS of our days together,"[149] but he answered immediately and unequivocally.

> Nothing wd . . . make me leave out the Cewri, or make them a Dream, or tamper with them as they are here in any way. Nothing also wd induce me, persuade me, or make me, leave out or turn into anybody's dream, the Miracle of the Owl-Girl Blodeuwedd. . . . I won't launch into a metaphysical or mystical or even a poetic-imaginative defence of this element of the marvellous in this book. I'll only say that in these things I really am a "Medium" and that my autumn of the year 499 is my vision of what Reality really was then to the people of that Age. To leave out Marvels & Wonders wd be to make the whole thing false, to make it ring untrue & unreal, to make it a tiresome & tedious transferring of our present pseudo-scientific & narrowly exact scientific attitude to life & the cosmos into the brains of the people of that time. . . . I treat them as real not as dreams & who can dogmatically be sure they're not real OR never happened? Well!! anyway in the world I have always lived in & shall always live in till I'm dead.[150]

He told a friend that he could understand Denny's difficulty: "It is a little *too* real for I have a *Dark Ages* Mentality.[151] For Powys, boundary skipping between worlds was natural and normal, and both worlds are real in the *niwl*, in the magic mist, of Wales. Dorothy Richardson wrote him a long letter in 1944 asking him, "Isn't it time, wouldn't you like, to get back to England? Or do you feel at home in an undiluted Celtic twilight?" He responded to her question in a revealing postscript:

No you see
I've got a
a curious mania for
antiquity in
continuity in one
spot of the
earth's surface
if I can claim with
<u>almost</u> <u>absolutely</u>
<u>certain</u> <u>certainty</u>
a share
  by
blood-heredity
        in
this particular
  continuity
  &
it goes
back
to
Total Obscurity
  and
Mythology
 fading
  away
  too
slowly to be
 caught at any
point for certain
  between
reality & unreality
  and
between history
  and
  legend.
This ever receding
  landscape
     &
  mirage
(reality & unreality!)
  I can pursue
  here
  as
nowhere else[152]

Porius, with its fusion of history and legend, landscape and mirage, reality
and unreality, the quotidian with the fantastic, was, sadly, before its time. Fifty
years later, who knows whether Powys's view of "reality" or Denny's is more likely

to appeal to readers who have by now been initiated into the wonders and marvels of magical realism?

John wrote defiantly to Littleton, "I actually am so certain that this book is my masterpiece and far the most original & exciting I've ever written that I am sure (without any pride or vanity or conceit) that the fault is with this particular generation of young critics & not with me!! Can several publishers editors & readers be wrong & one old author, who may, too, be in his Second Childhood, be right? Yes I think it is possible!"[153] However, when, on December 26, he received another letter from Denny indicating that he would only recommend *Porius* to the Bodley Head "if I consent to cut it to one thousand typescript pages," Powys agreed to do it.

Powys described himself as a "master-cutter"[154] and he certainly had a good deal of experience at cutting his long novels by the time the demand for cuts came from the Bodley Head. Anyone studying the original typescript and noting the firm crossings-out and skilful bridging passages can only marvel at his craftsmanship. However, as always with this writer, *what* he takes out is always illuminating. He told Ross that if they made him cut it he would have to do so "by shutting my eyes and chip-chop."[155] In fact, he was very deliberate in what he cut and, most unusually, he wrote in the back of the 1950 diary exactly what cuts he *did* make. He cut out some of the pages he himself had found "tiresome," and some of the long conversations. Whether or not at the publisher's specific request or his own discretion, he cut out almost a complete chapter which dealt with Brochvael's homosexual infatuation with the servant, Drom. Much more seriously, he was forced to cut out many of the sections to which Denny had particularly objected. Unfortunately, these are the crucial alchemical chapters, which were his "foundation." The entire chapter about the magical child was deleted as well as innumerable other passages referring to alchemical symbolism. He did stubbornly insist on keeping the Cewri giants and the owl resurrection but their context, and much of the imagery that buttressed them, were also eliminated, which is why, until the novel was finally published in full so many years later, this "secret" *werk* remained more secret than Powys had intended.

He also cut many of the scenes in which he explores the hero's affinities with Nineue, and virtually the whole of the chapter in which he and Nineue make love. After the cuts Nineue became more simply a force for evil and much of the marvelous tension between them is eliminated. Although Phyllis is most obviously Morfydd, in his diary he says she is also Nineue to his Merlin.[156] As in *Wolf Solent*, the cuts here raise more questions than they answer. Many of Porius's reveries, ecstasies, and horrors were also eliminated. In the process, whether deliberately or not, Powys makes Porius more a man of action, more a hero in the usual sense, and much less a portrait of himself. But other cuts appear to have been a deliberate elimination of aspects of himself which simply were, viewed in cold blood, too revealing. Most often, what was carefully cut were passages, sometimes even sentences, that reverberate with memories of what had been most destructive in his own childhood.

Powys knew himself that he had "all the long-winded faults full of rhetorical purple patches of a speaker who has by a *tour-de-force* become a writer."[157] But cutting this novel of a lifetime by one-third was another "tour-de-force." It took him two and a half months, but by March he had cut the five hundred pages demanded by the Bodley Head. Phyllis read through the whole book after the cutting, cried, then set to work typing "all the mixed up muddled amended passages!!" For the next two weeks he could hear her: "Tap! tap! above my head in the little room upstairs yes she is typing with MUCILAGE & SCISSORS those 'joinings up' where I have cut out things—all too many things!"[158] Both were bitter about the whole process, feeling that he had had to "scrape Porius into a Skeleton," adding, "though this may be for the publisher's good and my good and the general reader's good."[159] The mutilated book, "now just 999 pages," was sent to Denny on April Fool's Day, 1950.

A month later, Denny had read the revised novel and sent it to the Bodley Head "with my blessing." It was not until August that Powys finally heard from the publishers, who by then had had the book under consideration for a year.[160] The offer was an insulting £100. Powys felt like the beggar that Gertrude had once turned away at Montacute and who froze to death in the field below, but he decided that "no beggar wd be satisfied with this. It is an insult! but even if they had said—here's 300£—it would not even keep me while they have had the book!!!!"[161] For once he could express his anger, not only to his diary, but to relatives and friends. He wrote Gertrude: "I have just formally rejected & refused the Bodley Head offer of Porius—they thoroughly fool me as if I were a silly old man who can be ordered about as they like! . . . But I am in an obstinate father-like rage!"[162] He never forgave Denny, the "Turner Down of my Jabber Work" or "the publisher to whom I shall never return."[163]

His businesslike sister Marian was equally furious with Pollinger, who "should have got it out of them some months back." She wrote that she had already alerted Malcolm Elwin (by then a senior editor for Macdonald) of events and asked John to send the abridged typescript to Elwin, which he did that same day.[164] Elwin sent in a glowing reader's report, calling it "a work of great genius," and *Porius* was accepted. Powys records that on October 13, 1950, "there was an offer from Harvey of Macdonald to give me £200 down & 50£ on publication. . . . The T. T. went down to town in pouring rain & posted my acceptance of offer." It was published in August 1951. After much further negotiation on Marian's part, the plates were bought by the Philosophical Library in America for £70 and *Porius* was published there in 1952. Gilbert Turner had advised him as far back as December of 1949 to "leave the Bodley Head & to try Macdonald, Malcolm Elwin's firm, with Porius rather than cut out so much,"[165] but Powys had decided to cut rather than change publishers. Macdonald might well have taken the original *Porius* had *he* taken Turner's advice, and for a brief while

Powys hoped they might do so now, but instead they decided to take the abridged version.

The Macdonald *Porius* was not, therefore, the *Mabinogion* he had written. In the novel he is many selves—he is Porius, the young hero; he is Brochvael, the old scholar; he is Taliesin, the poet; he is, above all, the Henog—the man who is writing the Vita Merlini. None of these selves particularly like the other, and while to the Henog Powys gave some of his most carefully thought-out ideas of what he had been trying to accomplish, to his Porius self he gave the opportunity to castigate the professional writer who is "absolutely self-centred and self-sufficient," and whose "satisfaction in his own performance was a lonely and solitary thing and completely independent of all outward response or recognition."[166] Porius decides, "The fellow's quite mad, or he is the most original chronicler of events there's ever been!"

> "He's alone in Space," Porius thought, "and only Space has the power of reflecting his stories in such a manner that all their faults are lost and all their virtues remain. In the eternally empty Space round him he sees the perfection he aimed at and gives himself the credit for having attained it; and maybe, in some cosmic ideal sense, he *has* attained it."
>
> "Everybody who listens to the Henog," he thought, "is resolved into this paradigm or perfect pattern of an ideal myth; and, by becoming a part of it himself, is transformed into the very perfection of which in his critical hostility he refused to see so much as the fragment of a shadow! Thus while the Henog's hearers . . . may actually be tearing to pieces the tale he is telling them, they are themselves, as far as the story-teller is concerned, irresistibly compelled to assume the role of small and unimportant portions of the perfect pattern of his vision."[167]

This is a superb hit back against the Dennys of the world, and all those readers who are too impatient or too fearful to find their way into the myth. Powys was indebted to Macdonald for publishing his *chef d'oeuvre* at all, but he knew it was a mutilated masterpiece. Too tired, too poor, too sick to insist on all or nothing, he let it go. But Marian retrieved the original complete typescript from Simon & Schuster and kept it safe, convinced that one day a farsighted publisher would give it that "reflective space" so its perfection might be seen. And so it has happened.

"She talked at breakfast very, very, imaginatively and eloquently about manuscripts as opposed to Print and how they were a world in themselves. We came to the conclusion that all my writings belonged to the Manuscript Class."

—JCP Diary, 28 December, 1930

"And after giving me Sherborne & new cap . . . she gave me my gloves
& sent me off. After climbing the Tiny Lane & the 5 steps then I came
gollumping back."
                                                        —JCP Diary, November, 1960

"Here at the Window I look at the Mountains & such folk as may pass."
—JCP Diary, 15 January, 1959.

CHAPTER FOURTEEN

CLOUD CUCKOO LAND

1950-1963

W HEN POWYS HEARD THAT ERIC HARVEY, THE DIRECTOR OF MACDONALD, had accepted *Porius*, he exclaimed, "There's a Publisher to have found!"[1] A few years later he was still grateful, telling a friend, "It really has been the staunching and healing of all the wounds to my pride, vanity, and conceit that I've ever had in my long life—this perfect treatment from my last publishers."[2] Harvey of Macdonald coming along in old age was rather like Simon & Schuster suddenly appearing in his middle age. These two publishing firms were at once the best thing that ever happened to Powys as a writer and the worst. Simon & Schuster not only published his finest novels, they encouraged him in the writing of the philosophical tracts that added little to his reputation. Macdonald published not only *Porius*, but all the rest of the books he wrote until his death. Harvey's generosity took Powys & Phyllis out of the slough of total poverty, but at the same time his permissiveness allowed Powys to write without any editorial restraint whatsoever, and for much longer than perhaps he should have. Powys never fully recovered from the effort of writing his *Porius* or the trauma of hacking it up. During the writing, he made the occasional joking remark about entering his second childhood, but somehow, by concentrating his whole mind on the novel, by *living* it, he held himself, his erudition, and his memory intact. Now, at the age of seventy-eight, that control began to fail him. Increasingly, the present resembled a thin veneer of ruined civilization over a strong intact past.

Although he began a new story in March 1949, it was not until he had sent off the truncated *Porius* a year later that he could concentrate on it. He then wrote very quickly and finished the novel, *The Inmates*, by February 1951.[3] Not for the first time, the germ of the idea had come from Phyllis, who, at Hillsdale more than twenty years before, had begun to write a story about "the two Inmates of an Asylum—one is mad about making the world happy and the other is mad in thinking the other to be a Puppet, in fact to be the puppet Petrushka."[4] Characteristically, she did not finish it, but thereafter John would occasionally refer to himself and Phyllis as "the inmates." In 1949 he was also corresponding with a young man, Bill Gillespie, who had been diagnosed as schizophrenic and incarcerated.[5] The more immediate spark for the novel may have been Redwood Anderson's "mental trouble" in December 1949. Powys professed a great hatred for psychiatrists, and the novel was a chance to attack once again "the sophisticated experimental processes of our modern doctors' treatment of us when helpless in their hands."[6] Despite this, he longed to "have a try" himself at Redwood, "since Dr. Satchwell says he wants a Psychiatrist at Mental Healing."[7]

The plot of *The Inmates* is simple. John Hush is an orphan of twenty-two and has "no relations at all."[8] (Powys's heroes have been getting younger and younger, and casting off ever more family.) Hush has developed a minor sexual fetish and begs his guardian to have him committed to an insane asylum, Glint Hall. There he meets and falls in love with Tenna Sheer, who has murdered her father. After a few months, most of the inmates are rescued by John's guardian, who whisks them off in a helicopter to America. The novel begins on March 25—the day he and Phyllis misremembered as the day they met. Hush looks out the window of his room and sees beneath a tulip tree a "prostrate form" that "enshrined so absolutely the essence of all the maddening femininity he craved in his distraught idolatry" that he thinks he has beheld "an Elemental."[9] The attraction between them is immediate and mutual. He stares at her "in speechless enchantment," and she realizes that for the first time in her life she has someone who "belongs to her" although that person most reminds her of her doll—a puppet-doll. Hush and Tenna are undisguisedly John and Phyllis and in the novel their excited talk the first evening is a charming recounting of John and Phyllis's feelings in that long-ago encounter at Joplin.

Powys says in a preface that every one of the other inmates is "a symbol of some important aspect" of the "truth" of the "Philosophy of the Demented"—a philosophy based, he asserts, on "the theory of William James that we live in a multiverse rather than a universe." For instance, a character, improbably named Zeit-Geist, is "an epitome of those lonely sensations when we feel ourselves to be isolated consciousnesses at some uncertain point in boundless space and time. It is at the emptiness round us all that this mad creature points his horribly wagging finger."[10] Powys appears to be saying now that the acceptance of his philosophy of the essential loneliness of every human being will drive a person insane, and that the various forms of insanity are, in essence, the different responses of individuals to that loneliness. It is an intriguing idea but in fact, his inmates remain for the most part only "symbols." In this novel, he creates characters mainly to use them as mouthpieces for his own beliefs and manias, or as an excuse to air an ancient wrong. For example, Hush's "protector" (the one who puts him into the asylum in the first place) and the protector's American fiancée, seem to have been created for no other reason than to rehearse once again Powys's feelings about Louis Wilkinson and Frances Gregg. Although Hush protests that he is "completely devoid of every sort of homosexual vibration,"[11] when he sees his guardian *with that girl*," it is the "most hateful moment of his life" and he feels "an indescribable jealousy." "Does he think he can hand him-self over to that girl and keep me too? Not on your life, heart of my hell!" These are indeed what Hush calls "the private thumb-screws of the mind."[12]

The Powys-hero has any number of sexual fetishes and phobias but he is per-fectly sane, managing to arrange to free all the inmates, albeit with the help of his protector and a highly unlikely helicopter.[13] With the exception of Tenna, the rest of the residents are at most neurotics, certainly not certifiable psychotics. Powys had absolutely no idea of what went on in a lunatic asylum. However, he presumably thought that by setting the novel in an institution for the insane, he could allow his old obsessions, his fiercely repressed sadism, his desire for freedom and his desire for containment, all simply come out—in the guise of madness. Many of Hush's manias are those Powys already described as his own in the diary. What makes *The Inmates* interesting is that Powys explores, as a "psychologist of the soul" must, the possible origins of the manias. This is something he had not done even in the frank diary. Powys equates his hero's "imaginary difficulty in breathing" with a terror of "the black darkness round him," which he "mentally tries to push away with both hands."[14] In one sense this is a response, or a reac-tion, to the philosophy of aloneness, but Powys is hinting here at a more primal fear. In *Porius*, Prince Einion's last words arre, "Mother! Mother! Mother!' . . . She *will* turn out the lamp!" We are suddenly back in childhood and the fear of the dark.

He explores too the putative inception of his voyeurism, which Powys now sees as the flip side of "that blind sick horror of everything feminine." John Hush explains to Tenna that the reason he asked to be incarcerated was because "the only thing that gave me a real ecstasy" was to cut off a tiny lock of a girl's curls, but he goes on to say that this is only a recent manifestation of a lifelong mania for staring "like a crazy hypnotised vampire at some particular girl whom I dis-covered I could watch without attracting hostile attention."[15] What he calls "that old boyish mania about femininity" is, on the one hand, being "thrilled" by everything about women; on the other hand, it is "his boyish terror of growing . . . not into a man but into a woman." Powys gives, through Hush, such a bizarre explanation of the origin of the mania that it quite possibly had a basis of truth. John Hush recalls a conversation he had with his old nurse who had been with his mother at his birth. She witnessed "the performance of what was an ancient custom . . . when by chance the infant's feet appeared first." An "ancient crone," to hasten the birth, had rubbed the child's emerging feet with a "particular kind of pebble-stone." A breech birth has been known to cause special terrors in babies beyond the birth trauma itself, but Powys makes the association between this and his fear of turning into a woman.

> His mother, the nurse told him, had set her heart on the infant being a girl, "And if you, Master John," she had added, "be soft where women be soft, you may take it from me 'tis that pebble-stone fixed it—first in *her* mind, and then, half-born though ye were, in *yours*."

The possibility that this insane dread in his boyhood of developing certain feminine attributes and necessities which was so oddly associated with a horror of going bare-foot might be explained by this incident . . . came back to him now with revealing force.[16]

Hush always wears heavy boots, otherwise "he felt his breasts beginning to grow and their nipples to distend . . . get so long in fact that he could wave them about in the air! . . . Why, he could take hold of those window-bars with his elongated trunk-like nipples, nipples made of that warm, intimate, flexible, baby-smelling, rubber-like stuff, that seemed to have been stripped off the very secretest organs of warm nature-hidden life."[17] This absurd but rather horrifying passage is grounded in an existential terror—only one of many Powys (who also always wore heavy boots) was attempting to keep under control at this time. There are word-salad descriptions in the diary which appear more authentically crazy than in the novel:

> It was a peculiar sort of walk. I had my Tortured Stick & I wore (Though the Snakes of my Unknown Sex burst out of my Nipples to hear me be so exhibitionist like the bearded Gents in that night cafe in Paris where this murdered man went who our paper says where Existentialists cultivating not old but bearded "despairists" cultivating despair burst out into their evocations of Beaudelaire) wore I say my new Tie sent by Marian.[18]

In this novel Powys also returns to his exploration of the contraries of freedom and containment, so beautifully expressed in *Porius*. The simplicity of the plot reveals more clearly than ever before the diastole-systole rhythm of Powys's "mythology." Hush begs his guardian for the security of the asylum, not so much to guard the outside world from his mania as to protect himself from the "real world." Inside its walls, he feels as if he were back in the protective cocoon of childhood—even the iron bars at the window remind him of his "nursery-window." The first morning he awakes with "a vague sensation of extraordinary happiness," as if he were a "child of eight," at the seashore with his nurse in East Anglia.[19] But almost as soon as he is in, he wants to get out. Hush escapes from the asylum, but he does not go back to "the outside world that's liable to hurt us."[20] Instead of accompanying the other inmates on a plane, he and Tenna join a traveling circus as a horoscope reader and a palmist, to live happily ever after in the anonymity of its tents. Whether Tenna wants this freedom is debatable. She has already been in the asylum a couple of years and tries to explain to John that "they can't do anything to us as long as we're *both* certified, both under control!"[21] Perhaps the most unsettling aspect of this novel is Powys's depiction of Phyllis as Tenna. Tenna hates her father, "a great arch builder," and hates his "devoted struggle to become rich."[22] Powys before hinted in *Morwyn* that Phyllis and her father had a difficult relationship. Whether this was true or not, he now takes the idea to its ultimate conclusion. Tenna thinks her mother killed herself to escape her father and "left me alone with him."[23] She tried to "kill her dad";

in fact, the homicidal hatred now extends toward all old men. The father had her incarcerated because she has "a passion for violence . . . for physical violence."[24] Tenna is much closer to being truly mad than John Hush. If the portrayal had any connection with real life (and his fictional fantasies usually did) then this was an expression of his real fear that Phyllis was always on the edge of violence toward "old men" such as himself. Because of her love for him, Tenna follows John out of the asylum, where she feels protected from her own violence, but it is Hush who obviously will have to spend the rest of his life taking responsibility for restraining her violence.

Despite his manias, John Hush always appears to be in command of himself and others; the controls of his author are less obvious. There is so much chatter from his characters about their philosophical stances that the reader can be forgiven for not noticing that the talk about being "oneself" goes on midst the most flagrant violence. Powys allows himself to punish (there is no other word for it) all those who are "guilty," and he expresses the punishment in the most extreme images. He was still convinced that Puckle died as a result of Deacon's bullying, and while he was writing the *Inmates*, he had fantasies of killing Deacon with an iron bar.[25] Despite, or because of this, he kept on writing, transforming the energy called up by the raging fantasies into a prose illuminated by electrifying imagery. The sadistic guard, Gewlie, is disintegrated by the mental/magical powers of Esty, a Lama from Tibet, who is visiting England "in his escape from the Communists."[26] Another guard, the good Cuddle, shoots the psychiatrist in the head because the psychiatrist is a "maimer of dogs." Cuddle tries unsuccessfully to hide the body in the rhododendrons, so Esty destroys the body by pressing the faces of two clerics into it. The authorial voice suggests that in this way "the death . . . had been lifted out of the sphere of the criminal and tragic into the sphere of the fantastic and miraculous."

A long section of *The Inmates* circles around John Hush's maniacal obsession with Nancy Yew's possessive love for her halfwit son—"it makes anyone *murderous*."[27] Nancy feels that her son has "no right to have any life save me . . . who grew him in the dark depths of my being like a ripe, sweet, lovely round obedient little bulb!"[28] We are back to the womb and containment, love and death. For John Hush, the eye of love has become a devouring snake.

> He couldn't expel from his consciousness that possessive, in-drawing, insucking, maternal eye of the mother of Seth . . . that eye wherein this much-praised "love" could be observed, in the serpentine coils of its devouring insatiability, swallowing its offspring's freedom to live a life of its own and exciting itself to swallow the more voluptuously as its own pity for the helpless thing's struggles draws forth more maternal saliva to smooth the path of its re-enwombing.[29]

Hush makes sure that the idiot boy flees with the rest of the inmates in the bizarre helicopter escape at the end of the novel. Seth's mother tries to follow, but "the unlucky woman fell backwards from the deck of the plane, struck a twisted, sharp-edged six-foot iron stanchion fixed among the reeds. . . . The hurt to the cattle-woman's spine would alone have been fatal, even if her skull had not also been hit."[30]

A lifetime of suppressed aggression explodes in these pages. Powys tries to cover his tracks, so to speak, by suggesting in the preface that "the genius of great artists has always been in their unearthly and startling imaginations allied to madness."[31] *The Inmates* is at times a novel frightening in its violence, but by no means is it a novel of genius.

In tandem with the novel he was writing another book, *In Spite of: A Philosophy for Everyman*.[32] Rambling and perfunctory, it is the weakest and, mercifully, the last of his philosophical essays. However, one chapter, "In Spite of Madness," is of particular interest for it is, as he says in his diary, "about my own madness."[33] In this he advises those who are "insane" not to fight their madness but to hide it. "Everyone in the world, even your nearest and dearest, is a doctor desirous of curing you—while *your* purpose, absolutely alone as you are in a world far madder than yourself, is to conceal your insanity."[34] He articulates a belief that he has held throughout a life of physical and mental illness: that "symptoms" are not something to be cured, but to be respected as daimonic powers at work in the soul, part of the *mythos* of the psyche. "By 'curing' us, what our doctors mean is killing our mania; but what *we* feel is that *our mania is us*, and that by killing our mania they don't cure us; on the contrary, they kill us by inches."[35] He then debases this profound intuition by offering two pieces of advice for "everyman." Take up the "devil's bundle" filled with your deepest horrors, and whatever hour of day or night, "set off at a run along the nearest highroad" and run until you "reach home exhausted" and "all the imaginations that have caused us most discomfort in our whole migration through life have been pounded into a stinking blot." He assures his reader that "there is nothing in the whole arsenal of psychological and psychoanalytical cures for madness that approaches in efficacy this panting race."[36] Perhaps this supercilious nonsense is no worse than today's advice to laugh your way to happiness or to jog your way to health. His second solution is to take a "Pantagruelian quest for a pleasanter life"—a particularly ironic and increasingly desperate piece of advice when, as he was writing this, his own particular private devil, "Diabolos Morbidus" had his "claws into my mind"[37] as never before. For much of 1952 and 1953 he struggled with "my demons . . . those mad dreams of the mind."[38] He tries to keep control by noting on his walks the flowers that are coming out, hearing a meadow pipit, seeing three heifers, a telephone pole that reminds him of a rake and then a cross. But: "On the way Back—Beware Mad bare naked eyes & beware milk-weeping nipples!!!!"[39] This terror goes on constantly until, on the twentieth of June, he records: "I saw Forget-me-not in the water of the Devil's Stream. . . . So I am ready to face eye balls & nipples of my very own & madness too & to forget & let time & events & Nature erase their loathsome & appalling memory!"

It was while he was writing *In Spite of* that Gertrude died. This eldest sister had always been, Powys said, the "Head Nurse of our Zoo or our Asylum," and she gave succor to "her fellow Inmates of the Unknown Glint"[40] until the end. She continued to visit Littleton, who was badly crippled by arthritis, to protect Katie, and to concern herself with the various ailments of her brothers until she booked herself into Weymouth Hospital on April 22, 1952. She died the next day of leukemia. The apparently sudden death took them by surprise, but when Powys went to visit Chydyok for the last time in October 1941, he wrote in his diary that he had had a private talk with Gertrude in the kitchen: "She told me of a dream she'd had of her own death—in a gorse bush—and people came & she cried 'can't I even have my Death to myself??'"[41] After a life of serving others, Gertrude had this at least. In remembrance, Powys dedicated to this eldest sister a "flourishing Thorn Bush in full light Green leaf."

Phyllis's mother died exactly one year later. It was a slow death: "the poor dear Mistress seems always dying & then recovers again." Since a fall in November 1952 she had been "in confusion of mind & of body," and Phyllis had to nurse her day and night. Powys wondered if caring for someone who "lies on her back like a corpse" was upsetting, but "the T.T. tried to explain to me that it was not any crazy crazy-hazy-dazy Horror for Excrements or Anatomical projections or macabre Sights and Monstrous Vignettes of Bodies going to Bits & to pieces and to formless jelly and back to sea plankton . . . that spoils her satisfaction in life but but the perfectly appalling appalling effort she has to make to Cook & prepare food and to go to Door or the Doors & distribute it."[42] Phyllis may have been as violent as Tenna in *The Inmates*, but in real life she was matter-of-fact sane.

During these long months Powys was attempting to write another novel, although, as he frankly admitted, "my memory grows more and more confused under all these terrible agitations."[43] Fortunately, he chose a subject he knew so intimately and an author he had studied for so many years that the necessary memory seemed to come more from the "deep wells of the mind" he once talked about than from a tired brain. He intended to write a prose version of Homer's *Odyssey*, but Eric Harvey tactfully suggested that instead he write a tale about Odysseus's last voyage. This proposal appealed to Powys, although he admitted to Ben Roberts that the romance would be more "in the style of Tennyson than of Joyce."[44] Shortly after he began the novel, *Atlantis*,[45] in January 1952, he saw something on a walk that impressed him "from a mythological point of view & so to have it explained I have today ordered from Heffers . . . Jung & my greatly admired Dr. Kerényi on Mythology."[46] This was *Introduction to a Science of Mythology*, by C. G. Jung and Carl Kerényi, published in 1951.[47] A few years before Powys told his friend Huw Menai that he was "very suspicious" of Jung "just because he is so much like myself . . . dealing with the poor bewildered human soul,"[48] but by this time Powys had decided he "loathed" Jung "as much as I love Freud."[49] However, he admired Carl Kerényi, an appreciation which initially may have arisen out of Kerényi's esteem for him. In 1947 Phyllis came across *Romandichtung und Mythologie*, the correspondence between Kerényi and Thomas Mann.[50] In it there are a number of references to Powys, and in one letter, dated February 7, 1934, Kerényi wrote, "Besides yourself, it is primarily from English writers that I have learned to perceive 'spiritual' realities in 'mythological' forms—notably from D. H. Lawrence and the great mythologist, J. C. Powys. . . . Both your Joseph novel and Powys' *A Glastonbury Romance* testify to the return of the European spirit to the highest, the mythic realities."

Phyllis reacted to this unexpected source of praise with "pleasure" and John with "anti-narcissistic inverted contraceptional Vanity,"[51] but he wrote an adulatory blurb for Kerényi's *The Gods of the Greeks*, which was translated into English in 1951.[52] In Powys's own copy of the book he wrote on the flyleaf, "John Cowper Powys / My chief Authority for 'Atlantis.'" Presumably he was referring to Kerényi and not to himself, for in the front of his 1955 diary he wrote, "this is the modern book that has influenced me more than any other & that was at the heart of my Atlantis."[53] He would have been particularly sympathetic to Kerényi's stated aim, which was "an experimental attempt to translate the mythology of the Greeks back . . . into its original medium, into mythological *story-telling*."[54] In his introduction, Kerényi quoted extensively from Thomas Mann's 1936 lecture "Freud and the Future."[55] Powys was almost as suspicious of his contemporary Mann as he was of Freud, which is somewhat surprising since there were remarkable affinities between them in novelistic themes. However, Mann's comments in the following passage would have resonated, neatly summarizing as they do Powys's most profoundly held beliefs:

> Psychology's thrusting back into the childhood of the individual soul is at the same time a thrusting back into the childhood of mankind—into the primitive and the mythical. . . . The depths of the human soul are also "Primordial Times," that deep "Well of Time" in which Myth has its home and from which the original norms and forms of life are derived. For Myth is the foundation of life; it is the timeless pattern, the religious formula to which life shapes itself. . . . The moment when the story-teller acquires the mythical way of looking at things, the gift of seeing the typical features of characteristics and events, that moment marks a beginning of his life.

There is little doubt that *Atlantis*[56] is written by a storyteller who has acquired "the mythical way of looking at things." Powys now took the "wonders and marvels" of *Porius*, so castigated by the Bodley Head's editor, to their ultimate stage. There are singular scenes involving gods, goddesses, monsters, and legendary creatures. As well as his usual huge cast of human characters, Powys gives life and speech to inanimates such as a stone pillar, a wooden club, and an olive shoot. The novel is only nominally about the Tennysonian Ulysses and his last journey "to the West." Although the old Odysseus eventually leaves Ithaca to sail beyond the Pillars of Hercules to visit the sunken continent of Atlantis, the novel is mainly concerned with a revolution. The Olympian Establishment that represents the Power of Order is threatened with an insurrection of the old gods—the giant, animal, female gods (for "the older times were matriarchal").[57] The Powers of Disorder are exploding the cosmos into chaos, so that a Second Age of Cronos might begin. Powys's favourite dream of earlier days—of a world of magic rising again—he now makes into a fictional reality. He then proceeds to demolish his own dream. Odysseus is portrayed as a tired old man who is forcing himself to begin another journey not for any heroic reason but because, as he admits to himself, he wants to "escape" from having to deal with the new chaotic life that is struggling to be born. Another character, Telemachos, is the bearer of the Powysian philosophy ("You are a lonely individual. . . . You are surrounded by things that are made of the four elements. . . . You have the power of embracing these things.")[58] But as Telemachos expounds this life philosophy, he too feels "an inexpressible longing to escape from the whole business; . . . yes! from the ancient earth herself, mother of us all . . . from it all!"[59]

Young Nisos is not tired, but he too bears the marks of a shift in Powys's world view. Nisos wants to think from himself "outwards," unlike Enorches, the priest of Eros and Dionysos, who "thinks towards himself inwards."[60] Enorches asserts that through ecstasy he gains the power of touching that which is beyond normal awareness. He worships Eros for the "Secret behind life" and Dionysos for the "Secret behind death."[61] Zeuks, "an evenly balanced middle-of-the-road Achaean, moderate in all the imponderables,"[62] insists that Eros and Dionysos really represent "Not-Being" and that Enorches worships them because he hates life. Zeuks is Powys's new magician. His Rabelaisian philosophy is a life of sensation and of defiance toward a cruel First Cause. Significantly, his philosophy changes in the course of events and, as it does, another favourite theory of the author's is discarded. Zeuks comes to realize that "only a very few heroic human souls, and they probably already half-crazy, could possibly practise my philosophy of . . . defiance of the whole of existence."[63] Zeuks, who is "at one and the same time, a god, a man, a beast, a bird, a fish, a worm and an insect,"[64] has the long-sought-after "ichthyosaurus-ego." Like Myrddin Wyllt, he has the power of remembering past existences, but unlike Myrddin, Zeuks has decided that he must force himself to "forget," even though "his whole taut skin drums from within to the tune of 'remember.'"[65]

In 1949 Powys had written an essay for the *Occult Observer* on the unconscious. It is a confused piece, but in it he appears to reject everything he had spent a lifetime exploring. He calls the unconscious "a receptacle for horrid memories, like a psychic kangaroo's pouch, which each of us is doomed to carry about." He then insists that this, "the black Acheron of our mythological selves," does not really exist, and that "we have forgotten all the dreadful things that happened to us as babies, as children, as boys."[66] The illogic is necessary for Powys now. As Zeuks says, to remember is to "be sent raving through Arima like a naked madman."[67]

Eventually, Zeuks, Odysseus, and Nisos set off in their ship to the newly sunken Atlantis. Odysseus and Nisos descend, as all heroes have descended, to find the island beneath the sea which the Gods of Order have destroyed. The wondrous city is the concrete fulfilment of Powys's complex vision, "one vast musical composition in marble and stone,"[68] just as the "completely bi-sexual and androgynous"[69] ruler of the city is Powys's former "god within." Shockingly, when the creature speaks, it asserts the complete domination of science, and Odysseus's club, of its own volition, smashes the "indescribably beautiful face" to bits. The heroes sail on but never reach the Isles of the Blest, that age-old symbol of the centre. Ironically, it is the coast of America that they finally reach, and Zeuks dies laughing "at this big, bloody, beggarly joke of a world."[70] It is the old Powys, who knows a periphery when he sees one, who is laughing at his own joke.

Kerényi praised Greek mythology for its "archaic massiveness and freedom, the monotony and desultory extravagance of that unsurpassably spontaneous documentation of human nature." Powys's *Atlantis* in that respect is pure mythology. A moth and a fly that inhabit a crack in Odysseus's club act as a chorus in the play.[71] They speak a "long-hidden language"—the "universal language of matter"—in which "the sensations that certain words convey to us are [more important] than the precise nature of the words used or the number of the syllables they contain."[72] Powys believed as profoundly as did Kerényi that mythology is "an activity of the psyche externalised in images,"[73] but the language of the psyche is not easily conveyed. Although it sold fairly well, 2,000 copies, *Atlantis* was not one of Powys most admired books. An anonymous reviewer wrote that the book "may have an allegorical significance, . . . in fact, it must have an allegorical significance, for otherwise it would signify nothing at all." But Powys was now well beyond attempting to justify his storytelling to the critics of the world. As Kerényi says, "in mythology, to *tell* is to justify."[74]

Powys had known Evalyn Westacott for some time. She was involved in the Anti-Vivisection Society and wrote on the subject of vivisection. She was also interested in Paracelsus and had written about the seven alchemical processes. So when in October 1953 she sent him her *Roger Bacon in Life and Legend*, Powys considered that either Chance or "Aunt Atropos" had "chosen for me my next book."[75] However, he had only begun thinking about this "new Historic Romance" when Theodore died in November 27, 1953—not of another stroke but of bowel cancer. What effect this death had on John is difficult to tell. He reported it in his diary: "DEATH of Theodore. I cut my toenails. I saw One Carrion Crow I saw one Partridge I heard one Jay I heard one Grouse." And that appears to be that for the person who had always roused such ambivalent feelings in John Cowper. He makes no further mention of Theodore in his diary, except to report that Louis wrote him that Theodore's last words about his brother were "John's Happiness depends on his Demons."[76] How uncomfortably well Theodore knew his eldest brother! John's daemon *was* inoperative without his demons.

John Cowper's son died two and a half months later, after a long illness.

Following the death of his mother in a nursing home in Bath in 1947, in lieu of a helicopter Littleton Alfred celebrated his freedom by buying a motorcycle. In July 1949, while visiting his uncle, Harry Lyon, in Devon, he had an accident with the bike, hurting his right arm. A curate for six years after his ordination as a Catholic priest, Littleton Alfred finally obtained his first senior post at Dursley, Gloucestershire, that same year. He appears to have been very happy there, but two years later he was moved to Peasedown St. John, Somerset, then a poor mining village in the Mendips. He was there less than a year when, in September 1952, he went to a nerve specialist in London who ordered complete rest. Powys assumed that it was the "hard conditions of his work at Peasedown" that "have knocked his nerves to pieces" but decided that "it's impossible to have him here—we have all we can deal with in our own situation." It was "Old Littleton" who took the son to his own home in West Pennard, although he was himself now almost totally incapacitated with arthritis.[77] In December, the "luckless son," as Powys now referred to him, went into hospital in Bath, but it was not until the following March that the "monstrously weird mysteriously unique affliction" was diagnosed. By April 1953 it was reported that his "arms & hands are useless, his legs are tottery his speech thick & even his swallowing not easy to him."[78] Littleton Alfred had to hire a man to carry him around and look after his bodily needs. Friends brought his "wounded and erratic son" to see John in August for a few hours and "he was much worse than I ever thought he would be." His son left behind him "Bill Bruin the Human Doll I bought for him in Arundel when he was 3." In December, Harry Lyon died. Littleton Alfred was supposed to have inherited Lyon's considerable estate; in the event, for whatever reason, Lyon disinherited him and left everything instead to a favourite pupil. Possibly Harry was loath to have the money eventually to go to John Cowper, his old enemy. Littleton Alfred died on the sixteenth of February, 1954.[79]

Six months later, Powys and Phyllis made the momentous decision to leave Corwen, their home for twenty years and the landscape in which he had written two of his greatest novels, where practically every stick and stone of his walks was consecrated, named, filled with his prayers. There is very little in the diary about the process by which they came, or he came, to this pivotal decision. It is in his letters to "Old" Littleton that the reasons—some practical and some totally bizarre—become apparent. The official explanation was that although their small enclave had began with only a few houses and quiet neighbors, over the years many council houses were built in the immediate area and Cae Coed itself had more families with small children move in. Inevitably there were also more cars, the sight and sound of which irritated Powys. More logging was being done on the mountainside, and he became troubled that his solitary walks there were being overlooked by Peter-like foresters. However, there is no mention of a move in the diary until September 5, 1954, when he wrote: "We have definitely decided to GO." That is all that is said that day. The next day he wrote Littleton: "Best of Camerados I have now got an exciting bit of news for you. . . . Phyllis & I have decided to change our abode in North Wales! . . . We are—Phyllis is—going to look first at <u>Blaenau Ffestiniog</u>! . . . We hope to find a little flat above a shop there."[80]

On that same day he wrote in his diary, "This is a momentous day in the life of the T. T. & her old Man for we are now boldly and frankly confessing to everybody that we intend to leave here." Some friends were understanding: "Morrie has just come and we have told her all and she agrees that as neither of us are able to fight for our rights the only thing to do is to <u>run</u>!" Other friends, however, regarded them "as a bit crazy as <u>indeed we are</u>!"[81] On the tenth of September, Phyllis made the first trip of many trips to Blaenau on the 8:20 a.m. train. She reported that "she has no hope of our settling in Blaenau." Three days later they were both driven to Blaenau, which apparently John had never seen before: "I was thrilled by BLAENAU. Yes, I will be obstinate to live there. The T. T. left me seated on a bench with Bay Bushes behind me. And whichever way I looked it was Cloud Cuckoo Heaven. I was deeply content. . . . Resolut zu Leben in Blaenau is my Goethean Motto now!"

At this point they were still looking for a flat, but on the sixteenth his sister Lucy, her daughter Mary, and Mary's husband, Gerard Casey, came to help them in their search, and it was Gerard who found a house he thought would be suitable. The Caseys went off with a carload of their possessions, leaving Phyllis to make the arrangements with the solicitor and the first of many inspections with the surveyor and the sanitary inspector. Littleton had written to caution them against this impulse to buy, to which John responded, "We came to the conclusion that if we wanted to live in Blaenau this was the only way. I want very <u>very much</u> to live there; & we had reached the point of feeling we must leave here— so there it is!"[82] At the very end of this letter and in very small writing, there is something that had never been referred to before, and never mentioned again. After the death of Admiral Cotton, the new owner of the Cae Coed houses decided that it was more lucrative to sell them than rent them. By 1953 theirs was the only house that was still rented. In this letter to Littleton he spells out what he thought were the implications of this. "Phyllis couldn't have stayed on here after my death for the man who owns this house wh is the last of the 8 houses of Cae Coed unsold is naturally keen to have possession of it to sell. The rentbook is in my name and as long as I am alive he can't put us out but the moment I'm dead he can turn Phyllis out." This was not only incorrect, it was self-delusory. According to American law at least, she was already his common-law wife;[83] the simple solution would have been for them to marry after Margaret and his son died and then the landlord/owner could not have evicted her. Alternatively, she could have done the same thing when he died as she was doing now—that is, looked for another place. Given her predilection for warmth and culture, it would not likely have been Blaenau. Phyllis summed up the Blaenau climate to Francis Powys some years later: "It has been stormy and bitterly cold—and now that it is warmer—it rains and rains—48 hours once sans cesse—with dense mist as the only variation."[84] Even John recognized this quickly enough after they moved there and constantly referred to the bitter winds which they had been protected from in Corwen by the Berwyns.

Why Blaenau? Why did they not consider returning to Weymouth, which both he and Phyllis loved? Or to the seaside town of Rhyll which he often mentioned in the diary as a place they both would like to retire to? Or they could have stayed in Corwen where their close friends at Dee Bank were thinking of making a house on their property into flats. There are several hints in his letters to Littleton why he developed what he describes as his "peculiar & special mania" to live in Blaenau. Its quarries reminded him of the Ham Hill quarries of his Montacute childhood. More importantly, if obscurely, he thought it was the place where many events in his beloved *Mabinogion* took place. To move impulsively to a place neither of them knew for the sake of a myth is sufficiently outré to ring true. The even more eccentric possibility was this: he had recently been reading Aristophanes with a view to making a translation of it for publication, and he decided that Blaenau was the Cloud Cuckoo Land of Aristophanes's play *The Birds*. A translator describes *The Birds* as "literally escapist, in that its heroes, wearied of the Athenian atmosphere, decide to build a utopia which they call Nephelococcygia (Cuckoonebulopolis) in the sky."[85] Only Powys could consider Corwen an Athens or Blaenau a utopia.

One reason for moving that is never verbalized was that, now that her aunt and mother were dead, Phyllis finally had the freedom to do some of the things she enjoyed. He never understood, or professed never to have understood, that venturing into the outside world, if not exactly the "sophisticated life" she had once craved, only made her realize how bound she still was.

> Yesterday the T. T. had one of her mysterious fits of Misery so that she could hardly bear it after visiting Mrs. Morgan of whom she is particularly fond. Why is it that her plunges into the outer life of the world send her back to find her normal life so miserable when really left in it she is often quite happy? It is a mystery & I do not like it.[86]

Phyllis had become very close to the next door neighbor, Edith Jones, who as a nurse had provided her with great emotional and physical support during the mother's illness. The two of them were now going off together to the movies, to shop in Llangollen, Ruthin, Wrexham, even to Shrewsbury. He began to complain in his diary that he never knew where she was going. John Cowper hinted to friends that the move to Blaenau would make things easier for Phyllis. It is true that the bank, the main shops, the butcher, and the laundry lady in Corwen were a long steep trek away for Phyllis who, lugging several heavy baskets, had to do this three or four times a week. But by this period she was usually given rides by her friends and Edith, her husband, or son often did the shopping for her. It is also true that Phyllis complained that she wished she did not have so many people pressing in on her. John interpreted this to mean their neighbors, not his visitors who were particularly numerous that summer of 1954. The truth is that she enjoyed her involvement with the community and was obviously respected and liked by her neighbors. By moving to Blaenau he removed her from people she had come to know and depend on, as he did when they moved from Hillsdale to Dorset. His visitors, however, kept coming, in ever-increasing numbers, after their move to Blaenau.

Phyllis *did* long for a flat smaller than the Cae Coed house, but the house they bought, 1, Waterloo, had only one room downstairs, one room upstairs, a scullery, and an outside toilet. Every penny they had as well as the money they received from Littleton Alfred's tiny estate went into making it habitable. It was five months more before they could move in, during which time Phyllis was constantly back and forth by long train ride to Blaenau, supervising the renovations. The cottage backed against a slate wall and was next to a waterfall, so there were major problems with sewage and damp. They had electricity and an indoor toilet installed but there was no room for a proper bathroom. Phyllis knew that the cottage was not suitable, but it was all there was available in Blaenau, and she realized that he was determined to move there and nowhere else. At Cae Coed she began disposing of the possessions of twenty years which could not possibly fit into the tiny house. A good deal went into storage, but much of his library and many of his most valuable manuscripts went to help Francis Powys, Theodore's son, who had opened a bookshop in Hastings. It was at this time they drew up new wills and made Francis their literary executor and heir. George Sims, a book dealer, bought other manuscripts that she found in the attic and eventually sold them on to American universities and to private dealers. Powys was pleased to receive £125 for the manuscripts but found it was "a weird experience reading my own prose & poetry of half a century ago."[87] The money helped to pay for the "Half-Cottage of Stone," for which they paid £165, although the renovations cost three times more.

1, Waterloo was finally ready in May, and on May 3, 1955 he went for his first walk in this new landscape and named his first rock. Then he took up the long-delayed *Brazen Head*. By July he was two-thirds of the way through but finding it onerous. He felt that his mind was "disintegrating in so many ways at once that I find it hard to steer it in the direction I desire to go." He was grateful to the considerate and kindly Eric Harvey, who suggested ways "to make the book more exciting & adequate," and even more to Phyllis, who gave him "wonderful help in the difficult business of connecting the characters with the plot of the story."[88] When it was published, he sent off a copy to Westacott, with the inscription "without whose scholarly book on Roger Bacon this rambling tale could never have been written." He dedicated the novel to Gilbert Turner, who had sent him numerous books on the subject and loyally, if illegally, traversed dangerous military bombing ranges in Dorset in search of requested local color.

In *The Brazen Head* Powys explores the alchemical theory of magnetism, according to which nature or matter houses a self-creative energy—*energeia akinesis*. If it can be tapped, this force, sexual in nature, has the power for good or for evil. Powys creates two different magicians, Roger Bacon and Peter Peregrinus, to represent these dualities. Roger Bacon, a "notorious magician," has invented and constructed a brass Head that has the potential to "think as a man, and speak as a man."[89] Although mechanically complete, it apparently needs a virgin to "to make it its real self."[90] Bacon asks a young Jewess, Ghosta, to straddle the head and press it between her naked thighs. She is willing to do this because she has always been "fascinated by the word *Parthenogenesis*." During this ritual, the girl experiences an "erotic ecstasy" and draws from "the inmost depths of herself a dewdrop of living creation."[91] The head is thus given life by parthenogenetic creation and acquires a "unique power of revelation" which is ostensibly a power for good.

Bacon's old friend, Peter Peregrinus, "a great student of magnetism," has for twenty years been embarked on a similar quest and invented a magic lodestone which also has the immense potency of *energeia akinesis*. But unlike Bacon's sex-in-the-head (or on the head), Peregrinus's lodestone is activated through contact with his own "naked organs of generation."[92] His lodestone is referred to as "the Wand of Merlin,"[93] and his life—like that of Powys's other magicians, Uryen and Geard—has been a "frantic quest" which was "much more like a quest for the Sangraal than any ordinary alchemistic pursuit."[94] However, Peregrinus is explicitly considered a "demonic spirit," intending "nothing less than the deliberate manipulation of his own sexual force, by means of this powerful magnet, for the domination of the souls and wills and minds of other entities."[95] He wants to use his "magnet of universal destruction" to "injure whatever universe or multiverse there might be outside and beyond our world."[96] This "mania" in his friend troubles Friar Bacon because although he was "always aware of the presence of an almighty force behind . . . infinite space and infinite time," he feels that Peregrinus's attitude to this "remote and ultimate power" reduces not only his own life but "the lives of all other entities . . . to the level of lonely, desperate, lost souls, clinging to each other in a boundless, godless, cavernous nothingness, in fact to what he had heard a travelling Welsh tinker call *Diddym*, 'the ultimate Void.'"[97]

It is this *diddym* that was now fascinating Powys. He had written in his essay on the unconscious, "Why are we so constantly lured into its dim purlieus? . . . From fear lest the dark should truly prove to be Everything."[98] Shortly after her encounter with the head, Ghosta meets and mates with Peleg, so that "when their union had been fully achieved, there was no residual reservoir left of *energeia akinesis*."[99] Afterwards, they sit side by side with their backs to a wall of wet dark stone which has clefts of "incredible depth." These fissures lead "to the very centre of the whole planet, where such an explorer would be liable to be devoured by that fabulous creature called the Horm, the legends about whom were evidently so appalling, and so likely to be disclosing a horrible reality, that, long before any written chronicler existed, they must have been deliberately suppressed by the self-preservative consciousness of the human race."[100] As always, Powys's imagery is ultimately more hauntingly powerful than his philosophical expositions. At the end of the novel he returns to the theme of man's desire to defend himself, if not from that non-human void, at least from acknowledging it. The Wessex of this novel is not the West Country of *Wolf Solent* or *Weymouth Sands*. Here the landscape seems to have disappeared and the characters travel through an eerie country of spatial silence, where the only sense of solidity is offered by three isolated castles and a priory, pinioned, as it were, at the four points of the compass. A company of men going through the darkness of the thirteenth century Dorset forest suddenly hears a wild husky voice singing a ditty which clearly is a "howl of defiance to everything they had all been accustomed from infancy to venerate."

> It was like a voice from the depths of the earth replying to a voice from uttermost space. . . . It seemed to be appealing desperately to earth, air, and water, not to allow the sun-rays that were so life-giving to all, to fool them by their warmth.
>
> It was the sort of defiance such as the ghost of a baby of a million years ago, a baby or "baban" whose skull, "penglog," had been discovered in the grave of an antediluvian giant, "gawr," might have uttered to all oracles and prophets and announcers of revelations.[101]

Powys seldom linked happenings from one novel to another, but this "baban" is still howling in his mind from *Porius*. Porius had wanted to "beget a child on the gigantically sweet body of some Creiddylad of his own finding,"[102] but with her death the "barely conceived offspring . . . that shapeless baban-y-gawr" is also "so abortively drowned and lost forever."[103]

> Where leaf do fall—there let leaf rest—
> Where no Grail be there be no quest—
> Be'ee good, be'ee bad, be'ee damned, be'ee blest—
> Be'ee North, be'ee South, be'ee East, be'ee West
> The whole of Existence is naught but a jest—
> Penglog y Baban yr Gawr!

The response of the company to this ditty, Powys now seems to be saying, is but the necessary response of the human being: "Every single one of them pretended . . . that he had heard nothing."[104] The little skull of the foetus that Porius had implanted in his giantess Creidyladd is lost forever. Just as now Powys's only son is lost. No quest—just a jest. The time for playing magician is over. From now on he hears nothing. And sees nothing.

From the beginning, Powys believed that the gods had given him "imagination" which he defined as "an actual tapping of some great reservoir of planetary, if not cosmic experience," and that this was the "secret of the most significant poetry of our race."[105] It was also the "secret" of the alchemists who were convinced that a magical power dwelt in the human mind which, if it could be tapped, could "cause things hidden in the shadow to appear, and to take away the shadow from them. . . . All these things happen, and the eyes of common men do not see them, but the eyes of understanding and of the imagination perceive them with true and truest vision."[106] Powys was equally sure that the thing hidden, the "secret," was both in matter and in the depths of the mind: "It is all in nature; and it is all in our individual consciousness."[107]

For the visionary novelist, as for the alchemist, this interpenetrating world could only be adequately expressed by symbols or images. Powys knew that he was so made that his imagination inevitably converted every mental process that was important to him "into a ritualistic symbol." "All our secrets," said the alchemist Ripley, "are formed from an image."[108] But *what* are the images that are revealed? When Powys was a child, it was a vision of a golden world; by pressing his knuckles against his eyes he would be "transported into Elysium." The deeper into the underworld of his mind that he went, the darker the images became. He saw with the eye of the imagination, but the "true vision" in the centre of the depths, in the middle of the maze, filled him with a terror that only increased as he grew older and perceived the vision more clearly. Gradually, the symbol of the magician looking unafraid into the "diddym" is supplanted by the menacing image of *eyes looking back*. In *Porius*, there are the eyes of the dead Teleri—"those terrible watchers, judges, and condemners [of] . . . the light of that sun they *had seen through*."[109] There is "the eye of matter itself" that stares back at Morfydd "in sub-conscious or perhaps super-conscious indifference to the eye in a human skull."[110] There are the eyes in the half-devoured body of the young Mabsant "staring up at [Porius] from among the delicate ferns where he'd been flung" that have "the horrible *damned* look of the eyes of some hunted creature brought, head and all, to a human feast, impaled on a platter."[111] There are the eyes of the Cewri staring back at Porius, "those two pairs of eyes staring up at him through clotted blood and drowned hair." Finally, there are the eyes of Styx that had "seen the roots of the earth and the fountains of all the seas," and having seen all this, "there remained but one thing, one thing only, only one thing. . . . And that one thing was death."[112]

By accepting "on behalf of all the beasts in the world the sentence of the slaughterhouse,"[113] the magician succeeds in unloosing the bonds of imprisoned matter. Myrddin can release the "lost and condemned" owl maiden from her captivity; his cloak can become "the magnet, the centre, the cynosure, the loadstone," the "maternal womb," and he can bring back into being Blodeuwedd. But when Morfydd meets the begging eyes of this newly freed creature, what *she* sees is that "this strange creature craved pitifully for some human touch to give it confidence in its inhuman loneliness."[114] The magician can look inward "with the two eyes" and gain a mystical sympathy with all the suffering in the universe, but even for a magician, the destiny is "almost too heavy to endure."[115] For the hero to attempt to see this, Powys seems finally to be convinced, is madness. The secret of the cosmos is "unendurable." Porius, when he has a sudden memory of "the bloody and mangled head of an ox he had once seen in a butcher's shop," feels that it has become "part of himself." And "this link with the chained, the devoured, the tortured, the sacrificed, weighed him down to the bottom. . . . With that beast-head and those lost eyes he felt as though he saw everything in the world exactly as it was; yes, in all its unendurable reality."[116]

Many years before he wrote *Porius*, Powys knew the dangers. At Phudd Bottom, Gladys Ficke painted his portrait, and he told her that "I look like Faust when he could not bear the sight of the Earth-Spirit he had conjured up."[117] Like Faust, he had "built his inward world . . . intent on rising to the level of spirits." He would be the magician whose triumphant act was to summon up the earth spirit, the earth mother—the creative being at the centre. The earth spirit answered Faust's call with the words: "I have felt a mighty pull from you, you have long been sucking at my sphere." Faust averts his face, "Schreckliches Gesicht." Terrifying Vision.[118]

In his lifelong search for the "secret" at the centre, Powys often lost courage and escaped to the periphery, the place of exile, but the heart of the maze had an inexorable fascination and always drew him back with its power. However, in *Porius* it is as if the hero and Powys himself came close enough to the centre to see that the eyes of the earth mother are Creiddylad's eyes "staring up at him through the blood-clotted greenness"—"*That* was the terror and horror of the truth of Nature."[119] "All these things happen," says the alchemist, and the human mind cannot bear too much truth, too much reality. Powys's last novels are a final flight to the circumference, an unwinding of the spiral, a search for a way out of the maze.

He finished *The Brazen Head* in August 1955. On September 14, Old Littleton had a fall, and he died in hospital on the twenty-seventh. John recorded his death.

> 28th September 1955: Littleton died yesterday at 8.10 am. . . . I lay under a stone between Ghost-Tree & the drive. And I did think of Old Littleton being with me there. . . . Today I did not think of Littleton at all.

Yet his body was thinking of Littleton, and immediately after his death, John suffered "a serious loss of vitality in my legs in my shoulders and above all in my heart."[120] He became aware that the physical collapse was accompanied by "such a quaint collapse mentally—for instance I found myself spelling the word many, meaning a lot, with two n's Manny, just as if I'd put Nanny and spelt it with an M vaguely thinking of Mummy!! for it must be that old gents have a tendency to revert to being babies & want their Mummy!"[121] He gradually regained strength, the "heart-weakness" disappeared, and he resumed his walks. He may have taken comfort from reading Kerényi's quote from Goethe, writing to Eckermann:

> 11 March 1828: If the entelechy is of a powerful sort, as is the case with all whose nature is akin to genius, then, in its vital penetration of the body, it will not only strengthen and ennoble the corporeal structure, but also,

through its spiritual dominance, continually seek to assert its right to an eternal youth. That is why we may see in highly gifted individuals ever renewed periods of unusual productivity, even into old age; they seem to undergo a temporary rejuvenation over and over again, and it is this that I would call a recurrent puberty.[122]

"Recurrent puberty" certainly seemed to be the case with Powys, as he now began writing, almost frantically, fantasies about children. His heroes become the adolescent John Cowper of Sherborne School, and it is as if now, at the age of eighty-two, he was re-living all the sexual anxieties and fantasies of that troubled age. But if the hero is a boy, the message is that of an old man, struggling with his anger and his loss. The juxtaposition is disconcerting. In the first of a series of short tales, "Up and Out,"[123] there has been a nuclear explosion and the hero, Gor of Blaenau, his girl Rhitha, a monster called Org, and his girl Asm, find themselves floating in space on a circular fragment of earth. They make a "Declaration of Independence," which is to withdraw "from the whole horrible and appalling play."[124] This resolution is directed at Time which appears before them like an "enormous black slug." Their "coracle from Wales" slices the slug in half, whereupon Eternity comes along and swallows the severed pieces of Time. Then Eternity turns inside out and swallows himself. The hero and the girl next meet the stars who have been holding "a multi-cosmic conference for several million years." The stars have decided that "all this praise of life . . . is a wicked, cunning, crafty, treacherous, tricky, abominable *lie*!" and they too opt for "universal cosmogonic suicide."[125] The hero and the girl meet other wanderers— among them Mathonwy and Kwangtze. When they announce their decision to withdraw from life, Kwangtze asks if they have "fully realized all the hidden implications in their momentous decision."[126] Mathonwy points out that "since all of us will then be reduced to non-entity and non-existence, and since the whole cosmos will be nothing but empty space, or what we Ancient Britons used to call 'Diddym,' or the ultimate Void, things will have returned to their original condition before the creation of the World. No! I must not say 'things will have returned,' for there will be no 'things' there! . . . All that is anything will then be nothing."[127] God comes along and makes an offer to "make a new world." The hero proposes that instead of these alternatives of suicide, or beginning all over again, they "boldly make a desperate leap"[128] into another dimension. They all take the plunge into this "death-ocean." First they feel "incredible comfort," and then indignation, and then—nothing.[129]

If Blaenau was Cloud Cuckoo Land, then the landscapes of the last tales are increasingly like the lunar landscape of that town. Indeed they are not about earth at all but, in more ways than one, up and out. Powys hoped rather optimistically that they were mythical skits "on the Space-adventure Tales of today's fashion,"[130] but of course they are not. They grew out of his private mythology, as did all his stories, only now it is harder and harder to follow him. The next tale he called "The Mountains of the Moon."[131] At this time, whenever he saw the sun, he would write in his diary above the day's date, "Helios Lulu! Lulu!" and when he saw the new moon, he would add, "my son! my son!"—"who I now think of as much in the Moon as Lulu in the Sun."[132] He may have meant this next little piece as a kind of epitaph.

The sixteen-year-old Rorlt, heir to a kingdom situated in the centre of the moon, is looking for his lost sister Lorlt. His sister has run away after Rorlt had "begged her to marry me" like his ancestors who had "imitated those beings whose name was Pharaoh." His predecessors, as well as practicing incest, had other peculiarities: "the ancient King of Zed was sexually so abnormal that he preferred embracing trees to embracing women." Rorlt encounters the monster Oom, who reassures him that his sister is heading for the Mountains of the Moon to find his own son Yoom to be her lover. As the story begins, so it goes on. There are more giants, a "moon-passioning old maid," a group of talking "terrestial milestones" (Eve's apple core, King Alfred's Crust, the heel of Achilles, and so on) and the inevitable philosopher who lectures the young people on the differ-ence in method between earth and moon dwellers: "theirs is all machinery," whereas "ours is all magnetism." Rorlt is too late to prevent his sister and Yoom from making love and, feeling rather left out of it, he climbs up "the final ridge of the Mountains of the Moon" to see if Death is on the other side. On the edge of the ridge, he hears a chorus of human voices making "tragic music," and he watches the "weird procession" as it dances by. He is tempted to join it but some-thing impels him to leave this "mysterious harmony" behind. Climbing the last slope, he sees a "real living girl"—"the daughter of the Moon," coming toward him. "She was his completion. She redeemed him from insane loneliness. . . . And at their union all the divided halves of all the divided things in the universe that still cried and wailed and wept to be united, like that procession of desper-ate ones he had watched float past him, would be united by the pure magic force of what he felt for the maid."[133] They die in each other's arms, but "out of this instantaneous fusion," which is *energeia akinesis*, "a new being came into exis-tence." This androgynous being "alone makes the world's future possible."[134]

When "Mountains" was finished in June 1956, they had been in Blaenau for two years. The one-up-one-down terrace house proved much too small and inconvenient, and there were constantly recurring problems with sewage, elec-tricity, and serious damp. Ironically, this place, to which they fled to be away from cars and children, was teeming with both. After almost being run over sev-eral times in the town, Powys began to feel like "a Magyar surrounded by Russian tanks."[135] As the townspeople became accustomed to seeing him rescuing leaves from out of drains or on his way to post letters, they would watch out for his safe-ty: "A handsome lady stopt me to say my scarf was hanging and trailing yes drag-ging & trailing on the road under my feet as I walked and she came up to me & like a Pretty Wife with a difficult old Dad she fastened it yes! she fastened it twisting it twice round my neck."[136] Phyllis fought an ongoing battle with cars parked in front of their house, having decided that she did not want to be "driven out of Blaenau as we were driven out of Cae Coed at Corwen."[137] They began to ask themselves "why did we leave <u>Corwen</u>???? & . . . why did we come to Blaenau???????"[138] Corwen friends came often, as did Louis and Gamel. The visitors would take Phyllis off for the day, perhaps to Criccieth, Porthmadog, or Portmeirion and then return to have tea with John. Phyllis re-established the Dorchester habit of going out several times a week to the local hotel for her meal and sometimes to a movie, but increasingly his needs required her presence, or rather, the reassurance of her presence. "The sun and the T. T. have both of them gone & what do I feel? I feel alone!"[139]

Phyllis had a series of debilitating illnesses in 1956 which at times left her semi-invalid. By 1957 he was wondering "how on earth are we going to carry on when this little house & <u>all</u> the <u>rest</u> is getting too much for her—too much."[140] He knew he was "all the rest." As happened in the past, Phyllis pulled herself together for another long haul and accepted what John called her "Atropian destiny."[141] She had written no more diaries after 1931, but one small notebook exists, in which a few entries suggest that she intended to begin again. It is uncertain how many of these false starts are now lost; this one lasted for only five days in May 1955. There is little in these few days except a reiteration of her exhaustion and the terrible wind and rain, but two entries are revealing. It did not take long for John to acquire new disciples, who expected her to provide the tea but who otherwise ignored her.

> 18 May 1955: In the middle of the visit I felt such a wave of rebuff that I drew into myself and became a ghost. . . . It must be because I am in another country. I must not let it matter. I must be a ghost. I must not get <u>hurt</u>. I began writing this with such a feeling of absolute futility—and it is surely a waste of time and to no purpose.

She always felt a stranger in this land. There is a forlorn letter extant, written from Wales to a friend in 1957, twenty-three years after they had left America. In it she says, "I remain obdurately alien and drawn into myself and I am convinced that this country is <u>not</u> a good place for Americans to live. Some of course like T. S. Eliot and Henry James . . . like it for the very reasons I don't like it I guess."[142] Ironically, in Powys's search for a sense of place, any possibility of finding hers was lost. Certainly by this time she had long given up hope of a sophisticated life in a large city, or of much life at all. Her pathetic stimulation came in a Watteau-dictate of small measure or none.

> 17 May 1955: When the street light comes out at the corner—it is a marvel to look out of this window. It answers all the longings of my soul.

Music helped. She would stand in their little hallway late at night listening to the neighbor playing waltz records. Then, with the bequest from Littleton's estate, she bought a "hi-fi" and got her records out of storage. In death, as in life, Littleton looked after his older brother. John received almost £2,000 from the will—much more than he had received from his writings since he had returned to Great Britain. The financial ease allowed him to continue to write virtually anything he pleased.

Possibly encouraged by the surprisingly good sales of *Atlantis*, Powys told Marian that he was going to write "a Freudian Paraphrase of the Iliad."[143] *Homer and the Aether* is hardly that, although he had no difficulty remembering the *Iliad* itself. He could still quote much of the poetry he had learned in his youth, including his Sherborne prize poem. He could still remember what his father had told him in 1892, but not to whom he had written that day. Sometimes humorously, often wretchedly, the diary documents his loss of short-term memory: "We can't find <u>where</u> I forget what <u>is</u>!"[144] Putting a brave face on it, he told Louis, who was now visiting fairly often, that he must "get my analysis of Second Childhood written now, for it grows vivider & vivider each day. It is wholly & utterly different from—what was that book? 'The Art of Growing Old.' The Art of—*nothing*."[145] There is a touching reminder in *Homer and the Aether* of the important part that "the goddess of memory" had played in his life. The Aether reminds Homer that "the poetry of all your days . . . comes from memory." It is "particular objects in their daily life, in their dwellings and along the waysides that lead to their dwellings, rocks on banks, stones on paths, fallen trees in the copses, broken masts by the edge of the sea, that call up the memories, sometimes almost too wistful and poignant to be borne, by which the poetry of life is created."[146]

The blessing that came with "the art of nothing" was that the acids and ulcers that had plagued him his whole life disappeared about the same time his memory went. The last diary entry that reports a possible ulcer was during Phyllis's mother's last illness when Phyllis could not give him the attention he needed. He wondered occasionally where his ulcers, his "lifelong companions," had gone. His bowel also became regular about this time. Although he insisted that "the one thing I live for now my one ideal & my one life-purpose namely a good action of the bowels. Selah! whatever Selah means,"[147] he stopped needing enemas, or even laxatives. Gone too were the manias. Phyllis wrote thanking a disciple for sending E. B. White's *Charlotte's Web*. She wasn't sure whether his horror of spiders would not put him off it: "Probably not, for all his manias seem to have dropped away now—with so much else."[148] However, the bad dreams remained and only Phyllis could stop them. "I had an odd Terror in the night and called out loudly 'Where is the T. T.' & there she was at my back and she put her arm round my neck to show where she was."[149]

He was eighty-six when he wrote *All or Nothing*, a fable about four teenagers—John o'Dreams Nu and his sister Jilly Tewky, and Ring and Ting, children of the giant Urk. They make three voyages to outer space: to the heart of the sun, to a star in the Milky Way, and to a newly created planet. The two preoccupations that have always been present in his writings, sexuality and violence, are now given the full freedom of a mind that has cast off any remaining restraints. Ring and Ting's father is "gigantic and hideous" and has a mouth like a dragon "who has come up from some abyss below to gorge himself upon every morsel of flesh covering the skull of the last creature alive upon the earth." Urk could be any frightening monster in a fairy tale, but when Bubble urges Urk to "gobble up" the heart of the sun, the response of John o'Dreams to this comes straight out of the Pandora's box of Powys's own sadistic fantasies. When Urk "buried his flesh-devouring snout in that calm beautiful face," John seizes a "sharp-edged piece of adamant" and goes on hammering Urk's skull until he "had become a headless giant, with a bleeding neck ending in a mask of bones and brains and blood."[150]

There is the usual assortment of grotesques and space monsters and through them the omnipresent sexual fantasies are met, occasionally with a certain drollery. Bog, the King of the Milky Way, makes sure the end of his penis is "decently slung over his left shoulder." Masturbation in the service of the imagination is given another airing: "In the matter of sex, Bog taught me that . . . masturbation—that is to say, the excited emission of semen by the use of our imagination—is a much more important and creative act than ordinary and natural fornication. . . . Bog used to tell me that I always ought to be thinking sufficiently erotic thoughts to keep my penis in a state of erection."[151] The incest theme also resurfaces. Marian and John still referred sometimes to Peter as "our son," "as if we belonged to the Royalty of Egypt where 'twas the strict rule & custom!"[152] John o'Dreams dreams of ravishing his sister, so that they were "the parents of a child." He was sure that "to gain this desirable end" the "so wise and so calm" Jilly would "make herself shiver and shake with a deliciously created masochistic yielding; and she would stir up in me an equally delicious sadistic frenzy."[153] Their parents discuss the fact that the brother and sister are "very much in love with each other" and while they agree that "the division between the feeling of lovers and the feeling of brother and sister . . . is a thing so criss-crossed with emotional complications that it requires extremely cautious and careful handling,"[154] they get the rector to marry off John to Ting and Jilly to Ring posthaste.

In July 1958, Powys was presented with the Bronze Plaque of the Hamburg Free Academy of Arts in recognition of his outstanding services to literature and philosophy. The only other novelist ever to receive it was Thomas Mann. In an accompanying letter, the president of the Academy wrote, "In you we worship, besides the writer, the man: your very being is contained in all your writings." The secretary, Rolf Italiaander, journeyed to Blaenau to present the plaque to him and noted the irony that the first award of Powys's life was a foreign one.[155] John seemed more interested in his walks with his stick "Sherborne" than in the award, although the unexpected honor may have accounted for the fact that suddenly he was "accompanied by the Holy Ghost which in the form of a tremendously large white sea-gull went round and round my head."[156] When Hanley's son Liam visited, he painted an oil of the Blaenau landscape for them, which Powys refused to accept until Liam had painted in the Holy Ghost.[157] They continued to get many papers. It is difficult to know how much he was taking in, but they read to each other Nabokov's *Lolita* ("dull beyond words"), finished Alan Sillitoe's *Saturday Night and Sunday Morning* ("so now we can go back to Chaucer!"), and Tolkien's Ring Cycle ("got tired of"). A reading of Beckett's novel *Murphy* in 1958 may have faintly affected his last tales. However, there was a further mental deterioration in 1959. He had noted several years before that he had "several times acted rather queer with the T. T. & had to implore her to for-give or to analyze my queer conduct,"[158] and Gamel's frequent visits to Phyllis that summer seem to have roused some of the old jealousy. "I have just behaved shamefully crying angrily to the T. T, 'Hit me! Hit me!'"[159] Other visitors contin-ued to come, but he seldom made any comment about them in his diary, other than to record their coming and their going.

Powys wrote six more tales during 1959 and 1960—"You and Me," "Real Wraiths," "Two by Two," "Topsy Turvy," "Cataclysm," and "Abertackle." Phyllis typed up three of them but did not send them off to Macdonald, and probably they should never have seen the light of day.[160] They are what Yeats has called the "last poems" of a soul who now speaks "what's blown into the mind." Of the two rooms in the house, the one upstairs became his study, where he spent most of his day, except for increasingly brief walks. His meals, still consisting of milk, tea, stale bread, and olive oil, with the addition of Complan, Phyllis brought up to him on a tray. She placed more and more photographs of his brothers and sisters on the broad windowsill next to his couch until it became a picture of the past. The room down-stairs was her "parlour" and there they still slept together at night. Powys's "first pub-lic literary triumph" was an essay he wrote at prep school entitled "A Voyage round my Chamber"[161] which was "a rambling description of our own drawing-room" at Montacute. Since 1956, Powys had begun writing similarly detailed descriptions of the contents of the rooms at 1, Waterloo, as if the iteration of things was reassuring. At the back of the 1959 diary there is a strangely evocative list:

> Grey Armchair   Brown Armchair
> Black Sofa   White Bookcase
> Top shelf <u>Bewick</u> and <u>Lempriere</u>
> Fire-Place and Poker
> Red Curtains   Wooden round table
> White Window Sill   White Door
> Picture of Weymouth Bay
> Picture of old Mister
> Store Cupboard   Stairs
> The Lantern on the Telegraph Post
> The Blue Globe
> Boy Toddler out of Window
> Girl Toddler out of Window
> 1st Cut Glass and 2nd Cut Glass
> The Clock ticking in Parlour
> The Bed in Parlour Below

The Kitchen and Scullery
The Bank in the Rear
The Road in the Front
The field the hill
The Mountain
The House near the
Telegraph Post
Bokhara Rug
Door-Handle
and
Girl's Dance with Black Boy with Coffee
Topsy & Turvy the Girl's Dance and the Hand.
The Whirlwind and the Water-spout.

Although this reads almost like a prose-poem, it appears to be an aide-mémoire for "Topsy Turvy," a tale to illustrate his belief in the "amount of living-ness that comes to exist in every piece of furniture that has been for many years the background of human lives."[162] The inanimates become animate and, having absorbed the deepest feelings and the fears of the man upstairs, proceed to voice them one last time. The fable begins with the various objects in Powys's upstairs study discussing whether Whirlpool would swallow Topsy. But other matters are being argued in the parlour below. On January 30, 1960, John recorded that "The T. T. dreams that she has a child after my Death." This is transposed as:

Big Doll-Bibabug is explaining to Little Doll-Sillysuck: "I don't want a child,"said Big Doll. "You are the only child I'll ever love. . . . Surely we can be happy, loving each other and playing together, like we do, I with my what-do-you-call-it, and you with your what-do-you-call-it, both deliciously excited and tossing up and down, without going to this awful extreme of rending your virginity."
"But I want a baby! Oh how I want a baby! Take me! Take me!"
"Well, you can't have one, Sillysuck, you just can't have one."
Sillysuck wonders if she let someone else rape her "couldn't we both pretend that Bibabug had done it?"[163]

After many adventures, Topsy and Turvy fly off with a naked Galatea the Sea Nymph to a fourth dimension. Bedlam breaks loose as they return and the armchairs and the poker "come clattering downstairs to see what on earth had happened." Bibabug and Sillysuck, "as they lay side by side on their bed, were engaged with their usual topic," but suddenly

During this incredible hubbub, roused to activity as he had never been in his whole life before, Bibabug seized Sillysuck, pulled her down upon the rug and there . . . violently, shamelessly, recklessly, desperately, ravished her and did so with such success that her muffled cry was a mixture of blood and tears and crazy exultation. "I shall have a baby, a baby, a baby."[164]

Powys over a long lifetime had become, like his hero Porius, "a successful adept in a thousand self-healing tricks," but they work no longer and the last, deepest, bruise spurts blood.

In March 1960 Powys and Phyllis both got Asian flu. On the fourth of April all he could write in the diary was "Flu hovers over us" with a sketch of a bird with long claws. A few lines of poetry became part of his fever and burned into his brain. From then on until his death, on many days the only diary entry is from Longfellow's "The Saga of King Olaf." "I am the God Thor / I am the War god / This is my hammer / Miolnir the Mighty / Giants and Sorcerers cannot withstand it." There were days of lucidity, and other days when he had difficulty recognizing people. He wrote "Abertackle" while he was semi-delirious with this influenza. All his lifelong physical and mental ailments come into it, as well as Squire Neverbang, the clown Ooly-Fooly, a space-horse, Arch-Eagle, and other assorted oddities. For the first time, his parents are undisguisedly introduced as Mr. Charles Po and Mrs. Mary Po. They have a long discussion about their son Gor. They agree he is "essentially such a peculiar and original youth and the motions of his mind were so deeply born and so violently outflung that nothing could make you sure what he would be up to next." They also refer to the incestuous love of their daughter Nelly and Gor. Bringing his parents in so directly allows him, albeit through his mother, to burst out with: "We were too severe with them, too narrow with them, too traditional and conventional with them."[165]

John Cowper was still in bed downstairs and very weak in July 1960, but gradually he spent more time in his study.[166] In October, Phyllis began to take him for very short walks to the low wall by the waterfall next to their house. Then, in November, she encouraged him to go alone. In a very shaky hand he wrote down:

> The T. T. SHAVED me beautifully
> Then she put on my Boots
> And my Red Scarf & my cap
> And gave me after washing my face
> And after washing my hands
> And after cold-creaming my chin
> And after giving me Sherborne & new cap
> to carry and after washing my back
> And helping me with my trousers
> She gave me my gloves & sent me off
> I sat on my new cap on the low wall
> After climbing the Tiny Lane & the 5 steps
> Then I came gollumping back.

Many of the last pages of the diary sing the song of a helpless child, an only child, once again the centre of his mother's undivided attention: "She washed my face, she washed my hands she washed my front, she washed my back." "Oscar is so nice and warm."

His long-ago hero, Wolf Solent, felt "as if he searched in vain for any escape into the silences of the earth."[167] Powys spent his whole life in a search for that solitude and silence—from New York to Phudd to Dorset to Corwen then, when the cars came, to Blaenau Ffestiniog—his back now literally against the wall. Having found the silence, he feared it. He has the young hero of *Up and Out* say, "All my life I've only wanted two things—to enjoy myself . . . and to lecture somebody else on how he or she can enjoy whatever's happening! I want to perform, or act, to play the clown, to show off as a philosopher; and how can I enjoy all this when I am nothing and there's nobody there!"[168] By 1960, the diary has become a litany of woe:

> I met not one living
> Creature not one
> not one & I saw
> no Cow no calf
> no Sheep no lamb
> no dog no Cat
> I rescued Nothing
> from anything[169]

In December 1960 he decided not to walk anymore. To comfort him, Phyllis hung in front of his bed a painting of the Migneint. It is an abstract oil in tones of brown, gray, and bluish white—the moorland, the mountain beyond, and then the sea. As he looked at it, past merged into present and neither any longer held terror.

> Revisiting today
> my old familiar Weymouth
> I struggle to revive my
> nursery memories
> waning as they are of the hours
> when my recollections of
> both my Parents and what
> they liked me to do when
> lying in Tiny Thin's soft.
> Bed under the big picture
> there of the mountains including
> Snow — Donia
> Revisited often by both
> my Mother and my Father &
> each full of separate memories
> of the Weymouth Mountain of Snow
> surrounded by Sea-&Sand.
> Under which deep Descents
> Went Down inviting visitation

John Cowper Powys died the June 17, 1963. Phyllis lived on until the March 10, 1982.

EPILOGUE
"The Grief and the Rage and the Ashes"

〜

IN NOVEMBER 1960 POWYS LOOKED OUT OF HIS UPSTAIRS WINDOW AT Blaenau into the "fantastic entanglement of boughs and leaves" of the sycamore tree across the way. It reminded him of a game which he loved "better than any other to play for the bewilderment of my brothers and sisters," and he wrote *Whatsoever*.

> As a boy I was intensely fond of drawing mazes with my pen or pencil. These consisted of pictures of narrow little paths which could be followed if you looked at them carefully until they either ended by entering their own track or by coming to a circular destiny resembling a lake or a pond. [Trees] can make a Maze with their boughs and their twigs. Such a Maze can be followed in and out, and out and in, just as though its tiniest twig were hollow and from its inside you had to encounter a network of similar passages, some of which led to towers in a castle and others to lakes in a park.[1]

A maze has been defined as "a complicated artistic structure with a circuitous and ambiguous design whose confusing toils are intended by their clever architect to entrap or enlighten errant maze-walkers, denying or controlling access to a centre that may contain good or evil, and leaving the maze-walker with higher knowledge or in chaotic limbo."[2]

The paper mazes that he drew as a child and the metaphorical mazes he charted as a writer were equally equivocal. That "lake in a park" into which so long ago he had thrown the stick was a "circular destiny," but whether it brought birth or death, freedom or imprisonment, was the fairy-tale conundrum he posed in his novels again and again. Some of the mazes he drew *in malo* were inextricable, with no exit; others were impenetrable mazes which had no entry. The mazes he drew in his own head were those in which he had found the centre, and that centre was a prison. And on Peter Powys Grey, his son who was not his son, he imposed a similar destiny.

In 1991, Peter asked me to come to New York to see him. He wasn't in his flat; eventually I found him in a closed-ward psychiatric hospital. He wanted me to tape our conversations and for two days he talked with intensity, with rage, with defeat. I could only slip into my alternate role of therapist and listen. He told me the following story amongst so many stories.

John Cowper would come to see Marian and little Peter always felt at such times that he was shut out from some magic place. Then John would notice the child and draw paper mazes for him, instructing him to find his way out from the centre. Invariably the little boy would end up crying in sheer frustration and (Peter remembering vividly) in terror. One day Theodore Dreiser was there and for some time watched with amusement his friend making diverting little games for his nephew. Then Dreiser grew still and roared out, "Christ, Jack, there *is* no way out!"

Peter told me to take away his diaries. After reading some of them—so totally different from John's and yet so alike—I knew I must write.

23rd June 1991

My dear,

I have been thinking of you constantly. How can I not? Your pain tears at the human part of me; your mythic role absorbs my non-human analytic self. I had to write you tonight, for time is short, is it not, to tell you a little of what I have been thinking. I am an outsider in the Powys myth, but I think I understand better than most what you were saying. I have been watching, word by word in those diaries of John Cowper, what he did to Phyllis. He made her into an image in the mind; she was the sylph Nineue that Merlin met in the forest of Broceliande. There he entertained her with a magic game: he broke a twig and drew a circle, then taught her the unbreakable spell which would imprison them both in the blossoming whitethorn bush. Phyllis could rage; she could collapse; she could comfort herself with music; but she could not escape. Maybe she did not want to.

You used an important phrase in the tapes: "to entrance." "To entrance me John created mazes." Paper mazes for a little boy with the twist that you had to find your way out of the maze, not into it. There is the greatest of all ironies here, Peter. He entranced you and *gave you entrance. He wasn't keeping you out, my dear, he was keeping you* in. *He showed you the magic centre, he placed you in that sacred place where you so desperately wanted to be and you were trapped, with no way out. I wonder if, when your mother and Daddy Jack contemplated your forthcoming birth, they willed you to be Theseus? Or was it Pentheus?*

I saw by your bedside the Viking chess queen I gave you so long ago. You had glued her to a flat stone and you showed me what you had written on the base of the stone.

Reine de la Couronne Brissé

Guide

pour tous Pèlerins

Fous et Obstinés

My *maze-walker, I cannot be your guide; it is even too late to be your Ariadne. But if you wish it, I will tell the story of the house of Powys. You have given me all your journals but the last one. When you are finished with that, send it to me. Someday I will make sure that the dismembered is remembered. My dearest Peter, sleep sweetly in the forest of Broceliande.*

In *Whatsoever* the old magician found the fairy clue to escape his nightmare darkness.

> But the wonderful thing about the Mazes made by the boughs and twigs of trees is their complete disappearance when it grows dark. This event has to be prepared for and allowed for and this has been done in a fairy tale manner. In all directions when you have followed one of these hollow twig-paths through a certain entanglement you come upon a little square retreat with a thin chimney leading to the open air. . . . You can wait in agreeable seclusion and even enjoy a little sleep if so you wish.

The centre of JCP's own maze, that was his terror, became his escape. Merlin's magic circle was now a refuge with a little chimney that led to the open air, allowing him to breathe. His breathing terror—all his terrors—were over. John Cowper Powys died, aged ninety, apparently a happy man. In October 1992, the doomed Peter sent me his last journal and committed suicide.

ACKNOWLEDGMENTS

I T GOES WITHOUT SAYING THAT THIS BIOGRAPHY MIGHT NOT HAVE BEEN written, or at least, not in the form it has taken, if John Cowper Powys and Phyllis Playter had not had an attic, or had Francis Powys not kept safely the contents of that attic—manuscripts, letters, diaries, memorabilia of a long life—and bequeathed them to the present copy-right holders, John, Amanda, and Will Powys, who generously allowed me to use the material without hindrance or proviso.

Otherwise, succor to a biographer comes in many guises. Friends have often proved the most help simply by being there. I think especially of Roger Peers, Janet Machen, Nola Baldwinson, John and Eve Batten. The most inspiring conversations about Powys have been with people sadly now dead. Wilson Knight, Bob Blackmore, Oliver Wilkinson, and especially Joseph Percy Smith, always sparked off new lines of thought. Jeff Kwintner, very much alive and invariably insightful, could be said to have planted the seed for this biography by giving me some years ago microfilm and photocopies of unpublished material that he had accumulated as the estimable Village Press publisher. Librarians and Keepers at University archives have been helpful, but Dafydd Ifans at the National Library of Wales and Carl Peterson at Colgate University exceptionally so. More immediately and personally there are three people for whom I feel deep gratitude. Mel Ankney, reference librarian at The Ohio State University Libraries, has been, in effect, my personal research librarian. Living far from any academic library or large city has the advantage of no distractions, but has made the routine kind of work necessary in a biography extremely difficult. An email to Mel in America sorted out problems and questions that would have otherwise required much time and expense. For three years he has been my constant, and never failed in his assistance. The second person to whom I feel very grateful is Judith Bond. She has transcribed most of the JCP diaries from 1945 onward; scanned many documents in order to make them available to me on disk; patiently helped me with my many computer glitches; and generally has been an immensely supportive and understanding friend. Lastly, I owe a debt of gratitude, as well as much else, to Chris Gostick. He it was who told me that I must write the biography, "to get Powys finally out of your system." It was wise advice. Hopefully, the necessary magic has been performed, and John Cowper is now lodged instead in the imaginations and psyches of the readers of this biography.

NOTES

ABBREVIATIONS

The following abbreviations have been adopted for frequently recurring names of publications, places, and people. Otherwise, for printed sources the usual convention has been adopted of a full citation in the first instance, followed by a recognizable shortened form. Manuscripts are cited by location.

NLW	National Library of Wales, Aberystwyth, Wales.
HRHRC	Harry Ransome Humanities Research Centre, University of Texas at Austin.
Beinecke	The Beinecke Rare Book and Manuscript Library, Yale University, New Haven, CT.
Syracuse	George Arents Research Library, Syracuse University, New York.
DCM	The Powys Collection, Dorset County Museum, Dorchester, Dorset. (This collection is owned by the Powys Society.)
Colgate	Everett Needham Case Library, Colgate University, Hamilton, NY.
OSUL	Lloyd Emerson Siberell Papers, Rare Books and Manuscripts Library, The Ohio State University Libraries, Columbus, OH.
M. K.	Material bequeathed to Dr. M. Krissdóttir
PR	The Powys Review
PJ	The Powys Journal
Private Possession	Material owned by the copyright holder, John Francis Powys, in the safekeeping of Morine Krissdóttir. (Please note that in 2006, after the completion of this book, some of the material was sold to the National Library of Wales.)

Unless otherwise indicated in the notes, the vast majority of letters and diaries quoted from in this biography are to be found in archives or in private possession.

UNPUBLISHED SOURCES

Diaries of JCP: The originals are at the NLW.
Diaries and stories of Phyllis Playter: The originals are now at the NLW.
Letters from JCP to Phyllis Playter: The originals are at the NLW.
Letters from JCP to Littleton Alfred: The originals are now at the NLW.
Letters to Marian: The majority are at Colgate, however a substantial number of those written in later years remain in the possession of the copyright holder.
Letters to Gertrude: At HRHRC. Some originals in possession of copyright holder.
Letters JCP to Theodore and from Theodore to JCP: A few have been published but the majority remain unpublished. A significant number are in the Powys Collection, DCM: others in private hands, yet others scattered in university archives in America.
Letters from cousin Father Hamilton Johnson: copyright holder.
Letters to Gilbert Turner: NLW.
Letters from Philippa Powys to JCP and Phyllis: copyright holder.
Letters from Gertrude Powys to JCP and Phyllis: NLW.
Letters from Marian to JCP and Phyllis: NLW.
Letters to Elizabeth Myers from JCP: Powys Collection, DCM.
Letters from Littleton to JCP: NLW.
Letters from JCP to Littleton: Powys Collection, DCM.
Letters from JCP to Huw Menai: Powys Collection, DCM.
Letters from Alyse to JCP and Phyllis: NLW.

PROLOGUE

1. From "Branwen the Daughter of Llyr" in *The Mabinogion*. John Cowper Powys's preferred translation of this cycle was by Lady Charlotte Guest. (London: J. M. Dent and Co., 1802).

2. John Cowper named Phyllis Playter his literary executor and copyright holder. In her will she appointed Francis Powys to this same role. When Francis died, his son John, John's wife Amanda, and his son William became the copyright holders.

3. Diary, 14 August 1930.

4. John Cowper Powys, *Suspended Judgements* (New York: G. Arnold Shaw, 1916), 84.

5. John Fowles, "Hardy and the Hag," *Wormholes*, edited by Jan Relf (London: Jonathan Cape, 1998), 137.

6. John Cowper Powys, "Finnegans Wake," *Obstinate Cymric: Essays 1935-47* (Carmarthen: The Druid Press, 1947), 24.

7. John Cowper Powys, *Wolf Solent* (New York: Simon and Schuster, 1929), 512.

8. Letter from Llewelyn to Littleton, 25 April 1939. *The Letters of Llewelyn Powys*, selected and edited by Louis Wilkinson with an introduction by Alyse Gregory (London: The Bodley Head, 1943).

9. *Porius*, TS.1470-71. A new and complete edition of this novel will be published by Overlook Press. In the meantime, page references are to the typescript at Colgate University.

10. Diary, 11 January 1945.

11. *Porius*, TS. p1472.

CHAPTER ONE: 1872-1882

1. E. A. Robinson, "Hillcrest," *The Man Against the Sky* (1916) in *Collected Poems* (New York: The Macmillan Co., 1937), 16. "And he may never dare again / Say what awaits him, or be sure / What sunlit labyrinth of pain / He may not enter and endure."

2. John Cowper Powys, "Whatsoever" (an unpublished piece written on Guy Fawkes Day, 5 November 1960. NLW (22810E).

3. There was once a king of Crete called Minos who lived with his wife Pasiphae and their daughter Ariadne in the house of the Double Axe. A beautiful bull was sent from the sea by Poseidon to Pasiphae and she bore a child, half-human, half animal. King Minos had Daedalus build a maze-like prison, with such a complexity of corridors and passages that no one who entered the building could find his way out again and he put the Minotaur into this labyrinth, to live forever hidden at its centre. Every nine years, a tribute of fourteen young Athenians was sent into the maze to lose their way and die of hunger or be eaten by the monster. When the third shipment came due, Theseus accompanied the sacrificial youths, and seeing him, a love-smitten Ariadne gave the hero a clew or ball of thread and told him to tie one end of the thread to the entrance of the labyrinth and unwind the ball as he made his way through the maze. Theseus found the centre, killed the monster, then followed the thread back to safety. Theseus and Ariadne fled to the island of Naxeos. They did not live happily ever after.

4. John Cowper Powys, *Autobiography* (New York: Simon & Schuster, 1934. London: John Lane The Bodley Head, 1934), 2-3. There are slight differences in the two editions. All page numbers refer to The Bodley Head edition.

5. *Autobiography*, 3.

6. John Cowper Powys, Diary, 21 June 1944. Powys began a diary in mid-1929 and continued to write one until 1961. The continuous run of thirty-seven volumes is held by NLW (2206-41B). The diaries for 1929, 1930 and 1931 have been published. A selection of the diaries from 1929-1939 was also published. See *Petrushka and The Dancer*, edited by M. Krissdóttir (Manchester: Carcanet Press, 1995). The annotated diary for 1934-1935 was edited by M. Krissdóttir and R. Peers as *The Dorset Year* (Bath: The Powys Press, 1998). All references to the diaries in the biography are to the originals, and Powys's somewhat idiosyncratic spelling, capitalization, punctuation, and underlining have been retained.

7. *Autobiography*, 6.

8. Diary, 9 October 1940.

9. *Autobiography*, 32.

10. *Autobiography*, 33, 8.

11. Jean Stengers and Anne Van Neck, *Masturbation: The History of the Great Terror*, trans. Kathryn Hoffmann (New York: Palgrave, 2001).

12. *Autobiography*, 33. The eremetical life was introduced into the Lower Thebaid in the valley of the Nile by St. Anthony. Born in 251, he embraced the ascetic life at the age of twenty; then, impelled by a love of solitude, he buried himself in the desert, where he withstood a series of temptations by the devil.

13. *Autobiography*, 11-12.

14. *Autobiography*, 29.

15. *Autobiography*, 12-13.

16. *Autobiography*, 12.

17. *Autobiography*, 38-39.

18. *Autobiography*, 14, 16.

19. *Autobiography*, 19.

20. *Autobiography*, 15.

21. *Autobiography*, 4.

22. *Autobiography*, 25-26.

23. *Autobiography*, 25.

24. *Autobiography*, 26.

25. *Autobiography*, 31-32.

26. Littleton Powys, *The Powys Family*. A talk given in May 1945; later privately printed in 1952.

27. Mary Barham Johnson, "The Powys Mother," PR, 8 (1980/1981).

28. Johnson, 61. Her mother, Catharine Barham Johnson, contradicted her daughter's assessment of Marianne Patteson in a letter to Littleton Powys, dated 11 November 1952, in which she states: "Aunt Marianne's personality permeated the house and kept everything calm and smooth. . . . The strength of [her] personality is shown by the fact that except Aunt Dora the Patteson temperament was most obvious in all the rest, gentle, efficient and very lovable." Letter in private possession.

29. In 1980, Johnson sent to Peter Powys Grey copies of all Mary Cowper's letters to her brother during this period, and he bequeathed them to M. K.

30. JCP to Gilbert Turner, 27 August 1944. NLW (23493-8E). He says his father was sent to Mappowder in Dorset, "his first boarding school (from Stalbridge) & hated it there & then went afterwards for he never went to Sherborne being a Backward Boy till he was privately tutored (with other backward boys one of whom was Mr Labouchere editor of 'Truth') at Yaxeham Norfolk by my maternal Grandfather."

31. Patrick Bury, *The College of Corpus Christi and of the Virgin Mary: a History from 1822 to 1952* (Cambridge: printed for the college, 1952), 80.

32. Letter to her brother Cowper from Etta, 26 May 1869, quoted in Johnson, "The Powys Mother."

33. Johnson, 62.

34. Unpublished undated reminiscences of Susie Maskery in the Littleton Powys archive, Powys Collection, Dorset County Museum.

35. Diary, 7 July 1950.

36. Littleton Powys, *The Joy of It* (London: Chapman & Hall Ltd., 1937), 14.

37. JCP to Llewelyn Powys, 2 June 1925. *Letters to His Brother Llewelyn*, vol. II 1925-1939, edited and selected by Malcolm Elwin (London: Village Press, 1975).

38. S. T. Coleridge, "Marginalia," *The Collected Works* (Princeton, N.J.: Princeton University Press, 1980), vol. I of part 12, (notes on Sir Thomas Browne's *Religio Medici*).

39. John Cowper Powys, *Confessions of Two Brothers* (Rochester, NY: The Manas Press, 1916), 31.

40. *Joy*, 27-29.

41. *Autobiography*, 38.

42. *Joy*, 26.

43. *Autobiography*, 39.

44. *Autobiography*, 53.

45. *Autobiography*, 6.

46. *Porius*, TS, 1131.

47. W. H. Auden, "Wandering Jew," *The New Republic*, 10 February 1941, 112. Reprinted in *The Complete Works of W. H. Auden, Prose*, vol. II 1939–1948 (Princeton: Princeton University Press, 2002).

48. *Autobiography*, 42.

49. Information from the various wills and probates in the private possession of the copyright holder.

50. Diary, 22 January 1940.

51. *Autobiography*, 56.

52. *Autobiography*, 61.

53. *Autobiography*, 62.

54. *Autobiography*, 69.

55. *Autobiography* 58.

56. *Autobiography*, 44–45.

57. Diary, 22 April 1949.

58. *Autobiography*, 51, 52.

59. *Autobiography*, 48.

60. *Autobiography*, 49.

61. *Autobiography*, 50–51.

62. Diary of Sylvia Townsend Warner, 19 April, 1930. Sylvia Townsend Warner/ Valentine Ackland Archive, D.C.M. Warner writes that Theodore went on to speak of "the pains of death, the struggle to breathe, the suffocation," and Warner told him that "he might find Death's hand less experimental."

63. *Joy*, 34–35.

64. *Autobiography*, 62–63.

65. *Autobiography*, 64–65.

66. *Autobiography*, 63.

67. *Autobiography*, 50.

68. Theodore Powys, "This is Thyself" (written circa 1915. Manuscript at HRHRC. A transcription of it was published in PR, 20 (1987): 9.

69. *Autobiography*, 355.
70. *Autobiography*, 68.
71. *Autobiography*, 44.
72. Carl Jung, *Memories, Dreams, Reflections*, recorded by Aniela Jaffe, trans. Richard and Clare Winston (London: Collins, n.d.), 37.
73. *Autobiography*, 64.
74. *Autobiography*, 62.
75. *Autobiography*, 76.

CHAPTER TWO: 1883-1893

1. *Autobiography*, 63.
2. *Autobiography*, 47.
3. *Autobiography*, 77.
4. *Autobiography*, 78.
5. *Joy*, 38, 59–60.
6. *Joy*, 67.
7. *Autobiography*, 79.
8. *Autobiography*, 82.
9. *Autobiography*, 86.
10. *Joy*, 61.
11. *Autobiography*, 86.
12. *Autobiography*, 87.
13. *Joy*, 60, 62.
14. Information in unpublished letters from William Cowper Johnson to C. F. Powys, dated 29 August 1880 and "Tues aft." Letters owned by Marian Powys, given to M. K. by Peter Powys Grey.
15. C. F. was installed 5 November 1885. The succeeding vicar, John Craigie, was installed 10 May 1918.
16. *Autobiography*, 95.
17. *Autobiography*, 134.
18. Diary, 26 May 1947.
19. William Acton, *The Functions and Disorders of the Reproductive System* (A popular Victorian medical manual, first published in 1857 but still being reprinted as late as 1894.) Quoted in Steven Marcus, *The Other Victorians* (New York: Basic Books, 1966), 20–25.
20. Philip Roth, *Portnoy's Complaint* (London: Vintage, 1999). The tongue in cheek definition given: "A disorder in which strongly felt ethical and altruistic impulses are perpetually warring with extreme sexual longings, often of a perverse nature." Roth's Jewish hero, growing up to believe that almost everything was an offense to God Almighty, speculates, "Imagine then what my conscience gave me for all that jerking off! The guilt, the fears—the terror bred into my bones!"
21. *Autobiography*, 139.

22. *Ally Sloper's Half-Holiday* was a penny weekly comic paper published without break from 1884 until 1916. It was designed to appeal to the widest possible audience, and Ally Sloper, the eponymous hero with picaresque adventures, became a cult figure with artists like William Morris and Burne-Jones as well as the working classes. Part of its appeal was that Sloper is a minor deviant challenging Victorian pretensions of respectability. However, the paper was also an early pin-up magazine, Ally being accompanied in his social rounds by his daughter Tootsie and the girls from the Frivolity Theatre. "The girls who appear in the main cartoons are all of a type—enchanting yet remote, alluring yet daunting in the perfection of their stylised voluptuousness. They belong to a fantasy world, idealised and distant." Peter Bailey, *Popular Culture and Performance in the Victorian City* (Cambridge: Cambridge University Press, 1998), 70–71.
23. *Autobiography*, 123.
24. *Autobiography*, 114–115. In later years he wrote to Dorothy Richardson, "The public School 'Greek' eroticism is, at once, much more brutal & much more emotional and romantic. It grows vicious at the university. . . ." Unpublished letter to Richardson, 19 January 1930. Beinecke.
25. *Autobiography*, 139.
26. *Autobiography*, 131–32.
27. *Autobiography*, 139.
28. Alec Waugh, *The Loom of Youth* (London: Richards, 1917), 80. Although Waugh refers to another boy who was "bunked" for a homosexual affair, he does not mention in his book that he was also expelled from Sherborne in 1915. He became a cadet at Sandhurst, finishing the course just in time for Passchendaele. Alec's father was Arthur Waugh, a publisher with Chapman and Hall. He had been at Sherborne in the early 1880s, just before JCP and Littleton entered in 1886. Littleton went to him with his book *The Joy of It*, which Waugh published. Although he stoutly told Arthur Waugh what he thought of his son, Littleton was not averse to using the old-boy network.
29. Waugh, 84.
30. *Autobiography*, 113.
31. *Autobiography*, 125–26.
32. *Joy*, 66.
33. Diary, 10 June 1956.
34. *Autobiography*, 143.
35. *Autobiography*, 152–53.
36. *Joy*, 69–70.

37. *Autobiography*, 142.

38. *Joy*, 71. According to the Sherborne Register, Puckle entered Sherborne School at the Summer Term, 1885. Deacon entered at Michaelmas Term, 1886, the same time as both the Powyses. Both Deacon and Puckle left in 1889. JCP left in 1891.

39. *Autobiography*, 135.

40. *Autobiography*, 144.

41. *Autobiography*, 69.

42. *Autobiography*, 137.

43. *Autobiography*, 83.

44. *Autobiography*, 132.

45. *Autobiography*, 7.

46. *Autobiography*, 299.

47. For some reason, Theodore was not sent to Sherborne Prep when it would have been logical to do so, as both John and Littleton had been there since 1883. Instead he was sent off by himself to Dorchester Grammar School in September 1886, when he was ten. He was there for three terms but ill with jaundice for one term of those terms. When he was finally sent to Sherborne Prep in January 1888, he was twelve. He told his sister Gertrude many years later that he was at the Prep for another three terms but had measles in the last term and was sent to Weymouth to recuperate.

48. Letter to Littleton, 29 June 1928. JCP's letters to Littleton are in the Powys Collection, Dorset County Museum. The letters from Littleton to JCP are at the National Library of Wales. Both sides of the correspondence remain unpublished. Note that the original underlines have been retained.

49. Fanshawe was the head of an old landed family in Co. Durham and was married to C. F.'s cousin Bertha.

50. Bury, 96.

51. *Autobiography*, 159–60.

52. Littleton stayed on at Sherborne for two more years to play cricket, leaving in the autumn of 1893.

53. *Autobiography*, 161.

54. *Autobiography*, 172.

55. Theo Dunnet, "John Cowper and Littleton Powys: Cambridge in the 'Nineties, and a Wedding," PR,16 (1985): 4–20. Mr George Barlow, the archivist at Corpus, supplied Dunnet with copies of various photographs of the Powyses at Corpus which are in the Corpus Christi College Archives, and they are reproduced in this article.

56. In a letter to her sister Dora, outlining some of John's activities, Mary Cowper ends, "He is well & full of life & hope. What a

blessing youth is, it is so buoyant." Letter dated 5 January 1895, in the Powys Collection, DCM.

57. *Autobiography*, 158.

58. *Autobiography*, 165.

59. *Autobiography*, 167.

60. *Autobiography*, 163.

61. *Autobiography*, 186–87.

62. *Autobiography*, 163.

63. *Autobiography*, 188.

64. *Autobiography*, 168–69.

65. Autobiography, 182.

66. *Autobiography*, 53.

67. *Autobiography*, 157.

68. *Joy*, 46. This was their mother's phrase: "You must remember the Vicarage is a house set on a hill."

69. Letter to Llewelyn, mid-August 1912.

70. *Joy*, 47.

71. Louis Marlow, *Swan's Milk* (London: Faber and Faber, 1934), 235. Note: Louis Wilkinson used the pen name Louis Marlow.

72. *Joy*, 95. "In these days her life would have been saved, for there is little doubt that she was suffering from appendicitis, which was afterwards followed by peritonitis."

73. Llewelyn Powys, "Threnody," *Ebony and Ivory* (New York: Harcourt Brace and Company, 1923), 145–152.

74. Mary Cowper Powys's diaries, not a continuous set, are in the Powys Collection, DCM.

75. *Autobiography*, 195.

CHAPTER THREE: 1884-1901

1. Miss Heatley's Girls' School and Miss Walder's Girls' School. Diary, 10 September 1957.

2. *The English Men of Letters Series* included Scott, Dickens, Spenser, Sterne, Carlyle, Swift, Hume, Keats, Hawthorne, Carlyle, etc. It combined critical and biographical essays by well-known scholars. JCP wrote a friend, Boyne Granger, 4 August 1931, "I used to read these little books with an almost lascivious greed. For in them you get the essence of the writers' lives and work gathered up and interpreted by someone who is himself a writer of note." Quoted in Boyne Grainger, *We Lived in Patchin Place.*(London: Cecil Woolf, 2002).

3. *Autobiography*, 216.

4. Johnson, PR8, 62–63.

5. John actually witnessed the child's death. He reminded his sister Marian in a letter dated 12 July 1932 that "Our Nelly is the only one I've ever seen die."

6. Diary, 1 April 1939.

7. Diary, 8 September 1932.

8. *Joy*, 96-7.

9. *Autobiography*, 248.

10. Four times in his life William Cowper suffered extended periods of manic depression when he had hallucinations and heard voices. He tried on several occasions to commit suicide. Mary's father also suffered from depression. See further: David Cecil, *The Stricken Deer: The Life of Cowper* (London: Constable, 1929).

11. *Autobiography*, 222.

12. JCP to Nicholas Ross, 9 October 1939. *Letters to Nicholas Ross*, selected by Nicholas and Adelaide Ross, edited by Arthur Uphill (London: Bertram Rota, 1971). Note that by this period Powys was using capital letters liberally in his letters.

13. *Autobiography*, 239-40.

14. Powys is characteristically very vague about dates, but there is a rare letter to Gertrude dated 26 April, Court House, in which he refers to Littleton being there. It appears from the mother's diary that Littleton and John went to Middlecot, Devon, on 11 April, which was when he proposed to Margaret Lyon, then the brothers returned to Sussex to find Court House.

15. Mary Cowper notes in her diary that "26 July: John comes home" and "8 August 1895: JCP goes away with Mrs. Curme to Court House." The mother, father, Gertrude, and Littleton followed later in August to help settle him.

16. *Autobiography*, 251.

17. *Autobiography*, 259.

18. *Autobiography*, 223.

19. *Autobiography*, 257.

20. *Autobiography*, 255–56.

21. *Autobiography*, 252.

22. Diary, 19 December 1930.

23. *Autobiography*, 241.

24. *Autobiography*, 205.

25. Karl Pearson, "Woman and Labour," *Fortnightly Review* 129 (May 1894): 561.

26. Andrew Wynter, *The Borderlands of Insanity* (London: Robert Hardwicke, 1877), 276.

27. Maxe Nordau, *Degeneration* (London: Heinemann, 1895). Nordau considered modern styles in the arts as evidence of extreme hereditary degeneration and attacked as "degenerate" Symbolism, Tolstoism, Naturalism, Realism, "the Richard Wagner cult," Schopenhauer, Nietzsche, Blavatsky, etc. virtually all forms of modern culture.

28. *Autobiography*, 184.

29. Thomas Carlyle, *On Heroes, Hero Worship and the Heroic in History* (London: Chapman and Hall, 1841, Centenary Edition, 1897), Lecture 4, 24.

30. *Autobiography*, 237.

31. *Autobiography*, 174, 175.

32. *Autobiography*, 283.

33. *Autobiography*, 277.

34. *Autobiography*, 282.

35. *Autobiography*, 261.

36. *Autobiography*, 260.

37. The "Circle," like members of London Clubland—the Omar Khayham Club, the Athenaeum, the New Vagabonds Club, the Rhymers Club, the Savile Club, the Rabelais Club of this period—were bachelors or, as some wit put it, "married men who spent a large part of their lives as if they were bachelors." English clubs were primarily extensions of the public schools and universities, and with the possible exception of de Kantzow, all the members of his circle shared the assumptions and terrors of those male communities.

38. *Autobiography*, 315.

39. Diary, 22 March 1954. The bookseller first heard of the Powyses through Louis Wilkinson, who first wrote Sims in October 1949 about his catalogs of Baron de Corvo and Aleister Crowley. In 1952, Sims asked if he could buy Llewelyn Powys's letters to Wilkinson, which were then with Alyse Gregory. In August 1953, he offered to sell Llewelyn's manuscripts for Alyse, and they subsequently went to the University of California. Sims would issue a catalog "in the hope that some university library would provide a permanent home for them" and, presumably, a profit for himself. The Rauner Special Collections Library, Dartmouth College Library, New Hampshire, holds the correspondence from Phyllis Playter to G. F. Sims regarding the manuscripts.

40. "How Philip Warton Came to Godbarrow," (manuscript is at HRHRC in Notebooks 1897–1900, MS Hanley Collection). M. K. is grateful to Jeff Kwintner who gave her a photocopy and his own transcription.

41. One of the earliest and the most perceptive of Powys's critics, G. Wilson Knight, coined the phase "Powys-hero." In *The Saturnian Quest* (London: Methuen & Co., 1964), 24, he says that the hero in *Rodmoor* "with his heavy stick, is the first of Powys's succession of obvious—the reservation is needed—self-reflections, whom we shall

henceforth call the 'Powys-hero.'" Knight was not aware of these earlier unpublished stories; however, the term is applicable to even JCP's earliest heroes.

42. In his "Threnody," Llewelyn remembers his tomboy sister Nellie coaxing him to the topmost twigs of the walnut tree at Montacute.

43. The "Philip Davenant" fragment is in a notebook along with other prose fragments and drafts of poems at NLW, 22809E.

44. *Autobiography*, 314.

45. Sir Richard Burton, *A Plain and Literal Translation of the Arabian Nights Entertainment, now entitled The Book of the Thousand Nights and a Night*. With an introduction, explanatory notes and a terminal essay upon the history of the Nights by Richard F. Burton. 16 vol. (London: Printed by the Kamashastra Society for private subscribers only, 1885-1888). This remains even today in the restricted "cupboard" of the British Library, as does Krafft-Ebing.

46. *Autobiography*, 275.

47. Lewis Carroll to Mrs. N. H. Stevens, 1 June 1892; Carroll to Mrs. J. Chataway, 28 June 1876, in *The Selected Letters of Lewis Carroll*, ed. Morton N. Cohen (New York: Pantheon Books, 1982).

48. Francis Kilvert, Diary, 13 July 1875. *Kilvert's Diary, 1870-1879* (Middlesex: Penguin, 1977).

49. *Love's Tell-Tale; or The Decameron of Pleasure*. Quoted by Henry Spenser Ashbee, (pseud. Pisanus Fraxei) *Catena Librorum Tacendorum* (London: privately printed, 1885). Ashbee produced three volumes in all—the first bibliography in the English language devoted to writings of a pornographic nature. See Steven Marcus, *The Other Victorians: A Study of Sexuality and Pornography in Mid-Nineteenth-Century England* (New York: Basic Books, 1964), 59.

50. Vladamir Nabokov, *Lolita* (London: Weidenfeld & Nicholson, 1959), 23.

51. *Autobiography*, 358.

52. Nabokov, 20.

53. *Autobiography*, 221.

54. The play is in various draft forms scattered in notebooks 1, 2, and 7, Syracuse. Powys scholar Paul Roberts patiently collated the unnumbered pages and in its reconstructed form the play was produced and acted at a Powys Society Conference.

· 55. J. K. Huysman, *Against the Grain* (À rebours), 1884.

56. Charles Baudelaire, "Spleen de Paris," *Les Fleurs du mal* (1857) in *Oeuvres complètes*, (Paris: Bibliothèque de la Pléiade, 1951). "La femme est le contraire du Dandy. Donc elle fait horreur. La femme a faim et elle veut manger; soif, et elle veut boire. Elle est en rut et elle veut etre foutue. Le beau mérite! La femme est naturelle, c'est-a-dire abominable."

57. *Autobiography*, 222-23.

58. *Autobiography*, 204.

59. Constantine Cavafy. The title of the poem, "Who made . . . the great refusal," (1901) is borrowed from Dante's *Inferno* iii, 60. At the very gate of hell, home of the "wretched people who have lost the good of the intellect," Dante spots someone in limbo who made "il gran refiuti"—the great refusal. It was probably Celestine V, who was made pope at the age of eighty, but after five months on the job, concluded that the pope's palace was no place for a saint. Celestine threw in the apostolic towel to return to full-time asceticism. The church later canonized him, but Dante, who thought that vigorous Church reform was more pressing than further private navel gazing, put him in hell.

60. With the exception of the Philip Warton fragment, all these other pieces are at NLW, 22809E.

61. Syracuse. My thanks to Mark Weimer, Curator of Special Collections, for making microfilm of the relevant material available to me.

62. *Autobiography*, 217.18.

63. *Autobiography*, 293.

64. *Autobiography*, 299.

65. In 1915, his future lecture manager, G. Arnold Shaw, in a publicity blurb indicated that "the City Government of Hamburg sent a special representative to England to secure the man best fitted to interpret English Literature to the Hamburg public," and chose Powys. Shaw tended to hyperbole but it is possible that something of the sort happened.

66. *Autobiography*, 303.

67. *Autobiography*, 230.

68. *Autobiography*, 304–05.

69. Sir Phillip Sidney, *Astrophel and Stella*, Song v.ii.

70. James Halliwell-Phillipps, *Books Of Characters* . . . (London: printed by J. E. Adlard, 1857), 56. Title page: "The Wandering Jew telling fortunes to Englishmen: now reprinted from the very rare edition which was published in London A.D.. 1649." The quote comes from the "Roaring Boy's Fortune": "your life

being a continuall Warre, what peace can attend your death? This is all I can say to you, the path to Heaven is a milky way; not a bloudy."

71. Antoine LeGrand, "Man without passion, or, The wife stoick, according to the sentiments of Seneca," "written originally in French, Englished by G.R." (London, Printed for C. Harper, 1675).

72. *Autobiography*, 304.

73. The announcement in the *Western Gazette* of two lectures by JCP in the National Schoolroom, Montacute, "Coleridge the Poet" and "The History of Montacute," on Friday, April 12, 1901. Powys Collection, DCM.

CHAPTER FOUR: 1902-1911

1. *Autobiography*, 202–03.

2. See Stuart Marriott and Janet Coles, "John Cowper Powys as University Extension Lecturer, 1898–1909," PJ4 (1994): 7–50.

3. *Autobiography*, 294.

4. His fee had increased to double the rate of his first two schools—a pound for an hour's lecture.

5. Marriott, 11.

6. *Autobiography*, 245.

7. *Autobiography*, 284.

8. When Powys was ill in the summer of 1909, he got Louis Wilkinson to take his Oxford Summer Meeting lectures and gave him lots of good advice, concluding: "But believe me, my dear, it is important that you should have so excellent an advertisement as this would be—an audience composed of Secretaries of Centres from all over England." Louis Marlow, *Welsh Ambassadors* (London: Chapman and Hall, 1936), 129.

9. *Autobiography*, 286–87.

10. See Thomas Kelly, *Outside the Walls: Sixty Years of University Extension at Manchester 1886–1946* (Manchester: Manchester U. P., 1950).

11. *Autobiography*, 279.

12. *Autobiography*, 246.

13. *Autobiography*, 319.

14. Kelly, 33. This was Sir Bernard Pares.

15. *Autobiography*, 325.

16. *Autobiography*, 287.

17. *Autobiography*, 324.

18. Letter from Littleton to C. F., 22 April 1905, in the Powys Collection, DCM.

19. *Autobiography*, 330.

20. *Autobiography*, 343–44.

21. *Autobiography*, 330.

22. *Autobiography*, 50.

23. Letter to Llewelyn, late January 1923.

24. *Autobiography*, 309.

25. Letter to Louis Wilkinson, 9 October 1957, Colgate.

26. *Autobiography*, 397.

27. Letter to Glyn Hughes, 26 July 1957. HRHRC.

28. Letter to Phyllis, 4 May 1923, in which he quotes from a letter he has received from his son.

29. *Autobiography*, 206.

30. Ibid.

31. Letter from Hopkins to Richard Watson Dixon, 30 June 1886. *Gerard Manley Hopkins: Selected Letters*, edited by Catherine Phillips (Oxford: Clarendon Press, 1990).

32. Llewelyn entered Sherborne Big School in January 1899 and left in 1903. His friend, Lionel Mylrea, entered in the 3rd term of 1897 and left in 1902.

33. JCP to Llewelyn, October 1902. *Letters to his Brother Llewelyn*, vol. I 1902–1925, edited and selected by Malcolm Elwin (London: Village Press, 1975).

34. Letters from Llewelyn to Littleton, November 1937; 20 June 1937. *The Letters of Llewelyn Powys*, selected and edited by Louis Wilkinson with an introduction by Alyse Gregory (London: The Bodley Head, 1943).

35. *Autobiography*, 379.

36. *Autobiography*, 383.

37. *Ibid.*

38. *Ibid.*

39. *Autobiography*, 364.

40. *Ibid.*

41. *Autobiography*, 379.

42. *Autobiography*, 357.

43. *Autobiography*, 225.

44. *Autobiography*, 315.

45. Letter to Littleton, 12 February 1905.

46. Both manuscripts are at Syracuse. Some of the Keats material was published as *Powys on Keats*, edited by Cedric Hentschel (London: Cecil Woolf, 1993).

47. Diary, 31 March 1952: "Holiday House about Harry & Laura. It was this latter book that 'Lily' my pet whore who when she stayed with my wife & me at Burpham our servant from Birmingham refused to wait upon—read all the time she was in the House!!"

48. *Autobiography*, 327.

49. There are four "chapters" at Syracuse, and two at the Homer Babbidge Library, University of Connecticut, Storrs. In PJ4 (1994) 62-90, Paul Roberts has put the chap-

ters together and called the story "Owen Prince" after the hero. Having examined the Syracuse manuscripts and the fragments at NLW, my sense is that the chapters about the prostitute were written after 1905, but the chapters about Runnymede and Owen Prince were written much earlier, circa the same time as the Wales fragments, then taken out in 1906 and rewritten. Given the confused state of the early material when it was found in the attic and outhouses at Corwen, and given the fact that different archives bought different bits, it seems unnecessary to try to make much more of them than simply evidence of his struggle to become a writer and, incidentally, as an undisguised exposition of why he married.

50. *Autobiography*, 266.

51. Louis Marlow, *Seven Friends*, introduction by Oliver Wilkinson (London: Mandrake Press, 1992), 14.

52. *Swan's Milk*, 173.

53. *Swan's Milk*, 187.

54. *Swan's Milk*, 234.

55. *Autobiography*, 374.

56. Bury, 137.

57. The text is in five notebooks at Syracuse. A transcription of "The Entermores" by Paul Roberts was published in PJ10 (2000): 60–125. Roberts speculates that the play was written in 1905, but I think it was more likely written in the summer of 1907 when the subject of his son's education had become a vexing issue and Powys was voicing his concern in letters to relatives and friends.

58. Letter from JCP to Louis Wilkinson, August 1907. In Louis Marlow (Wilkinson), *Welsh Ambassadors*, (London: Chapman and Hall Ltd., 1936).

59. Louis Wilkinson, *The Buffoon* (New York: Knopf, 1916). Edition quoted from is the Village Press edition, 1975.

60. *The Buffoon*, 49.

61. *The Buffoon*, 86.

62. *The Buffoon*, 11.

63. *The Buffoon*, 43.

64. *The Buffoon*, 51–52.

65. See Alyse Gregory Papers, Beinecke (YCALMSS 163, Series IX, Llewelyn Powys Papers). In Llewelyn's diary for 1911, he has copied the letter from Lyon to Wilkinson, dated 22 December 1901, in which Lyon refuses to help, pointing out "the loss to me would be great, for the clergy are my most hopeful clients." This was undoubtedly true. In 1911 Lyon was offered his greatest chance

as an architect, a commission to rebuild the chapel of Sidney Sussex College. He also did a good deal of work on Corpus, no doubt through Pearce, not only on the chapel, the combination room, and the attic rooms above New Court, but stripped the ivy from Old Court (which JCP says his grandfather planted). He also built a student block for Peterhouse.

66. *The Buffoon*, 56.

67. *The Buffoon*, 75–76.

68. *The Buffoon*, 332, 344.

69. *The Buffoon*, 418–19.

70. *The Buffoon*, 72–73.

71. Letter to Llewelyn, 21 January 1908; 7 March 1908 in *Letters to His Brother Llewelyn*, vol. 1, 1902–1925, edited and selected by Malcolm Elwin, (London: Village Press, 1975).

72. Marriott, 32.

73. Letter to Littleton, 25 April 1908.

74. Letter to Llewelyn, 15 May 1908. See *The Pearl. A Journal of Facetiae and Voluptuous Readings*. London-Paris: Printed for the Society of Vice, 1879,1880. The original edition appeared in eighteen parts, published monthly from July 1879 to December 1880.

75. John Cowper Powys and Llewellyn [sic] Powys, *Confessions of Two Brothers* (Rochester, NY: The Manas Press, 1916), 220.

76. Llewelyn Powys, "Symonds and Stevenson at Davos Platz," in *Swiss Essays* (London: John Lane The Bodley Head, 1947), 105.

77. JCP to Llewelyn, 16 April 1908.

78. Louis Wilkinson, *Welsh Ambassadors*, 108.

79. Letter to Littleton, 1 June 1909.

80. *Swan's Milk*. Wilkinson is vague about dates, but it was probably about this time, probably shortly after he began with Arnold Shaw in 1910. It seems Louis had his Litt.D. by 1916 when Shaw published "Blasphemy and Religion," because he has the title after his name on the title page.

81. *Welsh Ambassadors*, 110. Letter from Llewelyn to Louis, early July 1909.

82. JCP to Llewelyn, September 1909. The stories remained unpublished until long after his death. The originals are in a manuscript notebook in the Powys Collection, DCM. In 1974, a small press in Guernsey, Toucan Press, published them under the title *Romer Mowl and Other Stories*, edited by Bernard Jones. Jones renamed "The Incubus" on the basis that the main character was named after Herbert Mole and Frank Romer, both of

whom were at Sherborne during Powys's time there.

83. *Autobiography*, 217.

84. Diary, 2 August 1937, in which he remembers this period.

85. *Autobiography*, 624.

86. Llewelyn's Diary, 23 September 1909. Transcript of the 1909 diary by Alyse Gregory. Diary No 14 (1909) Beinecke. Llewelyn's 1909 diary was copied out by Louis Wilkinson and published in *Welsh Ambassadors*, 212–216.

87. *Skin for Skin* (London: Jonathan Cape, 1926), 3–7.

88. 1909 Diary, quoted in *Welsh Ambassadors*, 213.

89. Letter to Llewelyn, 11 November 1910.

90. *Autobiography*, 394.

91. JCP to Llewelyn, 16 December 1909.

92. JCP to Llewelyn, 19 May 1910.

93. "This is Thyself" Manuscript at HRHRC. A transcription, introduced and annotated by J. Lawrence Mitchell, edited by Belinda Humfrey in PR 20 (1987): 16–26.

94. "This is Thyself," 20.

95. "This is Thyself," 22.

96. Llewelyn Powys, "East Chaldon," *Skin for Skin* (New York: Harcourt Brace, 1924), 90.

97. Theodore (Dicky) was born in 1906 and Francis was born in 1908.

98. "This is Thyself," 7.

99. Letter to Llewelyn, early May 1910.

100. Letter to Llewelyn, 19 May 1910.

101. Letter to Littleton, 17 October 1910.

102. *Swan's Milk*, 281.

103. *Swan's Milk*, 286.

104. Letter to Llewelyn, 7 March 1908.

105. Information about Arnold Shaw from Paul Roberts, *The Ideal Ringmaster: A Biographical Sketch of Geoffrey Arnold Shaw* (Bath: The Powys Society, 1996). For information about the WEA, see Marriott and Kelly.

106. According to C. F.'s will, he lent Lucy £550 on 27 April 1911, five days after her wedding.

107. Marian Powys, "The Mabelulu," PJ 4 (1994): 161–168.

108. The Chautauqua movement flourished between 1920 and 1924 and thereafter declined. The Great Crash of 1929, for all practical purposes, ended the circuit Chautauqua movement. See John E. Tapia, *Circuit Chautauqua: From Rural Education to Popular Entertainment in Early Twentieth*

Century America (Jefferson, North Carolina, 1950). Also Joseph E. Gould, *The Chautauqua Movement: An Episode in the Continuing American Revolution*. (New York: State University of New York, 1961). Gould writes, "Through the activities of the Chautauqua Institution, the great world was opened up to the incredibly isolated communities of our then new Middle West. Inaugurated for the purpose of training Sunday School teachers, the Institution rapidly expanded its course offerings and its popular appeal until it reached into thousands of culture-starved communities. . . . One of several waves of mass enthusiasm for self-improvement, social betterment, and reform that have periodically swept over the nation, the Chautauqua movement left behind changed tastes, changed laws, and changed social habits."

CHAPTER FIVE: 1912-1915

1. See Frances Gregg, *The Mystic Leeway*, edited by Ben Jones, with an account of Frances Gregg by Oliver Marlow Wilkinson (Ottawa: Carleton University Press, 1995). This poem is still unpublished in full but partially quoted in the introduction, 4.

2. Frances to JCP, September 1925. *Jack and Frances: The Love Letters of John Cowper Powys to Frances Gregg*, vol. 1, edited by Oliver Wilkinson. Assisted by Christopher Wilkinson (London: Cecil Woolf, 1994). Two volumes of the letters between Frances and John Cowper have been published, extending from 1912 to just before her death in 1941.

3. *The Mystic Leeway*, 100.

4. *Jack and Frances*, vol. I, xxx.

5. *Autobiography*, 411.

6. *The Mystic Leeway*, 155.

7. *The Mystic Leeway*, 65.

8. Barbara Guest, *Herself Defined: The Poet HD and Her World* (NY: Doubleday & Co, 1984), 24.

9. *The Mystic Leeway*, 109.

10. *The Mystic Leeway*, 153.

11. *The Buffoon*, 301–302.

12. *The Mystic Leeway*, 155.

13. *The Mystic Leeway*, 157.

14. *Swan's Milk*, 316–317.

15. Llewelyn Powys, "Venice," MS.2, Powys Collection, DCM.

16. See Malcolm Elwin, *The Life of Llewelyn Powys* (London: The Bodley Head, 1946), 99. Elwin says that between the end of February and 19 March (when Llewelyn was

crossing the Furka Pass from Arosa to Davos) "some of John's letters at this time were destroyed—doubtless by Llewelyn after copying into his diary." This letter is not in the Letters of JCP to Llewelyn. The Llewelyn diaries, some originals, some transcriptions, are in the Alyse Gregory Papers, Series IX, Beinecke. In the archive are copies of 1908–09; "A Consumptive's Diary"; 1910; 1911; 1912; "Africa Journal" (1913–18); 1914; 1919; 1928-29; 1933.

17. Elwin, 100.

18. Ibid. The letter has been omitted from Wilkinson's *Welsh Ambassadors*.

19. Guest, 37.

20. *Jack and Frances*, vol. I, 29 April 1912.

21. *Jack and Frances*, vol. I, late June 1912.

22. *Autobiography*, 405.

23. *Autobiography*, 411.

24. Typescripts in Beinecke. Both were written circa 1921 and remained unpublished until 1992. Hilda Doolittle, *Asphodel*, ed. Robert Spoo (Durham, NC: Duke University Press, 1992). *Paint it Today*, ed. Cassandra Laity (New York: New York University Press, 1992).

25. Letter to Frances from Ezra Pound, dated 3 December 1912, in the private possession of her grandson Christopher Wilkinson.

26. "Venice," MS. pp 17–19, Powys Collection, DCM.

27. *Autobiography*, 407–8.

28. *Autobiography*, 241.

29. *Autobiography*, 410–11.

30. *Mystic Leeway*, 61.

31. *Autobiography*, 410.

32. *Jack and Frances*, vol. I, 16 July 1912.

33. *Jack and Frances*, vol. I. Footnote by Oliver Wilkinson to letter of 18 July 1912.

34. See Angela Pitt, "Passions that Disturb: The Diaries of Katie Powys," PJ2 (1992):10.

35. See Christopher Scobie, *Fisherman's Friend: A Life of Stephen Reynolds* (Tiverton: Halsgrove, 2002).

36. *Jack and Frances*, vol. I, 27 August 1912.

37. Brislington was founded by Dr. Edward Long Fox, and the first private "humane" lunatic asylum in England.

38. "Phoenix," typescript, HRHRC. third version. Written circa 1927/28. It has remained unpublished except for a small section published in the *Dial*, August 1928, and another section in the *Powys Journal*, X (2000). Peter Powys Grey also had a copy of a version of "Phoenix," which is now in the possession of M.K.

39. *Jack and Frances*, vol. I, 27 August 1912.

40. *Jack and Frances*, vol. I, 22 August 1912.

41. *Jack and Frances*, vol. I, 24 August 1912.

42. *Jack and Frances*, vol. I, 13 February 1913.

43. *Jack and Frances*, vol. I, I 5 May 1913.

44. Letter to Llewelyn, 31 May 1913.

45. Letter to Llewelyn, 28 August 1913.

46. *Jack and Frances*, vol. I, 12 April 1914.

47. Letter to Llewelyn, 4 January 1914.

48. Letter to Llewelyn, late March 1914.

49. Dates in *Autobiography* for this period are vague or non-existent. However, a series of letters from Mary Cowper to her daughter Lucy verify my dating. She writes in a letter dated March 31, 1914: "John is expected to arrive at Liverpool on the 13th & he will come here via Bristol for one night on his way home to Burpham." Then in a letter of May 3, 1914, she wrote Lucy: "Your brother John is going to Paris tomorrow, en route for Spain. He will stay 2 days in Madrid & see the pictures, & then go on to Seville to join the Wilkinsons, who are there, he will be away for about a month; he has to lecture next winter on Spanish Art so it will help him to go there." June 3 to Lucy: "John and Bertie are home again, having much enjoyed their time abroad." They plan to go to Seaton 16 June and "Marion Linton is coming to stay with us next Monday for a week."

50. *Jack and Frances*, vol. I, 21 June 1914.

51. Oliver Wilkinson was born 28 January 1915 in Sienna. They sailed for the USA in July 1915 with the baby and a fifteen-year-old Italian nurse, "Lala." JCP lent Louis £15 to tide them over until December, when his lectures began. Oliver, writing of his mother, believed that "to Frances, having a child was the greatest achievement in life. To Hilda Doolittle, having a child was an interesting development."

52. Quoted in Elwin, 113.

53. Letter to Llewelyn, 30 July 1914.

54. Letter to Marian, 7 August 1914.

55. *Jack and Frances*, vol. I, September 1914.

56. Letter to Llewelyn, 17 November 1913.

57. Letter to Marian, 4 June 1914.

58. Letter to Marian, 6 September 1914.

59. Letter to Llewelyn, 28 October 1914.

60. *Jack and Frances*, vol. I, September 1914.

61. Letter to Llewelyn, 17 August 1914.

62. Quoted by Christopher Wilkinson, who dates the letter 16 August 1914, in *Powys Newsletter*, no 48.

63. Letter to Llewelyn, 9 September 1914.

64. Letter to Llewelyn, 22 October 1914.

65. Letter to Llewelyn, 8 November 1914.

66. *The War and Culture: A Reply to Professor Munsterberg* (New York: G. Arnold Shaw, 1914), 38; 48–49.

67. See Robin Patterson, "Powys in Canada: John Cowper Powys's Canadian Lectures," *Powys Notes* (1994/95): 33.

68. Patterson, 50.

69. Letter to Llewelyn, 28 November 1914.

70. *Boston Sunday Globe*, 29 November 1914.

71. Letter to Littleton, 8 December 1914.

72. *Autobiography*, 581.

73. Powys kept several of Shaw's publicity blurbs. One calls him "the most brilliant lecturer in the world," with an "international reputation," and a "supreme genius of the spoken word." Another announces a weekly lecture series in Carnegie Hall, New York, "with its seating capacity of 3,000 persons required to accommodate the crowds desirous of hearing his lectures."

74. See the unpublished biographical work by David Weiss, *Letters to the World*, in the David Weiss-Stymean Karlen Papers, Special Collection Department, Paley Library, Temple University. In it, Weiss quotes from his mother's diary and dates the meeting with Powys as 27 May and 28 October 1912. On 27 May 1912, JCP was in Venice with Louis, Frances, and Llewelyn. He was on board the "Baltic" on 28 October. The dating may have been a simple transcription error. Mrs Weiss says she took her "three-year old son" David to the lecture. David was born 12 June 1909, and would have been three in 1913. In May 1913 Powys was once again in England, but he was lecturing in the Philadelphia area in March and October of 1913, hence my dating. David Weiss died in 2002 and left everything to Temple University but the cartons, presumably including the diary, are still in the preliminary process of examination and inventorying.

75. Letter to Marian, 2 July 1915.

76. Letter to Marian, 29 May 1915.

77. T.F. Powys, *Soliloquies of a Hermit* (London: Andrew Melrose, 1918), 62.

78. "A Smuggler's Path," *Skin for Skin*, 111–12.

79. "Charlie" written in 1913, typescript in the Powys Collection, DCM. See also J. Lawrence Mitchell, "T. F Powys in East Anglia," *The Powys Review*, 23 (1989), 3–24.

80. "This is Thyself," 14–15.

81. Letter to JCP from TFP, 19 November 1917.

82. Letter to JCP from TFP, n.d. 1917.

83.Letter to Llewelyn, 29 February 1915.

84. It was published in an edition of 3,000 copies on 5 November 1915, with a second impression of 5,000 copies appearing the following month.

85. John Cowper Powys, *Wood and Stone* (New York, G. Arnold Shaw, 1915), vii.

86. *Wood and Stone*, 590.

87. *Wood and Stone*, viii.

88. *The Spot on the Wall*, ed. Bernard Jones. (St Peter Port, Guernsey: Toucan Press, 1974), 17, 18, 20, 19.

89. *Wood and Stone*, 415, 393, 12.

90. *Wood and Stone*, 202, 203.

91. *Wood and Stone*, 672.

92. *Wood and Stone*, 427–28.

93. *Wood and Stone*, 85, 82, 305, 306.

94. *Wood and Stone*, 651, 653, 660.

95. *Wood and Stone*, 686, viii, 701.

96. *Letters of John Cowper Powys to Louis Wilkinson*, 2 January 1953. "I often think of the difference between Theodore and me. He is original, I am not. My earliest story brought him in as an original character."

97. *Autobiography*, 515, 50, 238–39. Evangelicalism insisted that the despised of the world were more acceptable in the eyes of heaven than the great, which presumably was why C. F. preferred "the company of the most disreputable . . . members of his parish to the company of smart, clever, new-fangled persons."

98. *Autobiography*, 513.

99. Carl Sandburg, "Chicago," *The Oxford Book of American Verse*, intro. by F. O. Matthiessen (New York: Oxford University Press, 1950).

100. See Humphrey Carpenter, *A Serious Character: The Life of Ezra Pound* (London: Faber and Faber, 1988).

101. *Little Review*, editorial, vol. 2, no. 1, March 1915.

102. *The Correspondence of Ezra Pound*. ed. Thomas L. Scott and Melvin Friedman. (New York: New Directions Books, 1988). Letter dated 26 January 1917; second letter dated 3 August 1917. See also Edward de Grazia, *Girls Lean Back Everywhere: The Law of Obscenity and the Assault of Genius* (New York: Random House, 1992), 7–8: "Quinn provided financial support for two years to *Little Review* giving Pound a salary of $750 a year; he also

often gave Anderson and Heap donations from his own pocket."

103. Letter to Llewelyn, 17 November 1913. A poem addressed to Pound, never published, made his feelings even plainer, three lines of which are: "Always upholding Now 'gainst Yesterday / The commonplace is ever his loathed prey / Eating false Laurel foliage like a weevil." The University of Buffalo file reference is B359F17A, and it carries the following annotation: "John Cowper Powys to Ezra Pound Original unpublished mss poem. Not dated, but c. 1920. One page 4to. A sonnet." G. F. Sims. The name of Sims is evidence that it was part of the assignment of unpublished manuscripts bought by Sims from Powys in 1954.

104. See *The United States of America v. One Book entitled Ulysses by James Joyce: Documents and Commentary—a 50-Year Retrospective*. Introduction by Richard Ellmann (Frederick, MD: University Publications of America, 1984), xvii–xviii.

105. "Ulysses in Court," *Little Review*, vol. 7 (January–March 1921): 22–25.

106. Cloyd Head, "The Chicago Little Theatre," *Theatre Arts Magazine*, vol. 1, no. 3 (May 1917).

107. Browne's ideas eventually were formalized in the essays or credos: "The Temple of the Living Art," *The Drama: A Quarterly Review of Dramatic Literature*, 3 (November 1913) and "The New Rhythmic Drama," *The Drama*, 4 (November 1914). Browne's aims are most succinctly summed up in a promotional brochure "The Little Theatre of Chicago" in Scrapbook 10. "The sole aims of the management have been beauty, dramatic illusion, and simplicity; no conventional footlights or conventional scenery are used and staging of each play is designed in all its details by one person so that a perfect unity of effect is obtained. The atmosphere is that of intimate and uncommercial theatre, situated for the creation and production of poetic drama and for the free discussion of life and the arts." Quoted in Donald Tingley, "Ellen Van Volkenburg, Maurice Browne, and the Chicago Little Theatre," *Illinois Historical Journal*, vol. LXXX, no. 3 (Autumn 1987), 135–36. See also: Bernard Dukore, "Maurice Browne and the Chicago Little Theatre." (Ph.D. thesis Urbana: University of Illinois, 1957). Arthur Feinsod, *The Simple Stage: Its Origins in the Modern American Theatre* (New York: Greenwood Press, 1992).

108. *Autobiography*, 513.

109. *Autobiography*, 648.

110. *Autobiography*, 475–76.

111. *Autobiography*, 648.

112. "The New Rhythmic Drama."

113. *Little Review*, vol. 2, no. 1 (March 1915): 5–10.

114. Reginald Hunter, *A Chance-Taker's Memoirs*. Unpublished, Lloyd Emerson Siberell papers, OSUL.

115. Henry Miller, "John Cowper Powys: A Living Book," *The Books in My Life* (Norfolk, CT: New Directions Books, 1952), 136. Miller met Powys in 1917 at one of his lectures in the Labor Temple, New York.

116. *Autobiography*, 513.

117. *Autobiography*, 648.

118. Letter from Phyllis Playter to Frederick Davis, 9 October 1962. "Hers was a very beautiful gown very voluminous of grosgrain silk with bands of black velvet and it was much more dramatic and effective than the authentic one." NLW.

119. Will & Ariel Durant, *A Dual Autobiography* (New York: Simon and Schuster, 1977), 92.

120. Boyne Grainger, 19.

121. Maurice Browne, *Too Late to Lament* (London: Victor Gollanz, 1955), 109.

122. *Little Review*, vol. 2, no. 8 (November 1915), 35.

123. *Autobiography*, 448.

124. *Autobiography*, 525.

125. Claude Bragdon, *More Lives Than One* (New York: Alfred A. Knopf, 1938), 256.

126. Letter to Llewelyn, 10 November 1910.

127. *The Mystic Leeway*, 79, 81.

128. *Autobiography*, 527.

129. *Autobiography*, 522–523.

130. Burton Rascoe, "Contemporary Reminiscences: Some Literary Backfire from a Recent Visitor," *Arts and Decoration*, August 1926.

131. "King of Salamanders," later published in A. D. Ficke's *Selected Poems* (New York: George H. Doran, 1926).

132. *Confessions of Two Brothers*, 136-37.

133. *Autobiography*, 527. In 1939 a disciple asked Powys to "send a word to all those speakers who will come after you." JCP wrote a one page statement, in which he advised, "Above all exploit your own nerves. Exploit all your weaknesses, your maliciousnesses, your hatreds, as well as your adorations. . . . Never mind about logic and reason. A born

speaker is an artist; and art like love and hatred and religion and like Nature herself has nothing to do with logic." Letter to Harold Van Kirk, in private possession.

CHAPTER SIX: 1916-1920

1. Letter to Littleton, 31 January 1916: "If by chance I did have to have an operation over here there are 1st rate surgeons called the Mayo brothers at a place called Rochester Minnesota. . . . The X-ray exam revealed what they called 'a permanent deformity & fixation of the duodenum along with duodenal adhesions & possible ulcer.'"

2. Letter to Llewelyn, 3 January 1916.

3. Letter to Llewelyn, 28 February 1916.

4. Louis Wilkinson, *Blasphemy and Religion* (New York: Arnold Shaw, 1916).

5. T. F. Powys, *The Soliloquy of a Hermit*. Presumably with tongue in cheek, Theodore dedicated the book to Shaw: "Dedicated to a publisher whose humor is as kind as his judgement is honest."

6. *Welsh Ambassadors*. Letter from Theodore to Louis, 3 February 1916.

7. Letter from Llewelyn to John, 11 October 1915. Beinecke, Alyse Gregory Papers. Not in the published *Letters of Llewelyn Powys*.

8. Letter to Llewelyn, early December 1913.

9. *Confessions*, 11.

10. *Confessions*, 34, 131, 123.

11. *Confessions*, 42.

12. *Confessions*, 35.

13. *Confessions*, 118–19.

14. *Confessions*, 135.

15. John Cowper Powys, "Reversion," *Wolf's-Bane Rhymes* (New York: G. Arnold Shaw, 1916).

16. Frances Gregg, "Two Brothers," *The Forum*. August 1915.

17. Letter from Theodore to Louis, 16 December 1916.

18. *Confessions*, 110–111.

19. *The Buffoon*, 143.

20. *San Francisco Bulletin*, 6 September 1919.

21. Letter to Llewelyn, 28 April 1916.

22. *Welsh Ambassadors*, JCP to Louis, 11 September 1907.

23. Letter to Marian, 10 May 1935, reminding her of that time. About the only thing he liked was the name of the lake which he modified only slightly to provide him with a title for his novel.

24. John Cowper Powys, *Rodmoor: A Romance* (New York: G. Arnold Shaw, 1916), 180.

25. *Rodmoor*, 220.

26. *Rodmoor*, 85.

27. *Rodmoor*, 49.

28. *Rodmoor*, 313.

29. *Rodmoor*, 318–323.

30. Letter to brother Littleton, 1 July 1902, telling him of the impending birth.

31. *Rodmoor*, 458.

32. *Rodmoor*, 422.

33. *Rodmoor*, 427–28.

34. *Rodmoor*, 99.

35. *Rodmoor*, 437.

36. *Rodmoor*, 251-2.

37. *Rodmoor*, 254.

38. *Rodmoor*, 340.

39. *Rodmoor*, 367.

40. *Rodmoor*, 429. E. A. Robinson, "Richard Cory," *The Children of the Night* (1890-1897) "And Richard Cory, one calm summer night, / Went home and put a bullet through his head." Powys knew Robinson and his poetry, but this was surely an unconscious echoing, indicative of his astonishing memory for verse.

41. *Rodmoor*, 458.

42. Letter from Llewelyn to Louis Wilkinson, 28 January 1917.

43. *Bumbore* was not published until 1969, after the death of both Powys and Wilkinson. The publisher, Kenneth Hopkins, referred to it as a "little jeu d'esprit" and "in the nature of a family joke."

44. Letter to Llewelyn, 17 December 1916.

45. *Suspended Judgements* (New York: G. Arnold Shaw, 1916), 3–4.

46. *Rodmoor*, 289–90.

47. *Suspended Judgements*, 284–85.

48. *Suspended Judgements*, 286.

49. *Suspended Judgements*, 94.

50. *Suspended Judgements*, 123.

51. Letter to Littleton, 24 April 1917.

52. Letter to Llewelyn, 20 January 1917.

53. Letter to Llewelyn, 9 September 1917.

54. Letter to Llewelyn, 26 October 1917.

55. Letter to Littleton, 22 February 1918.

56. Letter to Littleton, 17 October 1917.

57. Letter to Llewelyn, 31 December 1917.

58. Letter to Llewelyn, 8 January 1918.

59. Letter to Llewelyn, 21 May 1918.

60. Letter to Llewelyn, 18 November 1917.

61. Powys kept this telegram and showed it to Nicholas Ross, a young friend, in 1943. See *Letters to Nicholas Ross*, ed. Arthur Uphill (London: Bertram Rota, 1971), 60.

62. Margaret Hooks, *Tina Modotti: Photographer and Revolutionary* (London: Harper Collins, 1993), 22, 37. In 1923 Powys also wrote an unpublished introduction to Robo's writings, collected posthumously in *The Book of Robo*. In it he referred to Robo's "immature talent" which found expression "more quickly, more easily, in cynical and satirical ways, in destructive ways, than in positive creation."

63. Letter to Littleton, 22 February 1918.

64. He continued to give war lectures, alternately praising France as "representing the truest form of culture," and condemning the German civilization as " a state-worshipping vulture," and in the process, rousing his audience, an Institute of Teachers convention, to "a condition bordering that of frenzy." His lectures were reported in the *San Francisco Examiner* through April 1918.

65. *Autobiography*, 584.

66. Letter to Llewelyn, mid-August 1914.

67. Letter to Llewelyn, 28 November 1914.

68. Letter to Frances Gregg, July 1918.

69. Letter to Marian, 2 July 1915.

70. Letter to Gertrude, undated but probably the summer of 1916 when he was forty-three.

71. Letter to Llewelyn, April 1918.

72. Letter from Powys to Duncan, quoted in the appendix of Fredrika Blair's *Isadora: Portrait of the Artist as a Woman* (New York: McGraw-Hill, 1986).

73. Letter to Llewelyn, 21 May 1918.

74. He kept the "Certificate of Rejection" Serial Number 3130, issued by the British-Canadian Recruiting Mission in New York, for the rest of his life. While it does not say why he was rejected, it gives some useful information. He was at that time 5 ft 10½ inches, with hazel eyes and brown hair, and weighed only 136 lbs. In private possession.

75. Letter from Llewelyn to Louis, 20 February 1907.

76. In *Skin for Skin*, p 43, Llewelyn talks of the "chamber at the end of the north wing, where, as boys, we used to sleep . . . and was always regarded as damp by my mother." In her diary, Mary Cowper often refers to John's terrible colds and bronchitis as a child.

77. *Autobiography*, 587–89.

78. Letter to Llewelyn, n.d. but early September 1918.

79. Louis Marlow, *Forth Beast* (London: Faber and Faber, 1946), 105–106.

80. Frances's grandson, Christopher Wilkinson, gave me the following informa-tion: "Betty was mentally handicapped from birth. When she was at the Vineyard School in Manchester in 1936, the principal . . . sent Frances a report: Betty Wilkinson: Chronological age 17 years 4 months, mental age, 7 years, Mental ratio or Intelligence quotient 50." [email: 22 November 2001]

81. Letter to Marian 10 May 1919.

82. Letter to Frances, 8 May, 1919.

83. Letter to Marian, 4 June 1919.

84. The telegrams from Frances and Louis and the receipt for the money were found folded in an old wallet belonging to JCP.

85. Letter to Marian, 23 June 1919.

86. Letter to Marian, 23 June 1919.

87. *Jack and Frances*, vol. I, xxv.

88. Letter to Marian, 14 August 1919.

89. John Cowper Powys, *The Complex Vision* (New York: Dodd, Mead, 1920) 134–35.

90. Letter to Llewelyn, 1 November 1919.

91. Letter to Llewelyn, 11 January 1920.

92. Letter to Llewelyn, 1 November 1919.

93. For various reasons, the novel was not published until 1980 and until his letters to Frances became available, it was unclear when he actually wrote it. He began to write it 17 February 1920 and finished it by October. Much of it was probably written that summer at Burpham where he could meditate at close quarters on the personality and character of his wife, who is, at least in large part, Nelly. He wrote Frances, accurately, "Its chief fault is long-windedness. It isn't fantastic at all."

94. John Cowper Powys, *After My Fashion* (London: Pan Books, 1980), 89–90.

95. *After My Fashion*, 53.

96. *After My Fashion*, 56, 132.

97. *After My Fashion*, 157.

98. *After My Fashion*, 158–9.

99. *After My Fashion*, 162.

100. *After My Fashion*, 121.

101. *After My Fashion*, 165.

102. *After My Fashion*, 176–77.

103. *After My Fashion*, 171.

104. *After My Fashion*, 214.

105. *After My Fashion*, 226.

106. *After My Fashion*, 247.

107. *After My Fashion*, 216–18.

108. *After My Fashion*, 220–22.

109. *After My Fashion*, 250.

110. *After My Fashion*, 261–62.

111. *After My Fashion*, 263, 285.

112. *Autobiography*, 513.

113. Powys first lived with Marian at 11 Charles St., which is virtually on the corner of Greenwich Ave. and Charles St.—four

blocks from Washington Square. They then moved briefly to 82 W. 12th St.—five blocks from Washington Sq., then in 28 November 1914 they moved to 12 W. 12th, further down the block. On 4 December 1919 they moved to 17 St. Luke's Place, on the corner of St. Luke's and 7th Ave. three blocks from Varick and Charleton, which is where he locates the flat in *After My Fashion*. Later he and Llewelyn moved to 148 Waverley Place, which was between 7th Ave and Ave. of the Americas—one block from Washington Sq. If 7th Ave. marks the western boundary of Greenwich Village, then they were literally on the edge of it from 1914 to 1919 and in it from 1920 to 1930: [15 October 1914] "You may think of us slipping out, of an evening, after a Montacute eat, and strolling down our street, which is a really a nice quiet old-fashioned Henry James one—into 5th Ave, and down that past two red brick churches and the Lafayette-Breevort Hotel . . . into Washington Square. . . . That particular corner of New York has a curious charm of its own different from anything else anywhere."

114. *After My Fashion*, 224.

115. *After My Fashion*, 163.

116. *After My Fashion*, 162.

117. Arnold Shaw wrote him in December 1920, saying that he thought the novel "would not help us much," and urging Powys to write another book of essays: "Don't aim this time over the heads of average fools. Why not general topics—'life in America,' 'English psychology.' Come on now, let loose a bit of rollicking fun out of your system even if it is not great literature." Powys did not take up the suggestion. Letter in private possession.

CHAPTER SEVEN: 1921-1924

1. Letter to Marian, 10 May 1919.

2. Letter to Marian, 7 February 1919.

3. Letter to Marian, 14 August 1919.

4. Letter from Gertrude to Marian, 11 January 1918.

5. Letter from Llewelyn to John, dated "Sunday 1920," but would be in March 1920. In *The Letters of Llewelyn Powys*.

6. Letter to Marian, 7 May 1920.

7. Letter to Llewelyn, 23 November 1920.

8. Letter to Phyllis, 5 April 1926.

9. Diary, 12 February 1934: "She did come to barn in her grey suit—the familiar one wherein she was when I first laid hand on her maiden zone & said "will you be—?" Powys

was fond of the expression, and used it often. 30 October 1931: "Read the line about Poseidon ravishing Tyro that beautiful girl. . . . Poseidon hid Tyro in a purple wave and 'Luse Parthenieen zooeen rata Hupnon ekaien' loosened her virgin zone and poured sleep upon her."

10. Letter to Phyllis, 18 October 1921.

11. They kept both sides of their correspondence until 1951 (Diary, 13 June 1951: "She has been Burning all her old letters to me when we were Courting.") Phyllis kept his to her, and after her death they were sold to the National Library of Wales by the copyright holder, Francis Powys.

12. All the extant Phyllis material was found in storage in Barmouth after her death in 1982. It was with other JCP material that the copyright holder kept in his attic until 1992 when he asked M. K. to sort it and preserve it in safe keeping.

13. In later life, Playter told a newspaper reporter that "conservative estimates in 1890 were that I could close out my holdings at $250,000." This amount today would have a "purchasing power" of more than five million dollars. Other information about Franklin Playter was found in various papers and newspaper clippings kept by Phyllis.

14. Diary, 27 November 1932.

15. Written at the front of JCP's 1957 diary in his hand: "this poem was written by Phyllis when she was 18."

16. Diary, 19 September 1933.

17. All the above fragments are written in Phyllis's hand on flimsy paper. Presently in the biographer's keeping.

18. *Jack and Frances*, vol. I, 10 March 1921.

19. Helen Dreiser, *My Life With Dreiser* (New York: The World Publishing Company, 1951), 55–7.

20. Llewelyn Powys, *The Verdict of Bridlegoose* (New York: Harcourt, Brace, 1926), 34. Llewelyn's biographer, Malcolm Elwin, put it thus: "He lived according to his philosophy of making love while the mood was warm and saying farewell before mutual attraction faded." 151.

21. Sara subsequently had a breakdown and tried to poison herself. Wood told John that he was no longer welcome either. See letter from John to Llewelyn, September 1922, Yale Archive. Letters considered too indiscreet were omitted from the published *Letters to Llewelyn*.

22. Letter to Frances, 6 May 1921.

23. He sent each of them £1 every week, which was the equivalent of about £27 in 2002.

24. Letter to Phyllis, 28 May 1921.

25. Letter to Phyllis, 1 December 1921.

26. Letter to Phyllis, 7 November 1921.

27. An untitled manuscript of one hundred and fourteen pages, NLW (21928D), 66, 125–126.

28. *After My Fashion*, 110.

29. Letter to Phyllis, 22 September 1922. Note that both John and Phyllis frequently used dashes of various lengths in their correspondence to indicate variously a break in thought or a parenthesis and occasionally to indicate the end of a sentence.

30. Letter from Scofield Thayer to Alyse Gregory, 22 October 1922, in *Dial*/Scofield Thayer Papers. Beinecke.

31. *The Verdict of Bridlegoose*, 73.

32. Letter to Phyllis, late November 1921.

33. Unpublished letter from Peter Powys Grey to Derrick Stephens, 2 December 1981.

34. Catherine Sinclair, *Holiday House*. Originally published in 1839, 1843 and as late as 1909 in Glasgow.

35. Letter to Frances, 1 November 1921.

36. Letter to Phyllis, 7 November 1921.

37. Letter to Littleton, January 1922.

38. Letter to Phyllis, 1 April 1922.

39. Letter to Phyllis, 25 May 1922.

40. Letter to Marian, 6 March 1922.

41. Letter from Frances, 8 February 1924.

42. Letter to Phyllis, 15 June 1922.

43. Letter from Theodore to John, 16 February 1919.

44. From an unpublished partial biography of Theodore Powys, "Eikon Animae," by Sylvia Townsend Warner. On the title page of one of the drafts, Warner has written: "Preliminary draft of a study of T. F. Powys—discontinued at his request. Typescript drafts are in the Sylvia Townsend Warner/Valentine Ackland Collection, DCM.

45. Letter to Marian, 19 March 1934: "Will you still leave me as Guardian to our Peter?"

46. Letter to Phyllis, 11 September 1922.

47. Found in the letters to Phyllis, undated but probably written in January 1923.

48. Letter to Phyllis, 10 September 1922.

49. So far as I know, the only play of his that saw the professional stage was a long-delayed production of his adaptation of Dostoevsky's *The Idiot*, in New York in May 1922, and that was accomplished only after Reginald Pole (who produced it and acted as Prince Myshkin) had substantially rewritten it, or, as Powys put it, "meddled" with it.

50. Letter to Llewelyn, 7 November 1922.

51. Letter to Phyllis, 13 September 1922. The typescript of "Paddock Calls" is at NLW. A carbon is in the safekeeping of M. K.

52. *Sherwood Anderson's Memoirs: A Critical Edition*. ed. Ray Lewis White (Chapel Hill: The University of North Carolina Press, 1942), 339.

53. Letter to Frederick J. Hoffman Frederick from Floyd Dell in "Freud and the Radicals: The Sexual Revolution Comes to Greenwich Village" by Leslie Fishbein, in *Canadian Review of American Studies*, vol. 12, no. 2 (1981), 173–189.

54. Theodore Dreiser, *Hey Rub-A-Dub-Dub: A Book of the Mystery and Wonder and Terror of Life*. (New York: Boni and Liveright, 1920), 131, 134.

55. John Cowper Powys, *Psychoanalysis and Morality* (San Francisco: Jessica Colbert, 1923), Oddly, it was re-published recently in Croatian: *Psihoanaliza I Moralnost*, trans. Marko Gregoric. (Zagreb: Naklada Jesenski I Turk, 2001).

56. *Psychoanalysis and Morality*, 5, 31, 10, 11.

57. Powys wrote to Dorothy Richardson in January 1930: "We really think and feel with the stomach almost more than with the brain."

58. *Psychoanalysis and Morality*, 12, 17, 18, 22.

59. Louis Berman, MD. *The Glands Regulating Personality: A Study of the Glands of Internal Secretion in Relation to the Types of Human Nature* (New York: The Macmillan Co., 1921).

60. Berman, 22-24.

61. Berman, 26-27.

62. *Psychoanalysis and Morality*, 26-27.

63. *Psychoanalysis and Morality*, 28-29.

64. Berman, 13–14.

65. Berman, 13.

66. *Psychoanalysis and Morality*, 31-4.

67. *Psychoanalysis and Morality*, 35.

68. Letter to Phyllis, 27 December 1922.

69. Ibid.

70. Letter to Phyllis, 23 December 1922.

71. Letter to Phyllis, 26 December 1922.

72. Letter to Llewelyn, December 1922.

73. Letter to Phyllis, 22 December 1922.

74. Letter to Marian, 15 November 1922.

75. Letter to Llewelyn, late January 1923.

76. Letter to Phyllis, 10 February 1923.

77. Letter to Llewelyn, late January 1923.

78. £1 0s. 0d. in the year 1927 had the same "purchase power" as £40.69 in the year 2002 (the latest year for figures).

79. Letter to Littleton, 11 April 1923.

80. Letter to Phyllis, 6 March 1923.

81. Letter to Llewelyn, 1 October 1922. Unpublished. Beinecke.

82. Letter to Phyllis, 21 March 1923.

83. Letter to Phyllis, 17 March 1923.

84. Letter to Phyllis, 12 May 1923.

85. Letter to Phyllis, 9 March 1925.

86. Letter to Phyllis, 2 December 1925.

87. Letter to Phyllis, 8 May 1923.

88. Letter to Phyllis, 30 April 1923.

89. Joseph Conrad, *Chance* (London: J. M. Dent, 1949 collected edition), 237, 201.

90. *Confessions*, 11–19.

91. *Chance*, 224.

92. *Chance*, 208.

93. Letter to Phyllis, 14 April 1923.

94. *Chance*, 426–27.

95. Letter to Phyllis, 23 April 1923.

96. Letter to Phyllis, 23 November 1923.

97. Letter to Phyllis, 10 May 1923.

98. Unpublished letter to Dorothy Richardson, 19 January 1930. Beinecke.

99. John Cowper Powys, *Ducdame* (New York: Doubleday, 1925), 249. He wrote his son, 26 February 1924, that he called it *Ducdame* because it is "a nice romantic enigmatic equivocal pantagruelian sort of title for a story."

100. *Ducdame*, 188.

101. *Ducdame*, 85.

102. *Ducdame*, 303.

103. *Ducdame*, 306.

104. *Ducdame*, 73–74, 80.

105. *Ducdame*, 87.

106. Otto Weininger, *Sex and Character* (New York: Putnam, 1914. First German edition, 1903).

107. David Abrahamsen, *The Mind and Death of a Genius* (New York: Columbia University Press, 1946).

108. *Ducdame*, 310.

109. John Knox,"The First Blast of the Trumpet Against the Monstrous Regiment of Women." pamphlet, 1558.

110. *Ducdame*, 3.

111. *Ducdame*, 264.

112. *Ducdame*, 426–27.

113. *Ducdame*, 288.

114. *Ducdame*, 154, 155.

115. *Ducdame*, 290.

116. *Ducdame*, 444.

117. Letter to Phyllis, 12 July 1924.

118. Letter to Phyllis, 13 July 1924.

119. Letter to Phyllis, 25 July 1924.

120. Letter to Phyllis, 2 July 1924.

121. Letter to Phyllis, 20 July 1924.

122. Letter to Phyllis, 7 August 1924.

123. *London Mercury*, January 1924. In the July 1924 edition, Priestley reviewed Theodore's *Mark Only*, which was, he wrote, "filled with dreary old tricks, the devices of ancient rural melodramas, such as stolen wills, elaborate seductions and rapes, and endlessly repeated catch-phrases and gestures. It is sad to reflect how a little reshuffling of the worn old pack can delude so many apparently intelligent reviewers, if not readers, of fiction, into imagining that they are being given something new."

124. Sylvia Townsend Warner, who knew both Theodore and Katie well, wrote perceptively in her diary, "Between sanity and madness there is a territory like a darkened moor, full of peat-bogs, & mists, with no perceptible water-shed or frontier. ... It is only a few who are transported to madness, the rest have to stumble towards it, over the soggy misleading ground, & through the obstacles of being a nuisance to those who love them & a laughing-stock to strangers. Philippa's indifference to being comical and conspicuous shows how far she has been along that road." Diary, 25 July, 1949. STW/VA Archive, DCM.

125. Letters to Phyllis, 6 & 7 September 1924.

126. Letter from Theodore to JCP, 16 March 1918.

127. Letter to Phyllis, 10 October 1924.

128. The cottage was at Montama, near Woodstock, Vermont.

129. Letters to Phyllis, 4 October; 6 October 1924.

130. Letter to Phyllis, 10 October 1924.

131. Letter to Phyllis, 12 October 1924.

132. Diary, 1 September 1931.

133. Diary, 4 March 1930: "There came Mr. Keedick's cheque for $15 about but the T.T. say that $180 has been lost like lost feathers. She feels very strongly that this is the end of our servitude to Keedick whereby we make only 1/3rd."

134. Letter to Llewelyn, 18 January 1925.

135. Letter to Llewelyn, 7 February 1925.

136. Powys's letters to Phyllis contain much information about Patchin Place and its environs. Of its inhabitants he says less, but in the 1920s it was a popular place for poor artists, musicians, and writers to live.

One, Boyne Grainger, wrote a remembrance of Patchin Place which has been published, *We Lived in Patchin Place* (London: Cecil Woolf, 2002).

137. Letter to Phyllis, 16 July 1924.

138. Ibid.

139. Letter to Phyllis, 18 July 1924.

CHAPTER EIGHT: 1925-1929

1. Letter to Llewelyn, 13 March 1925.

2. Letter from Llewelyn to Gertrude, 10 March 1925. *The Letters of Llewelyn Powys.*

3. Letter to Llewelyn, 13 March 1925.

4. Letter to Phyllis, 13 July 1925.

5. Letter to Phyllis, 16 July 1925.

6. Letter to Phyllis, 26 July 1925.

7. Letter to Phyllis, 2 December 1925.

8. Letter to Phyllis, 16 November 1925.

9. Letter to Phyllis, 29 November 1925.

10. Letter to Phyllis, 21 November 1925.

11. Letter to Phyllis, 28 November 1925.

12.Letter to Phyllis, 12 December 1925.

13. Letter to Phyllis, 16 July 1926. Powys was convinced that his zodiacal sun sign was Sagittarius, and Phyllis's was Libra ("with her balanced critical mind," Diary, 3 August 1940). It was only much later in life that he discovered *he* was the Libra and she was Sagittarius, but by then the myth of Chiron, the archer, was firmly embedded in his mind. It is true that his moon was in Sagittarius, and he or cousin Ralph might have decided that the moon was more important in his chart than the sun.

14. Diary, 25 November 1925: "Right in the middle of the worst of 'em my voice reaches you—listen thin Jill!—saying 'now enough of that—now stop!' and you know how when I kneel on the floor by your streaming abject's face so that those splashing tears fall on me I <u>can</u> stop you & make it all right, & then the dear thin says 'I ask you to forgive me'. . . & smile at your Jack thro' your tears & put vanishing cream on your face & be my dear Thin again. . . . Oh I love you so."

15. Letter to Phyllis, 16 November 1925.

16. Letter to Phyllis, 13 November 1925.

17. There are two versions of this letter— the heavily expurgated one in *The Letters of Llewelyn Powys* and the one which Powys quotes in its entirety to Phyllis. 11 April 1926: "Lulu has written me one of his startling letters of reproach & grievance. . . . Lulu talks . . . of my not treating my inmost friends—you & him I suppose he means—as well as others and . . . that I take everyone 'for

kind little walks in turn as I did when they were children'. . . . Lulu doesn't hesitate to speak of money too, in his attack & says I ought to 'reward my entourage' with the money I make & not fling it to others. . . . Lulu says he could manage it in my place & yet be honourable. . . . I don't care about appearing honourable or dishonourable as long as I keep people happy & avoid violent & agitating scenes. . . . It is really just simple & touching jealousy. Just as it really was over you in that other famous letter." In another letter omitted altogether from the *The Letters of Llewelyn Powys*, Llewelyn follows up this criticism with: "Your soul feels at peace under masks, you, disguised under a Jesuit's hood are content to offer false wafers to a false congregation." (11 April 1926, Beinecke.)

18. Letter to Phyllis, 17 April 1926.

19. Will Durant was struggling himself to finance the building of a new Labor Temple for which he was in charge, but he became for Powys "a secular saint": "Durant, in the manner of Ferney, had fed me when I was penniless." (*Autobiography*, 613). Durant writes of this time: "It was an imposition to ask this volcano to come and erupt punctually at a stated hour each week for a few dollars. Learning that he was badly in need of three hundred dollars, I forced that sum upon him as an advance against the fees his classes would give him." *A Dual Autobiography*, 91–2.

20. Letter to Phyllis, 1 August 1927.

21. Letter to Phyllis, 12 July 1926.

22. Letter to Phyllis, 17 February 1927.

23. In fact, the son got his curacy in the time-honored fashion of the Powys and Lyon family, with a curious downward twist. The vicar of Folkestone had stayed with Littleton's old nurse, Fanny Stevenson, who took lodgers and she "talked all the time of her darling Master Littleton." "This worthy priest" remembered their conversation when he read the list of neophytes for ordination, wrote to the son, and Littleton Alfred got the job.

24. Letters to Phyllis, 26 & 27 January 1927.

25. The "American lady" is Gertrude Stein who used the phrase in *The Making of Americans. Being A History of A Family's Progress* (New York: Albert and Charles Boni, 1926), 137.

26. Letter to Phyllis, 20 February 1927.

27. Letter to Littleton, 6 February 1927.

28. Letter to Phyllis, 3 February 1927.

29. Letter to Theodore, 3 December 1926.

30. Letter to Llewelyn, 3 December 1926.

31. Letter to Phyllis, 23 February 1927.

32. Letter to Phyllis, 16 August 1927.

33. Letter to Phyllis, 11 July 1925.

34. Letter to Phyllis, 18 October 1928.

35. Letter to Phyllis, 20 & 21 April 1928.

36. Letter to Frances, 1 February 1927.

37. Letter to Littleton, 12 May 1927.

38. Letter to Phyllis, 27 July 1927.

39. Letter to Phyllis, 4 August 1927.

40. Letter to Phyllis, 2 July 1927.

41. Letter to Phyllis, 1 August 1927.

42. Letter to Frances, 18 May 1928.

43. Letter to Phyllis, 9 August 1924.

44. John Cowper Powys, *Wolf Solent* (New York: Simon and Schuster, 1929). There have been many subsequent reprints, reset with slightly different pagination. The edition quoted from is New York: Harper & Row, 1984.

45. *Wolf*, 2–3.

46. *Wolf*, 7–9.

47. *Wolf*, 36.

48. *Wolf*, 87. Diary, 27 February 1941.

49. John Cowper Powys, "Song" in *Odes and Other Poems* (London: William Rider, 1896).

50. *Wolf*, 53.

51. *Wolf*, 61.

52. *Wolf*, 231-32.

53. *Wolf*, 70.

54. *Wolf*, 250-51.

55. *Wolf*, 340.

56. *Wolf*, 336.

57. *Wolf*, 159.

58. *Wolf*, 333.

59. Letter from Theodore, 12 May 1917.

60. *Autobiography*, 356-57.

61. *Wolf*, 335.

62. Letter to Llewelyn, 26 June 1925.

63. Letter to Llewelyn, 9 May 1916.

64. *Wolf*, 124.

65. *Wolf*, 289-1.

66. *Wolf*, 508.

67. *Wolf*, 386.

68. *Wolf*, 389.

69. *Wolf*, 414.

70. *Wolf*, 41–43.

71. *Wolf*, 90.

72. *Hamlet*, act 1, scene v. "Well said, old mole! canst work i' the earth so fast?"

73. *Wolf*, 369.

74. *Wolf*, 408.

75. *Revelations of Divine Love* by Julian of Norwich.

76. *Wolf*, 311.

77. *Wolf*, 597.

78. *Wolf*, 553.

79. *Wolf*, 517.

80. *Wolf*, 333.

81. *Wolf*, 345, 346.

82. *Wolf*, 411.

83. *Wolf*, 442–52.

84. *Wolf*, 460–61.

85. *Wolf*, 473.

86. *Wolf*, 527–28.

87. *Wolf*, 598.

88. *Wolf*, 612.

89. Diary, 14th August, 1930: "It will be wonderful to me to see the rugged face of my Lulu. The wise corrugated face of Lord Carfaxe."

90. *Wolf*, 594.

91. *Wolf*, 530.

92. The original manuscript of *Wolf Solent*, less the deleted chapters, is at NLW (22373–7D). The six chapters excluded from the manuscript are held at the George Arent Research Library, Syracuse University. The typescript of the six chapters are in the safe-keeping of M. K.

93. MS. p. 1027d, TS. pp. 729–30.

94. MS. p. 1008-09, TS. pp. 711–12.

95. MS. p. 1011b, TS. p. 714.

96. Theodora Scutt, "Portrait of T. F. Powys by his adopted daughter." 1965. Produced by Count Potoki, Theodora's putative father, who had a small printing press at Lovelace Copse in Dorset where he lived for a time with Theodora and Violet after Theodore's death.

97. JCP had finished fifteen chapters of *Wolf Solent* by August 1926 and by December had written the next four chapters, including the one in which Gerda's accident is described.

98. MS. p. 993b, TS. p. 702.

99. MS. p. 1011a–1012a.

100. TS. p. 714.

101. MS. p. 1132b, TS. p. 817.

102. Letter to Phyllis, 3 February 1927.

103. Letter to Phyllis, 28 February 1928.

104. For example, Letter to Phyllis, 5 August 1927.

105. Letter to Phyllis, 14 February 1926.

106. According to Will Durant, the secret of the future success of "Essandess," as they were known, was "the unceasing search for new authors, the exploration of new subjects, the risking of great sums on editorial judgement and widespread advertisement, the active effort to find and develop new markets for books, new techniques for distributing

them." *A Dual Autobiography*, 103.

107. Letter to Littleton, Good Friday, 1929. G. F. Sims subsequently sold Garnett's report on *Wolf Solent* in which he had said, "You really hypnotize us so wonderfully that at the end we feel like a fly who finds himself free of a most beautifully intricate web." Catalogue 25, Item 228. Quoted in George Sims, *A Life in Catalogues and Other Essays* (Philadelphia: Holmes Publishing, 1994), 22.

108. Letter to Theodore, 21 May 1929.

109. Letter to Phyllis, 15 May 1928.

110. John Cowper Powys, *The Meaning of Culture* (New York: W. W. Norton, 1929).

111. Letter to Phyllis, 12 June 1929.

112. Letter to Phyllis, 3 August 1929.

113. Letter to Llewelyn, 11 June 1929.

114. See Kenneth Hopkins, *Bertrand Russell and Gamel Woolsey* (North Walsham, Norfolk: Warren House Press, 1985) for details of Gamel's early background.

115. Alyse apparently suggested to Llewelyn's biographer, Malcolm Elwin, that she had connived at Llewelyn's seduction of Gamel. This interpretation of events is not recorded in Alyse's unpublished journal, but her sadness in a long entry for 9 April 1928 makes it evident that it was at this time that the seduction—if that is what it was—occurred.

116. Llewelyn Powys, *So Wild A Thing: Letters to Gamel Woolsey*, ed. Malcolm Elwin (Dulverton, Somerset: The Ark Press, 1973), letter dated 7 June 1928.

117. Letter to Phyllis, 3 July 1928.

118. See Jonathan Gathorne-Hardy, *The Interior Castle, A Life of Gerald Brenan* (London: Sinclair-Stevenson, 1992), 252.

119. Betty Burroughs and Reginald Marsh were divorced in 1933. By a second husband she had three children.

120. Letter from Alyse Gregory to Phyllis Playter, 23 May 1929, in which she writes: "Did you know that it was John's plea that made L. write the letter that brought her over?" Private Collection.

121. The unpublished typescript journals of Alyse Gregory are at Yale. Copies of them are in the Powys Collection, DCM. Entry dated 30 November 1928.

122. Letter to Phyllis, 4 November 1928.

123. Letter from Phyllis to Gamel. Internal dating early May 1929. Private collection.

124. Letter to Phyllis from Gamel, 26 July 1954. Private collection.

125. Journal, 2 January 1929.

126. Alyse Gregory, *King Log and Lady Lea* (London: Constable and Co, 1929).

127. Letter to Phyllis, 20 July 1929.

128. Diary, 31 July 1929.

129. Gamel Woolsey, *One Way of Love* (London: Virago Press, 1987), 76.

130. Woolsey, 266. Phyllis reminded Gamel of this time in a letter (9 February 1931): "Fragments of sentences—words—echo in my mind long afterwards—with a heart-breaking significance—as those words of yours once—do you remember Gamel— . . . after the accident to the first child— . . . and in a strange half-laughing way you said 'you know I don't know Llewelyn very well—I have hardly seen him.'" Private Collection.

131. Woolsey, 281.

132. Powys noted more than once in his letters to Phyllis how his voice would get higher-pitched and his accent more obviously upper-class when he became irritated. In a later novel, *Maiden Castle*, he gave the Powys-hero the same characteristic.

133. Letter to Louis Wilkinson, 19 October 1955.

CHAPTER NINE: 1930-1931

1. John Cowper Powys, *In Defence of Sensuality* (New York: Simon & Schuster, 1930), 259. All page references are to this edition.

2. Letter to Phyllis, 9 November 1929.

3. *Sensuality*, 172; 270; 117.

4. *Sensuality*, 8.

5. *Sensuality*, 103.

6. *Sensuality*, 29.

7. *Sensuality*, 37.

8. *Sensuality*, 210.

9. *Sensuality*, 226.

10. Letter from Theodore, 12 May 1917.

11. *Autobiography*, 13.

12. Letters to Phyllis, 6 and 14 January 1930.

13. Diary, 15 February 1930.

14. Letter to Phyllis, 7 January 1930.

15. *Autobiography*, 512.

16. Letter to Phyllis, 11 January 1930. Powys wrote Keedick on 6 January 1930 (draft of letter in private possession) agreeing that arbitration was better than lawyers and courts, but urging that they settle the dispute themselves. He then goes on to suggest that, concerning the word "option," they retain "the right to interpret the original contract in our individual ways." Powys's inability to understand contracts was the cause of his

much more serious difficulties in 1934.

17. *Autobiography*, 540–41.

18. *Wolf Solent* made $5,000 for the year ending 1929. In terms of purchasing power for 2003, that is approximately $54,000. "I sent the statement of royalties for Wolf Solent from Jan 30th to Dec 31st $5,000. O if only we can put it all away safe in an annuity or government bonds."

19. Letter to Phyllis, 13 February 1926.

20. Letter to Phyllis, 21 July 1927.

21. Letter to Phyllis, 23 June 1928.

22. Letter to Llewelyn, 4 January 1926.

23. Letter dated 22 January 1929 to Arthur Davison Ficke. Beinecke.

24. Letter to Llewelyn, 19 April 1929.

25. According to Ficke, he did not lend Powys the money but sold the manuscript of *Wolf Solent* for him. Ficke got $2,000 for it, instead of the $100 JCP was asking. See A. D. Ficke, letter to L. E. Siberell, 27 December 1943. In the Lloyd Emerson Siberell papers, OSUL.

26. Phyllis's diary, 18 November 1929. Phyllis Playter's diaries are in private possession.

27. Phyllis's diary, 21 January 1930.

28. Letter to Phyllis, 24 January 1930.

29. Phyllis's diary, 17 March 1930.

30. Phyllis's diary, 26 February 1930.

31. Many friends urged Powys to continue lecturing. Tom Jones, for example, wrote: "You leave something which comes easy and natural to you, for work which will cause you much more strain and anxiety & consequently prejudice to health. You will have twice the work for half the monetary result. I also doubt whether you can write badly enough for the coarse appetite of the British Philistine. . . . This 'giving up lecturing' seems a shocking tragedy to me."(No date, letter in private possession.)

32. Phyllis's diary, 23 February 1930.

33. Phyllis's diary, 24 March 1930.

34. Letter to Phyllis, 25 July 1925.

35. Letter to Phyllis, 7 January 1930.

36. Diary, 28 February 1930.

37. Phyllis's diary, 20 April 1930.

38. Phyllis's diary, 19 April 1930.

39. Letter to Marian, 15 November 1922.

40. Peter Powys Grey bequeathed his diaries to M. K.

41. Diary, 5 June 1930.

42. Diary, 23 June 1930.

43. Letter to Phyllis, 18 June 1928.

44. Diary, 12 August 1930.

45. John Cowper Powys, *The Owl, The Duck, and—Miss Rowe! Miss Rowe!* (Chicago: The Black Archer Press, 1930).

46. Letter to Phyllis, 20 September 1922.

47. Gregory, Journal, 29 November 1929.

48. Diary, 5 December 1930.

49. Diary, 10 September 1931.

50. Diary, 23 August 1930.

51. Gregory, Journal, 31 December 1930.

52. Diary, 30 July 1931.

53. Phyllis's diary, 9 January 1931.

54. Phyllis's Diary, 14 January 1931.

55. Diary, 26 October 1930.

56. Letter to Phyllis, 15 January 1930.

57. Diary, 29 January 1931.

58. John Cowper Powys, *A Glastonbury Romance* (New York: Simon & Schuster, 1929; London: The Bodley Head, 1933; London: Macdonald, 1955). The preface was added to the Macdonald edition. Page references are to this latter edition. xi.

59. *A Glastonbury Romance*, xiii.

60. Diary, 11 June 1930.

61. *A Glastonbury Romance*, ix.

62. John Rhys, *Studies in the Arthurian Legend* (Oxford: Clarendon Press, 1890).

63. Diary, 25 August 1929. Everything turned into symbols in his myth-making mind. One day as I sorted through another garbage bag of material I came across a bill dated 20-8-29 "Slop Basin (Sil plated on copper) 18/6 bought from one M. Emanuel of Southampton, Unredeemed Pledge Warehouse." I wondered why they had kept that particular bill all those years until I recognized what it was. It gave me a strange feeling to realize that now I was probably the only person in the world who did. Before he left England on his 1929 trip, he bought a tray and a basin as gifts for Phyllis and Olwen. On board ship he read Rhys's book on the Arthurian Legend over and over until "by degrees it becomes clearer to me what the Graal was—the Mwys of Gwydion Garan-hir; the Cauldron of "the Head of Hades." Then on 27 August he noted in his diary: "I have suddenly realized that the silver tray I have bought is like the dish at Carbonak and the basin I have bought for Olwen is like the Cauldron of Gwydno-Garanhir—which is a microcosm or an original of the Graal itself."

64. Jane Harrison, *Prolegomena to the Study of Greek Religion* (Cambridge: Cambridge University Press, 1903). also *Ancient Art and Ritual* (London: Butterworth Ltd., 1913).

65. Francis M. Cornford, *From Religion to*

Philosophy (London: Edward Arnold, 1912).

66. Gilbert Murray, *The Classical Tradition in Poetry* (London: Humphrey Milford, 1927). "Excursus on the Ritual Forms Preserved in Greek Tragedy," in J. Harrison's *Themis*. The "Cambridge Ritualists," as they were called, were influenced by the work of James G. Frazer, *The Golden Bough: A Study in Magic and Religion*. 2 vol. (London: Macmillan & Co, 1890).

67. Roger Sherman Loomis, *Celtic Myth and Arthurian Romance* (N.Y.: Columbia University Press, 1927). Diary, 30 January 1930: "Read the Green Book of Loomis about the mythology of Love and sank into it."

68. W. E. Mead, ed., *Merlin, A Prose Romance* (London: Kegan Paul, 1897).

69. Alfred Nutt, *Celtic & Mediaeval Romance*. n.p.,1899. *Studies in the Legend of the Holy Grail*.

70. *A Glastonbury Romance*, xii–xiii.

71. Jessie L. Weston, *From Ritual to Romance* (Cambridge: Cambridge University Press, 1920).

72. Letter to Phyllis, 8 January 1930.

73. Diary, 3 January 1931.

74. Phyllis's diary, 27 January 1931.

75. Phyllis's diary, 11 February 1931.

76. Letter to Phyllis, 10 March 1931.

77. Diary, 2 May 1931.

78. Phyllis's diary, 26 May 1931.

79. Diary, 1 June 1931.

80. Phyllis's diary, 10 June 1931.

81. Phyllis's diary, 29 June 1931.

82. Diary, 29 July 1931.

83. Kenneth Hopkins, *The Powys Brothers* (London: J. M. Dent, 1967), 157.

84. *A Glastonbury Romance*, 403.

85. *A Glastonbury Romance*, 405.

86. Diary, 22 December 1931.

87. G. R. S. Mead, *Thrice-Greatest Hermes*, 3 vol. (London: The Theosophical Publishing Society, 1906), vol. 1, 125.

88. Phyllis's diary, 22 September 1931.

89. *A Glastonbury Romance*, 936.

90. *A Glastonbury Romance*, 938–40.

91. Diary, 4 August 1929.

92. See William James, *A Pluralistic Universe: Hibbert Lectures at Manchester College on the Present Situation in Philosophy*. Includes "Concerning Fechner." (New York: Longmans Green & Co, 1909). See also Stanley Hall, *Founders of Modern Psychology* (New York: Appleton & Co.,1924) which includes a chapter on Fechner. However, he most likely began reading him in 1929 when he was visiting Lulu and Alyse—Alyse owned a copy.

93. Diary, 21 August 1931.

94. Diary, 9 February 1933.

95. *A Glastonbury Romance*, 109.

96. Diary, 10 November 1930.

97. *A Glastonbury Romance*, 618.

98. *A Glastonbury Romance*, 614.

99. *Swan's Milk*, 229–231.

100. *A Glastonbury Romance*, 1063–67.

101. *A Glastonbury Romance*, 1117–19.

102. Preface to the 1955 edition.

103. Jocelyn Brooke, "On re-reading A Glastonbury Romance," *The London Magazine* (April 1956).

104. Diary, 7 August 1932.

105. Letter to Durrell, 2 April 1957. *The Durrell-Miller Letters 1935-80*, ed. Ian S MacNiven (London: Faber and Faber, 1988), 315-16.

106. Diary, 12 July 1932.

107. John Cowper Powys, *A Philosophy of Solitude* (New York: Simon & Schuster, 1933), 43.

108. *A Philosophy of Solitude*, 45.

109. *Sensuality*, 59.

110. *A Glastonbury Romance*, 370.

111. *Sensuality*, 93.

112. *A Philosophy of Solitude*, 127–28.

113. Gregory, *Journal*, 9 April 1940.

114. *A Philosophy of Solitude*, 176.

115. Diary, 7 May 1933.

116. Diary, 8 January 1931.

117. Diary, 4 July 1932.

118. Diary, 30 June 1932.

119. *Autobiography*, 641.

120. *The Complex Vision*, 132.

121. Friedrich Nietzsche, *The Birth of Tragedy*, trans. F. Golffing (New York: Doubleday, 1956), 97.

122. *Sensuality*, 10.

123. Herman Hesse, *In Sight of Chaos*, trans. S. Hudson (Zurich: Seldwyla Verlag, 1923). D. H. Lawrence, *Apocalypse* (London: M. Secker, 1932).

124. *From Religion to Philosophy*, ix.

125. *Autobiography*, 55.

126. William James, *A Pluralistic Universe: Hibbert Lectures on the Present Situation in Philosophy* (New York: Longmans Green & Co, 1909), 321–323.

127. *Confessions*, 48–49.

128. *Confessions*, 159.

129. *Sensuality*, 131.

130. Llewelyn Powys, *Impassioned Clay* (New York: Longmans, Green and Co., 1931), 25.

131. Llewelyn Powys, *So Wild a Thing:*

Letters to Gamel Woolsey, edited as a narrative by Malcolm Elwin (Dulverton, Somerset: Ark Press, 1973). Letter dated 10 November 1930.

132. *A Philosophy of Solitude*, 108.

133. *A Philosophy of Solitude*, 109.

134. Carl Jung, *Wandlungen und Symbole der Libido*, translated by Beatrice M. Hinkle as *Psychology of the Unconscious* (New York: Dodd, Mead and Co, 1916).

135. Diary, 17 August 1932.

136. *The Occult Review*, ed. Ralph Shirley (London: William Rider & Co.) Advertised itself as "a monthly magazine devoted to the investigation of super-normal phenomena and the study of psychological problems."

137. *Autobiography*, 24.

138. *Autobiography*, 435.

139. *Autobiography*, 278.

140. Diary, 12 June 1931.

141. Diary, 3 December 1931.

142. Diary, 20 June 1933.

143. Diary, 31 May 1933.

144. Diary, 24 January 1932.

145. Diary, 28 October 1928.

146. Diary, 25 November 1933.

147. *Sensuality*, 87.

CHAPTER TEN: 1932-1934

1. Diary, 25 January 1932.

2. Diary, 9 February 1932.

3. Diary, 11 May 1932.

4. Letter to Llewelyn, 15 December 1931. Beinecke.

5. Diary, 9 February 1932.

6. Diary, 10 February 1932.

7. Diary, 4 July 1932.

8. Diary, 28 August 1932.

9. Diary, 4 November 1932.

10. Diary, 6 & 7 November 1932.

11. John Cowper Powys, *Weymouth Sands* (New York: Simon & Schuster, 1934). Since then there have been many reprints. The edition referred to is the Macdonald edition published in England in 1963. 32.

12. *Weymouth Sands*, 33.

13. *Weymouth Sands*, 36.

14. *Weymouth Sands*, 20, 478, 36.

15. *Weymouth Sands*, 120, 121.

16. *Weymouth Sands*, 272, 388.

17. *Weymouth Sands*, 330.

18. *Weymouth Sands*, 271.

19. *Weymouth Sands*, 412.

20. Alexandra David-Neel, *With Mystics and Magicians in Tibet* (London: John Lane The Bodley Head, 1931). She had also written *Initiations and Initiates in Tibet Land*, first

English edition, 1931.

21. Diary, 6 April 1932. Charles Potter subsequently wrote about Bernard, "The Omnipotent Oom of Nyack," in *The Preacher and I* (New York: Crown Publishers, 1951).

22. *Weymouth Sands*, 230.

23. *Autobiography*, 336.

24. *Weymouth Sands*, 271–272.

25. *Weymouth Sands*, 336.

26. *Weymouth Sands*, 383.

27. *Weymouth Sands*, 334.

28. *Weymouth Sands*, 402.

29. *Weymouth Sands*, 504.

30. *Weymouth Sands*, 507.

31. *Weymouth Sands*, 523.

32. *Weymouth Sands*, 382.

33. *Weymouth Sands*, 383.

34. *Autobiography*, 104.

35. Letter to Phyllis, 3 August 1929.

36. *Weymouth Sands*, 163.

37. R. R. Marett, *The Threshold of Religion* (London: Methuen, 1909, republished 1929). Powys so liked the name that he called Sylvanus's Punch and Judy girl "Marrett."

38. *Weymouth Sands*, 70.

39. *Weymouth Sands*, 162.

40. *Weymouth Sands*, 41.

41. *Weymouth Sands*, 311.

42. *Weymouth Sands*, 478.

43. *Weymouth Sands*, 26.

44. *Weymouth Sands*, 115.

45. *Weymouth Sands*, 118.

46. *Weymouth Sands*, 312.

47. *Weymouth Sands*, 37.

48. *Weymouth Sands*, 312.

49. *Weymouth Sands*, 565.

50. *Weymouth Sands*, 133.

51. *Weymouth Sands*, 476.

52. *Suspended Judgements*, 323.

53. *Weymouth Sands*, 282.

54. *Weymouth Sands*, 461.

55. *Weymouth Sands*, 490.

56. Diary, 14 March 1933.

57. Letter to Llewelyn, 7 May 1933.

58. Letter to Marian, 17 May 1933.

59. *Autobiography*, 53.

60. *Weymouth Sands*, 39.

61. *Weymouth Sands*, 551–53.

62. Diary, 28 January 1931.

63. Diary, 20 March 1933.

64. Diary, 24 January 1932.

65. Diary, 27 April 1932.

66. Diary, 14 January 1933.

67. Diary, 14 January 1933.

68. Diary, 23 January 1933.

69. Diary, 23 January 1933.

70. *Weymouth Sands*, 197–98.

71. Diary, 21 September 1931.

72. *After My Fashion*, 173, 176.

73. *Weymouth Sands*, 298.

74. *Autobiography*, 278.

75. *Weymouth Sands*, 486.

76. Diary, 1 March 1933.

77. Diary, 4 December 1933.

78. Diary, 22 December 1929.

79. Diary, 14 July 1930.

80. *Glastonbury Romance*, 312.

81. Powys took delight in teasing his friends, especially his conspicuously heterosexual male companions like Arthur Ficke, Louis Wilkinson, and Llewelyn, that "save for that one single serious and consequential and gravely responsible Lapse from my Natural Normal and Incurable ways tastes inclinations preferences and prejudices—I have never, so help me God and my dear redeemer, ever committed the Notorious and often referred-to, ORTHODOX ACT OF COPULATION." Letter to Arthur Ficke, 3 May 1936. In the Lloyd Emerson Siberell papers, OSUL. Although he admitted to "a somewhat un-Browningian Aaron's Rod," and there is some possibility of a slight birth defect making intercourse difficult, innumerable diary entries make it clear that when he so chose he could "à la Lulu."

82. Diary, 16 April 1934.

83. Letter to Benson Roberts, 28.

84. *Autobiography*, 636.

85. In the medical literature, use of enemas for sexual stimulation has been named klismaphilia, a form of anal masturbation. One article states, "In a case study of the unusual sexual behaviour of taking enemas to induce sexual response, the practice seemed the inevitable result of a pathogenic childhood environment. This included excessive administration of enemas." Joanne Denko, "Klismaphilia: Enema as a Sexual Preference," *American Journal of Psychotherapy*, 27 (1973): 232. Another article adds, "The gratification of anal eroticism may be perfectly unconscious." *American Journal of Psychotherapy*, 36 (1982): 564.

86. Diary, 27 April 1933.

87. Diary, 6 July 1933. "But Revisions are a struggle for a nature like mine, born to walk on, & walk on, & walk on & walk Past!"

88. Diary, 19 June 1933.

89. Diary, 26 September 1933; 6 November 1933.

90. Letter to Llewelyn, 9 February 1933.

91. Walter Benjamin, "The Image of Proust" in *Illuminations* (New York: Harry Zone, 1969).

92. Vladimir Nabokov, *Ada or Ardor: A Family Chronicle* (London: Weidenfeld and Nicholson, 1969).

93. Diary, 31 July 1930.

94. Although officially the translation came out in 1935, he says clearly that he bought "Gide's Autobiography" in September 1933.

95. Yeats's *Reveries over Childhood and Youth* was included in his *Autobiographies* (London: Macmillan, 1926). Powys read it in October 1928.

96. Letter to Phyllis, 15 October 1928.

97. Roy Foster, *W. B. Yeats: A Life*: Vol. 1. *The Apprentice Mage*, (Oxford: Oxford University Press,1997), 512.

98. Foster, 4; 8.

99. Quoted in Foster, xxvii.

100. David Hume, the Scottish philosopher who was a close friend of many of the Paris philosophes. Rousseau became obsessed with the idea that Hume was involved in a plot to discredit him. The Scot published his own account, *Concise Account*, in which he remarked that "although he thinks himself 'very infirm,' Rousseau is one of the most robust men I have ever known." (Correspondence, xxviii, 203). Rousseau could spend months (usually in the winter) confined to his room but remained a vigorous walker until his death at eighty-two. Hume also said that in spite of Rousseau's mania for self-knowledge, "nobody knows himself less." See Peter France, *Rousseau: Confessions* (Cambridge: Cambridge University Press, 1987), 6–8.

101. Powys read Goethe's autobiography, *Dichtung und Wahrheit*, in 1931, in which he describes his happy and sheltered childhood.

102. *Suspended Judgements*, 98.

103. Letter to Marian, 23 July 1933.

104. Letter to Littleton, 12 August 1933.

105. *Swan's Milk*, 237.

106. *Psychoanalysis and Morality*, 38.

107. *Welsh Ambassadors*, 3.

108. Letter to Lloyd Emerson Siberell, an early collector, 12 August 1933. In the Siberell papers, OSUL.

109. The funeral of the youngest, Lucy, was remarkable, even bizarre, in the sense that there were no flowers on her bier as it was carried solemnly to the grave, only a tiny doll—a black coated clergyman! Lucy Penny died in

November 1986. Her funeral was held in the Church of St. Peter & St. Paul, Mappowder, Dorset.

110. Juvenal, *The Satires of Decimus Junius Juvenalis Translated into English Verse by Mr. Dryden and Several other Eminent Hands* (London: Printed for Jacob Tonson, 1693), Dedication, xlii.

111. Diary, 31 December 1931.

112. Diary, 11 October 1932, referring to Book Six of Rousseau's *Confessions*.

113. Sigmund Freud, *The Psychopathology of Everyday Life*, trans A. A. Brill (New York: The Macmillan Company, 1914).

114. *Psychoanalysis and Morality*, 29.

115. *Autobiography*, 13.

116. John Cowper Powys, *Dostoievsky* (London: The Bodley Head, 1946), 179.

117. *Autobiography*, 46.

118. Yeats, "The Statues," from *Last Poems* (1936-1939) in *Collected Poems of W. B. Yeats* (London: Macmillan & Co, 1965). "That knowledge increases unreality, that / Mirror on mirror mirrored is all the show."

119. Diary, 8 October 1933.

CHAPTER ELEVEN: 1934-1935

1. *Autobiography*, 640.

2. *Autobiography*, 645.

3. Diary, 7 May 1933.

4. Letter addressed to Alyse, 13 August 1933, in *Letters to His Brother Llewelyn, vol. 2 1925–1939*, edited and selected by Malcolm Elwin (London: Village Press, 1975).

5. Diary, 17 June and 29 October 1933.

6. Diary, 2 March 1933.

7. Diary, 17 May 1933.

8. Diary, 19 December 1930.

9. Diary, 9 October 1933.

10. Diary, 26 July 1933.

11. Diary, 28 May 1933.

12. Diary, 29 August 1933.

13. Diary, 4 October 1933.

14. Diary, 4 March 1934.

15. Diary, 13 December 1933.

16. Diary, 28 February 1934.

17. Letter to Marian, 31 July 1933.

18. Diary, 10 July 1933. Powys was particularly pleased that *Glastonbury* was published by John Lane The Bodley Head, as it was the firm most closely associated with the literary style of that era. When the founder, John Lane, died, control of the firm passed to his nephew Allen, who became chairman in 1930. Allen's brothers, John and Richard, also became members of the firm.

19. Diary, 14 February 1934.

20. Diary, 27 February 1934.

21. Samuel Beckett, *Molloy, Malone Dies, The Unnamable* (London: John Calder Ltd., 1959), 86.

22. André Gide, "Philoctetes," act 2, sc. 1, in *My Theatre: Five Plays and an Essay*, trans. Jackson Mathews (New York: A A Knopf, 1951).

23. Letter to Gertrude, 10 March 1934.

24. Letter to Dorothy Richardson, 22 June 1934. Beinecke.

25. Diary, 19 April 1934.

26. Letter from Llewelyn, undated, omitted from the collected letters. Beinecke.

27. Diary, 26 April 1934.

28. Letter to Littleton, 30 April 1934.

29. Letter to Phyllis, 8 January 1930.

30. Diary, 5 March 1934.

31. A newspaper article in the *Sunday Chronicle*, 27 September 1936, described Susan as "the perfect child" and quotes Theodore as saying, "When we lost our only son in 1931, it left a great emptiness in our lives." Presumably this was a slip rather than a deliberate blow at Francis, but Theodore and Violet took a strong dislike to Sally and refused to allow her access to the child. Theodora grew up not knowing who her mother was—or her father for that matter.

32. Alyse Gregory, "A Famous Family," *London Magazine*, March 1958.

33. Letter to Llewelyn, 1 April 1934.

34. *The Notebooks of Henry James* (New York, Oxford University Press, 1947), 26.

35. Letter to Dorothy Richardson, 16 November 1934.

36. Powys kept all the letters and documents relating to the libel case. After Phyllis Playter's death they were transferred to the attic of the copyright holder, Francis Powys, eventually to be found and sorted by M. K.

37. Letter to Marian, 16 June 1934.

38. This declaration, made 9 July 1934, swears that: "As a resident alien in America I was treated there for all purposes as separated from my wife. About the year 1903 or so I bought a small house at Burpham Arundel Sussex. . . . When I went to America as above I gave this house to my wife Margaret Alice Powys and also my valuable library. My wife has always treated the above house as her own and when it was sold she took the proceeds for herself for her own purposes." He also swears that he "did not wish to take any of the benefits (money securities furniture sil-

ver or anything) I was entitled to under my Father's Will but that I wished them all given and handed over to my Wife for her own use absolutely." The last clause is: "The money I believe she invested with other moneys of her own she received from her own Father's Estate in her own name. I do not know what she invested the same in. I confirm that I gave her for her sole use and benefit the whole patrimony I received from my Father's Estate in 1923–1924 and I have never since made and do not now make any claim whatever to any part of it."

39. Letter to Marian, 11 July 1934.

40. Letter to Marian, 19 March 1934.

41. Diary, 4 July 1934.

42. Letter from Dorothy Richardson, 17 July 1934, in *Windows on Modernism: Selected Letters of Dorothy Richardson*, ed. Gloria Fromm (Athens, Georgia: University of Georgia Press, 1995). The original letters are at the Beinecke. A considerable number of letters from Powys could not be included and Gloria Fromm gave copies of these to M. K. Unless *Windows* is specifically cited, the letters are unpublished.

43. Letter to Dorothy Richardson, 18 July 1934. Beinecke.

44. Letters to Marian, 16 August 1934 and 25 September 1934.

45. Diary, 21 June 1934.

46. Diary, 23 August 1934.

47. Sixty-nine discarded holograph pages, numbered but not sequentially, and the only surviving copy of the typescript are in the Powys Collection, DCM. There appear to be five separate starts, the fifth start consisting of forty-four pages and quoted from here.

48. Diary, 11 October 1934.

49. Diary, 15 October 1934.

50. Diary, 17 November 1934.

51. John Cowper Powys, *The Art of Happiness* (New York: Simon & Schuster, 1935), 99.

52. *The Art of Happiness*, 94.

53. *The Art of Happiness*, 96.

54. *The Art of Happiness*, 127.

55. Diary, 15 December 1934.

56. *The Art of Happiness*,133–34.

57. *The Art of Happiness*, 135.

58. *The Art of Happiness*, 137.

59. *The Art of Happiness*, 170.

60. *The Art of Happiness*, 132.

61. Diary, 24 December 1934.

62. *The Art of Happiness*, 166.

63. *The Art of Happiness*, 174.

64. Diary, 4 January 1935.

65. Letter to Marian, 12 November 1934.

66. Diary, 21 July 1934.

67. John Cowper Powys, *Maiden Castle* (New York: Simon & Schuster, 1936; London: Cassell, 1937). Note: pagination refers to the Macdonald edition, published in 1966.

68. Diary, 25 January 1935.

69. *Maiden Castle*, 109.

70. Diary, 14 March 1935.

71. *Maiden Castle*, 20.

72. *Maiden Castle*, 23.

73. Forty-four pages in the Powys Collection, DCM.

74. Diary, 16 April 1935.

75. *Jack and Frances*, vol. 2. Letter from Frances Gregg, April 1935 (Letter 195). Oddly enough, his friend, Arthur Ficke, wrote him along much the same lines on 21 April 1936 after he had read *Welsh Ambassadors*. In it he refers to JCP's "utter indifference to the welfare of others which usually disappears by the time a child is ten years old. But it will never leave you. . . . You have the dreaming innocence and the blind cruelty of the child. . . . you have managed in your development to circle completely around that stage of growth which in normal people is called maturity, and there is in you no trace of normal adulthood." (Letter in the Siberell papers, OSUL).

76. The phrase is in a letter from H. D. to Silvia Dobson, dated 28 February 1934. Quoted in "A Friendship Traced: H. D. Letters to Silvia Dobson," edited by Carol Tinker with notes by Silvia Dobson. *Conjunctions*, No. 2 (Spring 1982): 117. "These things happen. 'Love terrible with banners' only emerges or materializes once or twice in a life-time and my 'terrible with banners' is being lived down. . . . But if I materialize you, I firmly and neatly super-impose you on that Frances." Possibly H. D. got the phrase from The Song of Solomon vi. 4, 10. "Terrible as an army with banners."

77. *Jack and Frances*, vol. 2, viii.

78. Diary, 26 November 1935.

79. *Maiden Castle*, 146.

80. *Maiden Castle*, 218.

81. *Maiden Castle*, 58.

82. *Maiden Castle*, 62.

83. *Maiden Castle*, 228.

84. *Maiden Castle*, 129.

85. *Maiden Castle*, 168,169.

86. *Maiden Castle*, 247.

87. *Odyssey*, Book IX, l.19; l.366.

88. *Maiden Castle*, 249–50.

89. *Maiden Castle*, 167.

90. *Maiden Castle*, 249.

91. *Maiden Castle*, 18.

92. *Maiden Castle*, 174-75.

93. MS, 18.

94. MS, 31.

95. MS, 20.

96. *Maiden Castle*, 469.

97. *Maiden Castle*, 537-38.

98. Diary, 19 March 1940.

99. *Maiden Castle*, 11.

100. MS, 154 -155.

101. *Maiden Castle*, 339.

102. *Maiden Castle*, 127.

103. *Maiden Castle*, 138.

104. *Maiden Castle*, 141.

105. MS, third start, 9.

106. *Maiden Castle*, 456–57.

107. *Maiden Castle*, 296.

108. *Maiden Castle*, 29.

109. *Maiden Castle*, 257.

110. *Maiden Castle*, 383.

111. *Maiden Castle*, 485.

112. *Maiden Castle*, 387, 388.

113. *Maiden Castle*, 388.

114. *Maiden Castle*, 266.

115. *Maiden Castle*, 358.

116. *Maiden Castle*, 440, 441.

117. *Maiden Castle*, 486.

118. *Maiden Castle*, 488.

119. *Autobiography*, 70.

120. Letter to Llewelyn, 1 November 1919.

121. Diary, 23 July 1935.

122. Diary, 12 July 1935; 11 August 1935.

123. Diary, 22 July 1935.

124. *Maiden Castle*, 388.

125. Letter to Littleton, 12 May 1927.

126. Letter to Littleton, 2 June 1935.

127. Diary, 24 May 1935.

128. Diary, 8 April 1936.

129. *Psychoanalysis and Morality*, 42.

130. Diary, 16 October 1934. JCP kept all the reviews of his works that his publishers sent him, including this one.

131. Llewelyn to JCP, Autumn 1934, *Letters of Llewelyn Powys*.

132. *Autobiography*, 150.

133. Letter to Llewelyn, 11 November 1910.

134. "The Mabelulu," PJ, vol. 4 (1994), 168.

135. *Autobiography*, 85.

136. *Porius*, TS. p. 1062.

CHAPTER TWELVE: 1935-1943

1. Letter from ARP to JCP, 19 July 1935, PJ, vol. 6 (1996): 184-187.

2. "Wales and America" in *Obstinate Cymric; Essays 1935-47* (Carmarthen: The Druid Press, 1947). 55.

3. R. S. Thomas, "Welsh Landscape," in *R. S. Thomas*, selected and edited by Anthony Thwaite (London: J.M. Dent, 1996).

4. Letter from Phyllis to Ruth Suckow, 17 October 1935. In private possession.

5. Her mother arrived Christmas Eve 1935; the aunt 25 May 1936. Powys called Mary Playter, inevitably, Mistress Mary or more often simply "The Mistress."

6. Diary, 16 May 1940.

7. Diary, 4 December 1935.

8. Letter from Maxe Schuster, 24 November 1936, in the keeping of M. K.

9. Diary, 22 September 1936.

10. Diary, 1 September 1935. L. H. Myers, *The Root and the Flower*, a trilogy published between 1927–1935 (London: Jonathan Cape, 1935).

11. Diary, 15 August 1933.

12. Diary, 12 September 1936.

13. Diary, 1 October 1933.

14. *Weymouth Sands*, 435.

15. Diary, 4 February 1936.

16. John Cowper Powys, *Morwyn*. (London: Cassell, 1937), 87; 165; 178; 170; 180; 199; 233; 209.

17. Diary, 27 October, 1950: "I felt a tiny bit cold round my navel, my sensitive spot wh shows what a born Oedipus I am!"

18. *Morwyn*, 235, 32, 254, 270, 268, 3

19. *Morwyn*, 23–24.

20. Diary, 10 March 1936.

21. Letter to Frances Gregg, 4 April 1936.

22. Llewelyn Powys, *Somerset Essays* (London: John Lane The Bodley Head, 1937), 167.

23. Diary, 18 May 1936.

24. Chris Gostick, who is writing a biography of James Hanley, says that Hanley appeared more surprised than Powys by being made a bard, but he makes the point that it was "a singular honor, recognizing the deep interest both writers took in Welsh history, language, and culture."

25. Diary, 20 June 1937. The original will, in private possession, is dated 8 July 1937. In it he confirms that his wife Margaret has the property, money, securities, and furniture referred to "in the Statutory Declaration

made by me." In clause 3 he bequeaths to Miss Phyllis Playter "all my manuscripts, diaries, writings and other literary copyright." In clause 4 he bequeaths to her "all the residue of my real and personal estate."

26. Diary, 25 June 1937.

27. Diary, 26 June 1937.

28. Llewelyn to JCP, 29 October 1937, *The Letters of Llewelyn Powys*.

29. Diary, 9April 1937.

30. Diary, 15 January 1938.

31. Diary, 15 August 1937.

32. Diary, 24 August 1937.

33. Diary, 16 April 1936.

34. Diary, 17 November 1935.

35. Diary, 15 December 1935.

36. Diary, 21 June 1946.

37. Diary, 19 October 1935.

38. Diary, 22 June 1944.

39. Diary, 13 February 1941.

40. Diary, 7 January 1938.

41. Diary, 5 June 1938.

42. Diary, 8 June 1937.

43. Diary, 30 May 1938.

44. Diary, 4 June 1938.

45. Diary, 21April 1938.

46. Diary, 27 June 1938.

47. Diary, 12 July 1938.

48. Llewelyn to Lyn Ward, Summer 1934, in *The Letters of Llewelyn Powys*.

49. Llewelyn to Van Wyck Brooks, 1 August 1938, in *The Letters of Llewelyn Powys*.

50. Diary, 7 August 1938.

51. Diary, 15 August 1938.

52. The passport issued in 1938 lists his profession as "lecturer and author" and his height as 5 feet 11 inches, his eyes gray.

53. Diary, 16 August 1938. Llewelyn sent a further check for £50 on 21 November 1938, and another a year later. On the transfer form that accompanied the latter, Llewelyn had written as the purpose of the transfer: "To support ART and give myself pleasure." John never cashed either; M. K. found them in his wallet where he must have kept them, along with a letter from his son, until his death.

54. Diary, 9 July 1939.

55. This is part of a long letter from Gertrude Playter, Phyllis's sister-in-law, who arrived in Corwen on 2 November 1938, detailing the situation she found at Corwen. Manuscripts Department, Lilly Library, Indiana University, Bloomington, Indiana.

56. Letters to Benson Roberts, 3 November 1938; 23 November 1938. *Letters to C. Benson Roberts* (London: Village Press, 1975).

Benson and his family soon became friends; they occasionally visited each other and corresponded until the end of 1959.

57. Letter to Louis Wilkinson, 9 December 1938.

58. Diary, 25 December 1939. His letters to Huw Menai are in the Powys Collection, DCM.

59. Diary, 30 March 1939.

60. Diary, 29 March 1939.

61. John Cowper Powys, *Owen Glendower* (New York: Simon and Schuster, 1940). A number of other editions have been published, the latest by Overlook Press (2003), 12. The pagination refers to the Simon & Schuster text.

62. Diary, 26 August 1939.

63. Diary, 31 August 1939.

64. Diary, 14 September 1939.

65. According to Malcolm Elwin in *The Life*, "The autopsy revealed 'a chronic ulcer in the descending part of the duodenum.' At the base of the ulcer were 'multiple necroses, extending as far as the head of the pancreas' and affecting a medium-sized artery 'which had become eroded'; there was also 'the open stump of a blood vessel, from which at the lightest pressure blood was sickering.'" 270–71.

66. Diary, 2 December 1939.

67. Diary, 24 April 1947.

68. Letter to Littleton, 6 January 1942.

69. Diary, 22 June 1950.

70. Diary, 13 October 1939.

71. Diary, 25 May 1938.

72. Letter to Louis Wilkinson, 24 June 1940.

73. Diary, 25 May 1938.

74. Diary, 3 October 1939.

75. *Owen Glendower* (New York: Simon & Schuster, 1940).

76.The copyright holder has a charming drawing done by JCP. In the middle of the page is a magnificent sea serpent with Arthur's sword, Excalibur, in its teeth, pointed at Hitler (complete with mustache) in a boat, who is holding up his hands. At the top on Mynydd-y-Gaer is Owen Glendower holding his Welsh flag, with the caption, "Owen Glendower returns & is puzzled by the New War." At the side is a drawing of JCP holding a tablet of stone on which is written "Owen Glendower an Historical Novel," and the caption, "Owen's Modern Biographer tries to reach him to tell him about the New War."

77. Diary, 4 December, 1940.

78. Letter to Marian, 21 April 1937.

79. *Owen*, 767.

80. John Redwood Anderson, *Dublin Magazine*, April–June, 1942. Originally sent as a long letter to JCP, 23 December 1941. Powys Collection, DCM.

81. *Owen*, 925.

82. Diary, 3 June 1939.

83. *Owen*, 938.

84. Diary, 19 February 1940.

85. Diary, 4 January 1940.

86. Diary, 10 August 1938.

87. Diary, 4 January 1940.

88. Diary, 16 February 1940.

89. Diary, 18 February 1940.

90. Diary, 22 May 1940.

91. John Cowper Powys, *Mortal Strife* (London: Jonathan Cape, 1942), 7.

92. Diary, 15 August 1940.

93. Diary, 26 June 1940.

94. Gregory, Journal, 5 April 1940.

95. Diary, 19 January 1940.

96. Diary, 11 September 1940.

97. The letters that Alyse decided should not go in were, without exception, ones which dealt with ticklish family matters, particularly Llewelyn's trenchant opinions about his brothers and sisters. Omitted letters are at Yale in the Beinecke Library.

98. Diary, 11 April 1940.

99. Diary, 29 March 1941.

100. Diary, 18 January 1941.

101. Malcolm Elwin described Allen Lane as "always courteous, but smooth, shrewd and discreet—made for material success." In 1935, Allen Lane "achieved a brilliantly successful innovation by publishing paperbacks." Penguin Books began but shortly thereafter The Bodley Head declared bankruptcy. Elwin says that "by one of those convenient curiosities of commercial law Penguin Books turned out to be a separate concern from the Bodley Head, and while Allen Lane increasingly prospered as a paperback publisher, the authors published by the Bodley Head were the losers by its bankruptcy." See "John Cowper Powys and His Publishers," *Essays on John Cowper Powys*, ed. Belinda Humfrey (Cardiff: University of Wales Press, 1972), 286–294.

102. Diary, 16 May 1941. By this time three other publishers combined to keep alive the Bodley Head imprint, appointing C. J. Greenwood as manager, but Phyllis was correct in being dubious about the firm's viability.

103. Diary, 7 May 1941.

104. Diary, 8 September 1941.

105. Gertrude wrote them regularly throughout the war, giving detailed information about their welfare. For example, 21 October 1940: "We don't go walking at night on the terrace as we have a feeling we might get shrapnel on our heads because there are large guns to the left and to the right which fire at the Germans going over our house."

106. Diary, 9 July 1940. Katie wrote in her diary that she could not believe that after thirty years Theodore would leave "his chosen home," but in retrospect realized that "it was undoubtedly through the scare and distress of the Bombing Germans."

107. Gregory, Journal, 30 August 1940. Alyse was full of praise for Gertrude, writing Marian 6 October, 1940: "Gertrude is so brave and so high-spirited and so resourceful—storing up provisions for the winter from the garden and looking after the bees . . . and getting all the first aid things in readiness and thinking of everything. When we have battles over us we go out to our garden dugout. . . . It is a world of mad men and it gets madder all the time." Peter Powys Grey Collection, DCM.

108. Letter from Gertrude to JCP, 29 April 1944.

109. Letter from Katie to JCP, 12 April 1942.

110. Letter to Louis, 23 October 1940. *Letters of John Cowper Powys to Louis Wilkinson, 1935–1956*, ed. Louis Wilkinson (London: Macdonald, 1958).

111. Diary, 11 July 1940.

112. Letter to Nicholas Ross, 30 October 1940.

113. Letter from Gertrude, 5 November 1942.

114. Diary, 21 July 1951.

115. Letter to Louis, 3 June 1946.

116. *Porius*, TS, p. 1005.

117. Diary, 8 July 1941.

118. Diary, 17 July 1941.

119. Diary, 24 June 1944.

120. Diary, 31 May 1941.

121. Diary, 8 August 1941.

122. Diary, 11 August 1941.

123. Diary, 19 August 1941.

124. Diary, 10 August 1941.

125. Diary, 10 October 1941.

126. Diary, 19 October 1941. Note that increasingly in his diary Powys was using double and triple underlines as well as capitals for emphasis.

127. Diary, 11 August 1941.

128. Diary, 5 August 1941.

129. Diary, 18 October 1941.

130. Diary, 3 April 1942.

131. Diary, 7 September 1943.

132. Diary, 14 August 1942.

133. Diary, 12 August 1943.

134. Diary, 22 April 1942.

135. Diary, 9 September 1942.

136. Diary, 17 November 1942.

137. Letter to Nicholas Ross, undated, July or August, 1942.

138. Diary, 11 September 1942.

139. Letter to Louis Wilkinson, 13 May 1942.

140. Diary, 5 October 1943.

141. Letter to Benson Roberts, 17 November 1943, in John Cowper Powys, *Letters to C. Benson Roberts* (London, Village Press, 1975).

142. Diary, 23 July 1942.

143. Diary, 10 February 1942.

144. Diary, 15 February 1942.

145. Letter from Marian, 5 September 1942.

146. Letter to Littleton, 6 January 1942.

147. There are 162 holograph letters to Elizabeth Myers from JCP, dating from 14 March 1941 to 10 December 1946, in the Powys Collection, DCM.

148. Letter to Elizabeth, 1 December 1942.

149. Letter to Elizabeth, December 1942.

150. Diary, 22 September 1942.

151. Diary, 26 October 1942.

152. In ten years JCP had written the following gratis: Introduction to Bertie's book *From the Ground Up*—1937 ; preface to Alyse Gregory's *Wheels on Gravel*—1938; preface to Gamel Woolsey's *Death's Other Kingdom*—1939; forward to Reginald Hunter's *Porlock*—1940; introduction to Llewelyn's *A Baker's Dozen*—published posthumously by Bodley Head—1941;introduction to Harlan McIntosh's *This Finer Shadow*—1941; introduction to Eric Wilson Barker's *Planetary Heart*—1942; foreword to Jacob Hauser's *Future Harvest*—1943; preface to Huw Menai's *The Simple Vision*—1945; foreword to John Redwood Anderson's *The Paris Symphony*—1947; foreword to Marjorie Tilden's *Star Crossed*—1947.

153. Letter to Iowerth Peate, 19 July 1944, in *John Cowper Powys: Letters 1937–1954*, edited with introduction and notes by Iowerth Peate (Cardiff: University of Wales Press, 1974).

154. Letter to Benson Roberts, 16 October 1944.

155. Diary, 31 December 1946.

156. He took *Y Cymro* (a weekly), *Brython* every Thursday, *Y Faner* and *Seren*. Welsh scholars were also making available new translations of the White Book of Rhydderch (*Llyfr Gwyn Rhydderch*) the Red Book of Hergest (*Llyfr Coch Hergest*), and the *Hanes Taliesin*.

157. Letter to Gilbert Turner, June 1947.

158. Diary, 13 January 1943.

159. Diary, 4 August 1945.

160. Letter to Louis, 17 September 1942.

161. Letter to Benson Roberts, 21 October 1939.

162. Diary, 4 December 1940: "Why cannot I even understand my pacifist critics of the war? . . . Because of Aytoun's Lays with those pictures!"

163. Letter to Louis, 4 February 1942.

164. Letter to Louis, 28 November 1939.

165. From Nicholas Ross's notes on the letters of JCP, 169.

166. Diary, 7 July 1943.

167. Diary, 29 October 1943.

168. Letter to Elizabeth, 29 October 1942.

169. Letter to Elizabeth, 10 July 1943.

170. Stevie Smith was an admirer of John Cowper. She wrote a number of adulatory reviews of his books and even a poem, "Souvenir de Monsieur Poop." She also wrote an approving review of Myers's *A Well Full of Leaves*. When she read Littleton's account of his marriage night in his 1956, *Still the Joy of It*, she subsequently wrote the poem, "I Remember." In it, the tubercular bride asks her seventy-three-year-old groom if the German and British aeroplanes overhead ever collided, and he replies that he doubts that "it has ever happened, / Oh my bride, my bride." *The Collected Poems of Stevie Smith* (London: Allen Lane, 1975).

171. Eleanor Farjeon, *Elizabeth Myers* (Aylesford: St Albert's Press, 1957), 14.

172. Letter to Elizabeth, 15 December 1943.

173. Diary, 17 February 1944.

174. 21 December 1943. This letter was found by M. K. in a bag of miscellaneous material that survived after the death of JCP and Phyllis.

175. Elizabeth Myers, review of *The Letters of Llewelyn Powys*, in *New English Weekly*, 20 January 1944.

176. Marianne Moore, "The Dial: A Retrospect," in *Life and Letters Today*, December 1940.

177. Alyse Gregory, review of *A Well Full of Leaves*, in *The Adelphi*, October–December, 1943.

178. Diary, 25 December 1943.

179. Letter to Elizabeth, 26 December

1943.

180. Bibi and Bebi are both African female names, but bebi was an English/African term meaning girlfriend, or an attractive young woman.

181. Letter to Elizabeth, 1 January 1944.

182. Letter to Benson Roberts, 18 May 1940.

183. Letter to Iowerth Peate, 6 November 1943.

184. Letter to Louis, 28 August 1944.

185. Letter to Gilbert Turner, 28 September 1944.

186. Diary, 4 May 1945.

187. Letter from Marian, 5 July 1945.

188. Diary, 1 January 1944.

189. Diary, 7 January 1944.

190. Letter from Elizabeth sent by Alyse to JCP, dated 29 January 1944. In private possession.

CHAPTER THIRTEEN: 1944-1949

1. Diary, 2 January 1944.

2. Diary, 6 January 1944.

3. Diary, 7 January 1944.

4. Diary, 20 January 1944.

5. *Autobiography*, 623-4.

6. Theodore was awarded a Civil List pension of £60 per annum in March 1935 "in recognition of his services to literature." Although it was David Garnett who steered the application through, he was helped by many including Mrs. Hardy. Signatures on the application included Bertrand Russell, Augustus John, Virginia Woolf, and E. M. Forster.

7. Letter to Louis, 25 December 1943.

8. Letter to Louis, 13 February 1944.

9. Letter from Littleton to JCP, 19 February 1944: "I would much prefer to help you myself than that sort of financial help should be organized by Louis Wilkinson for you." NLW (21931-6E). On 26 February 1944 Littleton wrote again, offering to give him another £100, saying, "To me it is all important that your mind should be free to write your Boethius book and any other book you may want to write."

10. Diary, 25 February 1944. On 13 May 1958, Pollinger wrote JCP reminding him that "It was James Hanley who told me how desperately short you were of cash and it was immediately following that that I got to work on Greenwood, Cape, Stanley Unwin, Newman Flower and in America." Letter in private possession.

11. Letter to Louis, 27 June 1944. Powys later discovered that the gift was from "some admirers of his genius," including George Painter and Angus Wilson. Letter in private possession.

12. Diary, 17 April 1944.

13. Diary, 5 December 1945.

14. Diary, 6 August 1946: "I must remember Gwrthevyr the Blessed was the Father of the friend of the youngest princess!!"

15. Diary, 25 November 1946.

16. John Cowper Powys, *The Inmates* (London: Macdonald, 1952), 24.

17. Diary, 11 October 1940.

18. *Porius*, TS. p. 1563. To avoid confusion between the expurgated *Porius* and the complete *Porius*, pagination refers to the corrected typescript which is at the Everett Needham Case Library, Colgate University.

19. Diary, 1 May 1940.

20. Diary, 21 February 1939.

21. Diary, 11 April 1947.

22. Diary, 3 October 1944.

23. Diary, 8 March 1939.

24. Diary, 1 October 1944.

25. Letter to Louis, 5 March 1945.

26. Several versions of this play were lent to M. K. by Frances's grandson, Christopher Wilkinson, along with his valuable comments. He does not entirely agree with my own interpretation of the play.

27. Letters to Louis, 18 February 1945 and 5 March 1945.

28. Letter from Littleton to JCP, 27 April 1937.

29. Diary, 12 May 1940.

30. Letter to Iowerth Peate, 20 July 1945.

31. Letter from Marian to JCP, 19 September 1946.

32. Diary, 9 November 1945.

33. Letter to Gertrude, 1 March 1946.

34. Diary, 5 October 1944.

35. Diary, 13 March 1946.

36. Diary, 2 March 1946.

37. Diary, 23 May 1946.

38. Diary, 6 March 1946.

39. Diary, 21 March 1946.

40. Diary, 1 April 1945.

41. Diary, 12 January 1946.

42. Diary, 21 November 1950.

43. *In Spite of: A Philosophy for Everyman* (London: Macdonald, 1953), 134.

44. Diary, 17 July 1946.

45. Letter to Gilbert Turner, 22 June 1946.

46. Letter to Gilbert Turner, 3 September

1946. Littleton had a successful cataract operation and urged John to have one also, offering to pay for it. John refused.

47. Diary, 19 August 1946.

48. Diary, 27 December 1946.

49. Diary, 4 February 1947.

50. Diary, 3 February 1947.

51. Diary, 20 February 1947.

52. Diary, 1 March 1947.

53. Letter to Gertrude, 27 March 1947.

54. Letter to Gilbert Turner, 21 February 1945.

55. Letter to Gertrude, 17 March 1945.

56. Diary, 26 April 1950.

57. TS. p. 96.

58. Diary, 23 April 1949.

59. Letter to Louis, 2 August 1945.

60. *Autobiography*, 73.

61. Diary, 2 December 1948.

62. TS. p. 1485.

63. TS. pp. 952–53.

64. TS. p. 1086.

65. Diary, 22 January 1940.

66. Letter to Benson Roberts, 2 November 1941.

67. Llewelyn Powys, "Paracelsus," *Swiss Essays*, 73.

68. Letter to Gertrude, undated but in an envelope postmarked 30 April 1896, thanking them for the wedding presents. "Once for all be pleased to forgive my messages to dear Mother. Thank her more than words can easily express for the splendid Paracelsus and also again tell dear Father how much I like Matt Arnold."

69. The first specific mention of Paracelsus in his prose work is in an unpublished fragment, "The Hunchback's House" written circa 1923, about a "professional Mesmerist and Spiritualist," " a man who has a mania for the works of Paracelsus & other Occult writers." NLW (22810E). By the time he came to write *Porius*, there were many alchemical texts, originally in Latin, available either in translation, or quoted extensively in books on alchemy. The most popular was A. E. Waite's translation of *The Hermetic Museum Restored and Enlarged*, which came out in 1893 and which contains twenty-two of the most celebrated ancient alchemical texts. Most of the alchemists' writings were accompanied by graphic drawings which in themselves would have conveyed much to Powys's image-making mind.

70. He began lecturing on *Faust, Part II* in 1928. In his study of *Faust*, Powys says he found the notes of one translator in particular "very exciting all about mythology and Swedenborg and Paracelsus and cabalistic mysticism." (Letter to Phyllis, 2 December 1928.) This was W. H. Van der Smissen, *Goethe's Faust Done into English Verse in the Original Metres with Commentary & Notes* (Toronto: J. M. Dent, 1926).

71. Letter to Nicholas Ross, 9 February 1940.

72. Letter to Gertrude, 12 October 1951.

73. Diary, 30 April 1948.

74. Diary, 17 April 1945.

75. Diary, 28 October 1947.

76. TS. p. 5.

77. TS. p. 977.

78. TS p. 850.

79. TS. p. 201, 213.

80. TS. p. 115.

81. TS. p. 727.

82. TS. p. 242.

83. Diary, 24 June 1946.

84. TS. pp. 490–532.

85. TS. p. 787.

86. TS. p. 906.

87. TS. pp. 876–77.

88. TS. p. 896.

89. TS. p. 888.

90. TS. p897. In the *Hermetic Museum*, vol. 1, Tract VII, there are a number of references to the hen hatching her chicks. For example, "The spirit and body are first separated, then again joined together by gentle coaction, of a temperature resembling that with which a hen hatches her eggs. Such is the preparation of the substance, which is worth the whole world, whence it is also called a 'little world'."

91. TS. p. 955.

92. TS. p. 980, p. 1013.

93. TS. p. 1044, p. 1014.

94. Diary, 9 May 1947.

95. Diary, 23 April 1947.

96. Diary, 27 March 1947.

97. TS. p. 1118.

98. Diary, 26 March 1947.

99. TS. p. 1011.

100. TS. p. 1012.

101. TS. p. 1122.

102. TS. p. 1148.

103. TS. p. 76.

104. TS. p. 1148.

105. TS. p. 1131.

106. TS. p. 1117.

107. TS. p. 1130.

108. TS. p. 1268.

109. TS. p. 1269.

110. TS. p. 1304.

111. TS. p. 1291.

112. TS. p. 1362.

113. TS. p. 1358.

114. TS. p. 1410.

115. TS. p. 482.

116. Diary, 15 September 1947.

117. TS. p. 1411.

118. TS. p. 1212.

119. TS. p. 1436.

120. TS. pp. 1438–39.

121. TS. pp. 1442–43.

122. Diary, 25 November 1948.

123. Diary, 31 October 1948.

124. TS. p. 1442.

125. TS. p. 1518.

126. See C. Jung, *Psychology and Alchemy*, The Collected Works of C. G. Jung, vol. 12, trans. R. F. C. Hull (London: Routledge & Kegan Paul, 1952), 302. The Jung lectures on which this volume was based was first translated into English by Stanley Dell and published in *The Integration of the Personality* (London: Routledge & Kegan Paul, 1940).

127. TS. p. 1549.

128. See Robert Graves, *The White Goddess* (London: Faber and Faber, 1961), 439.

129. TS. p. 1265.

130. TS. p. 1563.

131. TS. p. 1275.

132. TS. p. 1238.

133. TS. p. 1275.

134. TS. pp. 1570–74.

135. TS. p. 1574.

136. Paracelsus, *De Vita Longa*, quoted in Jung, *Alchemical Studies* (London: Routledge & Kegan Paul, 1967), 175.

137. TS. p. 1575.

138. TS. p. 1583.

139. TS. p. 1588.

140. TS. pp. 79–80.

141. Letter to Iowerth Peate, 25 April 1945.

142. Diary, 19 November 1944.

143. TS. p. 908.

144. TS. p. 909.

145. Diary, 22 October 1943.

146. Diary, 28 October 1943.

147. Letter to Louis, 18 August 1949.

148. Correspondence at Syracuse University. Denny's letter was dated 4 December, but possibly because of Aunt Harriet's cremation on the sixth, Powys appears not to have responded to it until 7 December. The correspondence with the Bodley Head reader/editor began in 1946 and ended in June 1950. Denny's rejection must have been particularly hurtful because by this time they were on intimate terms.

149. Diary, 7 December 1949.

150. JCP to Norman Denny, 7 December 1949. Syracuse.

151. JCP to Boyne Grainger, 13 December 1949, quoted in her *How We Lived in Patchin Place*.

152. Letter from Dorothy Richardson to JCP, 15 August 1944, published in *Windows*. Powys's letter, unpublished, at Beinecke, dated 23 August 1944.

153. Letters to Littleton, 11 & 12 December 1949.

154. Diary, 28 February 1941.

155. Letter to Ross, 17 July 1949.

156. Diary, 15 August 1951. He refers to the picture of them taken by Betty Evans which for many years he referred to as "Petrushka and the Dancer." By now it has become a picture of them as "Merlin and Nineue."

157. Letter to Nicholas Ross, 10 October 1945.

158. Diary, 24 March 1950.

159. Diary, 12 April 1950.

160. Diary, 22 August 1950: "Not one word yet about Porius not one word about me money for Porius & they have had the Book for a year."

161. Diary, 28 August 1950.

162. Letter to Gertrude, 24 August 1950.

163. Diary, 17 September 1950.

164. Letter from JCP to Elwin, 2 September 1950. HRHRC.

165. Reported in a letter to Littleton, 31 December 1949.

166. TS. p. 1019.

167. TS. pp. 1022–3.

CHAPTER FOURTEEN: 1950-1963

1. Diary, 15 October 1950.

2. Letter to Benson Roberts, 24 December 1952.

3. *The Inmates* (London: Macdonald, 1952). Macdonald paid him the same amount of royalty (£200) for this much shorter and greatly inferior novel as for *Porius*. Pollinger got his usual 10%—now a matter for Powys's resentment—while the hard-working Mrs. Meech got £10 for its typing.

4. Diary, 21 September 1930.

5. Letter to William Gillespie. JCP remarked in his diary, 25 October 1949, "It is queer having such a long, full, frank, well! comparatively frank—I don't talk of masturbation—correspondence with a Certified Inmate of an Insane Asylum."

6. *The Inmates*, viii.

7. Diary, 9 December 1949.

8. *The Inmates*, 84.

9. *The Inmates*, 32.

10. *The Inmates*, viii.

11. *The Inmates*, 80.

12. *The Inmates*, 311–12.

13. Powys calls the escape vehicle variously a helicopter and a plane. His brother Will may have put this idea into his head when he proposed to "rescue" them by taking them to Dorset by helicopter to visit their relatives—a suggestion which, needless to say, John thought little of.

14. *The Inmates*, 83.

15. *The Inmates*, 57–58.

16. *The Inmates*, 248.

17. *The Inmates*, 249.

18. Diary, 17 November 1949.

19. *The Inmates*, 85.

20. *The Inmates*, 60.

21. *The Inmates*, 60.

22. *The Inmates*, 124.

23. *The Inmates*, 89.

24. *The Inmates*, 295.

25. Diary, 2 December 1951. "I was too Cowardly to go down to the Dorm below & fight Deacon or really injure Deacon with something made of Iron yes!"

26. *The Inmates*, 307.

27. *The Inmates*, 211.

28. *The Inmates*, 293.

29. *The Inmates*, 199–200.

30. *The Inmates*, 311.

31. *The Inmates*, viii.

32. *In Spite Of: A Philosophy for Everyman*.

33. Diary, 12 August 1951.

34. *In Spite Of*, 156.

35. *In Spite Of*, 145.

36. *In Spite Of*, 155.

37. Diary, 16 October 1951.

38. Diary, 28 December 1952.

39. Diary, 17 June 1953.

40. Diary, 28 May 1952.

41. Diary, 30 October 1941.

42. Diary, 6 January 1953.

43. Diary, 29 March 1953.

44. Letter to Benson Roberts, 14 November 1951.

45. John Cowper Powys, *Atlantis* (London: Macdonald, 1954).

46. Diary, 26 May 1952.

47. C. G. Jung and C. Kerényi, *Introduction to a Science of Mythology* (London: Routledge, Kegan Paul, 1951).

48. Letter to Huw Menai, 1 September 1947.

49. Diary, 26 May 1952.

50. *Romandichtung und Mythologie: ein Briefwechsel mit Thomas Mann* (Zurich: Rhein-Verlag, 1945).

51. Diary, 27 April 1947.

52. Carl Kerényi, *The Gods of the Greeks*, translated from German by Norman Cameron (London, Thames and Hudson, 1951). Letter from Kerényi to Mann, 19 February 1952: "Old John Cowper Powys, that Celtic magician . . . confesses in a letter to the publisher, 'I have not read a book for years which I've found more exciting or more provocative or fuller of suggestions, in my most favourite of all studies.'"

53. JCP wrote Dorothy Richardson, 21 October 1952, "If you want to get an exciting book, though I can't lend my copy to you for I read it like the bible every day, do get 'The Gods of the Greeks' by C. Kerényi, published by Thames and Hudson."

54. *Gods of the Greeks*, 4.

55. Thomas Mann, "Freud and the Future," lecture delivered in the Konzerthaus in Vienna, 1936. Published in *Freud, Goethe, Wagner*, trans. Rita Reil (New York: A. A. Knopf, 1937). Quoted in Kerényi, 1–2.

56. *Atlantis* (London: Macdonald, 1954).

57. *Atlantis*, 217.

58. *Atlantis*, 236.

59. *Atlantis*, 239.

60. *Atlantis*, 99.

61. *Atlantis*, 143.

62. *Atlantis*, 130.

63. *Atlantis*, 209–10.

64. *Atlantis*, 287.

65. *Atlantis*, 289.

66. John Cowper Powys, "The Unconscious," *The Occult Observer*, (May 1949) 8, 11. The original manuscript is in the Powys Collection, DCM.

67. *Atlantis*, 288.

68. *Atlantis*, 433.

69. *Atlantis*, 436.

70. *Atlantis*, 461.

71. In 1951 Powys was given a new stick which he said was "almost a club." He associated it with Dokesis, the club of Heracles. A fly that alighted on his knee at the end of 1951 he called "Mouchy." His mythological tales continue to have a connection, however tenuous, with some chance reality.

72. *Atlantis*, 155.

73. *Gods of the Greeks*, 3.

74. *Gods of the Greeks*, 9.

75. Diary, 25 October 1953. Evalyn

Westacott, *Roger Bacon: In Life and Legend* (London. Rockcliff, 1953). See also Evalyn Westacott, *A Century of Vivisection* (London. C. W. Daniel Co Ltd. 1949).

76. Diary, 20 December 1953.

77. Diary, 29 November 1952.

78. Diary, 17 April 1953.

79. Littleton Alfred appears to have died from a form of motor neuron disease, progressive and invariably fatal, characterized by the gradual degeneration of nerves within the central nervous system that control muscular activity. Eventually all muscles under voluntary control are affected and patients lose the ability to move their arms, legs, and body. There is then an increasing problem with swallowing and speaking. The disease does not impair the personality or memory. Once it affects breathing and swallowing, it leads to death within two to four years of onset. Amyotrophic Lateral Sclerosis, or Lou Gehrig's disease, is the most common type of motor neuron disease. It usually affects people over age fifty and is more common in men. The first symptoms are weakness in the hands and arms.

80. Letter to Littleton, 6 September 1954.

81. Diary, 6 and 7 September 1954.

82. Letter to Littleton, 26 September 1954.

83. Diary, 24 March 1953: "30 years this summer we have lived together as if we were husband and wife . . . and so this summer by American Law that is her law she now is my Common Law wife & aye! how this does delight me."

84. Letter from Phyllis Playter to Francis Powys, 8 May 1969. Letter in private possession.

85. *The Complete Plays of Aristophanes*, ed. Moses Hadas (New York: Bantam Books, 1962), 229.

86. Diary, 13 November 1946.

87. Diary, 20 March 1954.

88. Diary, 14 June 1955.

89. John Cowper Powys, *The Brazen Head* (London: Macdonald, 1956), 131.

90. *The Brazen Head*, 207.

91. *The Brazen Head*, 211.

92. *The Brazen Head*, 240.

93. *The Brazen Head*, 278.

94. *The Brazen Head*, 239.

95. *The Brazen Head*, 239.

96. *The Brazen Head*, 279.

97. *The Brazen Head*, 239.

98. "The Unconscious," 12.

99. *The Brazen Head*, 147.

100. *The Brazen Head*, 149.

101. *The Brazen Head*, 246–7.

102. *Porius*, TS. p. 960.

103. *Porius*, TS. p. 1181.

104. *The Brazen Head*, 246–47.

105. *Autobiography*, 436.

106. Michael Sendivogius, "Novum lumen," in *Musaeum Hermeticum*, trans. A. E. Waite, *The Hermetic Museum Restored and Enlarged* (London: John M. Watkins, 1893), 153.

107. "My Philosophy," *Obstinate Cymric*, 153.

108. George Ripley, *Opera omnia chemica*, 9. Quoted in Jung, *Psychology and Alchemy*, 283.

109. *Porius*, TS. p. 1305.

110. *Porius*, TS. p. 858.

111. *Porius*, TS. p. 987.

112. *Porius*, TS. p. 529.

113. *Porius*, TS. p. 530.

114. *Porius*, TS. p. 1440, 1442, 1444.

115. *Porius*, TS. p. 530.

116. *Porius*, TS. p. 92.

117. Diary, 3 August 1933.

118. Goethe, *Faust*, act 1, sc. 2, lines 483–493.

119. *Porius*, TS. p. 1116.

120. Diary, 7 October 1955.

121. Diary, 14 October 1955.

122. Johann Peter Eckermann, *Gespräche mit Goethe in den letzen Jahren seines Lebens*, ed. H. H. Houben (Wiesbaden: F.A. Brockhaus, 1959), 513.

123. John Cowper Powys, "Up and Out," one of two stories in *Up and Out* (London: Macdonald, 1957).

124. "Up and Out," 32.

125. "Up and Out," 53.

126. "Up and Out," 58.

127. "Up and Out," 59.

128. "Up and Out," 107.

129. "Up and Out," 119.

130. Letter to Louis, 4 February 1956.

131. "Mountains of the Moon," in *Up and Out*.

132. Diary, 30 May 1954.

133. "Mountains of the Moon," 211–12.

134. "Mountains of the Moon," 214.

135. Diary, 21 May 1957.

136. Diary, 3 December 1956.

137. Diary, 7 August 1955.

138. Diary, 4 July 1957. Phyllis wrote a sad letter to Gamel dated 20 January, 1960, which sums up her feelings about Blaenau. "I thought our going down into these dark slate mountains would be like being together in Dis—in Pluto's realm—but I forgot about

Reality and all those people we went with and the darkness underfoot where we walked and I feared it was too frightening and painful an experience as it turned out. But of course what else could it be?"

139. Diary, 3 February 1956.

140. Diary, 10 April 1957.

141. Diary, 14 July 1956.

142. Letter from Phyllis Playter to Ferner Nuhn, 24 October, 1957. Letter in private possession.

143. Letter to Marian, 25 September 1956.

144. Diary, 19 September 1955.

145. Letter to Louis, 8 November 1956.

146. John Cowper Powys, *Homer and the Aether*, (London: Macdonald, 1959), 27.

147. Diary, 7 October 1955.

148. Letter of Phyllis Playter to Frederick Davis, 22 February 1963. Letter in private possession.

149. Diary, 14 May 1958.

150. John Cowper Powys, *All or Nothing* (London: Macdonald, 1960), 69.

151. *All or Nothing*, 192.

152. Letter to Marian, 2 April 1935.

153. *All or Nothing*, 148.

154. *All or Nothing*, 200.

155. *Elbe: Jahrbuch Freie Akademie der Künste in Hamburg*, 1958. The issue featured an account of his visit to Blaenau by Rolf Italiaander, small selections from various of JCP's writings, and his thank you letter: "This is the first time in my life that I have received any Public Honours and my gratitude . . . is boundless." The second award Powys received was an Honorary Life Membership from "The Society of Dorset Men," in March 1962, "as a token of our appreciation of your very distinguished services in the field of literature and in view of the very intimate connections which your family has always had with the County of Dorset." The letter was found amongst his effects. According to Iorwerth Peate, several attempts were made during the 1950s to persuade the University of Wales authorities to confer on Powys the degree of D. Litt. *honoris causa*, but it did not happen until 21 July 1962. Phyllis kept the certificate but sadly, by then he would not have realized that his native land and his chosen land had thus recognized him.

156. Diary, 6 July 1958.

157. Liam Hanley told M. K. this story when we met accidentally in an artist's supply shop in London in the 1970s and he noticed that I was having a copy of the Augustus John drawing of JCP framed.

158. Diary, 26 May 1952.

159. Diary, 11 June 1959. Powys wrote Gamel on 23 January 1959, thanking her for her gift of a bird book, and enclosed a poem, at the bottom of which he has written "The 'She' is G.W." The fourteen lines end:

O it is a pity
That she who pushes bull rushes apart
To find the old dew-drenched druidic stone,
Should only keep a drop of cuckoo-spity
Where common girls keep what is called
    a HEART!

The poem appears to have been written in 1929 or perhaps earlier, when he was angry at Gamel for not being "good" to Lulu and jealous of her friendship with Phyllis. He had kept this frankly unkind poem private all those years, and only sent it to Gamel thirty years later when once again he found the women's love for each other intolerable.

160. After Phyllis's death, Pollinger sent the three stories to Macdonald and they were rejected. The editor, Jock Curle, wrote, "I personally feel that [they] are self-indulgences, and really in the long run would do John Cowper more harm than good if they were published." Letter dated 3 December 1982 in private collection.

161. *Autobiography*, 83.

162. John Cowper Powys, "Topsy-Turvy," *Three Fantasies* (Manchester: Carcanet Press, 1985), 48.

163. "Topsy-Turvy," 13.

164. "Topsy-Turvy," 51.

165. "Abertackle," *Three Fantasies*, 78.

166. In a letter to E. E. Bissell dated 12 August, 1963, John's nephew, Francis Powys, wrote: "In his last years he was just as charming to visitors as ever, though he hadn't the faintest idea who some of them were; for his memory went completely at the end."

167. *Wolf Solent*, 558.

168. *Up and Out*, 121.

169. Diary, 10 February 1960.

170. Written on a scrap of paper found by M. K. in one of the sacks. The handwriting dates it to the time of his last diary.

EPILOGUE

1. "Whatsoever," MS. 22810E, NLW.

2. Penelope Doob, *The Idea of the Labyrinth from Classical Antiquity through the Middle Ages* (Ithaca, New York: Cornell University Press, 1990), 64.

INDEX

∽

diary, 246, 450
Llewelyn's description of, 335
visits Corwen, 335
believes JCP his father, 335
still referred to as "our son", 419, 425
death, 425-427
Guest, Lady Charlotte (see also *The Mabinogion*), 81, 430
Hagen, Magda, housekeeper at Phudd Bottom, 251, 253, 254
Haldeman-Julius, Phyllis works for, 187, 199, 281
publishes JCP's article on Longfellow, 209
Hamburg, Germany, visions experienced there by JCP, 76-78, 118
Hanley, James, asks JCP for money for his child, 298
libel action against, 301
invites JCP & Phyllis to Wales, 321-322
becomes Bard
(biography by Chris Gostick), 330, 456
recommends change of agent, 352
gets JCP commission to write on Finnegan's Wake, 354
suggests Civil List pension, 363
Hanley, Liam, paints oil of Blaenau landscape, 419, 465
Harrison, Jane, *Prolegomena to the Study of Greek Religion*
Ancient Art and Ritual, 252, 450, 451
Harvey, Eric, joint managing director of Macdonald, asks JCP to write introduction for *Tristram Shandy*, 371
accepts *Porius*, 392, 397
relationship with JCP & effect on his reputation, 397, 403, 410
Hattersley, Mabel, 177
trains under Jung, 267
Hesse, Herman, *In Sight of Chaos*, 265
Hillsdale (see also Phudd Bottom), JCP & PP move to, 242, 243
effect on his "magicianship", 297
reasons for leaving, 302
begins to name landscape features, 311, 364
Homer (see also *the Odyssey*), 241, 316, 338, 353-354, 403
homosexuality, homosexuality in public schools, 41, 432
in his "circle", 62
measures against, 65
in early writings, 67
in pornographic literature, 67
JCP not homosexual, 96, 349
in *Psychoanalysis and Morality*, 183-184
in *Glastonbury Romance*, 255
in *Porius*, 372, 391
in *The Inmates*, 398

Hopkins, Gerard Manley, "begetting one's thoughts on paper", 87, 436
Hopkins, Kenneth, *The Powys Brothers*, 255, 442, 451
horoscopes (See also astrology), 143, 188, 288, 299
in *The Inmates*, 400
Howe, Quincey, editor at Simon & Schuster, 331, 332

imaginary children (see also *The Owl, the Duck and—Miss Rowe! Miss Rowe!*), Glauk, 192, 282
Olwen and Falada in *The Owl, the Duck and—Miss Rowe! Miss Rowe!*, 247-248
the dog, 250
stone children, 282, 283
incest, in pornographic literature, 67, 70
regarding sister Nellie, 68
regarding mother, 182
regarding Phyllis, 187, 190
in *Wolf Solent*, 217, 219, 220, 225, 227
in *Porius*, 378, 379
in *Mountains of the Moon*, 416
regarding Marian, 419
in *Abertackle*, 422

Jack and Frances, The Love Letters of JCP to Frances Gregg ed. Oliver Wilkinson 2 vols, 112, 438
James, William, *A Pluralistic Universe: Hibbert Lectures on the Present Situation in Philosophy*, 451
pluralism and monism, 265-266
multiverse v. universe, 398, 411
James, Henry, 82, 209, 247, 417
as "eternal outsider", 304
one of JCP's favourite novelists, 304, 355
John Lane The Bodley Head, publish *Glastonbury Romance*, 300, 454
involvement in libel case, 302, 305-306, 312
publish *Owen Glendower*, 347, 458
commission "Introducing Rabelais", 356
reaction to *Porius*, 388, 389, 391, 392, 404
JCP refuses their offer, 392
Johnson, Mary Barham, describes Mary Cowper Powys as a young woman, family background, in *The Powys Mother*, 24, 431
Johnson, William Cowper, 24, 25, 39, 432
Jonathan Cape, publish *Mortal Strife*, 347
publish *The Art of Growing Old*, 364
Jones, Tom, 100
joins "circle" & introduces girls to JCP, 89, 290
urges JCP to continue lecturing, 450

The Joy of It, by Littleton Powys, 26, 88, 357
  describes JCP as childhood leader, 33
  Still The Joy of It, 459
Joyce, James
  work published by Anderson in the *Little
    Review*, complaint by the New York
    Society for the Prevention of Vice, 135
  JCP defends *Ulysses*, 135
  as exiled writer, 300
Julian of Norwich, *Revelations of Divine Love*,
    222-223
Jung, Carl, childhood fetish, 36
  Memories, Dreams & Reflections, 432
  "collective unconscious", 267
  *Wandlungen und Symbole der Libido/Psychology
    of the Unconscious*, 267, 452
  training of Mabel Hattersley, 267
  similarities with JCP, 267-268
  Jung's theories, 267
  theory of alchemy, 384
  Psychology and Alchemy, 462
  Alchemical Studies, 462
  Introduction to a Science of Mythology (with
    Kerényi), 403, 463
  JCP turns back to Freud, 403

Kantzow, Alfred de, 60, 62, 434
Keedick, Lee, becomes JCP's agent, 203-204,
    446
  fees, 205, 209, 212
  dispute with, 235, 240-241, 449
Kerényi, Carl, *Introduction to a Science of
    Mythology* (with Carl Jung), 403-404
  describes JCP as "the great mythologist", 404
  The Gods of the Greeks, 404, 463
  praise for Greek mythology, 406
Kilvert, Francis, *Kilvert's Diary, 1870-1879*, 67
Knopf, Alfred A., publishes *The Buffoon*, 147
Krafft-Ebing, 102, 435
  Psychopathia Sexualis, 57
  "Krafft-Ebing" fantasies, 62

labrys (double axee),, 18, 36, 430
labyrinth (see also mazes), 17, 18, 430
Lawrence, D. H., 134
  Apocalypse, 265
  libel action against, 301
  Kerényi links with JCP, 404
Lewin, George Lionel, 350
Linton, Marion, Llewelyn's proposal of marriage
    to, enters a nunnery, 123, 128, 439
  as character in *Wood and Stone*, 132
Little Review, literary magazine edited by
    Margaret Anderson, 134, 135, 137, 138-
    139, 142, 170
Lloyd, J. E., *Owen Glyn Dûr*, 330, 343

Loomis, Roger, The Fisher King
  Celtic Myth and Arthurian Romance, 252-253,
    451
Los Angeles, as artistic & intellectual milieu,
    154-155
Lyon, Margaret Alice (Mrs Powys), engagement
    to JCP, 69, 71, 434
  wedding, 72-73
  love poems to, 75
  running JCP's business affairs, 82
  relationship with depicted in JCP's early
    writings, 86, 94-95
  gives birth to their son, 87
  reasons for marriage, 90, 92
  invites JCP's "whore" to Burpham, 91
  relationship between Margaret, JCP & Harry
    Lyon, 96, 121
  JCP's payments to her, 106, 154, 160, 161,
    175, 182, 189, 210, 211, 298
  relationship with JCP during his affair with
    Frances Gregg, 121-122, 159
  portrayal in *Rodmoor*, 149
  in World War One, 155-156
  portrayal in *After My Fashion*, 165-166
  portrayal in *Ducdame*, 193
  portrayal in *Wolf Solent*, 217-218
  omits from *Autobiography*, 290
  tells about Phyllis, 177
  financial arrangements during libel case,
    304, 454-455
  JCP's will, 456-457
  JCP rejects idea of Civil List pension in case
    of worry for, 363
  death, 370
  in *Porius*, 373
Lyon, Thomas Henry, joins JCP's circle, 60, 69
  in early writings by JCP, 62
  as architect, 93, 94
  animosity with Louis Wilkinson, 95, 96-97
  character in *The Buffoon*, 95-97, 437
  in *Rodmoor*, 148, 151
  helps JCP with expenses, 153, 189
  influence on JCP's son, 199
  in *Porius*, 372
  death, 407

Mabinogion, The, Powys's favourite version
    of the Welsh folktales, 81, 82, 271, 326,
    336, 354, 364, 409
  Lady Charlotte Guest's translation, 430
  lectures on it in Bridgend, 336
  in *Porius*, 375, 379, 384, 388, 393
Macdonald (publishing house), 420, 462, 465
  Malcolm Elwin & Eric Harvey, 371, 392,
    397
  accept *Porius*, 392-393

physical attributes, 203
portrayal as Christie in *Wolf Solent* is as JCP
    unconsciously wanted her to be, 229
prefers death to life, 369-370
problems on arrival in England, 304-306
proof-reading, 281
psychological problems, 172, 175-176
reaction to *Maiden Castle*, 321, 325
reaction to Corwen, 324-325
reaction to visitors, 245, 410
reaction to Wales, 332
relationship with father, 282, 400-401
relationship with Gamel Woolsey, 233
self-disparagement, 208
settles into life in Dorchester, 308
suggests *Owen Glendower*, 325
suggests JCP keeps diary but does not keep
    her own for long, 230-231
takes over letter-writing, 351
the T. T., 249, 284
views on Hillsdale in diary, 242-243
violence towards JCP, 250-251, 356, 401, 403
wants a child & imaginary children, 282-283
Watteau sophistication, 272, 299, 347, 409,
    417
Poetry, literary magazine edited by Harriet
    Monroe; Ezra Pound & Hilda Doolittle
    contribute to, 134
Pollinger, Laurence, 305-308, 314, 325, 332,
    346, 347, 352, 356, 358, 364, 388, 392,
    460, 462, 465
Pollock, Rivers, friend of Llewelyn, 205, 312,
    334
Potoki, Count, 303, 448
Pound, Ezra, relationship with Frances Gregg,
    111-113, 116, 117
    contributes to *Poetry*, 134-135, 440
    views on JCP, 135, 441
    in *The Buffoon*, 146
    ridiculed by JCP in *Suspended Judgements*,
    152
Powys family, The, mother's family
    background (Johnson), 24
    father's family background, 24-25
    "Hydra-Headed Powys", 35
    names and nicknames, 51
    "insane family", 51
    clannishness, 35, 51, 122, 303, 322, 323, 353
    JCP protected & inhibited by family ties, 56
    at JCP's wedding, 72-73
    impact of mother's death, 124-125
    in World War One, 155-156
    JCP's view that they were "too many", 120-
    121, 350
    relationship between brothers in *Wood and
    Stone*, *Rodmoor* and *Ducdame*, 131, 196-197

characters in *Wolf Solent*, 219-220
effect on relationships of portrayal in
    JCP's stories, 219
Phyllis's criticism of, 282, 307
Phyllis meets, 303
reaction to *Autobiography*, 323
need for a "Powys Castle", 323
views on Llewelyn's biography, 360
effect of Elizabeth Myers on family unity,
    360
as shown in *Porius*, 372-373
Powys-hero, 18, 62, 67, 69, 73
    as defined by G. Wilson Knight, 434-435
    in *Wood and Stone*, 130
    in *Rodmoor & After My Fashion*, 148, 149,
    150, 165
    in *Wolf Solent & Glastonbury Romance*, 216,
    263, 269
    in *Weymouth Sands*, 274, 286
    in *Maiden Castle*, 313, 449
    in *Owen Glendower*, 341
    in *Porius*, 382
    in *The Inmates*, 399
Powys, A. R. (Bertie), architect, 73
    wedding, 92-93
    views on Venice trip, 115
    in World War One, 124, 129, 156, 157
    view on JCP's "lust for dramatic
    excitement", 189, 115
    Secretary of the Society for the Protection
    of Ancient Buildings, 201, 329
    desire for a "Powys Castle", 323
    reaction to *Autobiography*, 323
    reaction to JCP's move to Wales, 324
    family life, 214, 234, 322, 329
    death, 97, 329, 338, 340
    Winterborne Tomson church, 329
Powys, Charles Francis, vicar of Shirley, 18, 21,
    25, 39-40
    sexuality, 20
    as part of JCP's life-illusion, 23
    story of Fairy Sprightly & Giant Grumble,
    22, 372
    family background, 24-25
    meets Johnson family, 25
    marriage, 25
    early career in Church, 25-26
    moves to Dorset, 28-29
    business affairs, 29, 192
    JCP assumes mantle of, 33
    vicar of Montacute, 39, 169
    death, 192
    relationship with JCP portrayed in
    Weymouth Sands, 278
    in *Autobiography*, 291
    appears as a character in *Abertackle*, 422